About the Author

WILLIAM T. VOLLMANN was born in Los Angeles in 1959 and attended
Deep Springs College and Cornell University. He is the author of, among
others, *The Atlas* (winner of the 1997 PEN Center West Award), *You
Bright and Risen Angels, The Rainbow Stories,* and a series of novels entitled *Seven Dreams: A Book of North American Landscapes,* about the
collision between the native populations of North America and their
colonizers and oppressors. In addition, Vollmann's nonfiction includes
An Afghanistan Picture Show, which describes his crossing into
Afghanistan with a group of Islamic commandos in 1982, and *Rising Up
and Rising Down,* a seven-volume treatise on violence that was nomi-
nated for the National Book Critics Circle Award in 2003. His journalism and fiction have been published in *The New Yorker, Esquire, Spin,
Gear,* and *Granta.* In 1999, *The New Yorker* named Vollmann "one of
the twenty best writers in America under forty." He lives in California
with his wife and daughter.

Rising Up and

Rising Down

RISING UP and
RISING DOWN

Some Thoughts on Violence, Freedom
and Urgent Means

William T. Vollmann

AN  BOOK

HARPER PERENNIAL

NEW YORK • LONDON • TORONTO • SYDNEY

HARPER ● PERENNIAL

FIRST HARPER PERENNIAL EDITION PUBLISHED 2005.

Designed by Cassandra J. Pappas

The Library of Congress has catalogued the hardcover edition as follows:

Vollmann, William T.
    Rising up and rising down : some thoughts on violence, freedom and urgent means / William T. Vollmann.
        p. cm.
    ISBN 0-06-054818-5
    1. Violence.   2. Liberty.   I. Title.
HM1116.V65 2004
303.6—dc22

2004053243

ISBN-10: 0-06-054819-3 (pbk.)
ISBN-13: 978-0-06-054819-3 (pbk.)

05 06 07 08 09 ❖/RRD 10 9 8 7 6 5 4 3 2 1

In memory of Francis William Tomasic (1958–94)
and Will Brinton (d. 1994).
They chose danger in the service of charity and truth.
R.I.P.

. . . these subjects will certainly have to be discussed to some extent. But if they were to be covered in any sort of detail the book would be so long that only a dedicated student of insurgency would read it, and he would probably be an insurgent.

—Brigadier Frank Kitson,
Low Intensity Operations

Preface to the Abridgment

In its original form, *Rising Up and Rising Down* occupies seven volumes. The single justification which I can offer is that I believe it needed to be that long. This abridgment likewise has only one justification: I did it for the money. In other words, I can't pretend (although you may disagree) that a one-volume reduction is any improvement upon the full version. All the same, it's not necessarily worse. For one thing, the possibility now exists that someone might read it.

Moreover, since the only method I could think of to categorize excuses for violence was an inductive one, and since my conclusions are (I hope) the reverse of dogmatic, there seems no reason why you ought to inflict on yourself the tedious recapitulation of my own gleanings and concatenations; please make your own. I am grateful to Ecco for making this compact version possible. My paragraphs and punctuation have been conformed to house style.

The ultimate position of *Rising Up and Rising Down* is that moral values can be treated as absolutes in some respects, as relative quantities in others. I believe that every violent act refers itself back to some more or less rational explanation. To the extent that the explanations are irrational, they can be quickly disposed of. To the extent that they are rational, they do enjoy the *possibility* of absolute status, provided that ends, means and the intellectual-moral logic in between have all been correctly assembled.

For instance, the discrimination principle (see the Moral Calculus) proposes that noncombatants must not be deliberately targeted; since I have begun by assuming that each sovereign self possesses the absolute right to defend itself, but only in a situation of proven imminence, the noncombatant's status as someone who is not an imminent threat absolutely privileges his right to self-defense at the expense of any rights which I might have to practice proactive aggression. Therefore, the discrimination principle may be regarded as absolute. No wonder that a near synonym for "noncombatant casualty" is "victim."

To generalize, if we grant Presupposition A absolute status (example: *we each possess the right to defend ourselves*), then Justification B *(I invoked the right of self-defense in this situation, because . . .)* absolutely follows, or not. If B does follow, then B is also absolute.

On the other hand, any violent act may be supported by one plausibly absolute construction of justifications—for example, defense of homeland, with all the attendant logic just referred to—and invalidated by another, say, defense of authority. One of the many tragic cases of this disjunction is the civil war which ruined Yugoslavia. Authority's federalism, which just happens to have a Serbian flavor, mobilizes its defensive violence against Croatian defense of ethnicity and localism. Here is where the relativism comes in.

In short, you have the right to make up your own mind as to whose cause was more just, that of Croatia or that of Yugoslavia. On the other hand, I would strongly disagree if you chose to leave the merits of the discrimination principle open to question. How could you do this without rejecting what most of us hold dear, the fundamental sovereignty of the self?

My wish is that if you find anything useful in the categories I propose, and the simple if laborious inductive method employed, you will be able to arrive at your own moral calculus without feeling quite so burdened by someone else's. From this point of view, the abridgment now in your hands falls short of being short enough. Hopefully it will seem less dry than this introduction.

So much for the aim. Now for the means.

Rising Up and Rising Down comprises a series of almost self-contained essays. When is violent defense of gender acceptable? When is violent deterrence of violence permissible? We need not address either one of these questions in order to consider the other. This simplifies an abridger's task. The long version of *Rising Up and Rising Down* took me twenty-three years, counting editorial errands. The abridgment took me half an hour.

Shostakovich once said that a toothpick is an edited Christmas tree.

From a proportional point of view, this volume would seem to be a fence-post. About three-quarters of the tree has been trimmed away.

What you have here is (1) a selection of "when is violent defense of X justified?" chapters, which are each (I hope) interesting in their own right; followed by (2) the *complete* Moral Calculus, which contains my answers to every "when is" question considered in the long volume; rounded off with (3) several case studies from war zones, et cetera, along with some of the regional introductions to the case studies.

I shortened several chapters in the first group, to spare you a plethora of related examples. In a very few instances, transitional passages were added or altered in order to suture those cuts. In only one place, in the "Trotsky and Lincoln" section in "Defense of Authority," has the trimming been noted.

The annotated table of contents to the original has been retained. To save space all footnotes were deleted.

Thank you for reading this book. My sincere intention in writing it was to be helpful.

WTV
Sacramento
2004

Editors' Note to the Abridgment of
Rising Up and Rising Down

While it is our hope and belief that this abridgment retains the general sense and unity of the original, it should be noted that in attempting to preserve the heart of William T. Vollmann's seven-volume magnum opus, several compromises were made in the interest of both length and content. Perhaps the most noticeable is the absence of footnotes, which have been eliminated in accordance with the author's wishes. Readers should be assured that this absence does not harm the sense of anything included here. The reader may also notice several cross-references throughout the text which, in some cases, point to excised material. It was the author's intent that these references remain for the reader to follow back to the original edition. To aid in this effort, we have provided an annotated table of contents on page 707.

Preface to the Original Edition

This essay is intended as a companion piece to my memoir *An Afghanistan Picture Show* and to my novel *You Bright and Risen Angels*. In those books, much reference is made to do-it-yourself politics of an extreme character. *Rising Up and Rising Down* is a critique of terrorist, defensive, military and police activity, combined with some more general thoughts on when violence may be appropriate. I offer it to you, my unknown reader, in the hope that it may someday save a life or comfort a seeking mind.

> WTV
> *San Francisco*
> *New York*
> *Sacramento*
> *1982–98*

No doubt I have Osama bin Laden to thank for the fact that this work is getting published in my lifetime. People have advised me to "bring it up to date" by inserting references to the terrorist attacks of September 11, 2001. I feel no interest in doing that, although a footnote here and there (obviously deleted from this abridged edition) pays note to those grisly events. Nor did I alter any case studies, some of which are set in Muslim countries. (If you read them with that knowledge, you will see that even to a superficial observer such as myself some sort of attack was predictable and perhaps preventable. I can assure you that it will get worse.) What has been done (for fear that the book wasn't long enough) was to add a few more case studies, including one from Yemen, date-lined on and after September 11, 2002. (It was commissioned by the *New Yorker* and then rejected for not being "political enough.")

The text throughout has benefited from several new sources, and the various arguments are further puffed up and ossified.

It was said of Napeolon that "he held our imagination in his hand, sometimes a hand of steel, sometimes a hand of velvet; one never knew how it was going to be from day to day, so that there was no means of escaping." That is how this book has gripped me, year after year. I am very relieved to be free of it; I hate it. At the same time I am proud of it, and I hope that it can benefit someone.

WTV
Sacramento
2003

Contents

THREE MEDITATIONS ON DEATH

I.

CATACOMB THOUGHTS

Death is ordinary. Behold it, subtract its patterns and lessons from those of the death that weapons bring, and maybe the residue will show what violence is. With this in mind, I walked the long tunnels of the Paris catacombs. Walls of earth and stone encompassed walls of mortality a femur's-length thick: long yellow and brown bones all stacked in parallels, their sockets pointing outward like melted bricks whose ends dragged down, like downturned bony smiles, like stale yellow snails of macaroni—joints of bones, heads of bones, promiscuously touching, darkness in the center of each, between those twin knucklespurs which had once helped another bone to pivot, thereby guiding and supporting flesh in its passionate and sometimes intelligent motion toward the death it inevitably found—femurs in rows, then, and humeri, bones upon bones, and every few rows there'd be a shelf of bone to shore death up, a line of humeri and femurs laid down laterally to achieve an almost pleasing masonry effect, indeed, done by masonry's maxims, as interpreted by Napoleon's engineers and brickmen of death, who at the nouveau-royal command had elaborated and organized death's jetsam according to a sanitary aesthetic. (Did the Emperor ever visit that place? He was not afraid of death—not even of causing it.) Then there were side chambers walled with bones likewise crossed upon bone beams; from these the occasional skull

looked uselessly out; and every now and then some spiritual types had ornamented the facade with a cross made of femurs. There had been laid
down in that place, I was told, the remains of about six million persons—
our conventional total for the number of Jews who died in the Holocaust.
The crime which the Nazis accomplished with immense effort in half a
dozen years, nature had done here without effort or recourse, and was
doing.

I had paid my money aboveground; I had come to look upon my future. But when after walking the long arid angles of prior underground alleys I first encountered my brothers and sisters, calcified appurtenances of
human beings now otherwise gone to be dirt, and rat flesh, and root flesh,
and green leaves soon to die again, I felt nothing but a mildly melancholy
curiosity. One expects to die; one has seen skeletons and death's-heads on
Halloween masks, in anatomy halls, cartoons, warning signs, forensic
photographs, photographs of old S.S. insignia, and meanwhile the skulls
bulged and gleamed from walls like wet river boulders, until curiosity became, as usual, numbness. But one did not come out of the ground then.
Bonewalls curled around wells, drainage sockets in those tunnels; sometimes water dripped from the ceiling and struck the tourists' foreheads—
water which had probably leached out of corpses. A choking, sickening
dust irritated our eyes and throats, for in no way except in the abstract,
and perhaps not even then, is the presence of the dead salutary to the living. Some skulls dated to 1792. Darkened, but still not decayed, they oppressed me with their continued existence. The engineers would have done
better to let them transubstantiate. They might have been part of majestic
trees by now, or delicious vegetables made over into young children's blood
and growing bones. Instead they were as stale and stubborn as old arguments, molds for long-dissolved souls, churlish hoardings of useless matter. Thus, I believed, the reason for my resentment. The real sore point was
that, in Eliot's phrase, "I had not thought death had undone so many";
numbness was giving way to qualmishness, to a nauseated, claustrophobic
realization of my biological entrapment. Yes, of course I'd known that I
must die, and a number of times had had my nose rubbed in the fact; this
was one of them, and in between those episodes my tongue glibly admitted what my heart secretly denied; for why should life have to bear in its
flesh the dissolving, poisonous faith of its own unescapable defeat? Atop
bony driftwood, skulls slept, eyeholes downward, like the shells of dead hermit crabs amidst those wracked corpse timbers. This was the necrophile's

beach, but there was no ocean except the ocean of earth overhead from which those clammy drops oozed and dripped. Another cross of bone, and then the inscription—SILENCE, MORTAL BEINGS—VAIN GRANDEURS, SILENCE—words even more imperious in French than I have given them here, but no more necessary, for the calcified myriads said that better than all poets or commanders. In superstition the carcass is something to be feared, dreaded and hated; in fact it deserves no emotion whatsoever in and of itself, unless it happens to constitute a souvenir of somebody other than a stranger; but time spent in the company of death is time wasted. Life trickles away, like the water falling down into the catacombs, and in the end we will be silent as our ancestors are silent, so better to indulge our vain grandeurs while we can. Moment by moment, our time bleeds away. Shout, scream or run, it makes no difference, so why not forget what can't be avoided? On and on twisted death's alleys. Sometimes there was a smell, a cheesy, vinegary smell which I knew from having visited a field morgue or two; there was no getting away from it, and the dust of death dried out my throat. I came to a sort of cavern piled up to my neck with heaps of bones not used in construction: pelvic bones and ribs (the vertebrae and other small bones must have all gone to discard or decay). These relics were almost translucent, like seashells, so thin had death nibbled them. That smell, that vinegar-vomit smell, burned my throat, but perhaps I was more sensitive to it than I should have been, for the other tourists did not appear to be disgusted; indeed, some were laughing, either out of bravado or because to them it was as unreal as a horror movie; they didn't believe that they'd feature in the next act, which must have been why one nasty fellow seemed to be considering whether or not to steal a bone—didn't he have bones enough inside his living meat? He must not have been the only one, for when we came to the end and ascended to street level we met a gainfully employed man behind a table which already had two skulls on it, seized from thieves that day; he checked our backpacks. I was happy when I got past him and saw sunlight—almost overjoyed, in fact, for since becoming a part-time journalist of armed politics I am not titillated by death. I try to understand it, to make friends with it, and I never learn anything except the lesson of my own powerlessness. Death stinks in my nostrils as it did that chilly sunny autumn afternoon in Paris when I wanted to be happy.

In the bakeries, the baguettes and pale, starchy *mini-ficelles,* the croissants and *pains-aux-chocolats* all reminded me of bones. Bone-colored cheese stank from other shops. All around me, the steel worms of the Metro bored through other catacombs, rushing still living bones from hole to hole. In one of the bookshops on the Rue de Seine I found a demonically bound volume of Poe whose endpapers were marbled like flames; the plates, of course, hand-colored by the artist, depicted grue-somely menacing skeletons whose finger-bones snatched and clawed. I spied a wedding at the Place Saint-Germain, whose church was tanned and smoked by time to the color of cheesy bones; I saw the white-clad bride—soon to become yellow bones. The pale narrow concrete sleepers of railroads, metallic or wooden fence-rails, the model of the spinal col-umn in the window of an anatomical bookshop, then even sticks, tree trunks, all lines inscribed or implied, the world itself in all its segments, rays and dismembered categories became hideously cadaverous. I saw and inhaled death. I tasted death on my teeth. I exhaled, and the feeble puffs of breath could not push my nausea away. Only time did that—a night and a day, to be exact—after which I forgot again until I was writing these very words that *I must die*. I believed but for a moment. Thus I became one with those skulls which no longer knew their death. Even writing this, picking my letters from the alphabet's boneyard, my *o*'s like death's-heads, my *i*'s and *l*'s like ribs, my *b*'s, *q*'s, *p*'s and *d*'s like ball-ended humeri bro-ken in half, I believed only by fits. The smell came back into my nose, but I was in Vienna by then—whose catacombs, by the way, I decided not to visit—so I went out and smelled espresso heaped with fresh cream. The writing became, as writing ought to be, informed by choreographies and paradigms which mediated that smell into something more than its revolt-ing emptiness. I take my meaning where I can find it; when I can't find it, I invent it. And when I do that, I deny meaninglessness, and when I do *that* I am lying to myself. Experience does not necessarily lie, but that smell is not an experience to the matter which emits it. Death cannot be experi-enced either by the dead or the living. The project of the Parisian work-men, to aestheticize, to arrange and thus somehow to transform the objects of which they themselves were composed, was a bizarre success, but it could have been done with stale loaves of bread. It affected bones; it could not affect death. It meant as little, it said as little, as this little story of mine. It spoke of them as I must speak of me. I can read their meaning. Death's meaning I cannot read. To me death is above all things a smell, a very bad smell, and that, like the skeletons which terrify children, is not death at all.

If I had to smell it more often, if I had to work in the catacombs, I would think nothing of it. And a few years or decades from now, I will think nothing about everything.

II.

AUTOPSY THOUGHTS

It shall be the duty of the coroner to inquire into and determine the circumstances, manner, and cause of all violent, sudden or unusual deaths.

CALIFORNIA STATE CODE, SEC. 274911

Aldous Huxley once wrote that "if most of us remain ignorant of ourselves, it is because self-knowledge is painful and we prefer the pleasures of illusion." That is why one brushes off the unpleasantly personal lesson of the catacombs. But we can extend the principle: Not only self-knowledge hurts. Consider the black girl whom an investigator pulled from a dumpster one night. Her mouth was bloody, which wasn't so strange; she could have been a homeless alcoholic with variceal bleeding. But, shining the flashlight into that buccal darkness, the investigator caught sight of a glint—neither blood nor spittle sparkling like metal, but metal itself—a broken-off blade. In her mouth, which could no longer speak, lay the truth of her death. The investigator couldn't give her her life back, but by this double unearthing—the knife from the corpse, the corpse from the stinking bin—he'd resurrected something else, an imperishable quantity which the murderer in his fear or fury or cold selfishness meant to entomb— namely, the fact of murder, the reality of which would have been no less real had it never become known, but which, until it was known and proved, remained powerless to do good. —What good? Quite simply, determining the cause of death is the prerequisite for some kind of justice, although justice, like other sonorous concepts, can produce anything from healing to acceptance to compensation to revenge to hypocritical clichés. At the chief medical examiner's office they knew this good—knowing also that the job of turning evidence into justice lay not with them but with the twelve citizens in the jury box—what coroners and medical examiners do is necessary but not sufficient. Probably the black woman's family had figured that out, if there *were* any family, if they cared, if they weren't too stupefied with grief. The morgue would be but the first of their Stations of the Cross. (Afterward: the funeral parlor, the graveyard, perhaps the courtroom, and always the empty house.) Dealing with them was both the saddest and the most important part of the truth-seeker's job: as I said, knowledge hurts. Dr. Boyd Stephens, the Chief Medical Examiner of San Francisco, would later say to me: "One of the things I hoped you'd see was a family coming in here grieving. And when it is a crime of violence, when someone has her son shot during a holdup, that makes it very hard; that's a tremendous emotional blow." I myself am very glad that I didn't see this. I have seen it enough. In the catacombs death felt senseless, and for the investigator who found the black woman, the moral of death remained equally empty, as it must whether the case is suicide, homicide, accident or what we resignedly call "natural causes." Twenty-six years after the event, a kind woman who had been there wrote me about the death of my little sister. I was nine years old, and my sister was six. The woman wrote: "I remember you, very thin, very pale, your shoulders hunched together, your hair all wet and streaming sideways. You said, 'I can't find Julie.'" She wrote to me many other things that she remembered. When I read her letter, I cried. Then she went on: "I am tempted to say that Julie's drowning was a 'senseless death' but that's not true. I learned the day she died that there are realms of life in which the measure of sense and nonsense don't apply. Julie's death exists on a plane where there is no crime and no punishment, no cause and effect, no action and reaction. It just happened." Fair enough. Call it morally or ethically senseless, at least. (I don't think I ever wrote back; I felt too sad.) Only when *justice itself* condemns someone to death, as when a murderer gets hanged or we bombard Hitler's Berlin or an attacker meets his victim's lethal self-defense, can we even admit the possibility that the perishing had a point. Principled suicides also mean something: Cato's self-disembowelment indicts the conquering Caesar who would have granted clemency, and whose patronizing power now falls helpless before a mere corpse. But most people (including many suicides, and most who die the deaths of malicious judicial *in*justice) die the death of accident, meaninglessly and ultimately anonymously discorporating like unknown skulls in catacombs—and likewise the black woman in the dumpster. No matter that her murderer had a reason—she died for nothing; and all the toxicology and blood-spatter analyses in the world, even if they lead to his conviction, cannot change that. The murderer's execution might mean something; his victim's killing almost certainly will not.

From the White Hearse to the Viewing Room

In fiscal year 1994–95, slightly more than eight thousand people died in San Francisco County. Half of these deaths could be considered in some sense questionable, and reports on them accordingly traveled to Dr. Stephens's office, but in three thousand cases the doubts, being merely pro forma, were eventually cleared, signed off by physicians—that is, explained circumstantially if not ontologically. The remaining 1,549 deaths became Dr. Stephens's problem. His findings for that year were: 919 natural deaths, 296 nonvehicular accidents, 124 suicides, 94 homicides, 30 mysterious cases, 6 sudden infant death syndromes and 80 vehicular fatalities, most of which involved pedestrians and most of which were accidents (there were six homicides and one suicide). And now I'm going to tell you what his people did to reach those findings. In San Francisco they had a white ambulance, or hearse as I might better say, which was partitioned between the driver's seat and the cargo hold, and the cargo hold could quickly be loaded or unloaded by means of the white double doors, the inside of which bore an inevitable reddish-brown stain: anything that touches flesh for years must get corrupted. It smelled like death in there, of course, which in my experience is sometimes similar to the smell of sour milk, or vomit and vinegar, or of garbage, which is to say of the dumpster in which the murdered girl had been clumsily secreted. A horizontal partition subdivided battered old stainless steel stretchers into two and two. Because San Francisco is hilly, the stretchers, custom-welded years before by a shop just down the street, were made to be stood upright, the bodies strapped in, and rolled along on two wheels. "Kind of like a wheelbarrow in a way," one stretcher man said. This might be the last time that the dead would ever again be vertical, as they serenely traveled, strapped and sheeted, down steep stairs and sidewalks. The ambulance pulled up behind Dr. Stephens's office, in a parking lot that said AMBULANCES ONLY. Out came each stretcher. Each stretcher went through the door marked NO ADMITTANCE, the door which for those of us whose hearts still beat might better read NO ADMITTANCE YET. Inside, the body was weighed upon a freight-sized scale, then wheeled into the center of that bleak back room for a preliminary examination, and fingerprinted three times (if it still had fingers and skin), with special black ink almost as thick as taffy. Finally it was zipped into a white plastic bag to go into the fridge overnight. If the death might be homicide, the investigators waited longer—at least twenty-four hours, in case any new bruises showed up like last-minute images on a pale sheet of photographic paper floating in the developer, as might happen when deep blood vessels had been ruptured. Bruises were very important. If the body of a man who seemed to have hanged himself showed contusions on the face or hands, the investigators would have to consider homicide.

By now perhaps the family had been told. In the big front room that said ABSOLUTELY NO ADMITTANCE, I heard a man say, "Yes, we have Dave. I'm so sorry about what happened to Dave." If the family came, they would be led down a narrow corridor to a door that said VIEWING ROOM. The viewing room was private and secret, like the projectionist's booth in a movie theater. It had a long window that looked out onto another very bright and narrow room where the movie would take place, the real movie whose story had already ended before the attendant wheeled in the former actor. The movie was over; Dr. Stephens needed the family to verify the screen credits. They saw only the face. There was a door between the viewing room and the bright and narrow room, but someone made sure to lock it before the family came, because they might have tried to embrace this thing which had once been someone they loved, and because the thing might not be fresh anymore or because it might have been slammed out of personhood in some hideous way whose sight or smell or touch would have made the family scream, it was better to respect the love they probably still felt for this thing which could no longer love them, to respect that love by respecting its clothes of ignorance. The people who worked in Dr. Stephens's office had lost their ignorance a long time ago. They blunted themselves with habit, science and grim jokes—above all, with necessity: if the death had been strange or suspicious, they had to cut the thing open and look inside, no matter how much it stank.

A Solomonic parable: Dr. Stephens told me that once three different mothers were led into the viewing room one by one to identify a dead girl, and each mother claimed the girl as hers, with a desperate relief, as I would suppose. I know someone whose sister was kidnapped. It's been years now and they've never found her. They found her car at the side of the road. My friend used to live with her sister. Now she lives with her sister's clothes. From time to time the family's private detective will show her photographs of still another female body partially skeletonized or not, raped or not, and she'll say, "That's not my sister." I know it would give her peace to be able to go into a viewing room and say (and *believe*), "Yes, that's Shirley." Those three mothers must all have given up hoping that their daughters would ever speak to them or smile at them again. They wanted to stop dreading and start grieving. They didn't want to go into viewing rooms anymore. And maybe the glass window was dirty, and maybe their eyes were old or full of tears. It was a natural mistake. But one mother was lucky. The dead girl was really her daughter.

The Innocent Meter Maid

To confirm that identification, someone at Dr. Stephens's office had already looked inside the dead woman's mouth, incidentally discovering or not discovering the gleam of a knife blade, observed her dental work and matched it to a dentist's files. Somebody had fingerprinted her and found a match; somebody had sorted through her death-stained clothes and come up with a match. Starting with flesh and cloth, they had to learn what the mothers didn't know. The meter maid didn't know, either, and I am sure she didn't want to know. A young man eased some heroin into his arm—maybe too much, or maybe it was too pure (heroin just keeps getting better and better these days). He died and fell forward, his face swelling and purpling with lividity. The meter maid didn't know, I said. Even after he began to decompose, she kept putting parking tickets on his windshield.

"I'm a Happy Customer"

A stinking corpse, pink and green and yellow, lay naked on one of many parallel downsloping porcelain tables each of which drained into a porcelain sink. The man's back had hurt. Surgery didn't help, so he took painkillers until he became addicted. The painkillers proving insufficiently kind, he started mixing them with alcohol. When the white ambulance came, there were bottles of other people's pills beside his head. He was not quite forty.

"Everything's possible," said one morgue attendant to another, leaning against a gurney, while the doctor in mask and scrubs began to cut the dead man open. "You're limited only by your imagination." I think he was talking about special-effects photography. He had loaned his colleague a mail-order camera catalogue. Meanwhile the dagger tattooed on the dead man's bicep trembled and shimmered as the doctor's scalpel made the standard Y-shaped incision, left shoulder to chest, right shoulder to chest, then straight down the belly to the pubis. The doctor was very good at what he did, like an old Eskimo whom I once saw cutting up a dying walrus. The scalpel made crisp sucking sounds. He peeled back the chest flesh like a shirt, then cracked the racks of ribs, which could almost have been pork. His yellow-gloved hands grubbed in the scarlet hole, hauling out fistfuls of sausage links—that is, loops of intestine. Then he stuck a hose in and left it there until the outflow faded to pinkish clear. Beset by brilliant lavender, scarlet and yellow, the twin red walls of rib meat stood high and fragile, now protecting nothing, neatly split into halves.

The dead man still had a face.

The doctor syringed out a blood sample from the cavity, sponged blood off the table, and then it was time to weigh the dead man's organs on a hanging balance, the doctor calling out the numbers and the pretty young pathology resident chalking them onto the blackboard. The lungs, already somewhat decomposed, were indistinct masses which kept oozing away from the doctor's scalpel. "Just like Jell-O," he said sourly.

The right lung was larger than the left, as is often the case with right-handed people. Another possible cause: the dead man had been found lying on his right side, a position which could have increased congestion in that lung. Either way, his death was meaningless.

His heart weighed 290 grams. The doctor began to cut it into slices.

"This vessel was almost entirely occluded with atherosclerosis," explained the resident. "He used a lot of drugs. Cocaine hastens the onset of atherosclerosis. We get lots of young people with old people's diseases."

That was interesting to know and it meant something, I thought. In a sense, the investigators understood the dead man. I wondered how well he'd been understood before he died.

"God, his pancreas!" exclaimed the doctor suddenly. "That's why he died." He lifted out a purple pudding which spattered blood onto the table.

"What happened?" I asked.

"Basically, all these enzymes there digest blood. This guy was hemorrhagic. The chemicals washed into his blood vessels and he bled. Very common with alcoholics."

Out came the liver now, yellow with fatty infiltrations from too much alcohol. "See the blood inside?" said the doctor. "But the pancreas is a sweetbread. The pancreas is a bloody pulp. Blood in his belly. Sudden death. We got lucky with him—he's an easy one. This is a sure winner."

Quickly he diced sections of the man's organs and let them ooze off his bloody yellow-gloved fingers into amber jars. The pathology and toxicology people would freeze them, slice them thinner, stain them and drop them onto microscope slides, just to make sure that he hadn't overdosed on something while he bled. Meanwhile the doctor's knowledge-seeking scalpel dissected the neck, to rule out any possibility of secret strangulation. Many subtle homicides are misdiagnosed as accidents by untrained people, and some accidents look like murders. The doctor didn't want that to happen. Even though he'd seen the pancreas, he wanted to be as thorough as he could to verify that there was no knife blade in the mouth, that all the meaning had come out. —"Okay, very good," he grunted. Then the attendant, whom I should really call a forensic technician, sewed the dead man up, with the garbage bag of guts already stuck back inside his belly. His brain, putrefying, liquescent, had already been removed; his face had hidden beneath its crimson blanket of scalp. The attendant sewed that up, too, and the man had a face again.

"I'm a happy customer," said the doctor.

Of Jokes and Other Shields

If the doctor's wisecracks seem callous to you, ask yourself whether you wouldn't want to be armored against year after year of such sights and smells. Early the next morning I watched another doctor open up an old Filipino man who, sick and despondent, had hanged himself with an electric cord. I have seen a few autopsies and battlefields before, but the man's stern, stubborn stare, his eyes glistening like black glass while the doctor, puffing, dictated case notes and slashed his guts (the yellow twist of strangle cord lying on an adjacent table) gave me a nightmare that evening. This doctor, like his colleague, the happy customer, was doing a good thing. Both were *proving* that neither one of these dead men had been murdered, and that neither one had carried some contagious disease. Like soldiers, they worked amidst death. Green-stained buttocks and swollen faces made up their routine. They had every right to joke, to dull themselves. Those who can't do that don't last.

Strangely enough, even their job could be for some souls a shelter from sadder things. Dr. Stephens himself used to be a pediatric oncologist before he became coroner in 1968. "At that time, we lost seventy-five percent of the children," he said. "Emotionally, that was an extremely hard thing to do. I'd be dead if I stayed in that profession."

The thought of Dr. Stephens ending up on one of his own steel tables bemused me. As it happens, I am married to an oncologist. She goes to the funerals of her child patients. Meanwhile she rushes about her life. Embracing her, I cherish her body's softness which I know comprises crimson guts.

Evidence

The little cubes of meat in the amber jars went across the hall to pathology and to toxicology: underbudgeted realms making do with old instruments and machines which printed out cocaine spikes or heroin spikes on the slowly moving graph paper which had been state-of-the-art in the 1960s. But after all, how much does death change? Ladies in blue gowns tested the urine samples of motorists suspected of driving while intoxicated, and with equal equanimity checked the urine of the dead. Had they or had they not died drunk? The drunken motorist who died in a crash, the drunken suicide who'd finally overcome his fear of guns (in seventeenth-century Germany, the authorities encouraged condemned criminals to drink beer or wine before the execution), the drunken homicide victim who'd felt sufficiently invincible to provoke his murder—such descriptors helped attach reason to the death. Meanwhile, the blue-gowned ladies inspected the tissue samples that the doctors across the hall had sent them. I saw a woman bent over a cutting board, probing a granular mass of somebody's tumor, remarking casually on the stench. If the stomach was cancerous, if the liver was full of Tylenol or secobarb, that constituted a story, and Dr. Stephens's people were all the closer to signing off that particular death certificate.

In her gloved hands, a lady twirled a long, black-bulbed tube of somebody's crimson blood. On a table stood a stack of floppy disks marked PO-LICE CASES. Here was evidence, information, which might someday give birth to meaning. Kidneys floated in large translucent white plastic jars. They too had their secret knives-in-the-mouth—or not. They might explain a sudden collapse—or rationalize the toxic white concentration of barbiturates in the duodenum, if the decedent's last words did not. In San Francisco one out of four suicides left a note. Some of the laconic ones might leave unwitting messages in their vital organs. "I would say that about twenty-five percent of the suicides we have here are justified by real physical illness," Dr. Stephens told me. "We had one gentleman recently who flew in from another state, took a taxi to the Golden Gate Bridge and jumped off. Well, he had inoperable liver cancer. Those are *logical* decisions. As for the others, they have transient emotional causes. A girl tells a boy she doesn't want to see him anymore, so he goes and hangs himself. No one talked to him and got him over to the realization that there are other women in the world."

Look in the liver then. Find the cancer—or not. That tells us something.

"And homicide?" I asked. "Does that ever show good reason?"

"Well, I've seen only a few justified homicides," Dr. Stephens replied. "We handle a hundred homicides a year, and very few are justified. They're saving their family or their own lives. But the vast majority of homicides are just a waste, just senseless violent crimes to effect punishment."

And accident? And heart attack, and renal failure? No reason even to ask. From the perspective of the viewing room, it is all senseless.

Death Can Never Hurt You Until You Die

On that Saturday morning while the doctor was running the hanged man's intestines through his fingers like a fisherman unkinking line, and the forensic tech, a Ukrainian blonde who told me about her native Odessa, was busily taking the top of his head off with a power saw, I asked: "When bodies decompose, are you at more or less of a risk for infection?"

"Oh, the T.B. bacillus and the AIDS virus degrade pretty quickly," said the doctor. "They have a hard time in dead bodies. Not enough oxygen. But staph and fungus grow . . . The dead you have nothing to fear from. It's the living. It's when you ask a dead man's roommate what happened, and the dead man wakes up and coughs on you."

He finished his job and went out. After thanking the tech and changing out of my scrubs, so did I. I went back into the bright hot world where my death awaited me. If I died in San Francisco, there was one chance in four that they would wheel me into Dr. Stephens's office. Although my surroundings did not seem to loom and reek with death as they had when I came out of the catacombs—I think because the deaths I saw on the autopsy slabs were so grotesquely singular that I could refuse to see myself in them, whereas the sheer mass and *multiplicity* of the catacomb skulls had worn down my unbelief—still I wondered who would cough on me, or what car would hit me, or which cancer might already be subdividing and stinking inside my belly. The doctor was right: I would not be able to hurt him then, because he'd be ready for me. Nor would his scalpel cause me pain. And I walked down Bryant Street wondering at the strange absurdity of my soul, which had felt most menaced by death when I was probably safest—how could those corpses rise up against me?—and which gloried in removing my disposable mask and inhaling the fresh air, letting myself dissolve into the city with its deadly automobiles and pathogen breathers, its sailboats and bookstores; above all, its remorseless *futurity*.

III.

SIEGE THOUGHTS

And now, closing my eyes, I reglimpse tangents of atrocities and of wars. I see a wall of skulls in the Paris catacombs. Likewise I see the skulls on the glass shelves at Choeung Ek Killing Field. In place of the tight wall of catacomb skulls gazing straight on at me, sometimes arranged in beautiful arches, I see skulls stacked loosely, laid out on the glass display shelves in heaps, not patterns—although it would give a deficient impression to omit the famous "genocide map" a few kilometers away in Phnom Penh; this is a cartographic representation of all Cambodia, composed of murdered skulls. At Choeung Ek, they lie canted upon each other, peering and grinning, gaping and screaming, categorized by age, sex and even by race (for a few Europeans also died at the hands of the Khmer Rouge). Some bear cracks where the Khmer Rouge smashed those once-living heads with iron bars. But to my uneducated eye there is nothing else to differentiate them from the skulls of Paris. The Angel of Death flies overhead, descends and kills, and then he goes. The relics of his work become indistinguishable, except to specialists such as Dr. Stephens, and to those who were there. (I remember once seeing a movie on the Holocaust. When the lights came on, I felt bitter and depressed. It seemed that the movie had "reached" me. And then I saw a man I knew, and his face was very pale and he was sweating. He was a Jew. He was really there. The Nazis had killed most of his family.) *Before* the Angel strikes, of course, the doomed remain equally indistinguishable from the lucky or unlucky ones who will survive a little longer. Death becomes apprehensible, perhaps, only at the moment of dying.

To apprehend it, then, let's approach the present moment, the fearful time when they're shooting at you and, forgetting that your life is not perfect, you crave only to live, sweat and thirst a little longer; you promise that you'll cherish your life always, if you can only keep it. Thus near-death, whose violence or not makes no difference. A woman I loved who died of cancer once wrote me: "You will not be aware of this but it is the anniversary of my mastectomy and I am supposed to be happy that I survived and all that. Actually it has been a terrible day." She'd forgotten, like me; she'd shrugged death off again, not being godlike enough to treasure every minute after all. The first time I survived being shot at (maybe they weren't shooting at me; maybe they didn't even see me), I pledged to be happier, to be grateful for my life, and in this I have succeeded, but I still have days when the catacombs and Dr. Stephens's autopsy slabs sink too far below my memory, and I despise and despair at life. Another fright, another horror, and I return to gratitude. The slabs rise up and stink to remind me of my happiness. A year before her terrible day, the one I'd loved had written: "They had to use four needles, four veins last time. I cried as they put the fourth needle in. My veins are not holding up. I vomited even before leaving the doctor's office and then spent four days semi-conscious, vomiting. I thought very seriously about immediate death. Could I overdose on the sleeping pills, I wondered . . . My choices aren't that many and I would like to be there to hate my daughter's boyfriends." I remember the letter before that on pink paper that began, "I know I said I wouldn't write. I lied. I've just been told this weekend that I have invasive breast cancer and will have a mastectomy and removal of the lymph nodes within the week. I am scared to death. I have three small kids . . . I am not vain. I do not care about my chest but I do want to live . . . So, tell me. This fear—I can smell it—is it like being in a war?" —Yes, darling. I have never been terminally ill, but I am sure that it is the same.

In one of her last letters she wrote me: "There was definitely a time when I thought I might die sooner rather than later—it took me awhile to believe that I would probably be okay. It still doesn't feel truly believable but more and more I want it to be the case—mostly because I want to raise my interesting and beautiful children and because I want to enjoy myself . . . My hair grew back to the point that I no longer use the wig."

In another letter she wrote me: "Here are the recent events in my life. I am not unhappy with them but they do not compare with being shot at and losing a friend and perhaps they will amuse you. I set up a fish tank in my study . . . I got the kids four fish. They named only one. I told them once they had learned to clean and change the tank and feed the fish and explain how gills work, then they could get a guinea pig. I am not into pets, preferring children. The one catfish in the tank is in great distress and swims around madly looking for a way to die."

When I close my eyes, I can see her as she looked at seventeen, and I can see her the way she was when she was thirty-four, much older, thanks in part to the cancer—bonier-faced, with sparse hair, perhaps a wig, sitting on the steps beside her children. I never had to see her in Dr. Stephens's viewing room. I never saw her body rotting. I'll never see her depersonalized skull mortared into a catacomb's wall. Does that mean I cannot envision death, her death? The six million death's-heads under Paris weigh on me much less than her face, which you might call too gaunt to be beautiful, but which was still beautiful to me, which only in a photograph will I ever see again.

But—again I return to this—her death was meaningless, an accident of genetics or environment. No evil soul murdered her. I am sad when I think about her. I am not bitter.

I am sad when I think about my two colleagues in Bosnia who drove into a land mine trap. Their names were Will and Francis. I will write about them later. At the time, because there were two distinct reports and holes appeared in the windshield and in the two dying men, I believed that they were shot, and when armed men approached I believed that I was looking at their killers. Will I had known only for two days, but I liked what I knew of him. Francis was my friend, off and on, for nineteen years. I loved Francis. But I was never angry, even when the supposed snipers came, for their actions could not have been personally intended. We were crossing from the Croatian to the Muslim side; the Muslims were sorry, and such incidents are common enough in war.

But now I open a letter from my Serbian friend Vineta, who often had expressed to me her dislike of Francis (whom she never met) on the grounds of his Croatian blood, and who, after commenting in considerable helpful and businesslike detail on my journalistic objectives in Serbia, then responded to my plans for the Muslim and Croatian sides of the story (my items seven and eight) as follows: "You see, dear Billy, it's very nice of you to let me know about your plans. But, I DON'T GIVE A SHIT FOR BOTH CROATS AND MUSLIMS!" At the end of her long note she added this postscript: "The last 'personal letter' I got was two years ago, from my late boy-friend. The Croats cut his body into pieces in the town of B—— near Vukovar. His name was M——." Then she wrote one more postscript: "No one has a chance to open my heart ever again."

This is what violence does. This is what violence is. It is not enough that death reeks and stinks in the world, but now it takes on inimical human forms, prompting the self-defending survivors to strike and to hate, rightly or wrongly. Too simple to argue that nonviolent death is always preferable from the survivors' point of view! I've heard plenty of doctors' stories about the families of dying cancer patients who rage against "fate." Like Hitler, they'd rather have someone to blame. "Everybody's angry when a loved one dies," one doctor insisted. "The only distinction is between directed and undirected anger." Maybe so. But it *is* a distinction. Leaving behind Dr. Stephens's tables, on which, for the most part, lie only the "naturally" dead with their bleeding pancreases, the accidentally dead and the occasional suicide, let us fly to besieged Sarajevo and look in on the morgue at Kosovo Hospital, a place I'll never forget, whose stench stayed on my clothes for two days afterward. Here lay the homicides. I saw children with their bellies blown open, women shot in the head while they crossed the street, men hit by some well-heeled sniper's antitank round. Death joked and drank and vulgarly farted in the mountains all around us, aiming its weapons out of hateful fun, making the besieged counterhateful. Every morning I woke up to chittering bullets and crashing mortar rounds. I hated the snipers I couldn't see because they might kill me and because they were killing the people of this city, ruining the city in every terrible physical and psychic way that it could be ruined, smashing it, murdering wantonly, frightening and crushing. But their wickedness too had become normal: this was Sarajevo in the fourteenth month of the siege. Needs lived on; people did business amidst their terror, a terror which could not be sustained, rising up only when it was needed, when one had to run. As for the forensic doctor at Kosovo Hospital, he went home stinking of death, and, like me, sometimes slept in his clothes; he was used to the smell, and his wife must have gotten used to it, too, when she embraced him. (Meanwhile, of course, some people had insomnia, got ulcers or menstrual disturbances, went prematurely grey. Here, too, undirected anger might surface.) Political death, cancer death, it's all the same. The night after Will and Francis were killed, a U.N. interpreter from Sarajevo told me how she lost friends almost every week. "You become a little cold," she said very quietly. "You have to." This woman was sympathetic, immensely kind; in saying this she meant neither to dismiss my grief nor to tell me how I ought to be. She merely did the best thing that can be done for any bereaved person, which was to show me her own sadness, so that my sadness would feel less lonely; but hers had wearied and congealed; thus she told me what she had become. Like Dr. Stephens and his crew, or the backpack inspector at the catacombs, like my friend Thion who ferries tourists to Choeung Ek on his motorcycle, I had already begun to become that way. Sarajevo wasn't the first war zone I'd been to, nor the first where I'd seen death, but I'll never forget it. The morgue at Kosovo Hospital, like the rest of Sarajevo, had had to make do without electricity, which was why, as I keep saying, it stank. I remember the cheesy smell of the Paris catacombs, the sour-milk smell of Dr. Stephens's white hearse; after that visit to Kosovo Hospital my clothes smelled like vomit, vinegar and rotting bowels. I returned to the place where I was staying, which got its share of machine gun and missile attacks, and gathered together my concerns, which did not consist of sadness for the dead, but only of being scared and wondering if I would eat anymore that day because they'd shot down the U.N. flight and so the airport was closed and I'd already given my food away. Death was on my skin and on the other side of the wall—maybe my death, maybe not; trying to live wisely and carefully, I granted no time to my death, although it sometimes snarled at me. Ascending from the catacombs I'd had all day, so I'd given death all day; no one wanted to hurt me. But in Sarajevo I simply ran; it was all death, death and death, so meaningless and accidental to me.

I wore a bulletproof vest in Mostar, which did get struck with a splinter of something which rang on its ceramic trauma plate, so to an extent I had made my own luck, but Will, who was driving, discovered that his allotted death was one which entered the face *now*, diagonally from the chin. His dying took forever (I think about five minutes). Vineta said that I had been cowardly or stupid not to end his misery. I told her that journalists don't carry guns. Anyhow, had I been in his seat, my bulletproof vest would have done me no good.

The woman I loved simply had the wrong cells in her breast; Vineta's boyfriend had fought in the wrong place at the wrong time, and perhaps he'd fought against the Croats too ferociously or even just too well. For the woman I loved, and for me in Sarajevo, the Angel of Death was faceless, but Vineta's tormenting Angel of Death had a Croatian face; she hated "those Croatian bastards." Vineta, if I could send the Angel of Death away from you, I would. Maybe someone who knows you and loves you better than I can at least persuade your Angel to veil his face again so that he becomes mere darkness like the Faceless One of Iroquois legends, mere evil chance, "an act of war," like my drowned sister's Angel; and then your anger can die down to sadness. Vineta, if you ever see this book of mine, don't think me presumptuous; don't think I would ever stand between you and your right to mourn and rage against the Angel. But he is not Francis. Francis was good. I don't like to see him stealing Francis's face when he comes to hurt you.

The Angel is in the white hearse. Can't we please proceed like Dr. Stephens's employees, weighing, fingerprinting, cutting open all this sad and stinking dross of violence, trying to learn what causes what? And when the malignity or the sadness or the unpleasantness of the thing on the table threatens to craze us, can't we tell a callous joke or two? If I can contribute to understanding how and why the Angel kills, then I'll be, in the words of that doctor who swilled coffee out of one bloody-gloved hand while he sliced a dead body with the other, "a happy customer." Hence this book. For its many failures I ask forgiveness from all.

INTRODUCTION

The Days of the Niblungs

The hatefulness and hard-heartedness of humans are simply without limit. Calling upon Heaven and weeping in pain, I lament my fate.

LADY HYEGYONG (Korean Crown Princess), Memoir of 1805

We've become too accustomed to making overall judgments. Isn't that, after all, the root of our superficial intolerance and dogmatism?

SVETLANA ALLILUYEVA (Stalin's Daughter), *Twenty Letters to a Friend*

In 1962, with the texture of any post–Cold War world unforeseeable, and atomic mushroom clouds further darkening her crystal ball, Hannah Arendt nonetheless bravely asked:

> Is it too much to read into the current rather hopeless confusion of is-
> sues and arguments a hopeful indication that a profound change in in-
> ternational relations may be about to occur, namely, the disappearance
> of war from the scene of politics even without a radical transformation
> of international relations and without an inner change of men's hearts
> and minds?

I would have to say, yes, it is too much.

The Immutability of Violence

Putting aside any notion that the world is becoming a better place was neither easy nor pleasant for me; and I've not yet given up believing both that the world *ought* to be better and that we have a duty to construct methods of improvement. But since yesterday's hopes are today's wishful thinking, how could anyone be entitled to suppose today's hopes to be any more plausible? Consider, for instance, poor Peter Kropotkin, Russian philosopher, whose well-meaning attempt to establish a scientific basis for ethics now seems as far-fetched as those of his Marxist-Leninist rivals. Convinced as he was that mutual aid is more prevalent and significant among members of most animal species than competition, that antediluvian anarchist spent his final years upon an essay rancid with senile optimism:

> But if we consider each of these lines [of human social development] separately, we certainly find in each of them, and especially in the development of Europe since the fall of the Roman Empire, a continual widening of the conception of mutual support and mutual protection, from the clan to the tribe, the nation, and finally the international union of nations . . . notwithstanding the temporary regressive movements which occasionally take place, there is—at least among the representatives of advanced thought in the civilized world and in the progressive popular movements— the tendency of always widening the current conception of human solidarity and justice, and of constantly improving the character of our mutual relations. We also mark the appearance, in the form of an ideal, of the conceptions of what is desirable in further development.

The United Nations notwithstanding, the unpersuasive impotence of these words is as good a gauge of evil on earth as the front page of any newspaper. Isolationism, greed, anger, fear, ethnic nationalism, racial and class hatred, murderous coldheartedness and native human viciousness, once called original sin, now more politely known as the aggressive propensity, continue to narrow justice even as the few seek and struggle to widen it elsewhere. None of the triumphal events which Kropotkin, Arendt, Thoreau, Tolstoy and so many others longed for and awarded themselves faith in have ever come to pass; or, if they have, they've been corroded and perverted from *ideals* fondly held into mere *reality* with its leaking faucets.

Yes, we now have "laws of war"—but we inhabit a planet continually poxed and plagued by wars in which the commission of atrocities remains normal. In the eighteenth century, Edward Gibbon ventured to claim that institutionalized violence against witchcraft no longer stains our planet, but just last week I read of the massacre in Africa of some alleged penis shrinkers. And isn't the violent suppression of magic merely a subcategory of proactive defense of creed, which slew multitudes under Stalin as it did under the Inquisition? Which outrages upon freedom, safety and peace have vanished? Rape, murder, torture, slavery and compulsion, censorship, war and institutionalized tyranny—the marks of all these I've seen with my own eyes. To be sure, the *forms* of them do vary, and so do their relative proportions and frequencies. Human sacrifice, for instance, is at present much less common than assassination and genocide as expressions of religious praxis. Violence no longer hovers over the ballot box in American cities; it's in other lands. Institutionalized slavery is neither as widespread nor as overt as it was two hundred years ago, although it can still be found in the Sudan, Thailand, Cambodia, the Philippines and doubtless a hundred other habitats for sweatshops, forced prostitution and indentured servitude. "Whatever is universal is natural," argues a Confederate churchman, and I think he is right. "We are willing that slavery should be tried by this standard." If humankind throughout history has condemned it, then our clergyman is prepared to abandon it forever. "But what if the overwhelming majority of mankind have approved it?" he says. And, if we take the long view, they have. "What is more ancient and more universal than slavery?" cries that desperate antislaver, that anarchist Bakunin. "Cannibalism perhaps." There you have it.

Bakunin, however, possesses sufficient nobility to argue that ubiquity need not prove either inherency nor (as the Confederate clergyman was claiming) necessity; and Bakunin is not only good but correct. We must never allow ourselves to believe that progress is impossible. At the same time, we need not delude ourselves that "history" has accomplished much in the way of human improvement. This is why Bakunin begs us, "Let us, then, never look back, let us look ever forward; for forward is our sunlight, forward our salvation." Fair enough; maybe the improvements will occur someday. It is with the hopeful backward-gazers that I take issue—with the rosy present-assessors, once their printed documents get backward-swirled by time.

Robespierre's nineteenth-century biographer, Lewes, may be considered a member of that deludedly hopeful crew, for he points out the fact that torture used to be legal before the French Revolution as "sufficient to indicate the immensity of the progress that has since been made." But a century later, Frenchmen were torturing Algerians. Indeed, torture, now in its renaissance, is committed by a third of all the governments on this earth. While such statistics may provide nourishments to certain of those scholarly rodents who infest archives, the telling fact is the sameness of the calamities we inflict upon one another. (Yes, the forms change; the shapes of the wounds change.)

Gandhi's biographer was forced to conclude that "his troughs of depression and his ceaseless activity were the repercussions of unacceptable and inexpressible anger." Christ violently turns the money changers out of the temple. A shocked mother wrote me that when her son was two years old, "he put on a suit of plastic armor and wouldn't take it off for weeks (a gift from a relative that we decided not to give him because of the sword and we'd hidden it ineffectually in a closet). He played war, planned battles. Weaponry wasn't part of my kids' vocabulary. His elder brother's idea of war was to play chess. But he made both offensive and defensive weapons out of Duplos and the Duplo giraffe became a fire gun. I couldn't imagine where Mikey the tactical warrior came from."

Induction leads to the conclusion that human behavior winds on morally unaltered, and probably unalterable. "Now the earth was corrupt in God's sight," says the book of Genesis, "and the earth was filled with violence. And God saw the earth, and behold, it was corrupt; for all flesh had corrupted their way upon the earth." If violence is a kind of dust that lies inside the house of the soul, there does not seem to be any way to sweep it out the door. We can only sweep it into one corner or another. Go back fifty thousand years to the Neanderthal man whom archaeologists would find "frontally stabbed in the chest by a right-handed antagonist." To murder is not only human, but protohuman. A millennium and a half before Homer, the men of Uruk were complaining in their houses of clay: "No son is left to his father, for Gilgamesh takes them all, even the children; yet the king should be a shepherd to his people. His lust leaves no virgin to her lover, neither the warrior's daughter nor the wife of the noble; yet this is the shepherd of the city, wise, comely, and resolute." The gods listened, and what did they do? They created a companion warrior for Gilgamesh so that he'd leave his own city in peace and go with his new friend to slay the guardian of the Land of Cedars!

Causation and Justification

We can, if we wish, invoke a dialectical explanation. Thesis gives birth to antithesis. Lincoln's Emancipation Proclamation, combined with victory over the Confederacy, brings into being the Ku Klux Klan. Violent expressions of French and U.S. imperialism in Cochin China create the Vietcong. Nehru's secular modernization in India nourishes vicious Hindu and Muslim fundamentalism. And what is the resulting synthesis which dialecticians demand? It is *change by means of blood*. Administrations, bureaucracies, leaders, governments, nations, even whole peoples come and go; nobody, however, can change human nature. Some, like Prussian general Moltke the Elder, wouldn't want to. To them, eternal peace is a bad dream.

> So blossom the days of the Niblungs, and great is their hope's increase
> 'Twixt the merry days of the battle and the tide of their guarded peace.

Nor, for that matter, can the fact of *change* be changed. The dream of a Hitler or a Robespierre to create a New Man, the project of a Roger Williams to create a New Commonwealth, must be doomed a priori to supersession by somebody newer—in whom, we must grant, much of the old will remain. (Trotsky, having complained about Taine's parochial view of the French Revolution, went on to say: "A still greater perspective is needed to view the October Revolution. Only hopeless dullards can quote as evidence against it the fact that in twelve years it has not yet created general peace and prosperity." In 1929 this was a fair statement. In 1979 it would not have been.) History suggests, therefore, that whatever a revolution may achieve, its effects upon *morality* (unlike, say, its effects upon *culture*) will be temporary and local. Likewise, "the result in war is never absolute"— the same goes for the result of any act except perfect genocide.

The Mutability of Violent Forms

Someone will certainly invent new institutions for the mediation of human behavior. The Christian religion, the automobile, Communist praxis, Lincoln's Emancipation Proclamation and repeating rifles, for instance, have all altered their respective milieus considerably, and the number of such inventions is potentially inexhaustible. But, as that Neanderthal homicide proved, human violence itself cannot be altered without altering human nature. "Vice and virtue form the destinies of the earth," said Robespierre; and on the day that that is no longer true, there will be no more human beings as we understand them.

My premise may be quarreled with on the grounds that certain movements have in fact permanently and drastically altered the moral condition of entire societies. This is true and not true. In the Muslim countries which I have visited, for example, I generally feel safer from robbery and violent attack than I do in my own. This ambiance of safety—no, of outright helpfulness, of deeply felt hospitality and kindness (as long as a jihad has not been declared against me)—is in some measure due to the teachings of the Qur-'An. So many times I've heard: "No, no, I'm a Muslim; I *must* help you; you are a stranger in my country!" —Truthfulness, temperance and chastity, too (for some reason there are those who respect it), are more frequently met there than in non-Muslim countries such as Thailand and Madagascar. And yet, while I'll always prize my memories of the multitudinous undeserved favors which I've received in the nations of the Crescent, can I honestly claim that Muslims are more free or more moral ("better") than non-Muslims?

To a Muslim, one is either inside or outside the law. Certain generous souls may grant outsiders honorary status; thus to some Pakistanis, Afghans and Somalis, the fact that I had been born in a Christian country was sufficient to elect me; I was one of the "People of the Book." But what about Buddhists? They seem no less decent than anyone else. And yet most of the friends I made in Islamic countries regarded them almost as animals. (One old Afghan brigadier kept telling me: "They are *wild,* my dear son. Wild like horse, like donkey; they are not people.") There was a narrowness, an exclusiveness and sometimes a simple excluding-ness. And again, my friends were all men. We were excluded from the world of women. It would have been *shameful* (a common term of judgment) to have women friends. Because I had lived under other conditions, I knew what we and the women were missing in not being allowed to talk to one another. Perhaps the loss was justified; perhaps not. One could say, though, that a mind to whom some categories are prescribed and other categories are proscribed must be a mind prone to categorize, at least as far as those "others" are concerned, on the basis of insufficient information. I remember how in Egypt I was talking with some men about Salman Rushdie. They all said that the author of *The Satanic Verses* deserved to die for mocking Islam. None of them had read the book, and none planned to: a fine illustration of the vice of the committed mind—the revolutionary mind, if you will. After all, the more used one is to acting, the less time one has for thinking. As Solzhenitsyn writes disgustedly of the Soviet regime:

> Should we wrap it all up and simply say they arrested the *innocent*? But we omitted saying that the very concept of *guilt* had been repealed by the proletarian revolution and, at the beginning of the thirties, was defined as *rightist opportunism!* So we can't even discuss those out-of-date concepts, guilt and innocence.

The Muslims I met, in short, were in my opinion less likely than Americans to be violent thieves and more likely to be violent ideologues. Doubtless homicide, assault, rape and burglary rates varied: by such measures, one group would probably come out as more violent than another at any given time, or perhaps even (who knows?) for all time.

RISK OF BEING MURDERED (1995)

In Japan:	0.6 per 100,000
In the U.S.:	8.2 per 100,000

But that hardly proves that we won't find murder anywhere and everywhere . . .

Is Violence Displaceable, Eliminable, Sublimatible or Stimulable?

"Somehow or other, order, once it reaches a certain stage, calls for bloodshed." So does disorder. To deny that is to deny yourself. In Merleau-Ponty's words, "A regime which is nominally liberal can be oppressive in reality. A regime which acknowledges its violence *might* have in it more genuine humanity." Our society devours itself with violence because we are not completely homogenous (which means, according to the definitions of social insects, that we fail to entirely compose a society) and because we cannot devour others. The two go together: To devour others is to become homogenous, and to become homogenous is to devour others (or at least otherness). But that solution, the way of pogroms and invasions, doesn't appeal to our tastes sufficiently for us to kill more than a thousand in Panama, let's say a hundred thousand in Iraq (plus or minus uncounted thousands) and suchlike very occasional orgasms. —Good. —Another way might be the way of the Roman circuses. Were our future mass murderers given the chance to kill one another on television, the whole being government-taxed and glamorized, it is conceivable that the level of *uncontrolled* violence would sink. When Julius Caesar, pretended man of the people, furnished for the people's pleasure 320 pairs of gladiators whose armor was made of pure silver, did he therewith not only honor his dead father and buy goodwill for his tyrannical projects, after the fashion of the period, but also sustain civic tranquility through the sympathetic magic? —An affirmative answer presupposes (which might not be true) that the amount of death lust is finite at any one time, so that by opening a legitimate channel for it we leave less to flow into illegitimate channels. (In a carnelian intaglio from the first century A.D., we see a man in a fish-crested helmet holding in front of him a long slender shield which resembles a beetle's wing. He himself is buglike, the only remotely expressive part of him being his stance: resigned, bracing himself, one knee forward, his sword lost behind the shield. Like a friendly dog, a lion is jumping up into his face.) However, I have before me a monograph on gladiators which posits a negative answer. Dismissing what he calls "the dubious 'hydraulic' theory of violence," our scholar, Robert Wiedemann, cites evidence that (1) the Romans believed that gladiatorial spectacles hardened citizens to fighting and wounds, so that they'd be better soldiers; that (2) the trainers of gladiators sometimes drilled recruits; and that (3) Roman legions deployed in the distant provinces constructed their own arenas and sometimes actually owned troupes of gladiators, which apparently "reassured Roman soldiers far from home that they were part of the Roman community"—in short, that gladiatorial violence *stimulated, emblematized or facilitated* military violence. And did military violence diminish civilian violence? (Send our soldiers marching as far as their legs will carry them, an aristocrat advised shortly before the French Revolution. That way they can't return to cut our throats.) The case is almost impossible to prove. Meanwhile the games go on (Romans attended them for six hundred years). A Vestal Virgin sits in the front row, and the fourth-century poet Prudentius is watching her. "What a sweet and gentle spirit she has! She leaps up at each stroke, and every time the victorious gladiator plunges his sword into his opponent's neck, she calls him her sweetheart." Do her thrills make her more violent, or do they actually waft away her desire to pinch her fellow Vestals when they annoy her? The latter would seem to be

Trotsky's assumption: he claims that in Russia after the failed 1905 revolution, terrorist acts (assassinations) increased as the ability of the masses to strike weakened: one way or another, the revolutionary impetus must come out. All we have to do is decide how we want to express it.

The prevalence of infanticide in the U.S. has considerably decreased as a result of increased availability of abortion. And yet we read of a dead baby; the list of her bone fractures and dislocations, some old, some new, takes up almost an entire page. The mother explains that "two days prior to the child's death she had twisted its arms and legs because her crying had been so annoying." One gets the sense that her offspring had annoyed her often. Violence had become a habit. Could it have been directed against punching bags instead of human flesh? We don't know.

A woman gets raped in an elevator by a man she's never met. The police spokesman states the obvious: "It appears to be a crime of opportunity." Had a different woman ridden that elevator with that man, the chances are that she would have been the victim instead. It was not any particular victim but the rapist's *uncontrolled need* which provoked the crime. How could he have controlled it, then? Perhaps he could not.

A woman hires a contract killer to murder her husband. But by the time the killer (actually an undercover cop) comes to her home to discuss the details, she's decided to kill her boyfriend's wife instead. Had she not been arrested, who knows whom her wandering impulses might have chosen to murder next?

In all three of these newspaper cases, the victims seem to be mere placeholders, almost accidental outlets. Violence rises up and takes the sacrifices it finds. It employs the means that it finds. It even takes whatever motives it finds. How could some benevolent hyperrationalist cabal ever eliminate murder by eliminating the reasons for murder, when in different countries we find such different reasons—and varied objects? We read that "when Soga [tribespeople] and Philadelphia Negroes kill kinsmen, they kill spouses; when Danes kill kinsmen they kill their children." If we could ever stop Danes from killing their children, would they more or less stop all killing, or would they switch to killing their spouses, or their parents? The obvious (if presently unverifiable) answer is that they would switch. Homicide rates do vary over time and between populations, but they never reach zero.

Out of almost thirteen hundred murderers arrested in Japan in 1995, the two leading causes out of twelve (which were mostly quite specific) were, in this order, "grudge" and "other." There went two-thirds of the cases! In the United States during the same year, the most common murder circumstance was "unknown." Next came homicides committed in the course of a felony (robbery and drug offenses being the most common of these). Then came nonfelony homicides, of which the following two highly illuminating categories ranked first and second: "other arguments" and "other—not specified."

One American criminologist vaguely speaks of "defective ethical standards" as the causative agent in nonsociopathic homicides. But there have always been murders, no matter what the general ethical tone. If the general tone is defective, then we know only what we knew before.

In cases of strictly expedient violence, action is readily susceptible to expedient change. If only there were a good war . . . Do homicides in fact go down in wartime? The imprisoned anarchist Alexander Berkman describes how during the Spanish-American War "the patriotic Warden daily read to the diners the latest news, and such cheering and wild yelling you have never heard . . . The Warden admits that the war has decreased crime; the prison population is lower than it has been in over a decade." In fact, the data is wildly at variance on this matter also. In England, Wales and Scotland, for instance, per capita murder rates actually increased in 1943–45. Hence some people argue that violence stimulates itself, so that digging any legitimate channel only increases the scarlet flow through all the other creek beds that raddle our rock. (I have often noticed as I read the morning paper that certain kinds of homicide [drive-by-shootings, parental killing of children, et cetera] seem to occur in spates, as if the perpetrators had been reading the newspaper, too.) This question can be resolved only by experimentation (which we possess neither the courage nor the intelligence nor the malignant cold-bloodedness to permit).

Even more optimistic than this is our would-be wise and gentle guardian, the United Nations, which essentially follows the theory of placeholders, advising us to work against handgun possession, make cars more theft-proof, teach urban planners to design crime-unfriendly cities and generally to save ourselves through social engineering, my favorite being this:

> Further analysis of the relationship between violence and levels and types of alcohol consumption seems worthwhile to assess whether some governments should reassess fiscal policy with a view to discouraging the consumption of beer.

In other words, let's all become more hardened targets. This is the principle of arms races, but its practicality is not undisputed. If all cars become more theft-proof, then I believe all burglars will merely become better thieves.

I happen to own a wonderful volume called *The American Boy's Handy Book* (1882), whose purpose is as follows:

> Let boys make their own kites and bows and arrows; they will find a double pleasure in them, and value them accordingly, to say nothing of the education involved in the successful construction of their home-made playthings.
>
> The development of a love of harmless fun is itself no valueless consideration. The baneful and destroying pleasures that offer themselves with almost irresistible fascination to idle and unoccupied minds find no place with healthy activity and hearty interest in boyhood sports.

This is a laudable approach. Times have changed, of course. Of the various activities that the book suggests, most are out of fashion, either because Baneful & Destroying Pleasures & Co. can make and sell better items for less than we would pay if we made them ourselves, as with kites and water telescopes; or because our abuse of the environment has rendered them unethical, as with owl-stuffing, egg-collecting, mole-trapping, jug-fishing; or because we consider them too dangerous, as with blowing soap bubbles from gas pipes, or making lethal boomerangs, blowguns and spring shotguns. Up until very recently, most societies would have considered these activities innocent and rewarding. What do we teach our children to do instead? —I remember the boy who cried and screamed and punched his playmates because he couldn't put his robots together; his parents had to do it for him. He was not a rich little boy, and he wasn't poor; he had a pretty average toy chest, all things of someone else's invention, most requiring four batteries before they'd greet him, all doing things by themselves, leaving him only to sit and watch. He couldn't murder moles or build his own kite for the summer kite wars, so he punched his playmates instead. I knew him for several years, and I never saw him happy until the day his mother took him to the fort where every day at noon the soldiers "volunteer" people to load the cannon. The little boy loved guns. Seeing how rapt he was, the soldiers picked him among others, and gave him a job which one would have thought to be beyond his strength: to take the cannonball from another volunteer and insert it into the barrel of the great weapon. The boy, who almost never did anything his parents told him, obeyed the soldiers' loud curt orders in ecstasy. He tried to march like them; he listened and watched; he was a part of something at last. —*"Now, son,"* one of the soldiers shouted, *"if these other men are killed, your job is to DO YOUR JOB and KILL THE ENEMY. Understand?"* —And the little boy nodded and took the cannonball and staggered with it to the cannon, while the drums sounded and all the Americans clapped . . .

Toward a Moral Calculus

No credo will eliminate murder. But if we think about a sufficient number of cases we may be able to plant the seeds of a tentative ethics which others could consider, pick and choose from and hopefully benefit from even if they cannot improve. That is my hope for this book. I know that other people's advice has rarely made me better than I was. When it has, it was less often the advice itself than the spirit in which it was given which helped me, requiring me out of sheer respectful reciprocity to listen, search and consider, like Saint Ignatius being guided by an old woman to seek his own God as if he were a hunter employing all craft in a dark and wild forest. As it is, I wish that I were a more worthy person to embark upon this project called *Rising Up and Rising Down*. I am not a theoretician. Nor have I seen enough, suffered enough or thought enough about violence. I have never been tortured; I haven't *lived* in the mouth of violence; I've only paid a few visits. In a hopeful rather than confident spirit I close my research, and offer this book to you. My own life is also of value to me (this is an explanation, not an excuse), and I do not really want to see or suffer or think about violence any more than I have to—not that I can get away from it, either. In other words, the suffering of others shames me and awes me but does not invite my emulation. This essay will therefore be more broad than deep.

What Is Truth?

How does one begin an inquiry such as this? To describe universal forces, one must by definition take many excursions into alienness, where the pattern may be tested, but also where one's own ignorance makes it very easy to be deceived. A handbook for intelligence officers offers the following metaphor: "A cow can turn grass into milk, but a further process is required in order to turn the milk into butter." In other words, gathering data is hardly the same as interpreting it. If it were, how could Robespierre be described by Carlyle as a "sea-green tyrant" when Lenin depicts the very same man as progressive within the limits of his class and even historically necessary?

Regard the four photographs of bruised and beaten men. A man from a human rights organization in Sanzak, Serbia, took them. He told me that they were Muslims who had been beaten by Serbs. I personally believe that these Muslims probably *were* beaten by Serbs (it is well known that Serbs did and do beat Muslims; my Muslim friends told me that the men in the pictures looked Muslim, and, Serbian violence against Muslims was widespread in 1994). But the photographs are inadmissible—or, I should say, incompletely admissible. I was not given permission to interview the victims, on the very rational grounds that since I was being watched by Serbian police this might subject them to further abuse. An observer is free, of course, to make his suppositions. But it would be irresponsible on

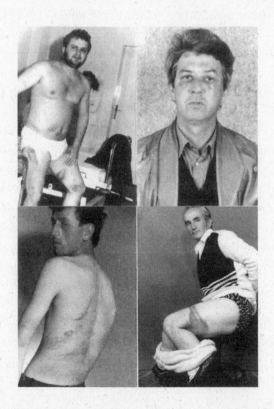

my part to claim anything definitive in this case, to claim even that these insufficiently identified men had in fact been beaten; the marks could be makeup. What would *you* do in such a case? Would you suspect, allege or accuse?

And what constitutes a large enough experiential sample to validate induction? My impression in 1991 of the Khmer Rouge cadres as scared, uneducated boys came from a single interview with captives in the presence of the prison's deputy director. Of course they would be scared. Only if I put myself into their power would I know for certain exactly how they tortured and swaggered. That is why I went back years later and sought to give myself into their hands (not that they would meet me except one or two on one, scared and uneducated again, lurking). My impressions hadn't changed. But I knew perfectly well that whatever I might find to substantiate or undermine my previous opinions of the "Khmer Rouge personality" would not be enough, would merely obligate me to return again and again, until I chose either to abandon the uncompleted work (for in this world no inquiry can ever be completed), or else to press on and pay the ultimate price, which I was unwilling to do. Subsequent interviews continued to confirm my perception of their scared ignorance. But how much did I fail to see? At border points, I was frequently advised by the Khmer Rouge themselves or their sympathizers that I was likely to lose my life if I proceeded in this direction or that direction, and I always heeded that advice. What do I know, then? Not what a Khmer Rouge cadre knows.

And Khun Sa, the Opium King—did he truly lead a Shan liberation movement? I saw only the tiniest piece of Shan State; I could not say for sure how many Shan supported and revered him. The fact that almost everybody I met praised him before he could possibly have known that I was coming suggests that he truly was well regarded. But again, he himself I met only once. Had I limited myself to writing about Khun Sa over the past decade, I would no doubt have known more about him than I do. But then I would have known less about the Khmer Rouge. As I said, I chose broad knowledge, not deep. Even had I chosen depth, my conviction that Khun Sa was a good man could never be demonstrated to anyone's satisfaction in the way that the fact of whether or not the men in the photograph were Muslims beaten by Serbs could have been discovered once and for all. For we human beings scarcely know ourselves, let alone others.

On the Pleasures of Making Authoritative Statements

Many traps have been prepared for the amusement of the gargoyles who overwatch the generalist's path. The common snare is that of casting inductions based on mere personal experience (as might be the case with my opinion of Khun Sa). I do not deny that experience is essential in this work. In fact, one cannot have enough of it. Sooner or later the intriguing things, the colorful things, the logical things pile up; one begins to feel informed, longs to fit them into a theory that will show them off to best advantage. Eventually the "big thing" happens. One gets permission at last to pass the secret way into Opium City, or one's friends are killed before one's eyes, or one witnesses something special on a walrus hunt. Certainly such occurrences impart knowledge of a sort, but only within a more or less local context. Yet to those even less well informed, one has become an "authority." An authority is by nature noxious, a windbag, a parasite, a professional vulture. One such bird of prey crowed: "The greatest moment of my professional life was standing in the Piazza Loretto, Milan, on April 29, 1945, literally amid the bodies of Mussolini, [his mistress Clara] Petacci, and the others." This is not only despicable but dangerous. This journalist standing over Mussolini's corpse (did he trail his toes in the blood?) might be inclined to pontificate on the nature and destiny of Italian fascism; and doubtless the experience would impart the sort of cachet accepted by sensationalists. But what would he necessarily know about Italian fascism, even were he Italian and a fascist? —More than I, but more is not enough. —They say that Soviet frontline officers in action against the Nazis thought that they had seen it all, but death in Stalin's prison camps was entirely a different sort of death. Solzhenitsyn was for eleven years a prisoner in those camps. He suffered, bore witness, had, one would think, the necessary experience. His account of the day-to-day struggle there, *One Day in the Life of Ivan Denisovich*, deserves our appalled respect. Yes, he can be called an authority, an expert. But Solzhenitsyn himself says that "the Kolyma was the greatest and most famous island, the pole of ferocity of that amazing country of *Gulag*." The man with the unhappy fortune to be an expert on Kolyma was Varlam Shalamov, and Solzhenitsyn asked him to collaborate with him on his grimly impressive three-volume history of the camps. Shalamov, old, sick and tired, declined. Solzhenitsyn writes of him in reverent terms, as if he, not Solzhenitsyn, had had the privilege of staring into evil's face. What did Shalamov pay for this opportunity? Seventeen years of his life, the ruin of his life, the destruction of his health, the wounding of his capacity for interest in life, trust and other human beings, of his very integrity. When the brilliant *Kolyma Tales* was published abroad, Shalamov was pressured into denouncing the people who'd sought thus to do homage to his genius. He possessed the authority; he had won it; keeping it was not worth his further suffering. His own translator wrote that this shocked "his former admirers so deeply that some literally removed his portrait from their homes. [Shalamov had] betrayed his own major achievement." If this is the price required for the sad knowledge that swarms between the lines of *Kolyma Tales* like lice, better to forgo it. Books like mine suffer as a result of just that decision to forgo, the attendant flaws being speculation in the place of certainty, ignorant misstatements, dilettantism and mere adventurism.

Statistical Niceties

There is a natural tendency on the part of any investigator to believe that "doing one's homework" will solve all these conundrums; but more often than we would like to believe, research will prove merely necessary, not sufficient. For example, a quick browse through one or two reference books ought to yield a reasonably consistent figure as to the number of Pol Pot's victims. One source gives the figure of "300,000+." Another proposes a number from 800,000 to one million. A third insists on "more than three million." Thus the first estimate differs from the last by an entire order of magnitude. Doubtless in ten or a hundred years the whole thing will be settled. (In 1995, when I first wrote this paragraph, not even the present population of Cambodia was certain.) In the meantime, if one wishes to interview living, breathing revolutionaries and then characterize them while one is still oneself living and breathing, the only way is to rely on contemporary data—a difficulty which would afflict even the Shalamovs, unless they somehow gained access to secret archives—and even then we may be dealing with the statements of those who, as Roosevelt remarked to Churchill, "do not use speech for the same purposes that we do." In the Kolyma, Shalamov saw corpses by the thousand. How many more didn't he see? "I realized that I knew only a small bit of that world, that twenty kilometers away there might be a shack for geological explorers looking for uranium or a goldmine with thirty thousand prisoners. Much can be hidden in the folds of the mountain." In fact, in the Kolyma alone several *million* prisoners died.

What "Really" Happened?

As for old and "settled" data, the dust has indeed settled on it, to the point of blurring its truth. Can we trust Herodotus? —As a teller of moral fables, certainly (and in an ethical treatise such as this one, the presentation of exemplary choices will occasionally suffice). —As a historian, only with qualifications. —We are free, as we are in considering the Bible, to ask: If somebody did in fact commit the stated act, is it right or wrong? We cannot, however, say with certainty: the named person committed the stated act.

No Context, No Judgment

And this is but the beginning of the problem. Not only can we not be certain whether violence has occurred, and to what extent, but *sometimes we do not even know what violence is*. Most often, of course, it is all too clear.

Arendt might well reject this argument entirely, insisting that Shalamov's uncertainty as to exact numbers, even orders of magnitude, remains irrelevant. She witnessed the Eichmann trial and described the audience as "filled with 'survivors,' with middle-aged and elderly people, immigrants from Europe like myself, who knew by heart all there was to know." In her sense, Shalamov, Solzhenitsyn, those frontline officers and perhaps even that vulture of a journalist were also in the know, and would have had little trouble in understanding the workings of, say, Buchenwald, although there were stylistic differences between Buchenwald and Kolyma: the former place employed a "factory" for mass shootings rather than the Arctic cold; and its punishments often took the character of sadistic public displays accompanied by music, instead of solitary starvation in some ice-house. The fundamental purpose of both institutions remained the same: to convert human beings into objects living and nonliving, extracting ideological, psychological and commercial profits along the way. —But differences deeper than stylistic remained. In the Kolyma camps, escape was quixotic, given the location: a prisoner wandering around in the Arctic vastness hadn't much of a chance. Still, it was a choice; it empowered, and it affected only the individual involved. At Buchenwald, collective reprisal was the policy. Hence an escape would bring punishment to the inmates remaining behind. In short, escape from Kolyma was suicide; escape from Buchenwald was homicide. One cannot simply be told that somebody escaped "from a concentration camp" and be ethically in the know.

One more example of the need to everlastingly expand one's knowledge, to seek, listen, qualify: What constitutes rape? We think we have it figured out. It is sexual knowledge without consent, or sexual knowledge of a person deemed unable to comprehendingly consent, such as a minor or a mental incompetent. And, like violence generally, its lineaments are frequently unambiguous. Here, for instance, we find both of these kinds of rape rolled into one.

FISHERMAN RAPED HIS OWN DAUGHTER

SINGAPORE: A fisherman and part-time medium, who raped his 15-year-old daughter on 3 occasions 2 years ago, was sentenced to 20 years' jail and 18 strokes of the cane by the High Court yesterday [which] rejected the accused's defence that the rape report against him was a conspiracy by the victim and her elder sister because he had been harsh with them and had often beaten them very badly.

No matter how one looks at this, it would seem that either the fisherman beat his daughter (by his own testimony), or else he beat her and raped her. In any case, he abused her. Regardless of what the circumstances might have been, I think that the High Court was correct in judging that the man had done wrong.

But many such determinations are not so facile, as even the FBI has concluded. I once had the dismal opportunity of hearing both sides of a rape story. To the woman, at least, it was rape. She told me that the man had cornered her and tried to kiss her while she kept pleading, "I can't, I can't." Her remembered terror, helplessness, humiliation and disgust crawled across her face as she told it. He had grabbed her breasts. He had started to do other things, but her entreaties finally stopped him. She said that she had never been capable of mentioning this to a soul before, and she was speaking of it now only two years after the fact, because I knew the man (he was my friend) and because she trusted me and needed to tell somebody. —To the man it had been no big deal. A rough fellow from a rough town, he was accustomed to casually aggressive methods of courtship. She had a boyfriend? So what? They were alone, after all. He gave it a whirl, but she wasn't in the mood, so that was that. Had he been told that what he had done was attempted rape, he would have shrugged incredulously. Hadn't he stopped when she said, "I can't"? Had he hurt her? Had he left marks? Call it an exploratory grope. Such divergence is to be expected, for when did victim and violator ever agree?

I think that given the norms of the area this was *not* attempted rape— merely insensitivity carried almost to brutality. To equate it with actual forcible penetration is to remove our ability to graduate in comprehension, judgment and penalty between these two very unhomogenous wrongs. But now reflect upon still another case, seemingly quite similar, for it, too, involves kissing and breast-grabbing.

COPS LOOKING FOR MOLEST CASE SUSPECT

PENANG: Police are looking for a factory bus driver who allegedly fondled the breasts of a 23-year-old woman in Air Itam here recently . . . It is learnt that the suspect also kissed the woman.

Malaysia being a Muslim country, what the bus driver did was very likely a terrible assault upon the woman's pride and sacred secretness. She must have been veiled, in which case his kissing her would have been as much an act of exposure, of humiliation, as his snatching her breasts into his hands. Call it rape. When I asked my Thai companion, D., how she would have responded had he done this to her, she said, "Me? Maybe I laugh. Don't like so much. Maybe little bit angry, but I try to talk to him. I think he need some girlfriend. Maybe I say to him, you very silly boy."

The conclusion I come to (one abhorrent to any local law, but agreeable to the contradictions of international customs) is that a major defining ethical constituent of violence is *the unique relationship between each victim and perpetrator at a given time.* That is why even the sternly consistent Martin Luther warns the sixteenth-century German princes that they must be guided by their own minds and consciences in any given case of legal judgment—and why it is permissible, for instance, for somebody to kill one person in wartime but not another, and neither one in peacetime. And if the motive and the context are so crucial, then we must ask whether one can with equal justification kill out of hatred, out of fear, out of rational self-defense or out of mercy?

Arendt, musing upon the "pale" and "ghostlike" figure of the accused Eichmann in his glass booth, insisted: "If he suffers, he must suffer for what he has done, not for what he has caused others to suffer." As a general rule this principle is demonstrably untrue. D., a live-and-let-live Buddhist from a sexually more easy country than Malaysia (the rural markets usually have on the walls colored advertising posters with photos of naked women), would not have suffered what the twenty-three-year-old Muslim woman presumably did. I know this because I know D. This is not to say that she would have suffered nothing; for in public life Thais are sufficiently modest that the public kissing of European lovers inspires them with disgust. Nor would that brute of a bus driver be any more justified in fondling her than he would have in the case of a Muslim girl. But D. never wore a veil. She would have been kissed without being uncovered. In short, she would have been humiliated, not raped. She would have shrugged it off and tried not to be shamed; the Muslim girl might well have been hurt to the core. And had, let's say, a man in Mexico City done this to D., and not a bus driver whom she could not get away from but a seatmate whose escalating flirting she had ignored; had the bus also, let's say, been filled with drunken soccer players who were groping giggling cheerleaders at least some of whom desired an orgy, I would, again, not excuse the brute, but I would be slightly less angry, thinking of him (as I do of my friend from the rough town) as someone who didn't know where to stop as opposed to someone who coolly initiated something. And I would think even worse of the Malaysian bus driver had he forced his attentions on the woman if no other passengers were on the bus than if the bus were crowded; for if the bus were empty the woman would feel more alone and helpless, the act hence more the vicious one of intimidation, domination and humiliation. If the same action can cause significantly different degrees of injury to different victims, then the deed itself cannot be adequately described without context.

Arendt gets around this by substituting the social fabric as a whole for the personal vagaries of any victim—a Kantian strategy which

> may be rendered by saying that the undeserved evil which anyone commits on another is to be regarded as perpetrated on himself . . . This is the right of retaliation (jus talionis); and . . . is the only principle which in regulating a public court, as distinguished from mere private judgement, can definitely assign both the quality and the quantity of a just penalty.

Thus Eichmann's genocide was in Nuremberg parlance a crime against humanity because it attacked human diversity, without which the whole concept of humanity becomes reduced to ethnicity or nationality. This argument is valid in Eichmann's case, and would remain so if his expertise had killed only one person instead of millions; who except the suicidally inclined (whose case will be taken up later in this book) would be at variance over the ultimate negativity of death? Had the Malaysian molester done his deed not with a kiss but with a dagger, then D. and the woman on the bus would have been more equally harmed. If not, then the merely normative approach fails to hold.

Interestingly enough, the importance of context from the other point of view—the aggressor's—was recognized up to a point even at Nuremberg. Just as the military court which tried and sentenced the assassins of President Lincoln endured (and probably instigated) experts' haggles on whether they were mentally or morally insane—in the end, they decided that the law didn't care—so too the Nuremberg tribunal ground through the motions of debate as to whether Rudolf Hess was sane enough to stand trial. In Churchill's memoirs he's implied to be mad; and the prosecutor Telford Taylor portrays a defendant rarely able to concentrate, listen or remember. The remarkable point is that the issue was raised at all. In the end, expediency, justice or perhaps vindictiveness won out, and Hess was tried. A decade and a half later, so was Eichmann, who displayed a different sort of madness. I wish that Kant had been there, for vis-à-vis the "I just followed orders" defense the philosopher expresses agreement: "The good or bad consequences arising from the performance of an obligated action—as also the consequences arising from failing to perform a meritorious action—cannot be imputed to the agent (modus imputationis poneus)." The implication is that the social medium in which one swims (or, as Kant probably would have preferred to put it, the institutional uniform in which one clothes oneself) automatically justifies the actions which it condones and commands. By conforming and obeying, the Eichmanns are exculpated. I would have loved to see the look on the chief prosecutor's face. —Well, if I'd been there when Eichmann was speaking, I guess I would have seen it; for this was precisely the argument which that monster used. Whether one agrees with his line or not (and I don't), it surely makes a difference to our moral or metaphysical understanding of his crimes ("I committed mass murder")—as opposed to our juridical comprehension ("I upheld my obligation to authority," or perhaps the very different "I violated the international laws against war crimes")—whether Eichmann donned the livery of the state in 1939 or simply flew the colors of a nonrepresentative cabal whose "agent" he was. In one case (the most likely one), the regime made him what he was. In the other, he would have done it regardless, like the opportunistic rapist in the elevator. Either way, let's hang him, but if the first cause is the dominant one, then we've learned that there's something very useful we can do with our lives: study Nazism in detail, in order to discover how to prevent it from coming to life again. If the second case gets privileged, it's more utilitarian to study the various Eichmanns.

Is Justice Objective or Passionate?

Hence perpetrator, deed and victim must all be considered—taking care, by all means, never to *underweigh* the deed, either, which might for an apologist (e.g., a Holocaust revisionist) be all too convenient in any case where the identity and circumstances of violence are clear, as they were for, say, Shalamov, no apologist in spite of his other sins, who looked silently on from within his scorched and frozen rags while the bulldozer transferred bodies to another mass grave. Here the individuality of victims and perpetrators remains immaterial to our judgment: by their very numbers, the dead in that pit constitute a silent scream of crime. We know all we need to know (except, of course, how to stop it next time). Understanding, even empathy, must not lure us into active sympathy. (I "understand" Eichmann—how pitiable he is!) Should I fail to come out and say that what happened there in Kolyma or Buchenwald was wrong, then I'll stand available for the friendship of all the killers I meet, in which case I can be worthy of Luther's sarcastic question to the easygoing Erasmus: "Perhaps you have in mind to teach the truth so that the Pope does not object, Caesar is not enraged, bishops and princes are not upset, and furthermore no uproar and turmoil are caused in the wide world, lest many be offended and grow worse?" The Soviet battle correspondent Ilya Ehrenburg remarked more bluntly still that all journalists who report a war objectively ought to be shot. Such a position is not only foul (presumably, it saves Soviet murderers from uproar and turmoil), it is also 50 percent likely to be wrong—a demonstration of which was left us by the bilious genius of Thucydides. Over and over in his pages we meet a city-state on the eve of decision. Two delegations come before the assembly, representing arch-foes. The web of their war has widened. Now it's reached this city previously neutral and exempt, and the grim drama begins. Soon, one of the two rivals will be the city's friend, and the other will be the enemy.

There'll be as little room for neutrality as in Ignatius's spiritual exercises, in which the meditator must choose between the army of Christ and the army of Satan. "In critical moments," a revolutionary warns, "to declare oneself neutral is to expose oneself to the anger of both contending parties." This is not a moral judgment, nor a paraphrase of Ehrenburg, but a very practical and realistic social law. For expedient reasons alone the choice must be made. Ah, but who is Christ and who is Satan? In 1632, a Protestant landgrave, about to be dragged into the Thirty Years' War, asks the wise men: "If his princely Grace is forced to choose between one of the two warring parties in the Empire, . . . with which side must he unite himself?" The assembly listens anxiously, trying to decide that very question. In turn the competitors address them in all sweet reasonableness, justifying their actions, offering civil affection, threatening the reverse and, of course, denying each other's goodness and very legitimacy. Much in these speeches consists of the merest rhetorical garnish of expediency, and it is most likely on expedient considerations that this assembly will shortly decide which of the two city-states, spurned, its representatives stalking back to their waiting ship, will shortly send bronze-armored infantry to lay waste the houses, fields and vineyards it so lately visited in a state of suppliant or commanding neutrality; and which city-state will send relief and protection (or, if the assembly guessed wrongly, send nothing). —Which side is stronger? Make *them* our ally!

And yet for those who listen, worry and debate, whether or not we can be menaced or advantaged by either side, the issue of right and wrong remains. —If those issues were irrelevant, the Spartans, say (renowned for their practicality), would hardly bother to mention liberating the Hellenes from Athenian tyranny; they'd speak merely with arrow, javelin and sword. —But no, I forgot: An appeal to *justice* is most *expedient!* It can't hurt, and it may trick a couple of archons into voting for my side (if only the other side doesn't do the same!). Anyone who's still trying to make up his mind where justice lies ought to be shot!

Now the speeches of the first city-state are over. As the opposing delegates rise, the assemblymen of the host city, one can be sure, sit tense, because they *must* choose and this is their sole remaining chance to know both sides before it comes to a vote. Ehrenburg's sin is not that he has already chosen, but that he would deny us our right to choose, without which we bear no responsibility, without which we join the guiltless inhuman legions in whose ranks Eichmann enrolled himself.

Indeed the Ehrenburgian stance proves empirically as well as morally unsound, there being data which it absolutely cannot explain. Tito's former deputy, Milovan Djilas, admits that when he and other committed Yugoslav Communists were entertained by a British major in Iraq,

> in our doctrinaire way we could not understand how it was possible, much less rational, to sacrifice oneself "for imperialism"—for so we regarded the West's struggle [against Hitler]—but to ourselves we marveled at the heroism and boldness of the British.

Ehrenburg's position does have its place in a desperate war, for propaganda can help people to fight, and counterpropaganda, if effective, becomes treason; but there must be a clear understanding that at a specific moment the blinders will be pulled off—say, at the instant of the enemy surrender (or one's own). No doubt Ehrenburg approved of the procedure followed by the Nuremberg Trials, which years after the German defeat refused to admit evidence of Soviet atrocities comparable to those of the Nazis who were being hanged.

When I first got called for jury duty in California—and every other time, too—the judge, sitting high between flags, insisted again and again that we retain the presumption of innocence unless convinced otherwise by the evidence, and that we be persuaded by any reasonable doubt to refrain from conviction—a noble principle not in accordance with any instinct of human or social self-preservation; for even the lady who ushered us into the courtroom had said: "There's a defendant in there, so be careful." I believed and still believe that the twelve silent ones in the jury box were prepared to be fair. By Ehrenburg's maxim, they should have been shot. (I quote my Serbian friend Vineta: "That's so disgusting, the way you Americans presume those criminals to be innocent.") The court reporter, aloof and distinguished-looking, played the keyboard with long slender fingers, his words white upon the blue screen. He would not lie, and the jury, while they might be wrong, would do their best not to be biased. —"I'd like you to remember that there are always two sides to every question," the judge said, so Ehrenburg would have had to shoot him, too. In other words, as we already knew, expediency rules. Djilas's anecdote about his own failure, thanks to his moral system, even to *comprehend* British loyalty to the imperialist cause is a classic, showing how solipsistic subjectivity prohibits the very perceptions on which induction and analysis must be based. If we deny any moral basis whatsoever to the Other Side—the capitalist exploiter British, the horrific Eichmann—then each of them stands before our gaze merely silhouetted, creature of the same featureless moral velvet—*are* they the same? If we good Stalinists truly act and speak as though they are, we are liable to make some serious mistakes. This is the trouble with Ehrenburg's way of transacting ethical business.

Yes, the mass graves of Shalamov's world *remain wrong*. Justice can and ought to be passionate about that. But what else is wrong, and is it as wrong as they are?

Judgment Versus Respect

Back to "understanding" Eichmann again: For the author of this book, as for any reporter of living, uncoerced human words, passionate justice offers an additional practical difficulty: If I am not allowed to be objective, to point out that every evildoer has a good side and may even mean well, then there is no reason on earth why the Other Side which I am writing about should sit down to be attacked by me. The fact that I invade its privacy is bad enough.

This leads to one of the central ethical questions of biography, portraiture and journalism: Do I betray and humiliate those who have trusted me, or do I soften my conclusions? My policy will always be to treat with empathy and respect anyone agreeing to be studied, interviewed, exposed. I would have been courteous to Eichmann. My obligation, however, is to the truth. But again, what is truth? My study of literature and life has taught me that sometimes there isn't any—or that it has so many sides that one is permitted only rarely to condemn it. And what if there is more than one perpetrator of even the most clearly evident crime; what if one man orders, another signs, a third conveys and a fourth shoots? If there is any doubt, isn't it better not to condemn? If, on the other hand, doubt has nowhere to hide, as in Eichmann's case, then one *must* condemn, but never without respecting the human being inside the evildoer. I hope that it is possible to follow this muted course, and still answer, however gingerly, the question of when violence is and is not justified. Sometimes, as the reader will see, my condemnations are passionate in spite of everything; other times, you may conclude (although I hope you won't) that I have tried so hard to be respectful and fair that I have become an accomplice. I am not and never will be one of those journalists who actively does wicked things for the sake of deeper understanding. In Madagascar I twice paid bandits to stage their lethal activities for me rather than agreeing to observe the real thing; in Sarajevo I refused to involve myself in the execution of a Serbian sniper. But in Malaysia, when I met the chuckling old terrorist Hadji Amin, a man whose bombs have killed many innocent people, I tried to tell his side of the story, and I promised never to reveal where he is—a promise I have kept. (Anyhow, he is dead now.) I was always polite to him on the telephone; I asked after his health (it was heart disease that he died of), his wife, his family. It is my hope that you will encounter that politeness in what I have written about him, no matter that he horrifies me. In short, I would rather be a coward, and write a work of ornately descriptive ethics, than to be Ilya Ehrenburg.

The Structure of This Book

Rising Up and Rising Down, then, is divided into two parts. The first, being more theoretical and general, attempts through induction, common sense and consideration of the deeds of certain contemporary, historical and even mythic people who have behaved violently, or not—among others, Trotsky, Napoleon, Cortes, Christ, Lincoln, Jefferson, Stalin, Tolstoy, "Virginia" of the Animal Liberation Front, the Amazons, the Marquis de Sade, Martin Luther, Martin Luther King, Field Marshal Wilhelm Keitel, Lawrence of Arabia, Robespierre, Gandhi and the Heike prince Taira Shigemori—to arrive at a way of ethically categorizing violence. It is possibly the more valuable half of the book (assuming, despite all the caveats above, that my ship has not been entirely wrecked on the shoals of hagiography), and certainly the less likely to be read. It concludes with a "moral calculus" extracted from the foregoing. "Explanatory power theories for interpersonal and systemic levels will probably differ," and this goes for explanatory ethical theories also; thus you will find the "equations" in my calculus to be blurred and sometimes ambiguous approximations rather than strict identities, because some degree of mistiness is required when one endeavors to be personal, inclusive and systematic.

With the dubious exception of my discussion of John Brown's letters, this part of the book does not qualify as archival or even scholarly research. My intention was neither to uncover new facts about the doings of historical figures, nor to formulate new interpretations of them. What I tried instead to do was to lay out the received wisdom concerning Caesar's mercy, Joan of Arc's honor, Hitler's territorialism, etcetera, and then judge that. No doubt my reading of classical sources in particular betrays a sort of credulity. But who knows what Leonidas the Spartan really said at Thermopylae, or to what extent Thucydides, who was an actual eyewitness of the Peloponnesian War, might have subordinated literal accuracy to elegant pathos? No matter. The reader is invited to consider each of the moral decisions undertaken by our historical protagonists as the centerpiece of a parable. For our purposes it matters less whether Leonidas existed at all (although I've done my best to rely on scholars who can tell me that he did) than whether *we can imagine ourselves into the circumstances described.*

Hence this "theoretical" portion of the book comprises a set of what Wittgenstein would have called "thought-experiments." Future scholarship may prove that Stalin's drive against the kulaks enjoyed more or less popular support than my reading (largely of secondary and translated sources) has led me to believe. It may also very likely come out that Stalin never for a moment believed his own justifications. No matter. When is violent defense of class justified? We'll inspect the ogre's justifications as if they meant something, for he placed them on public record and his cadres invoked them in the process of starving peasants to death. We'll try to determine their context and their implications. Then we'll judge their merits.

In deference to the examples which inform it, each theoretical chapter is organized somewhat differently from the others, but the basic scheme consists of arriving at a definition (or sometimes a more open-ended understanding) of the category which is being defended, then (or simultaneously) considering the fairness of invoking violence for the sake of that category. Imagine that you are the judge in a courtroom. The violent act has already occurred. Napoleon stands in the dock. The witnesses have finished explaining to you how and why he defended his honor. You must decide: Is defense of honor a legitimate category at all? In due course you will judge Cortes and you may well decide, as I do, that his offered justification of defense of ground is specious. You have already judged Joan of Arc, and you have determined that Napoleon's honor is different from hers. Well, is it worth defending, and do you accept his means?

I invite you to read each "theoretical" chapter with the Moral Calculus volume in hand, because it is there that the chapter in question has been boiled down to its own verbatim skeleton. Were you to read only the

Moral Calculus, you might find the assertions to be more tendentious and peculiar than they are. There is almost nothing in the Moral Calculus which does not come directly from the theoretical chapters.

Methodological Weaknesses of Part I

1. A broad approach necessarily results in superficial and inaccurate treatment of many topics.

2. Therefore, a broadly comparative approach may well produce misleading overgeneralizations, or else reproduce the stereotyped conclusions of that mediocrity miscalled posterity.

3. In particular, a focus upon moral actors in positions of political leadership is bound to overpersonalize and falsely render monolithic their respective causes.

Although I have done my best to overcome these failings, I must sometimes have succumbed to them.

Justifications for Part I

1. My aim is, where possible, to let the reader briefly peep through each moral actor's eyes, and to exemplify universally human decisions. Their universality can be shown only through comparison.

2. If we cannot situate ourselves in history, if we cannot match ourselves against our moral peers now dead and gone, what good is history?

The second part of this book owes more to my own experience, and comprises a series of case studies in violence and the perception of violence: Inuit seal hunting and animal rights, the Khmer Rouge in Cambodia, and Cambodian gangs in the United States; the civil war in Bosnia, U.N. peacekeeping in Somalia, cattle rustlers and street robbers in Madagascar, child prostitution in Thailand (and how and why I kidnapped one girl engaged in that trade), teenage suicide on an Apache reservation in the U.S., opium politics and ethnic guerrilla movements in Burma, the Libyan-funded PULO terrorist organization in Thailand and Malaysia, the Guardian Angel movement in the U.S., the Christian Patriot movement in the U.S. (with some references to neo-Nazis and the Militia) the Baraku ("Untouchable") class in Japan, and voodoo and folk religion in the American South as a means of "dealing with" violence. This section ends with applications of the Moral Calculus to strike at a brief ethical evaluation of each of the situations described.

A Note on the Case Studies, and on Literary Aesthetics

Finally, it may be worth explaining why a work organized on a theoretical basis indulges so much in description (indeed, as I already said, ornate description). The colors of the Burmese jungle at twilight, or the scorched smell of a shelled city, do not of themselves further analytical understanding. In fact, it might be argued (as I have done in my remarks on authorities and experts) that their very particularity gets in the way of it. That don of military strategy, Liddell Hart, whose paean to Sun-tzu's indirect methods of warfare was studied religiously by both Patton and Guderian, put at the very beginning of his opus the following statement: "Direct experience is inherently too limited to form an adequate foundation either for theory or for application. At the best it produces an atmosphere that is of value in drying and hardening the structure of thought." And in his detailed recounting of the feints, swoops, ambuscades, tricks and deceptions which made various contingents, from the ancient Greeks to the Allies of World War II, kings of the hill for their own instants, he almost never employs the adjectives of verisimilitude. His task, however, is quite different from mine. Who won this battle, who lost and why? The answer may well have something to do with a certain general's digestion, but the *objective* cause of a result on the battlefield will be pegged by less than introspective men, hence will derive from that lengthy category of causes available to those who are not mind readers: mobility, communications, trenches and counterstrokes.

Meanwhile, even Liddell Hart approvingly quotes Napoleon's dictum that "the moral is to the physical as three to one." Morale is a subjective factor, which might as well be considered subjectively. Ethics, especially as I have presented above, comes even more from within—so much so that Liddell Hart's disparagement of direct experience does not hold: While we may not expect a parochial intellect to produce broad strategy, we would not fail to keep the person to whom that intellect belongs accountable for the good or evil that he does. The reason is that this keeping accountable is in large measure also local, parochial. That is why a Somali man can have four wives and be respected, while an American man cannot. What does all this have to do with the color of jungles? It is precisely because local conditions have such an effect upon a person's outlook that they ought to be described. I admit that I've behaved this way partly because it is my bent, and partly because I figured that if my theorizing were wrong or unpalatable, the reader might at least have some moments of pleasure (this especially goes for the case studies). There is another reason. Even the pious materialist Trotsky, to whom people and places were but the local expressions of collective force, went out of his way to praise

> the ability to visualize people, objects, and events as they really are, even if one has never seen them. To combine separate little strokes caught on the wing, to supplement them by means of unformulated laws of correspondence and likelihood, and in this way to recreate a certain sphere of human life in all its concrete reality, basing everything upon experience in life and upon theory—that is the imagination that a legislator, an administrator, a leader must have, especially in a period of revolution. Lenin's strength was chiefly this power of realistic imagination.

Trotsky and Lenin might not value my own visualizations, since collective force interests me only insofar as it relates to personalized ethical decisions about violence. Nonethless, I too in my way seek to recreate various "spheres of human life" in order to make identification with each moral actor more feasible. Descriptions of personalities, appearances and the settings in which people act and react will hopefully provide further means for the reader to make that re-creation himself, and thereby to evaluate my judgments.

In the theoretical half of this book I will attempt to define as vividly as I can the ethos of a homeland, the identity of a place and of an animal, et cetera. "A homeland is a language, the way that the streets curve and the color of the sky in winter, the fashion in which coffee is served, the tempo of traffic." It is this that people commit justified violence to save, and unjustified violence to aggrandize. I truly believe in the utility of such a conception of motivation—people kill for what they cry for—and I want you to believe it. How else can I convey the feeling of a specific place except through description?

Above all, the blossoming days of the Niblungs deserve vivid records. "Despite confusion and uncertainty," writes the military historian John Keegan, "it seems just possible to glimpse the emerging outlines of a world without war." Maybe so—if thermonuclear war exterminates all of us Niblungs.

PART I

Categories and

Justifications

Definitions for Lonely Atoms

In our salesroom, we have on view upwards of 1,000 Different Kinds of Guns, from the early matchlock, up to the present day automatic. What a story some of these old arms could tell, of victories and reverses, of heroism and valor, but they lie silent now.

Bannerman Catalogue, 1927

Guns are an interesting prop.

Abbie Hoffman, 1968

I.

ON THE MORALITY OF WEAPONS

Sedentary people have become used to laziness and ease ... They are carefree and trusting, and have ceased to carry weapons ... They have become like women and children, who depend upon the master of the house.

Ibn Khaldun, fourteenth century

When I enter a house, I want to be the only one with a gun.

Police Officer Micki Bashford, 1997

The handgun's primary purpose is to save lives, not take them.
                                        Chuck Taylor, 1982

*I sometimes laugh when people get emotional about our weapons. I'll
tell you something really emotional . . . the day we finally convinced the
people in the villages about the importance of boiling the water they
drink and cook with.*
                        Major Ana Maria, insurgent in Chiapas, 1996

Knife and gun provide three things: security, autonomy (which is almost the same thing, but active rather than passive) and power
(which is most active of all). Calling upon the Communist Party to arm
the Chinese proletariat against the invading Japanese (who ironically had
a tradition of denying weapons to their own lower classes), Trotsky
wrote: "A people that today, with weapon in hand, knows how to deal
with one robber, will tomorrow know how to deal with the other one."
By "the other one," of course, he meant the class enemy, but his logic
would apply to *any* "other one." In Pancho Villa's Mexican utopia, citizens would have spent three days a week working and three days a week
in military training. "When the Patria is invaded, we will just have to telephone from the palace in Mexico City, and in half a day all the Mexican
people will rise from their fields and factories, fully armed, equipped and
organized to defend their children and their homes." A gun in my hand
prepares me, transforms me. If I can accurately shoot paper targets from
a distance today, I have a better chance of being able to shoot my enemies
tomorrow.

The simple law of might accords respect to an armed individual, who
may well come to respect himself accordingly—another way of saying
that security is the precondition for autonomy. One long-standing labor
unionist and civil rights activist had to contend with the active hostility of
American police. In a certain town, Ku Klux Klan recruiting posters
adorned the police station. The activist recalls: "I am convinced that I'm
alive today because I traveled with firearms—and that this fact was generally known." Whether self-respect will nourish bravery and honor, as it
seems to have done in his case, or whether it will subsidize egotistical cruelty, must remain dark to our knowledge until deeds are done, or at least

until we can invent an X-ray machine for souls. But self-respect in and of itself can never be a bad thing, because timorousness and incapacity in and of themselves can never be good. Incapacity to do evil is of course a *relative* good, a least-bad, a good-by-default; but when we reduce the evildoer to that state we are doing the right and necessary thing *for us,* and only incidentally for him (by, say, preserving his existence at the price of rendering him helpless). We read that in ancient Athens the franchise was bestowed only upon those men who had or could get the implements of war. We do not read that it was granted to trussed and defanged men whose virtue was that they could not harm the polity.

The Amorality of Empowerment

Thus the capacity to do violence extends the self: it does not only arm it, it also "hands" it, awarding it extra fingers of choice. The weapon becomes a limb, a friend. American frontiersmen so greatly valued their rifles' ability to feed and protect them that some bestowed affectionate pet names on them: "Ol' Ticklicker," "Deer Killer," "Indian Lament." A Soviet lieutenant en route to ambush Afghan mujahideen "pats the cannon of his APC as if it were a faithful dog." In other words, no matter what an appalled examiner of the Pakistani pen pistol might believe, they solve some difficulties. "The intended victim is the only one in a good position to stop a criminal act," insists a gun writer. And, indeed, a U.N. study of fourteen nations decided that the greater the number of times somebody had been *victimized* by crime, disarmed and unhanded, the more likely he was to be or become a gun owner, which is to say, of course, either a blood avenger or a self-defender; but I would be inclined to give such people the benefit of the doubt (since they were aggressed against) and assume self-defense until proven otherwise. The gun possession figure for three-time victims attained almost 25 percent. (The weapon owner's maxim: *If authority cannot protect me, I must protect myself.*) Did these guns ever help their owners? An FBI report I opened for the random year 1995 acknowledged that most justifiable homicides were committed with handguns. Can we agree that justifiable homicides are another relative good? In 1995, in the U.S. and Japan, several hundred people seemed to have lethally saved themselves.

SELF-DEFENSE HOMICIDES (1995)

	BY MEN	BY WOMEN	TOTAL HOMICIDES
Japan	36	5	1,295
	(3.4 percent of	(2.0 percent of	
	male total)	female total)	

	BY POLICE	BY CITIZENS	TOTAL HOMICIDES
U.S.	383	268	20,694

COMPARISON CAVEATS: U.S. figures are for justified homicides and do not include felony homicides whose perpetrators claimed self-defense. Japanese figures are for homicides which may or may not be justifiable. In any case, the legal criteria for justifiability may not be the same in the two countries. Please note that totals and percentages are affected by rounding.

We need not set out to increase the number of justified homicides; a more worthy end would be to decrease the need for them. But if homicides must be committed, better that they be justifiable.

And what constitutes justifiability? Would it be broad-minded of us, or prudent, or merely evasive to assert the crucial relevance of the psychological context of any moral act? Those daredevils who reduce their purview to facts alone, like the Roman stonemasons who chiseled terse recitations into marble, excluding case and punctuation, will surely stride forward impatiently to brush away like cobwebs all the complex nuances revealed in the case of Bernhard Goetz, which we'll examine shortly.

Reread that gun writer's aphorism: "The intended victim is the only one in a good position to stop a criminal act." Shall we bring his axiom to imaginary life—which is to say, to death? In a 1922 advertisement attempting to bring Thompson submachine guns into the American home market, we see a cowboy type crouching against one of the pillars of his long, shaded porch, firmly grasping a Thompson in both hands while shooting down a rifle-waving bandit whose arms outstretch as—inevitably in this secular liturgy—he begins to fly off his rearing horse. Other rustlers gallop in toward the herd, two of them taking direct aim at the defender of self and property, who we can only hope will triumph—no, we'll hope with good reason, for only he has a Thompson. "The ideal weapon for the protection of large estates, ranches, plantations, etc.," begins the ad, which offers two versions of this lifesaver: a semiautomatic capable of discharging a mere fifty shots per minute (given four or five already loaded magazines, a Sig Sauer could better this), and a full automatic, "fired from the hip, 1,500 shots per minute." Who wouldn't prefer full auto? Certainly the rustlers would; in fact, they'd very likely consider a Thompson "the ideal weapon for attacks upon large estates, ranches, plantations, etc."

CRIMINALS PREFER HANDGUNS

WASHINGTON: About 1.3 million U.S. residents faced an assailant armed with a gun during 1993, and the use of semiautomatic weapons by juveniles is rising fast, particularly in murders, the Justice Department said Sunday. Of the victims of rape, sexual assault, robbery and aggravated assault by offenders carrying a firearm that year, 86 percent, or 1.1 million, said the weapon was a handgun, the department said.

Of Crimson Storms and Their Weathermen

There lies the obvious difficulty with violence's tools, which seem to have been distributed on this earth with the utmost carelessness: should we happen to be Indians, how "ideal" a weapon will we consider "Indian Lament"? Go back to Julius Caesar's day, when an officer in the African campaign warns that one side's war elephants constitute "a menace to both sides." Consider the old cliché: "a double-edged sword." Were it possible to create a weapon which would function only in self-defense, most of us would be all for it. *But what is self-defense? When is violence justified?*

When only an elite possesses weapons, the masses will be subject to active or potential tyranny. But when everyone owns weapons, then the climate becomes more prone to storms of undirected violence. Which is worse? It depends on the times. The American myth of the Minutemen, those self-reliant, decent fathers and brothers ready at a moment's notice to repel a common enemy with "Ol' Ticklicker," is out of favor, because nobody agrees on who our common enemy is; indeed, we are too often each other's enemies—and always have been, as a pioneer woman recognized when she wrote of thirsty cowboys who bought whiskey at her father's store in the 1870s: "they could not refrain from partaking too freely, with the result that generally they felt an irresistible impulse to draw their pistols and shoot in a frolicsome way at whatever might be around." Was it merely that the legislative and executive branches exerted insufficient control? The sixth-century historian Procopius describes the Constantinople of his day as a disorderly tyranny, weighed down not only by the fear of the ruthless

emperor and his favorites, but also by an ambiance of street violence, originally politically motivated by the Blue and Green factions, now transformed
into simple extortion. "At first practically all of them carried weapons
openly at night, but in the day-time they concealed small two-edged swords
along the thigh under their mantle, and they gathered in groups as soon as it
became dark and would waylay men of the better classes." I live in an atmosphere of inconceivably greater government control; and yet as I write, Procopius's words could be applied to almost any large American city. How
many single women do I know who are afraid to leave their windows open
even on the hottest nights? How many people have told me, "Oh, I don't go
to that area. That's a bad area; that's a gang area . . . "? How many people
have said, "I wouldn't advise you to go out after dark"? Instead of double-
edged swords, our Blues and Greens carry double-edged guns with which
they kill their enemies, their friends, strangers, lost souls, lost children. Take
their guns away, and at least some of them will go back to swords.

In Hindu-Muslim riots in India, people kill each other, as Cain killed
Abel, with stones. In the U.S., back in the middle of the twentieth century,
where guns were more widely available than in India—indeed, there were
far fewer controls on them than at the time of this writing—a sociologist
noted: "If Negro, the slaying is commonly with a knife, if white, it is a
beating with fists and feet on a public street." In Poland we find that as
American baseball enters against the protests of a dying communism, the
baseball bat becomes the murder weapon of fashion.

A Note from the Ambassador

How then can we take shelter from these inevitable crimson storms, much
less predict them? They *will* come, whether my neighbors and I wait
weaponed or weaponless. The common enemy will regularly be recatego-
rized, and the power of the Minuteman remains now and forever also the
power of the rapist-murderer.

The power of the murderer is now and forever also the power of the
watchful householder. Let us then consider not the weapon, however much
it may have been reified into "Indian Lament," but the degree of necessity.
Because *they* have guns, I want a gun. Once acquired, my gun then perhaps becomes myself, as in Plato's maxim "the actor's mask becomes his
face," but to consider only the psychology of weapons ownership belittles
ineluctable self-preservation: they will not disarm, so I will not disarm, either. Give place to Winston Churchill's eloquence:

We may ourselves, in the lifetime of those who are here, if we are not in a proper state of security, be confronted on some occasion with a visit from an Ambassador, and may have to give an answer, and if that answer is not satisfactory, within the next few hours the crash of bombs exploding in London and the cataracts of masonry and fire and smoke will warn us of any inadequacy which has been permitted in our aerial defences.

I myself was confronted by some of those ambassadors once in San Francisco's Tenderloin district. They had knives. They informed me that they were going to use them. I happened to be carrying a Browning, in regretful defiance of local law, so my answer was satisfactory—to me, at least, hence perforce to them. They apologized and went away.

WEAPONS USED IN HOMICIDES AND ROBBERIES (1995)

Japan		U.S.	
MURDER	**ROBBERY**	**MURDER**	**ROBBERY**
Edged tool (52.7%)	None (42.6%)	Gun (68.2%)	Gun (41.0%)
Misc. (27.4%)	Edged tool (30.2%)	Edged tool (12.7%)	Strong-arm (40.7%)
None (13.7%)	Misc. (25.6%)	Fists, feet, etc. (5.9%)	Edged tool (9.1%)
Sword (6.3%)	Sword (4.4%)	Blunt tool (4.5%)	Misc. (9.2%)
Gun (3.7%)	Gun (2.4%)	Unknown (4.8%)	
Poison (1.7%)	Poison (0.8%)	Strangulation (1.2%)	
		Explosives (.095%)	
		Fire (0.82%)	
		Asphyxiation (0.67%)	
		Drowning (0.14%)	
		Narcotics (0.11%)	
		Poison (0.06%)	

PERCENTAGE TOTALS (*which make one wonder*)

105.50%	106.00%	100.05%	100.00%

Mantras and Bloodstained Snow

The three goods of violence—security, autonomy and power—can also be provided (on occasion) by nonviolence. Having been a member of an antinuclear affinity group in the face of police violence (which, depending on how one weighs corporate business and property rights versus the dangers of nuclear power, might or might not be justified), I remember the security that came from the loving trust we felt, or at least sincerely tried to feel (or perhaps pretended to feel) toward one another in our AG, which was called Cost of Freedom. I remember the autonomy that came from making our own decisions and acting as we thought was right; and the power which our security and autonomy gave us. We did not feel invulnerable by any means (and we weren't). After all, our adversaries owned far more security and power than we: they were armed and in authority. From a personal point of view they might have had less autonomy, but they didn't seem to miss it. We were at Seabrook, New Hampshire. Our rhetoric: "Shut the nuke down!" Among the throng who blockaded the street gate, our AG was not hurt when authority made its move. It was May 1980. In the middle, not the forefront, I saw the National Guardsmen suddenly file out of the gate very rapidly; then as light made vertical gleams upon their face shields they stabbed nightsticks down upon the nonviolent ones who tried to protect their heads; I remember so many raised hands and scared, grimacing faces of people (mainly young and white) who were trying to be brave; on the Guardsmen's faces (also young and white) I saw mainly wary concentration, with the occasional rare tight-lipped smile. (On one weapon I saw the words RHYTHM STICK.) They dragged a limp, bespectacled, denim-shirted girl away by her long red hair; she screwed up her face in silent pain. Everywhere they were bending over to grab people, their motions not unlike those of snow-shovelers. A stocky green-clad cop, his handcuffs riding high and gleaming in the small of his back, grabbed somebody by her shirt-collar and wrists, dragging her along between his legs, her bottom all dirty from having sat on the pavement; she resembled the quarter of some cow carcass being hauled out of the slaughterhouse. But, while I've used the word "violence" in reference to authority's activities, I'm referring only to the smashings-down of nightsticks on wrists and heads: the dragging-off, arresting and citing of the limp is not violence. Authority intimidated and occasionally employed pain; it could have done worse. Should I mention that the protesters, frustrated in their objective of occupying the plant, had begun jeering abuse at the police, or that one policeman had been seriously wounded by a protester's grappling hook? Mainly what they did was to meet us *outside* the fence rather than behind it, as before, the result being that activists succeeded in cutting only about two hundred feet of fence. Those of us who crossed the marsh river on a makeshift bridge, approaching authority's cadres on the other side, those (they didn't include me) who in ponchos huddled under plastic groundsheets, waiting for the riot hoses mixed with Mace, even those who felt the nightsticks on their heads, were free to assume they wouldn't be summarily liquidated. All the more security, autonomy and power! Still, there is something about practicing what one preaches, and living it, that makes for serenity. Of course, who knows for sure that what one preaches is right? That is why, in my opinion, only a saint can practice nonviolence in isolation; the rest of us have to do it in gangs.

My Gun Was My Rosary

Anybody in possession of a weapon and the ability and will to use it immediately gains some security, autonomy and power, even if he is alone— as most people are in American cities; Thucydides remarks that "internal strife is the main reason for the decline of cities," and by cities he means city-states, nations. Internal strife is one reason (in "democratic" countries the only reason) that city-dwellers are afraid—afraid of violence. Such fear, like Churchill's, is based on *a perceived probability of harm*. One morning in early 1995 I was preparing to go on a long trip, and remembered that my pistols needed cleaning. As it happened, two nights previously a couple of people had been shot in a park very near my house. (Years later, I opened the newspaper to find the executioners finally arraigned in court. One of their victims had died. The other, although shot in the face, had kept some grip on life, no matter that his security, autonomy and power left much to be desired. While testifying in the courtroom, he had a seizure and began to vomit.) In my memory I also saw an elderly couple who lived a mile away in another direction; they'd been shot in the back while they were walking their dog. My friend Linda, who's lived in this neighborhood for almost thirty years now, often walks to the supermarket late at night. She has never yet been bothered. She describes her deportment on those strolls as cautious but not afraid. She knows the couple who were shot in the back. The husband told her that he saw the car come circling around the block the first time, and then it went on because the gang kids inside it had to get up their nerve. Perhaps it was an initiation mandate. When he saw the car coming the second time and then it stopped and the kids stuck their pistol out the window, he said to himself, "It's all over." —"They're doing fine," Linda said to me the other day. "As soon as they were out of the hospital they went out to walk their dog, and they've been doing it ever since." But someone else I used to know, a woman who is dead now, lived in Queens and wrote me a letter: "I'm a walking target, literally, since I like to walk late at night. No one out here walks at night.

The police know me, think I'm insomniac or something." She walked but was always afraid. (Actually she died from something else.)

The woman whom I would eventually marry was usually as fearless as Linda, but every now and then she asks me to keep her company when she must walk her dog late at night in that same park. The double shooting terrified her. She said that she would be getting home from work long after dark tonight, and it was going to be foggy; would I please, please go with her? I promised that I would. Then I made myself a bowl of cereal and opened the newspaper. More murders—maybe they'd happened a hundred miles away, but they made an impression. I had just finished breakfast when somebody else I knew well telephoned. Her car had broken down late at night; while waiting at a pay phone for more than an hour for the towing company to come (they never showed, and at last she called the police), she'd been harassed and terrorized. She had no answer ready for her ambassadors. She said to me: "There was this one young boy who kept circling the parking lot and honking at me. I'm pretty sure he was a gang member. I had the feeling he was going to hurt me, and if he did he wouldn't really have given a shit. I called my best friend and she said she couldn't come get me because she was naked right then. I saw this one couple pull out and I ran after them and begged them to help me but they just rolled up the windows and looked at me like I was crazy and got out of there. Finally the cops came." She was one of the people whom Cicero had in mind when he remarked that "when weapons reduce them to silence, the laws no longer expect one to await their pronouncements." The laws had been reduced to silence, all right, and she would have ignored their limitations on her right to stab and shoot if she could, but she didn't know how and owned no weapon. Since the cops did come, she ended up lucky, unlike the best friend of a woman I once sat beside on a plane. "I loved her so much," my seatmate said. "They came in through her window. She was raped and tortured and then they strangled her." But I never knew the strangled one. I thought of her, though, as I was cleaning my .45. I thought of my fiancée who was afraid to walk her dog (once, then twice, then again, because she is Asian, some black men yelled epithets at her and threw bottles onto the sidewalk where they loudly smashed and almost cut the dog's eye). —Was I overreacting? Almost certainly. That year it seemed that every morning when I took the rubber band off the newspaper and found the Metro section I'd met another murder! Yet when I actually looked up my home city in the FBI's *Uniform Crime Reports* I was amazed to find a total of only fifty-seven homicides for Sacramento itself, and exactly twice that for the three counties included in Sacramento's greater "metropolitan statistical area." In short, I had exaggerated the murder rate by a factor of three. To be sure, taking into consideration *all* violent crimes in greater Sacramento—rape, arson, aggravated assault and the like—the FBI counted almost twelve thousand "incidents," or over thirty-two a day. Undoubtedly these were sometimes reported in the Metro section, and then there was the occasional murder from Redding or Stockton, which I'd most likely conflated with Sacramento. Sacramento was dangerous, but not nearly as dangerous as I thought. After the episode of the thrown bottles, which would not even have been an "incident," for nobody reported it, and nothing had "really" happened, violence didn't visit her there in the park for over a year. But when she went out at night I remained afraid. It is only now, when I hope I've more or less finished going to wars (this book being long enough) that I realize how crazy-anxious I was all that time. The sound of the dog getting up in the night for a drink of water would awaken me, and my heart would pound with fear; I'd be certain that somebody was trying to break in. An hour later, a floorboard would squeak, and I'd be awake again, afraid but ready—ready for nothing. When you get to some of the case studies in this book, the accounts of the war places, it may be more clear why I returned from some of my trips full of fright; and compared to a real soldier or a professional war correspondent—or a civilian trapped in a war zone—I've seen nothing. In real danger, fear is a friend; afterward he may not be, but once he first makes your acquaintance, then, like violence, he visits as he pleases. —That was how it was with me. I thought of myself, of how my house stood exposed on a corner by a high school, of all the average little scares I'd had there, none of which would have scared Linda at all (but she was among those who closed her windows even on the hottest nights; she didn't live in a two-storey house), and I thumbed the magazine release, swung back the slide to unchamber the last round, rotated the barrel bushing an eighth of a turn or so and took my gun apart. (My next-door neighbors shook their heads. —"Don't shoot us by mistake!" they said. They liked me, but I was a nut.) The heaviness, the substantiality of those strange dark pieces, some cylindrical, some angular, some both—complex polygonal solids which fit inside one another in marvelous and obscure ways—and the smell of the nitro powder solvent, the rich blackness of dissolved lead on my fingers, the slickness of the six pieces after I'd oiled them; all these were overpowering sensory proofs, however delusional, that I could act; and the sureness with which I could disassemble my guns and then put them back together by memory (the Sig Sauer was the easiest; the DC Tec-9 Mini, whose fifty-shot capacity was offset by poor-quality cast and stamped parts, remained the hardest), the knowledge that when I'd finished, each barrel would be clean and every part, as far I could tell by inspection, in working order (of course there must always be a "so far as I can tell" because certainty does not go down to the molecular level)—these facts lulled and relieved me. All in all, call it easy, useful work whose commission always afforded me pleasure; and when I was through I felt slightly surer that my guns could keep me safe—a minor renewal of my faith in myself.

That night when I went out with the Asian woman to walk her dog (a lonely, foggy night when anything could happen), I did not feel afraid when two men sauntered toward us. I nodded at them, my hand on the loaded .45 most feloniously concealed in my coat pocket. They sneered back. They were ugly, intimidating men. But I didn't feel intimidated. They walked on, and the fog ate them.

But the Rosary Confers No Eternal Life

The self-confidence provided by weapons may be as fallacious as any other form of complacent puffery. How could I tell the anxious citizens of sixth-century Constantinople that if they only bought enough swords, they'd be home free? Violence, being a manifestation of misfortune and of death, can fall upon us in any number of forms. In March 1995, two or three days before my arrival in Tokyo, an organization with a high opinion of its own righteousness, called Aum Supreme Truth, released the nerve gas sarin into several subway junctions. Poor planning on the terrorists' part produced a less than spectacular number of casualties, but that was only the first of their attacks. What could the victims have done? Their government didn't allow them to carry guns; if it had, the result would have been identical, for the terrorists accomplished their purpose and escaped before anyone suspected violence. A newspaper blared: NERVE GAS NOT EVEN HITLER WOULD USE! Echoing that headline, every Japanese subway rider I talked to remarked on the cruelty of using gas, which Hitler, himself a trench-gas victim back in World War I, certainly gave a bad name to, and which had been banned as a means of officially legitimized mass homicide (which terrorism is not) by the Geneva Protocol on Gas Warfare back in 1925. But what I suspect the subway passengers were actually objecting to was the cruelty of attacking *them* rather than subway riders in some other country. Would machine guns have been any nicer?

The most terrifying description of chemical warfare I have ever read is Malraux's fictionalized account of his father's experiences during World War I, when gas was first tested upon some Russian trenches. (When Hitler became blinded by gas near the war's end, it was all more routine.) Malraux describes the spiders dead in their webs, the birds falling out of the sky, the monstrous putrescence, physical and moral, of everything in sight, the Russians horribly, bloodlessly dead. But he did not see it. How accurately did the father tell the tale to the son, and how much did the son embellish? His embellishment certainly deserves the accolades of great literature. Great literature could be composed about any battlefield. It is as if we had descended back into the catacombs of Paris and, overwhelmed by those galleries of six million skulls, let our feelings trick us into going beyond the only real lesson of death, the stale, useless principle that *Dead is dead*, to call for a ban upon catacombs. Gassed or shot, dead is dead. And the spiders and birds? And the old man whose hovel just happened to lie downwind? There might not have been one, because World War I consisted of a stationary murder process in a zone long since cleared of non-combatants, so poison gas hurt almost exclusively the belligerents alone—which would not be the case now that battlefronts tend to be so mobile. Still, who knows for sure which way the poisoned wind blows? Such considerations led to the Geneva Protocol of 1925. And yet as late as 1937 a Brigadier General in our own army wrote an essay from which some extracts may be of interest:

> The measure of humaneness of any form of warfare is the comparison of (1) degree of suffering caused at the time of injury by the different weapons; [(2)] the percentage of deaths to the total number of casualties produced by each weapon; and [(3)] the permanent aftereffects resulting from the injuries inflicted by each particular method of warfare.
>
> In general, gas causes less suffering than wounds from other weapons. It is unquestionably true that chlorine, the first gas used in the late war, did at first cause strangulation with considerable pain and a high mortality. But this was due mainly to the fact that the troops against whom these first gas attacks were launched were totally unprotected. Later when supplied with gas masks, chlorine became the most innocuous of the toxic gases and was least feared by both sides.

(That particular paragraph, I admit, was amusingly disingenuous—for our good brigadier would hardly recommend the deployment of a humane gas which causes no casualties—but read on.)

> Among those gassed the sufferings are less severe and of shorter duration than among those wounded by other war weapons . . . As to the ratio of deaths to total casualties, we have already shown that the mortality among those wounded by nongas weapons was over twelve times the mortality from gas . . . Gas . . . produces practically no permanent injuries, so that if a man who is gassed survives the war, he comes out body whole, as God made him, and not the legless, armless, or deformed cripple produced by the mangling and rending effects of high explosives, gunshot wounds, and bayonet thrusts.

(I think of my grandfather's friend, a World War I survivor, who went through life coughing, getting drunk to shut out the pain.)

> Chemical warfare is the latest contribution to the science of war . . . [It] is the most humane method of war yet devised by man.

In future wars gas projectiles might be less controllable with respect to their intended targets than in World War I, unless battlefronts once again become stationary. Surely a weapon's controllability enhances its humaneness, and gas can never be fully controlled except in an enclosed space. We condemn Severino Di Giovanni's anarchist bombings in Buenos Aires because (among other things) their destruction-power failed to be controlled: he killed innocent people and did not thereby further his political ends. (Controllability *ensures* nothing: at Auschwitz, gas was completely controlled, but no one would say that it was employed humanely there. Uncontrollability, however, uncouples the means from any end, justified or not.) The Japanese terrorists of Aum Supreme Truth did not much care about controllability. In their calculus, the strategy of the means was simply to diffuse death as widely as possible. Controllability mattered only insofar as it contributed to the terrorists' own safety.

Is poison gas reprehensible, then? Our Brigadier General didn't think so; and decades later another military ethicist argued that gas could morally be used if doing so would win the war and if the enemy had used it first and continued to use it; or even if the enemy had not used it at all but was known to be genocidal.

Thus once again we see, as so often in this study of violence, that principles can't be easily nailed down, that merely knowing the tool of violence employed is insufficient; we must also be apprised of the relation between victim and perpetrator. It is true that some weapons are more passive in nature, hence more likely to be morally validated for the purposes of self-defense (one example would be antiaircraft guns entrenched around a capital). But those same guns could be used, say, to shoot down harmless commercial jets overflying that city. There is also the fact that a nation relying on purely defensive weaponry forgoes quite a bit in a war—and thereby potentially victimizes that nation's own citizenry. As they say on the playing field and the battlefield, the best defense is a good offense.

In my opinion, the method chosen often hardly matters, because the victims of a given terroristic act are not only those who experience it directly—that is, those upon whose flesh it falls—but also those who hear about it when rumors or the media do their dirty work. That was why the newspapers called Tokyo a "city of fear." Here is the relevant part of a letter which a near-suicidal woman wrote me about another Aum Supreme Truth gas attack in April 1995:

> There was a rumor that there might have been another nervous gas [*sic*] incident this weekend, yesterday or today, so all crowded areas such as Ikebukuro, Shinjuku, Shibuya have been guarded tightly by the police force. I didn't believe that rumor. I didn't care if I die or not by the incident if it happened because I have less hope in my future. If I did, I would be satisfied with my short life. I think I survived it anyway because Sunday is almost over.

Obviously this attack didn't even happen. And the woman was so sad to begin with that it could scarcely depress her much further. But it did make her world a shade greyer; she was one of the many, many victims. (That is why a sociologist has proposed the notion that there are direct and indirect sufferers from every crime. If I assault you, your children get nightmares and your sister has to pay your hospital bills.) Call her one of the birds who fell from the sky, especially susceptible to violence's effects by reason of her sensitive, delicate spirit, poisoned already by sadness. Other victims, lucky enough to be born stronger, or to stand farther away, get but a whiff of the gas, whose toxic effect thus attenuates into the sub-tle contaminations of dissociation and masked anxiety. After the Okla-homa City bombing of April 1995, a girl wrote me:

> It's really very strange. I live about 5 minutes away from where it oc-curred, & I still haven't really grasped the whole thing. It's really a sad thing. I know of someone they haven't yet found, and a lot of my friends have been to funerals and stuff. The whole thing is just really bizarre. When you see it on the national news it's like looking at pictures of peo-ple you don't remember even though they know exactly who you are. And then there are the ribbons. People who are wearing them look at me as if I'm the one who set off the bomb just because I choose not to wear one. Did I say ONE? Most have about 30 on . . . I don't get it.

And of course there is nothing to "get," nothing to "really grasp." Atrocities leave only wounds, and a wound is a cavity, an emptiness. Am I belaboring the obvious in claiming that one reason for that emptiness is *helplessness*—that neither the Japanese woman nor the American woman could have done anything more to guard themselves against these storms of violence, which left them unkilled only by luck, than they could have done to deliver themselves from death in a traffic accident at the hands of some careless, rapid driver? The lesson of the catacombs: *No matter what you say or do, we skulls will see you underground.*

In short, violent self-defense, like the nonviolent kind, offers no guar-antees. Well, speak of the obvious! —But let's suppose that my attacker will use only a gun and that I own a gun, along with the knowledge and the will to employ it. I may be safer—or I may not be. One black market "organizer" in Zagreb told me in 1992 when we got on the subject of his side business, guns, that "last year the market for those was better because the government incited people to go to war. They constantly showed chopped-up bodies on TV, over and over. So they stimulated demand. Peo-ple wanted arms in their homes. They didn't know if there was going to be a military attack on Zagreb."

Many, though certainly not all, of the Croatians who responded to the fear and anger implanted in them by the television footage of dismem-bered corpses—responded, that is, by buying guns—might have arguably been worse off, because the Serbs were also getting guns at the behest of Serbian television. If I have reason to believe that my enemies stand both armed and implacable, then I must shoot first. (If they are merely armed, on the other hand, I need only concern myself with Churchillian preparedness.) This reasoning applies to both Serbs and Croatians, obviously. And yet, as in so many other situations, even when a factor increases the risk for a group, that same factor may well increase the safety of an individual within that group. Had I been a Croatian in Zagreb in 1991 and had many of my neighbors started buying guns, I would have wanted a gun, also. My not having a gun would not stop other people from arming themselves and hence becoming dangerous to me. Serbs would not know that I didn't have a gun, so the law of the preemptive strike would continue to work against me. Because I know how to use, maintain and store guns and over the years am even becoming a tolerable shot, my personal firearm would be more likely to help than to hurt me. But guns, or any weapons, by the very fact of what Plato would call their "virtue"—their function, their raison d'être, the thing they do best—increase the likelihood of killing even without intent. "Everybody carried guns and pistols constantly," recalls the pioneer woman, Lily Klasner, whom I've already quoted (did I mention that her father was gunned down?), "and as there was always more or less handling of them, often in a very careless way, it was natural that these should be frequently discharged accidentally." We see a photograph of French soldiers in a muddy trench, cleaning their Saint-Étienne machine gun, stripping it down to its complex parts, employing their box of *petits utensiles* with all due diligence to make certain that it gleams more than they do—because these mechanics need their lethal tool. For the sake of self-defense they'd better keep it ready to spray death across the horizon. Their enemies do the same. And so the Saint-Étiennes await events in trenches and shell holes from Switzerland all the way to the Atlantic. Accordingly, "it was natural that these should frequently be discharged accidentally," or at least discharged without a great deal of personal knowledge of the men from the opposing trench who approached at a run. The intent is to survive *their* guns. That means cutting them down. The more guns, the more deaths. We see a mass grave in a ravine of naked earth stubbled by scorched tree-stumps. They lie in sort of pavement, those war-slain men, with their boots against the wall of dirt soon to cover them. This is the Eparges front, 1915, where to be missing usually meant to be dead, "prisoners being much more rare than in Argonne." If we replace guns by nuclear bombs, the danger of this reactive conception looms fierce and naked; one psychopolitical text insists that *"the American preoccupation with national security began with our own atomic bomb,"* which came into being out of fear of Hitler's prospective atomic bomb, just as my desire to buy and retain guns is (partly) based on the guns of others. The consequences of misusing atom bombs are even more tremendous than those of abusing Saint-Étiennes, but for just that reason (thinks the statesman-strategist), how can I give up mine first?

The Rainbow of Le Chambon

My carrying the .45 when I went to the park with the Asian woman was the result of an easier calculus than that of Yugoslavia, there being no war civil or uncivil in my neighborhood. (A) Insofar as it increased my self-respect and self-confidence, insofar as it allowed me to protect the Asian woman, what I was doing that night was moral. (Indeed, as one medieval writer insisted, "if you should see your most dear mother or your wife misused in your presence, and not aid if you were able, you would be cruel and incur the opprobrium of worthlessness and impiety." Recently I had in fact seen her misused by a double carload of teenagers of another color who yelled profanities about her gook eyes and her gook language; I leaped out of the car and yelled back at them to stop, but definitely lost that argument; the medieval scribbler was correct: I found it inexpressibly painful to stand helpless when she was being insulted.) (B) Insofar as I was breaking the law, on the other hand, my carrying the .45 was immoral.

But these descriptors ignore the fundamental one. Writing about the French village of Le Chambon, whose people saved thousands of Jews from the Nazis, Philip Hallie addresses the distinction between being one of many soldiers and being one of many nonviolent civilians:

> I had been a combat artilleryman in the European theater and I knew that decent killers like me had done more to prevent the mass murders from continuing than this pacifist mountain village had done. And so I found myself wavering between praising military valor above all and praising moral valor above all. I could easily make these two points of view consistent with each other (one was a "public" perspective and the other was a "personal" perspective, etc.), but the questions that kept gnawing at me were: Where does your heart lie? . . . Who, in short, or what, are you?

This was the question which some antinuclear activists kept asking themselves at Seabrook. I quote from the unpublished account which I wrote a couple of weeks later:

As everyone helped assemble the wire-cutters, ropes, goggles, gas masks, helmets and other [items] which, it was hoped, would allow entry onto the site in the face of police resistance, there seemed to be a tension in the group born as much from the ambiguity of what was happening as from the fear of arrest or injury. The arranging and packing up of equipment, the businesslike preparations of the medics, seemed like activities preceding some commando mission, something different—and yet this action was to be non-violent. We felt this oddness everywhere: in the decorated helmets, the fingers inserted behind a friend's gas mask to see if it was properly adjusted, and the nervous faces exchanging looks, breaking into laughter as they met each other's gaze and then resuming their seriousness.

Hallie learns where his heart lies when a lady whose children were saved at Le Chambon tells him that the Holocaust was a storm and Le Chambon the rainbow.

Ever since the woman from Minneapolis witnessed to that hope, I realized that for me too the little story of Le Chambon is grander and more beautiful than the bloody war which stopped Hitler. I do not regret fighting in that war—Hitler had to be stopped, and he had to be stopped by killing many people. The war was necessary. But my memories of it give me only a sullied joy because in the course of the three major battles I participated in, I saw the detached arms and legs and heads of young men lying on blood-stained snow.

The story of Le Chambon gives me an unsullied joy. Why?

Anybody who does not feel a sullied joy in committing violence for even the most righteous reason is probably a sadist or an inhuman aesthetician. Unsullied joy cannot but be the rainbow, the end, the Good, which is why when I first began to read Gandhi's *Satyagraha,* a feeling of intense excitement struck me, and a giddy sense of hope. Here at last, I thought, was a revolutionary without hatred, a man of Christlike integrity who had not only the will to change his society for the better but also a practical program for doing so. The idea of explicitly taking upon oneself the suffering inflicted by an oppressive order, or performing a sort of aikido through which all the damage would be inflicted by the opponent upon oneself, in order that that damage be *used* to touch that opponent's humanity, thrilled me. How bold, loving, rational and good! And yet, as Hallie is honest enough to admit, violence may sometimes be necessary. The limitation (which the antinuclear activists at Seabrook had tacitly banked on) is this: there does have to be that humanity in the opponent to start with. Otherwise, he'll merely laugh and redouble his slaughter. Consider the message that Gandhi had for the Jews in Nazi Germany after *Kristallnacht*:

> If I were a Jew and were born in Germany and earned my livelihood there, I would claim Germany as my home even as the tallest gentile German may, and challenge him to shoot me or cast me into the dungeon . . . If one Jew or all the Jews were to accept the prescription here offered, he or they cannot be worse off than now. And suffering voluntarily undergone will bring them an inner strength and joy which no number of resolutions of sympathy . . . can . . . The calculated violence of Hitler may even result in a general massacre of the Jews . . . But if the Jewish mind could be prepared for voluntary suffering, even the massacre I have imagined could be turned into a day of thanksgiving and joy that Jehovah had wrought deliverance of the race even at the hands of the tyrant.

What might Hitler's reply have been? "They're ready to suffer voluntarily? Good! Send more boxcars to the Umschlagplatz!"

"The Stability Which Can Only Rest in a Fanatical Outlook"

No doubt Gandhi would have been the first to report to the boxcars if he could (he wrote two letters to Hitler offering to serve him in the cause of peace, neither of which India's British government permitted to be sent). Frail and joyous on the path to the gas chambers he would have gone, that strange, roundheaded, toothless little man with full-moon spectacles and full-moon ears, so willing to admit error, so excellent in his aspirations, so removed from his or any other time. He would have offered up his life as a sacrifice for *all* people, including the Jews; and that would have infuriated many of the Warsaw Ghetto fighters who wanted to die with violent dignity. It was for equivalent reasons that he would never be able to get on with Mr. Jinnah, the head of the Muslim League and eventual founder of Pakistan. Gandhi longed to represent everyone in India, and claimed to; Jinnah's cold reply was that Gandhi represented only Hindus. Partition would go ahead. —Gandhi, weary and almost desperate, cried that this was poison, not Islam. Nonviolence being usually as much (or more) a performance for others as it is a form of discipline for oneself, what can the moral actor do if the audience cries out, "No, we reject your drama and your gift; you do *not* stand for us!"? Christ's well-known solution was, firstly, to move on to another town and preach anew, and secondly, to suffer crucifixion. Gandhi suffered various crucifixions, too, including spells of imprisonment and finally assassination, but as a politician, a nationalist and a reasonably sincere self-improver he could not walk away from the rejecters: India was his only town; he had nowhere else to go. With Jinnah he ultimately failed, but his other opponent, the British Empire, he bested. Here is a photograph of him representing the Indian National Congress in London in 1931. Beneath the chandelier is a long rectangular perimeter of table, upon which folded name cards and carafes of water have been strategically placed. The great men gaze at the camera. The ones nearest have half turned themselves around in their chairs (a bit out of focus; what we mainly see of them is their uncomfortably positioned shoulders; they endeavor to appear serious, bland and pleasant. The rest have much the same expression. They are being very patient.) Here's a man caught in mid-applause, as it seems—unless he's just clasping his hands and looking wise: Come on, men, let's put on a good show! And in the midst of all these dark-suited ones rests Gandhi, wrapped in a blanket, gazing down and away. His formula of challenge, self-sacrifice and deliverance exasperates and blocks them. He is winning—not here, not right away, but their morals and their policies forbid them to liquidate him; and ultimately India will be freed. —Will the credit be all his? Of course not, but at times he will be pivotal. —He is the man of the mantra; they are the men of the bloodstained snow. We cannot necessarily call them bad men, although some were, and although their India policy humiliated and exploited India; they were simply the practical men of English power politics. Hitler stripped away the wealth of conquered territories; the British did that, to a degree, but they also built, and a free India inherited that infrastructure. On one of the occasions when they jailed Gandhi in India, and needed to negotiate, they actually commissioned a special train to bring Nehru and his father out of their prison cell to met him. Gandhi's biographer writes:

> It was an amazing demonstration of the nature of the raj that it was
> prepared to co-operate with its own prisoners in this way for the sake of

political co-operation with their self-professed opponents . . . As is so often and rightly pointed out, Gandhi's role and achievements would have been very different had he confronted a different type of imperialism.

This is putting it kindly. When one reads about Gandhi busily calling upon the Czechs to meet Hitler with satyagraha, and upon the English to do the same, one is forced to say that here nonviolence (which Hitler, ever charitable to his opponents, would have called "spineless submission") has met its match.

What precisely *was* the difference between the imperialism of the raj and of the Reich? According to that expert in the employment of extreme violence, Hitler again, the former type could be characterized by vacillation:

The very first requirement for a mode of struggle with the weapons of naked force is and remains persistence . . . as soon as force wavers and alternates with forbearance, not only will the doctrine to be repressed recover again and again, but it will also be in a position to draw new benefit from every persecution, since, after such a wave of pressure has ebbed away, indignation over the suffering induced leads new supporters to the old doctrine, while the old ones will cling to it with even greater defiance and deeper hatred than before.

This was the secret of Gandhi's success, as it would be of Martin Luther King's—although what Hitler insisted was defiance and hatred was sometimes noble steadfastness. Those British negotiators with their carafes, name cards and special trains, like the television-conscious American presidency of the 1960s, were mere alternators, hence ultimately forbearers: nonviolence counted on that. Hitler's solution: unremitting mercilessness, armored by rigid plates of ideology to guard it against any counterideology of the Other: "Any violence which does not spring from a firm, spiritual base, will be wavering and uncertain. It lacks the stability which can only rest in a fanatical outlook." And the result? Well, cities burned, of course, and whole armies exterminated. That we know. And we also know the toll paid by people who either forswore violence or else were incapable of it: children gassed, hostages shot, women burned alive in trenches, Jehovah's Witnesses sent to concentration camps . . .

But Gandhi would never agree that this meant that nonviolence had failed. Nor would he approve of my conflation of the forswearers and the incapables. In Jehovah's Witnesses publications written after the Third Reich, the experiences of that sect in the camps now prove their unswerving glory. Maybe for some of them those times became indeed, at least in retrospect, "a day of thanksgiving and joy." They were potent. "I have become disconsolate," Gandhi had admitted at the beginning of the Second World War. "In the secret of my heart I am in perpetual quarrel with God that He should allow such things to go on . . . But the answer comes at the end of the daily quarrel that neither God nor non-violence is impotent. Impotence is in men."

THE SUPERIORITY OF NONVIOLENCE
Gandhi's moral calculus (1920–46)

1. "It is better to die helpless and unarmed and as victims rather than as tyrants."

2. "The purer the suffering, the greater is the progress."

3. "It may be that in the transition state we may make mistakes; there may be avoidable suffering. These things are preferable to national emasculation."

4. "We must refuse to wait for the wrong to be righted till the wrong-doer has been roused to a sense of his iniquity."

5. "One must scrupulously avoid the temptation of a desire for results."

Source: Young India, *May 12, 1920;* Harijan, *March 17, 1946*

"Impotence is in men." This is precisely my objection, at least in regard to myself. What about the gassed children? Gandhi's "suffering voluntarily undergone" surely ought be read as "suffering for the sake of something." The famed Golden Rule, *Do unto others as you would be done by,* which is the rule of satyagraha, is practical in extreme situations only for martyrs. What if someone does not have the aptitude to be a martyr? I first got an inkling of my own deficiency in this regard when, as a child thoroughly propagandized by Sunday school, I met with my usual committee of bullies and was punched in the face. I decided to literally turn the other cheek. Now, nowhere did Christ ever promise that so doing would spare one from further violence; and my memory is not clear enough for me to say after so many years whether I expected such an outcome; I think my motives were evenly divided between those of a scientist testing a hypothesis and those of a young boy who wanted to believe in adults and goodness. The Sunday school teacher had assured us, perhaps too upliftingly, that turning the other cheek was the way. I, of course, immediately got punched again, this time in the nose, which began to bleed. I turned the other cheek. Another punch. I forget how many punches there were after that. "Spineless submission," Hitler had said. And Sade: *"My neighbor is nothing to me: there is not the slightest connection between him and me."* I wanted to be noble and loving, and maybe I was; maybe I should have continued as I began that day, instead of growing up to buy guns. Finally, satiated, the bullies let me go. The reason why as I trudged along home I felt a certain dissatisfaction with the Golden Rule was that the blows I'd received had not really been for any cause or reason. The martyrs one reads about are always turning the other cheek to prove their faith. I did not have enough faith, nor was I being punished for any faith. The bullies went to the same church that I did. Their punches afforded them a certain joy. By making it easier for them to punch me I had become an unwitting accomplice in their sadism. In fact, I am convinced that I made it easier for them to do what they did. It never occurred to me to hit them back, but I did start avoiding the bullies (which is the coward's method of nonviolence). That veteran of snowball fights, that murderer and Golden Rule invoker, Captain John Brown, would surely have defended himself with fists and stones, without regarding himself as being in the least unchristian. A Gandhian, on the other hand, would have let them do their worst until other likeminded souls had become inspired and lined up to be punched in their turn. I know my hometown, and I don't believe that anyone else would have come. Well, no matter; "one must scrupulously avoid the temptation of a desire for results." I am not saying that Gandhi was wrong; I honestly don't know. Probably it would not have been good for me, at least at that time of my life (maybe it would be a good thing now), to offer myself as their punching bag every Sunday. It would not have developed in me any strength or self-respect. It would only have made me feel even more foolish and worthless than I already did.

BECOMING STEEL
The moral calculus of Trinh Duc, Vietnamese revolutionary
(1954–64)

When I was young I witnessed a great deal of injustice . . . but that hatred wasn't ingrained in me. Later I saw how people I loved were brutally tortured, and I had more hatred. Since I had been in prison that kind of thing had been happening to me personally for many, many years . . . I felt as if I had become like hardened steel . . . I was more than capable of doing the same things to my enemies that they were doing to me . . . and worse.

Judged by Gandhi's moral calculus, I had two failings: my suffering was not pure, and I wanted results. *Do unto others as you would that others do unto you* is not at all equivalent with what we might as well call the Fool's Gold Maxim: *Do unto others as you hope and expect that others will do unto you.* The famous muckraker and do-gooder Lincoln Steffens learned that distinction in 1911 when as part of his experiment in applying the Golden Rule to labor mediation he persuaded two union bombers to plead guilty. Steffens had fondly believed that there would be a quid pro quo: lenient sentences for the bombers. One got life, and the other got fifteen years at hard labor. After that, he was scornfully known as "Golden Rule" Steffens. As Machiavelli wrote with his customary bluntness, "From among other evils which being unarmed brings you, it causes you to be despised . . . there is nothing proportionate between the armed and the unarmed." I myself followed not the Fool's Gold Maxim but the Golden Rule, but I did so without understanding the implications. I was a child, vulnerable to others' impressions of me, and I had almost no friends. If the violence is purely opportunistic, has no intellectual expedient or ideological basis, then, it seems to me, nonresistance is meaningless, unless the moral commitment of the nonresister makes up for the lack of moral commitment of the assailant.

In short, satyagraha is correct only if the sacrifice is *for* something, and only if the oppressor will eventually be moved to cease his aggression should the sacrifice become of sufficient magnitude. If one or both of these conditions remains unmet, then counterviolence is justified.

Emotional Attachments, or the Pursuit of Sullied Joy

A few months after that foggy night in the park with the Asian woman, her dog and my .45, there was an article in the paper about a lady who barely escaped being raped in broad daylight in the parking lot of a nearby restaurant which the Asian woman and I often went to, and I didn't say anything about it but the Asian woman saw it and was a little shaken up. That evening she went out with the dog. It was a hot bright evening. She had been feeling unwell for the past day or two, and as I watched her go she seemed slow, tiny, awkward, weak—a victim. The excited golden retriever snapped up the leash, pulled her around the corner and then she was gone. I sat working upstairs and a long time passed and it grew dark. I thought of satyagraha and I asked myself whether her rape or murder would serve any purpose, and I was not able to see that it would—because *she* quite reasonably did not want to be raped or murdered! I asked myself whether there would be any fewer rapes and murders in Sacramento if somebody preyed upon her, and failed to be convinced that there would. If anything, there might be more. Satyagraha is the best means of self-defense, insisted Gandhi, who was sometimes more radical than Buddha himself; but it now became clear to me that satyagraha ought to be undertaken and followed to the end only by somebody who has renounced all attachments. (How strange, that extreme nonviolence agrees with extreme violence in this! "The revolutionary is a doomed man," writes the infamous terrorist Sergey Nechaev, and we can imagine Gandhi nodding in agreement. "He has no interests of his own, no affairs, no feelings, no attachments, no belongings, not even a name." The difference, of course, is this: Gandhi would be proud of the Asian woman, and joyous, if she chose willingly to sacrifice herself to the thugs; if not, he'd happily sacrifice himself for her. Nechaev would indifferently kill her himself, should that advance his ends.) As for me, I had no right to ask her not to defend herself, nor any right not to defend her—nor any desire for either such negation.

There was the .45 on my desk. I seemed to have it near me more and more these days. In one out of every two households in America there lay at least one gun like mine, maybe a smaller one like my 9 millimeter Sig Sauer, maybe a larger one like my .50 caliber Desert Eagle, but still a gun. I had a gun, I was not alone in having a gun, and right then I did not feel comforted. (Gandhi commented on that phenomenon, too.) The ugliest thing about daily anxieties is that they keep recurring. Rosary beads break. One can be brave one time, and the next, and maybe the next, but sooner or later, I suppose, something will happen for which one is simply not ready. As I said, she was not well. The black boys with bottles had unnerved me; the white woman in San Francisco who called her "fish-breath" when she wanted to use the pay phone merely made me angry; the blocked intersection (not far from our neighborhood) with the police cars and the yellow crime scene tape made me nervous, but my rosary beads had not broken yet. After all, if you break what can you do? What right had I to even think about breaking? These were the ordinary annoyances and hazards of life.

The books that I read and the things that I saw while writing this book affected me more than I wanted them to. I wanted to become deader inside, so that the smell of skulls in Cambodia or the hungry woman with the long knife who crouched in the stairwell in Madagascar (she was merely posing for my camera that time, but her pose demonstrated what she did for a living) would not return together as kinesthetic echoes. Near the end of the twenty years that I spent writing this book, I began to suffer frequent nightmares of violence. I saw an evil ape with a pistol ascending to a judge's bench. (This was ridiculous, but it terrified me. I had that dream while writing about Stalin.) I was trapped in a burning plummeting airplane which had just been hit by a missile. Someone had tortured the Asian woman to death. People had moved into the house, stolen my guns and unmasked themselves as my ideological judges and executioners. I was hiding in a mass grave, the sole survivor, waiting for the murderers to discover me. I was released on bail but would have to return for my execution in thirty days. I was lured into my basement (I have not lived in a house with a basement for years) but found only darkness and fear down there. Ascending the stairs, I saw a man with a knife in his hand, plotting to kill me. I shot him and threw him into the basement. Then I fled, knowing that I'd soon be arrested for murder. In those dreams I was always running. They were not normal sights that I'd seen—or were they all too normal?—and these were not normal thoughts, and I knew this and sought to dampen the vibrations of my paranoia, but it had been dark a long time now and the Asian woman was not home. Well, of course, such thoughts might have seemed quite normal to Bernal Díaz, one of Cortes's sixteenth-century conquistadors, who until the end of his life could not sleep securely unless he was in his clothes, and even then he but catnapped. "I am so used to it that, thank God, it does me no harm. I have said all this so that my readers shall know . . . how accustomed we became to our arms and to keeping watch." It was seeing his comrades get captured and sacrificed by the Aztecs that had taught him how to fear; after that, he was always a little strange. A woman I know well, who barely survived an arson fire, slept in her clothes for years after the event. She said to me that even when she lay down to make love she couldn't forget how she'd almost died in her bed, so she couldn't relax, couldn't have an orgasm. A decade or so went by, and she finally overcame this problem but continued to be rootless, moving from house to house, not finishing projects, restlessly packing and unpacking. The Asian woman had not returned. It was dark outside. Ilya Ehrenburg's vicious

aphorism boomeranged back to me: Any journalist who reports a war objectively should be shot. I did not feel in the least objective. If anyone tried
to hurt her, I would gladly kill that person if necessary to help her. Many
times I'd discussed such imaginings with my friend Ben in San Francisco,
who also had them, and considered them baneful; they alighted in his mind
like dark moths; he believed (as I occasionally do) that to prepare for evil
overmuch invites evil—and yet in Bosnia my two colleagues had chuckled
at me good-humoredly for wearing my bulletproof vest on that hot quite
warless day; they died and I lived. A Gandhian, perhaps, would have died
smiling gratefully, confident that his unprovoked murder would somehow
do its mite to reduce violence. My colleagues died anguished, terrified.
Epictetus scorned to fear for his body, and declaimed:

> If, then, a man has the same opinion about his property as the man
> whom I have instanced has about his body; and also about his children
> and his wife, and in a word is so affected by some madness or despair
> that he cares not whether he possesses them or not, but like children who
> are playing with shells care about the play, but do not trouble themselves
> about the shells, so he too has set no value on the materials, but values
> the pleasure that he has with them and the occupation, what tyrant is then
> formidable to him or what guards or what swords?

I had once been that way; I'd been alone. But the freedom of which he
speaks carries a high price: not only loneliness but also a certain egotism,
carelessness about others, an ideological indifference bordering on disrespect toward others who love one and who trust themselves to one's care.
Because the Asian woman would never read or agree with Epictetus, I did
not feel that I had the right to treat her as a seashell. I did not want her to
be dying in some dark place screaming uncomprehendingly for me (or just
screaming). And she was late. Out of the corner of my eye I saw the .45 lying heavy and black upon the work table, shining, on safe but loaded and
chambered with Golden Sabre cartridges, whose jackets are slit so that
when lead strikes flesh those scorings will tear into flanges destabilizing
outward into claws which twist and grab and maim as the bullet shears
whirling through the growing wound—after all, self-defense is not a sporting matter—Golden Sabre, they said, was even more effective than Black
Talon, whose sale was now banned to civilians since a murderous idiot

had misused them on the Long Island Railroad; my gun was well loaded, but it lay here with me, not with her, so it was useless. If it had been in her purse it would still have done her no good, because she feared guns and was ignorant of their use. On the other hand, I knew the general route she took with the dog. If she hadn't returned in another hour, say, I'd slip the gun in the pocket of my light windbreaker and go out looking for her. If somebody was hurting her, I'd hurt him to stop him. What else could I do? I preferred sullied joy to impotent fear.

II.

WHERE DO MY RIGHTS END?

> *The urgent consideration of the public safety may undoubtedly authorise the violation of every possible law. How far that or any other considera-tion may operate to dissolve the natural obligations of humanity and justice, is a doctrine of which I still desire to remain ignorant.*
>
> EDWARD GIBBON, ca. 1776

Four Murdered Children

What else could I do? —There's the bedrock justification for violent self-defense, and occasionally it even rings true. But Gandhi didn't think so. (Of course, Indian custom protected his wife from random violation by prohibiting her from going out alone.) I made a choice; Gandhi made a choice. And there are four choices that the self in extremis, regardless of its actual *capability*, retains the conditional right to make:

JUSTIFIED CHOICES OF THE SELF

1. Whether or not to violently defend itself against violence;
2. Whether or not to violently defend someone else from violence.
3. Whether or not to destroy itself.
4. Whether or not to help a weaker self destroy itself, to save it from a worse fate.

CONDITIONS:

1. No attachment to nonviolent creeds. (Nonviolence condition.)

2. No allegiance to collectivity or authority which might prohibit the self from removing itself from "the line of fire." (Allegiance condition.)

   CAVEAT TO (1) AND (2): *So-called involuntary attachments are not binding.*
   Voluntary attachments may likewise be withdrawn at any time. In short, both conditions may be overridden—at which point one returns to the state of nature. [First draft. This caveat will be modified somewhat in another chapter.]

   EXAMPLES: By the rights of the self one may justifiably refuse to fight a war, or one may renounce nonviolence in order to defend oneself, or one may violently rebel against authority provided that one's cause is just, etc., etc. Of course there may well be dire consequences to the decider.

3. An accurate understanding of circumstances and consequences. This is why we wouldn't allow a small child to destroy himself by drinking household poisons or to carry a loaded pistol for self-defense.

These are my axioms, my starting points, and as such cannot and will not be proved. Agree with them, or not. Evaluate what follows accordingly. I make no claim that they are the self's only rights. I do assert that they are the rights most germane to this study of violence.

Of the four conditions, the second is the heaviest, applying—or made to apply (in violation of the caveat)—to army deserters, arrest-resisters, plotters of palace coups, and so many more state-of-nature types that although we'll rarely refer to this condition in such a simple form from now on, we'll not be done with it for the rest of this book: —If I deserted, then my allegiance to authority wasn't voluntary. —Oh, yes it was, replies authority; haven't you enjoyed all the benefits of citizenship until now? You used my roads and bridges, didn't you? That means you signed on my dotted line, which now gives me license to execute you for treason.

The allegiance condition thus hovers like a winter fog over this entire inquiry. I see no way to begin, however, without imagining, as do classical physicists with their inventions of perfect vacuums, frictionless planes and the like, a self "in isolation"—like Thoreau in his ramblings around Walden Pond—or the Asian woman in the park at night, calling her dog, wandering into ever lonelier places beneath the winter fog. The dog does not hear. A car glares yellowly upon her. The car follows her, passes, makes a sudden U-turn, stops. The door opens, and three men get out. Nobody will help her.

A Mother's Sovereignty

FIRST MURDER: I read recently about an activist who was tortured in a political prison by being forced to watch her child being tortured in front of her. Authority explained, no doubt in tones of odious rationality, that even in this secret empire of glaring lights and capricious but inescapable physical agony, predestination did not entirely apply—for look! Behind a pane of glass she saw a struggling little figure. Perhaps they opened a vent, so that she'd hear its cries; almost certainly they arranged for it to see *her* there (ashen-faced, supported in two policemen's arms), in order to confirm that mutual attachment which can be so ingeniously utilized in games whose object receives that bitter gift called free will: If she did not betray her comrades (authority said), on her child would now fall the torments she knew so well. Which loyalty would the desperate woman then betray? She kept silent, and watched her child die screaming. No one will ever know how she actually chose. We know only that she did *not* choose to save her child—a choice, indeed, which might well have been spurious; after she'd talked, mother and child might both have been dispatched. Here were her possible courses of action:

1. Speak, and hopefully preserve her child.
2. Refuse to speak, and thereby protect others.
3. Refuse to participate in authority's scheme (asserting, in effect, that if they murdered her child it was all their doing).
4. Vacillate; make no decision.

(A fervent Gandhian might have made a fifth choice, adhering to the master's almost inhuman standard, whose slogan reads: "Truth, which requires utter selflessness, can have no time for the selfish purpose of begetting children and running a household . . . If a man gives his love to one woman, or a woman to one man, what is there left for all the world besides? . . . The larger their family, the farther they are from Universal Love." A mother's Gandhian act: Lovingly invite them to do their worst to oneself and one's child.)

Only the first act would have revealed the woman's true moral calculus—a valuable lesson for moral medal-pinners and stone-casters. All three other non-Gandhian possibilities must produce the same primary result—silence—and the same secondary result—a dead child. But to the protagonist herself, the exact reason she closed her lips might have mattered a good deal. Did she allow her child to die for some arguably good reason, or did she simply allow it to die? If she did have a reason, then she, like the Warsaw ghetto mother who suffocated her crying baby so that the Nazis would not discover the people in her bunker (in which case the baby would have died in any event), was a true heroine. Had she chosen to save her child at the expense of her comrades, she would also be a heroine to me. Either way, I'd bow down to her because she made a choice in an intolerable situation. (By extension, this license to choose either alternative may also apply to certain issues of animal rights.) Necessity gave her two alternatives each of which might have destroyed her. Plato describes the greatest folly of all as being "that of a man who hates, not loves, what his judgment pronounces to be noble or good, while he loves and enjoys what he judges vile and wicked." The mother's torturers sought to force that folly on her, to transform what she loved and enjoyed, her child, into a vile implement of traitorousness. They sought to make evil and dishonor inevitable. Let's hope that the mother did not turn away, that she did not make her decision by default.

Another Mother's Sovereignty

SECOND MURDER: In wartime in ancient China, a poet met a woman in a meadow heaped with human bones. The woman was starving. She'd left her baby to die and was walking away weeping. She said to the poet: "I know not where I myself will die. I cannot keep us both alive." The poet, who probably also could do nothing for either of them, galloped away. "Such words I could not bear to hear." He was no hero, she no heroine; they took their natural rights (which Robespierre calls "the sacred duty imposed by nature on all living beings"). I can brand neither one of them wrong.

The Confession of Bukharin

However forlorn and bitter the soul, however hellish the violence of material reality, such moments, by presenting alternatives—even if both horns of the dilemma are unspeakable—command us to be ethically human in the highest, extremist sense. Who would not willingly forgo such hideous "opportunities"? But it matters not what we will. Choice, like all of life, comprises not only action but reaction. No one escapes it. The absolute monarch and the criminal innocent or guilty en route to the electric chair must each decide who and how he'll be in his remaining moments of life— struggling or serene; righteous, forgiving or even penitent; selfish or other- ish. Thus Nikolai Bukharin, a vacillating, less than admirable fellow traveler along the Stalinist road, and now one of the chief defendants in Stalin's show trials, compelled, like the first mother we read about, by threats against his child, and probably by torture, to denounce himself, trans- forms his plea to the court into defiance no less noble for its heartbreaking obliqueness:

> I admit that I am responsible both politically and legally for the defeatist
> orientation, . . . although I affirm that personally I did not hold this
> position . . . I further consider myself responsible both politically and
> legally for wrecking activities, though I personally do not remember
> having given directions about wrecking activities.

He will be shot—and so will all his fellow defendants, whether they groveled, recanted or not. He possesses no power over his fate. But (within the stiflingly narrow limits of terror, and the partially overlapping bound- aries of the allegiance condition) he can still act.

But when? If your existence is as justified as mine, then mine must be as justified as yours—but no more. Do I injure my own goodness (commonly called my "humanity") in refusing to sacrifice myself for you? —Possibly, but the only practical remedy in some cases—namely, forcing me to sacri- fice myself for you—is equally unjust. Hence the first right of the self, self- defense (of whatever kind: in Bukharin's case only moral self-defense offers any practical hope, the biological kind having been ruled out, de- spite authority's lying oath: "Conduct yourself well in the trial—I promise you they will not shoot you"), becomes almost tautologically unarguable. Bukharin will not conduct himself well, and we admire him for it.

Even if, like Bukharin, our faith, careers, experiences, habits compel us to grant some legitimacy to the authority now bent on pulverizing us, self- defense takes moral precedence over civic obedience, other factors being equal. (Authority shouts: They never are!) Just as in the American Consti- tution all rights not explicitly ceded to federal power remain claimed by the states, so even under the allegiance condition any right of authority to demand my destruction for its good must be understood as explicitly localized, and elsewhere voided by my own superior right.

Consider again the right of a government to draft someone for military service. We have seen how an immediate tug-of-war develops between the right of the officer to order him into almost certain death in a battle and the enlisted man's right to survive. Which side is correct depends on whether the judge is Hobbes or Tolstoy. But only the extremist authoritarian would assert that the same officer could in peacetime order the man to march over the edge of a precipice. And, in fact, since authority desires to harness our rationality to its ends, it must accordingly reason us into obedience, which in turn implies that we can reason ourselves out of it. Saint Thomas Aquinas's view is representative.

AQUINAS'S MORAL CALCULUS (*BEFORE* A.D. 1256)

WHAT IS A MAN'S VIRTUE?
The good of a man . . .

1. As a man: "Consists in the perfection of his reason in the cognition of truth and in the regulation of his inferior appetites according to the rule of reason, for a man is man by his rationality."

2. As a citizen of earth: "Lies in his being ordered to the good of all within a commonwealth."

3. As a citizen of heaven: "Cannot be acquired by his own natural powers" and hence must come from grace. (Plato would claim that it could come from sincere meditation, discourse and study.)

These three types of virtue do not necessarily agree.

Source: Aquinas, pp. 96–97, "On the Virtues in General."

A rational person will be an obedient citizen—but only if authority is itself rational and does not infringe his heavenly citizenship. Hence Gandhi: "A Satyagrahi obeys the laws of society intelligently and of his own free will, because he considers it to be his sacred duty to do so. Only then does the right accrue to him of civil disobedience of certain laws in well-defined circumstances." Hence also the Basic Law for the Federal Republic of Germany: "The dignity of man shall be inviolable. To respect and protect it shall be the duty of all state authority." In both of these cases, a strong residue of self-sovereignty thus remains irreducible even by government's most violent acids of coercion.

THE MORAL CALCULUS OF THE CHRISTIAN DEMOCRATIC UNION/CHRISTIAN SOCIAL UNION GROUP IN THE GERMAN BUNDESTAG (1977):

"THE CLASSICAL FREEDOMS"

1. Life, freedom and safety of the person.
2. Effective legal protection against arbitrary measures by the State.
3. Freedom of opinion.
4. Freedom of conscience and religion.
5. The right to marriage, family life and the education of one's children.
6. Equal treatment and protection from national discrimination.
7. Freedom of movement and emigration.

"Violations of these rights are unlawful encroachments upon the individual's innermost freedom and strike deeply at human dignity."

Source: CDU/CSU, p. 24.

Even that worshipper of discipline Moltke the Elder relaxes the allegiance condition far enough to grant the right of a soldier to live off the country—that is, to pillage—if he is not properly fed by his own army: "He not only *can but must* take from the resources of the land what is necessary for his existence." —No matter that Moltke, who, gaunt, rigid and piercing-eyed, wears authority's eight-pointed star below his collar, indulges this necessity only because it accords with his war aims—an ill-fed soldier cannot fight as well as a nourished one, no matter what compulsion presses upon him. On the other hand, the necessity of self-preservation which the deserter pleads will never be allowed. —The fact remains that under extreme circumstances Moltke will tolerate deviation from "behavior appropriate for parade." "Willful deviations from the established arrangement may in no case be tolerated, for the disintegration of discipline spreads like a virus." The commanding officer lets them off the leash; they break down the peasants' doors. In such a case, responsibility will be laid not at the hungry soldiers' doors but at the threshold of the Supreme Command itself, where quite possibly the generals have just sat down to a sumptuous roast.

As for Gandhi, his nonviolent soldiers follow him not by compulsion but by faith. Each Satyagrahi "must carry out with a willing heart all the rules of discipline as may be laid down from time to time," it is true; but should his heart be unwilling, he may depart the cause in peace.

The Republic, *or Systematized Justice*

In Plato's time, the time of the Peloponnesian War, the hoplite soldiers formed shield walls whose every member needed to keep his place for the good of all. Discipline ostensibly maintained itself as much by faith and solidarity as by compulsion; but the goal was not the Gandhian one of benefiting all by dying smiling deaths of violence, but the more customary Moltkeian one, rather, of self-preservation and civic enlargement by means of victory. Gandhi believed that everyone possesses a moral faculty; he fervently prayed that wrongdoers might improve theirs, but he'd force nothing. Plato legislated differently, because, assuming that most souls are ignorant of the Good, he preferred to apply the allegiance condition *unconditionally* wherever possible. In his ideal army, "no man, and no woman" (for he allowed female soldiers)

> should be ever suffered to live without an officer set over them, and no soul of man to learn the trick of doing one single thing of its own sole motion, in play or in earnest, but, in peace as in war, to live ever with the commander in sight . . . in a word, to teach one's soul the habit of never so much as thinking to do one single act apart from one's fellows . . . Anarchy—the absence of the commander—is what we should expel root and branch from the lives of all mankind.

What if the officers fail to look after the soldiers? Plato's answer seems to be: That will never happen. —And indeed, were it somehow feasible to bring his republic into being all at once, most everyone would fulfill the tasks of his assigned position, either out of obedience, loyalty and compulsion (among the lower orders), reverence to the showy dictates of honor (in the middle orders) or knowledge, which is virtue (in the master class). —As for me, I think that Plato refutes himself; because the system which he demands to oversee human goodness can only operate if its pawns already possess that goodness. But however flawed it is, Plato's conception of the self in society remains well worth musing on, because while his proposals may sometimes offer only limited plausibility, his darkly skeptical evaluation of the self in isolation is based on all too realistic premises.

Plato requests that we look into the justice of the self by examining first the justice of the commonwealth, thus calling on us to assume that the state is composed of the same elements, in the same proportion, as the individual, the only difference being that in the former all is magnified (hence, he says, easier to see and to begin his inquiry with). From this premise, he neatly proves that since any just state must demonstrate order, restraint and the separation of powers, a just individual should do the same—and, ideally, in the same way. Indeed, who could deny that a perfectly just individual and a perfectly just community of whatever kind must either have the same goals, or else be able to harmoniously marry their differences? The allegiance condition would either be as voluntary as love or as innate as breathing. Between the self and the group we'd see no war. Plato, architect and worshipper of consonance, visualizes glowing Forms: perfect essences of everything, whose divine light—if we could only see it always—would bathe each moral act in the pleasures of unchanging logic: What's good for one is good for all.

PLATO'S MORAL CALCULUS (CA. 350 B.C.)
How sovereign is the individual?

All things in proportion. In practical life, where no Philosopher-King can be found, authority must be shared between the ruler and his magistrates. Autocracy destroys "national feeling," but "an unqualified and absolute freedom from all authority is a far worse thing than submission to a magistrate with limited powers." The moral decisions of a Gandhi—or of any other soul untrained in his particular school—would in Plato's estimation be very hit-or-miss—although he would still want one to make those decisions, provided that they were not in conflict with the laws of his republic. Were his system ever to come into being, the self-doubting contemplation of which he is so fond would certainly be illegal.

1. "The wellborn have a title to rule the worse-born," parents to rule
   their children, elders to rule the younger, masters to rule slaves,
   the stronger to rule the weaker, the lucky to rule the unlucky, and
   "the supreme claim": the wise to rule the ignorant.

However,

2. "A community should be at once free, sane, and at amity with itself."
   How can these two things be justly accomplished?

3. By requiring both rulers and ruled to obey the laws.

Source: Laws, iii.690a–c, 691c–692c, 693b, 697c–698b, iv.715d–e.

Rarely self-interested and never mendacious, Plato becomes incontrovertible when he argues that there is such a thing as justice, that some people are juster than others and most people feel little inclination to seek out
what justice is, that some form of authority is inevitable (hence the allegiance condition; and even if allegiance is conditional, from a practical
point of view the self can only transfer it to another sovereign object, not
withdraw and then withhold it forever), and that the individuals most qualified to exercise authority are the justest. Alas, not everyone agrees that justice is what Plato says it is; nor can any of Plato's regulations (or any others
I can imagine) prevent individuals from violently oppressing one another.

The early Platonic dialogues offer us the gently subversive inspiration
of Socrates, whose life ends with a nobly challenging act of satyagraha: he
submits himself (in a spirit of witty defiance, it would seem) to the law,
provoking a death sentence which he might have expected and which even
at the end he could have escaped through exile. (He will not: he prefers to
honor the law.) But Plato, though he continues to employ to the end the
so-called Socratic method, gradually transforms his Socrates (now that the
original is dead) from an ironic and passionate arguer, almost a nihilist, a
freewheeling apostle of selfhood's freedom, into a lecturer, nay, a hectorer
of his inquirers, the mouthpiece of a system. (Christians made the same
thing out of their Christ.) Plato feels that moral actors *may* be correct in
what they do, but since morality is such a tricky business it is better to have
it legislated. The Platonic conception, in its reliance upon equal proportionality between the leaders and the led, becomes troubled by those who
don't know their place—and that place is determined by philosophic laws
at which the majority who are not lawmakers would be ill-advised to carp.
Hence the rights of any self to express itself, educate itself, reproduce and
even hear music of its choosing—much less to launch a revolution—have
been carefully circumscribed by class and, again, by constituted law. (Plato
was a man of his times. H. G. Wells writes that any modern scientist in

ancient Greece "would have been in constant danger of a prosecution for impiety. The democracy of Athens would have tolerated Darwin as little as the democracy of Tennessee.")

In his *Laws* (whose Socrates is now simply called "an Athenian"), we look in vain for acknowledgment of the predicament of this world's Bukharins and necessity-trapped mothers. The magistrates will lead everyone toward apprehending the unity of courage, purity, rectitude and wisdom. They being wiser than the rest, Gandhi's opposition politics won't be needed. How could there arise any benign or utilitarian issue from granting the self permission to create justice and virtue in its own proportions, when those proportions follow unvarying rational-mystical principles? "Fear," Plato explains, "was cast out by confidence in supposed knowledge, and the loss of it gave birth to impudence. For to be unconcerned for the judgment of one's betters in the assurance which comes of a reckless excess of liberty is nothing in the world but reprehensible impudence." ("The present era is liquidating itself," wrote his half brother Adolf Hitler. "It introduces universal suffrage, shoots off its mouth about equal rights, but finds no basis for them.") Gandhi and Bukharin, if they are wise enough, will join the ruling class in its benignity and guard the constitution.

Another Mother's Sovereignty

Hence in Plato's ideal city-state, the right to physical self-defense, as with other rights, may formally apply to any full citizen, but the right to determine when and how to employ it will be limited to the privileged Guardian class and the Philosopher-King at their head. Masters and parents being natural leaders, the slave may not kill the master, nor the child the parent, *even in self-defense.* "The law's command will be that he must endure the worst rather than commit such a crime." In effect, Plato is asserting (as enfranchised Greeks and Romans generally would) that there exist prohibited persons, upon whom laying violent hands must in every case result in impiety. In the classical world, such assertions might literally be graven in stone.

EXCERPTS FROM THE TWELVE TABLES: TABLE IV
(*Rome, 451–49 B.C.*)

1. "A notably deformed child shall be killed immediately."

2a. "To a father . . . shall be given over a son the power of life and death."

In Cicero's day, Roman schoolchildren were set to memorizing the Twelve Tables.

Plato, then, was not reasoning in some abhorrent moral vacuum—a fact that increases our obligation to consider his proposals fairly. —Well, what can be said? —I respect his end—the consecration of ties of social obligation—while rejecting his means, which fetters the self unjustly.

THIRD MURDER: In a photograph, we see the naked corpse of a four-year-old girl whose legs kink outward to the knee and then in again, forming a diamond shape like a frog's. Legs and arms resemble bird bones. The face has been turned sideways on the coroner's sheet; or maybe she died that way. The eyes are closed, the mouth slightly open. She weighed fourteen pounds at death. "Fatal starvation at this age is rare," notes the forensic pathologist, "and can be explained only by a combination of failure to feed the child at home and forcibly restraining her to get food *outside her home* from neighbors." If there be such a phenomenon as social impiety, the parents committed it; and had this child been lucky enough to be succored by a brother or sister old enough to resist them, by violence if need be, I fail to see the wrongness of any such action. Was her case simply unimaginable to Plato? —Not at all. —Because for him not all selves are a priori equally worthy, unless proven otherwise by their deeds, he sees infanticide quite differently than we do:

> The offspring of the good, I suppose, they will take to the pen or crèche . . . but the offspring of the inferior, and any of those of the other sort who are born defective, they will properly dispose of in secret, so that no one will know what has become of them.
>
> That is the condition, he said, of preserving the purity of the guardians' breed.

We would condemn the slow murder of that four-year-old girl not only because it was cruel but because it was infanticide. Presumably Plato would also condemn its cruelty; he might then go on to condemn it (depending on the class of her parents) for being infanticide *for no good reason*.

If we overlook the radical divide between Plato and ourselves regarding what percentage of the population ought to be ethically enfranchised (for Plato, only a few; for us, all who have not transgressed against our relatively mild social contract), a serious difference still remains: for us, the enfranchised self may do whatever it likes, so long as it does not directly hurt the state, or another member of it; for Plato, the self is, in addition, positively enjoined to do only what will benefit and improve the state. I am past the maximum age for sanctioned baby-making in the state, and I wish to form a liaison? The state allows it—but I must destroy any offspring without a fuss. If I refuse to give my child over to be strangled, I'll become guilty of treason—not against the huddle of my Jewish neighbors in our deep cellar already filled with smoke from German flamethrowers, but against some infinitely broader conception of collectivity: the abstraction of my republic, to which I am obligated to present only perfect offspring (perfection's precondition, a youthful parent, having been legally codified). —Do you feel for the bereaved? Plato feels for the state.

Self-Sovereignty and Choice

My argument against Plato so far has been one of restless self-assertion: I declare that I am sovereign over myself because I want to be; I refuse to be otherwise. There were times when I would rather die than be told I must do one thing and not the other. And if I feel so strongly about my own autonomy, how can I trample down the choices of others, except in the extreme cases (described in this book) when those cause unjustified suffering? It is, perhaps, the latent narcissism of my attitude which most deeply offends Hobbes when he runs shoutingly to Plato and Moltke's side:

> I observe the Diseases of a Common-wealth, that proceed from the poyson of seditious doctrines; whereof one is, That every private man is judge of Good and Evill actions.

For this moral philosopher, we enter into an irrevocable covenant with authority in our beginnings (or else our ancestors have done it for us); having done so, we lose our right to determine what is just. This doctrine, so appealing to tyrants, leaves us with no means of evaluating the behavior of the Sovereign (be that a king or a state). Perhaps it is only because I was raised in easy circumstances (the United States of America; twentieth century; white; middle class) that I have the luxury of rejecting Hobbes's position and deciding for myself, thus: *That every private man is judge of Good and Evill actions, not already and otherwise judged by the state which I have chosen by my citizenship to support.* But there is already a very simple justification for refusing to be bound by received philosophies: They do not agree.

More and more it seems to me that out of all the possible actions in the world, only a few are categorically evil. The majority we must permit others to perform if they wish, looking on in not unsympathetic silence. I propose, therefore, that a worthwhile ethical procedure for a citizen is:

1. To follow his own inner logic in order to postulate laws of conduct which seem to him good;
2. To follow those laws if they correspond to local norms, and reconsider them if they violate those norms; but
3. Above all, to choose the right regardless of local authority or custom, and then act accordingly.

This comes close to Trotsky's definition of revolutionary superiority (which is also a good modus operandi for journalists): "a complete and in-grained independence of official public opinion at all times and under all circumstances." Joan of Arc had that, too. She could say: "I would rather die than do what I know to be sin." She did die for her opinions, and so did Trotsky.

The Machiavellian Caveat

My position is based on the optimistic postulate that the self, if left to its own devices, will usually choose the good. And Plato from his crystalline heights of elitism agrees—only, he adds that what we *think* to be the good (such as present pleasure) may not be so. Hence, crime and evil are the re-sult of misapprehension. —What about that starved four-year-old child, whose corpse resembled that of a little quail or sparrow? —Well, her mother evidently mistook sadism or convenience for the Good, that's all—it happens all the time! . . . Machiavelli insists that precisely because it happens all the time, the self cannot simultaneously protect its interests and be good, for (call this the Machiavellian Caveat):

how one lives is so far distant from how one ought to live, that he who ne-glects what is done for what ought to be done, sooner effects his ruin than his preservation; for a man who wishes to act entirely up to his professions of virtue soon meets with what destroys him among so much that is evil.

In other words, never turn the other cheek or they'll take your head off: the ascription of any significant amount of moral sovereignty to the self becomes as poisonous a gift as the tortured mother's ostensible freedom to save her child. Machiavelli was himself tortured when his city lay under the rule of the Medicis. He confessed to no spurious treason, but, like a certain friend of mine who was also tortured, his release failed to prevent him from turning bitter. Unlike Plato, Machiavelli never seeks in his writings to tell us how to live, only how to achieve. (The tortured mother, too, whether she betrayed her child or her comrades, must have felt that "how one lives is so far distant from how one ought to live.") Bird-faced, with a tight, narrow mouth, he sought to save his city by pragmatic means against powerful, ruthless enemies. Plato began with what ought to be, but never told us how to get there; Machiavelli begins and almost always remains with what is; although in certain lines of his infamous essay *The Prince* one senses a wistful craving to dwell amidst the luxuries of goodness. Like Lenin, however, he had to be a pragmatist, a military politician in wartime, a cautious preparer and insurer in peacetime; and, like the Marquis de Sade, he received a destiny of disappointment and disenfranchisement, and accordingly hammered out aphorisms of monstrous anger. If the Machiavellian Caveat is true, then authoritarian coercion—or any kind of violence—becomes just another natural law, like gravity—nothing to rail at, no matter how one may be feeling deep in his scarred heart. By all means, treasure your noble end, but keep it secret. Just means to that end you'll often find irrelevant; certainly others won't use them on you! By the Machiavellian Caveat, Bukharin should have conducted himself more obsequiously at his trial; he might have lived (although we know he wouldn't); his wife and child could have fared better, and—who knows?—such cunning might have rewarded him with a new opportunity to strike for his political aims. (And the mother who starved her four-year-old to death? We have no reason to think that Machiavelli was ever writing any advice to her. He wouldn't have instructed her to hide the body. She would have figured in his thinking only as an illustration of the weary, selfish, foolish wickedness of humankind.)

By contrast, remember that crucial axiom in Gandhi's moral calculus: "One must scrupulously avoid the temptation of a desire for results." (We don't know whether Plato would have agreed, or simply sidestepped the entire issue of praxis.) We already know that practically speaking the application of Gandhian satyagraha is quite limited. This in no way discredits satyagraha as an ethical choice. Gandhi's reply to Machiavelli, then, would be that there is nothing wrong—and a great deal right—about being destroyed by one's evil fellow beings, that voluntary self-sacrifice will benefit the self morally; and, if sufficient fortitude, intelligence, compassion and integrity are marshaled, then many other selves may be improved both materially and morally. —Which view is correct, then? —Why, both Gandhi's and Machiavelli's—but not to the same person at the same time. —Returning to the example of the mother forced to watch her child being tortured, we can fault her neither for following Machiavelli by making lying declarations to the torturer, in order to save both her child and her comrades, nor for being a Gandhian and prayerfully offering herself for torture, too. What is her end? If it is purity, or martyrdom, then the means is obvious. If it is the preservation of the one she loves above all—a goal which, like self-preservation, is not at all ignoble; indeed, it's at least minimally righteous—then the means of Machiavelli looms. As long as the danger to her child (or her Party) stands imminent, she has kept within bounds. It is when violent deeds become proactive or wanton that the limits of the rights of the self are reached.

The Ik, or Unsystematized Injustice

Behold such a case: The anthropologist Colin Turnbull spent two years— unhappy ones, by the sound of them—among a tribe called the Ik, who lived (I use the past tense, for I am not sure whether they still exist) in the mountains where Kenya and Uganda meet the Sudan. The government considered his report on them "extreme," and I must concur, for in one of the concluding chapters he writes, "I am hopeful that their isolation will remain as complete as in the past, until they die out completely." Rather strong words for an objective social scientist! But Turnbull insists:

> The surface looked bad enough, the hunger could be seen and the trickery perceived, and the political games were well enough known, but one had to live among the Ik and see them day in and day out and watch them defecating on each other's doorsteps, and taking food out of each other's mouths, and vomiting so as to finish what belonged to the starving, to begin to know what had happened to them.

Which is the state of nature—precolonial Tahiti, whose naked easy grace gave Rousseau his stereotype of the noble savage, or the land of the Ik? Or could it be both? Do these antipodes represent merely the old dichotomy of heaven and earth, theory and practice, Plato and Machiavelli?

Unless we can employ some minimal degree of precision in discussing people's actual capacity for good, it will scarcely be practical to draw up any moral calculus. We'll therefore want to give at least passing attention to the state of nature and the social contract. To Hobbes, the state of nature equals the state of war; and such comprised the state of the Ik. During his sojourn in their steep, dry land, Turnbull met a people who, having lost both love and conscience, existed only as social atoms. Shocked, repulsed, beleaguered, at first he did what little he could to help the weakest victims of malice and indifference. His efforts inevitably proved futile, and the Ik got a good laugh, for they scrupulously obeyed the Machiavellian Caveat in almost everything. Husbands stole from wives, and vice versa. Mothers laughed when their babies crawled into hearth flames. They more or less discarded their children when the latter became three years old—high time by then to make their own way, or die. (By comparison, the American parents who starved their daughter to death seem almost merciful; she was four; she got an extra year.)

FOURTH MURDER: Perhaps the saddest tale Turnbull tells is of a weak little girl named Adupa, whom other children loved to torment by literally snatching the food from her mouth. Weakened by hunger, she dared to return to her parents' house, but they owned neither the ability nor the inclination to feed her, so they walled her up until she starved to death, then dumped her rotten carcass.

What can we say, aside from exclaiming in horror, or, like Machiavelli, half-cynically theorizing and describing in order to get distance, or once again attacking Plato's absurd laws of self-defense, or indulging in the game of searching for a cause—as if any cause could justify such cruelty? —First of all, Adupa's death reminds us once more, like Bukharin's trial and the tortured mother's nightmarish, half-involuntary voyeurism, that while every self, such as Adupa, has the right to live—in other words, the child would not have been immoral had she gained her subsistence by whatever means necessary—one has no guarantee that the exercise of a right will be successful or uncontested. In short, the word "right" is but an exemplary fiction. —Second, while Adupa's story might seem to prove the Hobbesian thesis that any social contract, even the most despotic, is better than this state of "natural right," later on in this book we'll meet an eerie parallel to it but of the most anti-Hobbesian nature: namely, Stalin's collectivization of the Ukraine, which starved millions. Parents ate their children, and children were trained to spy on their parents from watchtowers in the cornfields, the picking of a single ear of corn being punishable by imprisonment or worse. (Did this constitute a social contract? —By Stalin's, Hobbes's and almost everybody else's definition, yes. By the same gap in logic which always takes my breath away, law and government of any kind—even if the dispossessed are self-professedly conspiring to overthrow it—implies consent!) Nature and despotism, anarchy and absolutism, are thus capable of accomplishing the same evil result. Gazing into these twin abysses, who wouldn't second Plato's plea for civic temperance? For me to exercise my four justified choices of the self as I see fit, and for you, Bukharin and my other neighbors simultaneously to employ theirs, we must have a just social contract.

Huddling Against Monsters

Very well. Enact the contract. Well, then, what is our taste? What is the highest political good? What is a good government?

Let us imagine our collective beginnings as Locke, Hobbes and even Gibbon did: scared, murderous brutes hunching somewhere out of the rain, afraid of the brutes across the river, afraid most of all of one another. Probably history never began that way, probably we dwelled already in ape bands before we were men, but let it be. What does their fear teach them? I suppose they've lived hiding from the archetypally monstrous bandits in the legend of Theseus, the untrammeled ones who wrenched their victims' limbs apart by tying them to upswinging pine tops, or kicked them over cliffs as they were washing their murderers' feet, or cut them to fit spiked bedsteads. "That age produced a sort of men in force of hand . . . excelling the ordinary rate," says Plutarch, "making use, however, of these gifts of nature to no good or profitable purpose for mankind," since justice "in no way concerned those who were strong enough to win for themselves." (Machiavelli knows about that; he remembers how Florence's conquerors endungeoned him and racked him.) Well, do we have a quorum? Not everyone is here, but I suppose that not everyone will be coming. Some prefer to rob and rape; others merely want to be Ik; a few, too weak and terrorized to come above ground, continue on in the safe course of dying alone. But most of us are here. Among today's delegates I even see some who yesterday were bandits. They've realized that when they get old, other bandits will get them. I see also the bandits' neighbors, weary of tolerating rapes. I see many a lonely, gregarious human being, hoping to get a friend or a spouse. I see the holders of credos, each with his own message: to the medieval Christians, for instance, the state of nature is a state of wounded imperfection; only by gathering together in communities of doctrinal purity may they hope to stop being or serving Plutarch's bandits. I see sly fence-jumpers and crowd-followers, to say nothing of slyer crowd-pleasers, hoping to legalize their banditry: I see the ancient Athenian tyrant, Peristratus, who will wound himself and claim that enemies did it; the people grant him a bodyguard of club-bearers, which seizes the Acropolis. Against his son the procedure of formal ostracism will be invented. Here gather the right-wing and left-wing murderers of present-day Colombia. I see Stalin, who figures prominently in this book; he's going to order that his rival, Kirov, be secretly murdered; then he'll blame "wreckers" for it and set the most murderous species of martial law to work. Moltke is there, ready to secure the enemy side of the river for us, provided that we render him due obedience during the course of the campaign. His aphorism: "Our diplomats plunge us forever into misfortune; our generals always save us." Machiavelli longs to ford the river beside him. I see the apathetic, the mercurial, the evil and the weak; maybe there are some good people, too—isn't everyone good by his own lights? I see Lincoln, who will try sincerely to keep all his promises, even if he shouldn't have made them. Gandhi's telling everyone that society ought to be organized on the basis of love, not fear; were I a Gandhian, this allegory would be very different. I see Robespierre, whose credo of a utopian state of nature, catalyzed by violence, will contribute to "bring about the grosser disappointments of which the first French Revolution was fertile." I see Julius Caesar, who, more ambitiously urgent than Moltke or Machiavelli, raging at being shut out of supremacy, will try to win favor by conquering the people across the river, and then, that purpose accomplished, cross back again, his army now directed at our capital. (Of his like, Robespierre speaks in a draft of a clause to the new French constitution: "Kings, aristocrats and tyrants, whoever they be, are slaves in rebellion against the sovereign of the earth, which is the human race, and against the legislator of the universe which is nature.") Most of all I see families. Homer says: "They dwell in hollow caves on the crests of the high hills, and each one utters the law to his children and his wives, and they reck not of one another." Plato says that each such clan consists of "one flock, like so many birds," and that each flock is "under patriarchal control, the most justifiable of all types of royalty." Robespierre's "sovereign of the earth" is unknown to them, and no threat to them—yet. In their private hollows, one must assume, most have come to some necessary accommodation with authority, personified in the father or the elder brother; now they must widen it, to block the bandits out. Leaders, followers and in-betweeners, there they squat, about to join together now—fearing, hating, coveting and lusting—and hoping. Lincoln hopes; so do Gandhi and Trotsky; even Stalin hopes—if only for himself. Whether fear or hope saved them, in either case, what they've learned is this presupposition of the Golden Rule: Just as each is, so others are. We all bleed; we all avoid pain. "Respect for man is the supreme law of Humanity," says Bakunin; that maxim follows, indeed, from the acknowledgment of otherness, but it has not been voted on yet, much less ratified. Still, these people have set out toward it; maybe they will get there someday. That is why although their hands twitch and sometimes clench when they gaze upon the objects of their ugly passions, they close upon air, since by agreement spears were left outside the commons. That was the first step. They do not yet concern themselves with inheritance, river traffic and the care of orphans. They understand only this much: *Since I myself cannot dominate all, nor can anyone else, better for me to be a part of that all, so that no one can dominate me.* Robespierre means just this when he so earnestly insists that "the interest of the weak is justice. It is for them that humane and impartial laws are a necessary safeguard." The dictum is nonetheless true, for all that Robespierre himself forgot it. We can all be numbered among the weak. Indeed, we have our interest. This is government. This is pragmatic humankind. Time to forge the allegiance condition—and, if possible, to consecrate it, which is why the Swiss constitution begins: "In the Name of All-Powerful God!"

The latecomers have finished creeping out of the bushes now, having hidden their treasures in cavelike canyons thickly ferned and glistening with snakes and newts where others can't see; they pretend to possess nothing more than what they show to one another on this open field of trust, kin greeting new kin with handclasps and shy smiles, women sharing food, children playing together. They're afraid. Rousseau tries to reassure them by saying: "Each of us puts in common his person and his whole power under the supreme direction of the General Will; and in return we receive every member as an individual part of the whole." They don't quite believe him, because behind him walks Robespierre, insisting that he embodies the General Will and knows who the traitors are. They fear that the General Will may impose sudden taxes, confiscating their most precious things, prowling ever in those canyons until it's found every last cache. Spreading their hands wide, gazing into everyone's eyes, they swear most solemnly that they have nothing. The General Will gesticulates ingratiatingly and swears with equal mendacity that that isn't a problem. Plato insists that "a society in which neither riches nor poverty is a member," by which he means the Flood's surviving remnant, or a group living essentially in the state we now imagine, "regularly produces sterling characters, as it has no place for violence and wrong, nor yet for rivalry and envy."

That was the beginning, their pact to be one family. Gandhi prayed and fasted to keep it so. He failed; mass loving-kindness perishes; but maybe violence, wrong, rivalry and envy can be sublimated into emulation. Hence this Spartan definition of the best government: "The one in which the largest number of citizens are willing to compete with each other in excellence and without civil discord." But a child stole another child's pretty rock, as he would have done before people came together. A woman liked somebody's else's husband. I ask you, Plato: Who is too rich or too poor for that to happen? And you, Spartans: Tell me how she can leave one man for another without civil discord? —A family feared, hence hated, another family's God. A man kept pretty cattle, and he knew that other men wanted him to die so that they could get them. Meanwhile, Julius Caesar's bodyguard was growing ominously large. It was time for government. Unfortunately, it is always time for government.

My Servant, My Executioner

No doubt Plato, Trotsky and all authority's other moral mathematicians will require that throats be cut only with the best possible motives—that is, they'll shed the blood only of the ungovernable, who've been threatening their fellow governed or menacing the governors. And good motives grow still better. In the book of Matthew we read that Christ said: "You know that the rulers of the Gentiles lord it over them, and their great men exercise authority among them. It shall not be so among you; but whoever would be great among you must be your servant." After the French Revolution, many a mass leader presented himself as the people's servant: the chief executive was but the loyalest drudge and slave. (King Itzcoatl would never have said so.) Yes, here's the highest good of government—if government's conception of good deeds corresponds with mine. My slave taxes me for my own good. He protects my soul from bad books, sends my father to the guillotine for crimes against me of which I was unaware.

III.

WHERE DO MY RIGHTS BEGIN?

Your good and my good, perhaps they are different, and either forced good or forced evil will make a people cry with pain. Does the ore admire the flame which transforms it?

PRINCE FEISAL, 1917

How to Erase Signatures

What can I do about it? —We heard Hobbes insisting that since my great-grandfather once agreed to form a commonwealth, I thereby agreed and will always agree to every new act of government; hence "no Law can be Unjust;" but I cannot remember giving my consent to anything so sweeping, and if Hobbes did it, I beg him to bind only himself, not me, nor my comrades who are likewise discontented; like Ivan Karamazov, who found himself dissatisfied with an order of divine providence under which any child on this earth might be tortured, we must be able to announce that we reject our entrance ticket; like the pseudonymous commanders of an insurgent group in Mexico, we must be able to say whenever and to whomever we will: "Our objectives are for the people, *with the people and against the government.* We are ready for anything." By the Machiavellian Caveat, mostly we are not. "No government can exist for a single moment without the cooperation of the people," says Gandhi, but he then adds the bitterly necessary qualification, "voluntary or forced." Force may partake of outright violence, craft or mutual obfuscation. Possessing all little power in their popular assemblies, the Roman plebeians, for instance, knew not how to reject the whole ticket, although by means of riots an ill-omened corner of it might be torn away, and they could shout demands at gladiatorial shows. When were they the sovereign people, whose demands constituted sacred commands, and when were they but a mob? Well, of course, authority decided that . . .

Suicide

An acquaintance of mine who was very high-strung and often talked about his enemies suffered politico-academic reverses and blew his head off. I remember visiting him one hot summer night when everything smelled like fresh trees and it was too humid to sleep, so we sat drinking mineral water at the kitchen table and he was telling me about some Greek and Sanskrit texts which he was reading in the original. He hadn't been forced to withdraw from the university yet. He went and got the books, and as soon as I saw the Sanskrit characters so mysterious to me I began to feel that he knew some secret that I didn't, and if I only paid enough attention I would learn it, something maybe as important as eternal life or the philosopher's stone—a feeling that I often get alone on a summer night reading and thinking in one of those insomniac times when the silence and sleep of others brings answers closer; I drink iced tea and work things out until dawn. That night J. G. seemed to me to be already arrived at apodictic understanding, probably less on account of his own being— although he was very intelligent, possibly even brilliant—than as a result of the night itself, that time of omens, and although I can't remember much he told me (it happened more than a decade ago now), I do remember how our concentration increased by the moment, as in those evenings before a New York thunderstorm when the air is so heavy that your face is covered with oily sweat no matter how often you bathe or mop it, a wind finally comes, wet and cool, and flashes as you begin to surrender to something. I later understood that all the while, J. G. was negotiating his surrender, preparing to give himself to something which at that night hovered yet faint and directionless; but I didn't see him for a year after that. Although the first roll of thunder was audible to me then, when at the party, newly severed from the university, he kept talking about those enemies of his—although, in other words, rain had begun to fall on his mind so heavily as to sound like wind, I didn't do anything because we were not close and anyhow you never know and he was proud and what would or could I have done? Now I think I would have invited him to come stay with me for a while, and I would have stayed up late with him and talked about Sanskrit—but probably I wouldn't have; I owned troubles, too. So the lightning went off inside his skull, charging that darkness with slate-blue light for an instant until everything became dark again; then again that surge, shocking and horrible light between darknesses, like the gaze of the Gorgon's head—what color was it really? Not slate blue, not dead white, not blinding grey; it was always the same color but it was indescribable . . . and so one of those flashes, the last one, was the flash when the bullet breached the cranial vault and for that one quarter-second his dying brain lay exposed to the light of the world as it had never done from womb-time to skull-time to now, and never would after now from tomb-time to dust-time; that was the light of the terrible answer he'd learned, or taught himself. I am sorry that he is dead. But I believe that he had the right to do what he did. One's self is one's own. The enemy of an unhappy self is that self. The self is within its rights to destroy itself, whether to flee itself or (as perhaps in J. G.'s case) to escape an unbearable social contract. He'd been falsely accused of sexual harassment.

THE MORAL CALCULUS OF A SUICIDAL CHEMIST
The question of suicide and selfishness to close friends and relatives is one that I can't answer or even give an opinion on. It is obvious, however, that I have pondered it and decided I would hurt them less dead than alive.

Source: Etkind, p. 81.

Assertion and Control

Plotinus, whose philosophy lay strangely close to Buddhism at times, rejected suicide on the ground that it was an action of the passions. "If everyone is to hold in the other world a standing determined by the state in which he quitted this, there must be no withdrawal as long as there is any hope of progress." And yet we can admire someone who offers himself up to certain or almost certain extinction for the sake of a cause, as did that earnest gadfly Jose Rizal when he returned to the Philippines, a nation then emiserated by the abuses of Spanish rule which he had satirized in *No Me Tangere*. He was executed, as he perhaps expected. In 1892, four years before facing the firing squad, he'd written in a letter "to the Filipinos" that "I prefer to face death and give my life joyfully in order to free so many innocents [from] such unjust persecution." This decision was thus also an act of the passions—or at least of the affections. If one can consider noble what Rizal did, and not what J. G. did, it must not be the passions themselves which we condemn, but their particular object or attachment.

Why should we call a bankrupt who blows his brains out a coward, and a conscript who exposes himself on the battlefield to overwhelming enemy fire a hero? Because the first death is chosen and the second compelled? One might equally well say that he who bowed to compulsion was the coward—a thought highly offensive to patriotism and soldierdom; better not to think the word "coward" about either, since only J. G. himself, and the soldier *his* separate self, saw their own respective flashes of skull lightning. From his sufferings in the Kolyma labor camps, Varlam Shalamov concluded that "a person could consider himself a human being as long as he felt totally prepared to kill himself, to interfere in his own biography. It was this awareness that gave me the will to live. I checked myself—frequently—and felt I had the strength to die, and thus remained alive." Later he decided that such comfort was illusory, since when the threshold was crossed his resolve might well fail. Fortunately, this is an unfounded objection.

The virtue of suicide is control. No one knows the future. If one feels control over one's life in the present, why, then—one has control in the present, no matter what happens later. I reiterate: If the self has any rights at all, those must include the basic right to continue, to constitute itself over time, to will itself—hence the corresponding right to unwill itself, or, as in the case of a soldier-volunteer or a Gandhian martyr, to offer itself to be unwilled. The point is that to be justified, suicide must be an act of assertion. In medieval Japan, "the grand style, rather archaic and exaggerated, was to take one's entrails in both hands and give them a vigorous throw in the enemy's direction." What could be a more emphatic statement of will than that? No right has any meaning if it be to make but one choice—precisely the situation which one finds both laughable and pitiful in totalitarian countries, when the forcibly assembled people are assigned the right to vote for a single candidate on a single ticket. Another nonvoter is the woman whose photo shows her hanging with her swollen face canted backward, a patterned housecoat belt wound tightly over her eyes and mouth, a towel around her head mimicking the turban of an Oriental harem girl (she was white), then a window-sash cord wrapped tightly around her waist and up in what the forensic write-up described as "a figure-eight pattern" around her engorged breasts, then down to press through her underpants between the lips of her vulva. This is a "sex hanging," an autoerotic accident. We can say that her death was no more meaningless than it would have been from the breast cancer which murdered the woman I loved. Indeed, at least in a sense the hanged woman participated in her own death, and it is quite possible that she died enviably, that is, feeling extreme pleasure. —Unfortunate, to be sure, if it was an accident. Whether her act should be defined as carelessness or suicide, call it, like the declaration of some new African nation's independence, sovereign self-determination.

But it was all chance, you might object—mere stupidity, like a traffic accident! Well, where does chance end and will begin? Let's call sister to her the young woman who, gamepiece of a sister fate, happened to be born in Hiroshima at the wrong time—that is to say, after the atom bomb, and so played, perceived, learned, loved and was loved, grew up and one day fell ill, and discovered despite her doctor's well-intentioned efforts that she had leukemia—in those days almost invariably fatal. Did she use the sash of her obi or did she find a rope? (Another example of cultural relativism: the largely Anglo-American Hemlock Society in its suicide manual remarks that "people who have hanged themselves have often done so as an act of revenge against someone else, for the shock of finding a garroted person is one of the worse experiences that could be inflicted by one human being upon another.") There she hangs, black in the face. "Whenever I hear such stories," writes the novelist Kenzaburo Oe, "I feel we are fortunate that ours is not a Christian country. I feel an almost complete relief that a dogmatic Christian sense of guilt did not prevent the girl from taking her own life." Had she been an eighteenth-century Prussian, the town executioner would have buried her dishonorably beneath the gallows.

Belly-Ends, Dagger-Means

Because it does not directly or necessarily harm anyone other than its perpetrator, the suicide's blood runs into a boundless sea of messages, signs, themes and motives: cowardice, hatred, vengeance, release, coercion, kindness, reconciliation, even self-expression. This act of violence truly cannot be comprehended without a context. Even if we limit ourselves to but a single incarnation (if such be not too frivolous a word to be applied to death) of suicide—namely, the famous self-disembowelments of the Japanese historical chronicles and legends—we can gather an almost inexhaustible harvest of causes from the melancholy vineyards of others' scholarship.

TRADITIONAL REASONS TO COMMIT SEPPUKU
(Medieval Japan)
Hara o warra hanasu [literally "to open one's stomach and speak"]: to speak sincerely

1. To prevent being captured in battle.

2. To make amends or express apology.

3. To assume responsibility.

4. To add emphasis to advice to a superior.

5. To correct a disciple.

6. To criticize a superior or an enemy; to express hatred. By the legal code of 1536, the person thus criticized in a suicide note would be punished.

7. To follow one's lord in death. Prohibited in 645 and again in 1633, but still followed as late as 1912. Arguably followed by Mishima in 1970.

8. To follow one's husband in death. Usually a wife would not cut her belly open but rather slit her jugular vein or drown herself. Never legally prohibited.

9. To become a guardian spirit by dying inside the foundation of one's lord's new building.

10. To receive a warrior's capital punishment. The property of such a one would not be lost to his family.

11. To retain one's honor when accused—guilty or not.

The Utility of Suicide

Thus one code; thus some of honor's fashions. As for suicide which has an explicitly political motivation (which, of course, might include many of the species of self-evisceration listed above), we may fairly appraise through the lens of a moral calculus not just its context but (turning away from the Gandhian code) its effects. *Does it accomplish results?* Did Thich Quang Duc, the South Vietnamese monk who in 1963, following an ancient tradition permitted to the enlightened, poured gasoline on himself and struck fire, thereby decrease the persecution of the Buddhist clergy? We read that on that very day, his government remitted the siege of a celebrated pagoda, allowed Buddhist flags to be flown and even

promised punishment for those good Catholics who (probably on its orders) had massacred Buddhists in Hue. Perhaps the corrupt President felt,
as Caesar surely did upon learning of Cato's suicide, an angry, bitter awe at
the dead man's resolution, at his now unpunishable withdrawal from and
denunciation of a rotten social contract. The monk's superior, the Vener-
able Giac Duc, "believed then and I believe now that Thich Quang Duc
was a Boddhisatva [enlightened one]." As might have been expected, the
government reneged on its guarantees, so after Thich Quang Duc's funeral (attended by a million), a Buddhist nun burned herself. However
temporary the relief which these suicides purchased for the persecuted,
they surely succeeded in mobilizing and radicalizing people by laying
bare the government's policy of deceit and atrocity. The Iroquois, who
carefully studied and practiced the art of torture, concluded that a death
by burning may well be unsurpassed in physical pain—although of course
they stretched it out on their victims much longer. By voluntarily taking
upon themselves such agony, the Vietnamese fire-suicides in effect accused
the regime of laying torments upon others. Their moral and political
effect was incalculable. As strategy and as moral choice, they were brilliantly justifiable.

    Seven decades earlier, when the Russian inmate M. F. Vetrova preceded
Thich Quang Duc along the same fiery path in order to protest the conditions of her imprisonment, a direct result was an improvement in the lives
of other female prisoners. Indeed, several unwell women obtained the
supreme blessing of an early release—among them Nadezhda Krupskaya,
Lenin's wife-to-be; for authority, under Tsardom both more "chivalrous"
and more susceptible to public opinion than it would be under Lenindom,
now felt compelled to preclude the potential embarrassment of having a
second woman die in custody during the interval (doubtless calculated by
political bureaucrats) in which Vetrova remained in everyone's memory.
Her goal must therefore be counted as accomplished; and her means
harmed only the proud and desperate militant whose life belonged to herself to destroy. As is usual in such cases, the dry opacity and brevity of our
source documents prevent us from following Vetrova down the long dark
corridor of her moral calculus; at best we can see her indistinct silhouette
through the cell window before, as in J. G.'s case, a flash of light illuminates her only in order to draw her once and for all into that darkness unknowable to any of us until we go there. Thus we'll never be able to

determine to what extent Vetrova's suicide constituted, like Thich Quang Duc's, an ascetic, perhaps even devotional act of public protest, and to what extent it was simply a personal escape. Arguably, most self-violence directs itself toward precisely this end. A beautifully multivariate graph of twentieth-century Japanese suicides (represented as a ratio between self-homicides and other sorts of deaths) resembles a kinked and fraying bundle of cords. Each strand of cord indicates a year. The axes plot age versus frequency of suicide. Between ages ten and twenty-five all the cords rise to peaks. In the year 1950, and even more so in 1960, those peaks were stunningly steep and high for persons in their mid-twenties, with an equally sharp decline for those survivors who rejoined the main body of the cords in the early thirties. What could have made all those young people kill themselves? —For both men and women of all ages, out of the various possible states of marital relationship, marriage was by far the safest. For men, divorce and widowhood were the most dangerous, whereas for women everything seemed less clear-cut. For people of both sexes aged twenty to twenty-nine, however, a single pillar of suicidal risk loomed immensely over the others: continued singleness. Surely suicide became in many cases an escape from the despair of that lonely state. —In 1975–80, the Japanese men most likely to kill themselves were jobless. For many of them, suicide was surely an escape. —In the 1970s and '80s, youth's suicide peak practically amounted to a low plateau which stretched on and on through self-killers' low- and mid-thirties, bottoming out at around age forty, where life's halfway mark perhaps projects an aura of absurdity upon suicidal calculations—better to die early, or late. (But in the year 1975, suicide's rise commenced shortly before the thirty-fifth birthday—who knows why?) After one's fortieth birthday, the general trend was upward; 1987 produced a strange spike in people's early fifties; suicides for that year then declined until past age sixty, whereupon they began to reascend and suddenly steepened to catch up with all the aging Japanese of other times who'd rushed pell-mell to do themselves to death—very probably, I'd say, a reflection of the loneliness and decline that curses most people's final years. By and large (which is to say, leaving out 1975 and 1987), one finds no valley of life satisfaction after age forty; the suicide ratios shoot up at an inexorable fifty- or sixty-degree angle, overtowered by the immense rise of 1950; and so it goes until the population reaches its eighties and dies, their fraying, upsloping strands of life then breaking off in midair.

Defiance, Loyalty and Escape

Undeniably there are times when (again, as perhaps for J. G.) suicide offers the only way to freedom. The grimly inspirational tale of Masada tells of one of those times. After a long siege, the Romans now stood on the verge of capturing that desert fortress, whose Jewish defenders, knowing full well that their destiny on the morrow would be slavery at best, ended their lives. "Judge not, lest ye be judged." At Masada, three souls chose not to die; and we ought not judge them, either.

The end of World War II was another such time. In a hideous photograph by Margaret Bourke-White, we see a desk table with its black telephone, a calendar open to the thirteenth, stamps, pens, an ashtray, papers, all in disarray; and then we see like a dark shadow the track where an elbow has swept the dust away. We see the elbow, and the man attached to it, or the back of him, at any rate. His almost bald skull lies at an angle at the edge of the desk—a wonder he hasn't fallen off. His slumped and folded body clings; perhaps the elbow helps—that and rigor mortis. Across the room, in a corner of a leather armchair, lies a young girl, her pale face oriented ceilingward, her eyes and mouth not quite closed, arms folded across her chest, the long, pale fingers of the left hand open and dangling; she is wearing some kind of official armband, and her slip is showing. In a chair lies another body, perhaps her mother or sister; the face dangles backward over the arm of the chair, so that one can't make out much of it. The caption reads: "The suicide of a minor Nazi official and his family in Leipzig, April 1945." (Around the same time, Magda Goebbels, preparing to poison her six children, writes in a last letter from Hitler's bunker: "The world to come after the Fuehrer and National Socialism will not be worth living in, and that is why I have taken the children along with me. They are too good for the sort of life to come after us." In atom-bombed, surrendered Japan, numbers of officials were preparing to follow the same path; occasionally their wives adhered to the old code and followed them in death, but it was hardly the rule for them to kill their children. The Goebbels family chose to flee; the Japanese, to die responsibly, as it were, at their posts. But before the armistice, as we'll soon see, all too many followed the Goebbelsian paradigm.) What ought we say? Seneca already said it: "Caesar's troops beset the city gates, yet Cato has a way of escape; with one single hand he will open a wide path to freedom." I am sure that this is what J. G. thought. A Caesarian officer will claim that although the local people "hated [Cato] for the side he took," they still gave him a funeral in recognition of his immense courage—for Caesar would have saved him, not tortured him; and after he first cut his belly open, the doctor would have saved him, too; but he ripped the stitches open with his fingernails, and died as stubbornly as he had lived.

Cato had ever so many brothers and sisters. Vetrova might have been one—or not. Here's another, a twenty-two-year-old kamikaze who left behind this haiku too unsubtle for us to worry that the meaning vanished in translation:

> Like cherry blossoms
> in the spring
> let us fall
> so pure and radiant.

We would be foolish to believe unreservedly in the sincerity of his sentiment; for the failing empire of which he was a subject had in 1944, broken by Allied air and naval power, set out deliberately to fabricate for utilitarian ends the Catonian suicides of human air-bombs and human torpedoes. (Cato had fabricated himself.) And yet the testimonies of surviving kamikazes asserts that on the chosen day they were proud to die—no matter that Vice Admiral Onishi had asked them; Onishi would also kill himself, and by the prestigiously agonizing method of disembowelment. They died honored by the military social structures which had formed them, and some of them expected to become minor gods. "Was it really necessary to go so far?" wondered the Emperor after he was told of the first kamikazes. "Well, it was a noble deed." *Suicide is right whenever it is not coerced.* To the extent that we can peel away from their self-sovereign purposes the velvety fabric of odious persuasion (their squadron leader called upon them to die or not, one by one—how many of them were brave enough *not* to volunteer?), likewise the evil political ends which suffused them but which they'd never created, we can, I think, honor these men. Five thousand of them died thus.

As for the Nazi functionary, he probably did evil with both path-breaking hands; certainly he participated in it. Cato, we said, died in order to proclaim and defy. The kamikaze died likewise to proclaim, and also to strike a war blow. The Nazi family, like the families at Masada, might also have died to proclaim, but one assumes that the father died in order to flee. He must have known that he faced arrest and internment, possibly worse.

Based on my presuppositions about the rights of the self, my moral calculus advocates that *suicide is permissible whenever uncoerced.*

Euthanasia

And the two female corpses beside him? Did *he* coerce them or, like Magda Goebbels, did they volunteer? What did they believe the Allies would do to them? We don't know. In Japan we do know. "Japanese soldiers gave us women hand grenades and told us to die with them if the time came," recalls a survivor. "They also gave us cyanide . . . with the admonition, 'It would not be good for a Japanese woman to get raped.' " —In Gibbon's voluminous pages we can find mention of a Roman matron who violently saved her chastity from the Emperor Maxentius; somehow this act of self-will, or perhaps even self-help, fails to repulse me as does authority's "helping" its subjects to do the same. A few months before Hiroshima and Nagasaki ended the war, the American enemy formed a beachhead on Takashiki Island. Self-defense of creed, homeland, honor and, above all, of itself impelled authority to gather together the Japanese civilian population for mass suicide. The euphemism: "crushing of jewels." One searches in vain for any remnant of whatever justification the kamikazes possessed. Such meaningless, useless, coerced public death inspires only pity and horror. Might it be that if we'd seen Masada's final night, we would have felt the same? Did everybody sign the social contract? If so, what were its clauses? Did I kill my mother because she and I both preferred death to tomorrow's changes, or because authority compelled me to? "When we raised our hands against the mother who bore us, we wailed in our grief. I remember that. In the end we must have used stones. To the head. We took care of Mother that way. Then my brother and I turned against our younger brother and younger sister. Hell engulfed us there." In the battle of Tarawa, only a hundred prisoners were captured out of 4,700 Japanese defenders.

Yes, we might compare Tarawa with Masada. But here's a more apt equation: The Athenians besiege the Persian-installed governor of Eion. The governor will defend his honor to the death—fair enough, but why can't he stop at his own death? "When all supplies were consumed," reports Herodotus, "he made a huge pile of timber, set it on fire, and then, cutting the throats of his children, wife, concubines, and servants, flung their bodies into the flames," then threw his treasures into the river and burned himself up. "For this behavior his name is still mentioned in Persia with respect, and it is right that it should be," but I wonder how his doomed dependents felt about it. Did he wonder? Well, they were his property, as Isaac was Abraham's; the governor could do as he liked.

A woman decides to leave an abusive husband. According to the later testimony of a homicide detective, he responds by loading his gun, "telling his wife she had ruined his life 'and he was going to kill himself and the two boys, and she was going to have to watch' "—which indeed she did, helplessly, uselessly screaming. The husband's assertion thus never even pretends to be euthanasia; it's only revenge-killing. Unlike a Masadan father, or even a propaganda-deluded Nazi or Japanese father, the husband will not by killing his six-year-old and his four-year-old save them from any situation which might arguably be worse for them than death. "She was going to have to watch." That declaration of triumphant malice could have come right out of one of Sade's novels. Alongside his case, set that of the young mother who prepared a birthday party for her seven-year-old twins, wrapped presents, invited other children, then drowned the boys in the bathtub, canceled the invitations due to "illness," unwrapped the presents and turned herself in. What was she thinking? Had the entire course of events been planned, or did an invincible dybbuk impulse seize her after she'd issued the invitations? Here talk of justice or injustice would not be extraordinarily relevant; the only judgment we should pronounce is: "acute psychosis."

Loving-Kindness

Sometimes, however, the justice of euthanasia becomes not just possible or probable, but shiningly certain—an act of kindness. Lawrence of Arabia, later to figure in this book in a far worse light, tells the tale of his servant Farraj. It is 1918. Mortally wounded by a Turkish bullet, Farraj lies helpless. To lift him causes him to scream with agony. Lawrence's band is but sixteen, and fifty Turks are approaching.

> We could not leave him where he was, to the Turks, because we had seen them burn alive our hapless wounded. For this reason we were all

agreed, before action, to finish off one another, if badly hurt: but I had never realized it might fall to me to kill Farraj.

I knelt down beside him, holding my pistol near the ground by his head, so that he should not see my purpose; but he must have guessed it, for he opened his eyes and clutched me with his harsh, scaly hand . . .

Anyone who believes that what Lawrence did to help this man he cared for was wrong is a hypocrite, a dogmatist or just plain unrealistic. *Families or comrades may legitimately coerce the deaths of dependents to spare them from loneliness, death by torture or dishonor sufficient to compel future suicide.*

Likewise, when the Yugoslav Partisans were desperately seeking to break out of German encirclement in the Sutjetska in 1943, they could not take the seriously injured with them. The enemy killed everyone they found. They were, for the most part, too busy to torture; but that doesn't imply that to die at their hands wouldn't have been worse than perishing, as did Farraj, at the hands of those who loved them. (In the same war, a Japanese army doctor volunteered to shoot any of his comrades who considered themselves too weak to retreat from the Allies. "This I consider 'sacred murder,'" recalled an eyewitness.) And so one badly injured Partisan woman begged her husband to kill her; he did, in her sleep. "It was then also that a father fulfilled the same request by his daughter," Milovan Djilas tells us. "I knew that father, too. He survived the war, withered and somber, and his friends regarded him as a living saint." So do I.

IV.

MEANS AND ENDS

I do not deny that among an infinite number of acts of violence and folly, some good may have been done. They who destroy every thing certainly will remove some grievance. They who make everything new, have a chance that they may establish some thing beneficial.

BURKE, 1790

Here you have the morality of the rightists: they say, let us find an expla-
nation for needless cruelty; we must be humanists, and laws must be
obeyed. But this morality is not revolutionary; it does not advance the
cause.

MOLOTOV, 1976

The previous chapters might be entitled "Weapons and the Citizen." In that case, much of the remainder of this book ought to be called "Weapons and the Revolutionary." We shall not, however, neglect the soldier, the prosecutor or the armed racist, all of whom justify whatever violence they commit by going beyond the rights of the self to invoke the rights of the group to which they actually or hypothetically belong. Identity is always sweet, and likewise the smoke of identity's sacrifices: every Moloch owns graciously accepting nostrils. For any cause in the name of which you wish to slaughter me, you can find your happy justification— although straightforward souls forgo such trash to save time. One might say that the more highly regulated a society (or a person), the more possibilities of breaking laws, hence the more guilt, hence the more need for justifications. But never mind. They lie like pebbles upon the beaches of cunning, ready to be scooped up by the fistful. First comes your justification. Afterward you may remand me to the secular arm.

Collective Violence

My argument so far is the less than original one (most often disputed on religious or legalistic grounds—disputed, in short, according to stone-carved moral codes) that it is the right of the self to defend itself, or not defend itself, or even end itself, as it sees fit; that the self is, in short, the basic indissoluble element of autonomy; that whoever attacks another unprovoked imperils those rights, and, therefore, in the course of being repelled, may forfeit them on his own account, should circumstances require it. —"Good thing this won't be read by social insects," responds one reader. "Even so, it's possible to think, 'How American!' or whatever." And most likely my formulations, if they are ever seen, will bring smiles now and a century from now, such being the lot of universalist pretenses. Well, our sketch of the individual's rights is completed. And now let us go to that beach of pretty pebbles, and ask: What else constitutes self-defense? —The immensity of this inquiry is so daunting that I can only begin to hint at it by raising various cases. For instance, is self-defense for me the same as self-defense for my nation or clan? Evidently not. Suppose that as a revolutionary I act violently or nonviolently to break laws with which I disagree (Trotsky once wrote that disobeying a law should be considered no more and no less important than missing a train). The consequence may well be that the nation of which I was once a part will invoke self-defense to hunt me down and kill me. And the government which pays my killers, is it a "legitimate" government or a mere "regime"? Who decides that? Even if it is but the latter, isn't a regime a collection of selves each with the right of self-defense? Does my breaking "their" law harm them individually? If not, how could I be harming them collectively? Are Marxists and anarchists reasonable in calling for self-defense based on class? ("All means are justified in the war of humanity against its enemies. Indeed, the more repugnant the means, the stronger the test of one's nobility and devotion. All great revolutionists have proved that.") How justified is violent defense of honor? What about "ecodefense"? We can bedazzle ourselves with such questions as long as we like (and in this half of the book we shall look at all of them). Naturally, we shall not answer any one of them as well as we should: each issue deserves a life's work. The tale of Joan of Arc, for instance, by partaking of so many categories at once—national self-defense, self-defense of authority, of creed, of honor, proactive self-defense—reminds us how problematic it is to fit real life into even one's best-constructed pigeonholes: "You, Englishmen, who have no right in this Kingdom of France," she writes on a sheet tied to an arrow and shot out of besieged Orleans, "the King of Heaven orders and commands you through me, Joan the Maid, that you quit your fortresses and return into your own country, or if not I shall make you such *babay* that the memory of it will be perpetual." How would you categorize that? And when we turn from the historical illustrations of this book's first half to our actual case studies, our dipperfuls of water from the murky well of experience, we'll rediscover the same difficulty, that within any given Joan (who's already distorted by our vision) lie dissolved and commingled her Kingdom of France, her King of Heaven, and all the other multitudinous treasures which she, in defending her own being, must also defend. This is one of the main reasons that great literature possesses the power to fascinate: it presents a whole person, offering him up on an introspective platter like a sort of omelette of mixed motives. This I hope to do in the case studies, whenever portraiture is appropriate. But first we must begin by defining the questions themselves. Answering them requires sincere induction, which must in turn be preceded by description. Let us then construct a pretty little natural history of mass violence, of rising up and burning and purifying in the name of the greatest good.

An Anarchist Comedy

And now we have arrived at the central matter of this book, the metaphor which revolutionaries, conquerors, patriots and other violent movers so often use. Ethics is the evaluation of justifications. Justifications are the links between ends and means. "Everything is moral which assists the triumph of revolution," wrote Sergey Nechaev in his infamous "Catechism of the Revolutionist" (that cold intellectual mask over an enraged face); if this assertion is true, then no justifications are required for any action, and we cannot judge any other person except on the basis of his stated ends (will this murder assist the triumph of my revolution or not?)—which actually leaves Nechaev in a bind, because if incumbency, calmly oppressing and massacring, states that it does so, like Nechaev, to "benefit the people," then how can revolutionary activism denounce it? Let us therefore grant our authority as human beings, as citizens, to judge each others' means, even when those means do not directly affect the rights of our sovereign private selves.

A means no one can be sure of in advance, because it belongs to praxis, to implementation, to the interaction between strategy and an unpredictable world. Maybe that nonviolent rally which you wish to lead will turn violent when the police start shooting your picketers down. Weaponless yourself, you must acknowledge the responsibility. (Gandhi had to do this; so did Martin Luther King.) "Behold, I shall raise up evil against you out of your own house." Or perhaps your assassination attempt will fail, and you'll be treated as a nonviolent lunatic with a toy gun instead of as a murderer-martyr. Say it succeeds, and your victim's successor carries on the old policies. (After all, not so many assassinations achieve their ultimate political object.) Then it has *not* succeeded. Perhaps, worst of all, you'll kill the wrong people, as did the anarchist Severino Di Giovanni— repeatedly. Two of his apologists shruggingly explain:

> when the violent act, decided by a militant or group of militants, is carried out with opportune analysis and guarantee; when its political

opportunity has been considered and is carried out with the maximum possibility of comprehension by the mass; and the militant or group are really part of the armed minority of the exploited; then if the action causes an "accident" and someone dies during the course of it, we cannot condemn the action and the comrades who carried it out.

The three conditions proposed by the apologists are thus, translated into our terms: careful consideration of ends, determination of the practicality of means and membership in the revolutionary elite (this last ad hominem postulate let us bury without a funeral). Now it becomes apparent that this formula is really a genteel form of Nechaev's, its cruel arrogance dressed up in pseudo-utilitarian rationalism, like some army's murderous pikes whose poles have been segmented with repeated crosshatched or floral designs: rather than asserting we have the right to commit premeditated murder in pursuit of a perfect end, it claims that we may commit any number of manslaughters. In 1920, the fanatical Communist John Reed tells Emma Goldman that shooting five hundred people was nothing, just a "stupid blunder on the part of overzealous Chekists." Di Giovanni's actions can equally well be classified as mere escapades, errors, not wickedness. In 1927 he commits his first known homicide, a double one, by means of his trademark suitcase bomb activated by a marriage of acids. What could be the most worthy target for an anarchist at the time? Why, of course—an American bank! But neither the nineteen-year-old clerk who had just finished planning her honeymoon nor the itinerant vendor have ever exploited anyone. Better to deny these globs of flesh—into the grave with them! Twenty-three other souls are wounded. Inspired (so it would seem) rather than remorseful, Di Giovanni proceeds to the Bank of Boston, planting another suitcase which fortunately fails to explode; if it had, it might have done the same sort of work.

A year later, impelled by his justified hatred of Mussolini, he and his accomplice Romano enter the Italian consulate. In this case I might have been willing to accept the label of "opportune analysis and guarantee," but because the two anarchists cannot bring their suitcase within range of Consul Campini, they resort to incompetence's cowardly expediency, opportunism, and set it down by the service desk. Nine dead, thirty-four injured. Fire, blood, rubble, broken glass. Once again, Di Giovanni accomplished nothing, except the writing of his murky message in other people's blood. Mussolini, whose evil of course incomparably surpasses Di Giovanni's (his moral calculus: "I need several thousand dead to be able to take my place at the peace table"), will not be stopped from giving Italy two decades of Fascism. Di Giovanni will have been long dead by then—strapped to a prison chair by the government and executed. As for Argentina, that nation will avoid declaring war on the Axis until March 27, 1945, a mere five weeks before Germany's surrender. Forty-odd top Nazis will find hospitable refuge in Argentina after the war. With regard to Italian fascism, then, Di Giovanni's ends are as germane and justified as his means are vain and atrocious. His own conclusion: Time for more fire and blood. But when he leaves a suitcase at the pharmacy owned by the chairman of the Fascist subcommittee of Boca, a curious child disarms the mechanism, so that only frightening flames burst out. Di Giovanni, one begins to see, is organizationally as well as ethically deficient. Another child, chasing a pet rabbit, inadvertently discovers his headquarters, which the killer, of course, has booby-trapped. But—here the tale begins to seem almost a comedy—we now find proof not only of poor organization but also of slovenly craftsmanship: the boy opens the door, the bomb goes off—and, once again, without accomplishing more than attracting the police. I would like to believe that were it not for the meager documentation available to me on Di Giovanni I'd find at the least a statement of sorrow, confusion, regret—but if, as the cliché runs, actions speak louder than words, then we need not admit despair in trying to reconstruct his state of mind; for later that same year he plants a bomb on a merchant vessel in support of a dockworkers' strike . . . A traitor calls the police, who flood the bilge area, so that one more time his mechanized mayhem fails. That bomb would have killed many people. Di Giovanni writes to his fifteen-year-old mistress, with a sort of intoxicated incoherence: "Do I perhaps do evil? But is that my guide? In evil lies the highest affirmation of life." This is aesthetics, not politics. Aesthetics may easily justify suicide, even double suicide—but never murder. Not long after that letter, amidst public demands for the release from detention of the anarchist Radowitsky, a young Argentine finds on the sidewalk a suitcase which feels strangely warm. His last words to an onrushing policeman: "Look what I have here!" Then flames, thunder and broken windows. The policeman is lucky enough to survive, though seriously wounded; he was not as close to the suitcase as its discoverer. In this instance Di Giovanni had planned to blow up the cathedral but, as usual, accomplished something entirely different (if random murder be an accomplishment).

"A Mean Between Excess and Defect"

The means, then, one reads about *afterward,* in history books and newspapers. We call it a result, and no one can ever apodictically know a result beforehand. But the end, one would hope, remains constant, whether or not it is ever achieved. Indeed, an inconstant end is a sure sign of deceitful or outright evil expediency, as when Di Giovanni switches from Italian fascists to dockworkers, or Julius Caesar leaves a Roman garrison in Egypt to prop up his new puppets, Cleopatra and her cipher of a brother, with this alleged justification: "He thought it important for the prestige of our empire and for the common good, if the rulers were to remain loyal, that they should have the protection of our forces, while if they proved ungrateful, these same forces could constrain them." Caesar's end, then, *cannot* have been "the common good." Call it what it really is: the good of Rome. We can see it then; we can judge it. —"In evil lies the highest affirmation of life." —Not for me. —Fix the end; lock it; raise it; present it; preserve it. If it is truly good, be faithful to it. It hovers in the sky like the dreams of most religions. It offers itself, seeing and seen: the prospect of improvement, of amelioration or of complete remaking (depending on one's temperament)—of reform, of revolution, of salvation, of security, of coming out of the cave and into the light, of rising up into the empyrean to marry the ideal forever (or at least until the next ideal comes along), of merging with the Good. One guerrilla poet in a Catholic country even wrote of *resurrecting* the peasant masses from their grave of poverty. This was the same as their "rising up as one." The stone is rolled from the tomb! We who look in upon the inspired ones gather courage at last, enter the grave and, like Christ's disciples, "saw and believed; for as yet they did not know the scripture, that He must *rise* from the dead." Verily now, the revolutionary does arise, stands on tiptoe, reaches toward the end; he longs to embrace it. He craves to fly up into that oneness. The fact that he may not be able to do so does not defile his longing. If he is revolutionary enough, he will never give up. "To life one should give the exquisite elevation of the rebellion of arms and the mind," Di Giovanni had written in his typically turgid style. Elevation, now—what's that but a rising up?

Go back to the commencement of his career, when after the Americans execute his fellow anarchists Sacco and Vanzetti he begins to set off his bombs in Buenos Aires. The first, directed against that city's Washington monument, sends up what is later described as a pillar of flame. The second does considerable damage within a four-block radius of a Ford dealership. Di Giovanni has not killed anyone yet, but, as we know, he will—oh, he will. We have not the space to list all the man's victims. In his underground magazine *Culmine* he offers—my God, what could be more literal than this?—a drawing of a man carrying on his back and shoulders, Atlas-style, an immense bomb whose fuse burns ominously. The hero is ascending a mountain at whose summit Di Giovanni has printed the word UTOPIA. Our ends fly overhead like the red banners of Marxist-Leninist clichés. Speaking of "those great and beautiful things," Bakunin, the power of whose yearning must be respected, since on account of it he spent years of his life in detention, fiercely declaims:

> Let it be known to you that our love for them is so strong that we are heartily sick and tired of seeing them everlastingly suspended in your Heaven—which ravished them from earth—as symbols and never-realized promises. We are not content any more with the fiction of those beautiful things; we want them in reality.

This courageous, angry, impractical man, in his person an embodiment of the anarchist stereotype with his wild beard and moustache, his fluffy sideburns and his wide sad eyes, could have had beautiful things as his class defined them, but he burned his bridges to the nobility, rejected God for being a slave master, praised Satan for being "the first rebel, the first freethinker, and the emancipator of worlds." Bakunin rose up in Dresden in 1849 (Richard Wagner knew him and rebelled beside him), joined the First International and was expelled by Marx's faction of authoritarians. He called them "impotent, ridiculous, cruel, oppressive, exploiting, maleficent." Maybe they were some of these, but not impotent; for they won and Bakunin lost. What did he accomplish? He fought; he suffered. He kept the beautiful things before his eyes. "When the people *rise*," demanded Robespierre of his Jacobins, "should they not have an object worthy of themselves?"

And Di Giovanni? In spite of his vacillations, he perceived a worthy object, too. Perhaps that fact was the very source of his wicked errors. The great bomb, the mountain called "utopia," the targets and objectives of his bombings themselves, all bespeak a farsighted (in the ophthalmologist's sense), almost poetic vision. He saw the mountain but not the people who unknowingly blocked his way.

A woman in Stalinist times wrote in her diary:

> The nausea rises to my throat when I hear how calmly people can say it: He was shot, someone else was shot, shot, shot. The word is always in the air, it resonates through the air. People pronounce the words perfectly calmly, as though they were saying, "He went to the theater." I think that the real meaning of the word doesn't reach our consciousness—all we hear is the sound. We don't have a mental image of those people actually dying under the bullets.

Di Giovanni's mental image was only of the mountaintop.

Martin Luther in the Heidelberg Theses of 1518 had warned that too vivid an apprehension of the beautiful things would give a moral actor confidence—which by Lutheran definition must be unwarranted—in his own moral capacity. "The works of men are all the more deadly when they are done without fear," he wrote, "and with pure and evil assurance." (A modern restatement: "When it comes to revolutionaries, trust only the sad ones. The enthusiastic ones are the oppressors of tomorrow.") —From this proposition, which was already pessimistic enough, Luther, frowning and pale in his black Augustinian habit, derived one still gloomier: "It is certain that a man must completely despair of himself to become fit to obtain the grace of Christ." —Then how can that man be a revolutionary? Luther's answer: He can't. And I suppose that it was for just this reason that Luther turned upon the peasant rebels who invoked his name as justification. His views are accurately summed up by the title of his broadsheet of 1525, *Against the Murdering and Thieving Hordes of Peasants*. The murdering peasants lost, and were murdered by state authority. No beautiful things for them—at least not in this life! After all, said Luther, how could there be a Christian rebellion when hardly any of us were decent Christians? This is the opposite pole from Di Giovanni's freewheeling ruthlessness, and to me it is just as unsatisfactory.

I'll take the middle road, then. In the thirteenth century, Saint Thomas Aquinas said:

evil . . . in human operations lies in someone exceeding the measure of reason, or falling short of it . . . moral virtue consists in a mean between excess and defect—excess, defect, and mean being understood in relationship to the rule of reason.

A little manual I own which rather sketchily describes how to attack airfields, blow up trains, kill sentries and occupy cities says: "Our example must be of a nature that leaves no person unconvinced of the sincerity of our goal. That goal is a society of freedom and a world of true liberty." Fair enough—not to Luther, but to us. Di Giovanni could have said that, and so could Gandhi. Violence with the noblest end may or may not be wrong; violence without an end can never be justified. Of Di Giovanni's ends we have said that they waver. Strike at the Americans, strike at the Italians—well, in his system both nations are oppressors, and he is arguably right. He shotguns the face of a police inspector who employs torture, and I might be persuaded to applaud him. But now he gets embroiled in factional fights with other leftists who call him a Fascist agent. Defense of the oppressed gives way to defense of honor. The director of the periodical *La Protesta,* under whose auspices the charge had been published, receives three lead pills in the heart—good medicine for that organ's disease of counterrevolutionary obstructionism. Di Giovanni has become a Nechaevian: he kills as he pleases, and since only he is allowed to define righteousness, why, then, he must always be right.

Rising Up and Rising Down

Rising up, rising down! History shambles on! What are we left with? A few half-shattered Greek stelae; Trotsky's eyeglasses; Gandhi's native-spun cloth; Cortes's gamepieces of solid gold (extorted from their original owner, Montezuma); a little heap of orange peels left on the table by the late Robespierre; John Brown's lengthily underlined letters; Lenin's bottles of invisible ink; one of Di Giovanni's suitcases, with an iron cylinder of gelignite and two glass tubes of acid inside; the Constitution of the Ku Klux Klan; a bruised ear (Napoleon pinched it with loving condescension) . . . And dead bodies, of course. (They sing about John Brown's body.) Memoirs, manifestoes, civil codes, trial proceedings, photographs, statues, weapons now aestheticized by that selfsame history—the sword of Frederick the Great, and God knows what else. Then dust blows out of fresh open graves, and the orange peels go grey, sink, wither, rot away. Sooner or later, every murder becomes quaint. Charlemagne hanged four and a half thousand "rebels" in a single day, but he has achieved a storybook benevolence. And that's only natural: historiography begins before the orange has even been sucked; the peeler believes in the "great and beautiful things," or wants to believe; easy for us to believe likewise, since dust reduces truth and counterfeit to the same greyness—caveat emptor. But ends remain fresh, and means remain explicable. Rising up and rising down! And whom shall I save, and who is my enemy, and who is my neighbor?

"We *rose up* in arms," wrote the leader of the Zapatista Army of National Liberation in 1995. "This is how we pulled away the veil of falsehood and hypocrisy which covered our soil." If the metaphor is not merely mixed, then we must see (as the guerrilla poet in the Catholic country did) earth-encrusted wretches, buried alive, panting, digging themselves out, throwing aside—what? the oppressor's flags, draped over their tortured graves?—leaping to their feet; they can breathe again! They gaze upward at Bakunin's "great and beautiful things," raise their machine guns to heaven; then, like the People's Uprising Committees hopefully imagined by the North Vietnamese, they begin to march, trampling underfoot that veil, that untrue flag of misbegotten authority. The revolutionary whom the Zapatistas drew on—namely, Emiliano Zapata himself—had written back in 1915 that "if I *rose up* in arms, it was not to protect bandits or cover abuses, but to give full guarantees to the pueblos, protecting them against any chief or armed force that violates their rights." He saw the beautiful things but showed his peasant origins by being mistrustful of speech, especially flowery speech. Why rise up into the sky like Bakunin? For him, it was sufficient to help his friends and neighbors clamber out of the dirty pit of debt to stand on firm ground and be farmers.

"The waves of the folkish movement will continue to flow through the German land," wrote Alfred Rosenberg, not yet suspecting that the atrocities for which folkishness will be partially responsible would get him hanged. "And if we turn our attention to other countries we see that everywhere organic forces are *rising up* against the same deceit which surrounds us." Deep underground, the grave of freedom is not just veiled but roofed with rock, but the magma of violent praxis will overboil, erupt, dissolve everything. There is perhaps a sexual connotation as well in Rosenberg's description; let it be; rising up is ecstasy. It is also contagious. In Moscow in 1905, the munitions workers say to the soldiers, "As soon as you *rise,* we'll *rise,* too; we'll open up the arsenal for you."

The Zapatistas and the Nazis both had ends and means. Possibly both experienced the same feelings in the course of their risings. Power entered them; they acted. Later on there would be time enough for the world in its dusty superciliousness to weigh upon their orange peels. All uprisers sink back into the grave at last. "The Torah holds, 'If someone comes to kill you, *rise up* and kill him first.'" Here peace is slumber; homicide, the means, is wakefulness, and the end is to resume one's sleep.

Explaining how the law that kills, the secular arm, the executioner's law, can only grate to bits our flesh, not our spirits, Martin Luther utters these words of stern comfort: "As the grave in which Christ lay after that he was *risen again* was void and empty . . . ; so when I believe in Christ, I *rise again* with him, and die to my grave, that is to say, to the law which held me captive: so that now the law is void, and I am escaped out of my prison and grave, that is to say, the law. Wherefore the law hath no right to accuse me, or to hold me any longer, for *I am risen again.*" This stirring, almost heartbreaking echo of Christ could almost be the credo of any revolutionary or titanic actor, like one of the "extraordinary men" to whom after solitary confinement and a mock execution Dostoyevsky was finally compelled to renounce his allegiance. "The law hath no right to accuse me." Luther means this only in the sense that no matter what crimes I have committed, after I have rendered satisfaction, my mangled, tortured corpse thrown down into the grave, I am, if in life I believed in the Good, no longer accursed; nobody can hurt me anymore. It was Luther's misfortune during the peasant rebellions to see these words taken literally, instead of as the arcana he meant them to be. He turned upon the desperate uprisers who had believed, and he would not stand with them or solace them; they were rebels who dared to rob authority. But what if *I* still believed? What if I believed that the law had no right to accuse me even in this life, that not only my soul but my very body, like Christ's, was exempt? What if to my way of thinking I had committed no crime? —"Our nation shall *rise* against the enslavement of Europe by National Socialism in a new, true burst of freedom and honor," wrote Hans Scholl of the White Rose group. He was saying to Hitler, "Your law hath no right to accuse me." He and his sister got executed for their pains, the latter hobbling up to the guillotine in crutches, her leg broken by torture. Those who condemned the Scholls doubtless used the term as Cortes did when, leading his wavering conquistadores onward, he'd warned: "It would clearly be wrong to take a single step backward, for if these people we leave behind in peace were to see us retreat, the very stones would *rise up* against us." He knew whereof he spoke. Everybody knew. Against the Spartans, their slaves "the helots *rose up*—until Kimon heard their supplication and saved them," slaughtering the helots' leaders and returning the survivors to their miserable bondage. One summary of the old Athenian constitution explains that "when . . . the many were enslaved to the few, the people *rose [up]* against the notables." It was in this same sense that we must interpret a much older homicide: We read in the book of Genesis how Cain said to Abel, whose offering to God had been accepted, " 'Let us go out to the field.' . . . And when they were in the field, Cain *rose up* against his brother Abel and slew him." Cain's revolution was one of envy and bitterness, but for his pains he did not succeed to his brother's honors; he got only fugitivehood, and a mark upon his forehead. As for Cortes, he succeeded in crushing the Aztec empire. When a Spaniard named Alonso de Zorita came to Mexico a few decades later, he found the native hierarchy in a shambles, and wrote: "No harmony remains among the Indians of New Spain because the commoners have lost all feeling of shame as concerns their lords and principales, because they have *risen up* against their lords and lost the respect they once had for them." Risers-up and lords alike, what did they win from the Spaniards? Poverty at best; otherwise, a mark similar to Cain's—the mark of slavery, literally branded on their foreheads.

Cicero cries to the judges of a man on trial for parricide: "Bid this man who is your suppliant . . . to *rise up,* at long last, from the ground where he is lying." This rising up has not the slightest revolutionary tinge, being predicated merely on the judges' compassion (which is to say their supposed justice), but it is kin to other risings up in this important respect: We are upright animals. When we rise up, when we stand up, we come into our own; we come into our rightful and natural inheritance—which is exactly the sense in which both the Zapatistas and "the Cambodian people *rose up.* They themselves toppled the Pol Pot–Ieng Sary executioners totally, established a government truly of the people, their sole legitimate representative." This is almost untrue. The Pol Pot regime was destroyed by Vietnamese military intervention—granted, with some Cambodian assistance. The government then established was not representative at all but a hated foreign imposition. As described, however, the process certainly sounds majestic. It almost always does. That is why thousands and hundreds of thousands more have risen up over the millennia. When are they right?

Judging "Correctness" ad Hominem

This is the militant's way, the extremist's and the sadist's. It was, at times, Di Giovanni's. It was Nechaev's. The formulation is: *The fact that you say X makes it wrong. The fact that I say it makes it right.* Put this way, of course, it sounds absurd. But it was a founding principle of the Third Reich—and of the Soviet Union, too, as we see from:

> LENIN'S MORAL CALCULUS (1913)
>
> People have always been the foolish victims of deception and self-deception in politics, and they always will be until they have learnt to seek out the *interest* of some class or other behind all moral, religious, political and social phrases, declarations and promises.
>
> *Source: Lenin, vol. 1, p. 48 [article on K. Marx].*

In other words, your promise remains irrelevant to me—and likewise mine to you—but if my uprising triumphs, you'll be uprooted anyway from the earth your class sought to bury me in.

Setting Lenin aside, let us agree here and now that while the interest of a class or another group may determine the utterance of some ethical formulation, the formulation itself is not glorified or tarnished thereby. Whether Christ or Hitler says it, it is what it is.

Judging "Correctness" by Result

Begin anew, then, with the almost as expedient gauge of *success,* which we heard Gandhi categorically reject. Vengeance is mine, says the patriot whom we rise up against, and too often he has the means to obtain it seamlessly. It behooves us, then, in planning actions intended to increase our control over our lives, to determine whether in the long run we'll be rising up, and gaining self-sovereignty, or whether in fact what goes up will only come down the harder. The American Revolution was a rising up (to some—certainly not to the Indians, who abstained or participated on either side); the abortive head-rollings in central Europe in 1848 were risings down, since after they failed, authority tightened the screws. The concept, in short, is vulgarly simple, which means that it might be useful. A patient revolutionary might well disagree with given applications of the concept, arguing, for instance, that 1848 led to better things such as 1870 and 1905, which led to 1917, whereas I would tend to think about the crushed and ruined lives of 1849, but who could deny that some strategies build a movement while others destroy it? When the Burmese Communist Party followed the line of the Chinese Cultural Revolution in 1966–68, their ends might or might not have been praiseworthy, but they severely damaged their power base: most if not all of the leaders and cadres put to death by their own comrades died quite simply for nothing—which constitutes a rising down if anything does.

I remember that May night in 1980 when, after the police had rushed out of the Seabrook nuclear plant's gates and beaten people, a long tense hush ensued, broken finally by the bullhorns of police calling on the committed to "DISPERSE. LET'S GO. CLEAR THE GATE." There was a silence, and so the police bullhorn said: "CLEAR THE GATE. LET'S GO. CLEAR THE GATE PROPERTY OR YOU'LL BE ARRESTED." Then the protesters began to get up, and the bullhorn said: "C'MON, EVERYBODY DISPERSE." The two leaders of my supposedly leaderless affinity group, Tom and Rob, now rose. Tom returned a poncho which he had borrowed against Mace-infused firehoses and helped fold up the plastic sheeting which other protesters had placed over their heads. Rob just stood there. Tom said: "Man, I really want to stay here. I want to—" to which Rob wearily replied, "Yeah, but like the thing to do is to hit this place tomorrow with a . . . " and Tom dully asked himself: "How did they just get rid of us like this? How did they, how did they just tell us to go and just swatted us away like that?" —Rob answered: "We didn't have enough people to do anything. This whole action is just like fucking doomed. America is saying we can all die in a meltdown, in a fireball and that's it. Right now they have us where they want us. There's nothing we can do."

Rob was right. A violent or nonviolent rush upon the gate would have been literally beaten back; and the only other method of staying in the game, the Gandhian one of staying put, might have clogged New Hampshire's courts somewhat, at a price of inconvenience, intimidation, a financial burden and perhaps further physical harm, but . . .

"There may be avoidable suffering," runs Gandhi's moral calculus. "These things are preferable to national emasculation." And I agree. But even if, as Rob and Tom believed, and as I myself tend to believe even now, nuclear power was a wrong and dangerous course which the American plutocracy had no right to impose upon its citizens, national emasculation would have been achieved in any case. How can I be certain of this? Of course I can't; would-have-beens remain eternally unverifiable, but the antinuclear protesters at Seabrook possessed neither the will nor the popular support to rise up; and when they locked eyes with the National Guardsmen, they knew it. —"One must scrupulously avoid the temptation of a desire for results," says Gandhi. Yes, but what if the end is laudable but not essential? The ambiguously harmful "incident" at Three Mile Island (many of the frogs downwind of there are mutants now, I've read) and the unambiguous disaster at Chernobyl, which might in the end claim twenty thousand casualties, still lay in the future, and it is to Tom and Rob's credit that they could imagine them, and imagine worse. They will not figure much in this book about violence; and in the unlikely event that they ever see it, I would like them to know that my admiration for them has grown over the years. At the time I thought them needlessly abrasive and defiant, which they were; more actuated by ego than they pretended, which they also were, but that now seems to me forgivable, even harmless in this context. Like Gandhi, they could have chosen to be "comfortable." Instead, they took risks in the interests of a higher good. And they harmed nobody (except financially) in the service of that good. The industrial apocalypse from which they sought to save their country still hadn't occurred when I wrote this book, but maybe it would someday; still and all, on the rare occasions when I meet people now who were antinuclear activists then, I always ask them why they're not still antinuclear activists, and their answers come down either to being busy and tired or else to the call of another cause. Back in 1980, would these people have been willing to bring America to, say, economic ruin in order to end nuclear power? Would they have been willing to remain in prison forever? I don't believe so. Their attachment (I use this word deliberately) to the end wasn't as fanatical as Gandhi's. Therefore, results were essential to justify the anticipated sacrifices. Those results looking ever more unlikely, it was time to cut one's losses, avoid a rising down, fold up the tarpaulins and go back to our tents, case closed.

From this pragmatic standpoint, a guaranteed rising up requires merely sublime dedication, a perfect cause, ideal weapons, a complete organization and omnipotence. Since I have been unable to find any of those things today, there come to me only the following second-rate considerations: —To start with, we ought never to expect to see our purpose accomplished generally, and should be gratified with the success of small tactics in limited areas. Radical environmentalists, for instance, will not stop the mass extinctions of species by themselves. (It is precisely because this is so obvious that I've rarely met an activist who understood it.) Therefore, as in fascist and communist groups, we must have a division of labor in our organization between the propagandists, to keep the main goal in mind (for instance, "a safe natural environment"), and tacticians, who compromise the integrity of that goal sufficiently to accomplish snippets of it. This analysis may rouse antipathy because of resonances with the above-named parties, which ruthlessly sacrificed people to strategies because historical preconditions X, Y and Z for the goal had not yet been filled; and so those groups corrupted the goal entirely, becoming secular successes and spiritual failures, which must also be considered risings down. I can see no way to guard against this entirely, but one thing occurs to me: that such groups as lose (or never begin with) decency seem to have what American conservatives call an "ideology"—that is, a model into which the entire social order can be stuffed and stolen away. I propose to steal a mere few dinner plates, for my aims are modest; I'm a mere reformist. You who want to clean out the patriots' entire banquet set, with all the food in the refrigerator besides, should take care. You'll cook the rhubarb wrong, as meanwhile the bare-stripped patriots come after you. Your gorge will rise, and you'll be risen down.

Carry out your program, please, not your ideology. People have improved conditions in sweatshops, temporarily and in finite localities, but no one has ever "reorganized the means of production" with happy results, because it is difficult to know when to declare victory. It is precisely this difficulty which leads Trotsky to try to scuttle away from moral judgment altogether:

Do the consequences of a revolution justify in general the sacrifice it involves? The question is teleological and therefore fruitless. It would be as well to ask in the face of the difficulties and griefs of personal existence: Is it worth while to be born?

It is "as well" to ask both questions.

Kill people if you have to, but do it practically, for practical reasons. That approach has worked for your oppressors, and it can work for you. Above all, kill only in self-defense. (Ah, but what is self-defense?) Rising up requires saintlike extremism in one direction, and neutrality or prostitution in others. It might be necessary to betray the goal in small ways—in which case betrayal is the greater decency, as long as the war is limited:—limited war has limited liability, the price for which is limited reward.

Judging "Correctness" by Goodness

But ends must come before means, so before concerning yourself with expediency, with practical success, read the gauge of *justice*. The killer customarily has his reasons, as I've said. So does the victim. When John Brown's son Watson lay captured and dying, a proslavery South Carolinian asked him why he had participated in the raid on Harpers Ferry. —"Duty, sir," said Watson. The South Carolinian turned upon him and cried: "Is it then your idea of duty to shoot men down upon their own hearth-stones for defending their rights?" Both men would doubtless have justified their respective positions, if they'd been pushed, on the basis of self-defense. Watson could invoke self-defense of race through the Golden Rule (in other words, though he was not black, he was giving assistance to blacks in the defense of their human rights). The South Carolinian could invoke the basic right of any self to defend person and property (which latter category to his mind included the slaves he'd paid for).

Were you and I to dwell within the same social-moral order (the South Carolinian probably thought that he and Watson did; they shared the same nation, president and constitution; Watson thought they didn't, given their disagreement about slavery), and were I to choose to engage in violence against you, my justifications would be, in decreasing order of fairness:

REASONS TO DO HARM

1. What you've done. (You physically attacked me.)

2. What you are: allegiance. (You wear the uniform of the enemy army.)

3. What you haven't done. (You evince neutrality toward my behavior when I need your help.)

4. Whom you associate with. (Your best friend is in category 1.)

5. What you might do. (You could conceivably end up in categories 1, 2, 3 or 4.)

6. What you are: biological, religious or ideological identity. (You are a Jew, and I hate Jews.) What you have. (You are rich and I am not, so I'll rob and kill you.)

7. The fact that you are. (You exist, and any victim will do.)

By these criteria, whatever acts of self-defense the South Carolinian might have committed would have been more justifiable than Watson Brown's actions, because the former's excuse for violence was of the first rank: Watson had attacked him and his. As for Watson himself, had he injured the South Carolinian in any way he could only have appealed to a justification of the second rank: the South Carolinian had not threatened him personally, but he was a slaveholder, a member of the oppressor class. Again, through the Golden Rule Watson could have, should have and did put himself in the place of one of the South Carolinian's slaves, but now we approach a moral paradox akin to Zeno's of the hare and the tortoise: the South Carolinian's slaves were not likely *at that moment* in any great physical danger; the injury which had been done them must now have been a customary ache, so by this way of looking at things there was in the matter of their liberation no immediacy comparable to the urgency felt by the South Carolinian regarding this unprecedented threat. A government of constitutional law which has delegated to itself the right to use force will temporarily relinquish that right, as we have seen, only to a citizen in extremity. Harpers Ferry was being raided; it would not have done for the householders to wait for the matter to be taken up in the law courts. John Brown's party was clearly the aggressor. But Watson could have replied (had he not been weak and probably delirious with septic shock) that it would never have done for him to go to the law courts, either. No judge in Harpers Ferry was going to free the South Carolinian's slaves on Watson Brown's say-so.

Thus, comparing the means and ends of these two principals invokes the cliché about apples and oranges. The South Carolinian, like most citizens, was defending ordinary self-interest justified by civil custom and state law, with the blessing of the Constitution of the United States as then written and interpreted. Recently, being called again for jury service, I was instructed by the judge that whether or not I liked the law (and there were many laws which he personally disliked) I was required as a citizen to follow the law. Could I do that? I could; but at Harpers Ferry, slavery was the law. —It was Watson's conviction that such a law, legally and even democratically arrived at (according to the standards of the time) by the white adult males of the United States, was wrong. I admire Watson, who acted bravely and unselfishly. To him, the South Carolinian's ends were unjustified, which automatically contaminated the means (since we have agreed that violent means without ends are unethical, it certainly follows that means, even nonviolent ones, in the service of unethical ends cannot be approved). Or, to put it more concretely, Watson saw nothing defensible about slavery; and so the South Carolinian's self-defense hardly impressed him. To the South Carolinian, Watson's ends were, at the very least, offensive, although it is possible that if the raid on Harpers Ferry had never happened and the two men had struck up a friendly tavern debate somewhere on neutral ground, the South Carolinian, whose views we know only superficially, might even have allowed that slavery was, in the abstract, a bad thing—who knows?—but certainly Watson's means for expressing his difference were unlawful, despicable, wolfish, murderous.

The gloomy conclusion begins to appear that whenever violence defines my relationship to you, I must be an apple and you an orange, and only dust upon our peeled carcasses can make us one; that because the stakes can be so high (literally, life and death), violent confrontations tend to be predicated on *insoluble disagreement*. In the Socratic dialogues, a brash soul utters some proposition; the other, gently and sadistically wise, by cunning stages gets him to disavow it because (as suddenly becomes clear when the brash one's illogic has been completely dissected away) it contradicts a presupposition which both parties share. But beyond and before logic stands the vessel in which logic is contained—the *living identity* of one's intelligence. Socrates can win over Euthyphro because the only consequences to the latter will be a slight humiliation, a change of philosophical position and perhaps (but only perhaps, human nature being what it is) a change of behavior derived from that position.

But Watson Brown and the South Carolinian were armed not only with mutually exclusive righteousness but also with guns. To lose the argument, as Watson did, was a serious matter: Watson died. (As Carlyle would have said, the rights of man were vanquished by the mights of man.) Violence and counterviolence allow (though, as Gandhi and Joan of Arc proved, they do not require) both sides to invoke our first principle of the rights of the self, the preservation of the living vessel; and even if these rights are identically expressed—especially then!—they remain irreconcilable.

Imagine that Socrates and Euthyphro have both agreed on the truth of an axiom—say, Euthyphro's "piety is what is pleasing to the gods." Fair enough; concord is restored. But imagine two soldiers in hand-to-hand combat, each acting upon the selfsame credo:

1. My motherland must be defended. [*Moral*]
2. If I refuse to follow orders, I will be executed. [*Expedient*]
3. I have the right and the duty to defend my own life. [*Moral and expedient*]

These propositions, none of them anything but passive, which is to say unaggressive, bring the two enemies, through circumstances not of either's making, into a horrible de facto agreement: Each must try to kill the other.

This is why ethics, however universal it may be in principle, so often becomes subjective in practical application, because the very same means, in the service of the very same end, may well produce different and even opposing results. One of these soldiers will live; one will die. One regime gains the victory, one the bondage. We agreed to measure moral "correctness" by two yardsticks, the first of which was Hitler's favorite, namely, results. From the point of view of the South Carolinian, and states' rights advocates generally, the War Between the States was a definite rising down, because through it not only was the South bled and impoverished, but it lost the very right which it had seceded to defend, and had defended against the Browns: the right to own slaves. For President Lincoln, as we shall see in a subsequent chapter, the war was hardly a rising up, either, since he didn't want it, had acquiesced in the maintenance (though not the extension) of slavery and aimed only at restoring the status quo where military and political necessity permitted. For federalists it was a definite rising up: these days, what Washington says, more often than not, goes. To the Browns, of course, the result of the Civil War, had they lived to see it, would have occasioned hosannahs— and it would have made them proud to know that their Harpers Ferry raid, by exacerbating the friction between North and South, helped bring about secession and hence war. Yes, a rising up it was indeed, whose effects are still with us even after the crumbling of everybody's orange peels . . .

And by the second yardstick, that of goodness? The historian who called it "the fanatical and meaningless John Brown raid" was wrong. Fanatical, yes; meaningless, no. It simply had different meanings to the various participants. Morally it was *perhaps* a rising up, although we could not really decide that without researching who was harmed on which side at Harpers Ferry, and how and why they were harmed, and how the whole thing began. Beginning is often the hardest part. The South Carolinian would probably begin with the cold night moment when old John Brown said to his twenty-one commandos: "Men, get on your arms; we will proceed to the ferry." Watson might choose to begin with the year 1619, when a Dutch ship landed the first black slave in America. This choice might affect the final judgment just a hair. —Some commonplaces which could be offered are: the South Carolinian was right to defend himself, and wrong to defend slavery. Watson Brown was right (and brave) to attack slavery, and not necessarily right to attack anybody in particular. The problem with formulations like this, and books like this, is that after reading them we are not any better off *practically* than we were before. But it is better—far better!—to fail to act or judge, than, overstimulated by dogmatism, to behave irredeemably. Hence the First Law of Violent Action: *The inertia of the situation into which we inject ourselves must always be given the benefit of the doubt*—a fancy way of saying, "Look before you leap." (A corollary to this law is that no moral calculus should be too readily applicable.) We should not deduce from this that Watson was wrong—or that he wasn't. It does mean that if we ever find ourselves in Watson's place, we had better be awfully certain that we are right, and that we can foresee the likely consequences, both of our success and of our failure. Here is one of the places where I part company with the

Unabomber, who, driven by passionate despair, utters this Hitler-echoing cry: "It would be better to dump the whole stinking system and take the consequences."

The Calculus of Fanaticism

The reason that the Unabomber is wrong, and that John and Watson Brown *might* have been wrong, is that sweeping, unilateral violent action fails to respect the attachments of others. Gandhi and Buddha, as we have seen, warned their seekers that the life-and-death road could not be followed very far by anybody who held on to family, wealth or anything but the goal. Curtis Sliwa of the Guardian Angels and the terrorist Nechaev, whom I've already quoted, said much the same thing. The Browns had gone through with it; they were ready to die. But it does not follow that because for my own convictions I have put my right to defense in the keeping of providence, I may do the same with your right. Here the Golden Rule requires amendment. *Do unto others, not only as you would be done by, but also as they would be done by. In the case of any variance, do the more generous thing.* (Call this the Empath's Golden Rule.) Needless to say, this maxim is even more impractical than the Golden Rule itself. When the prosecutor asks for the death penalty, he may say to himself: "If I had murdered all these people, I would deserve to die," but, unless he is masochistic, arrogant or self-deceiving, he will not say, "If I had done that, I would *want* to die." Nor do we expect otherwise from him (Gandhians and their like excepted), because by violating the Golden Rule himself, the convicted criminal has prevented us from trusting him not to violate it again. And (it is important to state) the criminal has *deliberately* violated it. The fanatical revolutionary, on the other hand, does not pretend that all the people whom he wishes to harm have in fact knowingly and maliciously broken what he considers to be a universal law of justice and decency. Disregarding my ranking of reasons to do harm, the revolutionary gazes upon me without empathy and shoots me, because what I am is to him no feebler grounds for condemning me than what I've done.

The terrorist's Golden Rule: *Do as you need to.* Who cares about the rest? In his brilliant novel *Runaway Horses,* Yukio Mishima, whose description of the fanatical sensibility deserves credence on account of the terrorist theater of Mishima's own end, paints an assassin's portrait of the

victim, the brushstrokes simultaneously delineating defense of race, homeland, creed:

> The evil of Kurahara was that of an intellect that had no ties with blood
> nor with native soil. In any case, *though Isao knew nothing of Kurahara
> the man,* Kurahara's evil was vividly clear to him . . . And one clouded
> stream that never ran dry was that choked with the scum of humanism,
> the poison spewed out by . . . the factory of Western European ideals.
> The pollution from that factory degraded the exalted fervor to kill.

We cannot say on such evidence alone that Kurahara's killer is wrong,
because a passage like this, ominous though it may be, does not give us
sufficient information to decide whether Kurahara has in fact committed
deeds deserving death. But if no further ascriptions appear, if no further
logic is developed, then the assassin is as fanatical as Di Giovanni ascending Mount Utopia. Why? Because the murderer does not have enough information, either, and still he goes ahead.

A Lutheran Typology

What information ought he to possess? What data do most moral agents
go by? Here we would do well to adopt an approximation of the schema
laid out by Martin Luther in one of his sermons, circa 1519.

THE TWO KINDS OF RIGHTEOUSNESS
vs.
THE TWO KINDS OF SIN

PASSIVE

1. Alien righteousness	vs.	1. Original sin
Bestowed by God through grace,		*Transmitted from Adam*
baptism and perhaps faith.		*and Eve. We are born with this.*
"THE BRIDEGROOM."		

+   +

ACTIVE

2. Proper righteousness	vs.	2. Personal sin
Achieved by us through self-hate,		*Committed by us through*
neighbor-love, fear of God and		*desire, self-indulgence, etc.*
perhaps faith.		
"THE BRIDE."		

As I have implied by the left-hand "plus" sign, Luther employs the metaphor of marriage to describe the union of the two kinds of righteousness. Alien righteousness, being received from the Divine, is, according to the epoch's usage, the bridegroom, Christ generally being portrayed as the potent active principle, and the soul being receptive, subordinate, feminine. The soul's acquired or active righteousness, then, what the soul actually *does* to be good, receives the bride's label. The "marriage," in effect, is the union of the soul with God, or absolute goodness.

If we turn to the two right-hand quantities, we may draw a similar equation, although Luther does not. Received sin may be equivalently joined to the sins which the soul commits. The "marriage" of the two represents the sum evil of an individual, or, if we like, the extent of one's divorce from God and righteousness.

One need not be a religious believer to appreciate the simple utility of these two dichotomies and two marriages as a general representation of moral judgment. In effect, in calculating another human being's rightness or worthiness, we rightly or wrongly take into account both what he does and what he is, thusly.

The Two Kinds of Justice
vs.
The Two Kinds of Injustice

1. Received goodness *You are what I consider good.*	vs.	1. Received evil *You are what I consider evil.*
+		+
2. Active goodness *You do what I consider good.*	vs.	2. Active evil *You do what I consider evil.*

This simple form of analysis has the advantage of clarifying the interpretations and motives of moral agents, of dispassionately laying them out for us to judge and compare. Here are ten hypothetical uncoverings of the moral calculi of actors who play a role in this book.

CALCULUS OF RIGHTEOUSNESS: HYPOTHETICAL EXAMPLES FOR HISTORICAL JUDGES
HOW SHOULD THIS PERSON BEFORE ME BE TREATED? WHY DO I THINK SO?

MORAL AGENT*	PERSON JUDGED	RECEIVED GOODNESS	RECEIVED EVIL	ACTIVE GOODNESS	ACTIVE EVIL	JUDGMENT
1. Martin Luther	A Christian.	God's grace.	Original sin.	Follows the law, helps the poor, etc. All irrelevant.	None known.	Be his friend and servant; refrain from judging him.
2. Martin Luther	A Jew.	Little or none.	Original sin.	Follows the law, helps the poor, etc. All irrelevant.	Denies Christ's divinity.	Needs conversion through nonviolent persuasion.
3. Adolf Eichmann	A German Jew.	None.	Jewish origin.	World War I veteran.	None proven, but must be assumed based on received evil.	Extermination delayed, because of past services to state.
4. V. I. Lenin (pre-1917)	A Russian Jewish Communist, former landowner.	None.	None.	Is now a militant comrade.	Until recently, believed in a different "line" for the achievement of Communism, the common goal.	Work with him enthusiastically.
5. V. I. Lenin (pre-1917)	A Russian Jewish Communist, former landowner.	None.	None.	Has been a militant comrade.	Now believes in a different strategic "line."	Energetically denounce him, and if necessary break political and personal relations.

(continued)

MORAL AGENT*	PERSON JUDGED	RECEIVED GOODNESS	RECEIVED EVIL	ACTIVE GOODNESS	ACTIVE EVIL	JUDGMENT
6. V. I. Lenin (post-1917)	A Russian Jewish Communist, former landowner.	None.	None.	Has been a militant comrade.	Now believes in a different strategic "line."	Imprison or shoot him.
7. J. V. Stalin (1930)	A Russian Jewish worker, former landowner.	None.	Aristocratic origin.	None possible.	Must be assumed.	"Repress" through punitive labor, imprisonment or shooting.
8. J. V. Stalin (1950)	A Russian Jewish Communist, former landowner.	None.	Aristocratic and Jewish origin.†	None possible.	Must be assumed.	"Repress" through punitive labor, imprisonment or shooting.
9. M. Gandhi	A member of the Untouchable caste.	A fellow creature.	None.	None known.	Committed murder and theft.	Bring him home, let him steal, forgive him, offer him love and, if he desires it, instruction.
10. John Brown	A black American slave.	A fellow creature; one of the meek and downtrodden who "shall inherit the earth."	Original sin.	None known.	None known.	Liberate him, if necessary by doing violence to his master.

* Of course this table does not mean to imply that a given moral agent would necessarily act as shown in every instance of a given case; only that it would have been in character for him to act in that way.

† Mandel quotes data to indicate that by 1939, when the first of the two waves of Stalinist anti-Semitism was about to strike (the second involved the so-called "doctors' plot" of 1950–52), "40 percent of the heads of Jewish families were [Soviet] functionaries, against only 17.2 percent of the average Soviet heads of families. These facts made Soviet Jews, in Stalin's eyes, an easy scapegoat for the masses' hatred of the bureaucracy" (p. 155, n. 22).

If we were to subject the decision-making of Mishima's protagonist to the same procedure, we would uncover something like this:

MORAL AGENT:	Isao the terrorist.
PERSON JUDGED:	Kurahara, financier.
RECEIVED GOODNESS:	Unknown.
RECEIVED EVIL:	Soullessness, cosmopolitanism. (We could, if we chose, put this under "active evil," but Isao is the metaphysical sort.)
ACTIVE GOODNESS:	Unknown; irrelevant.
ACTIVE EVIL:	Degradation of Japan's traditional soul.
JUDGMENT:	Put Kurahara to death.

The Calculus of Selfishness

Most of us expediently rig our own moral calculuses in such a way that our actions become automatically justified in accordance with our own urgencies. I remember a man I once met who robbed warehouses. He explained that no violence was used, that the companies who took the loss were rich—no, he didn't hurt anybody! The fanatic merely increases the momentum of this tendency. A cabdriver I hired in Manila assured me that the New People's Army, a violent insurgent group with both Maoist and Islamic branches, "never hurt anyone"—yes, he used the same phrase! — "They only abuse the manipulators," he said. In a slum near Intramuros I'd just met a woman named Rosana, who lived without electricity on the second floor of a filthy tenement; she was so uneducated that although she loved the memory of the great martyr-patriot Rizal she didn't recognize *No Me Tangere,* his most famous book, an explication of which is compulsory for graduation in many if not most Filipino high schools. The NPA had killed two of her uncles, who came from like circumstances. I think once again of Di Giovanni's bank-clerk victims: How could they be "manipulators" in any structural sense? An "abuser," then, is anyone whose moral calculus I disagree with—and so (I admit) is a fanatic. The Vietnamese author Duong Thu Huong, one of three survivors of a forty-member Communist Youth Brigade which fought for North Vietnam, has a character cry out in one of her anguished novels that that great end of mass revolution, "the people," is but a flickering abstraction:

You see, the people, they do exist from time to time, but they're only a shadow. When they [the regime's vanguardists] need rice, the people are the buffalo that pulls the plough. When they need soldiers, they . . . put guns in the people's hands . . . when it comes time for the banquets, they put the people on an altar, and feed them incense and ashes. But the real food, that's always for them.

When the "they" who claim to exercise power for "the people" become distinctly materially or politically superior to them, then something is wrong with end or means, and we can speak of a rising down. When we begin to discuss the justifications of defense of authority, defense of the revolution, defense of the homeland and judicial retribution, we'll see over and over again that one of the central aspects of each case is the legitimacy of the authority which issues the order of violence—that is to say, the commonality of purpose and feeling between the leaders and the led. It is by no means the only factor (or this book would be much shorter), but it stands perpetually relevant. For whom are we rising up? Do they agree with us?

"Hoping that a feeling of the magnitude of the interests at stake; & of your own obligation to make personal sacrifice for the good of mankind & the glory of the Most High God, whose guidance in this matter we hope you will earnestly seek," wrote John Brown in an insurgency recruitment letter, "we subscribe ourselves Your friends; & co-labourers in the cause of humanity." But who is humanity here—the slaves or the slave-owners? It cannot be both. In this book we'll see many such definitional ambiguities.

"It would be better to dump the whole stinking system and take the consequences." Remember the First Law of Violent Action: *The inertia of the situation into which we inject ourselves must always be given the benefit of the doubt*. Accordingly, incumbency is innocent until proven guilty. Show us the proof first. Show us how and why the system cannot be saved.

"The First Duty of a Revolutionary"

My own aim in beginning this book was to create a simple and practical moral calculus which would make it clear when it was acceptable to kill, how many could be killed and so forth—cold-blooded enough, you will say, but life cannot evade death. Have you ever shot a cow in the head, slit her throat, cut her hooves off, skinned her, gutted her and quartered her so that you and others can eat? Have you ever been the doctor who must decide which one of ten patients gets the life-support machine? Surely it is better to have a rational and consistent means of doing these things than to do them trying not to think of what one is doing. —Suppose, then, that the calculus can prove that one ought never to kill. —Well and good. We are surely better off for seeing it proved.

So I began to write some notes to myself, called "Rising Up and Rising Down." Textbooks of insurgency and counterinsurgency presented ever so many of the beloved "scenarios" for various general cases, which in my grim state of mind seemed as if written on water in letters of ominous phosphorescence.

I wanted to find a base point below which we couldn't go—the "floor" of evil. I could then note that at least the fall could not be bottomless. I might hit it and die from the distance but at least I wouldn't fall forever. It was a way of seeking control. It was like seeing those two men come sauntering closer on that foggy dark night when I was with the Asian woman walking her dog, and the men came closer and because my gun was in my pocket I had the power to draw lines. (To quote Trotsky again: "To understand the causal sequence of events and to find somewhere in the sequence one's own place—that is the first duty of a revolutionary.") If they began to threaten her (or me) I could remain calm. If they began to inflict injury or if they menaced us with death, then I could shoot, so that I'd have at least a chance. But I did not have control over the political atmosphere I had to breathe, and neither did most people. I wanted to be able to say: *No, this is wrong, and I will not put up with it. If you force me to the wall I will defend myself.* I had not yet gazed left and right along the dizzyingly strange and unhappy continua of this book: What is self-defense? Ask whom you like, and you'll get the answer you like.

The more fundamental flaw in my thinking when I began, which I was too inexperienced to see, but which I'm sad to say I've seen in many another soul's moral calculus since, was a lack of decency and compassion. The Unabomber's treatise exemplifies this perfectly. When I first began to read it, I experienced what the cliché calls "the shock of recognition," because his obsessions were mine: the poisonous nature of uncontrolled technology and the shrinking freedom of the individual. But I am not accordingly inclined to go out and kill somebody. The Unabomber was. "One has to balance the struggle and death against the loss of freedom and dignity," he said, which was true; it was his way of resolving the balance that I didn't care for: "To many of us, freedom and dignity are more important than a long life or the avoidance of pain. Besides, we all have to die some time, and it may be better to die fighting for survival, or for a cause, than to live a long but empty and purposeless life." Good, as far as it went, but it did not go far enough because he'd left out the one kind of suffering that was highly relevant since most under his control—namely, that of his victims and their families. All he thought about were himself and his hypothetical fellow travelers. He was as selfish as Hitler. He'd lost himself. I respect life much more now—the lives of others and of myself. I try not to be deluded by the calculus of fanaticism, by ad hominem irrelevances, by uncontrolled means or by ends capricious or all-devouring. There are so many ways to go wrong! As Carlyle put it so well in his history of the French Revolution:

What a man kens he cans. But the beginning of a man's doom is, that vision be withdrawn from him; that he see not the reality, but a false spectrum on the reality; and following that, step darkly, with more or less velocity, downwards to the utter Dark; to Ruin, which is the great Sea of Darkness, whither all falsehoods, winding or direct, continually flow!

JUSTIFICATIONS

Self-Defense

I.

IN THE JUDGE'S CHAIR

O you who believe, keep your duty to Allah and be with the truthful.
QUR-'AN, ix.9.119

Please now imagine yourself in the judge's seat. Each of the remaining chapters in this first half of *Rising Up and Rising Down,* up until we reach the Evaluations section and the Moral Calculus, constitutes an excuse for violence—a defense, an invocation, a plea to be let off, held harmless, considered innocent.

These justifications necessarily overlap. Cortes's conquest of Mexico gets told twice, once as defense of creed, another time as defense of ground. Is defense of ground a separate defense at all, or merely a subcategory of imminent self-defense? What I have tried to do is what an ornithologist would: prepare a key of what I've observed in the world. Two differently colored birds may actually belong to the same species, but let's begin by giving difference the benefit of the doubt.

In my work as a journalist, the most common justification I've heard is the one we've already examined in "Definitions for Lonely Atoms," namely, imminence. By and large, imminence gets misused; the emergency is neither so stark or so immediate as is claimed. "I must reject an indictment for 'conspiracy,'" insists a Nazi defendant. "The anti-Semitic movement was only protective."

Behind imminence and futurity lives the onion's next layer, which can be any or all of the justifications which follow. For instance, the case studies in the second half of this book could be categorized thus (and since they come from the "real world," where everything is snarled up beyond mere complication, these are only the *major* excuses for violence invoked in each case):

JUSTIFICATIONS INVOKED IN THE CASE STUDIES

SOUTHEAST ASIA (1991–2001)

THE SKULLS ON THE SHELVES (CAMBODIA)

- Defense of revolution, class, authority, homeland; policy of deterrence, punishment, sadism.

THE LAST GENERATION (CAMBODIAN AMERICA)

- Defense of race, honor; policy of deterrence, retaliation, revenge.

KICKIN' IT (CAMBODIAN AMERICA)

- Defense of honor; policy of deterrence, retaliation, revenge.

I'M PARTICULARLY INTERESTED IN *YOUNG* GIRLS (THAILAND)

- No claimed justification. Imminent defense of others by right [Definitions for Lonely Atoms].

BUT WHAT CAN WE DO? (BURMA)

- Defense of race, homeland, ground; policy of deterrence.

YAKUZA LIVES (JAPAN)

- Defense of honor; policy of loyalty, deterrence, retaliation, revenge.

EUROPE (1992, 1994, 1998)

WHERE ARE ALL THE PRETTY GIRLS? (EX-YUGOSLAVIA)

- Defense of homeland, race, ground, war aims, authority; policy of loyalty, deterrence, retaliation, revenge, sadism, punishment; extenuation of compulsion, fear.

THE WAR NEVER CAME HERE (EX-YUGOSLAVIA)

- Ditto.

THE AVENGERS OF KOSOVO (YUGOSLAVIA)

- Ditto.

AFRICA (1993, 2001)

THE JEALOUS ONES (MADAGASCAR)

- Defense of class, race; policy of deterrence, revenge.

SPECIAL TAX (REPUBLIC OF CONGO, DEMOCRATIC REPUBLIC OF CONGO)

- Defense of class, race, homeland.

THE MUSLIM WORLD (1994, 1998, 2000, 2002)

LET ME KNOW IF YOU'RE SCARED (SOMALIA)

- Defense of race [clan], ground, authority; policy of deterrence, retaliation, revenge.

THE OLD MAN (MALAYSIA)

- Defense of creed, homeland, authority, war aims; policy of deterrence, retaliation, revenge, sadism, punishment.

"THE WET MAN IS NOT AFRAID OF RAIN" (IRAQ)

- Defense of homeland, authority, creed, war aims.

WITH THEIR HANDS ON THEIR HEARTS (AFGHANISTAN)

- Defense of homeland, authority, creed, race.

EVERYBODY LIKES AMERICANS (YEMEN)

- Defense of homeland, authority, creed.

NORTH AMERICA (1988–2000)

LAUGHING AT ALL HER ENEMIES (U.S.)

- No claimed justification. Suicide by right [Definitions for Lonely Atoms].

YOU GOTTA BE A HUNDRED PERCENT RIGHT (U.S.)

- Defense of ground, authority, creed.

WHACK 'EM AND STACK 'EM! (U.S.)

- Defense of creed, authority [of the self].

DEY BRING DEM BLOODSTAIN UP HERE (JAMAICA)

- Defense of ground; policy of deterrence, retaliation, revenge.

MURDER FOR SALE (U.S.)

- Policy of retaliation, revenge, punishment, sadism.

GUNS IN THE U.S.

- No claimed justification. Self-reliance and self-defense by right [Definitions for Lonely Atoms].

SOUTH AMERICA (1999, 2000)

"YOU NEVER KNOW WHO IS WHO" (COLOMBIA)

- Defense of creed, authority, ground; policy of deterrence, retaliation, revenge, sadism.

PAPA'S CHILDREN (COLOMBIA)

- Ditto.

PERCEPTION AND IRRATIONALITY

NIGHTMARES, PRAYERS AND ECSTASIES (U.S.)

- No claimed justification. Imminent self-defense by right [Definitions for Lonely Atoms].

OFF THE GRID (U.S.)

- Defense of creed, race, authority.

THICK BLOOD (JAPAN)

- Defense of race, class.

Take the last of these as an example: When a Japanese bride's parents hire private detectives to make sure that her fiancé is not of Burakumin ("Untouchable") ancestry, they do so to protect their race against "thick blood." The occasional result: suicide. Well, is defense of race ever justified? You'll find the evidence for and against in this section of *Rising Up and Rising Down.*

For another instance, in "The Jealous Ones," when poor people rob or harm people who are less poor, does the class-based aggression for which jealousy is a shorthand possess any legitimacy whatsoever? Trotsky would say yes; Burke would say no. What about you? It is your duty and prerogative to apply a moral calculus, mine or yours, as you see fit.

II.

DEFENSE OF HONOR

"Now listen to me," Nakayori said to the servant. "Get out of this fight. Go home and tell my wife and children how I have met my end."

Nakayori then dashed alone into battle and roared: "I am Shinano no Jiro Kurando Nakayori, the second son of the governor of Shinano Province, Nakashige, and the ninth-generation descendant of Prince Atsumi, twenty-seven years old. Is there anyone among you who thinks himself a great warrior? Let him stand forward."

THE TALE OF THE HEIKE

Young love, if you do not fall in the battle of Maiwand,
By God, someone is saving you as a token of shame.

MALALAI, PUSHTUN heroine, to Afghans fighting the British

The Charge of the Light Brigade is remembered for its "gallantry" — in other words, for its tactical idiocy. Six hundred and seven British hussars, dragoons and lancers rode against Muscovite guns. One hundred and ninety-eight returned. A London *Times* reporter wrote this obituary of Captain Nolan, Fifteenth Hussars: "I know he entertained the most exalted opinions respecting the capabilities of the English horse soldier . . . He thought they had not the opportunity of doing all that was in their power, and that they had missed even such chances as they had offered to them—that, in fact, they were in some measure disgraced." Disgraced! The word appalls me, just as King Xerxes was appalled by the Spartan defenders at Thermopylae; "the truth," writes Herodotus, "namely that the Spartans were preparing themselves to die and deal death with all their strength, was beyond his comprehension, and what they were doing seemed to him merely absurd." Captain Nolan would likewise be appalled by me: I ride a horse without elegance, and should anyone order me to my death I would hesitate. I have no honor. (In 1856, said a witness who idolized him, old John Brown, leading a charge against the proslavers of Kansas in 1856, "sprang his horse in front of the ranks, waving his long broadsword, and on they came." In 1996, President Bill Clinton upraised the receiver of a telephone, spoke into it and turned, perhaps, to his wife, or to the concerns of his reelection campaign, while at his command missiles came shooting down upon Iraq. The next day the military told him that there were still some targets left. He ordered another strike, just as any American might order a pepperoni pizza.) Captain Nolan, however, had projected himself into the old paintings of battles, where cavalry and infantry stand in squares and rectangles, bayonets aloft so that they resemble neatly sliced portions of spiny millipedes. Such clumps make ideal provender for cannons, let alone rifled firearms, which is why we rarely see them outside of paintings anymore. The reporter goes on: "A matchless rider and a first-rate swordsman, he held in contempt, I am afraid, even grape and canister. He rode off with his orders to Lord Lucan. He is now dead and gone." Why was Captain Nolan prepared to sacrifice himself and others to overcome some perceived ignominy?

Purity's Strange Defense

Bound in with the selfhood of the physical body, most of us believe, there lives a moral, mental, spiritual and emotional being. That is one reason why it feels so odd to me to gaze upon a corpse. Here is something with my form and shape. I understand the hinges of its bony joints; I know what parts of it ought to move (if rigor mortis does not interfere), and in which directions. This is my likeness. And yet if my duty requires me to lift the thing's wrist or head to inspect some wound, it's only that heaviness that I encounter, there being no volition to give it buoyancy. A sleeper will stir very slightly toward me if I raise her head to slip a pillow underneath; death leaves dead weight. Violence *toward* the actual pulp and mineral and water of such an organism is rare, although, like terrorism directed *at* a group *through* various unfortunate victims, violence quite frequently expresses itself by means of the destruction of flesh. The real aim of violence is to conquer, direct, instruct, mark, warn, punish, injure, suppress, reduce, destroy or obliterate the consciousness within the body. The anatomy of that self I've never seen in any atlas of medical cutaways of sliced yellow bone and pink stuff in the curvy channels between; charts of the nervous system perhaps come closest to what I imagine, with their slender, multiple branchings of sensation extending to the tip of every limb. But the self lies beyond them, or around them, or lives through them; it is the thing which experiences the pain the aggressor transmits through those nerves, and which bears it—or not. It is the *moral* anatomy of the self which determines (when choice is permitted) what the self chooses to bear, and how it bears it—to say nothing of what it actively inflicts upon itself and others.

Honor in our context will therefore be defined as the extent to which the self approaches its own particular standard of replying to or initiating violence. A saint might regard the highest honor as allowing himself to be bound, led away and (by worldly standards, ignominiously) executed by torture. A revolutionary might think it most glorious to assassinate as many of the executioners as he can, or, like the anarchist Nechaev, to employ any device and subterfuge, conventionally honorable or not, murdering to protect from murder his program of hopes. "You can't murder murder," Martin Luther King said—a sentiment which Nechaev shrugs disgustedly off. For Captain Nolan of the Light Brigade, honor meant subjecting oneself to violence as an act of faith: he and his men could overcome it through martial means—and if they couldn't, it would be better to die. To many if not most people, honor is simply and practically identified with the "right" of local norms: Catch as many of the enemy as you can and torture them to death. Never molest a fallen enemy. Kill as many of the enemy as possible, but use no gratuitous cruelty. Offer yourself to the enemy for slaughter. Refuse to engage the enemy.

These conflicting approximations having merely hindered our inquiry, I propose that we strip them away and try again, thus.

Four Types of Honor

Inner honor may be simply defined as the degree of harmony between an individual's aspirations, deeds and voluntary or involuntary experiences, and his conscience. As such, it remains unknowable to others. *Outer honor* is the degree of esteem in which someone is held. It derives either from his status, or from the amount of consonance between his *professed* aspirations and *known* deeds and the values of his judges. As Christ said,

"A prophet is not without honor except in his own country and in his own house"; this is why outer honor begins at home, and why people strive so hard to attain it: without deeds, creeds and uniforms, how can they impress the neighbors?

Honor may be cross-divided into *individual* and *collective*—my honor as a person versus my honor as a citizen of the Roman Empire, or the honor of that empire itself.

Outer collective honor constitutes the group's official face; inner collective honor is its esprit de corps as well as its degree of actual adherence to the ideals it professes.

The inner honor of a group, unlike that of an individual, approaches knowability, because the ideals are knowable, so that the members can accordingly evaluate those ideals in conference with one another. The inner individual honor of the members themselves, of course, remains a mystery. But outer honor demands and is determined by publicity—which is why Caesar's general Curio (himself, like Captain Nolan, soon to be a grand self-sacrifice to honor on the battlefield) sarcastically noted that

Individual and Group Honor

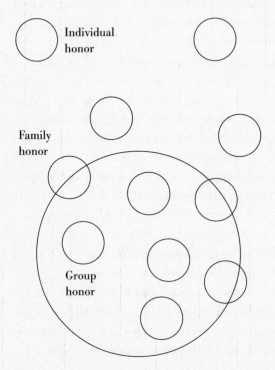

Individual honor

Family honor

Group honor

The lonely circles represent the honor of very idealistic or very selfish people (Tolstoy or de Sade).

The large circle represents group honor constructed by custom (say Christianity) or artifice (Napoleon's Grand Army).

The family honor circle represents one case of someone whose individual and group identities very strongly affect each other.

shame, which ordinarily acts to preclude the commission of faults, loses power in the dark. Given that phenomenon of ethical luminescence, we ought not to be surprised by the fact that outer honor of both sorts becomes expediently valuable, transformable into power, favors, goods and the like. Providential in every sense (Hesiod almost asserts its divinity), it is therefore what leaders and politicians strive for—and what the people they control kill and die for. Marx's bitter judgment that labor has grown "alienated" in consequence of undergoing objectification into a monetary value irrespective of its content could equally well be applied to the alienation of outer honor into the well-worn specie Shakespeare called "mouth honor." It was in recognition of the immense symbolic value of this commodity that Gandhi instructed his noncooperators to relinquish titles, medals and honorary posts. For the same reason, actresses with bedroom eyes sue for libel.

Thanks to that alienation, we cannot label outer honor good or bad without a context. It simply *is,* being as inevitably an aspect of persona as one's face. Nor can inner honor in isolation be judged a priori. Hitler's inner honor might well have been exemplary—which is to say, he probably acted in complete accord with his conscience. It is the radical disjunction between his outer honor (based on his actions) and posterity's conceptions of honorable behavior which causes him to be execrated.

Paintings of Napoleon

Napoleon well understood that soldiers' honor is a kind of empathy or identification. His method was to act the part of one of them—which he was; he'd risen from the ranks—sharing their privations, speaking directly to the enlisted men, even letting them approach him directly with grievances (this last must have been a carryover from the Revolution). As Madame Junot, who knew him well, has written, "But when the soldiers learnt that their chief had eaten of their bread, and found it good, who among them would have dared to complain?" (Thus the trick of George Washington's Prussian drillmaster.) Napoleon can fairly be called a man given to familiar warmness, who embraced the Emperor of Austria whom he'd just defeated, who clasped his arms around Tsar Alexander on their first meeting, who was known for pulling the ears of his valets, sentries and generals in direct proportion to his happiness and his fondness for them; who sometimes playfully sat upon the knees of his faithful secretary, Baron de Méneval, the man whose requests to join him in the final exile on Saint Helena would be refused by the English. (No doubt the Russian and Austrian sovereigns found such gestures less to their liking than the French, but isn't familiarity, however coarse, superior to coldness?) At the beginning of one of his eastern campaigns, he set out at such a rapid pace that his personal staff fell far behind, and so he had to sleep in Augsburg without any baggage; in the morning he greeted the laggards with a cheery laugh. That was the hero's way, the Roman Emperor's way. And the portrait grows more engaging by far. Like Joan, he bravely showed himself among the troops during many a battle, as if he himself were the standard; and at Regensburg in 1809, when he was struck in the foot by a spent musket ball, his first concern was to be rehorsed, galloping back into the view of as many soldiers as possible so that he could prevent any rumors of his death from disheartening those who killed and died for him. "The enthusiasm of the soldiers cannot be expressed when they learned that their Chief, though wounded, was not in dangerous condition. 'The Emperor is exposed like us,' they said. 'He is not a coward, not he.'" In the aftermath of an engagement, he'd generally be found picking his way among the fallen, holding up his hand for silence, so that the wounded could be located by their groans—again, something which one could imagine Joan doing. At Borodino, when one of the horsemen in his entourage carelessly permitted his mount to step on a man who cried out in pain, Napoleon was ready with a harsh reproof. Never mind, they said, it was only a Russian. But Napoleon replied that that didn't matter, and had the injured man carried out of the way. When his generals were mortally wounded, Napoleon would sit beside them and comfort them, often shedding tears. One biographer has particularly characterized the *Grand Armée*'s openness, easygoingness, even insubordination: "Napoleon thundered, but always proved more indulgent than the government . . . his great concern was that his men be eager for battle." (The Emperor used a democratic "people's army" to support extreme authoritarianism, while in the United States, strange to say, General William T. Sherman employed what he called "an animated machine" to defend a government of popular sovereignty.) Bonaparte was himself always eager, it seemed; he personified martial ardor. The military strategist Carl von Clausewitz, who in spite of his worship of cruel practicalities possessed a mystical streak, wrote rhapsodically of "the Will of the Commander . . . the spark in his breast." This describes Napoleon. Clausewitz might even have had Napoleon in mind: he knew the Frenchman's armies; he'd fought against him. Perhaps in some distant future, he writes, Bonaparte's battles "will be looked upon as mere acts of barbarism and stupidity, and we shall once more turn with satisfaction and confidence to the dress-sword of obsolete and musty institutions," a fate evidently worse to Clausewitz than death. Nothing musty about Napoleon, though! At Strasbourg in 1805 he rode alone to the bridgehead at five in the morning, an hour before the time he'd given as the rendezvous for his general officers, and awaited them calmly in a heavy rain. When they came, he gave them one of the most tranquilly confident greetings I can imagine: "All goes well, messieurs; this is a new step taken in the direction of our enemies."

His bestowal of the outward tokens of honor makes instructive reading:

> The Emperor would pull up in front of a regiment and calling the officers around him would address each by his name. He would ask them to mention whom amongst them they considered most worthy of promotion or such a decoration, and then passed on to the soldiers. Such testimony delivered by the peers bound the various regiments together with the bonds of confidence and esteem, and these promotions, granted by the soldiers themselves, had all the more value in their eyes.

Authority could hardly have condescended more graciously to mix the mortar of its own defense, but the decorations remained artificial. General Junot, who idolized Napoleon and hence, one would think, might have valued above all things the fruits of his esteem, once confided in his wife that "in the whole course of his career of honours, nothing ever threw him into such a delirium of joy as that which he experienced when his comrades, all of them as brave as himself, appointed him their sergeant, when their commander confirmed their appointment, and he was lifted on a tremulous platform still supported by bayonets dripping with the blood of the enemy." This had happened before Napoleon was anything but a highstrung youth with muck on his shoes. That youth himself got lifted into power on the trembling bayonets of popularity, which still dripped with the last blood of the French Revolution. Instigating this lifting was his own system of promotion (with, of course, a little nepotism thrown in). It flattered the masses; it soothed. In the first blush of *liberté, egalité, frater-nité,* it was even democratic and representative, like the soviets (workers councils) which sprang up during the First Russian Revolution of 1917, the mass revolution which overthrew the Tsar. The Soviets likewise elected their representatives by acclamation—precisely why the Bolsheviks suppressed them. Napoleon, however, kept the velvet gloves on: By all means let them pick their own officers. Let them control their representation. *I shall control the aims and means!* —One of his military maxims runs: *"The first consideration with a general who offers battle should be the glory and honour of his arms; the safety and preservation of his men is only the second."* In other words, you men are the currency I'll spend to enhance the stars upon my shoulders. In fairness to Napoleon, however, we must quote the rest of the sentence: "But it is in the enterprise and courage resulting from the former"—which is to say, the men's collective honor—"that the latter will most assuredly be found." This is the same advice that the ancient Greeks so frequently give one another in the pages of Thucydides: Stand fast, even against superior numbers, and our courage, ferocity and discipline will prevail. Retreat, and they'll pick us off one by one. Collective honor is *expedient.* Collective honor is made up of packets of individual honor all oriented in the same direction like magnetic vectors; therefore, your outer honor is also expedient; it will increase your chances of coming home. Cicero, that neo-Thucydidean to whom (as we have seen) collective honor was identified with prestige, and who always remained himself a desperate prestige monger, went further: Courage, ferocity and discipline must duly establish their own reputation. Slaves and pirates would then lay down their arms at the mere approach of the Light Brigade! Hence Cicero offered the expedient maxim that "there is no denying the extent to which the success of a campaign depends on what our enemies and our allies think of the commanders we appoint." (Napoleon could not have agreed more.) —In other words, when men grow sufficiently broken in to collective honor, the latter then becomes a kind of shorthand for collective preservation and even collective aggrandizement. That the shorthand may well be false writing, that honor of any kind is no substitute for strategy or decency, was proved long before the Charge of the Light Brigade.

We pause for a moment to gaze upon real life. The honor-infused Junot refused to obey his own traffic ordinances, which he'd signed in his capacity of Mayor of Paris. And the glorious legionnaires broke shopwindows, invaded homes, gang-raped prostitutes—they were thugs, many of them; in Hitler's Germany they might have become Brownshirts. That's why after the Moscow debacle, approaching Vilna on his long retreat, Napoleon writes despairingly: "Food, food, food! Without it, there is no limit to the horrors this undisciplined mass of men may bring upon the town." — Meanwhile, in the hagiographical paintings of his career, tokens of honor figure strongly.

We'll peer in upon him first in the gallery of the Château de Saint-Cloud, whose walls are clustered with tall, narrow paintings as night-gloomed as the waistcoats of the Senators approaching in a respectfully bowing crowd to present him with his mandate to be Emperor. (I wonder how similar are all such affairs? Does the mood of the French partake of the same ecstasy of worship and kissing that went on when Tito was elected Marshal of Yugoslavia by the Communist faithful?) He alone is dressed in forceful red. He stands out like a scarlet flame, or like that medieval emblem of French royalty, the salamander. Yes, one courtier's breeches are composed of that hue, and another's vest, but softened and darkened by the painter to an imitative lavender, these men being but embers to Napoleon's fire. A pale orange butterfly-like affair covers Josephine's breasts and marble shoulders, sweeping down behind her in a long tail, but the main impression she gives is one of whiteness like a bride. Her ladies-in-waiting embody woman-honor, appareled in pastels—in other words, almost midway in darkness between her colors and those of the Senators. And Napoleon himself, charismatic as Caesar, dwells at the center, as in almost all portraits: the brightest, the flag, the emblem. (In his memoirs he is always right, except when he exercises undeserved compassion or honor to others; this righteous infallibility of his becomes first absurd, then repellent.) He is honor itself. As such, he must safeguard the collective honor of these others; for while each of them may, as Adam and Eve did, choose of his own free will to do something disgraceful—grounds for expulsion from the community of honor—none can save the honor of all should their Emperor destroy it, as he indirectly acknowledges in his speech at the distribution of the army's colors in 1804:

Soldiers, behold your standards! These eagles will serve you always as a rallying-point. They will go *wherever your Emperor may judge their presence necessary* for the defense of his throne and of his people. Will you swear to sacrifice even your lives in their defense, and to keep them always by your valor in the path to victory? Do you swear it?

In other words, "Give yourself to me. I shall decide how to dispose of you." (He is already writing to Fouché: "The attention of the papers ought to be directed toward attacking England—English fashions, English customs, English literature, the English constitution.") That is why he passes out imperial communion: honor is not something merely to possess but an item of equipment for a cause. He who aims for the highest honor must be prepared to be the ultimate tool. Hence another of our toolmaker's military maxims: "All generals, officers, and soldiers who capitulate in battle to save their own lives, should be decimated." (The Roman Emperor Julian the Apostate had imposed the death penalty upon soldiers who lost their standards.)

In the painting of the fateful ceremony, whose significance people as alien as the Aztecs would have understood, we see gilded eagles above the red awnings at the Champ de Mars (need we mention that the old Roman legions adored their golden eagles, too?), while the standard-bearers lean forward, bracing their musket butts on the steps and raising aloft the eagle-headed poles upon which the regimental flags swim, each flag a square within which is inscribed a white diamond, the resulting border being two red triangles and two blue; thus the Tricolor is memorialized; and within the white diamond is embroidered in letters of gold the words L'EMPEREUR DES FRANÇAIS and the number of the regiment. Higher up the steps (but not as high as the Emperor, of course), and facing their standards, the regimental colonels raise decorated swords in Roman-style salutes. Honor has now come alive in these heavy, ungainly objects, whose vital force and destination, per oath, may be in the regiments' keeping but not in their control. This, I think, is what Emerson means when he says: "Every sentence spoken by Napoleon, and every line of his writing, deserves reading, as it is the sense of France. Bonaparte was the idol of common men, because he had in transcendent degree the qualities and powers of common men." (A century before Napoleon became Emperor, one French nobleman wrote that "our nation is so warlike that we can hardly conceive of any other kind of glory or of honor than those won in the profession of arms.") In those standards, then, the troops see themselves magnified. They need to be. Most people are sickened and exhausted by the French

Revolution's necessary defense of the nation and half-unnecessary defense of itself against the nation—the public squares still stink of blood. Why not don honor's new clothes? Why not enlarge, exalt, express their souls according to honor? For sooner or later politics must command them once again to dabble in blood. This ceremony cannot therefore be dismissed as procrastination—call it (as Napoleon pompously would) the commencement of national transformation. Indeed, Napoleonic honor marks the halfway point between ethics and pure aesthetics. Ho Chi Minh describes the process when he writes about the foundation of the Ku Klux Klan at the end of the American Civil War: "After big social upheavals, the public mind is naturally unsettled. It becomes avid for new stimuli and inclined to mysticism." And when is such sorcery well-advised? The question is worth considering, for sixty battles lie ahead! If I am certain of anything, it is, I repeat, that *collective honor ought never to be its own justification.* True honor, the only kind whose defense is justifiable, is that which allows one to evaluate the goodness of an end, and to make a judgment as to the ethical suitability of a means to an end. This is the honor that keeps one from becoming a rapist or executing unarmed prisoners of war, that tells when the time has come to kill and die in defense of one's country. It is this conception alone which allows me to comprehend and accept the statement of Milovan Djilas, who during the Partisan time of World War II lost his father, two brothers and a pregnant sister to war, murder and torture-murder, that "to lose one's life was necessary, as it always has been." Napoleon's conception was different, even if for a front-rank fighter it produced the same results: "I live only for posterity. Death is nothing, but to live defeated and without glory is to die every day." Djilas's honor partook of heroic collective defense and of struggle for a juster society; Napoleon's, merely of renown as the icing upon the cake of aggrandizement. When honor becomes, as it did for Djilas and for Joan of Arc, a bezel for the jewel of altruism—that is, when it impels us to recognize the rights of another self even at the expense of our own—we must respect and admire it, the rule of self-preservation being overfrequently extended to the point of abuse for anyone to withhold glory from the rule of self-abnegation—provided, as I hope I have made clear, that the sacrifice is made voluntarily, not coerced or manipulated, as it increasingly was with Napoleon's soldiers. Now, in plain fact most of us don't know where our opinions come from: I suspect that 90 percent of the thoughts I consider mine were insinuated there by the whispers of the newspaper, the postal clerk or the next-door neighbor; so the distinction I have been trying to make between my own inner honor and the inner honor of the collective I find myself belonging to is impossible to make in many cases. Authority knows this, and not only takes advantage of it but causes it wherever it can.

As we have seen, Napoleon was to a considerable degree gallant. He was also ruthless. To Tolstoy, who strove more or less honestly to bring him alive as an ethical actor, he was simply a fat, oafish, ear-pinching cad, a self-important little monster, who cast "now and then a glance of displeasure at the drowning Uhlans who had interrupted his thoughts." Emerson again: "He would steal, slander, assassinate, drown, and poison, as his interest dictated. He had no generosity, but mere vulgar hatred." —This is an exaggeration. Napoleon, as it happened, did possess a measure of intrinsic honor, especially in his younger years. When, for instance, he learned that the future Madame Junot's mother was hiding in her house a condemned man to whom she'd become obligated, but who was his personal enemy, Napoleon did not betray him, although the letter he wrote to the fugitive crows and gloats over his own rectitude: "Which of us stands in the preferable point of view at this moment? I might have taken my revenge, but did not." He could seduce the wives of his subordinates, or establish police spies to monitor his lieutenants, or massacre the entire male population of a tribe which had ambushed some French soldiers, or shoot howitzers at the ice on which Russian soldiers were retreating, drowning them by the hundreds. Meanwhile, one finds him painted upon the field of Eylau, in a portrait made according to his direction, saying, "If all the kings could see this horrible sight, they would stop making war." (One cannot imagine these words coming from the lips of Hitler, to whom he has so often been compared.) Smoke rises from burning villages in the background. In the foreground, snow-dressed corpses embrace one another, head upon breast. —"I imagine that you have arrested the Augsburg and Nuremberg booksellers," he writes to Berthier. "My intention is to bring them before a court-martial, and to have them shot within 24 hours. It is no ordinary crime to spread defamatory writings in places occupied by the French armies."

Perhaps none of his slaughters and trickeries were so far beneath the ethos of his time, or any time. And, again unlike Hitler, he did not have his citizens tortured. At any rate, here are the standards raised up, the representatives, the reifications, the idols of honor. They are believed in; they are invoked. "Soldiers, I am not satisfied with you," says Napoleon to Vaubois's division at Rivoli (1796). "You suffered yourselves to be driven from positions in which a handful of brave men might have stopped an army. Soldiers of the 39th and 85th, you are not French soldiers. Quarter-master-general, let it be inscribed on their colors, 'They no longer form part of the Army of Italy!' " As Bonaparte tells it, the veterans wept, cried out for a second chance and shortly thereafter "covered themselves with glory." Inner collective honor preserves the outer; both of them enlarge. Remember the mechanism when you regard that painting of him distributing honor's lineaments at the Champ de Mars. These are the same standards which the Emperor will command to be burned less than a decade later, during the retreat from Moscow,

> since he thought that fugitives had no need of them. It was a sad sight to see these men advancing from the ranks one by one, and casting in the flames what they valued more than their lives, and I have never seen dejection more profound, or shame more keenly felt; for this seemed much like a general degradation to the brave soldiers of the battle of La Moskva. The Emperor had made these eagles talismans, and this showed only too plainly he had lost faith in them.

Did it also demonstrate a streak of at least half-selfless humanity on Napoleon's part, being the destruction of his own honor-magic, done to lighten his men's burdens? —I suspect not. More likely he thought to prevent the Russians from seizing them, and humiliating his own prestige any further. In Japan at the end of World War II, General Tanaka, commanding the Army of the East, orders all regimental flags burned so that the victorious Allies can't get them, then shoots himself in the heart "to expiate this holocaust of the standards." Suicide is honor's last resort, when it is not the first. It will never be Napoleon's. We see him shortly before his abdication, fat, pale, sluggish and dejected, sitting in the firelight at Champaubert with his arms folded across his breast, resting on his heels. Shortly after signing the abdication document, he tries halfheartedly to poison himself, murmuring: "I cannot endure the agony I suffer, above all the humiliation of seeing myself surrounded by foreign emissaries! My eagles have been trailed in the dust! I have not been understood!" I cannot believe that this man who'd succeeded so brilliantly in his enterprises could not have ended his life if he'd really wanted to.

So much for the beginning; so much for the end, foreshadowed, perhaps, at burning Moscow, when we see the Guard supporting their scarlet-cloaked Emperor beneath the arms as, covering his face with his white-gloved hands, he strides into the flames. One helper gazes tenderly down to watch Bonaparte's footing, while the other stares ahead at the fire. Their master has become frail. The magic of the standards no longer strengthens and impels its adherents anymore; therefore it must be protected. Approaching those ancient gates, recalls one of his officers, he'd trusted in his men's "habit and thirst of glory"—which is to say, their outer honor, and their collective *esprit*. But their thirst cannot be slaked now; they'll drink only vinegar.

As for the narrative's middle, his portraits will show us that in profusion. Riding toward Berlin in 1805, he sits upon a white horse. The painter, with the usual determination or desperation to represent the Emperor's singularity, has rendered almost all the other mounts, and the very ground, by means of obsequiously inconspicuous ochers and browns. —Well, perhaps it was actually like that. —There he is, center stage, his horse a dazzling, luminous negation of muck, clouds and darkness, his face so resolute . . . —Next portrait: Astride his horse again, he pauses on a knoll, the *Grand Armée* facing round, at his back a strange old belfry with a cannon shot through it. He stretches out his arm parallel to the earth to cry: "The honor of the French infantry is at stake." He wins at Austerlitz. (By this time Madame Junot is belatedly using the word "despotism" to describe his regime, but the soldiers, we're plausibly told, continue to shout his name. After all, he personifies all four kinds of honor.) It is here that, in that scene made hideously memorable by Tolstoy, Napoleon's cannonballs break the ice upon which the panicked Russians are retreating; hundreds drown. Well, well, isn't war always like that? In the painting, folded corpses and the suppliant benedictions of the dying dog the horses' hooves, while a patch of golden sky opens above the waving standards, nature thus conniving with history after the fashion of the era. And along the walls of history's long gallery hang many other paintings. At Jena, for instance (1806), we see Napoleon, Murat and Berthier reviewing troops whose bayonets resemble the pickets of a dark fence, the Emperor's face here pale, almost eerie in intensity beneath the dark sky so autumnal and stormy. The abnormal rigidity of his soldiers at attention with their up-raised muskets gives an impression of straining potential energy like the clouds overhead: fate is about to let loose. Bonaparte, of course, makes the most dynamic figure. His chestnut horse shines, sweeping across the mucky earth. Afterward comes that painting of the battle of Friedland that same year, in which honor forms around itself a cool wet spring eve-ning, the sky already bleakly yellow as Napoleon on his pawing white charger points onward; his liege men lean toward him, staring into his face—the sinewy, alert officers, ready and determined. A wounded man lies covered up beside a wagon tongue; and by a gleaming cannon standard-bearers hold the colors which offer sad and resolute bands of rust and orange to that sad yellow sky, that sky almost as lurid as at Smolensk, which the retreating Russian army will set on fire (Tolstoy claims that the French did it). We see a man standing, blood streaming from his temple—emblematic, that casualty, for from Friedland on, as one commentator has put it, Napoleon will consider himself in "posses-sion of a blank cheque on the bank of man-power." Isn't that honor's right? He says to Fouché, who entreats him not to attack Russia, "Nowa-days Europe is only a rotten old whore who has to do just what I want when I have 800,000 men." Far away at Monticello, Jefferson, who'd once thought him decent, hears this or like remarks and calls the Emperor a *dishonorable* man, a ridiculer of honor, "the first and chiefest apostle of the desolation of men and morals." Had he penned these words on French territory, Napoleon might have had him shot . . . In the back-ground, a forest of men backpoint their rifles upon their shoulders, wait-ing for the next command. Napoleon has expelled the Russians from Friedland; they've fled across the Niemen River, 25,000 of them conve-niently drowned or otherwise dispatched. Here lies eternal honor as Napoleon would define it, or Julius Caesar, or Cicero—the honor of the goddess Victory, the spectacular end achieved which the bloodiness of the means can scarcely tarnish: "Ours are the trophies, ours the monuments, ours the triumphs." Napoleon sits upon his horse, a little older and stouter than he used to be, but everything within this painting's world waits upon him to whom the viewer's eye returns willy-nilly; he consti-tutes the sign and the guarantor of esteem's fire. (But after that comes Moscow.)

THE HONOR OF NAPOLEON (1801–12)

Inner Honor

INDIVIDUAL

Always followed his destiny, his "star," no matter what the cost.

COLLECTIVE

High initially, then low. Created and personified it to his soldiers and citizens.

Outer Honor

INDIVIDUAL

High at first. He was the Emperor, after all. But eventually his prestige and success declined.

COLLECTIVE

High, until his armies were defeated.

His version of collective honor proved both expedient and rewarding for most participants as long as there were victories—for Cicero and Caesar spoke well grounded in worldly reason: as Machiavelli notes, "nothing makes a prince so much esteemed as great enterprise and setting a fine example." In other words, in those spectacular years before Moscow, collective honor remained undifferentiable from profitable aggression. Ah, to relive the extortions of the Italian campaign! "Every public treasure was confiscated," said William Pitt later, invoking offended English collective honor in the cause of counteraggression. "The country was made the scene of every species of disorder and rapine"—surely one reason why biographers so often speak of the enthusiastic cries of Napoleon's army, as at the fateful battle of Borodino when he was "standing with folded arms, the sun shining full in his eyes, reflected from the French and Russian bayonets." Of course, that was not the only reason. In spite of Robespierre's theorem that "one can encourage freedom, never create it by an invading force," it seems to have been the case that egalitarian principles were carried beyond France's borders upon those selfsame bayonets. The destruction of a decomposing feudalism's unjust and unreasonable exactions had been an affair of which the Revolution, for all its own corruption afterward, could remain proud. The war against the counterrevolutionary coalition of nations had originally been self-defensive in nature: should Austria, England, Spain, Russia and Prussia triumph against France, the restoration of the Bourbons would become almost inevitable, and with it the extinguishment of all that the new mass armies had fought for. Their victories against the coalition, therefore, were intoxicatingly honorable. When Bonaparte came to the scene, he accordingly offered, with perhaps more fervor than sincerity or reason, a noble cause to fight for: the international extension of that revolution which he actually labored increasingly to undo, bringing back class hierarchy, Catholicism, paternalistic family laws. But above all, he offered victory. The historian Lefebvre, who calls him a terrorist, admits that "the overpowering vigour of the campaigns, and the faultless dexterity with which they were brought to a swift finish, evoke our romantic admiration to this day," which means that Napoleon did after all achieve some of that posthumous glory by which he defined honor. And to many of his contemporaries, up to 1812 and in some cases even after, he offered living fame. His equation: *All honor is honorable.* It was only after Moscow, when serving the Emperor could no longer be construed as an affair of evident self- and group interest, that the test came. At the commencement of the withdrawal from the burning city, Napoleonic honor still passed that test—no matter about domestic terrorism, spies everywhere, lettres de cachet. (The Marquis de Sade, whom we will profile elsewhere, was one of Napoleon's victims. Locked up by his mother-in-law under the ancien régime, reimprisoned by Robespierrists during the Terror, Sade now found himself, like a Soviet dissident a century and a half later, locked into an asylum for the rest of his days.) Bonaparte was as solicitous of his soldiers as ever during the retreat, perhaps even more so now that they were suffering so much. He and his staff gave up their mattresses to the wounded, and at least one injured man rode in every carriage.

But it was at Malodechno that dilemma struck. A coup had been attempted in Paris. The plotters announced that Bonaparte was dead, that he'd been slain in Russia. Napoleon was commander in chief, and the ethical system he'd created demanded that he continue to ride at the head of that shivering, snow-epauletted procession of hungry men, sharing their agony if he could not mitigate it, like the proverbial captain who goes down with the ship; for, as Napoleon's predecessors in nobility had been taught all too well by the Revolution, mere privilege and compulsion cannot create an ethos of collective honor; there must be kinship; the leader must be, or seem to be, loyal to the led. But Napoleon was also head of state, and the same requirements of visible leadership applied in Paris, which was far, far away. (As it was, even as commander in chief, he'd become fatally overextended, for the Spanish campaign, that famous "running ulcer," had turned against him, too.) The communications of his day could not make him ubiquitous like Orwell's Big Brother. If he wished to preserve the legitimacy and administrative authority of his self-awarded imperial mandate, as well as the instruments of it, namely, those staggering prisoners of "General Winter" now marching in his wagon tracks, he must return to the capital posthaste. After breaking the news to his marshals, however, "he felt the need of withdrawing; for he had been oppressed by the constraint of this interview, as could easily be seen by the extreme agitation his countenance manifested at its close." *"The presence of a general is indispensable,"* Bonaparte wrote in his own italics, *"he is the head, the whole of an army."* He departed early, secretly and rapidly. As for the line soldiers, they reviled him with unspeakable bitterness. The standards were ashes, and the captain had abandoned ship.

Now the lost battles began. To Metternich he said: "Someone like me doesn't care if he loses a million men!" He lost more. Having abdicated, he left Paris to the execrations of the widows and orphans created by the Napoleonic Wars. (People had begun to murmur against him ever since Austerlitz. Not at all irrelevant here is the hideous gore of Malo-Yaroslawetz, where the corpses' heads had been squashed by his cannon wheels. "In this scene, the Emperor, it was said, beheld nothing but glory.") His ex-Minister for the Marine said: "That terrible man enslaved us all. He held our imagination in his hand, sometimes a hand of steel, sometimes a hand of velvet; one never knew how it was going to be from day to day, so that there was no means of escaping." (We ought not to blame his aggressive imperialism for this entirely, however, for it has been truly said that "heroism . . . requires contradiction, a 'reality,' an 'is,' or an 'actuality' counterposed to the ideal . . . Without it there would be nothing against which to struggle.")

During his last gamble, the escape from the island prison-kingdom of Elba and then the ensuing Hundred Days, his subjects saw little to choose between him and the restored Bourbons—perhaps because the eagle talismans of both had been destroyed. If we were to make a list of "maxims for murderers," I would construct Napoleon's Maxim thus: *Reify collective honor into standards and monuments as needed. Then your pawns will have something to bleed for.* But his standards had burned. He tried to evoke in his tropes of honor the French Revolution which he had sprung from and partially dismantled. When the CIA published a sabotage manual for the contras of Nicaragua nearly two centuries later, it used the same ploy: "Take a decisive action toward the freedom of Nicaragua by incorporating with your arms, if possible, in[to] the ranks of your brothers, worthy heirs of Sandino." The real "heirs of Sandino" were the Sandinistas whose government the CIA sought to overthrow, but logic was not the point. Sandino was admired even by the contras; hence standards of collective honor could be manipulated for the good of the CIA's rather shoddy cause by urging thugs and mercenaries to join with him. Talk about honor among thieves! In Napoleon's case, the standards, once burned, could not be made to play phoenix. Possibly he himself no longer believed in them, if he ever had—surely he had! Exiled to Saint Helena, he dictated: "A good general, good officers, judicious organization, able instructions, good and severe discipline—these make good troops, independently of the cause for which they fight. It is, however, true that fanaticism, love of their country, and national glory are useful to animate young troops." These words might have been composed by the carefully professional Wellington who beat him, or by a tired bureaucrat, or by a cynic. Let Jefferson award the epitaph: "What a sample of the Bathos will his history present! He should have perished on the swords of his enemies, under the walls of Paris."

Needless to say, that isn't the epitaph he actually got. His tomb rises from a white well of pillars and figures, at the center of a gloomy sunburst inscribed with laurels. (Appalled, Tolstoy wrote in his diary: "Deification of a villain. It's terrible.") A sarcophagus of burgundy-colored porphyry, massive and strange, rises from darkness now interruption-riddled by the calls and popping photoflashes of tourists—but then, that is the fate of all monuments which linger unsmashed: to be appropriated by the present and by life with all its extraneous concerns. Napoleon's spell, such as it was, has been attenuated: it will continue to dwindle until his name becomes as remote as Tamerlane's. But, although the present generation does not attend him well, he lies attended by others who served France more or less well in life. Here in a private niche lies the hero of World War I, Marshal Foch, whose monument portrays in sculpture a man being carried on a litter or bier by dark soldiers. The sky backlights this place through myriad window scales, silhouetting those mournfully toiling figures even in the afternoon into pallbearers upon some ridge of evening. —But we slight the Emperor by lingering too long with Foch. Behind the glaring gold crucifix and its assemblages, we descend white marble stairs into the well, and arrive at the black crypt-arch flanked by two night-colored statues bearing crowns. Upon the wall we read HONNEUR ET PATRIE.

III.

DEFENSE OF CLASS

Soft, capacious, easy chairs, thick carpets, wide and long draperies, down pillows, all the refinements of the culinary art, which no other nation in Europe but ourselves know any thing about, were good for nothing but to send us to prison; and, because we lived in a fine hotel, situated at the bottom of a court yard, in order to escape the odious noise and stench of the street, we had our throats cut. This method of treating good manners somewhat disgusted people with them. For some time, therefore, they were abandoned.

THE DUCHESS D'ABRANTES

The wicked plebs take
slumber on patrician turf and inhuman soldiers
lie on couches spread for kings.

LUCAN

Nine out of ten of those of you who think yourselves the elite are traitors to your country.

Rizal's protagonist Simoun

To Dr. Jose Rizal, honest, passionate and good-hearted, the matter of class was simple. Social conditions had to be ameliorated by legitimate authority, not by revolution: "reforms in order to be fruitful, must come from *above* . . . those that come from *below,* [are] irregular and uncertain." The naiveté of this dictum is founded on its assumption that legitimate authority will always retain a modicum of civic decency, which, in combination with that natural efficiency of organization which is a virtue of incumbency, will ensure that its behavior is superior to that of a mob. (The authority which executed him was, as he and I would agree, illegitimate authority.) In the museum dedicated to his memory in Manila, one sees the implements of his profession: tarnished scalpels, then glass syringes, ampules and bottles of an antique shape, brittle and obsolete. Too easy, after this twentieth century which Stalin emblematized, to call Rizal's principles antiquated, too! And yet his mind was flexible, complex, clever. Like Tolstoy, he continually stated that the slaves of tyrants would, given power, become tyrants in their own right. Hence the gentle Rizalian prescription, not unlike Gandhi's: educate everybody; offer oneself in sacrifice; strive to make the tyrant become good; render the masses worthy of power—all the while proceeding steadily and without fear. That is why he never insisted that the Philippines get full independence from Spain. Practically speaking, his program called for redress from the abuses of the Spanish friars, full equality for Filipinos under the laws of Spain, proportional representation in the Spanish parliament. But what if, following Plutarch's line, authority believes that the masses, if too much relieved from oppression, will become dangerously unquiet? In 1896, the masses not being at all quiet, authority stood the doctor up against a wall, thus instantaneously elevating him in the public honor from gadfly to martyr; when I visited the Philippines a hundred years later, certain tribal cultists were still calling him God. His execution solved nothing for the elite of Spanish friars and generals, who (hindsight now shows) comprehended neither the practicalities nor the ethics of class self-defense. Nor, perhaps, did the native revolutionaries, who for their pains merely exchanged for Spanish masters American ones. Continued peonage showed once again the insufficiency of Plato's dictum that "no man whatsoever will prove a creditable master until he has first been a servant"—a conveniently quietist slogan, which class tyranny expresses thus: *No man will prove a creditable servant—unless we can keep him a servant for all time!* Thus is defense of class—the upper class. To the lower class there looms but one means of self-defense: rising up.

But the long century of Stalin (now finally at its end) opens its mass graves to us; within them we see literally millions of skeletons and corpses murdered in the name of class. Rizal never asked for this. Stalin did. When the slaves of tyrants become the masters, what then? We know Rizal's answer, and yet if slaves cannot become masters, what hope is there? Could true equality be possible or even desirable? *What is defense of class?*

Photographs from Russia

I have before me one ghastly photograph of a trial of "wreckers and hoarders" in Central Asia. In this outdoor scene, three good proletarians sit behind the table—Party workers, I presume. Two men sit on a bench before them with bowed heads. It must be cold, because they, and their trio of judges, and the standing crowd which rings them round (whose faces are grim and sad), have on caps and thick quilted jackets. Some wear scarves. Complexions seem pale and chilled. Each of the two accused has brought his sleeves together on his lap, in order to keep his hands warm during what has probably been a long harangue. The bystanders likewise keep their hands in their pockets. At the right-hand side of the table stands a fellow with a prosecutorial air, his accusing arm outstretched into one of the defendants' faces—stiff and ruthless, that arm, which could almost be said to form a Roman salute. Mussolini might have been proud of it, and likewise anybody whose calling consists of pushing people into abysses. One cannot see the outstretcher's face, nor the faces of the judges, because the photographer was standing behind them on that cold day in 1931, but the hunched submission and sorrow of everyone else cannot *but* be seen. If the two men are found guilty, as Stalinist norms press them to be, they'll get stripped of their belongings and sent north, perhaps to labor and perish in building another settlement, perhaps to be sent to Kolyma along with Varlam Shalamov. Maybe they'll be lucky and end up five or ten years hence as low-paid industrial workers more or less forgotten by the class authority. Regardless, this year they will be hungry, for this is the year of universal collectivization, class victory. "Officially the famine did not exist," says Koestler, who glimpsed it from his train windows.

In another photograph we see roll call at a collective farm: a long line of women, wrinkled and dirty, leaning on their hoes, hooded in the old peasant style. We see propaganda photos of flying dirt. We see Party activists in sheepskin coats and aviator-style caps dipping up peasants' grain from holes in the ground and pouring it into sacks to be taken away. We see a little lean-to hut with a red flag, and above it a crude, tripodal tower, two of whose legs form the sides of a ladder atop which a pair of Young Pioneers stand shading their eyes with their hand edges, watching vigilantly for grain thieves. (How hungry are *they?*) We see wrinkled, gnomish children whose flesh has imploded from starvation; one stretches out his hands. We see a peasant couple turned cannibal and caught at it, standing rigidly erect against what is probably the wall of their house, a severed head (eyes closed, mouth wry) and various joints of meat on the table before them. We see a child standing behind that table, his hands clasped upon a hunk of flesh, about to cry.

Preceded by red-flag wavers, pulling cargos of smiling children, the first tractors approach the new kolkhozes. Stalin says that we have never been happier. Defense of class has become war upon class. Had Rizal been one of these peasants, would he have salvaged his hope?

"Break Down All Barriers with an Iron Hand"

But if Rizal was naive, does that mean that we must follow the exactly contrary logic of the Unabomber, who insisted that "permanent changes in favor of freedom could be brought about only by persons prepared to accept radical, dangerous and unpredictable alteration of the entire system . . . in other words, by revolutionaries, not reformers"? —That fellow's murderous shallowness is proved by the fact that for all his hatred of authority, these words of his characterize Stalinist procedures all too well. —And yet (an upriser might plausibly reply), by what other means could those Stalinist procedures be overthrown? Well, what actually accomplished the event was a triad of events: first, Stalin's death; second, politic postmortem denunciations of the tyrant by the new regime, beginning with Khrushchev; and third, what were meant to be safe and predictable reforms nigh on four decades later: those quickly became a revolution, yes, a "dangerous and unpredictable alteration of the entire system." Once again, Plutarch was vindicated: give the people an inch and they'll take a mile! And the Soviet Union died. Now what? Certainly something better—or not. A new underclass seethes, and gangsterism rides where the secret police once led their cattle drives. In Kazakhstan I've met tired women snow shovelers who used to be college teachers; once Communism fell, they had to literally take to the streets. And all the old women there whose shanties were now getting bulldozed for the sake of capitalism, when I asked them who their heroes were, they shouted: *"Za Stalina!"* For Stalin! Of course it's better now; people aren't getting shot by the millions; but why did this new badness have to come? Are we then to believe that change from below and change from above both partake of perilousness? —As one of the confused, exasperated and defeated interlocutors in a Platonic dialogue would finally mutter, "So it would seem." —No means is infallible.

And how murky, how fallible might the end be? As with those nested pseudo-infinities of hand-painted Russian dolls, we open one question only to find another. The onion has no core. But if it did, it might be: *What is class?*

Four answers: Function, status, property, rank.

Function

For the ants such ideological matters must be as simple as for Rizal—or, I should say, they are immensely complicated, but (we are repeatedly assured by myrmecologists) the ants hardly possess the consciousness to know how complicated they are. Their astounding symbioses and specializations, and their random yet eminently purposeful movements, almost persuade me that they know what virtue is. But theirs constitutes the virtue not even of the bigot but of the sleepwalker.

Lessons of the Automata

Evolution leads gracefully (one scientist proposes thirteen stages) from the solitary female of some wasplike species who stings her prey, lays the egg whose hatchling will feed upon the paralyzed victim and then departs; to the Methuselah-foundress who outlives nest generations growing up around her; to the queen caste within the meaningful turmoil of the ant colony which itself continues to fission into subclasses. Or perhaps it began, they say, when sister ants shared a nest and laid eggs together, until one became dominant, literally standing above the others, those losers like Stalin's kulaks and Tolstoyans whom the workers dragged outside the nest forever. However the ant societies developed, they remain inspirationally troubling models for any human student of class to consider. Like the good proletarians in Henry Ford's Model T factories, they break tasks into subtasks each of which can be addressed by temporary or permanent specialists: food-regurgitators, digesters (the larval "metabolic caste"), larva-nurses, queen-lickers, foragers, leaf-cutters, soldier and reserve battalions. I wonder if Ford was consciously indebted to the ants? The treatise I referred to here cannot refrain from repeating the simile of a factory within a fortress to describe their colonies; but perhaps an even better analogy is with Plato's ideal republic, whose every division offers its own "virtue" or functional perfection—this is why I say that ants might know what virtue is—but whereas his is a republic of knowledge, of self-investigation and spiritual striving (at least among the higher orders; for we learned already that the lower classes will be lied to and tricked for the sake of smooth governance), the myriad republics of the ants are blind—not literally, for most ants do have compound eyes—but within the dark, moist nest, which practically oozes with antibiotic secretions exuded from their metapleural glands just as Stalin's republics oozed propaganda, one finds a system of ontogenetic rather than planned or voluntaristic specialization. Thus the best analogy of all is with imperial Rome. Patrician households might keep as many as four thousand slaves; the Emperor probably had twenty thousand: cupbearers, dwarves, buffoons, dancing girls, masseurs, barbers, silver polishers, gold polishers, rock crystal polishers, ushers, wardrobesmen of his undress military uniforms, of his parade uniforms, of his theater clothes . . . "Reading these [obituary inscriptions] without prejudice," remarks the historian from whom I borrow these details, "the student is dumbfounded by the extraordinary degree of specialisation they reveal, the insensate luxury and the meticulous etiquette which made this specialisation necessary." Are ants luxurious? Perhaps not, but insensate and meticulous they seem to be. Entering some burrow, perhaps we'll find ourselves among the honeypot ants, where from the ceiling hang like golden balloons the swollen bodies of the "repletes," into whom the returning foragers vomit up nectar and termite bits for storage. (Among other species, larval secretions help one's neighbors to digest their food and can even be a reserve food source. All ants employ the transformation of body tissues into eggs and food for their siblings.) Or perhaps we'll be guested by slaveholding ants, or fungus growers. In some species, giant soldier-guardians use their heads for gates. No one can enter the sanctum, until they draw aside. Tiny workers ride upon larger ones. Seed-millers, built like tanks, do their job with what science insists to be calm mindlessness. And so throughout life. We cannot imagine Joan of Arc as an ant. Why, for instance, will one particular egg become a queen instead of a seed-miller? (For the genes are the same in either case.) The answer, of course, cannot be choice, nor even command authority.

How can we know this? Somebody who could not understand human communication might be less impressed than we by the jaw-waggings of strategic and philosophical symposia. But myrmecologists have tabulated ant behaviors and found them to be limited, stereotyped (although again I reflect on the limited character of jaw-wagging). Experiments indicate so far that while ants can memorize the patterns of overhead foliage, or recognize extremely minute angles, they "cannot duplicate the mammalian feat of reorganizing their memories to construct a new system in the face of a novel problem."

Seed-Millers, Kulaks and Jews

Among the ants, then, caste results from "feedback." The size of the egg, the temperature of the egg chamber, the varying chemical signals transmitted by the queen at preprogrammed benchmarks in her life and suchlike agents determine one's destiny.

In case all this appears too far removed from human considerations, we might cite that valiant defense of race, Nazi eugenics, which sought to find biological Jewishness evinced in the shape of a nose—or Stalin's defense of class, which merely needed to know one's parents' occupations to grind out justice. For the moment, however, we'll do well to pursue the fact that in spite of all insects' evident facility for physical specialization (based, I suppose, on their brief life spans, which permit rapid mutation rates), anatomically divergent castes prove much rarer among the ants than what Hölldobler and Wilson have named "temporal castes." That is, if we define a caste functionally, as a group which carries out a specified type of behavior (here once again we find ourselves strangely close to Marxism), we find that as an individual ant ages she will substitute one set of activities for another. A young ant might begin by attending the queen and caring for her eggs, then proceed to groom the royal larvae when she is a few days older, and finally move to the necessary but suicidal reward of obsolescence: foraging and defense. What induces the ageing ant to change her occupation? Can we speak here of the merest shadow of choice? —Not at all. Whether she was physically fitted for her specialty as a result of nurture, or whether she simply carries out the sequence of tasks associated with her temporal caste, the mechanism remains biochemical.

Thus the class system of the ants. Lenin wrote truly in his *Granat Encyclopedia* article on Marx: "In any given society, the strivings of some of its members conflict with the strivings of others." Among the ants, genetic competition smolders on, as it does everywhere. But within the nest (until senescence, at least) the castes need each other and help each other. We may not want to be ants, but this has to be said: unlike Lenin, unlike Stalin, ant queens are not known to kill vast numbers of their own nestmates.

Status

Caste among the ants, then, embodies the most unequivocally rigid utilitarianism. In achieving the ideal which Plato hopes and pretends that human beings can approach, it reflects division of labor, not status. And how, after all, could status ever operate in the ant world? Within the hive, as in the novels of the Marquis de Sade, nestmates associate with each other only on an ad hoc basis. If there be any class hierarchy here, it must have to do with the queen. Indeed, they literally crave her (or, in the more alienated language of science, they demonstrate an attraction to her)—but a paper disk impregnated with her scent serves almost as well. No choice, then, no consciousness, so no status—but the case has not been closed, for can't we postulate a hierarchy of genetic determinism, or (more broadly) of outright necessity?

SIMPLIFIED CLASS RELATIONS IN AN ANT NEST

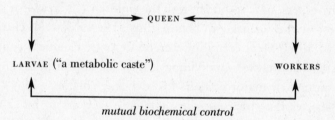

The Odors of Royalty

First and foremost, "the entire activity of the colony can be said to pivot on the welfare of the queen." When the queen dies, among most species the colony begins to die, too. For the queenless, all is lost. Statesmanship, Plato insists, stands "in charge of the rearing of a particular kind of herd"—precisely the queen's function. Continuously enveloped, fed and licked by her "courtiers" within the nest, or guarded by long columns of alert workers when on the move, she is supreme.

Alongside this basic principle stands a second: altruism. Workers do compete with one another to maximize their reproductive privileges, and so, as we've seen, do queens against queens, but in comparison to human societies the volume and proportion of what anthropocentric nineteenth-century researchers used to term acts of love is astounding. Returning foragers regurgitate food from their crops for their nestmates to share.

Ageing workers engage in perilous forage missions to save wear and tear on their younger nestmates. Most members of the worker caste offer up even the ability to reproduce. Late-twentieth-century scientists began to see this self-sacrifice as having genetic causes. If a worker's suicidal defense of a colony saves her biological sister so that the latter can reproduce, the allele which triggered that behavior may well be saved, since by Mendel's laws three-fourths of those two siblings' genetic characteristics will be common. Does chemically controlled behavior fall within the defining reaches of the Golden Rule? Be that as it may, the readiness of the various castes to aid one another to the ultimate extreme strikes a human being as, shall we say, Christlike, Communistic—and, again, blind.

Function or Exploitation?

Who benefits the most from all this? Is the ant mother enslaving her children and forcing some of them to sacrifice themselves to permit her to produce many others, or is it somehow in the children's interest—or rather, in the interest of their genes—to behave thus? The case is not clear. Those mothers of all mothers certainly exercise despotic chemical control, but only to create more life, subdividing it into the appropriate numbers of soldiers, minims or major workers for each stage of the colony's growth. In some species they pheromonally influence workers to bite the larvae which would otherwise become queens; in one case, as if in some classic Marxist parable, they subsist upon larval "blood" (hemolymph), though apparently without killing the larvae. *The queen is tempo, atmosphere, everything.* But her "virtue" cannot be, as for Plato's statesman, any form of knowledge. Plato's Philosopher-King lives and rules as an apprehender, being one of those highest-classmen with a "vivid pattern in their souls" who can "fix their eyes on the absolute truth." The ruler must study philosophy; the philosopher must rule. Can a queen ant be said to be a philosopher? Not she but intranest chemistry produces the optimal number of eggs for a given moment of the colony's life cycle, thus: foraging workers feed the larvae as much food of a specific kind as they can gather and the larvae will accept; the larvae then passively transfer secretions metabolized from that food to the nurse workers who lick them; the nurse workers in turn cluster about the queen and her eggs, giving off a chemical stimulated by the larval secretion and thereby helping to determine egg production. The queen regulates and is regulated. Except possibly over weaker rival queens, she possesses no "authority." That is why we are cautioned: "it is a mistake to interpret individual forms of interaction in terms of vertebrate behavior, where dominant individuals are able to raise their genetic fitness." When she becomes senescent, her workers may reject her and even seal her off to die. But this exemplifies no defense of class in any meaningful sense: the workers remove her from her position not in order to emancipate themselves from her but in order to gain a new queen who will regulate and be regulated by them exactly as the old one did before her functions failed. Among those species for which it occurs at all, the liquidation of the senile queen must be called normal, predictable, a stage in the cycle. Class remains function. The functionless will be discarded.

"Best Men" and Strangled Mothers

And the class system of our own kind? Let us briefly return to the state of nature, where in place of ant nests we'll find family bands living out (according to Marxist thinking) a quasi-communistic prehistoric idyll, not necessarily nasty and brutish à la Hobbes, but definitely short-lived, since susceptible to the dictation of more advanced means of production: farms whose steady produce can outstockpile any occasional hunt-harvests of nomads, factories which can turn out machine guns to exterminate aborigines, et cetera. In short, historical determinism claims that agriculturalists (say nothing yet of proletarians) form a productively superior class who can, hence will, supplant the nomadic class. So far, historical determinism has not been proven wrong. In the meantime, how idyllic is nomadism really?

It is almost as difficult for a modern urban observer to imagine the life of, say, an Inuit family circa 1900 as it is to envision the consciousness of a social insect superorganism. In one fur trader's photographs we see streaked and smeared parkas, children sitting amidst snowdrifts, standing and seated groups at the Hudson's Bay posts, eyes happy or not but somehow always faraway, dark faces, snow-clumped hooded skin parkas trimmed with lead and animal teeth, not uniform like machine-made clothes but nonetheless of a piece, like the numberless mudbanks and gravel-banks of the Arctic. We see motionless, intense children (who probably look that way because they are curious and because they have been instructed to keep still), tousle-headed whiskered hunters guarded by the hairy parka collars their wives have sewn for them; above all we find eyes gazing into our eyes with recognition rather than familiarity. To almost anyone sufficiently sedentary to read (or write) this book, the freedom and the hardship of nomadic life will be equally unimaginable. "We used to wear just caribou skin clothing and boots," says a ninety-nine-year-old Inuk lady. "They were so comfortable and very light. I could easily move about in them." How different this must have been from, say, French court dresses of the seventeenth century, from whose confines great ladies could not even escape to relieve their bladders unassisted! Mobility and self-sufficiency make liberty. If a nomad doesn't like the company in which he finds himself, he simply moves. No wonder that the Stalinists with their craving to enforce uniformity would find the lifestyle of nomads so irritating. They had to "eradicate the economic and cultural anachronisms of the nationalities." In the 1930s they killed about a million and a half Kazakhs out of a population of some four million—some by the usual "repressions," and the rest through Pol Pot's hallmark: inadvertent starvation. Of course, nomads left to their own devices have sometimes encountered the very same fate. Here is how the old Inuk lady introduces herself: "I am Jeannie Mippigaq. I was born in 1885. I have lived a long life. I have seen people die, I have seen people starve, but I am still alive to tell their story." But the people whose starving she witnessed died because they could not find anything to eat, not because the policy of another class killed them.

Well, are we to infer that nomadic society is classless? —By no means. —Every band, every family must surely display not only the functional specialization of the ants (women, for instance, bear babies and nurse them; men with their superior strength go seal-killing to feed the family) but also those internal divisions based on the inherently unequal capacities of human beings to meet any given goal or standard. Some, for instance, will prove better hunters than others. (Thoreau relates that the Algonquin Indians he knew referred to hunters as "the best men." Call this *status by function*.) Within the family some form of communism will prevail, as it generally does, always excepting the case of the Ik tribe: babies get fed although they cannot work, and the same might even be true of enfeebled grandparents, at least when seals and caribou are easy to catch. And, since reality is rarely simple, we have to remind ourselves that the grandparents might be, say, shamans, whose dreams about the locations of animals are given high productive value. For many a nomad family, I am sure, the Golden Rule guides and gilds life: as Martin Luther dreamed for his ideal Christian polity, each becomes the servant of the others—or, to use (as Luther does) an ancient and beautiful allegory, all live as members of the same body; when one member gets weak physically or even morally, the rest of the body helps it all the more. Once at the North Magnetic Pole I had to sacrifice my fingertips to frostbite, to save the rest, because it was impossible for me to light matches with my gloves on. My fingers quickly became white and numb. I felt a strange sense of love and compassion for them, as if they were beings in their own right, friends who loved me as I loved them; and now, when my fingertips lose feeling on chilly days or in a swimming pool, I baby them; I feel sorry for them; I try not to get impatient.

But I ask Luther, as a Stalinist might: What happens when one's fingers are gangrened? In our hunter-gatherer society, "the best men" will bring back meat; while others, the gangrened, will not. The "best men" give what they can. What can the gangrened give? Think back upon the ant nest, whose senescent members go out on dangerous foraging missions to aid their less expendable sisters. A Tagish-Tlingit woman tells the story of her ancestors who hesitated to negotiate a difficult glacier crossing: "Finally, two old men decided to go—to try it. Two little old men, ready to die, I guess. 'Send us through. We're old now. We're no good to you people. If we die, you won't miss us much anyhow.' " —Self-deprecation, I suppose—but also a portion of bitter truth. One turn-of-the-century ethnologist found that Inuit of the Ungava District (where Jeannie Mippigaq came from) acted in accordance with the ant ethos concerning senile queens: "Old and infirm people are treated with severity, and when dependent upon others for their food they are summarily disposed of by strangulation or left to perish when the camp is moved."

Strong and weak, then, is one division to be found in every family. What about male and female? The same source reports that regardless of their functional necessity, "women are held in little respect," and that around Fort Chimo "a woman is married as soon after puberty as a male comes along who has the requisite physical strength to force her to become his wife." This undoubtedly puts the case far worse than it was. Jeannie Mippigaq, for instance, lets us know that although she got married without her knowledge she loved her husband dearly. In my own experience, nomads more often than not heed Christ's parable of the vineyard: pay the laborers the same day wage no matter how late in the day they are summoned to work. But even if senecide or bridenapping occurred in only a single family, that's enough: that family is a society; and here germinate the rudiments of class. (Here also begins feminist theory.) Obviously, *defense of class prerogative is unjustified when class equals nothing but strength.* I have been told by my Inuit friends that the continuum from most expendable to indispensable used to run thus: children and old people, because the former could be replaced and the latter had already lived, while neither could contribute much; next, barren women; then fertile women, because "they could make new people," as several individuals remarked; then finally men in their prime, the hunters, because without them all the rest would starve. Among *Lasus niger* ants the ranking of ascending value goes: eggs, into whose maintenance the least amount of energy has been expended; small larvae; and in the highest ranking of all, the large larvae and pupae, which are almost ready to become functioning adults. As for the hunters, these, as we have seen, consist of superannuated workers, who literally expend themselves. All this is class.

Property

And now, while the nomads wander across the tundra, moving on whenever the animals move, why not go southward to meet the agricultural revolution, where, in Gibbon's mellifluous words, "the possession and the enjoyment of property are the pledges which bind a civilised people to an improved country?" In China, the First Mother steps in a god's toeprint and gives birth to Lord Millet, who covers the land with red- and white-leaved grains. He "reaped it and counted the acres." Hence boundaries, quantification, tabulation, written history, law.

The alien gazes of the Inuit and Cree in that fur trader's photographs testify to a divide from all that makes photography possible. Bride-rape, senecide, hunger, granted—but such a life also glows with such liberty, integrity and beauty that I used to long for it almost to the point of heartbreak, until I learned that I was not fitted for it, and that thanks to encroaching boundaries, quantification, written law, not many other people were fitted for it anymore, either—precisely the point (if we deduct my bitter regrets) of Marxist-Leninists, who claim that a farming society ranks not merely more technologically, hence politically, potent than a hunter-gatherering one, but also more advanced *historically*, since its more concentrated labor forms the womb of capital, whose divisions and emiserations will create the proletarian class which has the mission of rising up and creating an industrial classless society. (In 1976, speeding up his murderous class revolution in Cambodia, Pol Pot will explain: "We have said that in order to gain capital the important thing is rice.") But at the so-called dawn of history, which is to say the beginning to inscribed memories, that womb still lies within the womb of feudalism, itself yet an embryo.

CLASS-DIVIDED MODES OF PRODUCTION

A Marxist View

MODE OF PRODUCTION	OPPOSED CLASSES
[Communal]	[???]
Tribute-paying	State-class vs. peasants
Slaveowning	Masters vs. slaves
Feudal	Lords vs. serfs
Capitalist	Bourgeois vs. proletarians

Source: Amin, p. 23. (Bracketed items not in original.)

Begin with this truism: Within the community of farmers, the same family and social forces operate as for the hunters. People are people. But these empirical and open-ended "facts of life"—a man carries off his bride by force, *when he can;* a woman resists, *when she can;* man and woman, joined by sweet persuasion or not, achieve equilibrium (each choosing or being compelled to obey, respect, kill, cherish or contemptuously use the other)—now put down roots, and flower into codes. The ideology of Lord Millet demands harmonized propinquity. Thus the flavor of the crowd infects individual accomodation. Hence, for instance, the gender-class system: "In every age and country," writes Gibbon, not without exaggeration, "the wiser, or at least the stronger, of the two sexes, has usurped the powers of the state, and confined the other to the cares and pleasures of domestic life." The early Romans, like the Gauls whom Caesar conquered, assigned to the patriarch the power of life and death over his wives and children. Only male plebeians were eligible for free grain. I propose another obvious rule: *Defense of class is unjustified when class is merely status without functionality.* We might by analogy with our "best men" grant the right of an ancient Chinese husband to preference or even dominance over his wife were the conditions of existence so difficult that his gender's superior physical strength was essential for all parties' sustenance or defense. If not, then not.

In China, Japan, Korea we find ourselves guided (or imprisoned) by the "Five Relations" of Confucianism: lord and vassal, elder brother and younger brother, husband and wife, father and son, friend and friend. Where one person stands higher in status than the other, he'll receive service even unto death but must give his kindness and protection in return. "All things had a moral basis," says Mishima in one of his short stories, "and were in accordance with the Education Rescript's injunction that 'husband and wife should be harmonious.' Not once did Reiko contradict her husband, nor did the lieutenant find occasion to scold his wife." Between both parties, as in Gandhi's utopian India, love maintains homeostasis as does chemical regulation among the ants. —And if there's no love? Better not to ask. H. G. Wells in his *Outline of History* writes that

> a certain freedom and a certain equality passed out of human life when men ceased to wander. Men paid in liberty and they paid in toil, for safety, shelter, and regular meals . . . There was a process of enslavement as civilization grew; the headmen and leaderly men grew in power and authority, and the common man did not keep pace with them.

For better or worse, the struggle between peers has (officially) ended. This is class.

Cornfields and Class Shadows

And yet, although sedentary peoples more easily accumulate possessions than nomads, the mere circumstance of agriculturalism need not unduly privilege the property relation. (Again, remember the ants: their fungus-growing species share and share alike.) We read that in ancient German society, chieftans redistributed the land every year—a neat trick which Stalin failed to pull off in the Ukraine. Were those cases the only ones? By no means. Bypassing Canada's shallow lakes blue, brown and ruffled, we arrive at the Sweetwater Sea (as Lake Ontario used to be called), to find the Huron Indians with their longhouses, enemy-tortures and immense cornfields.

In place of the Five Relations, one lives here according to clan ties, matriarchal courtesies (we call the old woman in our longhouse "mother"), givingness, acquiesence. To make others follow my will, I must persuade them. Like Julius Caesar, I seek through generosity and good deeds to gain prestige. Unlike him, I can't collect clients; I can only make my neighbors love and respect me. Moreover, the means of production being so unspecialized, whatever I have to give—corn, beans, tobacco, deer meat, an enemy captive—my clan brothers and sisters can also give. It's not at all like trading money for shoes. With the exception of trading routes, curing songs and the like, my property remains entirely fungible, a sort of capital whose produce is goodwill. Hence, whatever I can give, I *will* give. Who but outsiders or revolutionaries with long-range goals could be against this sort of class?

CLASS DIVISIONS IN WENDAKÉ ("HURONIA," SEVENTEENTH CENTURY)

INSIDERS		OUTSIDERS
MEN	WOMEN	
1. Headmen	1. Clan mothers	1. Guests (envoys, trading partners, friends, Jesuits)
2. Proven old men (chiefs, traders, shamans)	2. Good hostesses, generous providers and preparers of food; good mothers	2. Enemies; captives to be tortured and killed
3. Generous men, good hunters, prestigious warriors	3. Stingy and incompetent providers	
4. Untried young men	4. Murderesses	
5. Stingy and incompetent providers	5. Witches and traitors	
6. Murderers		
7. Witches and traitors		

Source: Trigger, The Children of Aataentsic, *pp. 49–59, 66–68, 79–80.*

Competence, Tact, Merriness, Generosity

Referring to the brilliant group portrait by Trigger (whose integrity and trained precision steers him safely between the two perils of fictive individualism and inhuman "sociologism"), we learn that Huron labor differentiated itself along the usual lines of gender, experience and capacity—none particularly conducive to permanent class formation, except in the strictly functional sense of the ants. The salient fact that men and women never did each other's work need not imply (except perhaps to Marxists) that one sex exploited the other. Female labor sewed nets, made clothes, prepared food, sowed and reaped the corn, while male labor defended and aggressed, hunted, cut down trees and built new villages when the soil and the houses of the old became decrepit—this last task being a useful reminder of the Huron's seminomadism; little wonder that in their success in avoiding differentiation they resemble the Inuit. Almost all men (during their prime, at least) could do all men's work; the same went for women. Within a given gender, then, occupation could not determine class. —What did? As the previous table shows, the answer remained *individual capacity*. That is why not everyone could be a headman or a clan mother. Nevertheless, class privilege in the sense of status remained accessible to most Huron: a woman who fed people well, and a man who brought back enemy prisoners to be tortured or adopted, were loved and respected. Generosity enhanced status. In the old *Jesuit Relations* we read that even those possessions which their owners most valued—a favorite dog, say—would be given away to importuners. Why? Because kinship solidarity encouraged it, because the giver was admired as a result; and because jealousy acted as a leveling force.

I propose that *defense of class as status is justified when status is based on consensually defined merit*. Admittedly, in this Huron example prestige constitutes class in and of itself only in the most flexible and transitory way. —Nor could the seasonal nature of most tasks have encouraged specialization: Now might be the customary time when Huron women made new belts of deerskin which they'd use to to carry home firewood the following spring; next came the time for weaving fishing nets to be traded to the Montagnais that summer. No more net weaving this year, so no guild of net makers. —Against this, contrast the complex webs of specialization to be found, for instance, in ancient Rome, whose elite might employ slaves in capacities as abstruse as, for instance, commercial agents without personal rights or liabilities. These narrow life roles, so sadly akin to our own, would have been considered pitiably unwholesome in Wendaké.

The Privileges of Lonely Atoms

To be sure, we can find among the Huron a few individuals who practiced exclusive or even solitary callings, such as Tonneraouanont the Hunchback—but his shamanic profession informed individualism with the most ominous character. ("I am a demon," he explained to those who needed curing ceremonies; they'd pay him in presents. "Therefore I have never been sick.") He would have been feared and respected by most, emulated by few.

Self-assertion surfaced in any number of other places, as it must in all societies. Lonely atoms form molecules, but not always of their own volition; sometimes an elemental impulse wrenches someone out of bounds. A warrior might follow the dictates of a powerful dream rather than a consensus of his peers; and in spite of powerful modesty taboos, a sexually deprived old woman might successfully demand to have intercourse with a young man in order to be cured of her supernatural illness. Thus, desire or need could breach custom under certain circumstances, while custom prevented the assertion of desire and need from reaching antisocial extremes. This is the antithesis of class. Regarding property, class structures remained incipient (or basic), and the countervailing mechanisms of respect for givers and jealousy of nongivers continued intact.

Atomization and Hierarchy

Although some of his cousins might well express a certain nostalgia for such "precapitalist communalism," Marx would be unmoved by the Huron example. How can it be stable? Even if the process begins as communalism, he writes, it will sooner or later be privatized through forcible usurpation. In the Huron case this is sadly true. For where is Wendaké now? The Iroquois, the French and then the Anglophone Canadians appropriated every acre of that nation, which presently, with some nature-preserve exceptions, exists as a nexus of farms, motels and other reifications of the private property ethic. *The level of development of the productive forces, by determining the relative size of the surplus, conditions the level of civilization*, runs the Marxist axiom. What grimly neutral words! Is a greater surplus really of no benefit to the masses?

Alas, one need not be a Marxist to make the case that the swelling populations and burgeoning heterogenization characteristic of human sedentarism permit the accumulation of private wealth even as they weaken kinship solidarity, thereby fostering inequality. "The first man, who, after enclosing a piece of ground, took it into his head to say, *this is mine,* and found people simple enough to believe him, was the real founder of civil society," says Rousseau—going on to deplore the crimes, wars and murders which resulted. Aristotle lists four types of oligarchy, and they all derive directly or indirectly from property. The lonely atom no longer careers through space with happy or desperate freedom but finds itself now encased in an immense adamantine stratum, isolated among and even by its fellows, weighed down, locked away. —Lord Millet's priests say: You shall not go here. You cannot go there. You must do this. We rule you.

My neighbor's field is better than mine. He follows Lord Millet, respects the sacredness of borderlines. Therefore, he feels under no obligation to share with me.

The stage is set; history's curtain rises. Weather, war, debt, disease, science, anti-Semitism, nepotism, lucky or expedient marriages, primogeniture (or even inheritance generally, which Bakunin saw as the principal perpetrator of inequality), career specialization, topography, stupidity, arbitrary force and individual ability now interrelate to make some accumulators more successful than others. A few of us can be Druids; some will be knights; the rest must be commoners.

Well-meaning Plato, envisioning utopia, depends on command mechanisms to achieve what fraternity and jealousy did among the Huron. A productive surplus nourishes his ease. He sits writing while slaves and metics flash to and fro. This is class. Millennia later, a capitalist archaeologist writes with odious but justified smugness that "this societal division into 'haves' and 'have-nots' is the quintessential characteristic of civilization."

CLASS DIVISIONS AMONG THE GAULS (FIRST CENTURY B.C.)

The Official View

Caesar implies that similar distinctions exist among nomadic and sedentary tribes. The proportions shown are assumed; in particular, the number of Druids might be much smaller relative to the Knights.

Source: Caesar, Gallic War, *pp. 335-41 (vi. 13-15).*

When the Land Is Gone

Was he wrong? Was Plato? As soon as we've founded our own ideal republic we'll discover farmers staking out the best land they can, in the greatest quantities they can, until every arable inch lies in the possession of somebody. In the preambles of the medieval Icelandic sagas, one always reads such relations as: "Skallagrim took possession of everything between the mountains and the sea." This is utopia; this is Genesis. And what about the latecomers? This is the story not just of old Iceland but of many other places besides—the Mekong Delta, for instance, which began to be developed in the 1860s under French overlordship. By the

1930s, population pressure (and, of course, inequality) was forcing many Vietnamese into land tenancy and outright landlessness.

THE FIVE CLASS DIVISIONS OF NORTH VIETNAMESE VILLAGES (ca. 1960)

EXPLOITERS

1. Landlord (maintained entirely by hired labor; large field).

2. Rich peasant (works land but also hires labor).

3. Middle-upper peasant (rents land but owns cattle, etc.; produces surplus).

PROLETARIAT

4. Middle-lower peasant (rents land but owns cattle, etc.; barely sustains life).

5. Poor peasant (children must work and are sometimes sold).

> "When all of the denouncing was over, the cadres evaluated who were the worst landlords and they sentenced them to death. They had a quota they had to fill . . . The [poor peasant] woman I was living with appeared to be quite pleased with it all."
>
> *Source: Chanoff and Doan, pp. 115–16 (Testimony of Han Vi, cultural cadre).*

This is likewise the story of Elizabethan England, Easter Island and dust bowl Oklahoma. An unprosperous farm just might dwindle to nothing. Some Athenian *thetes* owned such farms, and, like lower-class Romans, struggled on the edge of that abyss of disenfranchisement. One summary of the Athenian constitution recalls the bad old days when

> all the land was in the hands of a few, and if the poor failed to pay their rents both they and their children were liable to seizure . . . officials were appointed on the basis of good birth and wealth; at first men held office for life.

The ruling class always claims that if there were no lower class, the labor couldn't get done, and the surplus would remain a mere potentiality. But whenever a so-called "labor-saving device" gets invented, no labor is ever saved! (We'll see why in a moment.) A Korean historian writes in a monograph about his country that the introduction of the iron sickle into rice-harvesting greatly improved productivity; but "doubtless," he says, the ruling class got most of the benefit. "Accordingly, the gap between the rich and the poor must have been further widened." Lord Millet does not care. In the seventh century an official record notes that "emoluments flow unceasingly into the houses of the highest officials, who possess as many as three thousand slaves"—the old Roman story. By the tenth century, we find the freeborn peasantry of Korea being tithed a quarter of all their produce whenever they harvest state land; when they work the lands of the nobility they are obliged to give up half. The conditions of baseborn peasants, of course, are worse. In the eighteenth century, Robespierre will insist that all resources *less than* the surplus ought to be common property; necessity decrees it. "History" will not listen.

In early twentieth-century Mexico, the ancient pueblos watch their fields falling to the sugarcane haciendas. They have title, in documents dating back to the Conquest, but no matter; productive forces have no time for such niceties. When the peasants resist, money's power dams their springs and drinks their rivers, leaving them literally high and dry. No kinship ties here! We read that "by 1908 the seventeen owners of the thirty-six major haciendas in the state" of Morelos "owned over 25 percent of its total surface, most of its cultivable land, and almost all of its good land." Once again, Marxist theory has been proven right: more efficient means of production supplant communalism—and always with increasing rapidity. To quote that malevolent deity Comrade Stalin, it took two centuries for feudalism to replace the slave system, and only one century for the bourgeois organization of production to crowd out feudalism. "Already in the depths of feudal society the bourgeois system of economy revealed that it was superior, far superior." (The devil knows what time and place he was talking about; it didn't matter; he was always right . . .)

"The Stronger Shall Now Prevail"

Recall this fundamental right of the self, which we've already entered in the Moral Calculus:

- To violently defend its property, or not, although:
    1. Proportionality must be maintained (see 5.2.F) The right to life supersedes the right to property. (Examples: Others may exercise their right to self-preservation by confiscating excess property if they are in dire

need. [See 5.2.B and 6.2.B.] A householder is not entitled to shoot a
fleeing burglar in the back.)

2. Legitimate authority (see 5.2.C.1) may confiscate excess property in
   the interest of the social contract (taxes, the Muslim zakat tithe, etc.).

In other words, *defense of class as defense of property is unjustified
when another's right to life supersedes the defender's right to property.*
One thinks of Marie Antoinette's apocryphal remark to the starving: "Let
them eat cake!" If only life were as black-and-white as this!

In fact, the consequences of property occur in increments and often with
seeming voluntarism. In medieval Japan, writes Maurice Pinguet in his ele-
gantly phrased history of suicide, "isolation was death; safety lay under the
dominion of an important clan." No doubt obedience shines as brightly
there as moonlight, compulsion being the sun—but in Iceland, where all
men not thralls or slaves theoretically enjoy equal rights, class despotism
will flourish equivalently, sending out its bloodsucking roots according to
the following laws: (1) each district gains its priest-chieftain to represent it at
the Althing law assembly; (2) no one has to render perpetual allegiance to the
priest-chieftain nearest him, but (3) if he doesn't, who will help with armed
men when his neighbor lusts for his richest meadow? The strong man chal-
lenges the weak, takes his land and wife. Better to shake hands with the
chieftain, gain his protection at the Althing (where, as anywhere, the most
powerful lawyer wins)—and cede him that meadow for his pains.

Is this class? Yes, but even now, lines have not yet become barriers. Marry
your chieftain's sister; foster his son. Then you'll gain family rights. (Plato's
class of Silver Guardians would never allow that.) If he's too hard, too
greedy, then depart from him—but search out another advocate then, because nobody can survive friendless—that is, without *powerful* friends, *political* friends—and for a powerful friend one must pay.

As it's said in *The Saga of Viga Glum*, "Whatever the law may be, the
stronger shall now prevail." That applies not least to those insidious ag-
glomerations of individuals known as *class.* By the twelfth century, Icelandic chieftains gain increasing concentrations of wealth—which is to
say, most importantly, land. A prosperous farm becomes both the token of
a higher status and the means for obtaining it, since more or better acreage
means greater likelihood of reaping a surplus, which constitutes power,
whether it is bartered, hoarded or even paid up in taxes—consider the poll
tax or the wartime levy upon a feudal lord, who's not oppressed because

he *must* pay but potent because he *can* pay. To pay signifies to vote, perhaps to command in battle—in short, to be the emblem, incarnation and instrument of the upper class. —Slaves didn't think so, but that was because they paid everything, got nothing. —Plato rephrases *Viga Glum*'s axiom thus: "Can you imagine," asks he, "that when the populace, or some other political party, or an autocrat, if you like, has got the upper hand, the victorious side will, of its own accord, enact laws with any principal aim but its own interest in the permanence of its authority?"

Property and Misery

The lawyer Clarence Darrow believed that "the jails and penitentiaries of every nation in the world are filled to overflowing with men and women who have been charged with committing crimes against property." He estimated that the proportion of persons arraigned in court who were there on suspicion of property crimes was as high as 90 percent. I think that he was right. Almost a century later, the FBI imputed the property motive to 91.2 percent of all index crimes (statistics for eighteenth-century Paris were almost identical), which figure almost certainly underreports the fact. Darrow continued: "Every time that the trust raises the price of coal some poor victims are sent to jail, and at every raise in the price of oil some girls are sent out upon the streets to get their bread by a life of wretchedness and shame." —What then could be more natural in any decent heart than the desire to nationalize the coal and oil trusts?

One may, indeed, be confounded by the fact that in my country rising crime rates have occured simultaneously with a rising standard of living—now the street girls I meet engage in a life of wretchedness and shame not for bread but for crack cocaine. Or does that rising standard of living simply translate into more property, which produces more greed, desperation, control? More fundamentally, *is poverty absolute, or relative?* —I would argue the latter. A statistician informs me that technology has now put the labor power equivalent of nineteen slaves, or nineteen megawatt-hours per year, at the average human being's disposal—whatever an "average" person may be. In 1860, the comparable figure was less than one megawatt-hour per year. A sweatshop laborer in Los Angeles has access to food, clothing and entertainment that ancient kings could never have hoped for. So why's she bitter?

In 1910 in England, 10 percent of the population owned almost 50 percent of the wealth; in the 1950s, in spite of reforms, the same was still true. The researcher concluded that "capitalism has in fact an innate tendency to extreme and ever-growing inequality."

Well, shall we take away all capital property from individual owners and live like Huron, then? One central question of this chapter will be: *When is class defense against* relative *inequality justified?* Maybe Lycurgus, the Spartan lawgiver (about whom more later on), was not far wrong when he proposed to limit and homogenize the number of goods available. That strangely radical moderate, or moderate radical, Jefferson, observing the last gasp of the ancien régime in France, was galvanized by sadness into concluding that while an equal division of property was "impracticable," nonetheless, since "this enormous inequality" made "so much misery to the bulk of mankind, legislators cannot invent too many devices for subdividing property."

But any attempt to impose a "device," "solution" or even a "system" upon property restricts *liberty*. Edmund Burke, one of property's fiercest champions, wrote against the Jeffersons and Robespierres of this world that "it is to the property of the citizen . . . that the first and original faith of civil society is pledged. The claim of the citizen is prior in time, paramount in title, superior in equity."

Why Potters Should Not Be Rich

Shall we simply restrict the *preeminence* of property? This was Plato's notion—and Robespierre's, too: "The right of property is limited, as are all other rights, by the obligation to respect the rights of others." But since wealth is power, we'll require at least one class above the wealthy in order to control *them*. For this office, Plato, like Thoreau's Indians, remembers "the best men." Who constitutes this class? Not hunters anymore. (Robespierre, striving ever to control them, quarrelling with them, insisting that he embodies them, will go to the guillotine.) For Plato, of course, they're the stringent, honorable philosophers, the men like himself.

PLATO'S MORAL CALCULUS
The Laws, 350 B.C.
The Three Classes of Citizens

Most honorable rank: "Good qualities of the soul," especially temperance.
Second rank: "Good qualities of the body."
Third rank: Wealth.

"Should any legislator . . . transgress these limits by promoting wealth to honor, or giving anything of a lower class the distinctions of a higher, the act is an offense alike against religion and statesmanship."

Source: Laws, III. 697 B.C.

In short, his equality operates less between classes than within them. Plato would make benevolently sure that all potters remained moderately unwealthy, because too great a surplus (of gold, grain or olive oil nicely sealed up in a potter's painted jars) might overcome the most wholesome upbringing: rich potters might be lazy potters, shaping fewer and worse pots. Likewise, defense of a wise class hierarchy demands that their poverty keep within bounds. Utterly propertyless potters, bereft of tools, could not do a good job, either. (Ants and Huron never had such problems: whatever a forager finds, she immediately delivers to the common storehouse.) Thus every Platonic potter finds himself the material equal of his brothers in the art—but how might he stand, I wonder, in comparison to the guardian class, or the still more honorable rank of temperate leaders? Temperance by choice defines a class of superior privilege to enforced temperance. Thus Marx, who readily admits that division of labor "improves" both product and producer, condemns *The Republic*—and I believe rightly so—as "merely an Athenian idealization of the Egyptian caste system."

Such idealizations are all too widespread. We find Plato's forebear, the lawmaker Solon, establishing a similar prescription for political power: the masses ought not to be too enslaved, or they'll suffer—nor too free, or they'll become proud and greedy. In 1790, Burke raises his pen to attack the French Revolution. The levelers have claimed that all occupations are honorable. Burke replies:

The occupation of a hair-dresser, or of a working tallow-chandler, cannot be a matter of honour to any person—to say nothing of a number of more servile employments. Such descriptions of men ought not to suffer oppression from the state; but the state suffers oppression, if such as they, either individually or collectively, are permitted to rule. In this you think you are combatting prejudice, but you are at war with nature.

Kindred formulations abound in ancient China and (as we shall see) twentieth-century Russia.

And what if the potters, strangely dissatisfied with such systems, want to be paid more, not to mention honored? Marx's answer will echo down the ages forever: "Between equal rights, force decides."

Rank

We've learned that the ant queen attracts her nestmates chemically; she is not "above" them but controls and is controlled by them. The ants' gloss on Marx is: "Our equal rights can never be in conflict, because altruism makes us one." The Inuk hunter of prior times who strangled his feeble old mother did so not because he was "above" her but because she was useless; he might even have done it out of kindness. But in Assyria, the new classes—priests, soldiers, administrators—did grow above the undifferentiated souls who fed them. Call them tall stalks in Lord Millet's field. Just now we saw the germination and flowering of property. Simultaneously it happens with status. The Icelandic chieftain whose lawsuit help I crave may not be better than I, but at the moment I need him more than he needs me. I'm on the way to falling below him, to being *valued* as less than he, not for what I don't have but for what I *am* not. We've just read what Burke thinks of tallow-chandlers. I'm sure this too occurs by increments. Pay a fellow Hebrew after seven years' service, says the Bible, and let him go. So far, at least the fiction of class equality persists: vassalage is revocable. "But if he says to you, 'I will not go out from you,' because he loves you and your household, since he fares well with you, then you shall take an awl, and thrust it through his ear into the door, and he shall be your bondman forever. And to your bondwoman you shall do likewise."

A Marxist could say that the bondman accepted enslavement less out of love than out of the bitter fact that he couldn't get work elsewhere; but what we may be misreading here as someone's alienation of himself, his new family read differently. And he himself, when the awl went into his ear, perhaps felt that he had achieved safe harbor at last—who's to say?

Regardless of what *he* thinks, we know what Burke's class thinks of him.

Regardless of what he *thinks,* adds the Marxist, "it is not the consciousness of men which determines their existence, but, on the contrary, their social existence determines their consciousness"—an argument which, however well meant, leads by mental and moral superiority's easy paths to a utopia whose citizens are not equals but sick patients. Unchecked (and who can check it? For everybody who disagrees with it suffers from false consciousness!), it will dangerously undermine the relevance of the bondman's own thoughts and desires—the central error in Lenin and Stalin's policy of collectivization. But we shouldn't write off this quick, clever aphorism so easily: Haven't we all seen degraded, broken individuals, some of whom *accept* their degradation and in their dullness or crushedness cannot imagine being better off? Perhaps they fear the process of improvement, like a blind child struggling against the operation which will bring him sight. The ones I know are mostly just tired. Social existence does more or less determine consciousness. Whether or not we condemn that fact, dependence—on the awl-wielding master, or on the Marxist—lies a very long way from the egalitarianism of hunter-gatherer nomadism . . .

Class-Branded Thinking

Or does it? If hunters are "the best men," then class has already been defined as status. And what is rank but status made inborn and perpetual? As for the idea which we seek to define, and others to defend, let us put it crudely thus: *class is either what you control or how other people treat you.* And here I want to reintroduce the standard human approximation of the Golden Rule: *do unto others as they do unto you.* Letting this axiom operate upon our practical definition of class, we should not be surprised to learn the result, that *people who live in a class hierarchy create and extend those divisions in their own minds.* Burke's an obvious case, but I also remember one very poor motorcycle driver I knew in Phnom Penh, a man who incidentally supported the Khmer Rouge. At the time about which I'm writing, motorcycle drivers represented an intermediate development upon the transportation scene—a new functional subclass (in the ant sense) doomed to live out all too rapidly what Marx would call its "historical mission." In 1991, with the whole country still deathly poor and broken from that spell of revolutionary delirium which had ended a dozen years since, I had seen only cyclo drivers—skinny men who pedaled their passengers in awninged vehicles which resembled baby carriages. Commuters who didn't want to ride in cyclos propelled themselves through the streets on their sky-blue Russian-made bicycles. Toward the end of 1992, reified by motorcycles, the internal combustion engine made its formal reappearance. By 1995 actual air-conditioned taxis had begun to show up—ubiquitous enough the following year that most foreign tourists elected for that comfortable isolation. From the standpoint of class as property, taxi drivers obviously stood highest and cyclo drivers the lowest. My motorcycle driver believed taxi drivers to be as a rule obnoxiously lordly, while cyclo drivers were oafs. Only motorcycle drivers such as himself could judge the individual merits of such folk. As the years went by, he eventually succeeded in buying a car— wonderful to see how his thinking then changed! Mao Zedong flatly states: "In class society everyone lives as a member of a particular class, and every kind of thinking, without exception, is stamped with the brand of a class."

If one believes in fighting the class struggle, then class-branded thinking writes its own license for Pol Pot's children to kill anybody with glasses, which brand their owners' eyes (at least to those who cannot afford glasses) with richness—no wonder Mao supported Pol Pot!

Emblems

By all means, condemn the killers of the bespectacled—for them there can be neither justification nor mitigation. But we might note that in Pol Pot's generation, in parts of China, the USSR and Southeast Asia, officials sometimes wore glasses simply in order to resemble officials. The "best men" of the Amerindians could be their own emblems. Rank, however, requires props. The Spaniards under Cortes would often encounter Montezuma's envoys strutting by "with cocksure pride," leaning on special crooked staffs as they went, and tranquilly sniffing the roses they bore in their hands. In the Three Kingdoms of fifth-century Korea, officials of infinitesmally graded ranks wore robes of purple, scarlet, blue or yellow to indicate their status, facilitating the expedient social equation between defense of class and defense of honor. If one had no robe, it was best to keep quiet and bow.

Because the "best men" are born with their muscles and keen eyes, the enfranchised may argue, in glib defense of class, that the name or skin he was born with likewise makes *him* best. One day in South Africa, Gandhi, dressed in full professional style, clasped his first-class ticket in one hand, his self-respect in the other, and entered a first-class carriage. The beleaguered white men within demanded that he leave. When Gandhi refused, a constable threw him off the train.

When People Become Objects

And so functional specialization grows into subordination, then official vileness, an instance being the bigotry which even now afflicts the "Untouchable" castes of India and Japan. We've told the tale in the language of creeping gradualism, but class domination also makes headway by that especially notorious means: the sword. Eight centuries before Christ, Ashurnasirpal II boasts of the people he's just annexed: "They embraced my feet." Few "best men" would demand that. Shalmaneser III crushes the Arameans, and crows: "They became afraid of the terror emanating from my position as overlord, as well as of the splendor of my fierce weapons, and killed their master." A hundred years later, Sargon II smashes the Samarians. "The town I rebuilt better than it was before . . . I placed an officer of mine as governor over them and imposed upon them tribute as is customary for Assyrian citizens." There goes some of their productive surplus! Sargon's defense of honor against the Samarians can now become defense of property.

In old Korea, where victorious commanders own prisoners of war outright, "the social compulsion to relegate large segments of the populace to unfree status constitutes a special characteristic of the aristocratic states of the Three Kingdoms period." —And of the Greek period, and the Roman period, too. Hence the Slavemaster's Maxim: *If I was born better than you, I have the right to your labor, to your very person.* The seed-miller has become her ant queen's inferior.

Charming Fellows, Living Tools

About these antique societies Marx wants us to believe (since his theory of increasing socioeconomic pressure requires it) that the seed-miller's life is better than it will become—if we overlook such ghastly exceptions as gold mining—because the exploiting classes have not yet become less concerned with the products of a worker's labor than with the worker as a product. I consider Marx's argument to be expedient to the brink of outright wickedness. Moreover, it is wrong. As Leslie White pointed out, slaves may be divided into European feudalism's "property-making machines"—the kind most familiar to Marxists—and their antithesis, Polynesian, Mesoamerican and Northwest American Indian expressions of rank's outward honor—which is precisely to say, products. "The noneconomic character of the institution of 'slavery' is revealed," says White, "when a Kwakiutl chief, for example, will kill a slave merely to demonstrate his high status." No matter what Marx writes, I am not sure that the slave is thereby better off. The Aztecs likewise expend their slaves on religious sacrifices when they see fit, or when authority calls upon them to do so; the Koreans of the old kingdom of Koguryo use up to a hundred at once to accompany their masters in death; the Roman householders torture them whenever they need to learn the facts about some insolence or insurrection.

As with the law of the bondman's ear, any generalization on the evils of a slave's life requires severe qualification. For some people, at some times, slavery may be preferable to freedom. One archaeologist claims that in and after the time of Juvenal, a rich man's slave was better off than a poor citizen, because to the former might be delegated the most lucrative and commanding tasks of administration, including the whipping of free citizens. What is mainly proved by such data is the fatuousness of *any* one definition of class: class as rank, class as wealth, class as prestige, et cetera. The obvious fact remains that, other things being equal, a slave is worse off than a free man. The slaves of the rich were sheltered and pampered for what we ought to call structural rather than personal reasons—no matter if their owners called them members of the family. In 61 B.C., Cicero writes his dear friend Atticus that "my reader Sositheus, a charming fellow, has died, and I am more upset about it than anyone would suppose I should be about a slave's death." —How nice—or is it?

When Unlawfulness Is Commited upon My Slave, Who Has Been Harmed?
The Moral Calculus of Roman Law (A.D. 533)[*]

1. "If anyone unlawfully kills a slave or servant-girl belonging to someone else, or a four-footed beast of the class of cattle, let him be condemned to pay the owner the highest value that the property had attained in the preceding year."

2. "If someone castrates your slave boy and thus increases his value, Vivanus writes that the *lex Aquilia* should not apply, but that you should

---

[*]Justinian, pp. 71 ("Concerning the Lex Aquilia," Book 9, Title 2, clause 2 [Gaius]), 86 (clause 27 [Ulpian]), 90 (clause 30 [Paul]), 91 (ditto), 127 ("Concerning Theft," Book 46, Title 2, clause 48 [Ulpian]), 136 (clause 61 [Africanus]), 154 ("Concerning Robbery with Violence and Riotous Assembly," Book 47, Title 8, clause 2 [Ulpian]), 173 ("Concerning Insulting Behaviour and Scandalous Libels," Book 47, Title 10, clause 15 [Ulpian]).

instead bring the action for insult or sue under the edict of the Aediles for four times his value."

3. "A man who kills another's slave caught in the act of adultery will not be liable under this lex."

4. "If a slave is wounded, but not mortally, and he dies of neglect, the action will be for wounding, not for killing."

5. "If a slave-girl is pregnant when stolen, or becomes pregnant while stolen, the child, when born, is stolen property."

6. "A runaway slave-girl is deemed to commit theft of herself and she makes her child stolen property by handling it."

7. "If a runaway slave of mine buys some things for his own use and they are taken from him by force, I can bring an action for robbery because those things are my property."

8. "If anyone is alleged to have beaten the slave of another improperly, or to have had him tortured without his master's order, I will give an action against him."

Cicero also tells us how one patrician lady puts a slave of hers to the question in hopes of making him bear false witness. He refuses; the torture continues until the appalled and disgusted spectators halt it. A couple of years later, she tortures him again, then cuts his tongue out and crucifies him, evidently because she fears he might recant. "Such treatment of slaves seems to have been common in Rome," says a twentieth-century scholar. Another account reports that during Nero's regime, the Roman city prefect was murdered by one of his four hundred slaves. *The assassin was known.* But the Senate followed ancient law and liquidated every last one of them, without distinction of age or sex. After all, two-legged chattels weren't rare (consider that appellation "the common people"); they made up a full third of the population. Wealthy patrician families might own so many slaves that they had to be grouped in tens to keep track of them. Caesar's friend Crassus calls them "lively cattle," "living tools." Tacitus speaks of "the slaves and those other inhabitants who need threats of force to keep them in order." He also calls them "articles for use."

The master of course lives immune to torture (at least until the decline of the Empire). He commissions statues of himself in marble and plates them with gold. He soweth not, neither doth he reap. Doubtless Cicero, Crassus, Caesar, Pompey don't see it that way; they plan, struggle, risk all, aid Rome, aid their clients, so let's rephrase the cliché: *with his own hands* he soweth not, his contribution being to set the tone, to establish, govern and coordinate—from the slave's point of view, to consume. —"Among slaveholding ants the worker caste degenerates and frequently disappears. Often slaveholding ants can scarcely feed themselves." Khrushchev with his good class outlook insists that it was the institution of slavery which sapped the Roman Empire. Perhaps he's right: slavery under his predecessor, Stalin, certainly undermined the Soviet Union and her founding revolution.

Lysias's Defense

And when official class relations stand thus, when the formal code of society refuses to regard the slave as a human being, then the most intimate social relations are poisoned. An Athenian defendant stands before the bar. The prosecutor has just finished. Now the water clock is dripping away the moments allotted for defense. How can he put his best foot forward? What argument will make the jurors drop their mussel-shell votes into the urn of acquittal? He'd owned a slave girl in common with another man, with whom he subsequently quarrelled. "She pretends to prefer me at one time, him at another, because she wants to be loved by both of us," he cries. —Is she then expedient, calculating, untrue? —Probably. Given her situation, who could blame her? —The defendant does. What are his feelings for her? Disgruntlement, it would seem, or rage, for she'd favored his rival, who freed her (if I'd been she, I would have preferred him, too). And so this very ordinary monster asks that she be tortured to confirm his statements. "She has been the cause of all our actions," he declaims. "Everything can be made clear by reference to her . . ."—and we know what that means. "I feel indignation, gentlemen, if on account of a mere prostitute slave-woman I find myself faced with the danger of losing all that is most dear."

How many kindred monsters must the Athenian system have created? Just look at the class basis of that "cradle of democracy," whose constitution specifically excluded laborers from officeholding.

Meditate on this sincerely, and you must admit that the Marxist goal of total classlessness, however impractical, unwise or evil it might be in execution, is nonetheless noble. If living Justice ever succeeds in taking off her blindfold and enforcing her conscience, then no one will ever be "a mere prostitute slave-woman" again. But that hasn't happened yet, and maybe it never will. On the eve of World War I, we find the socialists of the First International desperately arguing that class war ought to be a far more fundamental concern to the masses than conflicts over national sovereignty. No one listens. Twenty-three centuries before, Thucydides ascribes to the brutally frank Athenian surrender commissioners in his famous Melian Dialogue the adage that "a rival empire like Sparta, even if Sparta was our real antagonist"—they are at war with Sparta at the time—"is not so terrible to the vanquished as subjects who by themselves attack and overpower their rulers."

CLASS EGALITARIANISM IN ATHENS (MID FIFTH CENTURY B.C.)

	CLASSES OF CITIZENS
CITIZENS: 10%	1. Pentacosiomedimnoi = 500 measures of produce/year
FREE NONCITIZENS: 40% *(Resident aliens, Athenian women and children)*	2. Knights = 300 measures
	3. Zeugitai = 200 measures
UNFREE NONCITIZENS: 50% (Slaves)	4. Thetes = Lower-class citizens

Source: Thucydides (Strassler), Appendix A, pp. 577–78 (Alan L. Boeghold).

"Scourge Him to Make Us Even"

Once the notion of class expresses itself as worth instead of function, and once urgent self-defense commands ruthlessness, then the unworthy may be broken or destroyed on mere suspicion, or out of caprice, or for any reason. Under Charles V, a soldier who "regularly tarried and ate and drank in inns" without what we would now call "visible means of support" could be put to the torture on suspicion of robbery. As an expedient policy, this was probably logical, for how could a fellow in soldier's livery (as opposed to a man in a fine lord's cloak) indeed have funds or leisure without being a bandit? God knows, his pay was low enough! (The ants, I suppose, would reason the same, did they reason: idlers do not last long in their company.)

What then must Charles V's lackey-torturers, magistrates, constables and rich citizens have thought of their own country's soldiers, whose role was to defend their privileged lives? What must any soul feel toward its natural inferiors? We know Burke's sentiments. For more of the same, just read Plutarch's endless anxious sneers against "the people"; or consider how Mark Antony scourged Caesar's freedman and wrote to him: "If it offends you, you have got my freedman, Hipparchus, with you: hang him up and scourge him to make us even." Yes, this is class.

As a result of his noble birth, recollected the Marquis de Sade, "I believed, from the time I could reason, that nature and fortune had joined together to heap their gifts upon me." When his father died, he required of his mayors, consuls and deputies the ancient kiss of homage. That was his due; his honor; forgoing it would have constituted failure to defend his class. His sad and ferocious experiments with prostitutes remind us of the tale of the Athenian slave girl. In Marseilles he surreptitiously administered Spanish fly in candies to several women, who suffered great pain as a result and almost died. In lines which could have been taken from any of his novels, he referred to his exploit as one of

> these amusements, whose only drawback was at worst the death of a whore . . . Putting these vile creatures in their true place, people are beginning to feel that, since they are made solely to serve as victims to our passions, it is only their disobedience that must be punished, and not our caprices.

Sade was no sport of nature. When he was a child, his playmate's father, the Comte de Charlois, liked to shoot workmen on roofs, just for the pleasure of hitting his mark. (One is reminded of the Japanese warrior class, which at about the same time liked to test out new swords by chopping in two the first commoner who came to a crossroads.) All that Charlois had to do afterward was beg the king's pardon, which, the king had to admit, was "due your rank and quality as prince of the blood." In every age one can find such beasts, whose impunity is brought up short by neither obligation nor compassion. That is why Bakunin shouts: "It is the characteristic of privilege and of every privileged position to kill the mind and heart of men."

Why Vile Creatures Must Be Vile

What is class? we ask again. Is it rank, or wealth, or caste, or status? The local definition matters not. Class is, quite simply, the particular arrangement by which power and resources get unequally distributed within a society— no matter whether its divisions are attenuated over long gradations, as in the many-tiered hierarchies of ancient China, or sharply marked as in Greece, where (so the scholar Vernant has noted) the democracy enjoyed by the citizen classes defined exactly and was exactly defined by the slave class with its paucity of civil rights. *Class is the local determinator of social inequality.*

Burke's Reply

"All this violent cry against the nobility I take to be a mere work of art . . . Nobility is a graceful ornament to the civil order. It is the Corinthian capital of polished society."

From Feudalism to Capitalism

Now even the Greek demos with its noble rhetoric and its brutal foundations is long gone. Gone, too, the Huron warriors who followed dream-visions whenever they chose, paying as much or as little heed as they liked to the remonstrances of their Old Men. (In point of fact, medieval class hierarchies and what might be called "longhouse individualism" coexist in the seventeenth-century world, but that doesn't at all discomfit Marx's pretty schema of productive development: as soon as they meet, the former will gobble the latter.) With his nineteenth-century predilection for literary lights and shadows, Marx describes "feudal Europe, shrouded in darkness":

> Here, instead of the independent man, we find everyone dependent— serfs and lords, vassals and suzerains, laymen and clerics . . . But precisely because relations of personal independence form the given social foundation, there is no need for labour and its products to assume a fantastic form different from their reality [that is to say, the objectification of labor under industrial capitalism]. They take the shape, in the transactions of society, of services in kind and payments in kind.

Briefly, what he means by the objectification of labor, now creeping upon the scene, is as follows: In tribal, classical and feudal times, work possessed only a "use-value," but in capitalist times it acquires through the "cash nexus" an "exchange value" calculated in *money*. In Wendaké I brought a cake of tobacco for your curing ceremony when you were sick; you gave me a captive Iroquois for me to torture as I pleased. These were free gifts between equals, not exchange at all. In the Middle Ages, I dug a ditch for my lord when he commanded me, while you delivered to him the statutory proportion of your lambs and apples; no one thought of equating the two in absolute terms. But in Marx's nineteenth-century England,

I dig ditches for a fixed wage, while you sell apples for a fixed price. We can thus calculate the prices of ditches dug in relation to the prices of apples, or (as do class-pigeonholers) my hourly worth in relation to yours. By thus quantifying the value of our labor, we become susceptible to making money for someone else whose claim is merely that he owns the means of production. Again, I'm not sure I see the practical difference, to a slave dying in the gold mines of ancient Rome. Nonetheless, here lies the true meaning of the revolutionary adage that "property is theft."

As a factory worker, my productive power becomes potentially unlimited. New machines decrease the amount of time it takes me to make something, thereby allowing—that is, requiring—me to make more such items than before, for the same fixed wage. It is as if I suddenly found myself digging not one ditch for my lord but ten. I may expend no more effort than I did in completing a single ditch, and so in a certain sense opaque to Marxism am not exploited at all (or at least I'm not more exploited than I was), but thanks to capital, embodied in the new machine, the gap between my wage and my lord's profit has increased by an order of magnitude. The distinction between absolute and relative poverty suddenly becomes much more important. It is no longer what I make but I myself who am for sale.

And when the only work I can find is factory work, then the "cash nexus," the objectification of my labor value, is determined by the factory owner. I don't like it? Well, I'm "free" to refuse, unlike the Roman slave. How progressive this nineteenth century is! Another factory owner just might hire me—for even less! And soon new machinery will compel him to increase his productivity, in order to keep up with his business rivals, so that, desperate to lower his overhead (it's really not his fault), and needing fewer workers to operate the efficient apparatus, he can fire me. When it takes eight workers to accomplish what it used to take twenty, then my factory town holds too many souls: down goes every worker's labor value, and the capitalist, seeing another way to shave costs, pays accordingly. Hence Marx's shoe-banging descendant, Khrushchev, vehemently states that "the invincible law of capitalism is the law of the impoverishment of the proletariat and the ruin of the peasants." Robespierre says it with less cant: "Nature tells us that man was born for liberty, and the experience of centuries shows us man enslaved; these rights are written in his heart, and his humiliations written in history."

Rising Up and Rising Down

And what can we do about it? The underclass's answer has always been: "Revolution." The new middle class says: "Reform"—ever the bitterest joke to revolutionaries. Or perhaps it too whispers "revolution" if it thinks (as it did in 1789) that it can gain more than it will lose. The upper class in its turn may sigh: "Concessions." (One Marxist jeers that a feudal lord's "freeing" his serfs—the Marxist's quotation marks—is the same as proletarianizing them, turning them out of the land he owns, the land they've lived on for generations.) Or it cries: "Repression!" —"If a slave rises [up] against his master," runs a Hittite law from the fourteenth century before Christ, "he shall go in a pot" to be buried alive.

Prelude to Dekulakization

Like the tablets of Hittite moralists, Marx's pages crackle with hatred and menace. Anyone who reads *Capital*'s careful statistics of woe, to say nothing of the appalling accounts incorporated from periodicals and parliamentary "Blue Books" of mistreatment of the workers—starvation, disease and cold, weary forced idleness, death, death, death—cannot but feel his anger to be justified. "The hour of the machine had struck." It was the hour for surplus value to be extracted from the workers—and the hour for the workers to rise up. Marx himself was living on charity then (he had to borrow money for his daughter Franziska's coffin). I'm sure he would have reduced the members of the oppressor class to slaves if he could! In the *Manifesto* he told them to go ahead and tremble: the Communists were coming!

And in Russia, they came. "The government is already running big estates with workers instead of peasants, where conditions are favourable," said Lenin to H. G. Wells. "That can spread . . . The peasants in the other provinces, selfish and illiterate, will not know what is happening until their turn comes" —When their turn comes, they'll know it, those lousy kulak bastards! Those Party activists in their sheepskin coats and aviator-style caps will dip up their grain, and they'll begin starving.

Devils or Angels?

But leave that story for later; we haven't quite come to Stalin's century yet. Spartacus rises up and dies. So does Robespierre. Who exemplifies legitimate defense of class? —It depends on whom you ask, of course. —To

Trotsky, for example, Robespierre must be called a magnificent bourgeois forerunner of Communist revolution; to Carlyle, he's a wicked sea-green mediocrity, the eighteenth-century manifestation of Hannah Arendt's banality of evil. But risings up occur no matter what you think of them— likewise risings down. After all, says Stalin to H. G. Wells, who's come back for more, "the rich experience of history teaches that up to now not a single class has voluntarily made way for another class."

False Consciousness Again

Precisely because the upper class won't make way, the underclass always rises up, or seeks to. —So, at any rate, runs the paradigm. And yet most scholars agree on the irrelevance of "class consciousness" as a descriptor of, say, the Roman plebeians, who might riot when grain prices rose, but whose aim was not to take the mechanisms of distribution into their own hands, merely to get cheaper grain. About this stratum, whose hemmed-in lives in Rome's firetrap tenements now lie beyond our vision (if we except the patricians' brief, distorted notice, or the coarsely pixillated gaze of modern statistics), Erich S. Gruen writes bluntly, in a passage which might equally apply to the atomized family dependence of many women throughout history: "For most, their welfare was tied more closely to relations with powerful patrons than to members of their own class. The result was an enduring fragmentation"—which the rulers surely encouraged in self-defense. Here is how Cato the Censor ruled his slaves: "He would ever craftily make one of them fall out with another, for he could not abide they should be friends, being ever jealous of that." For similar reasons, owners of slave-gladiators preferred a hodgepodge of Celts, Thracians, Germans and the like, to hinder mutual communication, let alone class solidarity. After-proof of the prudence of their intentions: Spartacus the gladiator rises up (even if no plebeians join him). Marx calls him a noble proletarian; the historian Christian Meier calls him "a robber chief on a grand scale." He dies in battle; his slave army gives and gets no quarter; the ruling class crucifies all the survivors.

And yet what twentieth-century agitators would term the failure of "mobilization" and "class consciousness" among the plebs was never the result of any cunningly farsighted patrician defense of class. Appian, historian of the ruling elite, tells how the plebeians arrive at one civic assembly bearing daggers. —Ominous, to be sure, but he cannot see beyond the supposition that they've been murderously misled. How could they possibly embody, let alone offer, a self-contained purpose, a righteousness, a noble striving? And they probably don't. Some patrician or his tool will be trying to bribe them. For that matter, it never occurs to Appian that his class as such needs defending: *Rome* is imperiled by plebeian violence. Likewise, when the dictator Sulla gives fortuitous birth to himself, saving Rome from *her*self, by means of easy bloodshed, his tools demand "that the voting should be controlled by the well-to-do and sober-minded rather than by the pauper and reckless classes—there would no longer be left any starting-point for civil discord." Sulla and Appian do not conceive of mass revolution, only of mass disorder. That's why Sulla's victims (at least the ones we read about) tend to be senators, rich men, patricians who might prepare a credible opposition to him on the narrow power stage of Roman politics. For, after all, the plebeians are *needed*. Moreover, as the Roman centuries succeed each other, they gain a modest measure of civic power— all to the good; here's another way for a politician who flatters "the people" to manipulate the system, in defense of his own income and prestige, his dynamic private class! Under the ancient law of the Twelve Tables, commoners could not intermarry with the patricians, but this was no longer followed; and we read that in the last generation of the Republic the patrician demagogue P. Clodius succeeded (with Caesar's connivance) in getting himself adopted into a plebeian family so that he could stand for the plebeian office of tribune—evidence both of the practical fluidity of class lines and of the not insignificant civic powers of plebeian representation (however easily Clodius might have corrupted those to his ends). All to the good! Dole out grain, control the vote, prevent civil discord.

To Marx, this sentiment merely brings a bitter smile. Marx knows that civil discord in this context means simply "danger to one's class interest." Rank hath its privileges; and the more of them it hath, the more certain rank becomes that its existence is not exploitative at all, but as vitally functional as any ant queen. Call Marx correct. We see his logic now, when we see the Sullan formula for reconciliation repeated down the ages. For Edward Gibbon as he sat musing over the history of old Rome, the solution was as simple in its own way as the ants', or Rizal's: Let the rich have luxuries; they'll have to pay poor craftsmen to make them. This begs the question: What about the unskilled poor? —And here is the ruling class's answer, attributed to that moderately cruel emperor Tiberius: "If we are decent, we shall behave well—the rich when they are surfeited, the poor because they have to."

Pareto's Shell Game

Wait! Marx was wrong! insist those clever twentieth-century theorists, Pareto and Mosca. There *is* no ruling class in mass democracy—that went out with hereditary absolutism! What we have instead is a *circulation of elites*. (It sounds a little like the ants. The queen dies; a new queen takes over; nobody complains; the larvae grow on time.) The *most qualified* can rise to the top for a while. Wasn't capitalism—and feudalism, too, for that matter—the result of ideology as well as economics? And aren't elites often a collection of individuals at cross-purposes, not blocs and cabals? Gaze, for instance, at the following.

THE SIX CLASS DIVISIONS OF THE UNITED STATES OF AMERICA (1948)

"He defined his classes not only in terms of wealth and power, but in terms of people's consumption and sociability habits. [A fellow traveler] used the tossed salad as a more reliable indicator of a person's status than the size of his bank account."

1. Upper-upper ("old-line aristocrats").
2. Lower-upper ("the nouveaux riches").
3. Upper-middle (professionals, executives, etc.).
4. Lower-middle (white-collar workers, tradesmen, etc.).
5. Upper-lower (skilled and semiskilled).
6. Lower-lower (laborers and first-generation immigrants).

Source: Packard (pp. 97–98); after Lloyd Warner, Social Class in America.

The case could certainly be made that from the point of view of the last three classes, the first three constitute an elite. Among them they control a disproportionate amount of national income and power. But do, say, the aristocrats and the managerial professionals always agree? —Of course they don't, Marx would say. And, if anything, that fact only exacerbates their stranglehold over the fifth and sixth classes (the fourth one, white-collar workers and tradesmen, will be guilty of petit-bourgeois leanings until proven otherwise). As we've learned, competition forces individuals among the elite to squeeze their employees harder; otherwise they might

208 WILLIAM T. VOLLMANN

lose their market share. Anyhow, some Marxists reason, to typify class divisions on the basis of occupational or income brackets misleads. "Taking this method to extremes, one arrives at one category per individual, thus conforming to the individualistic requirement of the ideology that takes the place of social science. The dynamic of society then becomes incomprehensible."

For me, the most important point is this: Whether or not subgroups circulate in and out of the ruling class, the ruling class remains. People die, history devours nations, centuries blow away like dust and still our class divisions allow us to treat one another as ants would never do . . .

The Aspirations of Manjok

And now we're almost ready to return to Stalin and the kulaks. We understand the complexity and urgent *endlessness* of the class struggle. Ninth-century Korean rebels grow so numerous and anonymous that government records refer to them as "grass bandits." They rise again in the twelfth century, slaves and peasants both—thousands of them. In 1198, Manjok, leader of the Kaesong insurrection, cries out these words in defense of class:

> Why then should we only work ourselves to the bone and suffer under the whip? . . . If each one kills his master and burns the record of his slave status, thus bringing slavery to an end in our country, then each of us will be able to become a minister or a general.

Rizal, Tolstoy, Gandhi would have smilingly shaken their heads. I continue to think, for all that I admire those three, that their call for nonviolence patronizes the people who have to suffer the most. Why *should* Manjok's people endure the whip? Why shouldn't they kill their masters? The Kaesong uprising gets crushed, of course. —Anyhow, explain the Marxists, any slave rebellion in those times could not have advanced history by creating a new society, because the opposition between classes (that is, between masters and slaves) did not yet correspond with the "fundamental contradiction" of that mode of production. When the proletariat takes over a capitalist's factories, their joint ownership creates socialism. But when the Spartan helots rose up against their masters two dozen centuries earlier, all they could have hoped to do would be to seize and possess the farms which they'd been working for their masters' benefit.

The lack of mechanical aids to farm production—tractors, milking ma-chines, et cetera—would prevent them from giganticizing, concentrating and collectivizing that production. Thus the classical Marxist argument. (Thanks to Mao Zedong, however, the "peasantization" of classical Marx-ism has been a sort of acid bath, dissolving much of that half-dead body's theoretical skeleton.)

I remain less than convinced that "advancing society" is a necessary goal of class struggle. Spartacus and Manjok didn't give a fig about capi-tal. They just wanted the whip cracks to stop. —Nor, Rizal might add, did they want justice. They wanted only reverse injustice. True or not? They didn't triumph, so we might as well ask the dusty wind.

The Aspirations of Manjok (continued)

In the nineteenth century, the Korean peasants rise up again, first in small bands, as "fire brigands" and "water brigands," then coalescing into larger rebellions—all crushed. Official government slavery has been abol-ished by then, but property slavery continues to starve the farmers.

Halfway around the world, equivalent forces operate: first comes the French Revolution ("the common people have become bored with moral-ity," explains one of Mishima's Sadean characters, "and they'd like to en-joy for themselves the immorality that hitherto has been the exclusive prerogative of the nobility"); then the Paris Communards try to liquidate all property, and cobblestones glisten with their murdered blood. Marx and Engels shrill out, "Workers of the world, unite! You have nothing to lose but your chains!"

And finally comes the October Revolution. Oh, yes, the hour of the machine has struck! The productive forces stand ready. "There were bayo-nets at the edges of the room," writes John Reed, "bayonets pricking up among the delegates; the Military Revolutionary Committee was arming everybody" —In a woodcut made decades after Lenin's death, we see that leader standing in a long row among his Red Guards. Lenin himself has a hand in his pocket, perhaps preparing to whip out some gun or decree. Left to right, they gaze unflinchingly into our faces, capped or shawled (for on the far right there is one woman in long skirts, gripping a bayonet), high-headed, steady and still, with their holstered pistols, their rifles and bandoliers, their determination: formidable class fighters. We see them coming closer and closer.

The Last Gasp of Functionalism

Must it be revolution, then? Must we destroy the ruling class instead of bringing it into some lovingly *conscious* ant feedback system?

Gandhi, of course, replies that we need not. As uncompromisingly, nobly impractical as his violent brother Bakunin, he offers a magic remedy which Bakunin (and Stalin) would despise, proposing to divide Indian society into four kinds of occupations, none superior to the others. The cruel ostracism of the untouchable caste will have to be repealed, but Gandhi, unlike his disciple, Martin Luther King, hesitates to demand caste intermarriage or even interdining. Why? Because that's not necessary; it's not important. As for class relations mediated by the cash nexus, "why should not the mill-owners feel happy paying a little more to the workers?" he wrote in a letter to a mill-owner friend. "There is only one royal road to remove their discontent: entering their lives and binding them with the silken thread of love." This could be considered almost a Platonic view (although Plato's *Republic* with its example of the potters had put it rather more mean-spiritedly): in the anthill we all dwell in, the classes need one another.

Functionalism Denied

No, they do not, says Marx (for whom the Gandhian view would have been just another of Sulla's tricks of elite self-defense). We must *crush* the ruling class. And we'll accomplish that by temporarily installing a ruling class of liquidators. After they complete their job, then their power, too, can "wither away." Who will the liquidators be? The dispossessed, the wretched of the earth, the factory workers, the proletariat. They constitute the revolutionary class, because factory technology has sharpened and simplified the class struggle, rendering history a contest between the bourgeoisie, which has marshaled capital to reproduce itself and give off money, and the proletarians, whose exploited labor actually created that capital. The increasing power of the machines means that fewer and fewer oppressors control more and more resources, and therefore that the bourgeoise are becoming outnumbered, and that competition to keep up with newer technology will weaken them, throw more proletarians out of work and bring all the contradictions to a head. So the proletarians are the liberating class.

Defense of Class

As an official Soviet monograph explains, even though "the organs of pro-letarian dictatorship" ought to be, in Lenin's words, "open to all,"

> in the first post-revolutionary years the soviets [workers' councils] were not and indeed could not be open to all, because representatives of the ousted exploiter classes, who had unleashed a civil war, were deprived of suffrage. It was not until after the construction of a socialist society in the USSR that it became possible to remould the soviets from class or-ganisations into organisations of all working people. The Constitution of 1936 introduced universal suffrage.

This is the famous "Stalin Constitution," as empty as it was beautiful, issued during the year of the worst show trials, when the organs of prole-tarian dictatorship remain open to none but the new elite.

The Glow of Inspiration

But then, under capitalism itself, how many people enjoy the benefits of the now immense productive surplus? For all the historical missions completed by the various classes, has there been any "progress"? Has life gotten "bet-ter"? "The cleanly weeded land and the unclean human weeds of Lin-colnshire," says Marx, "are pole and counterpole of capitalist production." —This is class—oh, this is most certainly class! —In 1892, the anarchist Alexander Berkman goes to Pittsburgh in hopes of avenging by assassination the ruling class's murders of the Homestead strikers. Here is what he sees:

> In the distance, giant pillars vomit pillars of fire, the lurid flashes accen-tuating a line of frame structures, dilapidated and miserable. They are the homes of the workers who have created the industrial glory of Pitts-burgh, reared its millionaires, its Carnegies and Fricks. The sight fills me with hatred of the perverse social justice that turns the needs of mankind into an Inferno of brutalizing toil.

Frogs in a Pool

And so we find ourselves back again in Stalin's Russia, the October Revo-lution won, the Civil War won, but socialism still not quite built, kulaks unconquered, true communism unachieved. It is 1931. Peasants starve. In the 1920s we had reason to hope that western Europe would join us, but the ruling classes saved themselves: we're ringed round with enemies! (Don't forget the enemies at home.) How can we be secure, let alone supreme? Berkman's assessment continues to hang in the air: The smokestacks of Pittsburgh choke us with hatred—because they're not our own socialist smokestacks. Well, in Lenin's words, *What Is to Be Done?*

First, and as a means to an end, we need an agricultural surplus—food for our cities—so we can build those smokestacks. Heavy industry established, capital now producing *for us,* we'll mass-produce weapons to defend us against the international exploiting classes, which will buy us that leisurely safety so conducive to paving and electrifying our rural areas. —Oh, and we'll produce more goods for the people, of course. (Chekhov: "Those who are more stupid and more dirty than we are called the people.") But as a precondition we must consolidate the revolution. Trotsky impatiently explains:

> The gendarmerie of Tsarism throttled the workers who were fighting for the Socialist order. Our Extraordinary Commissions shoot landlords, capitalists, and generals who are striving to restore the the capitalist order. Do you grasp this—distinction? Yes? For us Communists it is quite sufficient.

He's still powerful and popular then. Stalin remains the half-obscure paper pusher, friend of mediocrities, lackey of Lenin. Trotsky slights him, fatally dazzled by his own magnificence. When the Red Terror begins in 1917, Trotsky says: "There is nothing immoral in the proletariat finishing off the dying class. That is its right."

Twenty-two years later, finishing off a dying Trotsky, Stalin will agree.

The Mission of a Doomed Class

But why must the peasants disappear? From our sketch of communist class theory, one might more readily imagine a small herd of fat, cigar-smoking capitalists in top hats being shoved against a wall by the myriad workers. —Ah, but class science isn't for tyros like us! It takes an expert to know that the enemy might wear a farmer's face!

In 1914 Lenin writes that of course we must follow Engels's prescription: the small peasants will never be expropriated, only led by example.

But this is merely Lenin the politician speaking, not Lenin the ideologist. During the 1905 attempt at revolution, he'd drawn the real line:

> In this struggle the peasantry, as a landowning class, will play the same treacherous, unstable part as is now being played by the bourgeoisie in the struggle for democracy. To forget this is to forget socialism, to deceive oneself and others regarding the real interests and tasks of the proletariat.

That dictum, which nowhere appears in Marx's *Capital,* informed Stalin's procedures and Soviet dogma everywhere. (A related class defense parable: in classical Rome, the dictator Cinna, needing manpower for his coup, frees those slaves who agree to join; but when a few employ that liberty to attack their masters, he liquidates them all.)

Why must the peasant be "unstable"? Because he loves the land he works, the land that sustains him. He owns it (or would if he could). We see a father and son standing on a boardwalk of logs and planks, so it must be autumn or spring—spring, most likely, for the trees behind them are in leaf. The street is but a long wide zone of mud. They wear fringed boots wrapped round with ankle-cloths. Baggily, heavily dressed, cap-brims just above eye level, they gaze patiently into the lens, the boy holding what might be a horse halter, his father with a cowbell and a crude harness slung over his shoulder. This evidence of livestock ownership brands them as kulaks. Of course their gear may serve an entirely different purpose, but I, an activist from Lenin and Stalin's Moscow, know whose side they're on merely by looking into their eyes . . . "Peasant life is a life committed completely to survival," concludes the author of a "peasant trilogy." —How natural, and to revolutionaries how selfish! —" 'Don't run away from anything,' says the Russian peasant proverb, 'but don't do anything.' The peasant's universal reputation for cunning is a recognition of this secretive and subversive tendency." In one of Chekhov's stories he's emblematized as Ignat Ryabov, "a sturdy, broad-shouldered peasant who never does anything and is everlastingly silent." This silence, as the anxious ruling class tries to forget, betokens not idiocy but stubbornness. Make of Ignat Ryabov a serf, a conscript soldier, or a laborer—no matter what, he thinks his own thoughts and will not tell class enemies what they are. But when at last he speaks, his voice booms. Throughout the Tsar's domains (soon to become "the country of the revolution") he makes war on the gentry whenever he can. In the first five years of Stalin's century we find 670 peasant uprisings in European Russia alone. There lies the peasant's historical mission: In his own class interest, he's doing what that bourgeois lawyer Robespierre did against the French aristocrats. When the gentry have all been liquidated as a class, his task will have ended. He'll be progressive no more.

The Thousand Years' War

Although he doesn't personalize the issue as Lenin will, nonetheless, in obedience to his bloodshot calculus of necessarily intractable oppositions, Marx asserts that *by their very nature, city and countryside must be at war.* (Here we might also quote the ominously relevant aphorism of one scholar that "the enmity between peasants and the state" is "one of the distinctive features of Russian history.") On the one hand, labor power and feeding power reside in the country, but, thanks to property, and property's new offspring, fathered upon industrialization—namely, capital—coercive administrative power (capital's political shadow) now builds up in the city with every new technological and bureaucratic advance. The country feeds us; but the city organizes us.

It is almost as if those two poles were rival ant nests to Marx, each with its own functional system of class—almost, but not quite, because that analogy would be too neutral; the urban hive actually contains the progressive class, with its various functional subclasses.

One of Lenin and Trotsky's favorite parlor games was to compare the history of the Russian Revolution they were making with events of the French Revolution 128 years before. French radicals had dealt ruthlessly with the *chouannerie,* or sporadic peasant rebellion which occurred in western France from 1793 onward. The Chouans resented new taxes and the loyalty oath required of priests. Many of them allied themselves with monarchists. They were accordingly slaughtered. The *chouannerie* of the Russian and Ukrainian peasants was about forced grain requisitions, and it began almost immediately after Lenin seized power. The people whom he called "profiteers" were, by and large, petit bourgeois storekeepers and rich peasants. How could they be anything else? If they had grain, if they were thus of interest to the hungry new regime, then they were by definition rich. Most likely they had gathered together their hoards by their own efforts; no doubt, people being people, some had employed foul means; almost certainly none of them wanted to yield anything up. (Gibbon repeated: "The possession and the enjoyment of property are the pledges which bind a civilised people to an improved country.") *That* morality was hardly revolutionary. Lenin believed that he had no choice but to take their food at gunpoint, and from the standpoint of his revolutionary aims he may well have been right. Anyhow, who are we to question him? For, as the Soviets assure us, he was "the most gifted organiser and leader history has ever seen." (I prefer an aphorism out of Tacitus: "The more distinguished men were, the greater their urgency and insincerity.")

There runs a socialist slogan (or cliché, if you prefer) which I have heard on the lips of Russians, Ethiopians, Burmese and ever so many others: *Land to the tiller.* The Leninists utter it (mendaciously) during the revolution and the civil war; but the Stalinists proclaim it a retrogressive irrelevance, for the city, not the country, has won Marx's war. The countryside must accordingly be broken and citified, so that in future there might be no city or country anymore.

Stalin's 1930s will offer the ironic spectacle of peasants who, hoping for such amenities as the eight-hour day which proletarians are much closer than they to receiving, ask the Party: "When will the boundary between town and countryside be wiped away?" But that can't happen all at once when a revolution is city-headed! The city must first extend tendrils of control into every haystack, in order to create its future superorganism of coordinated egalitarianism.

Draining a Stagnant Pool

For the moment, take Marx's stated aim of abolishing urban-rural distinctions at face value. Is it a good one? We already saw how those marvelously adapted survivors, the social insects, took the exact opposite course, subdividing into specialized labor castes, and adapting themselves with even more dramatic morphological variations from species to species, according to terrain and way of life: I repeat, city ants differ from country ants! Was it perhaps an error on the part of Stalinists, and Marxist-Leninists generally, not to have gone in the ants' direction? Of course they too had their specialists, their welders, war pilots, female shock workers, NKVD interrogator-torturers, tractor drivers, commissars; but the same system was to be everywhere imposed, local conditions being, in the long run, irritations. When they collectivized agriculture, some cadres imposed identical farm grids upon the terrain, be it pastureland or swampland. Well, they retreated from that; and in ant terms, survival terms, we cannot say they failed, not right away, for their USSR survived Hitler's worst—and Stalin's, too. But their colleagues in China a few decades later would prove that for the furtherance of class war one could equally well impose the country on the city as force the city on the country. Never mind. We all have our likes and dislikes. Burke despised tallow-chandlers, and Gorki contemptuously referred to "the flat, stagnant pool of the rural world."

Summing up, the proletariat makes up the vanguard class, while the peasantry's but the fat and lazy ally of inertia, hence of prevailing exploitation. It is our mission to level the world horizon and to prevent any further eruptions of inequality. Besides, we need their grain. Hence the peasants must submit to us.

Of the Fraternity of Workers and Peasants

If the Marxian paradigm of the eternal war between town and countryside was obviously self-fulfilling, still, at the beginning of the Bolshevik regime the peasants did have a weapon: without the products of their labor, everyone would starve. Pol Pot paid reverence to this very material necessity when in 1975 he launched his slogan: *When there is rice, there is everything.* His strategy, foiled by his own murderousness and incompetence, would be to make almost everyone into a rice producer, a peasant, until Cambodia had built up enough rice capital to begin industrializing, while murderous cadres urged the toilers on. Stalin's strategy, on the other hand, was to keep and empower his proletarians from the very first moment, not emptying the cities at all, since that would have lost the urban-rural war, but building new ones, fed by the peasants, who would be enrolled willingly or not into collectives. (More equality, less liberty! At least, that was how it had to be for now.) Objective: A city-controlled surplus. Any future threat of withheld production could then be dealt with by zealots who enjoyed full granaries.

It was an article of faith for Stalin, as it would be for Pol Pot, that the greater efficiency and comradely motivation of socialist agriculture would create that surplus. Poor peasants would benefit from joining the collectives. Rich peasants would lose—all to the good. Were they allowed to retain their cows and bushels of grain, they might not be so vulnerable to the state which employed fear to complete its revolution—the state, moreover, which required those cows and that grain.

Yes, the peasants must submit. But start with the landlords; that's good revolutionary strategy. Use the rich peasants to help tear down those plutocrats. Later we can use the poor peasants to crush the rich peasants . . .

A Jewish Aside

Trotsky, always as suspect as he is illuminating for his didactic literariness, assures us that as soon as the Tsar abdicated, the peasants commenced looting and sometimes burning the estates of the rural nobility, announcing to history's spectators: "He was our lord and all his goods are ours." Did Trotsky, whose enthusiasm avoided the fact that the peasants' first victims were often Jews like himself, experience any twinge of premonitory terror, like those Party cadres of the 1930s, loyal or not, who, hearing the telephone's scream late at night, expected a summons from the political police? Did he, a country boy, consider the peasants to be his personal enemies? During the Civil War, their counterrevolutionary manipulators seized on his Jewishness with gleeful ferocity. He tells us that he declined Lenin's offer to make him Commissar of the Interior, because "was it worthwhile to put into our enemies' hands such an additional weapon as my Jewish origin?" When we meet Trotsky in exile years after 1917, and find him shrugging off that genocide called collectivization, we may well suppose that his revulsion for the peasants does not follow solely class lines. In 1917, when he colored with obliging redness his account of the peasant expropriators, could he have predicted the anti-Semitism that Stalin would bring to official politics? Did he, in short, ever reflect upon the possibility that vis-à-vis the revolution, he himself, like the peasants, like Shakespeare's Moor who has done his duty and can now go, might constitute a member of a doomed class with a very brief historical mission?

A Clever Move on the Class Chessboard

Strangely enough, the peasants wanted their historical mission to continue! (Do you remember what Stalin said to H. G. Wells? "Up to now not a single class has voluntarily made way for another class.") The Ukrainian scholar A. Graziosi, writing eight decades after the revolution, admits to the baleful survival in the countryside of what she calls an "archaic nucleus" which attacked not only Jewish property but also that of "widows and lonely women, priests of 'alien' religions and owners with foreign names." Her phrase, if perhaps so delicately abstract as to approach euphemism, remains accurate as a delineation not only of age-old rural cruelty but also of rural class bitterness. "He was our lord and all his goods are ours." Whether or not the burners' utterance is verbatim, it deserves our attention here as a Marxist parable. It is just what any underclass uprisers believe. It is the revenge of the exploited, a fantasy of equalization come true. Lenin preaches it. As soon as the Soviet government is formed, he abolishes landed proprietorship "without any compensation," and the peasants receive millions of hectares of land—temporarily. Their delegates, writes that infatuated witness, John Reed, "went wild with joy."

"They Must Be Annihilated"

In terror, the monarchist landlords now pretend to be liberals; the kulaks, or rich peasants, who stand just below them in the class hierarchy, go a step further and pretend to be leftists. But they can't fool us! They're the same fat frogs in that repulsive bourgeois pool!

With his usual wearisome vindictiveness, Trotsky conjures up a vision of one of these fellows making up his mind to come along on a peasant raid: "The kulak maneuvered while he could, but, at the last moment, scratching the back of his head once more, hitched the well-fed horses to the iron-rimmed wagon and went out for his share. It was often the lion's share."

Right, then, comrades—drain the pool! First we'll skim the scum off; then we'll go deeper. We can't do it all at once—for look how vast its murky depths.

Now that we understand that even the poor peasants won't be on our side, why, it's 80 percent of the population that we have to conquer! —Maybe more, for in 1905, out of 150 million people, the Russian working class "in all branches of labor" numbers a mere 10 million, of whom only between 1 and 3 million can be sanctified by the label *proletarian*. We good risers-up, then, make up less than 1 percent of the masses whom Marxism has delivered into our power, and for whose sake we've supposedly risen up. Arise, ye wretched of the earth! Out with it, comrade—do these figures strike you as undemocratic? Well, no one said that the dictatorship of the proletariat would be gentle—how could it be? Comrade Zinoviev, himself to be liquidated by Stalin, announces to the fellow converted his own premonitory calculations: "We must carry along with us 90 million out of the 100 million of Soviet Russia's inhabitants. As for the rest, we have nothing to say to them. They must be annihilated." We mathematicians of hindsight now know this to have been an underestimate.

Mercilessness

The use of novels to illustrate a political or historical point must be conducted with extreme caution—for although any novel "represents" its own period, still, unless its intent is overtly political, like Thomas More's *Utopia,* George Orwell's *1984* or that racist tract poorly disguised as art, *The Turner Diaries,* how can we be certain that its paper world follows any laws in preference to the aesthetic ones of its creator? That self-styled "document in the form of a novel," *Babi Yar,* was, like Norman Mailer's brilliant *The Naked and the Dead,* written by an eyewitness to violence, and we might as well assume (as in this book I do) that when the authors of those two works describe jungle battles or the machine-gunning of Jews, they do so from knowledge. There is a certain faith one tends to keep with extreme events. Precisely because they are extreme, those who have suffered in them tend to try to describe them accurately. —Still, while novels of this kind may assist us in visualizing history, they make no oath before the bar. Were *Babi Yar* the only evidence of Stalin's famine and Hitler's Holocaust, how could I believe?

We now turn, however, to a novel of an altogether different sort. Nikolai Ostrovsky's *How the Steel Was Tempered,* written while the blind author, like his blind protagonist, lay slowly dying of injuries sustained in the Civil War, can only be described as a Bolshevik bildungsroman. Ostrovsky was laid in black Russian earth in 1936, the year of the Kirov affair and its subsequent show trials. His book had been composed, not without editorial help, in 1930–34, while collectivization and famine were performing their esteemed services to Soviet power. Collectivization thus receives a few glowing if elliptical tributes in its pages. The text of the 1979 Progress Publishers edition I own must have been tampered with according to the usual Soviet practice, for in it I find not a single mention of Comrade Stalin. But what remains is brutally partisan enough. This novel, written as an act of solidarity with the regime, and proudly distributed by it in 110 languages (it was, the paralyzed soldier explained, his last "offensive," his "victory," his "battle"), constitutes a hymnal, an official doctrinal parable. Its purpose is to tell us what to think. As such, we can rely on it far more than we could a work by an author for whom art comes first (I will not say a more honest writer, for who am I to call Ostrovsky cynical rather than devout?). Marx and Engels say in their *German Ideology* that "the ruling ideas are

nothing more than the ideal expression of the dominant material rela-
tionships." Ostrovsky and his publishers offer us those ruling ideas, in a
form crudely concrete enough to be apprehended by the uneducated
people in whose name Stalin reigned, hence also by us.

CLASS DIVISIONS IN RUSSIA (1914)

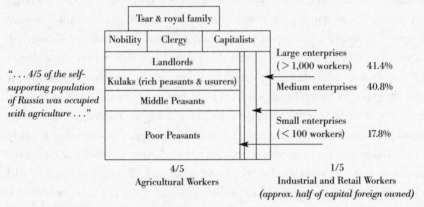

Source: Trotsky, History of the Russian Revolution, *pp. 7–15, 33.*

How the Steel Was Tempered opens in Tsarist times. "We work like
horses," cries young Pavel, "and instead of thanks we get blows—anyone
can beat you and there's no one to stick up for you." —His words read not
unlike those of the petition to Tsar Nicholas II in 1905, the words of desperate people who believed in their "Great Father" until brutal incompetence shot them down in cold blood. Unlike them, Pavel fights with his
fists for the right, beats down bullies. "You shouldn't be so merciless,"
says Tonya, the forester's daughter, who's sweet on him. (From her origins
alone we know that her advice can't be good! She doesn't want to rise up.
If this book were a Nazi parable, Tonya would probably be a Jew.) After
she dares to show up well-dressed at a Komsomol meeting, thereby revealing her essential elitism, Pavel realizes that he had better expel her from his
life. After all, he's surrounded by so many other alien elements! For Ostrovsky's blind vision now gazes upon that bitter year in a string of bitter
years, 1919, when Trotsky held the line in that famous armored train and
the Civil War approached resolution. (As a fighter, Ostrovsky must remember Trotsky's achievements. But he listens obediently to authority's

themes. Trotsky will not fare well in *How the Steel Was Tempered*.) "A fierce and merciless class struggle gripped the Ukraine," our author explains, just in case we hadn't noticed. "More and more people took to arms and each clash brought forth new fighters"—in perfect fulfillment of Marxist-Leninist principles.

Ostrovsky knows better than to paint the peasantry with his inky class stereotypes. After all, redeemed peasants, calloused comrades willing to be led, may read his book. Who then shall be the frogs in his stagnant pond? "Ex-officers of the tsarist army, Right and Left Ukrainian Socialist-Revolutionaries—any desperado who could muster a band of cutthroats" —and, needless to say, "kulak rabble." —Keeping this worldwide class conspiracy straight is all quite confusing, to be sure. But thanks to the mentorship of a certain grim, stern old sailor, "Pavel came to see that all this tangle of political parties with high-sounding names—Social-Revolutionaries, Social-Democrats, Polish Socialists— was a collection of vicious enemies of the workers, and that the only revolutionary party which steadfastly fought against the rich was the Bolshevik Party." It is the old sailor who, as he stands beside Pavel, watching through the window for enemies, most clearly articulates the book's credo:

> I can't stand the quiet, smug sort. The whole world's afire now. The slaves have risen and the old life's got to be scuttled. But to do that we need stout fellows, not sissies, who'll go crawling into the cracks like so many cockroaches when the fighting starts, but men with guts who'll hit out without mercy.

And in due course, his Party, the Party of Lenin and Stalin, liberates Pavel's town. A mechanic's helper at the sugar refinery promptly rises at a town meeting to shout that now self-defense of the working class can finally be instituted; now the gentry can be crushed: "This is the end of those vermin."

We find Pavel among the stout fellows, who confiscate the lawyer's house for their deliberations. A real soldier, like one of John Brown's sons raiding in proslave territory, he slays bourgeois counterrevolutionaries, acting in concert with "thousands of other fighting men as ragged and ill-clad as himself but afire with the indomitable determination to fight for

the power of his class." (Years later, in a scene of almost endearing absurdity, he'll encounter the lawyer's daughter on a train, and instantly see
from her ravaged nostrils that she, in obedience to the destiny of her class,
has addicted herself to cocaine.) Where must the lawyer's family go now?
Never mind. Inside their home, the Revcom (Revolutionary Committee),
decisive and dynamic, utters Lenin's dictum:

> The front must have supplies. The workers have to eat . . . We know very
> well that none of the profiteers are going to sell their goods at the fixed
> prices [because those prices, of course, are wretched: the Bolsheviks
> don't care about giving fair value to the bourgeoisie]. They'll hide what-
> ever they've got. In that case we'll make searches and confiscate the
> bloodsuckers' goods. This is no time for niceties.

We know what this means.

The Civil War ends with Soviet power conclusively established—but,
alas, new enemies have risen up or down against the revolution. The kulaks still try to hide their wealth—doubtless under the inspiration of what
Trotsky refers to as the "traitorous leadership of the aggressive Social Revolutionary type of *muzhik*." —Excuse me, comrades! Did I commit the error of mentioning Trotsky? Pretty young Comrade Talya steps to the
rostrum and says, "Today we are very glad to note that in our organisation
Trotsky's followers have been defeated." Ostrovsky's parable, ever consistent and coherent, obligingly presents us with a piggish Trotskyite character, whose every act confirms the wisdom which underlies Comrade Talya's
spontaneous gladness. The last we see of this fellow, he's drunk, his breath
smells of onions, and a fat whore lies in his bed. Pavel wants to give him an
ideological lecture, but the Trotskyite will not rise up against pleasure's
toils, so our hero, who reminds me of Wagner's Siegfried, stalks away forever, muttering: "The swine!"

Thus far, Ostrovsky has withheld his concern from "the agrarian question," which even as he writes is murdering millions. He knows who the
loathsome frogs are, but won't say. Presently, however, his narrative
reaches Lenin's death—a deliciously solemn moment for any Bolshevik
propagandist to employ for promises and covenants. Throngs of previously half-committed workers now decide to join the Party. Among these
we find Pavel's brother Artem, a perfect worker and militant in every respect but one: he's married a peasant wife, a frog if there ever was one,

when he could have allied himself with the more proletarian stonemason's daughter. (Just in case we might not have understood the distastefulness of that choice, Ostrovsky makes the stonemason's girl pretty and the peasant wife ugly.) Pavel visits him once, but, sickened by the spectacle of the peasant mother-in-law praying to her cobwebbed old God, performs his usual malediction-by-walking-away, without even saying goodbye to his brother. Since Pavel is perfect, we now know, in case we missed it before, that poor Artem has attainted himself. Ostrovsky cannot forbear to dig his readers in the ribs.

On the floor of the railroad shop, when Artem applies for Party membership, the issue inevitably comes up:

"Let Comrade Korchagin explain why he has settled on the land and how he reconciles his peasant status with his proletarian psychology."

But Artem was already replying:

"That's all right, Comrade. The lad is right about my having settled on the land. That's true, but I haven't betrayed my working-class conscience. Anyhow, that's over and done with from today. I'm moving my family closer to the sheds. It's better here. That cursed bit of land has been sticking in my throat for a long time."

Once again Artem's heart trembled when he saw the forest of hands raised in his favour, and with head held high he walked back to his seat. Behind him he heard Sirotenko announce: "Unanimous."

In my opinion, their jubilee bodes badly for Artem's wife.

Lenin and the Kulaks

Lenin, as we have seen, hoped simply to keep the middle peasants neutral during the revolution; afterward, the revolution would help them overcome their "vacillations." (But, as Ostrovsky's novel hints, they all too often stood on the wrong side of neutral.) Here he is, in the piously painterly 1950 reimagining of V. Serov, leaning forward, a pencil in his hand, frowning in utter concentration as he gazes into the face of an uncouth and gesticulating peasant deputy; they're conferring at a tiny round table which seems to be of mahogany, nationalized from the executed Romanoffs, no doubt; Lenin (who has assured the Scandinavian press that their liquidation was a capitalist hoax) rests his wrist on the table's edge, up close with his darling peasants. This conclave is as intimate as it is immediate. Next to the gesticulator sits another muzhik deputy, a young moustache-stroker who peers into Lenin's face, mesmerized (decades later, Ho Chi Minh, reading Lenin, will describe himself as "overjoyed to tears"), while behind them the third deputy stands, his fingers splayed across the back of the Romanoff chair in which the gesticulator is sitting; this chair, by the way, is still shrouded in white cloth, emblem of the royalist mothballers, whereas the cover of Lenin's chair has slipped down to the arm, on which our most gifted organizer of all time leans his left elbow. The standing deputy, who like his two colleagues wears a sheepskin coat, collar slightly undone in concession to the indoors (perhaps there is no heat in the former palace, or the peasants just like their jackets), muses soulfully upon Lenin. Like Ostrovsky's characters, Lenin has no time for bourgeois niceties. He has gone to the heart of things. On the table, between his wrist and the moustache-stroking deputy's hand, lies a little pad. In a second or two, once all has been clarified, Lenin's pencil will rise, then stab down upon the pad, issuing concise and masterful commands which will improve the peasants' lot by instilling classlessness.

Shall we call them kulaks? In the Ukraine, from April to July 1919 alone (a period over which Trotsky's memoirs glide with vague mention of anarchism, disorganization and other difficulties), there were three hundred more peasant revolts. Hence this pleasant document of Lenin's, never to be released from the secret Party archive until the collapse of the Soviet Union in 1991:

> Comrades! The uprising of the five kulak districts should be mercilessly suppressed . . .
>
> 1. Hang (hang without fail) so the people will see, no fewer than one hundred known kulaks, rich men, bloodsuckers.
> 2. Publish their names.
> 3. Take from them all the grain.
> 4. Designate hostages . . .
>
> Do it in such a way that for hundreds of versts around, the people will see, tremble, know, shout: they are strangling and will strangle to death the bloodsucker kulaks.

How to Create Bloodsuckers

And what was a kulak? —A rich peasant, we said. More technically put, a usurer; semantically, a "fist"—but never mind technicalities; didn't we learn from Ostrovsky that all rich people are exploiters?

A definition from the *Great Soviet Encyclopedia:* Kulaks aim to reinstate "a serflike method of exploitation." They are "the basic social force of petit bourgeois counterrevolution."

In Soviet historiography, the kulak was, like Hitler's idea of the Jew, something *other,* uniquely evil and unclean. Let us quote again from Vitaly Startsev's monograph on the formation of the soviets. Remember that Startsev was a professor at the USSR Academy of Sciences, and, by virtue of his participation in the "True Socialism" series which translated him for your and my benefit, a spokesman for the regime. Remember also that his book was published a full fifty years *after* the liquidation of the kulaks. Imagine for purposes of comparison some respected German historian publishing a half-century after the Holocaust a tract on the wicked subhumanness of Jews! (The difference: The Nazis lost the war and the Soviets won.)

Following Marx's general line, Startsev writes that the abolition of serfdom in 1861 actually lost Russian peasants their land tenure. If they wanted to own their farms, they had to overpay the landlord class. (The result was not dissimilar to what happened after the American Civil War, when blacks who thought they'd been freed from slavery now found themselves trapped by the economics of sharecropping. So far, Startsev is plausible.) Thus on Russian soil, which Marx calls "so fruitful of all infamies,"

> the process of class differentiation was accelerating. There appeared in the countryside a new and far more sinister figure than the landlord, namely, the kulak, who was from the well-to-do strata of the peasantry. The kulaks were properly called "blood-suckers" because of their ruthless exploitation of their fellow villagers and their unquenchable thirst for profit. By 1905 the kulaks had taken over three-quarters of all peasant holdings and more than half of the draught animals.

Here is how a Ukrainian scholar writing after the death of the Soviet Union interpreted the same data: "the vigor and impetus of the liberated peasantry . . ." and "the massive purchase of noble land . . ." "In fine, the land belonging to peasants almost doubled between 1877 and 1905."

What were they, then—rich bloodsuckers or liberated peasants? —It depends on how you draw your class lines. Again and again the conclusion bursts out on us: For Stalinists, a kulak could be *any* peasant. He might be poor or even landless, owning no draught animal whatsoever; maybe his uncle had kept a horse once . . . Former Tsarist policemen, children of prerevolutionary officials or the servants and relatives of kulaks could all wind up on the kulak list. So could artisans of any kind: millers, black-smiths, lacemakers and other small entrepreneurs. People in bad repute for other reasons, such as thieves, might be put on it by their peers. Village leaders were selected by the government. Lenin's answer, then, to the question "What is class?" is: "Whatever I want it to be."

Marxism Versus Ant Logic

But can't exploitation be quantified? Marx conceived of the notion of *surplus value,* which is to say the profit taken by the capitalist from the labor of workers. We can simplify the concept thus: If your work produces for me the dollar-value V, measured by the income I make from the product you've made for me; and if I pay you the wage W, and if my other overhead costs are O, then the amount of surplus value I make from you is V minus W minus O. This is value I am not entitled to, says Marx, for I did nothing but own the means of production. Justice demands that my workers share the surplus value, and own the means of production jointly, dispossessing me. If I am a kulak, if I have a cow and you don't, then it is expediently plausible (and maybe true) for you to claim that that cow reifies surplus value, extracted by me from you over time. The fact that I myself also work does not exculpate me; it merely makes me a hybrid, a man between capitalist and worker, a "small master." It stands to reason that I wouldn't pay you to dig potatoes for me if it weren't worth my while—which means, if I didn't gain more from the arrangement than I paid you. Thus for Marxists (and certainly for these Soviet vanguardists whom Marx would have called vulgar Marxists) the "cash nexus" is *by definition* a relationship of exploitation. And it becomes *coercive exploitation* if six or seven hours of your labor would feed or shelter you, were you working your own field, whereas I demand that you work ten hours on my field before I pay you enough for you to obtain that same food and shelter. I am a vampire. I have stolen at least three hours from you. And I have done so six days a week for ten years. I am a hardened expropriator.

The doctrinaire stupidity of this argument can be shown by any number of examples. Instance: If you have a horse and I don't, then circumstances compel me to hire you to plough for me. You are the rich one—you have the horse—but because I am your employer, a Stalinist will accuse me of being the little capitalist, the exploiter, the kulak. I in turn could denounce you for owning the horse, which, since class equals property, proves your wickedness to whichever Stalinists I bribe with vodka. What if neither of us exploited the other? That simply cannot be admitted. In Lenin's words:

> General talk about freedom, equality and democracy is in fact but a blind repetition of concepts shaped by the relations of commodity production . . . From the point of view of the proletariat, the question can be put only in the following way: freedom from oppression by which class? equality of which class with which? democracy based on private property, or on a struggle for the abolition of private property?—and so forth.

To the ants it wouldn't matter who owned the cow: we'd both own it; we all would. This is precisely the logic of the collective farm.

"From Each According to His Ability . . ."

The Marxist-Leninist penchant for collective farms is predicated on the following reasoning: Concentration of capital has been shown by capitalism itself to increase productivity, and hence surplus value. It is in the interest of any owner, be he a member of the "exploiting classes" or of "the people," to increase productivity as much as possible, and hence gain the highest possible surplus value. So far, so true, as attested by any number of examples in history:

JOINING THE VIETCONG
The expedient calculus of Nguyen Tan Thanh (1961)

Size of rice field leased: 1 hectare.

Quality: "Very poor, almost sterile. That was why the owner rented it out to us."

Yield: "Despite working hard all year round, we got only 100 gia of rice out of it."

Landlord's cut from that yield: 40 gia.

History of surplus value: "We lived a very hard life. But I cultivated the land carefully, and in time it became fertile. When it did, the owner took it back; my livelihood was gone."

A capitalist will keep that value for himself, whereas any member of a worker-owned (socialistic) enterprise may expect to enjoy his share of it, either by working less or by deriving more sustenance or material income from it. If, invoking self-defense of class, we confiscate the lands, cattle and equipment of kulaks, and share them all among us, they will create the most value if they are managed jointly, not scattered. Their farms in effect become an immense agricultural factory. This is what happened in the United States in the 1930s. The small farmers in Steinbeck's *Grapes of Wrath* are always talking about being "tractored out." They simply cannot compete against the combines. —Never mind, say the Marxists; we'll give the people combines!

But where will we get them in the first place? Russia was never capital-rich to begin with, and revolution, civil war and kulak "sabotage" (many slaughtered their own cattle rather than hand them over) have impoverished us further. Since we cannot at present increase surplus value by improving your means of production, you collective farmers will have to work harder instead. The state will extract surplus value from you *as it sees fit*. *When it sees fit,* it will reinvest that surplus value *where it sees fit*. A collectivized peasant complains that "the government now has all the rights that kulaks, landlords, and speculators used to have. For example, bread. The state takes grain at 6 kopeks a kilogram and sells cookies and so on at 75 kopeks. Isn't that pure speculation; isn't it exploitation?" Or, as an official historiography put it fifty years later: "The Great October Revolution in Russia opened up to the peasants the road to a free and happy life . . . Having gained the land, the peasantry took the road to socialism by uniting voluntarily in cooperatives."

Right around the time of the revolution, Russia had been suffering from an epidemic of lice. Karl Radek, the journalist, the climber, the counterrevolutionary (so he must have been, for Stalin would shoot him, too), was also a jester. His solution to the nuisance: Collectivize it! Half the lice would die; the rest would run away . . .

"The Liquidation of the Kulaks as a Class": First Round

By late 1918, while Trotsky rides around the circular front in his armored train, Lenin has already sent out a secret note recommending that all private property deeds be seized and pulped. But in 1919 he advises that "extraction of the [grain] surpluses from the Ukraine to Russia" be "delayed," no doubt for expedient reasons only, or he would have said "prevented." He goes on: "Use *any* extraction of surpluses to feed the local poor peasants" in the Ukraine "no matter what, giving them without fail a share taken from the kulaks." It is not yet time to drain the entire stagnant pool, and perhaps Lenin truly hopes (why not give him credit?) that some of them may be won over—which explains why in the Ukraine, the most activist villages, which all too soon will lead the doomed struggle against the collectivization of their zone, now furnish "an abnormally high proportion of socialist cadres." Lenin must be proud.

In a woodcut commemorating the October Revolution we see him, pale and schematized, gripping the lectern, gazing resolutely across the crowded world of agitators, arm-wavers, shoulders and gestures, to say nothing of the cylindrical-capped listeners who face him in attentive silence with their arms in the pockets of their greatcoats, while between their heads hover in thick darkly wide-spaced Cyrillic the words WAR FOR THE HOMELAND and, cynically enough, LAND. Lenin's famous words ascend over all: WE WILL NOW PROCEED TO CONSTRUCT THE SOCIALIST ORDER. The inner world passes the lectern and receives rifles from a boy who holds them in his arms like marsh reeds (we won't slow down the narrative here by describing the shadowy man in the dark hat). Then the empowered ones become shadowed themselves as, preparing to defend their class, the righteous class, they pass to the edge of the revolutionary world to face outward in the direction of Lenin's gaze, ready with fixed bayonets. Their shade-imperiled flag waves as they aim at the counterrevolutionaries who shoot at them, who fall back dying, who lie still, guns in hand, beneath their wavering skull-and-crossbones flag. One revolutionary already lies dead, too. But the counterrevolutionaries are outnumbered. Lenin knows that. His gaze holds stern fearlessness. In an inset we see his peasants, armed and waiting on a haystack, guns poking up through the straw. Lenin wins the victory.

What Really Happened

Richard Pipes estimates that "thousands" of peasants were shot down while fighting to keep their grain from being taken away. Graziosi evidently lumps together Civil War victims along with the directly repressed, for her summation works out to "hundreds of thousands."

The Puppets' Crusade

The Bolsheviks set out to pit the poor and middle peasants against the rich in every village. They said so explicitly. After all, that was a necessity of class warfare. (Trotsky crows, without elaborating on the substance of the lecture, that at this historic moment "I explained the importance of the question of the middle peasant" to "none other than Stalin.") They always followed that "line" as consistently as they expediently could. In 1919, when the Cheka worried that its twelve thousand hostages might fall into counterrevolutionary hands, it was instructed to shoot the richest ones first. This, my friends, is most definitely class.

Three Statistical Portraits

By the way, what is class?

I would call myself an open-minded nonacademic. When I began writing this chapter, I had no preconceptions about the class composition of the Russian peasantry during this period. Having read the work of people far more enlightened than myself—scholars, experts, theorists, class revolutionaries—I conclude that nobody knows it very well.

Judge for yourself. Herewith, Lenin's assessment, which pays due reverence to the classic pyramidal notion of class:

CLASS COMPOSITION OF THE PEASANTRY BEFORE THE RUSSIAN
CIVIL WAR (APPROXIMATE FIGURES)

Rich peasants (kulaks): 13%

Middle peasants: 20%

Poor peasants: 67%

Source: Computed from Lenin's figures of August 1918; quoted in Pipes, The Russian Revolution, p. 730.

Next consider this homage to the bell curve, a picture not without intuitive plausibility (which could also be said for Lenin's). Of the three, I find it most trustworthy simply on account of the number of its adherents, who include that middle-of-the-road leftist Deutscher, whose biography of Stalin some constituencies find too harsh, others, too sympathetic; the restrained and scholarly Fitzpatrick, who in her focus on strategies of peasant survival emphasizes their tenacity and strength; then both Conquest and Bullock, whose topic is the tyrant himself, leaving the peasants to appear as more passive victims:

CLASS COMPOSITION OF THE PEASANTRY BEFORE THE RUSSIAN
CIVIL WAR (APPROXIMATE FIGURES)

Rich peasants (kulaks): 4%

Middle peasants: 66%

Poor peasants: 30%

Sources: Bullock, p. 260, who agrees more or less with Deutscher, p. 323, Conquest (The Harvest of Sorrow), *pp. 74–75, and Fitzpatrick, p. 30.*

Finally, gaze through the eyes of the Harvard historian Pipes, whose long opus presents Lenin as a misguided monster, and whose statistics not very surprisingly show that "Lenin's notion that three-quarters of the peasants were 'poor' was pure fantasy":

CLASS COMPOSITION OF THE PEASANTRY BEFORE THE RUSSIAN
CIVIL WAR (APPROXIMATE FIGURES)

Rich peasants (kulaks): negligible

Middle peasants: $\leqq 96\%$

Poor peasants: $\leqq 4\%$

Source: Pipes, The Russian Revolution, *p. 738.*

When the supposed reality of class division shows such divergences, one cannot help but feel violent defense of class to be unjustified by insufficient analysis, especially when considering only a few of its gruesome applications in Stalin's century.

But enough. Return to 1918, as Lenin's cadres murder their mere thousands. We'll proceed by degrees to the logical outcome of dekulakization.

The Puppets' Crusade (continued)

The first trick was to sidestep each village's traditional peasant commune by creating a Committee of Unwealthy Peasants, who, if they failed to be good puppets, could always be infused with mercilessness by the central authority. In Graziosi's words, they shattered "the unity of the rural world by exploiting inner divisions which, though not of class origin, were certainly present." Think of fifteenth- and sixteenth-century witch-burners coming into a new town to spread judicial terror, nailing on the door of the parish church a general citation that all enemies of the faith must be reported within twelve days, upon pain of excommunication and that state's necessarily fiery consequences. In the Soviet Union, enemies of the faith were either arrested or robbed. —Whom do I envy? Whom do I hate? I'll denounce them. —And yet, in defense of Lenin and in spite of Pipes, some of those divisions must have truly reflected class: If I am jealous of your horse, because I have none, then my committee can arguably raise class issues: Why shouldn't I have a horse, too? Moreover, there *were* kulaks, as we see from the tables above—a good 4 percent, if Deutscher and his colleagues are right!—and some of them might have deservingly possessed enemies among the poor. Maybe Deutscher understates the situation. Let's say they made up 5 percent, or even Lenin's 13. An anarchist fighter (hence a foe of the Leninists) states in his memoirs that when the revolution first came to his part of the Ukraine, "whoever was strongest and had the most sons to help him" seized the best parts of the landowners' estates. He continues in Trotsky's vein: "Plainly these were mostly kulaks, whilst the . . . poor peasants got only the crumbs." Why shouldn't this be true? It certainly sounds like human nature.

DEFENSE AGAINST CLASS ENEMIES COMPARED

COUNTRY	CONTEXT	VICTIMS
USSR	Dekulakization, 1929–32	6.5 million
	Deliberate famine accompanying dekulakization, 1932–33	4.5–6.5 million
	Peasants sent to labor camps, 1929–36, dying later	3.5 million
	TOTAL =	14.5–16.5 million
VIETNAM	Executions of "rich landlords," 1955–56	40,000?
CHINA	Great Leap Forward, 1958–60	25–43 million
CAMBODIA	Pol Pot's class revolution, 1975–79	300,000–3 million

Having now ourselves thrown Lenin a crumb, we need not lose sight of the fact that Lenin's primary aim in the villages was not classlessness, at least not then, but forced grain requisitions. The result was therefore, in Graziosi's blunt words: "the biggest peasant insurrection since Pugachev's time." *Only 1 percent of the harvest was surrendered.* (There would seem to be considerable truth to Montesquieu's remark that "the soil is productive less by reason of its natural fertility than because the people tilling it are free.") The cadres countermoved proportionately. In 1919, in the space of several weeks, one group is said to have liquidated eight thousand Cossacks. Meanwhile, Lenin called for the execution of more rich hostages, and, presaging Stalin's measures, the confiscation of both surplus and seed grain. The peasants continued to resist. History records Lenin as an ironical intelligence. It speaks of the coldly mirthful sparkling of his eyes, of his secret notes and quick, pricking retorts. Maybe because the soul of the man swam in a sea of theory, shapeless, weightless and self-insinuating like an octopus, he seems to have been as insulated from his own failures as from the screams of his victims. (In the previous century, when he'd quarrelled with Stalin and Lenin's forebear Marx—and lost—old Bakunin had accused "men of science" of calmly vivisecting human rabbits "in honor of some pitiless abstraction." Bakunin was right.) I imagine Lenin, therefore, as grinning ironically when, the Civil War won, he shelved the agrarian question for the moment, letting the peasants continue to indulge themselves in their doomed historical mission while he declared victory.

"Infinitely More Slowly Than We Expected"

Thus he persevered in his stance of public moderation. Even before war's end, at the Eighth Congress of the Russian Communist Party (Bolsheviks) he'd warned of the dangers of haste and ruthlessness. (Could it be that he honestly didn't know what his own cadres were up to? That question is answered by that document from the secret archive: "Hang (hang without fail) . . . " Of course the kulaks had to go, he said. But the middle peasants were only vacillators, nothing worse—most of them. The murderer shook a finger: *"We shall not tolerate any use of force in respect of the middle peasants."* (Stalin agreed; how could Stalin go against his dear Ilyich?) As for the poor peasants, well, they were on our side; they were emiserated, hence progressive. With them there couldn't even be any question.

When Lenin addressed the Tenth Party Congress in 1921, he was admirably blunt. The interests of the working class and the peasant class "differed." Since the Soviet Union had to go it alone until worldwide revolution broke out, in defense of order—which was to say, in eventual defense of class—the peasantry must be conciliated—for now. (Easy enough, since, as he'd claimed in secret session, they'd already been "conquered.") Now beginning to grasp the true worth of his land decree, they were "dissatisfied and disgruntled, and legitimately so," he admitted, because the Party had been simply expropriating their grain. The Party had already shut down the Committees of Unwealthy Peasants (soon to be resurrected by Stalin), but that wasn't enough. The peasants must be offered some freedom of exchange. "What is free exchange?" Lenin asked, and one can almost hear the delegates drawing stunned breaths. "It is unrestricted trade, and that means turning back toward capitalism."

Stalin was there; Stalin was listening. Soon enough, in the second campaign against the peasants, he'd pull the same trick, attacking his own cadres in his "Dizzy with Success" speech (they'd only been following his orders).

So the Party turned back. —That it receded only out of expediency is shown by the fact that four months after this tolerant Tenth Congress, when past confiscation measures (interpreted by Lenin, hypocritically or not, as crop failures) had already brought about famine, Lenin and Molotov sent out a telegram to all provincial and regional party committees, ordering them to take steps "to provide the food agencies with the necessary authority and the total power of the state apparatus of coercion." Here our sources differ. We've already related that the grain procurement brigades secured only 1 percent of the harvest. Yet now we're told that there was no grain left to be seized, unless the regime wanted to fight a second civil war. Perhaps the best inference to draw is that the Bolsheviks and the peasants had fought one another to a standstill. At any rate, for seven years the vanguard left well enough alone. They replaced requisitions by a fixed tax in kind, and, in the end, by a monetary tax. Peasant landholdings were guaranteed. One thing must be said for Lenin: He was a master, not only of forcing others to swallow, but also himself of swallowing, bitter pills.

The New Economic Policy, as it came to be called, permitted the resurgence of bazaars, prostitution and other "capitalist vestiges" of which the elite disapproved, but it did raise agricultural productivity. The pill didn't taste so bitter anymore. In 1922, at the Eleventh Congress, Lenin offered a ruefully moderate formula: "Link up with the peasant masses, with the rank-and-file working peasants, and begin to move forward immeasurably, infinitely more slowly than we expected, but in such a way that the entire mass will actually move forward with us." The peasants were satisfied now, he told the Fourth Congress of the Comintern that same year. Last year they hated us, but now their uprisings had ceased—a vote of confidence for us and the NEP. Hopefully in future they wouldn't be able to stand against Soviet Russia . . .

One scholar believes that by the end of the NEP, both peasants and workers in the USSR were better off than they had been before the Revolution—and better off than they would be "for years to come." Had defense of class been justified thus far, then? Not to Trotsky, who with breathtaking callousness and mendacity could write a decade after the terror-famine that Stalin, that bourgeois centralist, was actually a friend of the kulak, who "was allowed to rent his land from the poor peasant and to hire the poor peasant as his laborer. Stalin was getting ready to lease the land to private owners for a period of forty years." In truth, it seems, Stalin was simply busy during those years consolidating his personal power. Meanwhile, the peasants, even if they were not expropriated, continued to be taxed.

In 1928, partly as a result of new crop shortfalls, partly as a means of destroying the power of his most serious remaining rival, Bukharin, formerly one of his best friends (Stalin's daughter lovingly remembers him as the man who always visited accompanied by hedgehogs and garter snakes, the man who taught her how to ride a bicycle and shoot an air gun), Stalin took matters in hand.

Stalin and the Kulaks

He was just then coming into his powers. Not yet the drunken old bully by whose crudities his Yugoslav apostles would be shocked at the end of World War II, no longer the self-effacingly indispensable assistant to Lenin, he now argued openly for his views in executive sessions, forced for the last time in his life to seriously address the opinions of his own countrymen, and for the first time, even if only a little, to reveal himself.

His way of dealing with a contrary opinion was to remove the opiner.

The frontispiece of Trotsky's unfinished *Stalin* reproduces the photo-portraits of the thirty-one members and alternates of the October Central Committee of 1917–18. By the end of World War II only Stalin himself and the marginalized Alexandra Kollontai remained in life. (And why didn't Trotsky finish *Stalin*? Because Stalin finished Trotsky.)

The long, careful rise of this man, of this stodgy, brutal, turgid, vain yet personally unpretentious, terrifying and sometimes companionable evildoer, can occupy us in this book only peripherally, because that rise grew out of expediencies rather than moral decisions. Like Sejanus, commander of the Roman Guard, he "concealed behind a carefully modest exterior an unbounded lust for power," which he now no longer needed to conceal. Thus Stalin in the Lenin years. His gloomy prime reminds me even more of the ascendancy of Nero, whose loyal or passive citizens were condemned solely for being the friends of the previously condemned; they obediently committed suicide when that most concrete of hints, a dagger, arrived through some discreet intermediary. In Stalin's time they killed themselves by accepting imaginary guilt at their show trials. (If they refused, they got tortured again.) "Line after line of chained men were dragged to their destination at the gates of Nero's Gardens. When they were brought to be interrogated, guilt was deduced from affability to a conspirator, or a chance conversation or meeting or entrance to a party or show together." At least Nero never pretended to be the great class-smasher, the altruistic egalitarian.

Less brilliant than Lenin and less quick-witted, Stalin liked to prepare everything in advance. He never debated as well as he sprang traps. Under his government, between forty and fifty million human beings were put to death. He is said to have been suspicious almost to the point of insanity. Unlike Lenin, who treated people with Olympian skepticism, Stalin listened eagerly, a credulous believer—if the assertion was *guilt*. Protestations of innocence didn't convince him, but any soul he'd cast into the waters could always pull others down to doom. At the end, in a senile rage against death and Jews, he turned against his own doctors, had them hideously tortured. His instructions: "If you do not obtain confessions from the doctors, we will shorten you by a head." There is, indeed, a lurking irrationality to many of his doings. That strain shows itself more obviously in Hitler's foaming charisma than in Stalin's dull, secretive busyness, but that's only natural, given the two men's differing political beginnings: Hitler created his movement from almost nothing and swept himself into power by acclamation as much as by trickery, while Stalin, forced to take as his starting point the dead Lenin's genius, had to creep into a spider's preeminence.

Having acknowledged the immense motivating force of what historians almost without exception refer to as Stalin's paranoia, it behooves us now to set it in the background. In this investigation we are interested in when defense of class is justified. Let us assume as best we can that

Stalin's solution to the agrarian question was motivated by a logical and moral calculus, so that it remains susceptible to discussion and analysis. And, indeed, by so proceeding we'll be far closer to some kind of truth than we would be if we summed it all up under the sterile rubric of "aberration."

We see him at his dacha, probably at Kuntsevo, sitting next to his pale, glum son Vasili, who wears a dark uniform. The picture is undated, but his second wife Nadezhda is not there, so perhaps it was taken after she shot herself in 1932. The public story will be that she always tasted her husband's meals to protect him and one day ate some counterrevolutionary poison. Collectivization is going on. It is over collectivization that this husband and wife had their last quarrel. Stalin wears his trademark cap and tunic. His face is a little fleshy. He clasps his fingers in his lap, squinting into the camera. Between him and Vasili stands his little daughter, Svetlana, the future memoirist, whose arms rest on each of their shoulders as she almost smiles, her head cocked, on her face an expression of luminous curiosity. Stalin and Vasili, on the other hand, seem merely resigned to the business of being portrayed. How many thousands of photographs has the General Secretary submitted to by now? As for Vasili, his blue mood might have another cause. He's always getting rebuked for indolence by his father, who treats him as strictly as his own father treated him. But Stalin adores his daughter. "Whenever I asked him for anything," she later remembered, "he liked to answer: 'Why are you only asking? Give an order, and I'll see to it right away.'" He never once visited Nadezhda's grave, because her suicide letter (which he destroyed at once) had attacked him both personally and politically. "People were a lot more honest and emotional in those days," thought the daughter. "If they didn't like life the way it was, they shot themselves." When the Nazis invaded in 1941, he withdrew from Svetlana, too; he had no time then for anything but defense of homeland. But now it is still high summer; tall trees are in leaf behind the family grouping. In light of Stalin's obsession with collectivization it is interesting to read in Svetlana's memoirs that his feeling for nature partook of "a profoundly peasant interest. He was unable merely to contemplate nature; he had to work it and be forever transforming it. He had fruit trees planted over large tracts."

In our next chapter, the one on Lincoln and Trotsky, we will consider this man's methods of repressing his erstwhile peers, the Bolshevik elite. Many of those victims deserve our pity. But at least they chose to be revolutionaries; they chose the life of struggle. The peasants wanted only to be left alone. With the vacillating exceptions of Bukharin and a few half-hearted fellow travelers, how many in the leadership turned away from Leninism so far as to pity *them?*

"The Liquidation of the Kulaks as a Class": Second Round

Admitting that attacks on the kulaks and the confiscation of landed estates had lowered grain production levels, the dictator proposed the solution in his breezy, genial way: Don't encourage the kulaks, but instead establish collective farms on socialist principles. In three or four years, the USSR will be grain-rich! The alliance between workers and peasants will then be consolidated.

Bukharin whispered to Kamenev (also soon to be shot) what Stalin's real policy was: "We have no colonies, we can get no loans, therefore our basis is tribute from the peasantry."

Centuries earlier, we find quoted in Gibbon's pages the maxim of the ancient Persian monarch, Artaxerxes: "The authority of the prince must be defended by military force; that force can only be maintained by taxes; all taxes must, at last, fall upon agriculture; and agriculture can never flourish except under the protection of justice and moderation." Why did Stalin follow all but the last clause of this prescription? —Because of defense of class, of course. —Tribute from the peasantry, yes; and that tribute must be extracted *mercilessly* (the favorite word): "The more socialism grows, the greater will be the resistance to it," which the intellectually patrician Bukharin went on to label "idiotic illiteracy." Maybe so, but illiteracy was now the law of the land—and the sentiment seems in tune with Marx's symphony of class oppositions. Stalin, we are told, never visited a single village after 1928 (perhaps for security reasons), but that didn't stop him from going forward. After all, he'd been born in the country; who knew more about rural problems than Comrade Stalin? And for rigorous laws of the land, call Comrade Trotsky back to the podium: "As long as class society, founded on the most deep-rooted antagonisms, continues to exist, repression remains a necessary means of breaking the will of the opposing side." Call Rosa Luxemburg back from the dead. In the words of that famous and in many ways appealing revolutionary, who if she hadn't been murdered by the German secret police would surely have been murdered by Stalin two decades later (her defining sin: she hated centralism):

the basic lesson of every great revolution . . . decrees: either the revolution must advance at a rapid, stormy and resolute tempo, break down all barriers with an iron hand and place its goal ever farther ahead, or it is quite soon thrown backward behind its feeble point of departure and suppressed by counter-revolution. To stand still, to mark time on one spot, to be contented with the first goal it happens to reach, is never possible in revolution.

I have to believe her. A revolution is by definition an overthrow, an imposition of the new upon the unwilling old. Her prescription is common sense. Therefore, it would seem, class revolutionaries must *themselves* heighten class struggle, in order to win it and end it forever. Thus, at the end of 1929, a year distinguished by over a thousand peasant "disturbances," Stalin spoke to "students of the agrarian question," explaining with his leaden, brutal trademark catechisms that now the Party was strong enough to proceed to a new phase:

we have passed from the policy of restricting the exploiting proclivities of the kulaks to a policy of eliminating the kulaks as a class . . . Now, the expropriation of the kulaks is an integral part of the formation and development of the collective farms. Consequently it is now ridiculous and foolish to discourse on the expropriation of the kulaks. You do not lament the loss of the hair of one who has been beheaded.

Naturally, he said, those bloodsuckers, expropriated or not, could never be allowed to join the collective farms, for they were class enemies. The so-called second revolution was about to begin. The stagnant pool would be drained at last.

Molotov, never one to lament over beheaded individuals, announced the arithmetic to those who needed to know: between 3 and 5 percent of all peasant households were to be dekulakized. What a precise-sounding, impersonal verb! That worked out to 150,000 families. In addition, 60,000 would have to go to what he baldly called "concentration camps." (In 1938, one prisoner asked another, a German woman: "Does Hitler take the land away from the peasants like they do here?") —How were they chosen? —By the "troika" system, apparently: one Party secretary, one local Soviet member, and one member of the secret police—a procedure which had been established and validated by Lenin's "de-Cossackization" of 1920. No doubt there remained some decent violence-minimizers, but they were outweighed by half-trained, ruthless enthusiasts, by careerists who knew that exceeding their quotas of victims would make them look good and by moderate professionals such as Belousov, drunken district Party committee chairman, who jumped upon a collective farm chairman, shook his revolver in his face and screamed obscenities at him. Thus the alliance with the peasantry. Belousov's treatment of *confirmed* class enemies can easily be imagined. And there were hundreds of thousands of Belousovs, who interpreted Stalin and Molotov's target figures as mere minimums: More than 381,000 households underwent the stripping process in 1930–31; by 1932, at least 1.4 million people had been deported.

Robert Conquest calculates that from 1929 through 1933, *10 to 12 million* kulaks were deported. About a third of them died in the process— usually the children. Refer back to the previous table if you wish, the table of comparative defenses against class enemies. The total dead (as opposed to the merely imprisoned, exiled, expropriated) from dekulakization itself he sets at 6.5 million, and the total dead from Stalin's collectivization policies of 1930–37 at 14.5 million. —This was all but an episode, of course. As I've said, Stalin must have killed at least 40 million people between 1929 and his death in 1953. When he passed on, Ukrainian peasants were still being rendered harmless in the Arctic. A Polish prisoner wonders: "But why had Soviet officers, interrogating seventeen-year-old girls, broken the girls' collarbones and kicked in their ribs with heavy military boots . . . ? They died with the medallions of the Virgin on their shattered chests, and with hatred in their eyes"—class hatred, no doubt; we never escape the thinking of our class, so they must have had it coming to them! And these crimes went on decade after decade. Solzhenitsyn describes how the wave of arrested kulaks "bypassed the prisons, going directly to the transit prisons and camps, onto prisoner transports, into the Gulag country . . . In sheer size . . . there was nothing to be compared with it in all Russian history."

What Is a Kulak Again?

"By 'kulak' we mean the carrier of certain political tendencies which are most frequently discernible in the subkulak, male and female."

"Philanthropy Is Evil"

And so we come once more to those photographs of roll call at the collective farm; of grain procurement brigades, grain spies, starving peasant children, cannibals. Faithfully, the activists followed Stalin's line. "Don't think of the kulak's hungry children," went one local directive; "in the class struggle, philanthropy is evil." Oh, yes, they were following

> The Marxist's Golden Rule: Do unto some others as you convince your-
> self they would be done by, and do to the rest whatever your end re-
> quires.

One easy, profitable trick was to assess huge taxes, and, if by some miracle the victims scraped together the cash to pay, to tax them again, right down to their clothes and samovars. When they couldn't pay anymore, the activists dekulakized them. That meant taking their houses, their last pot of porridge on the stove, everything, and then expelling them from the village, so that they became vagrants, exiles, factory workers without papers, prisoners or corpses. After all, how else could fledgling collectives compete with the bloodsuckers? Expropriate them! (Much of the spoils, of course, got kept by the spoilers.) "The women were sobbing—but were afraid to scream. The Party activists didn't give a damn about them. We drove them off like geese."

A certain district leader in the Urals would gather peasants together and say: "Those who are joining the *kolkhoz,* sign up with me; those who do not want to join, sign up with the police chief." And the police chief did his duty. (A peasant in Novgorod writes a relative: "They disenfranchised my brother Kolia, and on the night of March 28 somebody from the brigades drove up and took him from his house with his whole family to an unknown destination.") Another vanguardist burned the undecided with cigarettes, struck them, froze them. Others cut off men's beards and women's hair. Still others went in for revolver-waving. Presumably they had the same vision as Ostrovsky: the earnest mass meeting, the hands all shooting up, the Bolshevik voice announcing: "Unanimous."

By 1930 the aptly named "terror-famine" was in full swing. Agricultural production fell by 50 percent. Stalin himself drafted a law that anyone caught stealing grain from the collective farms would be shot. (Meanwhile, a woman submits a poster of "Stalin amongst the children," which gets rejected two times: "Not sufficiently benevolent." Finally she makes Stalin grin from ear to ear.)

242 WILLIAM T. VOLLMANN

"A Sort of Senseless, Crazy Peasant Strike"

As Bullock, Deutscher and others (including Stalin himself) have made clear, the purpose of this cruelty was not genocide in Hitler's sense but ruthless sovereignty, unbridled defense of class. Call it the dictatorship of the proletariat. No matter how obedient the Jews might have been, Hitler would have killed as many as he could. Stalin might not have been quite so vindictive, had the peasants become his good sheep. (In other words, he might have killed only thousands instead of millions. Poor peasants, at least, didn't have to be class enemies.) But sheep they were not. "Class-alien elements," defending their own alien class, refused to sow, especially in 1930–32. (Stalin's response: Take the seed grain, too, then. So what if those bloodsuckers have nothing to eat?) Bandits rose up in Siberia and the Don Cossack zone. One grain procurer concluded with reason that "everyone was a counterrevolutionary, and . . . the whole countryside was in full revolt against Moscow and Stalin." The great novelist A. Anatoli Kuznetsov recalls his father, a Party organizer, telling him that the peasants kept insisting: "Lenin promised us land; that was what the revolution was for." (Remember that land decree, the peasant-delegates "wild with joy"?) Kuznetsov's father went on: "They would keep repeating the same thing over and over again and wouldn't give in. It was a sort of senseless, crazy peasant strike, and there was nothing left to eat . . . " His father, of course, did his duty to Comrade Stalin. Starving, half-crazy peasants continued their struggle. In 1930, secret police statistics gave the figure of 13,754 "peasant disturbances" (not including four thousand acts of "terrorism")—an increase of ten times over the total for 1929.

CAUSES OF PEASANT REBELLIONS, 1930: OGPU STATISTICS

Collectivization	7,380	(54%)
Arrest/deportation	2,339	(17%)
Church closings	1,487	(11%)
Lack of food	1,220	(9%)
Confiscation of seed grain	544	(4%)
Requisitions of food	456	(3%)
Other	328	(2%)

Source: Graziosi, p. 52, citing Danilov and Berelowitch's compilation of secret police reports on peasant "moods."

The following year, the year of starvation, a full 40 percent of all collective farms in the USSR were attacked by bandits.

"The fact that the sabotage was quiet and overtly innocent," Stalin told Mikhail Sholokov, in one of his typical inversions, "does not change the position that the respected tillers of the soil in essence conducted a 'quiet' war against Soviet power. A war to starve us out, Comrade Sholokov." Defense of class demanded, then, that he starve *them* out. It was said that the peasant "wants the . . . grain to die in order to choke the Soviet government with the bony hand of famine. But the enemy miscalculates. We will show him what famine is." And they did. An official told his collective farmers: "If five people croak, that will teach you how to work, you idle bastards." That was in the Ukraine, where not five but five million peasants starved to death. (Ten years later, thanks to the Nazi occupation of the Ukraine, the Soviet Union would produce only a third of the grain it had in 1940—yet hunger was incomparably less severe than during the terror-famine of 1932.) Soldiers at the border stopped Ukrainians from going through to other republics where food might be found. A new law for that was already conveniently on the books: Just as in Tsarist days, travel was prohibited without an internal passport. Stalin and Trotsky's unauthorized biographer, Isaac Deutscher, happened to be traveling through the Ukraine at the time. One of his trainmates was a GPU colonel who cried out: "I am an old Bolshevik . . . Did I do all that in order that I should now surround villages with machine-guns and order my men to fire indiscriminately into crowds of peasants? Oh, no, no!" Oh, yes; this is class; this is not class; this is class.

In her study of collectivization, Sheila Fitzpatrick has written that in the 1930s

Decisiveness and a firm hand were highly valued . . . in many circumstances cadres in the countryside carried guns. Theirs was a harsh, frontier world where bandits—often dekulakized peasants hiding in the forests—were likely to take potshots at officials while sullen peasants looked the other way.

This was all straight out of Ostrovsky's novel.

Marx's slogan runs: *From each according to his ability, to each according to his needs.* Stalin rewrote it thus: *From each according to our requirements, to each according to how much we need them.* That is why the weak, the old, the sick got less than the strong, and died, and why the innocent who worked hard and produced well frequently also died. Who were the "best men"? The ones who were in Stalin's favor that day.

Calculations of Two Moral Scientists

As for Trotsky, that excellent schoolboy found the whole subject a bit awkward. Exiled now, hating, fearing and envying Stalin, he could argue that the dictator had handled matters badly, but not that he himself hadn't followed a similar line. Enough of his class-arrogant, class-vicious remarks about the peasantry have already been quoted. His magnum opus, *The History of the Russian Revolution,* published just as Stalin was decisively solving the agrarian question, maintained the same level of lethal abstraction against which Bakunin had once protested:

> In order to realize the Soviet state, there was required a drawing together and mutual penetration of two factors belonging to completely different historic species: a peasant war—that is, a movement characteristic of the dawn of bourgeois development—and a proletarian insurrection, the movement signalizing its decline. That is the essence of 1917.

His analysis of Stalin's famine follows logically from this premise. He couched his attack less in an ethical than an ad hominem form:

> To guard the nationalization of the means of production and of the land, is the bureaucracy's law of life and death, for those are the sources of its dominant position. That was the reason for its struggle against the kulak . . . The fight against the kulak . . . seemed to the workers . . . like the renaissance of the Dictatorship of the Proletariat. We warned them at the time: it is not only a question of what is being done, but also of who does it. Under conditions of Soviet democracy, i.e., self-rule of the toilers, the struggle against the kulaks might not have assumed such a convulsive, panicky and bestial form and might have led to a general rise of the economic and cultural level of the masses on the basis of industrialization.

In other words, under Trotsky it would have been good repression instead of bad repression. It would have happened more slowly. But Trotsky himself was never one for half measures.

And what did Stalin himself think about his famine? Given his secretiveness, we'll never know for certain, but, in Bullock's view, "economically it might be rated a disaster . . . but politically he saw it as representing a major victory," because the peasants could no longer thwart him. Publicly, he insisted that they were faking it: those kulak bastards were staging a hunger strike for propaganda purposes . . .

Solving the Agrarian Question
The moral calculus of Stalin, 1929–32

END: Eliminate all classes; build socialism.

MEANS: Govern the USSR through dictatorship of the proletariat.
  (a) Eliminate the power of the former possessing classes.
  (b) Ruthlessly control all economic and political activity.
  (c) Fill the power vacuum with Party cadres and proletarians.
  (d) Then let the dictatorship wither away.

JUSTIFICATION: Classes are inherently opposed. This opposition creates exploitation and violence. Defense of the emiserated classes demands the destruction of class.

END: Consolidate and expand my personal power without limit.

MEANS: Any and all.

JUSTIFICATION: None needed. My self-preservation is a factor.

Collectivization and dekulakization

IMMEDIATE ENDS:
  (a) Increase grain procurements.
  (b) Punish prior peasant resistance and prevent its recurrence.
  (c) Win the class war in the villages.
  (d) Socialize agriculture and discourage private property generally.

MEANS:

    (a) Increase procurements.

    (b) Exile, terrorize, monitor, liquidate.

    (c) Destroy the kulaks as a class.

    (d) Enroll the remaining peasants in collectives.

RESULTS:

1. Peasant uprisings, leading directly to

2. Decreased procurements and

3. Threats to my authority.

COUNTERMEASURES:

1. Increase the terror.

2. Increase procurements.

3. Take the seed grain. Starve them out.

JUSTIFICATION: None needed. Anybody who demands one is a class enemy.

Epitaph for Alexander Arkhipenkov

The injustice of the campaign against the kulaks lay in the failure to distinguish between unequal human capacity, unequal luck and unequal goodness. The seeming paradox of concentration camps, in which some prisoners get ground down and others elevated, despite the reduction of their personal effects to the equality of *almost*-nothingness, is explained by that "almost," by the very fact that because of proximity to absolute zero, inequalities almost indetectable to unreduced persons become decisive. An extra slice of bread or a way with words might save a prisoner. This is class. At Auschwitz, Primo Levi witnessed one strong man of crazed enthusiasms who on account of his muscle was promoted into a position of inaction, while other muscleless creatures worked themselves to death. Levi was forced to conclude that "to he that has, will be given; from he that has not, will be taken away." Difference cannot be eliminated. The "best men" are the born hunters. Moreover, among human beings the class relation can never be eradicated because *the power relation is indissoluble.* The presence or absence of that extra slice of bread defines us at certain moments. At other moments it doesn't. *Defense of class is unjustified when class is defined according to an inconsistent standard.* (This goes, of course, for defense of anything.) But that scarcely hindered the

Party activists, who were assigned their quotas of kulaks to uncover and repress. Should they fail, they themselves might be considered class enemies. On with the show!

"The young people on the collective farm in the village of Guta can barely remember the wealthy kulak Alexander Arkhipenkov," laughs an article in *Izvestiya*. "Arkhipenkov and his kulak brood are long gone from Guta; the waves of collectivization swept him up and bore him away from the village, never to return—he wouldn't dare!" Almost fifty years later, one reads in a tract called *The Soviet Way of Life*: "Such conceptions as 'poor peasant,' 'middle peasant,' and 'kulak,' which reflected the inevitable results of the isolated and individual life of peasants, have long been forgotten and lost in history." Arkhipenkov's "brood," then, is doomed to get "lost." No matter what they do, they will always be kulaks, just as in Hitler's Germany someone with a Jewish parent will always be a Jew. And *Izvestiya*'s gloating about that recalls Nietzsche's bitter epigram that "terrible experiences pose the riddle whether the person who has them is not terrible." Apparently *Izvestiya* thought so. No matter that Stalin himself had insisted that the son was not responsible for the father's sins! Stalin never let himself be hindered from punishing his enemies' sons . . . To have been born from the womb of a class enemy was to have been stained by original sin. (Perhaps every ideology requires a heaven and a hell.) Proof that Lenin and Stalin pulled us back into the Aristotelean age of natural slaves, the Roman age of Tacitus's "articles for use," is given by the case (one among many) of a man who, after waiting for days in "a small cramped and dirty hall smelling of fresh human sweat," finally learned that his mother, who'd been invited downtown by the NKVD for ten minutes, got an eight-year sentence for "concealing her social origins," about which she'd made no secret, and about which the NKVD has known for years. "Tears streamed down from her aged, wrinkled eyes," he wrote in his diary, "she had trouble getting the words out."

As for Citizen Arkhipenkov, he's sufficiently renowned to be punished not only for his origins but also for his last desperate achievement. Expelled to the forest, he manages over time to establish a new farm with six cows, three calves and a dozen pigs. To me this is a mark of enterprise. Here is somebody I would like to be in the forest with! To *Izvestiya* it just goes to show that he is an unregenerate exploiter. After all they've done to him, once again he owns more than the collective farmers! "These are not isolated cases," *Izvestiya* warns. Indeed they are not. Ask any prisoner who comes before a judge to petition for release and is told: "Refused, as a class alien."

Blessing Stalin's Name

"We did a pretty thorough job of carrying through collectivization," said Molotov in his twilight years. "I believe our success . . . was more significant than our victory in World War II . . . I personally designated districts where kulaks were to be removed . . . We exiled 400,000 kulaks. My commission did its job."

Stalin also used the Second World War as a basis for comparison, insisting that the struggle for collectivization had been even fiercer than the struggle against the Nazis (but this he said at the height of the battle for Stalingrad—which makes me think he said it to downplay current difficulties; why tell the truth when you can lie?). "It was all very bad and difficult— but necessary," he told Winston Churchill, who piously reflected for a moment upon the victims, then concluded with amazing naiveté: "A generation would no doubt come to whom their miseries were unknown, but it would be sure of having more to eat and bless Stalin's name."

THE TRIUMPH OF SOVIET AGRICULTURE

Statistics of the Ruling Class

"The farmers' general income has increased by twelve times" since Tsarism.

DATE	TYPE	COLLECTIVE FARM OUTPUT	HOME FARM OUTPUT
1937	Meat and dairy	<30%	70%+
(Capitalist	Produce	<50%	50%+
figures)			
1970	Meat and dairy	60%	40%
(Communist	Produce	70%+	"nearly 30%"
figures)			
	Commodities	86%	14%

That generation never arrived. As late as 1954, cattle and per capita grain production totals remained below what they had been before the revolution; and at the very end of the Soviet regime the situation improved to only the slightest extent. Why? Because politics got in the way of production.

Collectivization: The Experience

With their obligation of six days' unpaid labor every year, their other labor being miserably compensated as it was, and their liability to be abused verbally and physically by their overseers, who could arrest them, confiscate their property, fine them, et cetera, many peasants compared their situation to the bad old days of serfdom in the nineteenth century. (Molotov: "The fundamental principle of socialism [in contrast to capitalism] is fulfillment of norms of labor established by society.")

Throughout the 1930s, what little grain was available in the villages might never be ground, because it was difficult to find any millers, most of whom had been dekulakized. A full decade after Stalin's collectivization drive, by which time one might have expected conditions to be better, we find a Ukrainian describing his acquaintance thus: "Like all people who worked on the collective farms in the neighborhood, he had always turned up covered in mud and dressed in rags and tatters."

After it became clear that the kolkhozes were there to stay, however, resistance gave way to business. Hardheaded kolkhozniks realized that they might be able to keep themselves on the books of the collective farm by fulfilling the absolute minimum of labor-days, then spend the rest of their time at legal or black market wage labor. For a substantial minority, the minimum meant meant no labor-days at all.

COLLECTIVE FARMERS IN SOVIET AGRICULTURE

DATE	COLLECTIVE FARMERS	PRIVATE FARMERS
1917	0%	100%
1918	"a few hundred"	near 100%
1928	<2%	98%
1929	20%	80%
1930 (March)	50%	50%
1930 (May)	28%	72%
1930 (August)	21%	79%
1932	59%	39%
1933	55%	45%
1934	90%	10%
1937	>90%	7%
1950	(78m=39%)	61%
1970	99.86%	0.14%
1979	<40% (39 m)	>60%

NOTE: Some of these statistics lump collective farms in with the sovkhozes, or state farms, whose employees were often salaried and which produced directly for the government. Some do not. In her statistics for 1979, for instance, Fitzpatrick pegs collective farm membership at under 40 percent because a number of members had joined state farms instead. Between 1950 and 1980, the number of state farm workers increased by a factor of three and the number of collector farmers decreased by a factor of two (Fitzpatrick, p. 384, n. 22).

What was more, smart peasants began to realize how to work the institutional levers of coercion to their own benefit. Difficult individuals could always be gotten rid of by means of denunications. "It is hard not to feel that the Party, through its obsessive concern about kulaks, had become the peasants' patsy, being jerked and manipulated at will." Even some of the dekulakized got themselves back in the authorities' good graces to a sufficient extent to join the collectives. Many of the others (if they survived a round of mass murder in 1937) became good proletarians, in line with the growing urbanization of Russia, a trend entirely in the spirit of orthodox Marxism.

CLASS COMPOSITION OF THE USSR (1939–79)

DATE	POPULATION	URBAN	RURAL	AGRICULTURE	INDUSTRY
[1905	150 m			80%	20%]
1939	170.5 m	33%	66%		
1959	209 m	48%	52%	38.8%	60.3%
1966				24.6%	75.4%
1969				23.6%	76.4%
1970	241.7 m	56%	44%	21.6%	78.4%
1979	261 m	62%	38%		

From the end of World War II until Stalin's death in 1953, new grain procurements and taxes made the peasants' existence more miserable than at any time since the 1930s. (Meanwhile, as far away as Vietnam, a young recruit to the People's Army listened to his teachers tell "about Russia and the happy lives people led there and the social justice . . . Everyone wanted to become a Communist.") But in 1966 the kokholzniks were finally guaranteed a minimum wage. Literacy also increased dramatically in the rural areas. Collective farmers might occasionally get token consumer goods. Incompetence combined with sudden policy lurches created this official assessment from the late 1970s: "The fluctuation of manpower, which haunts some enterprises, means that there are people with no roots in the collective, no inward desire to work in the given collective, and not attached to it by creative or moral ties."

Collectivization: The Results

In 1961, Khrushchev's admittedly hostile English-langage editors noted that 9 percent of the American population produced agricultural surpluses, while 40 percent of the Soviet population produced too few crops. No doubt Khrushchev would have contested such figures, but I never remember hearing about the USSR selling grain to America. In 1974, Soviet statisticians admitted that uncollectivized agriculture still generated almost a third of the nation's produce and two-fifths of its meat and dairy output, but the official line still went: "As soon as the economic situation is ripe, home-farming will die out gradually without any need of compulsory or restrictive measures." This statement is a monument to stubborn blindness.

Following Lenin's tactic, Stalin had declared victory long before. There were no opposed classes anymore, the bureaucracy announced, merely functional castes as among the ants.

Everybody was equal. Chemoregulation, or at least Five Year Plans, did the rest. Citizen Arkhipenkov could no longer siphon off the surplus value.

"Act Like Bolsheviks Worthy of Comrade Stalin"

Were they just cynical loyalists? Maybe not. Arkhipenkov's persecutors must have been quite sure of themselves, one would think. So they were. As the secretary of the Union of Soviet Writers, a fellow who is known to have worked in a grain confiscation brigade noted about new people "raised up" by the Party: "It's hard to find the right words to express this confidence, but I'll try. It's a feeling of power, might, and serenity that comes from the realization that the mighty Soviet people, a hundred seventy million strong, is behind you." Joan of Arc, and those who burned her, could have said the same thing, substituting God for the Soviet people. They too were sure that they were right. And perhaps the secretary of the Union of Soviet Writers was right, too. Fourteen and a half million dead was less than 10 percent of the population . . . He could invoke the principle of proportionality: our violence is justified because it helps more people than it hurts. Besides, if one defines "people" properly—that is, as the group of human beings of one's own class origin, who share one's own doctrines—then confidence rises even more. When Milovan Djilas asked Stalin what the difference was between a people and a nation, the latter replied: " 'Nation?' You already know what it is: the product of capitalism with given characteristics. And 'people'—these are the workingmen of a given nation, that is, workingmen of the same language, culture, customs." Evidently, those who were not workingmen were not people. (A Roman slave at least stood a chance of being freed on the basis of loyal service. He stood a chance of being reclassified as a person.) Yes, confidence undoubtedly helped, especially when it was developed to the point of unflinching righteousness. The well-fed activists received directives on the spirit with which they were to expropriate the starving:

> Throw your bourgeois humanitarianism out the window and act like Bolsheviks worthy of Comrade Stalin. Beat down the kulak agent wherever he raises his head . . . Your job is to get the grain at any price. Pump it out of them, wherever it is hidden . . . *Don't be afraid of taking extreme measures*. The Party stands four-square behind you. Comrade Stalin expects it of you.

CLASS EGALITARIANISM IN THE SOVIET UNION AFTER STALIN

The Official View

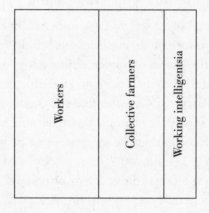

Source: Barghoorn, p. 48

Did Ostrovsky, lying blind and paralyzed on his deathbed, have any conception of what this rhetoric, which was his own, meant when applied to civilians? Quote his novel again: "They'll hide whatever they've got. In that case we'll make searches and confiscate the bloodsuckers' goods. This is no time for niceties." Did he know? For him as for Stalin, was it all worth it?

Origin

Assume for the moment that we are Bolsheviks whose hearts are steel as well tempered as those of Ostrovsky's heroes, that with our guns, grain bags, directives and Party cards we stand fully encouraged and empowered to liquidate the enemies of our class. Assume further that we feel justified in doing so. The question arises: Who are our enemies? Or, to reopen a sour can of worms, what exactly is class?

Bring that Athenian defendant back to the bar. Remember him? He was the one who'd whined: "I feel indignation, gentlemen, if on account of a mere prostitute slave-woman I find myself faced with the danger of losing all that is most dear." But the revolution broke out, and we won. We unshackle his slave girl and tell her: "Don't worry. No one's going to torture you. No one will ever be able to own you again."

Now for the master himself. What is his origin? He must be a *thete* or a *zeugatai*—a member of one of the poorer propertied classes—because he had to go halves with another man in order to own her, but he *could* own her. In other words, he's a kulak. Very good. Eliminate the *thetes,* the *zeugatais* and every class above them. Take their farms away; assign everybody to collective farms—masters and slave girls alike. (The slaves will probably do a better job, hence gain prestige like the Algonquin Indian "best men"; after all, they have lifelong experience.) Strip the fine clothes from the rich; make everyone wear the same factory-issue clothes. Aren't we finished? There are no classes anymore, right?

But what about the habits of thought (to say nothing of the superior entrepreneurial expertise) of the "former possessing classes"? They have experience, too—managerial experience. They'll find some way of getting their farms back if we don't watch them. Soon they'll be owning slave girls again. Worse yet, won't they pass those bloodsucking characteristics on to their children, through exhortation and example? —Well, take their children away! We'll bring them up ourselves . . . —But what if their characters were already formed? Then we'll just have to *settle accounts* with them, too (Nazis and Soviets both used that phrase). That's why the Leninists killed not only the abdicated Tsar but his wife, children, servants and even his pets. In North Vietnam, the son of a deputy village chief (who'd died when the boy was four) finds himself ominously classed as a "middle farmer element." A young girl from the same country tells us: "Like most children I wanted to go to the university so that I could have a good profession. But I belonged to a petit bourgeois family, so I knew I didn't have a chance." And because she didn't have a chance, all the more reason to spy on her, in case her resentment transformed her into an enemy of the people! (As Lucan so wisely remarked, "the poverty of slaves is dangerous not to themselves but to their master.") A Chinese factory executive, caught in the Cultural Revolution, prudently resigns and becomes a coolie, explaining to the Party Secretary that "my class status as a former capitalist rendered me unsuitable for a responsible executive position." *Defense of class is unjustified when it defines class solely in terms of origin.*

When some people are permitted what others are prohibited, solely on the basis of their possessions or social profile, then the class lines might have been drawn unjustly—not always, mind you, for we have no business meddling with, say, a closed, hereditary shaman class if the society which supports its existence is satisfied. Defenders of class privilege argue, by spurious reference to the ant model, that their kind performs functions for which privilege is merely a tool. And in a shaman's case (let's say that he needs to eat taboo foods in order to perform his rituals), or a general's, a policeman's, a Philosopher-King's, that argument might be justified. Hence Gibbon's notion, not far removed from that of the pimp or Mafia salesman of "protection," that armed and politically organized nobles form the best check against monarchical despotism. Indeed, he goes further:

> The superior prerogative of birth, when it has obtained the sanction of time and popular opinion, is the plainest and least invidious of all distinctions among mankind. The acknowledged right extinguishes the hopes of faction, and the conscious security disarms the cruelty of monarchs.

Recast hopes and opinions in biochemical terms, and those lines will certainly apply to the ants. But Gibbon's own tale, with its emphasis on the horrific accidents of royal personalities, condemns his claim of noninvidiousness. So too the tale of Lenin and Stalin. The ant queen's nestmates become her captives; whether she nourishes them tenderly or devours them, they have no say. In consequence, what she may consider a social contract may be renounced by slaves maddened to exasperation.

Then come faction's hopes, and insecurity's countercruelty.

Zapatistas and Bureaucrats

Another way of framing the same accusation is to say that the crime of Stalinist mercilessness was directed not only against individuals but against the civic bond itself. It need not have been. In the Mexican state of Morelos, for instance, we find the dour, beloved provincial revolutionary

Emiliano Zapata. It is one year before the Russian Revolution. Zapata had insisted with crazy or admirable fanaticism on his *Plan de Ayala,* which expropriated a third of the monopoly landlords' holdings with compensation. Now he leads a guerrilla war against the federal forces, the so-called Constitutionalists, who, even if they don't want to bring back the era of untrammeled haciendas which choked off pueblos' water and grazing rights, still crave accommodation with capital. Zapata will have none of it. He's out there defending class. But in spite of Zapatista rhetoric that the landlords deserve "war to the death," he does not stand them up against the wall. The people of Morelos idolize him; he'll die for them soon. He insists that "municipal liberty is the first and most important of democratic institutions." The pueblos of Mexico, like the mir of old Russia, are both sovereign and approximately fair. Chosen by those pueblos' elders, Zapata seeks to respect them. Like Stalin, he takes origins into his calculations. But what kind of revolutionary is this? He leaves it to them to decide whether their land will be parcelled out among individual farmers or held in common. To him, origin is not a stain but a reality, a working arrangement. If the elders are satisfied, then so are the people; so is he. His surveyors try to solve border disputes between villages; his guerrilla militias include local elders in their chain of command. He comes from the pueblos, owes his power to them and governs in their name.

Whom Was It For?

The Stalinists, on the other hand, might have come from the people, but they remained decidedly not *of* them. My Spartacist-Trotskyist acquaintances always used to refer to the Soviet Union as a "bureaucratically deformed worker's state," which is putting it charitably. Seven years after Stalin, strangling from a cerebral hemorrhage, black in the face, raised his left hand with what seemed to his daughter to be "a curse upon us all," fell back in his bed and died, the composition of the "party of the working class" represented his priorities all too well:

THE TRIUMPH OF THE BUREAUCRATS
Chances of Joining the Party in 1960:

 Collective farmer: 1 (index value)

 Blue-collar worker: 2

 White-collar worker: 6–7

By the time the Soviet Union fell apart, the Party would hardly have passed the test of origin which it had imposed on others for so many decades. —"But we're not *capitalist* officials, we're *people's* officials, antfunctionalist bureaucrats!" —All right, but ants keep nothing. How much did you take? How much did you share?

Lycurgus the Leveler

Consider now a parable. My *Oxford Classical Dictionary* informs me that our protagonist, Lycurgus, may have been either "purely legendary" or else "a historical person subsequently invoked as a charter for the [Spartan] regime." He has no face anymore, and his voice, his character, his very doings were carefully given an antique luster by the commentators who (socialist realists of another order) appropriated him in order to score moral points and titillate patrician collectors of curiosities. In short, he bears a distant kinship to the hero of Ostrovsky's novel. Never mind: After so many centuries, his existence has become far less important than his example.

Imagine a moral actor who unlike Stalin actually had a mandate to change society. (More likely, Lycurgus simply happened to be on the winning side of the class war between traditional elitism and helot egalitarianism.) Imagine further that he followed the ideals of justice, as Stalin professed to do, and that he desired no power for himself. Rousseau supposes him to have abdicated his royalty, in order to preserve the division between legislative and executive powers. His soul was so generous that the sacred oracle at Delphi called him godlike. (Eleventh in descent after Hercules, hence literally deserving of Delphi's appellation, he is said to have established the Olympic Games—twin tokens of his worthiness. Thus his class basis consisted of *origin* and *prestige*.) Harmed in an assassination plot, he took his would-be murderer in and made him a friend, a supporter, above all, a *citizen*. Imagine Lycurgus as a revolutionary of sorts, a lover of liberty. Herodotus tells us how he helped expel the tyrant Pisitratus from Athens. In short, he was sufficiently noble, powerful and respected to address the issue of class warfare *without coercion*. Unlike Lenin and Stalin, he enjoyed the luxury of justified methods.

The Orchard Keeper and the Ant Queen

How could he proceed? Well, I can think of two fair ways to nurture equality (which is the goal of the class struggle—well, isn't it?): (1) to redistribute wealth and status *periodically* but leniently, perhaps rewarding the surplus-producers with a little something; or (2) to *continually* monitor and prevent any unauthorized accruals on anyone's part, hopefully acting in a mechanistic rather than a punitive way. In the former case, recommended by Plato, a kulak who'd gained ten cows when everyone else had one would be entitled to keep between two and nine, depending upon authority's moral and expedient calculus. Thus the procedure of the mixed-capitalist welfare state, which taxes the rich heavily enough to gain good harvest, but lightly enough (ideally) to encourage them to continue to produce surplus value. Accordingly, this procedure will not abolish class divisions but mitigate them.

In the other case, the rich kulak's entire surplus would be confiscated, leaving him with a single cow like everyone else (not, as under Stalin, with no cow at all). But perhaps some ephor or district party chairman would present him with a laurel wreath or a Stakhanovite medal stamped out of tin . . .

Call these two choices the strategy of the orchard keeper, who plucks ripe fruits from time to time but leaves enough for seed; and the strategy of the ant queen, who brings production and consumption into equilibrium. The former would merely *constrain* inequality within certain limits hopefully humane both to the expropriated and to the poor; the latter would approach perfect equality, presumably at the expense of productivity. As a worst case of that, remember the collective farmers' laziness and despair. As a better case, consider:

The Utopia of Sparta

Now for the constitutional solution of Lycurgus, who, having sifted among the laws of Cretans, Ionians and Egyptians in his exile, returned home to enforce the most rigorous equality, first by creating a senate to help the king "resist democracy"—that is, mob tyranny—while simultaneously resisting despotism. "The commons have the final voice and decision." To this system, which embodies some notion of separation of powers, he added this clause worthy of Stalin: "That if the people decide crookedly, it should be lawful for the elders and leaders to dismiss" their assembly.

Equality of Property

Next Lycurgus subdivided the country into thirty-nine thousand equal lots of just sufficient size to maintain each family in grain, oil and wine.

The first Soviet collectivizers literally sowed disaster when they too imposed upon the countryside that grid of equal squares in revolutionary disregard for topography; but let us for the sake of argument suppose that the Spartan lands were homogenously rich—rich they certainly were. Plutarch tells us that at harvest time, "seeing the stacks standing equal and alike, he smiled and said to those about him, 'Methinks all Laconia looks like one family estate just divided among a number of brothers.' " —And of sisters, too, we might add; misogynistic Aristotle writes sourly that even as late as historical times, Lycurgus being long vanished into moonbeams, Spartan women still owned two-fifths of the land.

Lycurgus now bans spoliation in war, so that no one might become rich. He obliterates dowries, for the admirable reason "that none should be left unmarried because of poverty nor any pursued for their wealth, but that each man should study the girl's character and make his choice on the basis of her good qualities." As for dress, "the rich [shall] do their best to assimilate their way of life to that of the poor."

Like the Bolsheviks, he realized that kulaks and hoarders had not yet been defeated; so he replaced the gold and silver currency by iron, of so little worth that an oxenload of it would hardly suffice to buy anything. (Lenin, we're told, vented a cynical laugh when during the Civil War he forced his hated peasants to exchange grain for worthless government scrip. Meanwhile, in the Weimar Republic to his west, Germans trundled wheelbarrow loads of inflated currency to purchase their necessities. Savings and pensions were destroyed. Thousands starved, robbed, committed suicide.) The Lycurgan argument runs: "Who would rob another of such a coin? Who would unjustly detain or take by force, or accept as a bribe, a thing which it was not easy to hide . . . ?" The answer, of course, is: No one. They'll steal your jewelry instead! Foreseeing such eventualities, omniscient Lycurgus proceeded logically to the next step: "an outlawry of all needless and superfluous arts." For class, as we must keep reminding ourselves, is *relative*, at least once everyone has enough to eat. So away with all the silversmiths, fortune-tellers and harlot-mongers! Moreover, to the extent that class constitutes itself along ant-functional lines, what need had the Spartans for functionlessness? (Pol Pot agreed.) So there'd be no more monkey-shaped scent bottles, no ivory combs and reliefs of sterotyped mythic scenes, no bronze mirrors whose frames incorporated naked girls. (All these our archaeologists have found in the dust of dead Sparta—but from before or after Lycurgus who's to say?) Who could pay craftsmen now anyway? Why would they trade bronze mirrors for iron? Why steal when your neighbor had exactly what you did? We are back in the longhouses of the Huron Indians.

And in direct consequence of this new law, as if to prove the doctrine of socialism in one country by means of a wavy parallel, Sparta developed her own handicrafts of sober excellence: "Their cup, particularly, was very much in fashion, and eagerly bought up by soldiers, for its color was such as to prevent water, drunk upon necessity and disagreeable to look at, from being noticed; and the shape of it was such that the mud stuck to the sides, so that only the purer part came to the drinker's mouth. For this, also, they had to thank their lawgiver, who, by relieving the artisans of the trouble of making useless things, set them to show their skill in giving beauty to those of daily and indispensable use."

Equality of Austerity and Prowess

After presiding over the birth of that mud-colored cup, which would constitute a fitting metonym for any regime of workers' and peasants' austerity, Lycurgus next required his citizens to eat in common, in associations of about fifteen, so that those spiritual kulaks known as sumptuous diners would be seen and scorned for their effeminacy. "This would reduce to a minimum disobedience of orders." Every citizen contributed his share to the meal. Thus they supported and entertained one another. Their evening repast finished, they'd go home without torches, "that they might accustom themselves to march boldly in the dark," and visit their wives—who, of course, did not qualify to be full citizens.

Equality of Gender

Indeed, like servants, horses and hunting dogs, women might be loaned out—not habitually, as in Plato's utopia, but rather as occasion dictated, to worthy men who needed sons and might bluntly ask the husband's connivance. And yet we ought not to conclude from this that Spartan women lacked spirit and influence. Other Greeks were appalled by them because they, like the males, competed naked in public athletic contests. (In fact, virtually the only archaic Greek artistic representations of unclothed females come from Sparta.) We see a bronze figure, popularly called "the runner" but believed to represent a dancer: lithe and slender, she crouches on the balls of her feet, gripping the hem of her short tunic, her braided head facing backward, her elbows at the ready like weapons.

She personifies elegant alertness, combining femininity with pride. Several Spartan women are reputed to have won the Olympics in horse racing. Gorgo, wife of Thermopylae's doomed defender King Leonidas, watches a foreigner loll at ease while being shod by slaves. She makes a class-conscious quip worthy of Lycurgus: "Father, the stranger has no hands." An Attic woman asks her why Spartan women are the only ones who can rule men, and she replies proudly: "Because we are also the only ones who give birth to men." They also destroy them. We're always reading that some Spartan woman or other has killed her son or disowned him for being a coward in war.

Equality of Origin

What followed from the Spartan birthing process? Children became the property of the state to a far greater degree than of their mothers. Unpromising babies simply got hurled over a cliff. The survivors enrolled into bands where, unwashed and underfed, they slept outdoors, encouraged to steal nourishment to develop their mettle, on the understanding that they'd be whipped if they were caught—a procedure perhaps more ethically worthy of the Ik tribe than of a nation of sincere and honest men; but, like the custom of walking home at night without torches, it certainly contributed to the military virtues of initiative, craft and stoicism. (A subsequent Spartan king put some prisoners of war on the slave block stripped naked, with the desired result that their white and flaccid bodies were despised. Contempt for pleasure, and for its effect on the body, became a Spartan virtue.) In hoplite warfare, he who downs his shield and runs imperils the entire line; the best security in battle is unbrokenness. Accordingly, the ability to hold fast and endure punishment is privileged among the Spartan virtues. "I myself," glowingly remarks our author, "have seen several of the youths endure whipping to death." Any man could discipline any child; and, should a boy complain to his father that another adult had beaten him, "then it is a disgrace if the father does not give his son a further beating." Such was the life of the youths. Aristotle thought that their elders treated them like animals.

Those who did well must surely have been strong and proud, like Huron warriors. I can well believe Thucydides' report that when Athenian troops first set out against the Spartans in the Peloponnesian War, they suffered "slavish dismay at the idea of attacking Spartans." It may be worth remarking that of the many, many lead-cast votive figurines which archaeologists have picked out of Sparta's soil, the most frequent human representation, the mass-market ideal, is of the hoplite soldier.

We see a crude, squat bronze figure, his legs braced, his shield held almost at a horizontal against his breast, as if the edge were a weapon; his right hand is raised, clenched possibly around a stone or the haft of a spear broken off the statuette; and beneath his helmet he scowls: unhandsome, ungraceful, formidable—the hoplite ranksman, the common soldier.

Inequality of Rank

And his commander? The Spartans have left us a representation of him, too. In his parade dress, narrow-hipped, slender-waisted, corseleted and greaved, he stands beneath a tall plume which hangs over his forehead, runs over his skull-styled helmet in a fringed ridgetop, then crawls down between the shoulder blades while the man gazes straight ahead, confident, invincible. He's certainly of another class. If one of equality's defining virtues is equal obedience, how can it be otherwise? Shall we add that the Spartans (as Stalin essentially did) set up a shrine to Fear, because by it more than anything a state was held together?

Equality of Virtue

All these laws Lycurgus refused to write down (another Stalinist touch)—in order, says Plutarch, to better engrave them in the citizens' hearts.

His work was now finished; and, "being consulted how they might best oppose an invasion of their enemies, he returned this answer, 'By continuing poor, and not coveting each man to be greater than his fellow.'"

Lycurgus and the Kulaks

I see him as realistically benign—or, one might say, a hard man for hard times, but not unnecessarily hard. Spartan kings enjoyed the power of life and death only in combat; even there, disobedience was not unheard of. The Spartans generally had two kings at once, whose natural rivalry offered a sort of checks-and-balances system. Beyond that, unanimity of opinion was the polity's best safeguard. To Lycurgus, even functional specialization, no matter how useful it might be to the ants, remained suspect, a menace to equality. (The Delphic oracle had warned him that "greed for money and nothing else will destroy Sparta.") Therefore, all citizens had to do the same things, live the same sort of life—which implied that anything not everybody could do shouldn't be done at all, with the extremely important exception of kingship. Here is Lycurgus's haunting answer to those who wanted to establish democracy: "Begin, friend, and set it up in your family." The implication is that within the civic or national family there exists at all times a mass of individuals at different stages of capacity and development; and this we know to be true. (We see the five-year-old Spartan children beginning to learn the Pyrrhic dances, employing fennel stalks as they soon will be employing spears—drilling for war, in short. They must submit to the authority which drills them.)

The solution of Lycurgus to the human problem is to impose a super-consistent grid of law, authority and esprit de corps, leaving every citizen's political self within an equal cell of powers and constraints. Defense of authority, ground, homeland and honor will all be the same. It is, in many respects, an attractive and admirable vision, rigid only in order to be fair, productive of discipline, bravery and hardihood. When asked how much wine to serve, a Spartan king replies: "If plenty of wine has been provided, then as much as each requests; but if there is only a little, then give everyone an equal amount." This is the textbook Communist solution. It would be my solution.

"You Get Nothing for Your Work"

Equal levels in the wine cups are one thing, but Sparta begins to sound stultifying, like an eternal army barracks in which the majority of the things I love to do would be forbidden. Moreover, Lycurgus's equality and refinement of soldierliness becomes possible only through the sullen labor of helot slaves. (In Stalin's USSR, most people were helots, but the majority, who didn't constitute class enemies, were supposed to like it, because they were somehow working for themselves.) "It is confessed, on all hands, that the Spartans dealt with them very harshly," says Plutarch, who ventures to hope that this was not Lycurgus's doing but somebody's later strategem of counterinsurgency, following the helots' massive, doomed Messenian Revolt. Until then, it seems, the helots were not full serfs but merely conquered tenant farmers, which seems quite bad enough.

A Spartan king, come to sacrifice to the gods in Messenia, meets assassination at the hands of helot revolutionaries. Time for defense of class! "They shall fall back shattered before the destruction while struck by great boulders," exhorts an orator on the masters' side. "Their bronze helmets will ring." It will take two decades, however, before he can be vindicated by the rout of the Messenians. (The ferocity of the struggle may be imagined: Strabo remarks that Spartans who failed to fight were themselves reduced to helotry; and from the sons born during that time citizenship was withheld, they being called "sons of concubines.") But it was all worthwhile, for the Messenian farmland was now in Spartan hands.

Toward the helots themselves, who were forced even to mourn for the Spartan dead, punitive expediency grew into established usage and even ritual: Each new ephor, or magistrate, upon entering his office would renew a solemn declaration of war against the helots—what a parable for Marxists!—and "the ablest of the young men," by which I suppose is meant the most brilliantly aggressive, were sent every now and then to randomly assassinate helots by night or cut them down in the fields as they went about their day work.

Observing his own class sympathies, Aristotle deplores the frequency with which "helots attack the Spartans, always on the look-out for any mischance that may befall their masters." "One should also be very clear," says Xenophon, "that the practices of always walking about with spear in hand and of keeping the slaves away from weapons both have an identical purpose."

"They went to war several times because of the Messenian revolts," writes Strabo. That statement alone crushingly indicts the Lycurgan paradigm.

We are left with the melancholy question: Can true equality exist without declaring war against helots and kulaks? Or would the final victory of the industrial revolution in Russia have removed the necessity for serfdom; will future Spartans command robots instead of helots? —Necessity may or may not disappear, depending on techno-economics; but what will dispel the fear and retributive lust of the masters? "Oh, it's not easy on the collective farm," sighs an old peasant woman in a black shawl. "You get nothing for your work, there's nothing to wear, nothing to eat, everyone is just crushed." Beside her testimony I place this line out of Tyrtaeus, who describes the helots as "like asses worn down by great burdens, / bringing to their masters out of grievous necessity / the half of all the crop the tilled land bears."

The parable becomes more pointed. They made them wear dogskin caps in order to humiliate them, says Athenaeus. (This is relative poverty.) They awarded them "a stipulated number of blows every year apart from any wrongdoing so that they would never forget that they were slaves. In addition, if any exceeded the vigor proper to a slave's condition, they made death the penalty; and they assigned a punishment to their owners if they did not rebuke those who were growing fat." These words afflict me with eeriness, because they describe so well what Stalin did to the kulaks.

Specialization Versus Interdependence

Very well. Imagine Lycurgus's republic modified. We'll *all* be citizens— men and women, Spartans and helots. As in Pancho Villa's ideal Mexico, let's make everyone a collective farmer, a soldier and a voter. In our dinner groups of fifteen, we'll decide whether to invest our surplus value in newer tractors, save it, expend it on leisure time or trade it for the products of the tailors' and dressmakers' collective across the river. The efficiency of petrochemicals allows us to work less without helotizing anyone—and to hold more great debates, more martial athletic contests.

Every now and then a tractor will break, and most of us won't know how to fix it. How could we, given our many other duties? —Two choices: train some of us to be mechanics, or else pay surplus value to the mechanics' collective. The same principle applies to doctors, entertainers, cobblers.

To the extent that we depend on others, we wound self-sufficiency. Cosmopolitanism of any sort holds our autarky hostage. But to the extent that we depend on ourselves, we introduce creeping functionalism, which even Lycurgus couldn't get away from; he merely defined it away by decreeing that certain specialists (farmers and child-bearers) weren't citizens, and others (generals and kings) were mega-citizens. The result, despite his best efforts: three classes. Not liking this dilemma, we may choose to renounce all unneeded, post-Lycurgan specialization. The women will spin flax for our clothes. (Even this concession to enfranchised egalitarianism is radical: "But then how should girls brought up like this be expected to bear any strapping babies?" demands an admirer of the Spartan ideal. "In Lycurgus's view . . . clothes could be produced quite adequately by slave women.") The men will bring in grain and herd the cattle. Folk medicine will make us all doctors, as in Pol Pot's Cambodia (where medicine was administered by illiterate teenaged cadres, and the patients needlessly died).

Electricity, internal combustion engines, gunpowder and steel? Banned. No tractors after all! We'll retain our self-sufficient equality. Of course, when Hitler arrives with his tanks and dive-bombers, we'll become slaves. How now, defense of class?

Feeler-Taps and Gendarmes

To guard local equality (which is to say, to guard ourselves), we'll need to achieve a parity of force with the worldwide level, or else do better. One means to that subsidiary end would be to transform ourselves into a fierce, adept and dedicated weaponsmakers' collective, then take over the world to gain our oil, grain, land—in other words, to become Hitler. (In a sense, Sparta followed this path by winning the Peloponnesian War. Then better weapons makers came.) Such a course immediately introduces class differentiation all over again: us, and the conquered.

The only other possible solution is to accept specialization.

Who made those mud-colored cups, anyway? Surely not the citizen-soldiers, who were busy marching in the dark. And, in fact, we find in Sparta a group called the *perioeci,* who enjoyed some autonomy as long as they fought on command—and, more relevantly, as long as they did artisans' work. —Another class!

Well, then, shall we all become perioeci? Assume that economies of scale and technological efficiency empower everyone to work half-weeks; assume also, as Stalinists refused to do on the collective farms, that the half-week of a nurse, a farmer, a nursing mother, a general, a prostitute, a gunsmith and a garbage collector shall be counted as equal. Assume further that the other half-week can be devoted to civic duties and functions, duly subcommitteed by our associations of fifteen. We can still return home without torches, and loan each other our horses and hunting dogs. But our athletic contests must dwindle in inclusiveness, because the gunsmith won't have the physique of the garbage collector. —No matter what Plutarch says, I don't believe that it was entirely otherwise even in the days of Lycurgus. Consider that bronze Dodona figure found by those representatives of futurity, those antitheses of gravediggers, known as archaeologists. We see a man—a hoplite. His face is weathered, perhaps from centuries of interment, perhaps because war and austerity grizzled him in life. Old and grave, his face constrained as usual to skullishness by the helmet, his hair in six braided tresses, he grips pieces of shield and spear, but time's vandals have broken the rest off. The reason that he expresses and personifies hopliteness instead of mere humanness is because the majority resembles him neither in training nor in inborn physique. Recall the anatomically divergent castes of the ants. How could it be otherwise? Drill your doctor day and night, and where will he find time to learn his science? Some people will never be good soldiers anyway. (This is class.)

The more we specialize, the more indebted we'll become to oversight and coordination. When Socrates suggested that the happiest souls include those who will become social insects in the next life, he meant that the anthill's members *by nature* regulated *themselves,* just as his ideal of a virtuous citizen or polity would do. Lenin (whom we now know, ironically enough, to have been a hereditary noble) hoped likewise that the day of ants and bees would come, that classless day when police are no longer needed, and the citizens take turns spying on and punishing one another. Ants accomplish exactly this with their feeler-taps and their constant sniffing of each other's odors; strange ants, alien and unsocial elements, get expelled from the nest or liquidated. Suppose we try to regulate ourselves. My farming collective needs twenty new hoes. Someone will have to inform the blacksmiths, who in turn must contact the miners. Enter the bureaucrats, since I don't sit next to any miners at dinner. And how can I know whether the miners are working as hard and well at refining ore as I am at planting cabbages? The bureaucrats know. Knowledge is power, runs the proverb. Watch them become the master class. After all, when they uncover deficiencies and transgressions, won't they need a secular arm to enforce equality's laws? Don't we need roving secret police to ensure that nobody has started hoarding surplus value for personal enrichment? Unless they are thwarted, intelligent, industrious peasants tend to become kulaks, just like Citizen Arkhipenkov. Lenin knew that, and said it in so many words. Thus too with everyone else—including Lenin. "The communists will never be able to eliminate classes and achieve perfect equality as they have proclaimed," wrote a disgruntled Vietnamese in the 1980s. "The one endeavor left for everybody is to hustle and eke out a livelihood less wretched than that of his or her neighbor." Even if "everybody" doesn't act that way, the secret police will. That is why in the Soviet Union high Party officials and their like "went around in official cars, pampered their bodies at Caucasian health resorts, and regularly received secret supplements to their pay . . . For his frightful job of crawling around inside the drains my grandfather received a monthly salary which was only half the price of a cheap suit of clothes."

The Oracle's Curse

Hence Aristotle: "And so a state of affairs has come about which is just the opposite of the happy conditions envisaged by Lycurgus: he has produced a city which has no money but is full of citizens eager to make money for themselves."

The application of unequal ability to equal *or* unequal spheres of production *must* in the long run make for unequal results. Corporations, governments and religions seek monopolies, large estates have a tendency to get larger, and as each of these entities grows, it gains increasing power to preserve and enlarge itself—maybe not forever, since all things do pass (in medieval France, noble families kept their power for half a dozen generations or less), but certainly long enough to effect good and evil before the next wave of power rises up in an irresistible typhoon. —Again, make an analogy with ant society: Large eggs are most likely to become queens. And the others? Consider the lactating women in medieval and modern Europe who were "literally owned by wealthy families," who rented them out either as whores or wet nurses. People are selfish, or at least self-interested. The Delphic oracle meant just that when it warned Lycurgus that greed for gold would destroy Sparta; and, indeed, we read that when in due course the Arcadians, with whom the Spartans had deposited their silver and gold to keep it from corrupting their own city-state, became foes, that treasure had to be imported into Sparta—whereupon it immediately became subject to embezzlement. Aristotle informs us that the Sparta of his day was as full of bribery, illegality and hypocrisy as any other place, in part because Lycurgus's standard had simply been set too high, "so high indeed that they really cannot live up to it but secretly get round the law and enjoy the more sensual pleasures." The Spartan poet Alcman, though he prefers lentil soup, sustenance of commoners, bears witness to "seven couches and as many tables crowned with poppy-seed loaves and linseed and sesame, and among the cups dishes of honeycake." Meanwhile, a new Spartan elite swallows up most of the land; Lycurgus's equal plots have vanished with Lycurgus.

Well, then, in the interest of equality, which do we prefer—secret police, or blind chemoregulation? Or shall we simply say that complete and utter equality is poison?

We don't want to say that. Then we'll have to keep the kulaks down. There's no other way.

Stalin's Vindication

"Since today the Spartan domination is no more," says Aristotle, "it is clear that they are not a happy and prosperous people, and their lawgiver was wrong." And, indeed, Plutarch himself, in another one of his *Lives,* tells how an idealistic young Spartan king who sought to bring back the constitution of Lycurgus was tricked and strangled by the rich.

The Countess and the Clay-Eater

If total equality is impractical and perhaps evil, then don't the upper classes (or, as mass revolutionaries might say, the exploiting classes) have the right to defend themselves, too? Surely most kulaks possessed that right. If what defines a class as such—the underpinnings of its culture, if you like—are its privileges, and if these privileges are not innocuous ones (such as the exclusive right of the priestly class to say Mass), but measurable material and social benefits (property, rank, prestige, above all *power)* whose bestowal correspondingly impoverishes the unprivileged, then may that master class justly use violence nonetheless to ward off threats to its interest?

Marx addressed precisely this issue in the *Communist Manifesto.* His answer, of course, was no. (With reservations, I agree.) Turning then to the property of kulaks, he remarked:

> We Communists have been reproached with the desire of abolishing the right of personally acquiring property as the fruit of a man's own labor, which property is alleged to be the groundwork of all personal freedom, activity, and independence.
>
> Hard-won, self-acquired, self-earned property! Do you mean the property of the petty artisan and of the small peasant, a form of property that preceded the bourgeois form? There is no need to abolish that; the development of industry has to a great extent already destroyed it, and it is still destroying it daily.

That was how he answered—not with any justification but with that chilling jeer. We search the manifesto's pages in vain for any discussion as to whether or why peasant property *should* be destroyed. To him, the matter was obvious. In his essay "On the Jewish Question" (1843) he explains that the so-called rights of man aren't the rights of citizens in civil society but the selfish, egotistical rights of atoms, "namely, that each man shall without discrimination be treated as a self-sufficient monad." This is a breathtakingly revolutionary conception—breathtaking not only in its fearless reenvisioning of the social contract but also necessarily in its cruelty. He does not prove his case, because it cannot be proved. The fundamental ethical issue of defense of class remains this: When am I justified in guarding and preserving what I have, and when are you, who have less, justified in acting (violently, if necessary) to assure yourself an equal chance to possess, preserve, command, enjoy and guard?

Toward a Calculus of Class

The ethical question of this chapter is enormously complicated by the fact that there are more kinds of class than there are of, say, honor, and that these create grossly different entitlements, necessities and imminences, both real and spurious. Here is the best that I can do:

VIOLENT DEFENSE OF CLASS IS JUSTIFIED:

1. When it is truly defense against the exactions, impoverishments, oppressions and humiliations imposed by other classes—not proactive self-defense.

2. When it is directed against class structures and their active or official representatives, not against individuals who happen to be members of opposed classes only passively, through biological or social accident.

3. When class equals function or status by function, and when that function is essential as the society is currently constituted. For example, in a precontact indigenous band, violent discrimination against old or otherwise unfit people by the hunters, the "best men," may be justifiable if doing otherwise would harm the hunter class which feeds everyone else.

4. When class equals status by consensually defined merit.

5. When the result will increase both liberty and equality.

6. When the defense tends toward classlessness.

VIOLENT DEFENSE OF CLASS IS UNJUSTIFIED:

1. When it fails to distinguish between unequal human capacity, unequal luck and unequal goodness.

2. When it defines class solely in terms of origin. Owing to those first three inequities, equality of circumstances can be created and maintained only through unending repression, which requires a class of repressers.

3. (Similar to 2) When class is merely status without functionality.

4. (Similar to 2) When the thing defended is merely class privilege.

5. When class equals nothing but strength.

6. When class equals property, and another's right to life supersedes the defender's right to property.

7. When its end or means violates the fundamental rights of the self.

8. When it is predicated on any one definition of class.

9. When it does not steer fairly between liberty and equality.

VIOLENT DEFENSE OF CLASS MAY OR MAY NOT BE JUSTIFIED:

1. When it aims at "advancing society" (see the Moral Calculus on rules for revolution, 5.2.C.2, 5.2.M, 6.2.C.1, 6.2.M).

2. When its purpose is to benefit the most emiserated class.

3. When its aim is to end relative as opposed to absolute poverty.

4. When it increases equality at the expense of liberty, or vice versa.

Justifying these ends and effects would require adding to or modifying our axioms about the fundamental violent rights of the self (Moral Calculus, 5.1.1–3, 5.1.8).

A Nest of the Gentry

Personalize the issue one last time. Consider the case of a hypothetical Russian Countess, a cultured woman, talented on the piano, who dabbles in watercolors. See her in her white dress at boarding school. Let's suppose that her parents raised her to love the peasants on the family estates and even to pity their poverty. Maybe she's read Tolstoy, and, inspired, endows a little school for the peasant children. Blossoming in the cool shadow of gentility, she remembers well-rounded Levin in *Anna Karenina,* who gladdens and strengthens his noble blood by laboring alongside his nominally emancipated serfs. She reads that some student or agitator named Ulyanov tried to kill the Tsar and will be hanged. She feels horror, disgust, more pity—never connecting, as most certainly does the condemned man's brother, one V. I. Lenin, the terrorist act with the pauperdom around her. A drunken vagrant freezes to death in a pit, and she weeps. When a laborer gets sick, she brings him hot broth with her own hands. On the roadside she encounters a child chewing bluish clay—how frail he is! She gives him two kopeks. The child looks into her eyes. We'll see him again.

Let's say that she marries a decent member of the provincial nobility, and that for whatever reason the newlyweds settle on one of her estates, given as her dowry. The Countess is proud and happy to abide with her peasants. They doff their caps to her husband as he rides through his forests and fields. He is one of the kindest lords they've ever had. During the typhus epidemic of 1892 he brings in a doctor to treat the sick. The Countess helps them develop cottage industries, teaches them about sanitation. They bow to her, call her "little mother." Hasn't she been as good to them as she could practically be? —I say "practically" when I remember Kropotkin, who went from prince to jailed anarchist: he sacrificed *all* his class privileges in order to work for revolution. Have we the right to accuse the Countess of insufficient goodness? Isn't "practically" enough?

Or is it too convenient for her to believe herself loved by them, like Cortes five centuries before, who, conquering tribe after tribe in Mexico, always insisted that to become his vassal remained the best and only way to become his friend?

See the Countess and the Count at the Ball of the Colored Wigs in Saint Petersburg. To maintain one's bon ton at such events (as well as to express one's soul, and to advance her husband in his quest for new connections) she must dress properly, which costs money. Meanwhile, the boy at the roadside stuffs another wad of cold blue mud into his mouth.

And now it is 1905, now 1914, now 1917; and the Countess, middle-aged at last, with her husband and their brood of children whom she has raised to be good and kind like her (a boy, let's say, and two little girls in matching feathered hats), must face the revolution.

A Nest of Vipers

She finds that—with inevitable exceptions—the peasants are neither so friendly now, nor so respectful. She'd never dreamed that Nicholas would abdicate, then that Kerensky could possibly lose out to those bloodthirsty Bolsheviks. Her priest assured her that it couldn't happen. (Her priest has been shot.) Nor could she have imagined that when the people rose up, all her acts of service, around which she organized her routine, would be so quickly forgotten. Thus the practical realities of class division. (Sade had had a similarly unpleasant experience with "his" peasants after the French Revolution.) Oh, some weep for her, a few pity her and fewer still even want to help her, but what can they do? In the 1920s, one of Lenin's Committees of Unwealthy Peasants will dekulakize the local miller. Whether he deserves it "personally" is irrelevant to the representative of the victorious class who pulls his daughter's shirt off, crowing: "You've worn it long enough; now it's my turn." I imagine that the miller probably had friends, and that they stood quietly by, intimidated and ashamed, loathing themselves. Let's suppose he didn't deserve it. Nor does any given soldier deserve to die in battle. That fact leaves his killer no less justified. And the citizens stand by.

For now, the Countess and her family will be allowed to keep the parlor to live in. Soon enough the local soviet will "spontaneously" take over their entire home.

See her on the streets of an unfriendly city, standing in her shabby coat, offering for sale her silver thimble, her dancing shoes (once worn at the Ball of the Colored Wigs) and the medal which her husband received at a reception for the Tsar. She needs to eat. See the Count leaning over his shovel, removing Civil War rubble from a street while Cheka men stand grinning and looking on, hands tucked in the pockets of their long warm coats, pistols at their sides. "We are exterminating the bourgeoisie as a class," their commander has explained to them. "Do not look for evidence that the accused acted in word or deed against Soviet power. The first questions you ought to put are: To what class does he belong? What is his origin?"

"Yes, it was hard on those people," says Lenin to Gorki. "History is a stern mother, and it will freely use any means when it comes to retribution. What is there to say? . . . The more clever of them naturally realise that they have been pulled up by the roots and will not grow into the soil again."

The Crux

No one denies that the Countess accomplished good while she still possessed the power and the resources pertaining to any ruling class. The fact that "society" never compelled her to do so makes her, in my eyes, a worthy person. (Spartacus's slave rebels would have agreed. In that long-perished era of personalized relations, many a Roman was spared massacre for having previously shown kindness to his human cattle.) She wasn't obligated to help. That selfsame fact, from the standpoint of the boy who had to eat blue clay, justifies revolution.

The Clay-Eater

Who is he? I am thinking of one youth straight out of Ostrovsky, but a real youth (unlike the countess, who merely signifies a type), a member of the new class for whose benefit the dictatorship of the proletariat was intended. Under Lenin and Stalin he'd transform himself (not without a little direction) into a domineering *shock worker*, as exemplary producers were called in the militaristic parlance of the day. Later he'd become a mining engineer. He traveled, made discoveries, lived out his old age. But in the days before Lenin's "stern mother" weeded out the count and countess, he'd been a desperate boy. Two decades after the revolution, he recalled in his diary, in tones as passionate as Marx's, that bitter, bitter childhood of his, which indicts the Countess's class and goes far to explain the Bolsheviks' success:

> The primary source of my internal life was my experience of poverty in childhood. By the time spring came around every year we would run out of bread. We would go around the cupboards gathering up "mouse crumbs." During the "hungry year" we ate goose-foot plants, crows, and some kind of bluish clay. I went to see a rich peasant on the pretext of wanting to play with his son. When I hear that the son isn't home I just stand there until they give me a piece of bread. But then they stopped giving it to me.

But the Countess gave him two kopeks! Maybe she gave him bread also . . . With his customary fury, Marx quotes the following line from an English public health report: "Except in so far as they whom his labour enriches, see fit to treat him with a kind of pitiful indulgence, he is quite peculiarly helpless in the matter." So much for the Countess and her do-gooding. She wasn't obligated. That isn't right, that one person must eat clay and his well-fed neighbor isn't obligated to do anything about it. And the clay-eater goes on in his diary:

> The material violence committed against mental and moral freedom from generation to generation inculcated spiritual enslavement, feeble-mindedness, and weakness of will in people doomed to material poverty.

An inherited loss of the sense of one's own human virtues and of the faith in one's own virtues and their free development. This is what troubled my consciousness, and stirred my will to indignation and protest.

The Crux (continued)

And so once again we find ourselves brought up short by the fundamental undeniability of Marx's doctrine of the *opposition of classes.*

Here we might want to recall Gandhi's remark about the "royal road" of generosity, through which the rich mill owners might bind their employees to them by paying decent wages. Had such informal institutions of trust been sufficiently widespread in prerevolutionary Russia—had our Countess, in short, been a ubiquitous type, a swollen "replete" ready to disgorge on command to any and all other honey ants (and how can she be blamed that others weren't like her?)—then expropriating her might not have been necessary. But this is no more than to propose for the Russian nobility the saintly course of class suicide. We've overheard Stalin remark to H. G. Wells that that would never happen, and he was right. Likewise, Gandhian utopianism, or the magical affection of the Platonic guardians who care for the potters because they care for their pottery, has been proven by history—thus far, at any rate—to be akin to a delicate inhabitant of some tidal pool, which cannot survive either on land or in the open sea. Perhaps this is my practical objection to Lycurgus's utopia also. Communes, small rural enclaves, families, lovers and dear friends, charitable foundations, church groups, monasteries, blocs of political prisoners, insurrectionists at white (or red) heat, soldiers in battle together, strangers in common extremity—all these may on certain occasions form into antlike altruism, their privileged members being not parasites but leaders, teachers, healers, saviors. But the quotidian quality of social relations has always been and always will remain *selfishness,* however mediated by religion or other ideology it may be.

Of course, no revolution ought to be blamed for trying; both privileges and resources can be approximately "leveled." Again and above all, no clay-eater can be blamed for wanting to do something about his hunger.

Unequal luck and unequal goodness, yes; with shock troops everywhere and an efficient judicial system those difficulties might be controlled. Speaking of knowledge and understanding, and of the reward to come, Christ had said, as Primo Levi said about Auschwitz, and as the ant-god says to the inmates of big and little eggs: "To him who has will more be given, and he will have abundance; but from him who has not, even what he has will be taken away." But Christ did not have shock troops—at least, not until the Inquisition and the Crusades. The Stalinists did.

"Unquenchable Hatred"

Our clay-eater, as I said, would become a shock worker, a quota-overfulfiller, a leader, an inspiration, a bully. His kind was found everywhere, from the steel mills to the collective farms to the prison camps. Needless to say, they made many enemies among the underfulfillers, but Comrade Stalin held his protective hand over them. Why, they might even be invited to the Kremlin! "Thank you, comrade Stalin, our leader, our father, for a happy, merry kolkhoz life! He, our Stalin, put the steering-wheel of the tractor in our hand."

No need to follow the clay-eater's banal career of petty overlordship, just as we need not compliment the Countess's watercolor landscapes. But let's look in on him in mining school, not a real shock worker yet but soon to be, lonely and trying not to admit it, struggling on as we all must struggle in life. Now he's recording in a diary his impressions of the film *Kirov:*

> It convinces you that the oratorical art of the school of Lenin and Stalin is the most paramount, mighty, and delightful of all the arts. In this film, together with our dear, beloved government, you reexperience the enormous loss that inflames the columns of intrepid workers, millions strong, and their unquenchable hatred toward class enemies.

He was referring to Party boss Kirov's murder (and doubtless feeling that loss; why not call him sincere?). Kirov had been an enthusiastic class liquidator, who suffered from that dangerous disease called popularity. At the end of 1934, while Hitler was putting his own country's sufferers out of their misery, Kirov's ailment took a fatal turn. Delicacy being called for in cases of untimely death, shall we merely say that the shooting was an inside job? The dictator's daughter, Svetlana, who remembered Kirov crying after her mother's suicide, refused to believe what I am telling you. In her *Twenty Letters* she sometimes struggles to hide her love for her father, but it comes out in the denials that he committed this or that crime, at least of his own sole accord. In the case of Kirov, she preferred to blame Beria.

We see Stalin at the funeral, arms folded inside his long coat, steadfast and stern, the military cap pulled down to his eyebrows. He's one of the pallbearers. Is he thinking whom to kill next? For in the name of security, authority, creed and justice—that is, of self-defense of class—he'll now began to hunt down Kirov's supposed murderers. The more people his secret police arrest, the wider the conspiracy will grow. Thus begin the show trials, the Party and military purges, the Great Terror of 1936–38. (They had shock workers on the legal front, too. One of their victims remembered: "The prosecutor just gave me a nasty grin, leered and said, 'Don't worry, you'll survive till the trial.'") The most infamous year, perhaps, is 1937, when the clay-eater was at mining school. Stalin's daughter remembers the old servants gradually disappearing around then. "Finally our housekeeper, Carolina Till, left too. It was 1937, and her German ancestry probably had something to do with it." This period of repressions will be far more urban in character than that of the early 1930s. Now that the peasantry lies dekulakized and broken, Stalin can afford to arrest engineers, activists, Party delegates and the like. In 1937–38 there will be seven million arrests, as a result of which a million people will be executed and two million more will die in labor camps. Collectivization and dekulakization now make up little more than a sideline for the murderer in the Kremlin. —At Kirov's funeral, all is dark. The photographer has placed Stalin at the center, of course; the flash illuminates him above all. Immense, out-of-focus wreaths and flowers shine like the patches of light on the shoulders of the cordon around him. He stands between a hooded, dark-garbed security man, whose face has been washed out by the flash, and somebody's sly face which hangs suspended in blackness, gazing sidelong and shadowy at the camera. Was this image arranged before or after he kissed Kirov's corpse?

"The funeral procession floods the streets with a sea of people," wrote the clay-eater in his diary. "I'm studying the personality of Kirov as a revolutionary, a leader, and a speaker. An image that I consider my ideal." As for Stalin's speeches, they impressed him; they "mobilized" him.

"Those years have left an oppressive, permanent mark on the family— the mark of injury, poverty, oppression." The shock worker might have written that about Tsarism, or Marx about his own circumstances. But neither of them did. Those are the words of a dekulakized peasant, written in 1937. *Defense of class is unjustified when it supersedes defense of other rights.* Indeed, we can add to our moral calculus the general and fundamental maxim that *violence is unjustified when defense of a given right or issue supersedes all other kinds of self-defense.*

Rising Through the Ranks

He entered military training and increased his physical exercise. He became the brigade leader of a ballroom dancing class. "Only people who had passes or my permission were allowed into the hall." At geodesic fieldwork he did not get on with his brigade leader, so he took the Stalinist way: "I presented an accusation with which the triangle agreed. They voted. To exclude the brigade leader from the union. To strip him of his status as a shock worker. To remove him as brigade leader." The clay-eater was then promoted to assistant brigade leader. He became "a middle-rank commander of the revolutionary, proletarian Army." The Party sent in his candidacy as a political agitator. In 1936 he met his aunt, whom he hadn't seen in a decade; she cried out in joy that she never would have imagined "back then" that he could have studied in the institute. For all the institutionalized unpleasantness of this young man's character, there remains something good and just about his success. Before the revolution, he had to steal flour from the mill to feed his starving mother. As a child, he once had to walk forty kilometers without even a taste of bread. I do believe this: Lenin and Stalin saved him.

Self-Defense of Class

Back to 1917, or maybe even 1918. No matter. At some point, the Countess and the clay-eater would have had to meet. Liberty meets equality.

Suppose that in the threatening days after Tsardom dies, the clay-eater, still skinny and shy, enrolls in a Committee of Unwealthy Peasants. The taunting crowd smashes down the gate. They insult the Countess and steal her cloak, her fur coat, her wedding ring. She weeps. Later on, at school, the clay-eater will come to appreciate culture—not just Party culture, but Beethoven, for instance, who "made of me a victorious warrior on the battlefield of life" with "his optimistic revolutionary overture." But when a lecturer on Heine tells the audience that the German's poems moved her to tears in her very sleep, the clay-eater thinks, "This is indeed the sobbing of a sick soul, one that is familiar to me. Her crying is tender, dainty and high-pitched, but that made me dislike it even more." Wouldn't that be how the Countess's sobbing made him feel?

I said that Ostrovsky would have loved this young man, who told his diary:

> It is my fate to take cruel action against those who stand in my way. There is no opposing force of personality that would not be mercilessly destroyed by me. No sooner do I sense the presence of an oppressive force than it is doomed to perish. My view of the world is triumphant. I gain universal respect through both my modesty and my fairness even to those cast down by me.

What could "fairness" possibly consist of in this encounter between classes? What does fairness imply? Self-criticism sessions and show trials exemplified it: the cast-down ones had to denounce themselves in order to validate the acts of their new oppressors. Our shock worker, our clay-eater, wanted to have it both ways. He wanted to impose his will on the masses. But he also wanted them to agree that he was right—and more, incredibly enough. Here he is as brigade leader of a ballroom dancing class: "And with that powerful force of respect of the group I can confidently, boldly force those guilty parties to love me." Would our Countess have been able to love him? Moreover, would that have saved her?

Her moral dilemma was obvious. Her expedient dilemma was this: Denounce oneself in the hope of mercy from the self-styled merciless, and risk liquidation on account of open guilt. Plead innocent, and risk liquidation as a secret class enemy.

Imagine, if you care to, the Countess and her children huddled in the sitting room behind boarded-up windows, praying, frantically kissing their silver icons, while the Count strides out with loaded rifle to die defending their home from the mob. Imagine our future shock worker, the hungry boy, whose teeth are still bluish-grey with clay, running in the vanguard of these radicalized peasants, the tines of his pitchfork aimed at the Count's chest. A demobilized soldier shouts out: "If you destroy the wolves' nests, you must strangle the wolves, too." Everybody shouts approval. Now the clay-eater is almost upon the Count. Two pairs of eyes gaze upon each other, shining with hatred and resolution. Does the Count now fire, or does he hesitate, afraid to inflame them against his family once he is gone? Does the clay-eater feel pity? Do the two kopeks which the Countess once put into his hand soften him a little, or inflame him? Who is to blame? There can be but one definition of this confrontation: tragedy.

IV.

DEFENSE OF AUTHORITY

Anyone who shares profit with all the people under Heaven will gain the world . . . Sparing the people from death, eliminating the hardships of the people, relieving the misfortunes of the people, and sustaining the people in their extremities is Virtue.

T'AI KUNG, *Six Secret Teachings*, eleventh century B.C.?

What are you doing there? Die. Are you passing through the street? It is a crime. Why do you oppose the government? Government is a cutthroat. It has stated that it will do a certain thing; it has begun it; it must be carried out. If society is to be saved, the people must be destroyed.

VICTOR HUGO, *Histoire d'un crime*, nineteenth century

We must have faith in the masses and we must have faith in the Party.

MAO ZEDONG, *The Little Red Book*, twentieth century

Trotsky and Lincoln

Unlike Lincoln, who sought and prayed for reconciliation wherever possible, sometimes at the expense of justice, unlike even John Brown, who was capable of kindness to enemy prisoners and might spare the son when he executed the father, Leon Trotsky refused to distinguish between political and personal categories. Oh, we can't say he was unkind; he'd present some Red machine-gunner-hero with cigars, or encourage another emulation fighter with a lump of sugar . . . In Lincoln one sees, particularly during his Civil War, steadfastness; in Brown, grim determination. Trotsky by contrast presents us with *energy* above all: the mercurial turnings of a mind as intellectually ambitious—and capable—as it was eloquent and sarcastic—humorous, too, unlike John Brown; nor was Trotsky's the wooden, folksy humor of Lincoln which now sounds so heavy in our ears; rather, his wit was clever and sharp, lawyer-fashion, vanguardist-fashion, raking and slashing spontaneously like a cat's claw—and this is just the mind; we have as yet said nothing of the rushing hands that produced decrees and theoretical tomes by the score, or of that second body of his, the famous armored train, which traveled all over the front during a Civil War far more fearsome than Lincoln's, when both sides hanged, raped, flayed and shot with abandon: Trotsky's train would come and issue tobacco to the brave, death to the deserters and traitors, speeches to the wavering—yes, above all, speeches; he was a sort of winged Mercury of the revolution (he was, for a very short time, also her winged Victory). Then off he'd rush to the next desperate place. Through our standard-issue historiographical spectacles we see him almost as we do the journalist Camille Desmoulins, who claimed to spark off the French Revolution with one passionate oration: Here is Trotsky, ever standing at improvised podiums, at clench-fisted attention in his shiny knee-high boots, chin straight, little round glasses glittering as he gazes out upon the crowd and begins to speak. In the full-face photographs, his eyes are strangely round, the pince-nez sometimes a little askew. With the moustache, goatee and briskly controlled sideburn tufts, he resembles an owl. We see him at a snowy rally, saluting October's coup, snow on the visor of his military cap, snow on his collar buttoned up to the chin, snow on his wool-covered shoulders. He beams, points, smashes his fist down on the lectern, turns from side to side, making sure that he's gazed into all directions; he gestures, laughs . . . Generally, fittingly, we see him in crowds. In his great *History of the Russian Revolution* he writes that individuals are nothing except receptacles for history (just as both Lincoln and John Brown thought themselves to be instruments of God), while the masses are everything, omnipotent statistical particles whose movement will, in the end, fulfill the equations of revolutionary enlightenment. He knew those equations by heart, so he never hesitated. Sometimes he changed sides: first he was a Menshevik, then a Bolshevik; he was with Lenin, against him, then with him again—but always he remained certain he was right—as a revolutionary had better be! For him, tactics directed the quivering needle of the historical scale, whose oscillations this way and that, arbitrary though they seemed, were the necessary expressions of the zeroing process. Cross him politically, and he was dead to you personally; Trotsky must be considered an expert at severing relations. Run away from the certain death he ordered you to, and he'd shoot you. In his voluminous pages one meets an ironic coldness coupled with perfect lucidity of exposition—or, sometimes, with self-important pedanticism: this man with a provincial schoolteacher's heart has become Commissar of War!—but be not deceived; beneath the stylized Trotsky lurks a soul of passionate sincerity, raging against the established order of things, against hereditary hierarchies, serfdom, idiotic absolutism, illiteracy and all the evils of class society—he is, of course, the defender of class par excellence. But, because we have already peered into that topic a little we shall only incidentally consider him as the revolutionary he mostly was. Rather, because he was so sure of himself, so ruthlessly sure, and because for a time he had the apparatus to exercise that sureness, we ought to ask of him: When is it justified to make our fellow human beings obey us unto death?—or rather, more specifically and personally: For what end, and by what means, do you yourself exercise your authority?

For comparison's sake, we will then ask President Lincoln the same thing.

[In light of the longish selection on the Russian Revolution in the previous section, "Defense of Class," I have omitted my recapitulation of Trotsky's career from this excerpt.]

The Rights of States

Sallow in his portraits, after the necessary fashion of early photography with its high-contrast glass plates and long exposures, Lincoln stares out at us from the past not without grimness, his jaw clenched in a manner which affords his cheekbones prominence; this, too, might be an artifact of those long exposures, which required the subject to hold himself rigid. One needs but to compare a contemporary thirty-five-millimeter portrait with one created by the large-format camera to detect the latter's relative "seriousness"—in this case, the gravity of an authority whose defender believes it to be sacred. Lincoln, of course, was by circumstances as well as temperament a stern exemplar of federalism, which in the context of the Civil War meant executive centralism. The authority vested in him by the Constitution was not, like Trotsky's, a new and transcendent thing, to be enlarged and deployed without limit, for desperately limitless stakes, but the steady ordinary flame of a candle then almost a century old. Trotsky was a creator, Lincoln a preserver—although, as Lincoln would find, sometimes preservation demands engorgement. The formal authority which Lincoln's stump orations gained him was legitimized not only through the acquiescence of time but also by popular mandate (one of Hitler's "three pillars," you'll recall); for the Revolutionary War had been a people's war, whose victory established a republic of the people.

" . . . And Peculiar Jurisdictions Within Its Own Limits . . . "

That popularity shines through in, for instance, Benjamin Franklin's proposed Articles of Confederation (1775), and in particular in Article III, which states "that each Colony shall enjoy and retain as much as it may think fit of its own present Laws, Customs, Rights, Privileges, and peculiar Jurisdictions within its own Limits." Here we read the rights of the self writ large! Within this document there lurks much which now seems antique and strange: Article XI spells out a perpetual alliance with the Iroquois, who still possessed a measure of their ancient strength; Article XIII invited Ireland, Quebec, Bermuda and any other English colonies to join. There is much, too, that we hunt for in vain—in particular, any discussion of a mechanism for withdrawal from the Confederation. The proposed Articles state only (a) that the "League of Friendship" here described will be binding on future generations—exactly the sort of social contract that some members of those future generations, such as Bakunin (and, come to think of it, myself) will object to—and (b) that this League will dissolve in the unlikely event of reconciliation with the mother country, Great Britain, on prewar terms. "But on Failure thereof this Confederation is to be perpetual." Here, one feels, is a good-faith contract among equal principals. No reason to poison the atmosphere by tying off all eventualities, or even by considering the possibility that the marriage might someday be considered punitive entrapment. And why should it? Mutual advantage remains general advantage.

In personal deportment, the Founding Fathers acted the part: modest, accessible (the latter facilitating Lincoln's assassination). It is delightful to any republican soul to recall Jefferson's reception of the British minister, Anthony Merry, in 1803: the President wore faded corduroys, heelless slippers, and a dirty shirt. His hair had not been combed, and he needed a shave. In his lengthy *History of the United States,* Henry Adams insists on Jefferson's patrician-ness, on his seeming lack of ease in mass democracy. "With manners apparently popular and informal," says Adams, "he led a life of his own, and allowed few persons to share it . . . His instincts were those of a liberal European nobleman, . . . and he built for himself at Monticello a château above contact with man." The reception of Merry thus could be described, if one chose, as eccentrically indifferent or even snobbish rather than egalitarian. Adams's nature, one must remember, was a half-compassionate belittler's, his immensely intelligent pen too often that of satirist; after all, uneasy or not, Jefferson did choose to be a national leader; and if we grant that he was reclusive, such a quality gauges neither his effectiveness nor his legitimacy; Robespierre, like Jefferson an immensely popular leader while he lasted, never stumped or took to the streets, either. And from Jefferson's heart came words which it would be difficult to impute to a European nobleman, however liberal: "I consider the people who constitute a society or nation as the source of all authority in that nation, . . . free to transact their common concerns by any agents they think proper." Again Robespierre comes to mind—the early Robespierre, anyhow, who argued that the people were so sovereign that they should not even accept representatives, only agents ("commissares," the forerunners of Lenin's commissars—history so often inverts the meaning of a word!). Robespierre's spectacular failure had proved yet again that practically speaking, a people cannot exercise undivided power on its own behalf, that to collectivize and universalize participation leads to totalitarianism, whose grievous effects can scarcely be distinguished from those obtained when the people are systematically robbed of all their powers and presented with despotism. Jefferson and his predecessors therefore proposed that the people would *hold* power, but that in the course of political business power must be *delegated*. "The most powerful of all inducements to crime is the prospect of impunity," argued Cicero, and to render that inducement as harmless as they possibly could, the American Founding Fathers (following, among others, the precedent of Cicero's system, old Roman constitutional law) carefully applied the formula: *separation of powers*. When I was in high school, my government teacher taught me that this meant the division of the government into a legislative, an executive and a judiciary. Separation of powers between federal and state authority was hardly spoken of. But, of course, I went to high school after the presidency of President Abraham Lincoln.

The Tendrils of Centralism

Jefferson for his part had continued to insist that the several United States, despite having joined in a federal system, retained "each to itself, the other rights of independent government," which was why he protested the federal government's usurpations of state power: building roads and digging canals upon state territory, et cetera. (There was no national income tax, of course.) It would be a shame if the states were to have a falling-out, he wrote, a crying shame, but not the greatest misfortune of all: "There is yet one greater, submission to a government of unlimited powers." Jefferson wrote this complaint as late as 1825, which is to say, almost at the end of his life. And if that were all Jefferson recorded on the subject of states' rights, Adams's gently demeaning characterization would be entirely unjustified. Unfortunately, during Jefferson's administration, idealism, as it usually must, met with necessity.

Defense of Authority as Defense of Homeland

In spite of the embarrassing outcome of that late war with the American colonies, the British navy continued to engage in impressment of sailors from the new so-called United States. In 1807 they attacked the American frigate *Chesapeake* for harboring deserters, of whom they hanged one and imprisoned three. A few months later, responding to Napoleon's embargo of English goods, which had been passed the previous year, they invoked defense of homeland to issue an Order in Council requiring rigorous impressment of neutral shipping. On December 22, Jefferson, still convinced that economic coercion would prove in its effects practically equal and morally superior to war, himself signed an Act of Embargo against England, thereby usurping state power to an unprecedented degree. The irony of that assertion of authority is that he was seeking to *avoid* misusing the potency of his office; he meant to do what we might now call the Gandhian thing, the nonviolent thing, or at least the passive-aggressive thing of simply withholding, withdrawing from commerce instead of employing authority to take life. Jefferson had entertained this idea as early as 1793, when, noting the English blockade of revolutionary France, he wrote to Madison: "I think it will furnish us a happy opportunity of setting another example to the world, by shewing that nations may be brought to justice by appeals to their interests as well as by appeals to arms . . . It would relieve us too from the risks & the horrors of cutting throats." An embargo being nothing more than the government-enforced counterpart of a boycott, this would seem purely Gandhian, yes? —No. —Commenting on a proposal to boycott British Empire goods, Gandhi wrote in *Young India:* "From the standpoint of non-violent non-cooperation it seems to me to be

wholly indefensible. It is retaliation pure and simple and as such punitive."
(I'm ignoring his later campaign to use only Indian-spun cloth.) Gandhi's
response to the English, were he in Jefferson's shoes, might have been to
call upon as many sailors as possible to go to England, be impressed, smilingly refuse to work, and get hanged; because the true Gandhian, while he
may show his disappointment with his oppressor by boycotting *social* relations with him, may do nothing which hurts anyone but himself. This
point having been made, one must still credit Jefferson with a gentle idealism almost as extraordinary as Gandhi's—perhaps even more so, given the
social ethic out of which Jefferson sprang. Context is a great deal when
one judges somebody. It is easy for a twenty-first-century American to
fault Jefferson for extending suffrage only to free white males, forgetting
that before the American Revolution men without property could not
vote, while even propertied men found themselves barred from deciding a
number of political and religious questions which gravely pertained to
them. Vis-à-vis the embargo, then, one must credit Jefferson as an experi-
menter in the realm of international kindness. He refused to be violent
without both cause and necessity. He would not make of the United States
a sanguinary monster akin to other nations. And by so acting, he broke
states' rights asunder with a more insidious violence than he ever imagined; in an ugly twist of pseudo-Gandhianism, it was indeed the doer, the
embargoist, the United States which suffered—England, too, of course,
but also the American merchant seamen with nowhere to go (and no social
welfare system to recompense them, either), the maltsters and timbermen
forbidden to export their wares, the shipowners, tanners, farmers. One
Englishman wrote to the Governor of Lower Canada's secretary:

> The sensibility excited by this measure among the inhabitants in the
> northern part of Vermont is inconceivable . . . The clamor against the
> Government—and this measure particularly—is such that you may ex-
> pect to hear of an engagement between the officers of government and
> the sovereign people.

Thus matters also went in Massachusetts, Virginia, South Carolina.

Adams, before detailing the economic havoc which the embargo created throughout the United States, argues very convincingly that "no one
could doubt that under the doctrine of States-rights and the rules of strict
construction the embargo was unconstitutional." But a Massachusetts

district court judge, supporting the President, nailed down the doctrine that the federal government's power to regulate the commerce of the states could essentially be used to justify any encroachment desired. Here we find (in an alloyed form to be sure) the iron pragmatism beloved by Bolsheviks—in the words of the Soviet academician Startsev, "a break with bourgeois parliamentarism which was based on the separation of legislative power from executive power."

The Bolshevik ideal was the organization of all workers (who in their system would comprise all people) into collectives whose elected representatives would constitute super-collectives. "In the present Soviet system," Startsev continues (he is writing in 1982), "there is no opposition between local and higher bodies of authority," because class conflict has been eliminated, so all share the same interests. "The combining of general centralised supervision with local self-government ensures organisation of the entire political, economic and cultural life on uniform principles." Jefferson, needless to say, neither demanded nor aspired to such uniformity. Certainly he did not achieve it. In 1809, resented, denounced, despised by some of his own former friends, he was forced to repeal the embargo. "Fifty millions of exports," he admitted, "are the treble of what war would cost us; besides, . . . by war we should take something, and lose less than at present." The substitute: a face-saving "Non-intercourse Bill" allowing the U.S. to trade with neutrals who in turn were sure to trade with England; this marked the collapse of Jefferson's attempt to assert federal authority over the states. In any event, the embargo had been conceived of as an emergency measure, not as a precedent.

The year 1823 finds him writing to Justice William Johnson: "Can any good be effected by taking from the States the moral rule of their citizens, and subordinating it to the general authority . . . ?" Congress (as would Trotsky) had begun to think that it could—only to be discomfited when in 1816 Jefferson's friend and successor, President Madison, in one of his final acts in office vetoed a national improvements bill with the familiar words: "The power to regulate commerce among the several States cannot include a power to construct roads and canals . . . Such a view of the Constitution would have the effect of giving to Congress a general power of legislation." Thus states' rights continued in spurious health, fooling even the otherwise suspicious and prescient Tocqueville, who could report in his great *Democracy in America* that "the government of the States remained the rule, and that of the Confederation"—that is, the federal government—"became the exception." But Henry Adams's *History,* wealthy-wise in hindsight, concluded more accurately that "the favorite States-rights dogma of [1798] had suffered irreparable injury," because Jefferson, as we saw, got his way for a moment—no matter that the consequences of his actions had forced him to reverse them. "For sixteen years the national government in all its branches had acted, without listening to remonstrance, on the rule that it was the rightful interpreter of its own powers." As yet, little permanent change had been effected, but the possibility of justifying such change at any time now enveloped the White House in a golden glow of expediency.

Defense of Authority as Defense of Slaveholding

And so, back to Lincoln, who like Robespierre began as a mere lawyer seemingly uncalled to lead his nation in violence—but unlike Robespierre, he humbly, cheerfully rose through the established order: Abraham Lincoln, anti-Robespierre! To Walt Whitman, who blamed North and South equally for the approaching Civil War (but between the lines of this partisan I think I read the words "northern and southern Democrats"), the politics of the time was made by "crawling, serpentine men, the lousy combings and born freedom-sellers of the earth . . . The former Presidents and Congresses had been guilty . . . their hands were all stain'd." It is 1854, and our lanky, ugly, middle-aged Congressman and aspiring President seems to retain the views of Jefferson and Madison when he insists in his speech on the topic of the Kansas-Nebraska Act: "I trust I understand, and truly estimate the right of self-government . . . Here, or at Washington, I would not trouble myself with the oyster laws of Virginia, or the cranberry laws of Indiana." Indeed, Lincoln singles out Jefferson, "who was, is, and perhaps will continue to be, the most distinguished politician of our history; . . . withal, a slave-holder, [who] conceived the idea . . . to prevent slavery ever going into the north-western territory." For it is with slavery that the Kansas-Nebraska Act deals.

The Missouri Compromise of 1820 allowed Missouri to enter the Union as a slave state, but all the rest of that territory once French and purchased from Napoleon (who admitted laughingly in his memoirs that if he didn't sell it fast, then England or somebody else would grab it anyway) was barred forever from slaveholding. The unincorporated territory of Nebraska—a third the size of Lincoln's United States, hence now subdivided into the new regions of Nebraska and Kansas—lies north of the

Missouri Compromise line, and so the proslavers propose to declare the Compromise "inoperative and void," in order to bring two new slave states into the Union—or, to be more precise, to let the two states themselves (protostates, I should say; read on) choose whether to be slave or abolitionist. For don't states have rights? "The chandeliers flashed their brilliant lights again over the hall," recalls an eyewitness. "The clerks were hoarse with the continued roll call." Edmondson of Virginia, "inflamed by liquor," rushes toward Campbell of Ohio. "It was a fearful scene!" Edmondson has "his hand upon a bowie knife concealed in his vest." Olds of Ohio reports a false quorum to the House. And the measure passes by 113 to 100. The Missouri Compromise is dead.

Defense of Authority as Deference to "Universal Feeling"

Lincoln, we must begin by saying, hates slavery almost as much as John Brown, is sickened by the cruelty and sheer selfish unfairness of it. Among his papers a fragment from this period states that "if A. can prove, however conclusively, that he may, of right, enslave B.—why may not B. snatch the same argument, and prove equally, that he may enslave A.?" Unlike John Brown, however, Lincoln stands at a miserable loss as to what to do. Seeking, as the saying goes, to do well by doing good, one sometimes finds oneself—like the whole nation—at cross-purposes. Returning the slaves to the African coast might be their murder, for they know not how to live there; keeping them in subservience is unjust; as for granting them full equality, "my own feelings will not admit of this," he says, parting company with John Brown, "and if mine would, we well know that those of the great mass of white people will not. A universal feeling, whether well or ill-founded, can not be safely disregarded."

Regarding universal feelings I reiterate, as the Founding Fathers would have: *Consensus constitutes no guarantee of authority's justice.* Anyhow, the feeling Lincoln refers to was never in fact universal, even among whites; during the Civil War he'll receive occasional letters requesting him to emancipate and even to enfranchise the slaves. —However, far more with the opposite drift will come in. "Now you God damned old Abolition son of a bitch God damn you," runs one such encomium, followed by more of the same.

Shall we quantify that universal feeling a little? Consider Iowa, nominally a free state, which crawls with militias of both persuasions. In Dubuque in 1839 a few good citizens save one black man from being shipped back to his master under the Fugitive Slave Act, but on election day in 1856 a white businessman who dares to assert that blacks are as good as he gets knocked to the sidewalk and attacked. —Confusion, contradiction, brawling superiorities and ideologies! In 1848 another slave brought to Iowa, evicted by his master for bad behavior, settles down there, refuses a demand by the master's family to return to Saint Louis for sale and withstands the detective sent to kidnap him: Iowa declares him legally free. But just two years earlier, the black wife of a white man had been turned in by neighbors and arrested, told that she must show her free papers or be sold at auction. Thus—what? What does it all add up to? Well, if we want to quantify a so-called universal feeling, the result of the Iowa referendum of August 3, 1857, will do. Should blacks be granted equal suffrage? Eight thousand four hundred and seventy-nine people vote yes; 49,267 vote no; and 21,751 of those who that day cast their ballots on another matter don't vote on this one at all.

Lincoln is right, then? Well, after all, he'll soon get legitimately elected by people who (democracy presumes) know what he stands for— but then, what does he stand for? At any rate, disinclination for abolition is probably nearer universal than not in the circles he moves in: both Grant and Sherman admit as much about themselves in their respective memoirs; and the Supreme Court itself refuses to elevate the black man Dred Scott from the status of "an ordinary article of merchandise." During the war years, hundreds of black people will be murdered in riots by Northerners—a sure sign of the limits of Lincoln's emancipationist authority.

Defense of Authority as Defense of the Constitution

Besides, even were Lincoln's "feeling" disregarded, well, the Constitution remains sacred; harmony is sacred; the rights of the states which entered the original Union must be respected.

Nebraska, as it happens, is not yet a state but a grassy, sandy tabula rasa now federally inscribed. Lincoln demands:

> Again, is not Nebraska, while a territory, a part of us? Do we not own the country? And if we surrender the control of it, do we not surrender the right of self-government? It is part of ourselves. If you say we shall not control it because it is ONLY part, the same is true of every other part; and when all the parts are gone, what has become of the whole?

Thus there seem to be three distinct entities within the Union: free states, slave states and federal holdings—which last category has immensely complicated things, for when the old colonies unified, the federal government was given only the tiny District of Columbia in order to do its business without spawning the conflict of interest of operating within a particular state. The acquisition of Florida, the Louisiana Purchase and the annexation of Mexican territory have put the government into the canal-digging, road-clearing business with a vengeance. What would dead Jefferson say? No matter in our day that all three divisions of state will have achieved a hazy unity, thanks perhaps to the gunsmoke which would soon blot out the trees at Antietam. On this subject, the Constitution remains equally hazy.

Defense of Authority as Defense of Ground

The existence of these territories, vital to Lincoln's impending justification of violent force countercommitted against the South, will be similarly seized on by Ulysses S. Grant, then virtually unknown, soon to be Lincoln's supreme general and later his successor. Grant began by admitting the original basis for the Jeffersonian conception of states' rights, agreeing that "each colony considered itself a separate government" and that when the federation was first formed it would have been permissible, if not exactly desirable, for any state to bow out. But in his view "if the right of any one State to withdraw continued to exist at all after the ratification of the Constitution, it certainly ceased on the formation of new States, at least so far as the new States themselves were concerned." As for the old states, such as South Carolina and Virginia, which led the secession, Grant glossed those over. Federal power appeared to be supreme over one category out of three; therefore, it must be supreme over the others.

And in his speech on the Kansas-Nebraska Act, Lincoln adopts the same sophism: "Do we not own the country?" I take this to mean: "Do we not own the Territories, and therefore the free states and the slave states, too?" —Legerdemain!

"Stand with Anybody That Stands Right"

But what about states' rights? asks Lincoln derisively in his speech. Well, if the citizens of Nebraska can invoke those to keep slaves, then it is certainly within their rights to go to Africa to buy slaves, and we've already made doing that a capital crime! —Not that anybody's yet been hanged for it . . . —For Lincoln the struggle between state and federal authority can be resolved in only one way; we never hear him argue that the federal government ought not to have the power to regulate slave trading. (Oddly enough, however, when the issue of granting statehood to Utah comes up, he says that there is nothing in the Constitution which allows the government to prohibit polygamy there, which is precisely what the government ultimately does.) Trotsky and Tolstoy speak of natural law; and there does seem to be a natural law that authority enlarges itself indefinitely, whether by frenzied growth in revolution or by incumbency's subtler increase. Given the rights of the self, it seems to me that authority possesses the right to self-aggrandizement only through *imminence* or *incumbency*. Most of the time, it grows without right. What's done is done, continues the candidate, both on your side and on mine; and he proposes to calm the waters with what seems from my perspective here in the future to be oily expediency: "Stand with anybody that stands RIGHT. Stand with him when he is right and PART with him when he goes wrong. Stand WITH the abolitionist in restoring the Missouri Compromise; and stand AGAINST him when he attempts to repeal the fugitive slave law," which requires that free-state Northerners catch runaway slaves whenever they can, and return them to their Southern owners for reenslavement and probable violent punishment. "In the latter case you are with the southern disunionist. What of that? you are still right. In both cases you are right. In both cases you oppose the dangerous extremes."

States' rights hang by a thread these days, as we've seen from Jefferson's embargo, from the compulsion put on Utah, from the antislaving laws. The misery of the slaves troubles Lincoln's soul, but he will not cut that thread. His fear of the disunion of the many (and, perhaps, of the disfavor of the electorate) is greater than his pity for the torture of the few. He believes that the United States of America, while imperfect, remains in actuality or potentiality the most righteous country in the world; the beautiful justice that it strives for ought not to be lost in a vain struggle for justice for black people. (For a parallel, listen to Trotsky loudly and zealously submitting to the necessity for "repressing" people whose personal innocence nobody doubts.) Lincoln's authority's consensual basis is merely constitutional; slavery, being a preexisting evil brought into the original compact of states, is therefore a *necessary* evil which like Trotsky's dictatorship of the proletariat must inevitably wither away.

We've agreed that for incumbency, *legitimate authority is constrained by, but not solely defined by, law*. Slaveholding, while now limited and deprived of its basis in trafficking, remains the law. *The state exists not for its own benefit but for its sovereign citizens*. Some of those citizens are slaveholders. Slaves are not sovereign citizens.

Is slavery wrong? To go against it, we must flout both law and consensuality. In short, we must refashion ourselves into a revolutionary authority of sorts, expanding our dominance beyond tradition's limits.

Do we prefer to remain the faithful steward of preexisting authority? Then we'll have to wait upon a utopian future as distant as Trotsky's, a day when slavery will be abolished legally and with consent. Once again I quote from Lincoln's fragment on government:

> In all that the people can individually do as well for themselves, government ought not to interfere.

Abolitionists cry out: "What hypocritical conveniency!" The suppression of the African slave trade increased the market value of "black diamonds" from $325 per head in 1840 to $360 in 1850; by 1860, when secession begins, an African will go for $500. Slave-runners in Lincoln's time are like drug-runners in ours; the profit looms too high for the states' rights thread to be cut.

Like Jefferson and unlike Trotsky, Lincoln longs not to be a man of violence. Jefferson did not want to murder Englishmen, so he stepped back and trod upon the states with his executive heel. Lincoln will not pervert the Constitution any further by means of executive force; therefore he must abandon slaves to the lash. He will not create new slaves; he will not worsen the evil, but he will not pay, or make states' rights pay, the price to remedy it.

I cannot believe that he truly regards the Missouri Compromise and the Fugitive Slave Act as "right." If slavery is wrong, then those two bills must also be wrong. But dissolving the Union is most definitely wrong.

A year goes by, and to William H. Henderson he writes: "The political atmosphere is such, just now, that I fear to do any thing, lest I do wrong."

And as to withering away, he now admits to George Robertson that "there is no peaceful extinction of slavery in prospect for us."

To Joshua F. Speed he writes: "I confess I hate to see the poor creatures

hunted down, and caught, and carried back to their stripes, and unre-
warded toils; but I bite my lip and keep quiet."

He loses the election to his rival Douglas.

More Righteousness

Unlike Trotsky, he agonizes over principles. He writes a note on "section-
alism," which Stalin and Robespierre would have called "factionalism."
He is referring to the national division over slavery, of course. Here he
seems to be approaching the crisis. "*Who* can help it?" he asks. "Either
side *can* help it; but how? Simply by *yielding* to the other side. There is no
other way . . . Then, which side shall yield? To this again, there can be but
one answer—the side which is in the *wrong*." (Would the framers of the
Constitution have spoken in this way?)

He knows which side is in the wrong and has always known it. So did
Trotsky.

In the draft of his famous "House Divided" speech he insists: "To give
the victory to the right, not *bloody bullets*, but *peaceful ballots* only, are necessary." The following year he talks of firmness, but can he imagine how
firm he will have to be?

We find him receiving the presidential nomination in 1860, his face
strangely pale against the stained grey background of this salted paper
print, his lips almost puckered, his cheek creases sharper than ever—what
a strange, gaunt, homely man! His eyes are sad and patient almost to
glassiness; again, perhaps, it was the long exposure. He clasps his hands in
his lap. He appears gentle and crazed. To Mr. George T. M. Davis he
writes privately, confidentially and beseechingly: "What is it I could say
which would quiet alarm?"

He does not yet possess the supreme authority to which a person can
aspire under our system of government: executive power. Undoubtedly
both he and his antithesis Napoleon would agree with Cicero's remark
that "nothing in the world is so delicate and fragile and unstable and frail
as the popular attitude and feeling towards men who are standing for an
election."

The Elevation

William T. Sherman, the future ruthlessly successful Union general whose
name Southerners would employ as an epithet more than a century later,
was in Louisiana in the fall of 1860, teaching at a military academy he'd

founded. John Brown had scarcely been cut down from authority's rope; the South certainly had not forgotten his menace and violence. "The election of Mr. Lincoln fell upon us all like a clap of thunder," Sherman wrote in his memoirs. (The slaves, of course, had been praying for it.) Secessions followed—seven of them. By the following February, the Confederate States of America had their president one Jefferson Davis, who, a lady told Sherman, was not *Sherman's* president but *her* president. (W. E. B. DuBois had an even better description of him: "the peculiar champion of a people fighting to be free in order that another people should not be free.")

Sherman's president writes confidentially to James T. Hale: "We have just carried an election on principles fairly stated to the people. Now we are told in advance, the government shall be broken up, unless we surrender to those we have beaten, before we take the offices."

The outgoing president, Buchanan, a proslave man, menaces and reproaches him in the State of the Union address. Buchanan adds that in his view the federal government has no justification whatsoever for using force against a state.

Lincoln writes to Seward: "I am inflexible." But he is inflexible only in preserving the status quo. He does not want to aggrandize his authority or emancipate slaves. He has already written off his forts in Charleston Harbor, now seized. He loathes the coming war. So do many Southerners, who hope and believe everything's all over. One Confederate lady writes in her diary: "We are divorced because we have hated each other so." But others exult in the split. Robert Toombs, a Georgia state senator in the Union before the war, and then the Confederacy's Secretary of State, utters a gloating expletive and goes on, "animated by an almost fiendish malignancy": *"If I were to die tomorrow, I should care to have but one epitaph cut in my tombstone: 'Here lies the man who destroyed the Republic of the U.S.'"*

Defense of Authority Through Logic

Lincoln's propositions desperately multiply. Now he says that no state can secede because there were *never* any states, only dependent colonies—who became independent precisely by federating under the Constitution—and dependent territories. No state can secede because a government has never yet given the governed the means to destroy that government. (This goes against Jefferson's talk of all men's revolutionary right to overthrow their government. It also goes against the spirit of authority's legitimacy-through-consensus.) No state can secede because all states have benefited from federal moneys and services, which no state has ever repaid. No state can secede because all states joined together, so all must leave together. All these arguments of his are as the bent and jointed corpses soon to be wrapped around the boulders of Little Round Top, which is to say that they have no strength, no motive power, particularly from a man who insists that sovereignty comes from the people. Where does he actually stand? A tired old diplomatic historian remarks in another context that "there must always be a fairly wide gap between the arguments that governments use behind closed doors and their public defence of them"; the applicability of that aphorism to Southern secessionist discourse we shall shortly see, but it surely applies to Lincoln himself. I imagine that his personal impulse at this moment must simply be, as any other chief executive's would, to learn how to control this new machinery of power over which he's just now been temporarily set. He desires neither to mar it nor reduce its scope of operation; he isn't certain which levers to pull, or, in general, whether to slow it down to prevent a catastrophe, or speed it up to show his mastery.

Do you remember what Trotsky said? "What moves things is not the piston or the box, but the steam," the energy of human beings en masse. To be sure, seccession is a vast and consensual mass movement. What ought Lincoln to do about it?

He pontificates on. "Physically speaking, we cannot separate," he says, and, "can aliens make treaties easier than friends can make laws?" These are both worthy points. They prove the secessionists' hubris and stupidity. They do not, however, prove any absence of right. In her declaration of secession, South Carolina writes that "where no arbiter is provided" between a state and the federal union, "each party is remitted to his own judgment to determine the fact of failure, with all its consequences." This, I am afraid, is fair, just and right. There is only one valid moral argument which I can see for prohibiting secession, and the president does not make it, save by implication: namely, that secession would injure, perhaps to death, those who stayed behind, who therefore are justified by imminent self-defense in vetoing the dissolution. And, frankly, I don't see any imminence here.

But the South for her part has excellent reason to feel injured. First of all, Lincoln's against them. His "House Divided" speech, however purely rhetorical it might have been, is a call to action against her institutions.

His public attacks on Douglas have left a decidedly unpleasant taste. His opposition to the Supreme Court's decision that Dred Scott was not a man but a unit of cattle does not go down well in South Carolina. In short, either Lincoln means slavery no good or else he is a hypocrite. In either case, the South does not want him.

Secondly, even though Southerners never wanted Lincoln, they could not prevent him from being voted in. He's been imposed on them; he doesn't dominate them by consent; his authority over them therefore *is not legitimate.*

Violent Defense of Preexisting Authority Is Justified:

1. When the authority has not been proven unjust; and when failure to defend it will injure or destroy it. [Incumbency has a lower standard to meet than revolutionary authority, simply because overthrowing it would cause turmoil and violence. See Moral Calculus, 1.1.3.]
2. When mutual affection exists between authority and its subjects, and when the defense is motivated by that affection.
3. When the leaders' authority is peacefully revocable on the part of the led.
4. When authority directs its defense so as to commit the least possible harm. [In other words, when it obeys proportionality and discrimination. See 5.1.2.1, 5.1.7, 5.2.F.].

Violent Defense of Preexisting Authority Is Unjustified:

(in other words, one may fairly rise up against it)

1. When that defense in and of itself permanently aggrandizes the authority, as opposed to merely maintaining it. [Example: Lincoln's victory in the American Civil War was justified certainly by the abolition of slavery it brought about, and arguably by the fact that the South attacked first. But one result of his victory, and the main point for which he fought—federal control—was not justified.]
2. When the dispute does not imminently endanger authority and when authority nonetheless refuses to entertain the idea of reconciliation.
3. When authority has no "empathetic bridge" to the masses or the opposition.
4. When that defense aims at permanently excluding or debasing a portion of the governed.

5. When authority offers no release from obedience in the event of disagreement with it.
6. When self-defense constitutes mere defense of unity.
7. When it does not generally take place at a steady and moderate tempo [revolutionary authority, as we have seen, is briefly excepted from this].
8. When authority invokes more violent power than it needs to in a given case.
9. When authority is not legitimate in the first place. [See Moral Calculus, 5.2.C.1.4.]

INDICATIONS OF ILLEGITIMATE AUTHORITY

• When authority can unilaterally abrogate the social contract.
  [Note: Authority's subjects may, however, do just that. See Moral Calculus, 5.2.B caveat.]
  REMINDER: Authority cannot legitimize itself merely by refraining from violence, or even by rewarding its dependents. [Julius Caesar: "I myself am never happier than when pardoning suppliants."]

DESCRIPTIONS OF ILLEGITIMATE AUTHORITY

• When the officials are not assistants of the people but constitute a ruling class.
• When the government performs its duties by force, not by affection.
• When the state does not enrich its citizens but makes them poorer.
• When the state does not enhance liberties but restricts them.
• When people feel not safer under the government but more threatened.
• When the people cannot peacefully revoke the social contract.

From the standpoint of the South, Lincoln's administration failed conditions 2 and 3 of justified authority and met conditions 1, 5, 6 and 9 of unjustified authority. Moreover, from the descriptions of illegitimate authority immediately above (all of them derived either from our definitions of legitimate authority or else from Lincoln's fragment on government), it would seem that Lincoln's authority now partook of unjustifiability on every criterion: his officials constituted a ruling class, since they imposed on the South an unwanted social contract (this grievance gets recapitulated in the last item on the list); mutual affection was certainly gone; economic competition between slave and free states was in fact impoverishing the South; the South's right to secede was not upheld and its right to hold slaves undermined; hence it followed that Southerners felt threatened. Considerable wrong lay on Lincoln's side.

"Just Little Niggers"

Slavery itself I would have preferred to consider separately from secession, but unfortunately it is impossible to do so in this chapter at least. As Carlyle would say, ah, the rights of man versus the *mights* of man! All the grievances of the Confederate States, including their claims of constitutional violations, ultimately have to do with actual and perceived interference with this institution. What is more, we can peer forward a century and *still*, sad to say, find the phrasing of states' rights being pressed into service to encode racism! In 1958 the National States Rights Party, a friend and sometimes a rival of the Ku Klux Klan (the two organizations have overlapping membership), will constitute itself as a "white racist party" dedicated to expelling blacks and Jews from the U.S. In September 1963 a church in Birmingham, Alabama, will be dynamite-bombed, killing four black girls. The United Florida Ku Klux Klan will happen to have a rally that same month, and the featured speaker will be one Charles Conley "Connie" Lynch, minister of the gospel and incidentally associated with that same National States Rights Party. The well-named Reverend Lynch, whose categorization process functions very much like that of a good Party cadre rounding up kulaks in the Ukraine, explains why the white race is now better off:

> They ain't children. They're just little niggers . . . it wasn't no shame they was killed. Why? Because when I go out to kill rattlesnakes, I don't make no difference between little rattlesnakes and big rattlesnakes, because I know it is the nature of all rattlesnakes to be my enemies and poison me if they can.

Can we blame the Confederacy for Reverend Lynch, or Reverend Lynch for the Confederacy? Of course not. But when a term first sullied by slavery continues to be sullied a hundred years later by murderous bigotry, we ought to consider very carefully when we join an organization concerned with "states' rights" that we are in fact using that phrase, as opposed to letting something else use us. —Noted. Now, if we can set connotation aside and strictly consider denotation, we may, as stated, consider the concept of states' rights to be justified by social contract theory—but let's keep in mind what the Confederacy wants to do with those rights. They see the Missouri Compromise and its resulting legislation as their doom knell, for if future states conceived from the territories will not be permitted to have slavery, then sooner or later a quorum of abolitionist states will amend the Constitution in prohibition of slavery. Abolitionist sentiment in general terrifies and enrages them, evasions of the Fugitive Slave Act the same; the capture and trial of John Brown have given their spleen the proof of conspiracy that it yearned for: Republicans were behind it! The South in 1860 has much the same feelings as the U.S. would have had in 1960 had a Trotskyite President been elected and had he announced that the United States cannot stand half privatized, half nationalized; all private property must go sooner or later. This dangerous President, Abraham Lincoln, has said exactly that about the South's property; and they believe him to be far more energetic about the matter than he actually is. In Georgia, some are already crying for "resistance to the rule of Lincoln and his Abolitionist horde." —He has not even been inaugurated yet! —"Be it resolved by the legislature of the state of Mississippi that, in the opinion of those who now constitute the said legislature, the secession of each aggrieved state is the proper remedy for these injuries."

For this reason I am compelled to state: Lincoln was wrong to prohibit secession, but that secession was largely in the pursuit of an immoral end. The outcome, which neither Lincoln nor the South expected, was a good one: the formal destruction of slavery within the United States.

Lincoln's Echo (Serbia, 1993)

"It is logical to start with the fundamental crime—crime against peace, which is the origin of all other crimes. In the case of Yugoslavia this is a forcible secession of the republics and recognition of secessionist republics." Thus the Serbian federalists' explanation for the Yugoslavian civil war which began in 1991. The Serbs committed many, many war crimes, "because they had more bullets," as one Croat told me. They were widely condemned; they stood against the self-determination of Slovenia, Croatia, Bosnia. And yet their argument was Lincoln's. If they were wrong in their end (set their means aside), so was he.

Is There Any Alternative to Authority?

Here is a good place to pause, to step back and ask once again: *When is defense of authority justified?* We have already heard a number of answers. Now consider the most extreme position, the anarchist position. In 1894, less than halfway through his fourteen-year stretch in a Pennsylvania jail, Alexander Berkman decides that Robert Burns, once one of his favorite poets, "seems inadequate, powerfully as he moves my spirit with his deep sympathy for the poor, the oppressed." Why? Because Burns is blind to causes.

> "Man's inhumanity to man" is not the last word. The truth lies deeper. It is economic slavery, the savage struggle for a crumb, that has converted mankind into wolves and sheep. In liberty and communism, none would have the will or the power "to make countless thousands mourn." Verily, it is the system, rather than individuals, that is the source of pollution and degradation.

If the deep truth is economic slavery, then surely the literal enslavement of black people by white people in the antebellum South is "the system." (Here I recall again the Unabomber's desperate words—he would hate Berkman's "leftism," of course: "It would be better to dump the whole stinking system and take the consequences.")

Ask yourself this: To what extent are the words of Reverend Lynch his own, and to what extent are they those of "the system"? If there were no system, would Reverend Lynch be any different? I think he would not. How, therefore, would he be restrained from encouraging and perhaps inciting the murder of children? If we liquidated Reverend Lynch, wouldn't another Reverend Lynch be born sooner or later? If we imprisoned him or monitored him, wouldn't we need "the system" to do it?

"In liberty and communism, none would have the will or the power 'to make countless thousands mourn.'" It would be easy to say that Stalin, Lenin and Trotsky proved the opposite. Of course they did not. An anarchist would argue (as Berkman later did—and so did Stalin, Lenin and Trotsky in their separate ways) that the Russian Revolution achieved only an impure sort of communism. Very well. What would achieve pure communism?

Were Alexander Berkman presented with the means to suppress

slavery—weapons factories, plus authority's machinery of conscription—
what would he do with them? He once said—and here he sounds like his
enemy Trotsky—that "the individual—or any number of them—cannot
be weighed against the interests of humanity." Presumably, that means
that he would conscript the unwilling and defeat the slaveholders, which is
just what Lincoln did. In short, he would be—for the short term, at
least—a conventional head of state, the antithesis of an anarchist, indeed,
the target of the anarchist (during Berkman's prison term, an anarchist
killed President McKinley). If his anarchistic scruples were through some
unlikely chance to prevent this very militant man of action from proceeding against the South, then he would be guilty of maintaining "the system" in its worst form.

If I were Berkman, I would probably denounce this choice as a false
one. I would call it "everlasting pessimism." There *must* be a way to render the Reverend Lynches harmless forever, without institutionalized coercion! Give me an army, I'd say, and I would use it to carry out class warfare
throughout the United States. Destroy capitalism, and slavery-capitalism
must perish. —But again I say to Berkman: To do this on any significant
scale, you must employ authority.

The Rights of States (continued)

The quantitative political scientist Jack Nagel has pointed out in a dryly
excellent book reeking of equations the meaninglessness of referring to a
person's "power"; the questions to be asked are: Power over *what*? At what
time and in what place? Let us then concentrate Lincoln's degree of control
over two particular "dependent variables": states' rights, and slavery. Nagel
has coined another useful term: "autonomous preference," meaning one's
personal disposition to influence an outcome. This may always be re-
aligned, should other people or forces of power lean on one hard enough.

At Lincoln's inauguration, then, his official authority over states' rights
was deeply debatable. His autonomous preference was a very strong inclination to subordinate them to federal power—in other words, to prohibit
secession. Secession having already occurred, we would have to say that
his actual *power* over states' rights—his ability to affect them—must also
be considered very small. As far as slavery was concerned, his autonomous
preference for abolition, for all his private feelings about "those poor creatures," was nonexistent: he would not permit slavery to spread above the

line of the Missouri Compromise if he could help it; other than that (despite what some Southern demagogues claimed) he didn't mind sitting on his hands. For this reason, his power over slavery in 1861 was almost nil.

By 1865, like Trotsky, he had imposed his autonomous disposition by force (it helped that after his men were fired on and vanquished at Fort Sumter, he had collective honor in his war chest: defense of unity, defense against insult, defense of esprit de corps). His authority over states' rights was now very high; after Lee's surrender at Appomattox, Lincoln's dominance over the former Confederate States of America was almost unconditional. His authority over slavery had similarly and correspondingly grown, even though his autonomous disposition for abolition was not unambiguously zealous, thanks no doubt to his consciousness of the restraints of law and consensus upon his power. His advisers usually gave him military rather than moral arguments for emancipation, and the Preliminary Emancipation Proclamation was just that—preliminary. (In 1861 one of his generals, John C. Frémont, had issued an edict of emancipation in Missouri; fearing that neighboring Kentucky's rebel sentiments would harden, Lincoln had forced him to eat his words.) The lag between this statement of intent and the actual emancipation decree the following year shows that his power here (perhaps, too, his intention) was less than robust. The necessity to put pressure on the Confederacy, and the expectations of some but by no means all of the electorate, surely helped bring about this outcome, but it hardly occurred at a tempo which would have satisfied Trotsky.

There are two situations in which a politician's authority can exceed his actual power: weakness—as was the case at the beginning of Lincoln's first term, thanks both to popular discontent and to the manipulations of elites within his own party—and restraint, which marked the end of his government, and which, other moral considerations being equal, is always to be commended. Defense of authority is more likely to be justified when authority refrains from invoking all the power which it can invoke, because forgoing some power proves that power alone (i.e., despotism) is not its end. If we wished to qualify further, we could say that Lincoln's influence over state sovereignty was marked by great authority and power and by considerable restraint, while his influence over slavery showed great authority, and considerable power, with perhaps almost as much weakness as restraint.

In practice, both the authority which Lincoln claimed over the South, and the power he exercised, were limited. Having achieved his primary object of reunification, and his corollary one of emancipation, he was satisfied; he'd achieved his war aims.

The authority which Trotsky represented during the Russian Civil War, and the power which he expressed at the same time, were limited only by the forces opposing him. Moreover, his power, being arbitrary and lethal without appeal, was even greater than his authority, which had to pay lip service to proletarian consensualism. Thus in this respect the two men were opposites.

Defense of Authority as Military Command

"If you don't Resign we are going to put a spider in your dumpling . . . ," runs a letter to Lincoln from this period, "suck my prick and call my Bolics your uncle Dick god dam a fool and goddam Abe Lincoln who would like you goddam you excuse me for using such hard words with you but you need it you are nothing but a goddam Black nigger." Then comes the triumphant postscript: "Tennesse Missouri Kentucky Virginia N. Carolina and Arkansas is going to secede Glory be to god on high."

He grants that marching his armies into South Carolina would be invasion and coercion—but not if South Carolina seizes the forts and imposts he's received in trust for the Union. South Carolina insists that he surrender Fort Sumter. Secession has already been consummated; the Union retains no right to the property of this born-again sovereign state. (Old General Scott, commander of his armies, advises compliance for practical reasons. So do most of his cabinet.) He pleads in his inaugural address for all to think carefully and slowly upon the grave step they contemplate. Virginia still tries to keep out of it. Jefferson Davis sends envoys to arrange an amicable divorce, but he refuses to receive them, because in his mind their government is but pretended and he will not encourage any to believe otherwise. Toward the seceded states he forbears, saying only that he will hold his forts and collect his imposts. (Is he too busy to read his foreign dispatches? That most reactionary of autocracies, Russia, has just now freed its serfs from slavery. Meanwhile, in the shining democracy of Washington and Jefferson, they're still lynching uppity niggers.)

When two people in a small room are on the verge of a quarrel, they can sometimes delay or even avoid it by pretending not to notice one another. Should the Confederates simply refrain from attacking his forts, he'll let them be. But Fort Sumter needs provisioning quite urgently now.

The fulfillment of that task must involve federal movements, disembarkations of troops and porters who wear his hated federal livery, clatterings of wagons, draggings of bean sacks, rollings of hogsheads filled with salt pork—how will they be able to maintain their pretense of his nonexistence then?

To avoid alarming them, he announces the operation. It is not and will not be an attack. He even offers to be discreet about it, in order to avoid provoking further lawlessness. But his defense of authority now encounters their defense of fresh-born homeland. Insurgents fire on his troops and take Fort Sumter. Naturally, Jefferson Davis tells this story differently. We must, however, grant that Davis is accurate in relating that the Union commander of Sumter, Anderson, was sent home with all honors. The Confederate States of America have no wish to torment or humiliate their former government; they too would keep peace if they could—well, some of them.

The Maryland legislature convokes. Lincoln knows that they may well call their rebels to arms, but he will not violate their constitutional right to assembly. And they call to arms.

Walt Whitman will later remember the fateful moments of the war, and of Lincoln's career, as *silences,* from the very first time he sees Lincoln in New York City, Lincoln then unpopular almost to friendlessness, and this crowd which has cheered so many other dignitaries looks upon him with soundless hostility: Lincoln returns their gaze with pleasant curiosity, not apprehension. Is this mere hagiography? I think not. Whitman's writings breathe an eloquent calm. Comes the news from Fort Sumter. At midnight, a man reads out the telegram to a crowd of some thirty or forty people who listen beneath a hotel's streetlamps, stand wordlessly, then dissolve. Whitman is there. Perhaps he feels then what his President feels. Next the Union loses at Bull Run; and in the drizzle, exhausted, filthy soldiers march or straggle into fearful Washington almost in silence, "half our lookers-on secesh of the most venomous kind—they say nothing; but the devil snickers in their faces." Halfway through the war, Whitman goes to "look at the President's house" by moonlight, at "the palace-like, tall, round columns, spotless as snow." The sentries in their blue overcoats again are silent, "stopping you not at all, but eyeing you with sharp eyes, whichever way you move." Whitman remembers how for fear of assassination the President had to be smuggled into the Capitol for his own inauguration, and guarded at that ceremony by sharpshooters; with his earnest belief in popular sovereignty he hopes that this first such defense of highest authority in the United States will be the last; but one of history's many tasks is to prove to new nations that they are no more virtuous than anyone else. In the twentieth century, McKinley will be democratically approachable and die from an anarchist's bullet; Kennedy will be murdered at a greater distance by another of John Wilkes Booth's spawn, the righteous loner, sovereign of his own self and hence answerable to no authority but that which he chooses to recognize—this is freedom and manliness? God knows the self is sovereign and thus has the right to rise up against tyrants, but who exactly is tyrant here? —Silence, always silence precedes the fateful change; the *act* is not the change but its consequence. Silence at Lincoln's murder, says the chronicler-poet; Whitman's mother cooks as usual, but that day she and he cannot eat. Silence in the hospital tents; he becomes a volunteer nurse, distributing money, stationery, tobacco and berry preserves, writing letters and comforting those who would have him do so; when a soldier hangs between life and death the attendant puts a finger to her lips, warning others not to disturb him in his struggle.

And now another struggle is decided. Sumter is not the forgivable end (could Lincoln have forgiven even that?). I say again: The Maryland legislature have called disunionists to arms.

We see a picket fence, and trees painted white around their bases so that they resemble tombstones. Then, almost at the white horizon of the octagonally cupola'd courthouse of Natchez, Mississippi, we see a dark line of new Confederate recruits.

Lincoln announces a state of insurrection. "It was with the deepest regret," says his message to Congress, and I believe him, "that the Executive found the duty of employing the war-power, in defence of the government, forced upon him. He could but perform this duty, or surrender the existence of the government." Now the ethical reflexes of self-defense twitch Union authority's great limbs into forcefulness. Grant, soldier but not yet supreme commander, writes to his wife: "There is such a feeling aroused through the country now as has not been known since the Revolution." Unlike Trotsky, Lincoln will never have to shoot every tenth man, defense of his authority being both popular and well understood. Elizabeth Cady Stanton scribbles: "The age of bullets has come again; and a rotten aristocracy must be subdued by the only weapons they can feel . . . This war is music in my ears." In the South, of course, moustached, star-collared General Beauregard uses the word "invasion," calling Lincoln "a restless and unprincipled tyrant . . . regardless of all moral, legal, and constitutional restraints."

The people who've elected him send their President fresh butter, salmon, Dr. E. Cooper's Magnetic Balm, patented unfermented bread, countless poems, a dictionary, a sofa cushion, a specific against constipation, a pair of live eagles, an ox, an honorary degree . . . He is of them; he comes from them. (I wonder what gifts Trotsky got? Hadn't he already requisitioned everything?) But defense of the authority they've loaned him must inevitably become authoritarian. Start with authority's fists, the armies. Do you remember Napoleon's egalitarian, honor-bound braves? Napoleon, unlike Lincoln, cares not a fig for constitutionality or even for his own promises. But Napoleon owns (at the beginning, at least) superior striking force, as well as his own undeniable strategic genius. Besides, he is attacking in those early years, not defending. He can move fast to objectives of his own choosing; call him, if not the father, at least the grandfather of *Blitzkrieg.* And within his dominions he has secret police to enforce his authority. He can afford to urge his high-spirited young men on, to drag them by the leash of emulation. Lincoln's armies for their part begin with enthusiasm, not confidence. The Mexican War gave them some combat experience, but that was a while ago, and nothing compared to Napoleon's graduates of a decade of foreign and domestic struggle. Lincoln has no secret police; his recruits are unaccustomed to discipline. They had, therefore, better not be allowed to run wild. ("I had perhaps a dozen officers arrested for cowardice in the first day's fight at this place," writes Grant. "These men are necessarily my enemies.") With his usual elegant sourness, Sherman warns us how the wheels will turn:

> In the United States the people are the "sovereign," all power originally proceeds from them, and therefore the election of officers by the men is the common rule. This is wrong, because an army is not a popular organization, but an animated machine, an instrument in the hands of the Executive for enforcing the law, and maintaining the honor and dignity of the nation.

In the same spirit, Grant accepts buried Jefferson's point that the people have the natural right to rise up, but makes of this a mere tautological plaything: they have the right to rebel only if they succeed! In other words, might makes right. Having formed this self-serving and mediocre argument,

Grant abruptly bolts far to the assertive forefront of Lincoln to utter what, depending on one's perspective, is either a brave declaration of a statesman's free will or else a chilling justification of Napoleonic arbitrariness:

> The fact is the constitution did not apply to any such contingency as the one existing from 1861 to 1865. Its framers never dreamed of such a contingency occurring. *If they had foreseen it, the probabilities are they would have sanctioned the right of a State or States to withdraw rather than that there should be war between brothers.*
>
> The framers were wise in their generation . . . It is preposterous to suppose that the people of one generation can lay down the best and only rules of government for all who come after them . . . We could not and ought not to be rigidly bound by the rules laid down under circumstances so different for emergencies so utterly unanticipated.

This surely had been Jefferson's frame of mind in proclaiming the Act of Embargo against England—and, oddly enough, it will be by means of a sort of violent embargo that Lincoln, Grant and Sherman win their suppressive war against states' rights. Whenever they come into Confederate territory, the Union troops will be instructed to pull up the steel rails and bend them so that they can no longer convey enemy trains; they demolish, destroy, expel and strip. (If Jefferson had been opposed to the federal government's digging a canal or two in Virginia, I don't suppose he would have been any more pleased to allow it to literally burn his state's bridges.) "Suppress the entire press of Memphis for giving aid and comfort to the enemy," instructs Grant. As for one probable source of what a general in our epoch would call "leaks," "I feel a strong inclination to arrest him and trust to find evidence against him afterward." Meanwhile Sherman has "deemed it to the interest of the United States" to turn Atlanta into an unpeopled military depot, just as Pol Pot will do 111 years later with Phnom Penh. Pol Pot, however, drives out the citizens at gunpoint, their fate being to become starving slaves. Sherman at least lets them go where they will, and provides transportation for them and their personal effects at the commencement of their journey. General Hood, commanding the Confederate Army of Tennessee, addresses him by letter: "Permit me to say that the unprecedented measure you propose transcends, in studied and ingenious cruelty, all acts ever before brought to my attention in the dark history of war." Sherman stingingly begs to differ: "If we must be enemies, let us be men, and fight it out as we propose to do, and not deal in such hypocritical appeals to God and humanity." Sherman's sheer righteous mercilessness almost terrifies one in the reading, and one begins to think General Hood in the right until his response comes back: "You say, 'Let us fight it out like men.' To this my reply is—for myself, and I believe for all the true men, ay, and the women and children, in my country—we will fight you to the death! Better die a thousand deaths than submit to live under you or your Government and your negro allies!" ("I have sworn not to take a prisoner," writes a Confederate soldier to his wife, "and I want to go out and kill some of them, will probably go tomorrow if I can get off.") And now it is impossible not to comprehend what Sherman has always known, that war must be hate and measured cruelty, that the intransigence of the one is locked against the scorn and defiant bigotry of the other; and we understand why Lincoln in all his patient forbearance and sad hopeless hopefulness once stooped to accept the Missouri Compromise and the Fugitive Slave Act and even to call them right, not that they were; because compromise, however evil, having failed, the fruit was disunion, and disunion has bled the fraternity between these once United States as white as those twin ruts of dirt road, the Hagerstown Pike, which lies like two rib bones touching the low white horizon; alongside of those are the real bones, mostly but no longer unanimously within the flesh of the dead: a knee drawn up sharp and steep in rigor mortis (the other leg down), a headless man embracing earth, as if he strives to find a way under; no doubt a Samaritan will help him get there. A body in bloody grass lies on its back, one hand on its bloated bloody belly, the other half-open and away. Legs and backs and shoulders rest between the Pike and the rail fence, forming their own Pike of Murder to lead us again to the horizon. Imagine the smell. They're Stonewall Jackson's men, butchered fair and square by General Hooker on September 17, 1862, that day of more than twenty thousand casualties. A quarter mile away are more Confederate dead from that battle, crowded together in the long ditch called Bloody Lane, while from above, two silhouettes, Union men I suppose, look on.

This victory consolidates the President's moral authority. Four months previous he'd rescinded Major General Hunter's premature and narrow emancipation decree for the South just as he'd done with General Frémont's decree in Missouri. Hunter's decree, in other words, was conceived as punishment. But now that so many men have died by violence beside the Hagerstown Pike and in Bloody Lane, in that vast and ghastly battle called Antietam, Lincoln feels able to issue his preliminary *general* emancipation proclamation within the week. It's been written that he was the led rather than the leader in this, that Union soldiers especially were sick of aiding the "secceshes" particularly once they began to meet the legions of hungry and mutilated runaway slaves. This may or may not be so. It is incontrovertible that at Lincoln's level of command authority, the deed has to be forced through. Various delegations of law professors, ex–Supreme Court justices and the like pass resolutions of protest against emancipation, "both on the grounds of its UNCONSTITUTIONALITY and inexpediency." After all, how long has it been since the Secretary of War was writing to the Commander of the Department of Virginia: "It is the desire of the President that all existing rights, in all States, be fully respected and maintained"?

In 1861 states' rights were still an ideal to be striven for, or at least yearned for. In 1862 they must be offered up on the altar of federalism. By the autumn of 1863, Grant, who like Sherman began with no particular abolitionist principles, who indeed had referred contemptuously a few months before the Emancipation Proclamation to cowardly "negro stealing," will write that "slavery is already dead and cannot be resurrected." One slave freed by the proclamation calls it "the sublimest and most important State paper that had ever been sent out . . . to the American people."

The President is gradually finding his strength. He visits Antietam three weeks after the battle, curiously wooden in his stovepipe hat and dark suit, in profile with his hands at his sides (remember the long exposure). Detective Pinkerton stands behind him, button-columned in clusters of three, shorter than the President. Tents, a guy line and trees complete this banal image of the Union's highest authority. Usually a scene is banal because it is typical; in Lincoln's case, it is typical because it is banal. In Washington, for instance, Walt Whitman, who sees the President go riding by almost every day, often with his little boy beside him, has to grant that authority, accompanied by its obligatory security detail of a quarter of a hundred cavalry, "makes no great show in uniform or horses. Mr. Lincoln on the saddle generally rides a good-sized, easy-going gray horse, is dress'd in plain black, somewhat rusty and dusty, wears a black stiff hat, and looks about as ordinary in attire, &c., as the commonest man." Once again I see in my republican mind's eye old Jefferson receiving the English minister, Merry, in a dirty shirt and heelless slippers, and I feel proud. Lincoln, as we say, is no Napoleon. He wants no splendor about him; that is scarcely his way. He defends not his own power, except as needed to defend the power entrusted to him. Unostentatiously and steadily he does his duty as he sees it, making mistakes and apologizing for them as he recognizes them, eating his defeats, meditating his victories, laying waste. Untrimmed in luxury's mantle, and popular, and remorseless—this is Trotsky, too. But Lincoln remains the compromiser; Trotsky demands total victory. Does Trotsky meditate on the dead he's made? —"The question is teleological and therefore fruitless." Lincoln does meditate on them. He understands all too well that violence is forcing North and South even farther apart. And he has no itch to annihilate the South. At the commencement of hostilities he would have restored everything to the old arrangement—Missouri Compromise and Fugitive Slave Act—if he could. Now he has made this promise, partly out of morality, partly out of expediency (for why have blacks on the enemy side when they can be, as General Hood calls them, allies?), and he will never go back on it. In time the Confederacy will sue for the old terms, and Lincoln will refuse. Meanwhile he suspends the writ of habeas corpus, and civil war continues.

Here lies the field of Fredericksburg, where six times the Union troops attacked, and six times they were slaughtered. "Men fell almost in battalions . . . Late in the day the dead bodies, which had become frozen from the extreme cold, were stood up in front of the soldiers as protection against the awful fire to shield the living, and at night were set up as dummy sentinels." —A constellation of dead men displays war's astronomy on the meadows of Gettysburg, where fifty thousand fell. The Confederates approach the crimson, swollen-bellied Union dead to take their guns and shoes. Here stands a wagon wheel at a tilt, like the wagon itself, now lacking the other wheel; a shell landed there, killing the horse which lies dark and heavy on its side, its mouth a black gape. A Confederate sniper lies stiff and pale in the Devil's Den. Here flourish only corpse vermin and disunion unbridgeable—the empathetic bridge that Trotsky sneered at is nowhere to be found; had it existed, General Sherman would have been forced to burn it, or General Hood would have ordered it shelled. It is in Lincoln's temperament ever to search for one, which is perhaps why Whitman remarks upon the sadness of his eyes. And it is the task of Generals Sherman and Hood (those two being subordinates unempowered to negotiate) to be as Trotsky. "This is the conclusion of our correspondence," writes Sherman coldly to his enemy counterpart, "which I did not begin, and terminate with satisfaction. I am, with respect, your obedient servant." There remains to be dealt with the Mayor of Atlanta, who implores Sherman to revoke his order of expulsion. "Many poor women are in an advanced state of pregnancy . . . And how can they live through the winter in the woods—no shelter, or subsistence . . . ?" His tone, unlike General Hood's, is respectful and decent. He does not seek to enter into political quarrels with Sherman; his voice is but human and humane. He speaks to Sherman as one reasonable, compassionate man to another. And Sherman, who after all once had many Southern friends, responds to him not, as he did to Hood, with the anger of a medieval knight who's just slammed down his visor, not, like Pol Pot, with utterly untouchable, insane lethality, but with an explanation: "I . . . give full credit to your statements of the distress that will be occasioned, and yet shall not revoke my orders, because they were not designed to meet the humanities of the case, but to prepare for the future struggles in which millions of good people outside of Atlanta have a deep interest . . . The use of Atlanta for warlike purposes is inconsistent with its character as a home for families." Rising up and rising down! Two months later, beginning his unstoppable march to the sea, he abandons Atlanta, having first smashed and burned it.

Defense of Authority as Refusal to Compromise

Lincoln is equally unstoppable. Emissaries from the Confederacy offer to settle everything, as we've seen, if only he will allow them to keep their slaves. Some loyalists still expect the same. A blue-clad fighter-memoirist is shocked to learn that the brother of the famous abolitionist Henry Ward Beecher "even now, with the proclamation of freedom ringing in his ears, did not hesitate to declare that the negro girl in a log-house near my tent did not belong to the same human family with himself." In 1864 we find a white lady riding home in her buggy with two black women, one beside her, the other walking at the rear with her hands tied behind her back; the Union commander has given her a pass to bring these escapees back to servitude because "Mrs. Baker is a good loyal lady." We must always remember the existence of such people and their dragging weight before daring to sneer at this President, this would-be "Great Compromiser." Yes, he hesitates to use black soldiers. A hundred and seventy-eight thousand blacks will eventually fight for the Union—for lower pay at first— and forty thousand of them will die in that fight. We're told that during his own Civil War, Trotsky will be inspired in part by the example of these

black regiments to appeal to the peasant soldiers of the counterrevolutionary side: Come to us, and we'll emancipate you! Leave the Whites, join the
Reds, and we'll share our land with you! One of Trotsky's loyal biographers calls the formation of the black regiments "the decisive turn" in Lincoln's Civil War, and in retrospect it certainly was. But one can imagine
the hardening, the very fossilization of hatreds, when the proslavers grasp
that the Great Compromiser will no longer compromise. —Oh, he continues to think about sending all the Negroes back to Africa. He has no am-
bition of allowing colored suffrage or racial intermarriage. But his
promise to black people, however belatedly made, however insufficient by
the standards of the twentieth century, remains immensely progressive
by the yardstick of his own time, when white women couldn't vote, either;
moreover, it's a covenant which he'll never breach. This is the reason that
one Union man who for the sake of *Realpolitik* is willing to vote for Lincoln over McClellan in the 1864 election still wishes "heartily however we
had a new man in the place of Lincoln, a man who was not bound personally, as it were, in honor by the emancipation proclamation." In this voter
we have the human average: not evil, not base, merely self-interestedly callous. He exemplifies one powerful motivation for the cause of states'
rights.

Authority's Compulsion

What we can be sure of is that the soldiers Union and Confederate are not
dying for "states' rights" or any such murderous abstraction, but rather for
other abstractions equally out of their control. Defense of creed, ground,
homeland, war aims, don't forget those! Defense of honor, naturally, takes
its usual myriad positions: honor as renown, honor as careerist prestige,
honor as "doing the right thing" for country and personal pride, and, above
all, collective honor as expediently defined by mass politicians. And we
mustn't leave out simple coercion—authority's surest defense.

 Nor, as we've seen, does Sherman, more bleak and to the point than his
President and his commanding general, save much time for highfalutin
philosophizing about states' or revolutionaries' rights. "They were mani-
festly the aggressors, and we could only defend our own by assailing
them." (A countervailing opinion: "Abe must die, and now," runs a letter.)
But in the end Sherman's rationale for violent defense of authority is much
the same as his superiors'. Rules and rights must be held over the fire of
war and twisted ruinously like those steel rails—but only as an emergency

expedient, not as a precedent for twisting rights in the peacetime to come. "No President has carried the power of presidential edict and executive order (independent of Congress) as far as he did," a historian writes. It was nothing compared to what Trotsky dared.

In 1862 Lincoln receives a letter of bitter complaint because a reverend in Pennsylvania was arrested merely for complaining about the care of wounded Union soldiers; the President's response is no longer known to us. In 1863 the *Chicago Times* is arbitrarily commanded to cease printing; upon receiving a petition signed by the Mayor of Chicago, Lincoln rescinds the suspension. In the occupied portions of the South, other such rails do not get so easily untwisted. "Unfortunately," Sherman soothes the Mayor of Memphis, now fallen into his power, "at this time, civil war prevails in the land, and necessarily the military, for the time being, must be superior to the civil authority, but it does not therefore destroy it."

Defense of Authority as Rejection of Public Opinion

Defense of authority, though? If authority is predicated on prestige, as Napoleon's partly was, then the President has little by now. In his own party, "Bluff Ben Wade," Zachariah Chandler and Thaddeus Stevens are out for his blood. The *New York Herald,* jeering at his stereotypical humor, calls him "a joke incarnate." Here is a cartoon in *Harper's* from the year when he finally proclaims the general edict of emancipation. The war is still going badly. Desperate, white-robed Matron Columbia begs him: "Where are my 15,000 Sons—murdered at Frederickburg?" —Lincoln: "That reminds me of a little Joke." For all her enthusiastic bellicosity, Elizabeth Cady Stanton writes to Susan B. Anthony about the incapacity and rottenness of his administration, and says that all administrations are the same; every four years they ought to be swept out like pigsties. New York, Ohio, Illinois, Pennsylvania and Indiana, who'd once given him their electoral votes, grant them to the Democrats instead. One historian sums up contemporary opinion about him during the worst war years as "a President who offended moderates without satisfying extremists." Political historians, with all their interesting coefficients and ratios of power, could easily produce from public and private sources the portrait of an impotent do-gooder.

But Grant and Sherman, never a praetorian guard, will stand by him; and they care not overmuch for public opinion. Although Sherman begins by warning his troops that straggling and pillaging are capital crimes, he

soon begins to send them on organized "foraging" expeditions to strip the
South of whatever his remorselessly marching armies need. This they enjoy hugely; we can almost see in the air above them the ghosts of the not at
all organized robbing parties of Napoleon's troops, who'd been likewise
compelled to live off the country. And the war continues, and Union
prisoners-of-war starve to death in the Southern concentration camp
called Andersonville, whose commandant will after the war be hanged,
and emancipation continues. The president writes to a lieutenant-colonel
suspected of impressing blacks into the army by torture: "You must not
force negroes any more than white men. Answer me on this." Against the
wishes of "a large number of respectable citizens" in New York, he has already refused to commute a slave dealer's sentence of hanging; this will be
the first time in the United States that the statute penalty has ever been enforced on one of these monsters. And Sherman triumphs, Grant triumphs
and Lincoln triumphs.

Defense of Authority as Growth of Authority

Lincoln was a very consistent man, and I believe that I do him no injustice
in simplifying his position as follows: the wrong of slavery must not be extended (which slaveholders took as a threat to starve them out); its abolition would delight him, but ending bondage must take second place to
union and constitutionality. "Mr. Lincoln did not enter with reluctance
upon the plan of emancipation," insists Congressman Arnold, "if he did
not act more promptly, it was because he knew he must not go faster than
the people." Once the war had begun, it probably gave him gratification to
be able to proclaim emancipation without violating the Missouri Compromise or the Fugitive Slave Act, which the secessionists, by seceding, had
already annulled. I've said that other unconstitutional measures brought
about by military necessity, such as the suspension of habeas corpus, were,
like Jefferson's embargo, simply emergency measures, but their employment, and above all the victory of the Union side, brought about, through
the simple logic of "spoils to the victor," an immense expansion of federal
power; so that the right of a state to resist road-building and canal-digging
became less and less heard of. Arnold puts down as a "settled question" that
"no State can by secession, nullification, nor by any act short of successful revolution, absolve any citizen from that allegiance and the obligation
to obey the laws of the Nation." After Reconstruction, John Roy Lynch,
Representative from Mississippi, by his complexion and by his former

employment (a slave) walking proof of his own thesis, courteously disdained "impractical State rights theorists" who seemed "to forget that the Constitution as it is is not in every respect the Constitution as it was."

Should we be sorry? The federal government's murder of a woman who was doing nothing more threatening than holding her baby in her arms (Ruby Ridge, 1992) was simply a crime; the FBI sniper and his superiors should have been convicted of first-degree murder (or, at the least, negligent homicide) and sentenced like "ordinary" citizens. Of course, in 1862 a posse comitatus in one of the sovereign states might have proudly lynched any number of innocent black men, which federal authority now undoubtedly keeps some devotees of local right from doing. The new Constitution to which Representative Lynch was referring was something to be proud of when, in 1957, enforcing school desegregation in Little Rock over the violence of white racists, Arkansas paratroopers made "a show of federal power in a southern state."

I certainly am glad that the Union won the Civil War. Were it possible to leave slavery out of the equation (which it isn't), I still wouldn't be sorry. But the natural process by which successful authority enlarges itself depresses me. *Defense of authority is unjustified when that defense in and of itself permanently aggrandizes the authority.* But *defense of authority is justified when the authority is not proven unjust and when failure to defend it will injure or destroy it*—in other words, here is our old friend, the right to self-defense. Certainly it would be even sadder to have to fight the Civil War a second time; there can be no question of state secession anymore—as long as the federal government follows Constitution and custom, which is now an open question. State sovereignty was, as we've seen, never well defined in the Constitution; Lincoln's victory continued the process which Jefferson's embargo had begun of defining the usage.

Another way to say this is that from the point of view of the Founding Fathers, Lincoln's defense of authority was unjust. The consensus upon which authority justifies itself has, however, changed; and I suspect that nobody in Virginia really minds anymore when the federal government pays to improve their sector of an interstate highway.

Defense of Authority as Defense Against Authority

There remains only one last hope for states' rights: John Wilkes Booth. Call him the Confederacy's John Brown. (He was, in fact, one of the militiamen present at the hanging of John Brown.) Did he take time to justify, he might go back to that sixteenth-century justifier of tyrannicide, "Junius Brutus": "Seeing that the people choose and establish their kings, it follows that the whole body of the people is above the king." The whole body of the people elected Lincoln to the presidency, and Booth has not been given any letters patent by the whole body of the people; nonetheless, he might perhaps argue (were he given more to argumentation than declamation) that insulted sovereignty demands extreme measures for the removal of the federal stranglehold. Thus Booth and his fellow conspirators take upon themselves—arrogate to themselves!—the grand self-rights, and self-righteousness, of thousands. Booth crouches ready; how can he not see that his cruelty will be of vain effect, that neither ends nor means will serve? He stalks into Ford's Theatre, "his eyes like some mad animal's flashing with light and resolution," and shoots Lincoln in the back of the head. Silence for a moment, says Whitman, as always; then Mrs. Lincoln screams, and the President's security detail, authority's failed defense, come vainly charging and cursing.

Oh, a victory for states' rights indeed! A year later, one of the causes of the ferociously antiblack riot in Memphis is a confrontation between white policemen and drunken, demobilized colored soldiers who are cheering the memory of Abraham Lincoln. A policeman answers them with what Booth's shade must surely deem a witty punch line: "Your old father, Abe Lincoln, is dead and damned."

Grant, however, mourns his president, and gives him this elegy: "I knew his goodness of heart, his generosity, his yielding disposition, his desire to have everybody happy, and above all his desire to see all the people of the United States enter again upon the full privileges of citizenship with equality among all." And here is Sherman, whose summations of character often range from testy to contemptuous: "Of all the men I ever met, he seemed to possess more of the elements of greatness, combined with goodness, than any other." Scorned and despised though he often was in life, the dead Lincoln is sincerely mourned. A century later, he will be equally admired and quoted by the Vietcong and by the Vietcong's arch-foe, President Johnson. Lincoln never was a despot, although war required him sometimes to act despotically. Between himself and the people lay a degree of mutual regard, maybe even love. Perhaps it is just this which gives authority's self-defense its best guarantee of justifiability.

And now for authority's final retributive defense. In Alexander Gardner's photograph taken at the Old Arsenal Prison in Washington, D.C., one sees the line of troops upon the high brick wall, as many of them as teeth. Their shadows dangle downward on the wall. Next one sees the huddled shine of some strange, ribbed polygonal convexity: They've given Mary Surratt, the first white American woman to receive the honor of a hanging, a parasol against the hot sun. She sits gazing at the noose which limply waits in front of her. To her left waits Lewis Paine, the tall, grim youth who, yelling, "I'm mad, I'm mad!" stabbed the Secretary of State and injured his sons—he justifies violence "because it was my duty," and his defense attorney will call him "the legitimate moral offspring of slavery, State rights, chivalry, and delusion"; David Herold, who surrendered to the Sixteenth New York Cavalry (beside him, John Wilkes Booth had refused to surrender, and died of what was probably a self-inflicted gunshot wound); and then their obscurer accomplice George Atzerodt, who is equally memorable, witnesses have said, for his good-natured disposition and for his cowardice. He admits his acquiescence in the conspiracy to kidnap, but says he rejected any notion of assassination. The photographer's flash powder explodes. (Their nooses sway in the breeze during the exposure, so we see but rope-ghosts in this print.) A cluster of clergy minister about the doomed; one is whispering into each of Mrs. Surratt's ears. Then slanting beams lead the eye down to the shaded understory where soldiers await the order to break out the vertical beams without which the trap will spring. In the weedy grass, a knot of invited auditors stand ready to witness this first and final act, with many more soldiers behind them.

As for the South itself, Grant writes to his wife a few days after the president's assassination: "The suffering that must exist in the South the next year, even with the war ending now, will be beyond conception."

Trotsky and Lincoln

In his series of articles about California migrant laborers, John Steinbeck, using the word "dignity" not in any sense of individual aggrandizement but as "a register of a man's responsibility to the community," argued that "a man herded about, surrounded by armed guards, starved and forced to live in filth loses his dignity; that is, he loses his valid position in regard to society, and consequently his whole ethics toward society." It was 1936.

Halfway around the world from the pea fields and eucalyptus groves, from the lines at government water taps and the shanties made of Kotex boxes, from the gaunt, tired Americans in their dusty overalls and faded print dresses, the Soviet show trials were growing their bumper crop of heads. Steinbeck's words powerfully and simply explain why the measures employed by Trotsky, and to a far greater degree by Stalin, were wrong. Lincoln's defense of authority, as we have seen, was based on the very debatable premise that he had the right to prevent secession. Trotsky's aim was the infinitely nobler one of creating a better society. Lincoln got his hands dirty by compromising with slavery. Trotsky got his hands dirty by refusing to compromise with divergent opinion. Lincoln believed, as Trotsky did not, in a *preexisting and potentially universal* mutuality between the leaders and the governed, which ought to be continued—hence his mild prescriptions for Reconstruction. Trotsky also understood that that authority, to be legitimate, must create and maintain that mutuality; but whereas Lincoln proposed to maintain that mutuality by force—he would not let the South go—Trotsky proposed to exclude from it by force all active and potential counterrevolutionaries. His writings give us no certainty that he would not have treated the kulaks as brutally as Stalin did. Surely the Bolsheviks, having inherited a social contract of sorts with *all* the people in the USSR, including the peasants, who never overtly rose up on a mass scale (they didn't have the weapons to do so), but simply resisted forced requisitions and collectivization, should have respected that contract.

The destruction of Atlanta by Sherman can debatably be justified on the grounds of necessity. The destruction of millions of civilians over a period of decades by the Cheka and its successors cannot. Authority may or may not have the right to maintain itself by force. This right implies the right to temporary enlargement, just as a householder being threatened with death by an intruder has the right *at that moment,* and at that moment only, to kill the intruder if he can. Authority never has the right to unilaterally enlarge itself by force, maintaining that enlargement long beyond any reasonable definition of a crisis. (Trotsky insisted that authority now embodied the will of the progressive class; Hitler and Robespierre, that they embodied the general will. The fact that all three so frequently employed violence against their people proved that they did not embody any general will except in some potential phantasm of form.) This is why Lincoln was ultimately more justified than Trotsky, not necessarily in his goals but certainly in his methods; and why, when the two men were each assassinated, Trotsky was mourned only by the converted, but Lincoln became almost a folk saint.

V.

DEFENSE OF GROUND

So let each stand his ground firmly with his feet well set apart and bite his lip.

TYRTAEUS, fragment 10

But what's needed to fight our foes is a man who stands his ground, not one who runs away.

THE SPARTAN ANDROCLEIDAS, who enlisted
even though he was crippled

Could it ever have been intended that our Government could tell a semi-dependent and semi-barbarous power that it might defend boundaries which we had fixed without by implication conveying to it that we would assist in the defence of those boundaries?

LORD ETTRICK, UK Secretary of State for Foreign Affairs,
Speaking on the Afghan Question (1874)

Ethical Perimeters

Defense of authority typically takes place in sealed areas: the high-walled prison yard where the gallows gapes its trap, the closed borders of the Ukraine where authority introduces mass starvation in pursuit of perfect classlessness, the police barricades behind which the antiterrorist team raises its sniperscopes, the dry riverbeds outside of town where the Genji execute their Heike prisoners. "The Protective Strip is marked off from the Restricted Area by a metal trellis fence only half the normal height but with electric contacts on top. If they are touched an optical signal is immediately flashed to the nearest command post of the guard company on duty. A siren may also be sounded. This enables the alarm groups to take action from two sides to stop the person trying to escape." Help somebody cross the Restricted Area and surmount the wall, and you'll be convicted under Section 105 of the East German Penal Code, "anti-State trading in humans." Authority may well, for the sake of intimidating, appeasing or proclaiming, offer its violence as a spectacle, like the French Revolution's *journées,* the condemned in their tumbrils riding past silent or jeering crowds to the guillotine. But at the spot where the deed is done, whether or not there are any inanimate walls, authority will have posted its minions. When Louis XVI, standing already at Sanson's elbow (within weeks, Sanson would also behead his wife), sought to address the people, authority walled him off with deafening drumbeats, and his counterrevolutionary pleas were sliced away.

Walls of an Atom

War, on the other hand, is not merely public but almost wall-less—or, to be more accurate, its walls are unpredictable improvisations, which constitutes one measure of its fright. Where will the sniper's bullet come from? Who will die in this campaign, my brother, or myself, or no one whom I know? Are we safe here, or is this orchard an ambush? (Louis XVI knew very well where the guillotine was, and who would die that day.) "Grape rattles on the roofs of the houses and in the fields," writes Clausewitz;

> cannon balls howl over us, and plough the air in all directions . . . The young soldier cannot reach any of these different strata of danger without feeling that the light of reason does not move here in the same medium, that it is not refracted in the same manner as in speculative contemplation.

For confirmation, gaze into the farseeing, helmet-shaded eyes of a shell-shocked soldier in Vietnam.

These zones of concentration, which vary with time and place, and which are called battles, have their own concentric walls multiplied by the number of human beings. The threatened self lives within its fortress of flesh, which may be walled again with armor. In the medieval *Song of Roland* we are continually reading how that reified vector of force, the warrior's lance, passes first through the foeman's shield, next through the hauberk, that bodysuit of chain mail, and then through the final redoubt, the breastbone. "Through the man's back drives out the backbone bended / And soul and all forth on the spear-point fetches." In Lidiya Ginzburg's "blockade diary" of the Nazi siege of Leningrad, "a hostile world was on the offensive and pushing its outposts forward. The closest of these outposts had suddenly turned out to be one's own body . . . with all its new ribs and angles," for everyone was starving to death. (Three hundred thousand Leningraders died.) Beyond the body, and the bulletproof vest of the fortunate, loom brick walls and perimeters, within which it is the business of authority's self-defense to *confine and direct* violence, whereas it is the contrary business of military bellicosity to *smash* those walls. Should the army succeed, back to rib cages again for our protection—sometimes even the rib cages of our fellow creatures. During the final Spanish campaign of Julius Caesar's civil war, the Caesarians set up enemy "bodies in place of a turf rampart. On top were set severed heads on sword-points . . . they . . . thus encircled the town with a wall of corpses."

We are told that in 1941–45 "the ground war in the South Pacific was a war of perimeters instead of lines," but this has always been true for the individual. His body is his perimeter. In fear he huddles into himself, waiting for violence to strike his side or his back, his belly or his arm. He prepares, arms himself, strikes back, or not. He is a French sentry at Verdun, a man who wears a poncho, standing in a hole walled to his chin with snowy sandbags, and crazy circles of barbed wire above him. Maybe a shell will come straight for him from Enemyville, or maybe it will overshoot him and earth will fall upon his back, crushing him. His flesh, his bones and bowels await. He is a member of a British company encircled by Zulus. (Che Guevara has a name for the expression of a frightened person: "encirclement face.") The living wall of the Native Contingent having collapsed, the Zulus in their red tunics come rushing in. The surrounded Englishmen "held their ground in compact bodies, till, their ammunition being expended, they were overpowered, and died where they stood." One of the sixteenth-century Spanish conquistadors, receiving a charge of Indians, noted how "the stones sped like hail from their slings, and their barbed and fire-hardened darts fell like corn on the threshing-floor, each one capable of piercing any armour or penetrating the unprotected vitals." A terrifying German poster from a year or so after Leningrad shows a large-skulled skeleton riding through stormy darkness upon a fighter plane; he bares his teeth in glee, and in his skinny arm raises high above his pale round head a dark round bomb, ready to hurl it down upon a single half-lit building in a blacked-out German city. "The enemy sees your light!" screams the poster (and to English speakers, the German word for enemy, *Feind,* transforms a mere opponent into a fiend, a ghoul, a monster).

"*Verdunkeln!*" Turn that light out! For the careless householder in the poster, of course, it is already too late. The scene is one of fear and helplessness. The good Germans below are not aggressors, or even violent defenders, only human beings to be pitied. Their only hope in the face of the fiend's oncoming is to hide in that ominous darkness. The remark of a French commentator that soldiers at Verdun were "orphans who fought in isolation" is true of any human being alone or in company against whom violence is directed, for when we fear, we are always alone; this becomes incalculably more true when the enemy and his munitions are magnified from a group of subway muggers with sharpened screwdrivers to an army with a thousand 155-millimeter cannons. A hundred fifty-five millimeters? Old stuff! We see a soldier posing beside an unexploded 305-millimeter shell which comes almost up to his shoulders. I know the difference between a .22 caliber pistol cartridge and a 9 millimeter, between a 9 millimeter and a .45, between a .45 and a .50, which is almost the highest-caliber handgun I can legally own and shoot; from the barrel of my .50 comes a long fireball; the noise and the shock are unpleasant. I cannot imagine the sound of a 305-millimeter shell detonating. (What were they shooting at Sarajevo? It was loud; they never told me.) But here's a photograph to show me the 305: one struck a French battery—"literally crushed and buried," just as the caption says. Here comes another, and another. "Soon it's not possible to count the shots," says a foot soldier, "we're in the center of an uninterrupted roaring . . ." No matter what, at some point the spearpoint will ferret out that wretch's soul, and Lidiya Ginzburg's neighbors will begin to surrender as their fat and flesh get slowly breached by hunger, leagued with cold. (For contrast, consider the leitmotif in so many of the old Norse sagas: enemies surrounding one's house and burning to death everyone inside.) "A fortified place can only protect the garrison and arrest the enemy for a certain time," admits even optimistic Napoleon.

Walls of a Cohort

War destroys; war takes. Saint-Exupéry's bailiff must be paid. Will he demand our old clothes today, for use in the war effort, or will he burn us alive? In the officially inspired Assyrian reliefs we discover the usual bearded, huge-eyed profiles of Assyrian victors leading a procession of prisoners of war. Captive women sit above a high cartwheel, their hands upraised in wisely submissive gestures. War has won, the city wall overrun. Sennacherib's infantry files after siege engines up steep inclines, smashing the walls of Lachish; archers launch death from behind immensely wide shields (their own portable walls); two soldiers have impaled three naked men whose shoulders swell grotesquely like those of hunchbacks as they hang rabbit-limp—war takes; war does as it pleases; and as usual everyone is in profile, marching as seriously and as unaware of any observing eye as ants on their mission. Homeland contracts, like Trotsky's USSR during the Russian Civil War of 1918–21: "Our fronts had a tendency to close into a ring of more than eight thousand kilometers in circumference." Trotsky can thus deploy his Red Army along entirely internal lines. "But this advantage was available to us on the sole condition of complete centralization in management and command." His equation, we know, runs thus: Defense of homeland being a priori justified, repression being a logical necessity, then repression must be justified, too.

The selfsame Sennacherib, King of the World, King of Assyria, who seven hundred years before Christ uses "mines, breeches as well as sapperwork" to attack Hezekiah the Jew in forty-six of his strong cities, fortresses and the like, gleefully provides his scribes with still another reason why he ought to be deserving of our immortal reverence: "Himself I made a prisoner in Jerusalem, his royal residence, like a bird in a cage. I surrounded him with earthwork in order to molest those who were leaving his city's gate." The walls need not even necessarily be breached, you see; war can make a defensive wall, designed to keep me out, into an offensive one, by means of which I'll keep you in. Hezekiah is finally forced to surrender and remit great tribute, including his own daughters as concubines. He is luckier than Lidiya Ginzburg's fellow Leningraders. Sennacherib, unlike Hitler, does not demand to fetch out his soul on the swordpoint. Lines of cavalry with drawn bows and extended lances ride toward the enemy in still another of the frozen reliefs which a scholar has called "this series of pictorial war-records without equivalent in any country, . . . this almost monotonous display of horrors." Of course it was not only the Assyrians who thus pictorially recorded their sickening triumphs.

Walls Versus Vectors

Defense of authority is most often paradoxically directed against the unarmed or the relatively weak, authority by definition being incumbency, which is strength, armed strength, the strength of the clan, of the state, of the organization; and rebellion, beginning from subjection, must start as feebleness. (This applies equally to acts other than rebellion which authority chooses to repress: robbery, murder, rape, arson, idolatry, expression of unpopular opinions, racial self-defense, et cetera. The state is the strongest; otherwise it could not be the state.) When insurgency grows sufficiently, it becomes civil war (unless it can follow that secret ladder to power called coup d'état—a case we won't consider here). At this point, authority's walls cannot contain what authority's survival demands must be contained. Capital punishment's bullrings and ghettos may and probably will continue to be walled, but the frontier, the city wall and above all the wall of troops now take on the decisive role of determining whether the other walls can exist. Authority cowers, or sallies, from behind its walls, knowing that to keep what it has, it must break the enemy's mobile bulwarks. "If the enemy opens the door," says the great strategist Sun-tzu, "you must race in." That is the way Ramses II will get his pile of severed hands. From time to time, as we've seen, authority's customary rings of repression are duplicated in war: from a pure standpoint, the siege of Leningrad, or the "kettle" encirclement of German troops at Stalingrad, or the two-pronged Persian attack upon the narrow pass of Thermopylae, were but counterparts of Louis XVI's besiegement on the scaffold by the soldiers of the Revolution, or Che Guevara's strategic policy of making the enemy feel at "every moment . . . he is surrounded by a complete circle" of guerrillas. Diagrammatically, we might represent some of these situations (simplified) as follows.

TOPOGRAPHIC VECTORS OF FORCE

FIGURE 1: Defense of authority. The vectors of force are all focused inward, in a tightly controlled zone. Someone is being executed, or a rebellion is being put down. The circle represents either a permanent wall of some kind (say, the perimeter of the gymnasium at Nuremburg where the Nazi war criminals were hanged) or the easily replicable, and indefinitely holdable, perimeter of the zone of control (for instance, the series of roadblocks and other barriers established by the FBI and the Bureau of Alcohol, Tobacco and Firearms around David Koresh's "compound" in Waco, Texas). Of course, this diagram could also indicate a lone victim being surrounded by attacking thugs.

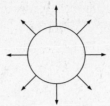

FIGURE 2: Defense of authority / potential defense of a nation. The vectors of force are all focused outward. The borders are sealed; perhaps mobilization has begun. Enemies are expected. Because the zone which these vectors are required to cover is infinite, this configuration is practical only if the zone within the arrows is relatively small, as would be the case if, for instance, merely a Prime Minister were in it, being protected by his bodyguards; or if the zone were a medieval city. Even in the latter case, the position is not tenable for long. In the case of a large nation approaching war, a more realistic diagram would be Figure 3. This diagram could also represent terrorists guarding a hostage (although if we wished to indicate their intimidation of the hostage we would have to include some inward-pointing arrows, too), or sentries monitoring a secret post in enemy territory.

FIGURE 3: Defense of authority / potential defense of a nation. The vectors of force are all focused outward, but in one sector. The nation is defending itself, or attacking, along a limited front. Where there are no arrows, there is (hopefully) no threat.

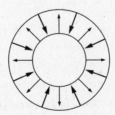

FIGURE 4: Defense of a nation. A city is under siege; or a nation has been drawn into a two-front war. (Bold arrows originating in the outer ring indicate the violence of the aggressors.) The defenders are fighting back. Of course, this diagram could also describe a rebellion, in which case the bold arrows would be

the lineaments of authority in the zone of repression; the other arrows would
express the force of the trapped rebels trying to hold the gendarmes at bay.

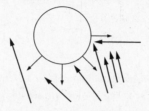

FIGURE 5: Defense of an individual in combat. (Note the similarity to Figure
3.) The bold arrows pointing upward represent the attacks of the enemy.
There are (let's hope) also bold downward-pointing vectors originating from
his own side, but this beleaguered soldier (or woman fighting a gang rape, or
rebel desperately seeking to avoid capture) cannot see them. Perhaps the
approaching arrows have no personal intent, but the lonely self stands in
their way.

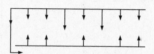

FIGURE 6: A pitched battle. This might represent one of the clashes of Greek hoplites described in Thucydides. The two lines of troops are facing each other,
more or less evenly matched—but the uppermost army has slightly more force in
the center, although it does not seem likely to break through, and it has initiated
a well-advanced flanking maneuver around the enemy's left. On a much larger
scale, this could be a modern battle, too, in which case the facing lines might be
fronts instead of troop lines.

Given the agreed-on right of the self to defense and preservation, it
would seem clear that the legitimacy both actual and perceived of violent
defense in the above situations would vary in proportion to the number
and intensity of force-vectors in one's path. Regarding Figure 1, we could
not blame the Nazi war criminals from exercising this right and using
lethal force to escape, if they could; of course, it was the responsibility of
the prison to make sure that they could not. They'd been outlawed and remanded to the executioner, like Robespierre; we had decided that they
were not entitled to live, but the struggles of the body to live must be taken
for granted just as much as the need to defecate; that is why there are soldiers, walls and manacles at executions.

Regarding Figure 2, an invading soldier, seeing that the city was on the offensive, would probably destroy its troops as much as he could; having breached the circle, however, he would be unjustified in slaughtering defenseless civilians. In 1582, Russian troops set out to conquer Siberia and encountered an "immense gathering of the heathen." With no irony whatsoever, the Russians' leader, Ermak, addressed the men as follows: "Oh, friends and brothers! Let us pray to God and to His Virgin Mother, and to all the heavenly powers, and to His saints, that they will protect us against invasion by the vile and cursed enemy!"

Figure 3 shows that the need for an attacker to shoot first and ask questions later would be higher in the southeast quadrant than in the north and northwest. Figure 4 portrays a life-and-death struggle, which looks absurdly tidy in this stylized diagram, but to somebody actually involved would resemble the writhing muddles of a Renaissance battlefield, with lances literally at cross-purposes, stabbing at shoulders and bellies; a man down grimaces; competing banners fly colorfully, high above it all. The painting by the Korean Pyon Pak (1760) depicting the "Heroic Defense of Tongnae City" against the Japanese in 1592 is laid out in just this way, with defenders massed upon the high dark curves of the city wall, steep fairy-tale mountains in the background and the Japanese all around in a girding, threatening rush. In the zone of battle between the two rings, almost any violent means would be justified.

The same license must be granted to the individual in Figure 5, who might be one of the grandly honorable and egotistical warriors whom we read about so often in the *Tale of the Heike,* a proud, self-doomed fighter who throws himself where the enemy is thickest, and hacks until he's cut down. Or he might be somebody who wants to keep his life. In either case, he is one against many and deserves to even the odds in any way that he can.

In Figure 6, the same goes for any of the fighters in the opposing lines; as for the flankers and the flanked, both of them are now at extreme personal risk, and can be legitimately expected to lash out all the more desperately. A grim Mesopotamian proverb runs: "You go and take the field of the enemy; the enemy comes and takes your field."

Simply put, *defense of ground is justified by imminent self-defense, even during unjust aggression.* A shivering French soldier in his snowy bivouac outside of Moscow shoots down the Russian homeland-defenders who try to kill him by night. His army, Napoleon's army, is wrong. But he has every right to defend himself. So does Napoleon—correct?

"Did I Want to Destroy Them or Protect My Own Life?"

When we meditate more seriously on the ethics of defense of ground, over us, like the fog from a chlorine gas shell, begins to steal a sense first of bemusement, then bewilderment, then uneasiness. Napoleon is a man like me. Napoleon has the right to defend himself. Yet Napoleon is also—Napoleon. A soldier loyal to his standards, I follow him to Russia and back, loyal but lost in a maze of walls of which I'm a single brick. I have no time to think. I march, I shoot or I run. Present arms! Forward march! About face! War breaches walls, yes; and to accomplish that, it builds temporary walls of its own—moving walls. "Do not attack well-regulated formations," warns Sun-tzu; they cannot be breached without paying too highly in blood. Sometimes the walls contain and protect the blood: these are the supply arteries—increasingly weakly walled in proportion to their length, which is one reason to build garrisons. My mind wanders to movement and tactics, away from ethics. I think of fluid dynamics, not of ends, means and morally colored expediencies. An analyst of Alexander the Great's campaigns reminds us: "It must be stressed again that a military route is not a mere line drawn on a map but a narrow corridor with sufficient agricultural and water resources in the immediate vicinity with which large numbers of men and animals can be supported." The corridor is life: the corridor is homeland. (All armies need to be mobile, or else require firm lines and bases of supply, in order to avoid exhausting the resources of a fixed area, be those of food or of ammunition.) In a wooden model we see Egyptian soldiers in a column four abreast, marching, barred and leopard-dotted shields at their left sides, lances vertical, the points above their heads, like cattails on the stalk, or that old simile applied to Charlemagne's invading army of iron cornfields; they are a narrow wall of death on the move; and by constituting themselves as such, they protect themselves and each other. Thucydides compares the terrified, disheartened Athenians in retreat from the battle of Syracuse (A.D. 413) as "a starved-out city, and that no small one"; and Nicias, their doomed general, seeks to encourage them by saying: "You are yourselves at once a city wherever you sit down, and . . . there is no other in Sicily that could easily resist your attack." They wall themselves with weakly wobbling spears and heavy bronze shields now almost unbearable to raise; only fear gives them strength; for a little longer, they constitute their own homeland, until their final scattering and defeat, dying in agony on

Syracusans' javelin-tips, drinking desperately from river water bloodied by
their own dead. Until then they are a wall. So are the Germans in France in
May 1940: a hollow square of tanks, with infantry inside. And in Russia in
December 1941, Hitler will command them to wall themselves against all
odds—don't give up an inch! The Germans' Sixth Army, suddenly in the
same situation as Nicias's hoplites, will now be supplied by building an "ice
railway bridge" across the frozen Dnieper. No need for bronze shields—in
the one month of its operation, the ice bridge delivers over 4,500 wag-
onloads of supplies: food so that the body can hold on, munitions to wall
away the enemy with all-round threats of lead and explosive shells. Although frozen rivers elsewhere imperil the Germans, because the Russians
can come at them over the ice, the Sixth Army maintains its line—at least
until that final day of javelins. General Tippelskirch recalls:

> The Russians always failed to break our front, and though they pushed
> far round our flanks, they had not yet the skill nor sufficient supplies to
> drive home their advantage. We concentrated on holding the towns that
> were rail and road centres, rolling up round them like "hedgehogs"—
> that was Hitler's idea—and succeeded in holding them firmly. The situa-
> tion was saved.

(The same general, however, admits that supplying those "hedgehogs"
by air in the terrible winter weather was a major cause of the downfall of
the Luftwaffe. And Hitler's doctrine of holding fast, continued in the winter of 1942 with weakened, diminished troops, allowed those troops to be
captured.)

This is war: Wall off oneself from the enemy, and surmount *their*
walls. If they cannot be breached, perhaps they can be avoided.

When one reads the American Revolutionary Army's drill manual, written by Baron von Steuben in 1794, one gets an eerie sense of how the army
liquefies as needed, creates its own temporary arteries of travel and flows
around walls. Indeed, Steuben's contemporary Napoleon defines its strength
as mass times rapidity. "Break off!" the commanding officer cries, and then
the files of troops swing right and left (or inward if the obstructions are on
the army's wings), then flow through the gaps they've found, as Blitzkriegers
will do a century and a half later, considerably more rapidly and aggres-
sively; then the organism reconstitutes itself: "In proportion as the ground
permits, the files will march up to their places in front, dress, and take step

with the colours." Much of military strategy consists in executing flanking movements, getting around and behind the enemy, as in Figure 6, in order to surround them as in Figure 4. *Take the offensive before you are surrounded,* Napoleon insists. (This would seem justified by defense of ground—but what else justifies it?) Quick—preserve our access, and cut *them* off! Hence one's own walls and arteries lengthen sideways—the story told by the bewildering, sickening ugliness of World War I trench maps, which begin by dividing up each landscape as usual into grid squares already transected by winding village roads; upon these, murderous and accidentally suicidal engineers have overlaid their communication ditches, their trenches which curl across the land like strands of spaghetti: "3' 6" d[eep] mud & water," warns the legend for one; another: "wet ditch," another: "passable—water,"—another: "passable for infantry" (poor bastards); then come the telegraph wires, the long, twisting streams of barbed wire, cheveaux de frises ("many iron posts," the map warns, "iron spikes," "probably abatis"), and then they've raised brickworks and breastworks and embrasures for machine guns; and the artillery cartographers have superimposed their target circles, whose results we see in later maps as shell craters, some of whom even have names: "New Year Crater 2-1-16." Lines of craters overlap like a necklace of half-melted, fused beads. "Breastwork 4' to 5' high at Point 59; it is said to be 15' thick." Trenches intersect, spew off pseudopods, as likewise occurred with Alexander the Great's lines of supply, which Alexander extended as he went by receiving (such was his capacity to intimidate, or to invoke the chimera of "liberation") the surrender, often with hostages, of local authority *in advance of his arrival!* After reaching Babylon, Alexander was, of course, in Persia proper, and the people became more hostile to him. No matter; what the Macedonians could not gain by threats, persuasion or market-dealing they received by force, dividing his army in proportion to the resources they could take from a given area, so that the expedient corridors multiplied. Thus the reduction of the Uxians in 330 B.C. Alexander himself labored alongside his men to smash a way through the ice of the Deh Bid Pass. And he went on and on, until the disasters in Afghanistan and southern Iran, where in 327 B.C. the failure of his supply fleet to appear resulted in the death of 75 percent of his army. And these trenches of World War I, they go on and on, also, but they get nowhere. Trenches parallel each other, for the enemy is close enough to hear. Can we flank him? No, we've already gone from Switzerland right across Europe to the sea! Napoleon proposes the following universal principles of victory: "to keep . . . forces united;

to leave no weak part unguarded; to seize with rapidity upon important points." His commentator suggests that the first of these may be obsolete, that mobility may be more wise than concentration. World War I is why he thinks so. Tanks and *Blitzkrieg* have not yet been born; they will save us from the trenches, so that we can commit new atrocities; meanwhile, trenches lengthen with the years, curving out new arms, connecting segments. They resemble nothing so much as crazy dark cracks in the landscape. "Hedge $4\frac{1}{2}$' high, not strong but wired." And then on some maps, after all this, we repeatedly find the letter "A," meaning: "Defensive works being carried out." At the third battle for Ypres there will be one gun for every six yards of front! The maps say: "Lateral. Defensive traverse. Tunnel. Dugout. Shaft to machine gun emplacement. Mine. Incline blown in. Blown in water. Brickfield, sunken. Holed through at 3 feet. Blocked. Blocked. Blocked." Dead men everywhere, in the mud and in the snow, curled or spread-eagled, headless or crushed, the only features of featureless craters, pounded into the dirt and dusted with dirt, dust to dust. A headless corpse hangs skewered in a scorched tree—sometimes the bailiff enjoys collecting his debt most freakishly. Here again comes death, in the form of chlorine. But self-defense is ready, and we find men lurking like crater-eyed ghosts in their pale gas masks. Or is it self-defense? Why must this trench be my homeland? (In Roman times, we heard Aemilius Paullus tell his legionnaires before battle that their entrenched camp is "a resting-place for the victor, a refuge for the beset. This military residence is our second fatherland.") In the 1980s, a Soviet journalist taking part in an ambush of Afghan guerrillas wonders afterward: "Was I shooting at the *dukhi* with an assault rife to attack or to defend? Did I want to destroy them or protect my own life?" More trenches now. Their names speak of fantasy, despair, homesickness and bureaucratic dullness: Madagascar Trench, Inverness Trench, Old Boots Trench, Harry's Cut, Lover's Lane, Tower Reserve Trench, French Central Trench, Incision Trench, Inch Trench, Incline Drive, Inadequate Trench, Created Trench, Ceylon Trench, Cesspool Trench, Covering Trench, Trenches Night, Novel and Necklace, Trench 38, Trench 39 . . . See the files of helmeted ant-men toiling forward in their chin-high zigzag grooves of earth. See the miners and sappers in their long dark tunnels. The battlefield drawing of Urs Graf (Basle, 1521) is no less gruesomely bustling than any of these scenes, but in Graf's time the soldiers are, with exceptions, fighting upright, in massed ranks; four centuries later, in the days of Cesspool Trench, the attacks will occur in "waves" of desperate scuttlers. Armies keep adding insets to their maps to keep up with new trenches, supports, dumps, redoubts and fosses. Dig in—armor yourself! Burrow into the ground and defend it! (Against what? Against the machine guns. The British, for instance, began the war with only two per battalion. By the end, they had one machine gun for every two platoons—to say nothing of the new Machine Gun Corps, and the cavalry, who now rode mechanical horses, armed with sixty-four machine guns per battalion. Their allies and enemies did much the same. Machine guns caused almost eight out of every ten casualties in World War I.) We see the dugouts, sometimes mere log-walled caves whose domed dirt roofs dimple the trampled forests, sometimes, as is the case with this Germanic marvel, real subterranean forts *"en maçonnerie,"* of masonry, complete with steps of brick or stone on which we see the German officers standing for a pose; beneath the smooth overhang of the earth-packed roof are shuttered windows similar to those one meets in bungalows, or (more to the point) shooting-blinds. War's jocularity, which attempts to laugh off horror, calls them "dugouts of the Crown Prince." By August 1917, when the German tunnel under Dead Man is captured, we can find a machine room twenty-seven meters deep, with dully shining engine wheels, a tiled ceiling with electric lights, a wall panel studded with controls; the entire tunnel has electric power! That must be why it, too, is called "Crown Prince." Spoils to the victor; the German mechanics will be replaced by French ones, and the war continues. "This warfare was often treated as siege warfare," writes a military historian. "But in fact it differed from a normal siege because new 'walls' could be created more easily and quickly than old 'walls' could be knocked down." —What are they like, these easy solutions? Read the poems of Wilfred Owen, the paeans to boys being delivered to annihilation, storming fixed positions which become more rather than less impregnable during the attack, because so many attackers are killed by the machine guns that their bodies form new obstacles. "The character of violence, of brutality and of rapidity must be maintained," ran the French instructions for the attack on Champagne; but the refrain in Owen's poem "Exposure" is: "Nothing happens." Caterpillar files of troops scuttle in and out of shellholes. The repulsed attack of "Spring Offensive," and the stench of dugouts where men have lived "for years" ("The Sentry") are brought to us by a poet in hell. Photographers tell us the same story as poets. Here is one image of sugarloaf-hatted Russian troops standing ankle-deep in water, in what appears to be a grave in the snow, a narrow, snaky grave with slanted sides; they stand there in their boots, and one soldier grips a corrugated hose which crawls out of that trench like a fat earthworm and meets a handpump at graveside where two other soldiers hold the long handle; this is a posed photograph, and so halfway down the side of the trench stands an officer (for whose benefit the image was probably taken), one hand on his hip, the other on a delicate little cane as he stares bluffly ahead, doing nothing; nobody else is really doing anything, either; after the photograph was taken they probably got to work in earnest, pumping out that sodden hole in which they would have to sleep, unless the officer commanded them to dig another one. Gas, and machine guns, and barbed wire; mass murders beyond measure. "At that time," writes the German eyewitness Remarque, "even one's parents were ready with the word 'coward': no one had the vaguest idea what we were in for." Those who still read Clausewitz could take spurious comfort, for that worthy explained through his "annihilation principle" that the object of a great battle was to destroy the enemy's forces. The only problem was that in trench warfare vast numbers of one's own troops seemed to get destroyed as well. No matter—pay the bailiff; fight on! Kill or be killed. Hence the strange equivalence of war posters: A World War I German, supported by his comrades, or fighting a heroic battle alone, is pushing Russian enemies off a cliff; failing to get their foothold in his country, they fall, dying and hating. A World War II Russian is pushing Germans off a cliff. It doesn't matter. The enemy's face is distorted, fiendlike; often we see him accompanied by monsters: hydras, snakes, octopi. From the standpoint of the powerless individual summoned by the bailiff, *the enemy is always the aggressor.* Attack in order to survive; survive in order to attack again— that's defense, as the generals and politicians define it, as homeland defines it; invoke, if you like, Jerzy Kosinski's dictum that "a community, threatened with destruction or with a break-up of its cultural forms, clings with renewed ferocity to the mythic; the stresses of war produce this group reaction, bringing added tension into both the communal and the individual consciousnesses"—but when we inspect a photograph of "a gallery of Vaux Fortress at the heart of the battle" we see rubbled darkness beneath a heavy arch; a man lies sleeping, wounded or dead on the sharp stones, with his boot-toes turned up; a bearded man with a hospital armband sits with his helmet askew, gazing down into nothingness—this is homeland? Incline Trench is homeland? Gaze into his eyes. He is tired. Perhaps for him—certainly for more and more men like him—there is no homeland, ground or war aim worthy of this agony anymore.

What ground is sacred? Ask its ultimate defender, invincible in creed and greed—the cruel rager, the sprightly gambler-conqueror, Cortes.

Gaming for Gold Pieces

I can never read without pity and horror the account of the captive Montezuma, erstwhile king of the Aztec Empire, now shadow-king, puppet-king, soon to die, and his civilization with him—commencing a round of *totoloque*, "a game played with small, very smooth gold pellets specially made for it." Opposite sits Don Hernando Cortes, citizen of Medellin, who has married well and intrigued in high places. With all the politeness of a cat undesirous of killing the mouse straightaway—in part because he knows that his military strength, in relation to that of his prisoner's as yet unsubdued warriors, stands not as cat to mouse, but rather the reverse—Cortes visits every day, after Mass. (What obscene blessings he receives from God I can only imagine.) It often happens that he stays for a round of *totoloque*—for he has a lot of time on his hands, being yet uncertain what to do next (more specifically, how to convert a perilously illegitimate defense of ground into an unvanquishable authority). They throw the pellets of gold, he and Montezuma, and on the fifth toss there is a winner and a loser. The stakes are gold and jewels. When Montezuma wins, he gives his prizes to Cortes's soldiers of the guard. When Cortes wins, he with symmetric graciousness distributes his stakes to Montezuma's attendants. Cortes, I am afraid, possesses neither gold nor jewels of his own; whatever he puts up must therefore be either his plunder from Montezuma's outer dominions, or else the treasure Montezuma has already given him. The games go on as do the days; Montezuma and Cortes assure one another of their mutually imperishable regard. (They're brother tacticians. They're both city-burners and book-burners.) Montezuma wishes to go hunting on his private island. The courteous destroyer assures him that he is "very welcome to go, but that he must remember what had been said to him before, when he went to visit his idols, that if he raised any occurrence it would cost him his life." On the occasion to which Cortes refers, the Emperor had indeed been allowed to climb the sacred pyramid—but surrounded by Cortes's men who stand prepared to stab him should he cry out. By now Montezuma knows the rules. So his jailers take him hunting, and he returns "very contented." "Finding him so frank and pleasant, we treated him with the respect habitually paid to kings in those parts, and he treated us in the same way." And why not? For the Spaniards are now kings also. They play *totoloque* again, king to king. Montezuma winning, he presents a golden gift to the captain of Cortes's guard, one Juan Velazquez de Leon, "who in every way showed himself Montezuma's true friend and servant." —No doubt, for this is the same Juan Velazquez de Leon who when they first seized the remonstrating Montezuma, cried out "in his usual high and terrifying voice": "What is the use of all these words? Either we take him or we knife him. If we do not look after ourselves now we shall be dead men."

"This Is Not an Assault"

There lies the crux of all the conquistadors' expedient syllogisms: We have the right to defend our ground. Our several diagrams have shown to what extent defense *and* ground are both accidental, circumstantial. Defense of ground constitutes the defense of a revolutionary peasant's nascent right to own that ground and the livestock on it—and defense of his landlord's established property rights to the same. Were I kidnapped, drugged, flown halfway around the world and deposited on one side or the other of some alien battlefield, I'd have every right to fight whatever enemy came charging toward me, whether I understood the cause or not. Thus the argument of Juan Velazquez de Leon. He is thousands of miles from home, his commander outnumbered; Montezuma will certainly kill them all if it can be done. —The rub, of course, is that the Spaniards brought their sacred ground with them as they pressed forward of their own will, that (I'm almost ashamed to mention) they invaded. Or, as the Conquest's lapidary nineteenth-century historian, Prescott, puts the question: "The difficulty that meets us in the outset is, to find a justification of the right of conquest, at all."

One of justification's props is defense of creed. In Cortes's time and place, deviation from orthodox Catholicism constituted a sin punishable by death. And Montezuma, unfortunately for him, did not happen to be Catholic. Prescott reminds us: "This doctrine, monstrous as it is, was the creed of the Romish, in other words, of the Christian Church—the basis of the Inquisition." From divine justification followed divine right: right of kings, right of the lieutenants of kings to impose correction in their name, right to proprietorship over heathen territory. In other words, defense of creed, finding itself successful, grew bold and simultaneously became defense of authority and defense of ground. Thus the tired old story: the tale of the French in Canada, which magically became New France; of the English in New England and, yes, of the Spaniards in Mexico, which became New Spain. But, no matter how weary (and wearisome) the theme, it will not die, so let's call it innately human; one finds it, for instance, murkily coloring the actions of my government at Waco, Texas, in 1993, when, having refused the possibly disingenuous offer of that gun-loving cult Messiah David Koresh to openly inspect his so-called compound for violations of firearms laws, the Bureau of Alcohol, Tobacco and Firearms sent agents disguised as students to move in across the street. The home of Koresh and his Branch Davidians to them constituted alien territory, an insult to their sovereignty which had to be redressed in the most brutal fashion: Koresh went jogging regularly, and his murderers could have arrested him without any fuss, *but they feared that he might be released too quickly*. Better, then, by the logic of authority's too proud self-defense, to violently retake this ground. To be sure, Koresh, following the "survivalist" fashion of that epoch, appears to have been equally too prepared to defend himself. His imminent self-defense, like a foreign nation's nuclear missiles, did indeed constitute a threat. So when I used the word "murderers," it shouldn't be understood in as unequivocal a fashion as for Stalin's cadres or the worst of Cortes's conquistadors—let's call them "manslaughterers." Their actions showed arrogance, clumsiness, deceitfulness, stupidity and, I think, malice—but the murder was not in the first degree. Their commandos came in military vehicles; nobody knows anymore who fired the first shot; people were killed on both sides. Then it was time for the FBI.

But all this is mere context, whose diffuse light bathes equally anxious fools, ignored negotiators, fanatics on both sides and evilly arrogant men. Begin the real tale on the fifty-first day of siege, when authority, no longer able to bear being balked, obtains the go-ahead from the U.S. Attorney General and prepares the Cortesian stroke. Juan Velazquez de Leon had indeed cried out, "What is the use of all these words?" but words always remain important. Before launching his final battle against the Mexican capital, Cortes will offer his honeyed ultimatums; and on this last morning that most of the Branch Davidians will ever see, history repeats itself when the FBI's chief negotiator, Byron Sage, master of converting black into white, telephones the besieged and politely announces that "we're in the process of putting tear gas into the building. This is not an assault. We will not enter the building." The time is one minute before six in the morning; for many of the past fifty nights the FBI's tactical team has been broadcasting the squeals of rabbits being slaughtered; nor is the logic of Mr. Sage any less dreamlike than Caesar's at besieged Massilia (summoning the Massiliote Grand Committee of Fifteen, the aggressor "urged them not to let the Massiliotes be guilty of starting hostilities; they ought rather to follow the lead of the whole of Italy than bow to the will of one man," that is, Caesar's enemy). Understandably, then, Sage's groggy, doomed interlocutor repeats in astonishment, "You are going to spray tear gas into the building?" —Sage, as smooth as Cortes or Caesar ever were, answers: "In the building . . . no, we are not entering the building." (Self-interest and self-preservation adore such inversions. When Bernal Díaz describes the siege of Tenochtitlan, he gives the impression that it is the *Spaniards* who are besieged, for the Aztecs rush their beachheads by day and by night. Under such circumstances, who wouldn't approve of Spanish self-defense?) Having thus (as he hopes) paralyzed and stupefied the Branch Davidians, our efficient Mr. Sage hangs up the telephone, switches on the loudspeakers and deafeningly broadcasts this incredible justification of the forthcoming defense of ground, whose logic is that since the government despite all appearances is not attacking, the Davidians had better not commit the aggressive sin of defending themselves:

"THIS IS NOT AN ASSAULT"
The FBI's Ultimatum of 5:59 A.M., April 19, 1993

We are in the process of placing tear gas into the building. This is not an assault. We are not entering the building. This is not an assault. Do not fire your weapons. If you fire, fire will be returned. Do not shoot. This is not an assault. The gas you smell is a nonlethal tear gas. This gas will temporarily render the building uninhabitable. Exit the residence now and follow instructions. You are not to have anyone in the tower. The tower is off limits. No one is to be in the tower. Anyone observed to be in the tower will be considered to be [*sic*] an act of aggression and will be dealt with accordingly. If you come out now, you will not be harmed. Follow all instructions. Come out with your hands up. Carry nothing. Come out of the building and walk up the driveway toward the Double-E Ranch Road. Walk toward the large Red Cross flag. Follow all instructions of the FBI agents in the Bradleys. Follow all instructions. You are under arrest. This standoff is over. We do not want to hurt anyone. Follow all instructions. This is not an assault. Do not fire any weapons. We

do not want anyone hurt. Gas will continue to be delivered until everyone is out of the building.

Gas will indeed be delivered, by means of booms smashed assaultlessly
through walls and windows, until suddenly, mysteriously—was it the gas
or did Koresh do it on purpose?—the Branch Davidians' home bursts into
flames and almost everyone dies, including seventeen children. In a report
issued years later by a House of Representatives subcommittee, authority
will decide that it was essentially David Koresh's fault.

The Pursuit of Happiness

Is defense of forward-moving ground hypocritical, then, or merely blindly
self-serving? Caesar moves deeper into Gaul. The Germans ask him to halt
until they can return with envoys in three days. But Caesar, like the FBI,
fears that the delay will allow them to reinforce themselves with cavalry.
He commands his legions on. "When Caesar was no more than twelve
miles away from the enemy, the deputies returned to him as agreed: they
met him on the march, and besought him earnestly not to advance further . . . their request was not granted," writes the conqueror. In the end,
however, he agrees to advance only four miles, to camp near water. This is
not an assault. The Germans fall suddenly on his vanguard. Caesar coun-
terattacks, driving men, women and children into the river, "there to perish," as he says, "overcome by terror, by exhaustion, by the force of the
stream." Exultantly he continues: "The Romans, with not a man lost and
but few wounded, freed from the fear of a stupendous war—with an enemy whose numbers had been 430,000 souls—returned to camp."

For a balder explication of the urge, turn to the Nazis—or the ancient
Greeks. Nearly two thousand years before Cortes, the Athenians, weakly
trying to evade or delay the Peloponnesian War, explain to the Spartans
that "the nature of the case first compelled us to advance our empire to its
present height; *fear being our principal motive,* though honor and interest
afterward came in." Balder still: Xenophon in his *Memorabilia* makes
Socrates toss off this chillingly casual aphorism: "Men fight in order to
live as happy a life as possible . . ." —that is, to gain security, prestige and
treasure. My own country's Declaration of Independence assures me that
I have the preconditional right to the pursuit of happiness. If, as in ancient
Greece, warfare is a routine way to obtain that happiness, then, as for the
FBI, who said they were doing it for the laws they broke and the children

they killed, aggression becomes self-defense, an easy doctrine which allows monsters to flourish like mushrooms after a rain.

VIOLENT DEFENSE OF GROUND IS JUSTIFIED:

By imminent self-defense, even during unjust aggression—but only by imminent self-defense.

VIOLENT DEFENSE OF GROUND IS UNJUSTIFIED:

When that ground may be shifted at will for the sake of expedient or aggressive advantage.

"We Had Begged Them to Keep the Peace"

Back to Cortes. Invoking the rights of the self, Bernal Díaz, the conquistador whose chronicle I quote, repeatedly explains in his memoirs that they've come to Mexico only "to take a look at the great Montezuma—in fact to earn our livelihood and make our fortunes"—that is, at Montezuma's expense. And that, indeed, is exactly what Cortes wrote to the Emperor. "As if they were monkeys they seized upon the gold," says the native account. "They starved for it; they lusted for it like pigs." "Send me some of it," runs Cortes's first message to Montezuma from afar, "because I and my companions suffer from a disease of the heart which can be cured only with gold." That disease is called greed. It differs but little from the malady which drove Caesar to conquer Gaul in the name of a less than enthusiastic Rome. Time to earn their livelihood, by all means.

Setting out on this most innocuous of errands, they encounter the Tlascalans, to whom (after a skirmish) they make noises of peace, for their country merely lies along the way; it can be subjugated later. But next morning a thousand Tlascalans appear, launching darts.

Like Byron Sage, Cortes will have only just war. Invoking all the proper rules of engagement, "Cortes made signs of peace and spoke to them through his interpreters, begging them to desist and warning them formally before a notary and witnesses (as if they could profit by it or understand what it was all about)," but with wise mistrust, the Tlascalans refuse to be friends, invoking defense of homeland as they gather their forces in hopes of eating the invaders' flesh and sacrificing their hearts. The Spaniards continue marching and riding toward Montezuma, beating off the attack. Soon the Tlascalan armies return, led by nobles in flamelike headdresses, robed and sandalled, waving long wooden swords striped or herringboned, studded with flint or obsidian teeth. In the old painting, the effect is not only menacing but also alien, birdlike. Cortes, who while not given to lyricism can express his purposes with considerable grace, commands the royal notary

> to watch what happened so that he could bear witness if it should be necessary, in order that we should not be made responsible at some future time for the deaths and destruction that might occur, for we had begged them to keep the peace.

The Tlascalans charge. Invoking, as always at this stage, self-defense of creed and self-preservation (New Spain not having been sufficiently conquered for self-defense of authority to apply), the Spaniards break the enemy line again and again. From the now brittle pages of Prescott's opus, as in the victors' memoirs, there arises a strange fragrance of glamour: However evil the means and ends, the actual *achievement* of Cortes and his troops compels my unwilling admiration. I know now that he'll press on, and on, and on, praying to his loving God, leading his men against vast hosts. "The steadfastness of our artillery, musketeers, and bowmen did much to save us," writes Díaz (which I can well believe), "and we inflicted great casualties on them." Another Spaniard compares the victory to that of Joshua in the Promised Land.

And so the Tlascalans perforce offer their friendship. —On to the city of Cholula, whose citizens, like so many others, are angry and fearful at the foreigners' coming. Dwelling in proximity to the Aztecs, they're already vassals: Montezuma and his predecessors fought many a flower war against them, intimidating them, killing off their noblest warriors in stylized combat: better, then, to be dependent Aztec allies—before the terms get harsher. Now they must compute rapid sums according to the following expedient calculus:

> (a) Break with Montezuma, and we'll be at the mercy of these unknown bearded men, who have just sworn friendship with our enemies the Tlascalans;
>
> *or*
>
> (b) Defy Cortes, and lose the war as the Tlascalans did.

Far better to invite them in to gain time (and, possibly, Aztec reinforcements). Meanwhile, one must presume, a messenger runs secretly to Tenochtitlan and back. What does Lord Montezuma command? —Murder by treachery, so that the Mexican homeland will be defended before they get any nearer. —But Cortes likewise has his observant satellites, not least his native mistress, Doña Marina, now perhaps already pregnant. (Years hence he'll marry her off to one of his drunken lieutenants.) Learning of the plot from a Cholulan woman who'd made the mistake of trusting to racial commonality, she rushes to whisper in her master-lover's ear. And he? Self-defense advises exemplary slaughter, for were no punishment meted out, other tribes and cities might resist yet more ferociously. Moreover, by his lights their device constitutes unscrupulous warfare. Therefore he may employ violence. (The Nazis will reason similarly about Partisans in eastern Europe.)

At his smiling invitation the Indians assemble; one must suppose that ignorance truly constitutes bliss. Away with ignorance now! They're surrounded! Cortes, righteousness's schoolmaster, now accuses, pronounces sentence, fires off the musket signal and justice begins. How can we begin to imagine the shouts and the screams, the desperate escape-seekers and crazy-eyed defiers all enclosed and doomed? "If we had not inflicted that punishment," pens the chronicler, defending Cortes's memory against allegations of gratuitous cruelty, "our lives would have been in great danger." By the rights of the self, indeed, Cortes is justified in defending the ground he stands on; otherwise indeed his heart would have been upon the Cholulans' bloody altar. At fault is only his first premise, that he can move his ground where he lists. His very restraint up until now, says Prescott (who, like so many, halfway admires him), leads us to believe that the treason of the Cholulans partook of actuality,

> yet who can doubt that the punishment thus inflicted was excessive,— that the same end might have been attained by directing the blow [merely] against the guilty chiefs . . . ? But when was it ever seen that fear, armed with power, was scrupulous in the exercise of it?

The Aztec version of the story, needless to say, awards Cortes still less credit, being a tale of Spanish atrocity pure and simple, carried out upon all the Cholulan leaders, who assembled in good faith, never expecting to be harmed; there was no murder plot, no order from Montezuma.

We at our disadvantage of almost half a millennium's dust can never hope to know the facts. But I accept Prescott's logic: Cortes is unlikely in his first season of weakness-inspired amity to have slaughtered the Cholulans without cause; either they were truly preparing his sacrifice, with or without Montezuma's dominating complicity, or else the Tlasacalans, who hated the Cholulans—or Marina, prudently or desperately seeking to become indispensable—cleverly convinced him that they were. As it happened, the deed was politic. "When Moctezuma heard what had happened, and about the troops who were marching against him, he began to shake like a leaf," says the Aztec account. Cortes leads his army on.

Montezuma (counseled, as I would suppose, by his most important adviser, Cihuacoatl or "Snake Woman") hastens to send word to the enemy that he had nothing to do with any conspiracy. This denial makes me suspect him, and perhaps it had the same effect upon Cortes. Prescott, confessing that all portraits of Montezuma are biased, goes on to say that "one cannot contemplate this pusillanimous conduct of Montezuma without mingled feelings of pity and contempt." He offers any tribute the Spanish Emperor would like, provided only that he be left alone. Cortes thanks him courteously and continues on.

Moctezuma then blocks the roads, preferring not to resort to open violence yet, since all others who tried it against Cortes were beaten. In Montezuma's terms, this is, however, a declaration of hostility, and Cortes's Tlascalan allies surely tell him so. (Bernal Díaz claims that Montezuma installed an ambush along an unblocked road; the Aztec account does not mention this.) Cortes's army marches around the barricades.

"I Go Forth About to Destroy"

In simple, Montezuma versus Cortes equals defense of homeland versus defense of ground.

In a native codex we see Montezuma, as it happens the second ruler of that name (which signifies *He-frowned-like-a-lord*), standing on a mat with his legs braced apart, leaning on an ornate spear as tall as he is, with a wide, bordered, carpetlike cloak sweeping across his body, and feathers the size of palm fronds blossoming from his left shoulder. A beard sharpens his spade-shaped face, whose outline is almost symmetrically doubled by his headgear. Left hand on his abdomen, he stares straight into space from under heavy eyelids. His conqueror's private secretary portrays him as "a man of middling size, thin, and, like all Indians, of a very dark complexion. He wore his hair long and had no more than six bristles on his chin . . . He was of an amiable though severe disposition, affable, well-spoken, and gracious, which made him respected and feared."

When Cortes arrived, he'd held the throne for seventeen years. He'd reorganized and conquered. He'd upheld the sovereign reputation of Tenochtitlan. In his manuscript of 1585, Fray Sahagún castigates the fashion in which "the lords of Mexico, Texcoco, and Tlacopan, united with all their troops, should go conquer some province, even though its rulers had never given any offense to these three lords or their domains. This indicates clearly that they were tyrants."

Our indictment of Cortes (crueler than Caesar, kinder than Hitler) hardly exculpates Montezuma. Whence came his empire? What justification had Montezuma for expanding it? One anthropologist concludes that "war *was* the empire. Halting war for too long diminished perceived Aztec power." As in the ancient Greek city-states, war defined not only economy and authority but also manhood. When an Aztec boy was born, his mother cut the umbilical cord, intoning: "You are a server and a warrior, you are the bird called *quechol,* you are the bird called *zacuan,* you are the bird and warrior of the One Who Dwells in All Places." Later the boy received a bow and arrow from his parents, "because warfare was so frequent among them." There was an excellent chance that he would use them—in wars of conquest.

Relying, therefore, on the deterrent power of his reputation, Montezuma probably never expected Cortes to march into Tenochtitlan—his native enemies would hardly have dared.

An Aztec war hymn runs in part: "I go forth, I go forth about to destroy, I, Yoatzin; my soul is in the cerulean water."

Meanwhile Cortes addresses his men at the very beginning of the expedition to New Spain: "We are engaging in a just and good war which will bring us fame." Doubtless he prays for his good success every day when he goes to Mass. "He was devout and given to praying," recalls his secretary; "he knew many prayers and psalms by heart."

Tributes, Ruses, Incantations

Montezuma's first campaign in the war of defense had been a magical one. (We might compare him with Leonidas the Spartan. Both kings probably sought to propitiate, to avoid, preempt or cleanse any religious pollution and to invoke divine aid in defense of homeland.) But the incantations failed. He was compelled to contend not only with the material reality of the Spaniards as greedy and dangerous usurpers, but also with a religious prophecy which equated Cortes with one aspect of the old Toltec deity To-piltzin Quetzalcoatl. (A certain chronicle based on Aztec sources insists that Montezuma, at the behest of his religious advisers, sent messengers to give tribute to Cortes upon his first arrival at the coast, and that Cortes dressed up in his finery and received them upon a makeshift throne. Supposedly the Spaniards told these envoys that Montezuma's gifts were insufficient, "and that when they went to Mexico, they would rob them of all they had and take it for themselves." This does not square with the polite Cortes of Díaz's chronicle but offers what might be called truth-in-hindsight.) Montezuma, like Cortes, is a man of ruses. He'd sent a noble to impersonate him, but the Spaniards, having been told of the trick by their native allies, merely took the puppet's proffered gifts and reviled him. His envoys had cut the throats of slaves to honor the Spaniards, who of course were merely disgusted by this literal sacrifice without transubstantiation. They had a countervailing advantage: nothing in *their* religious tradition disposed them toward making any particular accommodation with Montezuma.

His sorcerers tried new spells, only to be threatened by their god Tezcatlipoca. At that, Montezuma had said, "I pity the old men and women and the boys and girls who do not have feet or hands to defend themselves. As for the rest of us, we are now resolved to die in the defense of our homeland."

Cortes's men tramp on. Further complicating the matter was the fact that, being ignorant of the Mesoamerican laws of battle, the Spaniards entered the city during harvest season, without declaring war. The Aztecs knew neither whether to strike nor how to strike. When Montezuma was crowned, the enemy sovereigns in Tlasacala and Cholula were invited and secretly attended the ceremony. Could Cortes's purpose be similarly diplomatic? Better to await developments—especially since one could not prevent them.

And so at last they arrive in lake-girded Tenochtitlan, where Montezuma loads them with gold and fine cloaks—in hopes of buying them off, as they cynically suppose, which might mean the same thing as making them allies. The Aztecs in their conquests have always been satisfied merely to exact tribute. They find neither desire nor need to remake other city-states in their own image. We can be sure that to them Cortes's war aims remain incomprehensible.

Further Necessities

When the conquistadors first saw the Aztec capital, they were stunned. The place resembled "an enchanted vision," writes Díaz. "Indeed, some of our soldiers asked whether it was not all a dream." "But today all that I then saw is overthrown and destroyed; nothing is left standing." A song to the war god runs: "O author of life, your house is here! . . . Behold Mexico, palace of the white willows, palace of the white sedges!" (This evocation of homeland perhaps achieved the same effect as the patriotic French posters at the beginning of World War I.) Awed and dazed at first by the magnificence of the place, the Spaniards visit the market, then compel Montezuma to take them to the main temple, where, ascending a steep pyramid stained with blood, they revile the Aztec gods, thereby forcing upon their shocked host an expiatory prayer.

It seems that Cortes, like his colleagues, rivals and successors, cannot keep his troops in good order, and they immediately begin to loot Montezuma's palace, where they are being put up. Most of the foot soldiers will, as usual in war, end up with a minuscule share of the plunder.

Says the native account: "The king, Moctezuma, came out to welcome them as strangers because he was not able to offer resistance at that time; nevertheless, the Mexicans always considered this arrival as an act of violence and tyranny." So did the Cholulans; so did the Tlascalans. And the unwelcome guests know it. That is why they kidnap Montezuma. Another historian writes simply: "This act of treachery seemed the safest thing to be done, and therefore, with Cortes, it was the best." No doubt the logic is correct. Don't get the kidnappers wrong—it's nothing personal. Our chronicler calls him "a great and valiant prince," deserving of all respect. They merely need to make a living, you see. Does this make the deed better or worse? Montezuma asks them to take his children hostage instead, so that he will not be disgraced. But Cortes makes his usual reply, the reply of Trotsky: There is no alternative.

Cortes's Maxim

In order to secure and defend my ground, I have every right to conquer you.

The Honors Due a Sovereign

Thus Montezuma in captivity, throwing down the golden *totoloque* pellets. One of his guards calls him a dog in his hearing. Another audibly relieves himself. Montezuma, presenting him with a "gold jewel" to smooth the way, asks him to kindly refrain from showing such disrespect in the future. The next night, the guard relieves himself again, hoping for another gold jewel. The recipient of this treatment wears the honor-pride of any powerful political leader—he rules millions and has presided over the sacrifice of thousands (when his "captains on the coast" arrived to tell him of the approach of the Spanish fleet, they'd thrown themselves on the ground and said, "Our lord, we merit death for having come without your permission")—and the degradation is in proportion—in proportion also (as I assume) to his dwindling utility to the Spaniards. Well, they're all friends just the same. Cortes twice assures him that he is free to return to his palace. "The prince replied most courteously that he was grateful for this kindness. But he well knew that Cortes's speech was mere words, and that for the present it would be better for him to remain a prisoner." How could he not know? The hypocrite has just thrown him in chains and publicly burned alive seventeen of his captains for trying to reconquer territory lost to the Spaniards. (Their defense: The uprisings were by Montezuma's orders.) When Cortes's ruffians had first laid hands on him, it's said, he couldn't quite believe it. How now, when they manhandle him and clap him in irons, and he hears his captains' screams? As irrelevant, in a certain sense, as their executions might seem to one in whose halcyon days twenty thousand victims a year were sacrificed, especially to a man who with his kindred ate roasted prisoner flesh, and marked calendar cycles by lighting fires in the chest cavities of the heart-ripped, the shrieks must have nonetheless touched him in his fear and his dignity. What was being burned was his sovereignty, his authority, his godlike self.

In the Codex Mendoza, drawn by Aztec hands, we see a warrior, tall, disdainful and serene, holding his shield with one hand, while with the other he grips the topknot of a captured warrior who louts before him, small proportioned in everything, even in shield and weapons; he barely comes up to the Aztec's armpit. Such is his honor; such is his status. We see the conquest of Azcapotzalco. Dead bodies—commoners, from the look of them—lie on the ground, almost naked. Aztec jaguar soldiers clash with the Tepanec defenders, while others are already marching up the temple steps. They have won. It is 1428. Azcapotzalco will be razed. If such be the status of warriors, imagine the status due to kings. Can we see now why for a few moments enchained Montezuma might have gone mad? We read that he roared like an animal—with terror, desperation and rage.

All things pass, of course. "After the burning, Cortes went to Montezuma's apartment with five of his captains, and himself removed the chains; and so affectionately did he speak to the prince that his anger quickly passed away."

More captive days and nights. More rounds of *totoloque*. Montezuma offers Cortes one of his two legitimate daughters in marriage, as a token of his love. No doubt he craves alliance on almost any terms by now. (How can he ever forget the burning and those chains?) Cortes takes off his helmet in respectful gratitude but refuses, being already married. To Montezuma (who himself once had many wives, perhaps a thousand), this reply must be still another insult. Some thirty years later a Spanish judge will be apprised that "a daughter of Moctezuma [*sic*], having contracted an illness of which she later died, was thrown out to lie on a mat on the ground. She was so poor that she would have had nothing to eat if the Franciscans had not sent her some food." Why should we expect otherwise? The Aztecs' fortunes have fallen. Within a few weeks of being tendered the daughter's hand, Cortes, adopting his soldiers' usage, will refuse to visit Montezuma even when entreated. He keeps his helmet on now. (How many gold pellets does Montezuma have left?) He mutters: "Why should I be civil to a dog who was holding secret negotiations with Narvaez, and now, as you can see, does not even give us any food?" —Indeed, Tenochtitlan's market is closed, because it recently happened that at a festival of their god Huitzilopochtli, Cortes's deputy, unprovoked, massacred great numbers of nobles, soldiers and commoners. The Aztecs hate them now. Well, may they all be enchained! —True also that Montezuma did intrigue with Narvaez, Cortes's enemy; for factional strife among the Spaniards represents the Aztecs' last hope for defense of homeland. But Narvaez loses to Cortes; Montezuma makes politic haste to congratulate the victor, who refuses to listen to him.

"Like Water in a Heavy Rain"

That slaughter in the market marks a watershed—or bloodshed, I should say—in Spanish-Aztec relations. Up until then, mental and moral paralysis encouraged the hope (or pretense) that the Spaniards were guests, among whom Montezuma claimed to dwell by choice. Cortes had sworn that he meant no harm. But now it's undeniable: the white men mean to tread them down into the mud. (Here is Pierre de Gand on the Mexican character nine years after the Conquest: "They do nothing they are not forced to do; you can obtain nothing from them by mildness or by persuasion." That was in the sixteenth century. In a seventeenth-century engraving, we see a naked woman hanging in a doorway, her child likewise strangled by means of a cord tied around her waist. A broad, hearty Spaniard with a ruffled collar is dangling two naked little corpses before the jaws of interested dogs. Another dog is gnawing on the ankles of the hanged woman's baby. In the background, naked Indians are being hunted with dogs.)

Why did they kill those people in the market? Evidently they'd seen human sacrifices there—thus at least runs one justification for the atrocity. Or perhaps, like Stalin, they merely wished to make a cleaner sweep. "The greatest evil that one can do another is to take his life when [the victim] is in mortal sin," pens the chronicler Sahagún, who has access to Aztec sources but remains a Spaniard and a Catholic. Honest and true, he will not hide the fact that his countrymen, in defiance of their own professed moral calculus, "killed them, the greater part of whom were unarmed, without their knowing why." "Some had their heads cut off, others were cut in half, and others had their bellies slit open, immediately to fall dead." Blood ran "like water in a heavy rain." Can this possibly be defense of ground?

Cortes, who was not present at the time, will later claim in his duly notarized declaration of war against the Aztecs that the plan at this festival was to murder Spaniards, as in the case of the Cholulans. It is written that when he returned to Tenochtitlan and learned what had happened, his aspect was "*mohino,* an adjective which is applied to one who plays in a game against many others." By then he is not playing the game of *totoloque* with Montezuma anymore.

"This Whore of the Spaniards"

After that day of bloody rain begins the Aztecs' violent self-defense of homeland.

Montezuma entreats them not to take up arms, because the occupiers are invincible. —"What is he saying, this whore of the Spaniards?" The stones begin to fly.

The Spaniards say that he was killed by his own people, that a stone knocked his soul away. The Aztec source implies that the Spaniards garroted him.

Defense of Ground

The Aztecs rise up. No doubt they've gashed their tongues and ears in the temples, offering their own blood to the gods in hope of victory. They surround and besiege the usurpers.

Cortes cries: "The Mexicans and all their allies are now determined to kill us all. Let us then, with all our Indian allies, defend ourselves. Indeed we can do no less in our defense than kill them, take from them their kingdom, and make them our slaves." Then, the Aztec relation claims, they strangle all the Aztec nobles they hold as prisoners and throw them from the palace roofs.

In a copy of a Tlascalan painting, we see jaguar soldiers with their shields crowding about the Spaniards' redoubt, launching copper-headed arrows, copper-headed lances, while the Spaniards huddle together on horseback, clenching weapons, their cannon blazing out fire. They put up a good fight, like old Spartans defending their ground and biting lips: "This is the good soldier; at once he turns to flight the rough ranks of the foe, and eagerly he stems the wave of battle." (How strange, that Cortes, not Montezuma, should play Leonidas's role!) But the wave cannot be stemmed. Grizzled soldiers remark that they've never encountered "men so courageous as those Indians at charging with closed ranks." The wave rises, and that smooth, oval stone, stone of destiny, comes hurtling over the wall toward Montezuma's head. The Spaniards' frail pretext of legitimacy thus perishes.

The First Enslavements

By night they flee the Aztec dominions, getting engaged in battle and picked off along the way. Three hundred Spaniards drown in Tolteca Acaloco canal, along with two thousand of their native allies.

Cortes is desperate. Where can he defend his ground now? At the very beginning of the Mexican campaign, like the Roman general Asclepiodotus who invaded rebellious Britain, he'd burned his ships so that the men would have nowhere to go but forward. This deed is frequently styled heroic. But Cortes had lied to his men then, saying that the ships were worm-eaten. Expediency dictated that he do this; otherwise the men would have risen up. Now he's irrevocably chosen his ground, and theirs. Why not? For Cortes, the die had been cast long before. As the historian Arthur

Helps remarked, if he didn't capture Montezuma and return home, "he would but have returned to a prison or a grave; for the ambassadorial capacity which he assumed was a mere pretext." He must assert himself. Stumbling back and back through New Spain, he discovers that some of the conquered tribes have risen up against him. The penalty will be as expedient as it is (by his lights) just: Summoning his notary, he prepares a decree of enslavement and begins to brand his captives. From this date, perhaps, begins his greed for serfs as well as for gold.

"Cortes Offered Them Peace"

He regroups. Unlike Caesar, who drove himself by will-force (which was in his case composed of greed-force and honor-force) in order to attain his conquests, Cortes possesses the advantages of an athletic body. His personal secretary describes him as tall, great-shouldered, strong, although like Caesar he was pale. He never loses heart. He gathers together his pet Tlascalans, who scarcely consider rising up against him. Why? Because fifteen years earlier the Aztecs had increased the pressure on them, adding force to their flower war of intimidation so that it began to resemble an all-out war. The Tlascalans had won one flower war and lost the next. They were getting worried. Now Cortes, as they believe, will save them— if they help him. In their company he now approaches the capital. As always, he presents himself as the innocent self-defender. At Cuernavaca, "Cortes offered them peace; they answered with war." A Tlascalan having shown his men the secret path, he fires the town . . .

His ultimatum to the defenders of Tenochtitlan: "Therefore we come to make war on you as bestial, unreasonable people, from which we will not cease until we avenge our grievances and overthrow the enemies of God . . . This will be carried out without fail."

The Conquest of Tenochtitlan

"So they came on as bravely as tigers and fought us hand to hand," says that spirited trooper Bernal Díaz; and another Spaniard of equal gallantry wrote that "it is one of the most beautiful sights in the world to see them in their battle array because they keep formation wonderfully and are very handsome."

"We killed more than a hundred splendid chiefs," Cortes gloats, and the enemy countergloats. In an old drawing, we see Spaniards, grimly unbending, riding forth with lowered lances, trampling the dismembered bodies of the dead. The Tlascalans accompany them, raising narrow clubs and skull-adorned shields.

The chroniclers are pleased to inform us that when the troops encounter "women, children, old men, and other miserable creatures, overcome with hunger and sickness," Cortes usually "ordered his men not to harm the poor wretches." From time to time, however, he "slaughtered many of them, mostly women and children and unarmed men." Part of it is that he cannot always restrain his soldiers. (One thinks again of Caesar at Thapsis, powerlessly witnessing his soldiers murder all the enemy prisoners—and then their own officers.) The other part—as we now know all too well—is that he will not stop at cruelty, when other expedients fail to stick. In his second assault on the great city, "seeing that they were so rebellious and showed such determination to defend themselves to the death, I inferred two things"—first, and perhaps most important to his heart, that it would be very difficult to get the treasure back again, and second, that "they gave occasion, and forced us to totally destroy them. This last reason caused me the greater grief, for it weighed on my soul and made me reflect on what means I might employ to frighten them . . ." He burns the royal houses and aviaries. "Although it grieved me much, I determined, as it grieved them even more, to burn those edifices."

We see the Tlascalans crouching predatorially, gripping their shields like drums, some of them wearing jaguar skins, as they approach the suppliant and pointing defenders, in whose keeping rests a skull rack from which glares a fresh Aztec head.

Against these atrocities must be set Aztec counteratrocities, such as the sacrifice of prisoners of war, which the Spaniards had to watch helplessly. It was this sight which almost destroyed the self-assured battle courage of Bernal Díaz, who'd scarcely suffered fear until then. Out with the heart; smear its blood on the mouth of the god. Roll the opened man "down the steps, of which there were about fifty or sixty, his arms and legs breaking and his skull cracking, until he arrived at the bottom still twitching . . . another high priest cut off his head and thrust through the temple a long stake, which was like a hook." At first, fifteen or eighteen, and later fifty or fifty-three, Spanish captives will be thus sacrificed.

The Aztec capital fights on, surrounded by battle but still surviving it. "Every day the Spaniards were cornering the Mexicans more," writes Fray Sahagún, but "the Mexicans returned at night to open the canals and ditches which the Spaniards had filled by day." For their part, the Spaniards huddle in their armed camps, each of which resembles the hollow square in which blitzkrieg counters the web defense. At night, they must beat off rushes by the warriors with their device-adorned shields and their feather headdresses as lush as the tops of tropical trees. And yet *defense of ground has no justice when that ground may be shifted at will for the sake of expedient or aggressive advantage.* In an Aztec codex, we see a line of conquistadors waving long, stingerlike swords aloft, while shield-flaunting Aztecs (from their simplicity of costume, evidently commoners) hurl spherical stones at them. From behind approach the noble warriors in their striped costumes, leveling swords and long thrusting spears at the Spaniards' backs. Another conquistador wrote: "In warfare they are the most cruel people to be found, for they spare neither brothers, relatives, friends, nor women even if they are beautiful; they kill them all and eat them." For both sides, the order of the day is defense of ground.

The siege deafens, mutilates, desolates all—Díaz writes that it lasts for ninety-three days. Undeterred, however, by enemy ululations, or the thuddings of drums, the screams of trumpets, the whizzing of stones from maguey-fiber slings, Cortes continues self-defense. Specifically, he will starve the Aztecs out.

In the last campaign, he moves against Iztapalan. "More than six thousand souls, men, women, and children of the inhabitants, perished, for our Indian allies, seeing the victory which God gave us, had the sole idea to kill right and left."

At the end, the defenders try magic one more time, but their sacred serpent and owl will not come alive to help them.

Mexico falls. Falls a silence. When the fighting finally stops, many soldiers experience a ringing in the ears which drowns out all other sounds. Cortes gives thanks to God.

He finds corpses everywhere—by his estimate fifty thousand dead. As for the living, their condition excites pity. "Their excretions were the sort of filth that thin swine pass that have been fed on nothing but grass." He tries to stop his allies from killing them, but, in his usual phrase, "it was not possible to prevent it that day, so more than fifteen thousand persons were massacred."

Defense of Gold

"The city was put to the sack," runs Gómara's account, "the Spaniards seizing the gold, silver, and featherwork; the Indians, the clothing and other spoils." Cortes is said by one chronicler to have sought to disallow his troops from branding and enslaving the surrendered Aztecs, and by another to have "branded with the King's iron many men and women as slaves." Maybe he did both. Well, he's successfully defended his ground—or, as we should say, he's made the ground his. Defense of ground will hardly justify his violence anymore. Defense of authority must now be invoked; after centuries and traditions have bloomed, then defense of homeland will do. But first, we'll worship expediency.

"Ah, captain," says Montezuma's unhappy successor, Guatemoc (or Cuautémoc, or Guatemucin), "I have done everything within my power to defend my kingdom and deliver it from your hands. But as fortune has not favored me, take my life; it will be most fitting; and in so doing you will bring an end to the Mexican kingdom, for already you have ruined and destroyed my city and my people."

This is the man whose person the wily conqueror promises to honor and respect once he surrenders—comforting him after his usual honeyed fashion, insisting (as he did with Montezuma) that the sovereign will remained raised up—Guatemoc will rule Mexico just as before! Thus lulled and softened, and conveyed to a captured housetop from which he can be well heard, Guatemoc calls on the remaining seventy thousand defenders of homeland to lay down their arms. He'll be a good puppet, it appears. He'll help Cortes lead the Aztecs to walk in the ways of God. The war is over.

But, half drowned by the clamor of peacetime, Cortes now finds himself accused of hiding Guatemoc's treasures for himself. He denies it, so the other Spaniards, in the spirit of scientific inquiry, torture Guatemoc by burning his feet with boiling oil while "one of his gentlemen" gets roasted to death, his eyes on Guatemoc. Perhaps Cortes deserves no blame for this, being less an absolute leader than a swimmer fitfully treading water in a sea of factions; his captains continually mutiny, run riot and attack each other—but he ought not to have made absolute promises—not that Guatemoc believed them in any event; he never chose to surrender but was captured. As I meditate on this grisly scene, into my mind comes its double image, of Montezuma enchained while his seventeen loyalists die in the fire. A coincidence? Montezuma's ordeal was undoubtedly choreographed by Cortes—why not Guatemoc's? And, in the end, he himself had the authority to halt the torture of Guatemoc "either because he thought it degrading and cruel," or because Guatemoc told him that he had thrown everything into the water where it could never be recovered.

Guatemoc will live five years more, despised and feared, compelled to be always carried with the conqueror. In 1524, that glorious year when the tithes of Vera Cruz and Medellin reach a thousand gold pesos, he'll conspire with other royal hostages in hopes of rising up. Cortes pronounces his guilt—and to justice devotes still another troublemaker, one Tetepangueçal. "These two, therefore, were hanged, and I set the others free because it appeared they were to blame for nothing more than having listened to it, although this alone was sufficient for them to deserve death." Thus Cortesian generosity.

As always, the punishment has a salutary effect: the lord Apoxpaléon, whom our hero is at that moment busily intimidating, forthwith burns "an infinite number of idols."

A Brief History of New Spain

Just as Aztecs once divided up the body of a war prisoner, the captor getting the carcass and the right thigh, his helper the left thigh, so the Spaniards now divide up the place they call New Spain.

Cortes gives land and Indian slaves to his soldiers; organized serfdom begins. "It is a question, however," says his admiring editor, "whether this treatment was worse than they had suffered from their Mexican owners." —No question—it was worse. The Spanish judge Zorita, who spent ten years in Mexico in an official capacity, concluded "with certainty" that "one Indian pays more tribute today than did six Indians of that time." After all, that was the raison d'être—and, speaking of games and game-pieces, we might mention that while some human beings suffered in order that Montezuma could have his *totoloque* pellets, gold mining became far more terrible under the Spaniards.

What did the Conquest bring to the Aztec homeland? In the unabridged edition, we've tabulated its casualties in "Defense of Creed." Less quantifiable in any table: confusion, litigation over land, social unrest, forced labor on Spanish estates or in gold or silver mines, followed by fines for not working on the fields which they were simultaneously obliged to reap—always fines and taxes. Often the Indians found themselves required to pay in cash rather than in kind, which meant that *rurales* had to come to the cities to work for almost nothing, solely in order to fulfill this burden.

Return for a moment to the relation of the judge Zorita. As he tried (as benignly and altruistically as he could) to fulfill his function within the colonial machine, traveling to and fro on the roads, he often found Indians

straggling down the roads, pushed and pulled by conflicting corvée obliga-
tions, tired and hungry. Sometimes he'd see them dead, men, women and
"even their little ones, for they used them to carry food—something these
people had never before done." The conquerors seized them as porters,
just as the Burmese government would do with insurgent hill tribes four
centuries later. When they collapsed, rather than unchain them the
Spaniards might simply cut off their heads.

The population plummeting, the ingenious Spaniards added to the
taxes of the living the taxes of the dead.

In 1521, eleven million Indians lived in the heart of Mexico. Twenty
years later, less than six and a half million were left.

A reddish-orange man I met in a Chinese-Mexican restaurant in Mexi-
cali who told me that he was 100 percent Aztec (actually, he was Tlascalan
on his mother's side) said to me: "They brought horses. They brought
many fine things. But they hurt our pride."

His Golden Gamepieces Lost

At the century's end, Spaniards will still be torturing Indians to death to
try to get their gold. But we can't blame Cortes for that, because he's not
getting rich! Wondering just why it was that he defended this ground in the
first place, he complains to the King of Spain that he has spent more than
three hundred thousand gold pesos of his own money on the Conquest.
He asks for ten million, or for the interest on that amount. The king is
silent.

He proposes new projects—for instance, the conquest of the Chichime-
cas in the north. "By making slaves of these barbarians, who are almost sav-
ages, Your Majesty will be served, and the Spaniards greatly benefited, as
they will dig for gold, and perhaps through contact with us, some of them
may save their souls."

Now his true war aims shine through—or is it simply that bitterness
and unsatisfied greed etch away the last of his kindness? We read that he

> took Toluca for himself and asked the people for a tribute in maize . . .
> The next year he ordered them to cultivate a field for him, and this they
> did for many years. In addition, he sent them to work in the houses that
> he built in Mexico. Still later, he demanded slaves for the mines of Tle-
> tiztlac; the lords and principales gave him all the slaves, men and
> women, that they themselves had. On two occasions he took all those

slaves away and branded them on the face, and ordered that they carry maize from his tribute field to the mines. When new mines were discovered, he required sixty slaves every year for fifteen years.

Losing supreme authority over Mexico to a latecomer, he struggles to bribe the King of Spain with Mexican gold and a cannon made of melted-down Mexican silver. Accused of intrigue, concealment of the spoils, poisoning, arrogance, he mildly bows to the new Lord Governor.

He gets exiled from Mexico but replies to all: *"Thou shalt give thy life for thy loyalty and thy King."*

He was a very stubborn man, as a result of which he had more lawsuits than was proper to his station. He spent liberally on war, women, friends, and fancies . . . In his dress he was elegant rather than sumptuous, and was extremely neat. He took delight in a large household and family, in silver service and dignity.

After having undertaken an expedition to the Spice Islands in the King's service, he sails for Spain to obtain his rights, bringing with him, among other companions, one of Montezuma's sons, and "eight tumblers, several very white Indian men and women, and dwarfs and monsters. In short, he traveled as a great lord." He brings more Mexican loot to be employed "for gifts." This tactic succeeds. The King—now the Emperor—ennobles him, converting him into Captain General of New Spain, with a right of keeping one-twelfth of everything for himself. And so for Cortes all the battles begin to approach a happy ending. He marries well, returns to the New World, survives other intrigue-driven reversals of fortune, explores the Sea of Cortez, quarrels and litigates, loses his favorite Aztec jewels in a shipwreck and expires of dysentery, aged sixty-three—like Napoleon and Stalin, one of the few moral actors in this book who dies not by another's hand.

In his will, he asks people to look into whether he did anything wrong in enslaving the Indians, and to make whatever restitution is required. But "over his doors and on his coat of arms he caused to be inscribed . . . *The judgment of the Lord overtook them; His might strengthened my arm."*

JUSTIFICATIONS

Policy and Choice

I.

DETERRENCE, RETRIBUTION AND REVENGE

On the orders of an officer with the powers of at least a battalion commander, collective drastic measures will be taken against localities from which cunning or malicious attacks are made on the Armed Forces, if circumstances do not permit of a quick identification of individual offenders.
                                        FIELD MARSHAL WILHELM KEITEL, 1941

I think that the American Army as a unit will handle the 12th S.S., every unit they can get ahold of. They are the men that killed our people in cold blood . . . We hate everybody that ever wore a 12th S.S. uniform.
                                        GENERAL DWIGHT D. EISENHOWER, 1945

When Pancho Villa, that wide-sombrero'd, double-bandoliero'd, squinting, moustached swaggerer, resolved to shoot Señor Claro Reza in revenge for the latter's attack upon his hideout, it had to be done where all the people could see, "even in front of Government Palace—do you agree, *compadre?*" Reza was police and Villa that transitional life-form, a highwayman with an ideology. Having crawled out of the primeval sea of manifest self-interest, he could now evolve successively into each of the following creatures: guerrilla leader, general, statesman, underdog, martyr. No matter that self-interest nourished these incarnations, too: authority needs to act a rarefied part in order to legitimize itself. Reza's murder, then, would enact revolutionary justice. *Deterrence, retribution and revenge must all be didactic to accomplish their ends.* Somebody shoots Reza somewhere, and who cares? Villistas shoot him to teach a lesson; other Rezas might take fearful heed. So they riddled him in the marketplace— more dangerous for the killers than any ambush. Crowds witnessed this reduction of a human being into a bleeding corpse. Then the Villistas galloped away in broad daylight, pursued by cavalry, but not too zealously, because local authority was already getting frightened of them. They'd made their point, putting symbolic politics ahead of "pure" expediency— and thereby furthering long-term expediency, since they could count on more impunity on subsequent occasions.

When Stalin signed the death sentence of the trade unionist Rudzutak, the result must have been as routine as it was secret. Rifles boomed out, but not in any marketplace; their after-rings died muffled by stone walls. Rudzutak's corpse probably got heaved into a windowless lorry that night, landing on a bed of companion pale and bleeding limbs; then a couple of secret policemen climbed into the cab, lit cigarettes and drove off toward the newest pit. No witnesses—Moscow slept. Yet this execution was, if anything, even more symbolic than the murder of Reza, for *Rudzutak had committed no actionable behavior to speak of.* Expressing a doubt or two about policy, as most sincere moral actors do, he'd remained more than loyal to his Party. The silence of deterrence crashed down upon him. It reverberated not among "the masses" but among the people who counted, the ones who dictated in the masses' name. Along the darkened corridors of officialdom, Rudzutak's steps sounded no more: ominous echoes of his absence goaded survivors into the outer marches of enthusiastic abasement.

Is a public slaying any "better"—more honest, more subject to accountability—than a private one? In this book I have made the argument that it is. The Maxims for Murderers posted warningly in our Moral Calculus share the dangerous trait of *unaccountability.* Needless to say, if the slaying wasn't right in the first place, then making it public merely magnifies its effects without justifying it. The theatrical liquidations accomplished by Robespierre's guillotine or Mao's village hangmen sicken me no less than shootings under carefully controlled conditions in the Lubyanka cellars; the

spontaneity of the lyncher or the opportunistic sex murderer has its counterpole in the seemingly passionless foresightedness of an Eichmann.

Stalin, for all his private rages, took Eichmann's course, proceeding by
means of the NKVD, with malice aforethought. As for Pancho Villa, he
was one of those individuals called "mercurial." How many times would
he greet a man affectionately, then become convinced of treachery and order him up against the wall? Even then the story might not be over. Somebody might plead the laws of hospitality, appealing to Villa's outer and
inner honor: a great brave commander such as he had no need to execute
people! Then Villa dismissed the firing squad and weepingly threw his
arms around the condemned man now brought back to life, in tribute to
his own potency to make and unmake other human beings. The unkilled
man was Villa's own monument! Was that the end, then? Sometimes his
mind might change yet again; and the resurrected found himself re-
condemned. Here the goal of violence was but a will-o'-the-wisp, a fitfully
shining ball of nothingness. The same can be said of the characters in
Sade's books: After the orgasm, what remained but the vile puppet within
whose orifices the protagonist of the moment, solitary human in a world
of puppets, had masturbated? No matter what the murderer's heart rate,
or how grand or small his audience, the corpse lies bleeding.

The Turk Who Wept

In September of 1918, T. E. Lawrence and his Arab forces, being advised by
the British that a column of Mezerib Turks two thousand in number was
approaching, set out to meet it. By the time they did so, the Turks had already taken Tafas, where, Lawrence writes with dryly restrained anger in
the *Arab Bulletin,* "they . . . allowed themselves to rape all the women they
could catch." Upon perceiving the Arab attack, the Turks murdered every
inhabitant, including "some twenty small children (killed with lances and
rifles), and about forty women. I noticed particularly one pregnant woman,
who had been forced down on a saw-bayonet." Because of these atrocities,
his order was, for the first and only time in the campaign: No prisoners.

> The second and leading portions [of the enemy], after a bitter struggle,
> we wiped out completely. We ordered "no prisoners" and the men
> obeyed, except that the reserve company took two hundred and fifty
> men (including many German A.S.C.) alive. Later, however, they found

one of our men with a fractured thigh who had been afterward pinned to the ground by two mortal thrusts with German bayonets. Then we turned our Hotchkiss on the prisoners and made an end of them, they saying nothing. The common delusion that the Turk is a clean and merciful fighter led some of the British troops to criticize Arab methods a little later—but they had not entered Turaa or Tafas.

In *Seven Pillars of Wisdom* Lawrence adds other details, regarding both what the Turks did in Tafas, which I gladly omit, and what he and the Arabs did in return. For the latter, this elaboration of Lawrence's order and its results will suffice:

I said, "The best of you brings me the most Turkish dead," and we turned after the fading enemy, on the way shooting down those who had fallen out by the wayside and came imploring our pity. One wounded Turk, half naked, not able to stand, sat and wept to us. Abdulla turned away his camel's head, but the Zaagi, with curses, crossed his track and whipped three bullets from his automatic into the man's bare chest. The blood came out with his heart beats, throb, throb, throb, slower and slower.

Revenge at Tafas

What we have here is a form of capital punishment: a combination of revenge and deterrence which the Turks' atrocity called into operation. Of course, this is *collective* capital punishment, and knowing only as much about the weeping Turk as Lawrence told us—which is to say, only as much as he knew—we cannot determine the man's guilt or innocence vis-à-vis atrocities at Tafas. Nor did his guilt appear to be an issue for Lawrence. The military historian John Keegan insists: "There are no circumstances, in any code of justice which the British army recognizes, that justify the shooting of unarmed men, not convicted of capital crimes by a court of law, who have fallen into one's power." Of course the Turk who wept probably failed to qualify as unarmed; he hadn't surrendered his weapon— Lawrence and the Arabs would not let him. Was he then convicted of a capital crime? —Lawrence defined it so.

In war, definers abound. Pancho Villa regularly shot his prisoners if they fell into particular categories: (1) officers of the *federales* (if they were members of the lower ranks their fate was at the discretion of the individual Villista commander); (2) followers of his ex-ally Orozco, who'd turned on him; (3) Americans, in arms or not, after the Americans began to support his enemies (at Santa Isabel the Villistas killed sixteen American miners and engineers; then they rode across the border and murdered twenty-six Americans in Columbus, New Mexico, most of them civilians); (4) Chinese (when they captured Parral in 1916, they were shouting, "We are going to kill gringos!" but there were none, so they hung the Chinese instead). What the Villistas did, since they did it so often, was policy, however slapdash and unjustified according to other moral criteria such as discrimination and defense of race. At least they followed Walzer's Axiom: It is less important for the justice of a war that any particular item be on the list of limitations than that there *be* a list.

What Lawrence and the Arabs did might have been policy, since they usually did discriminate between armed combatants and unarmed prisoners. It might also have been sheer rage.

Unlike Villa and Stalin, Lawrence was not ordinarily a cruel man; indeed, at the successful conclusion of the Arab Revolt at Damascus he worked hard to remove decomposing corpses and sick filth from an improvised hospital for Turkish prisoners. We ought not to forget his statement, already quoted, that the Turks were not clean fighters. He made this assertion more than once, repeating that Turks never took Arab prisoners and that their methods of withholding quarter were less than humane. Tafas made his blood boil, and it should have. But should he have responded as he did?

An Executioner's Drolleries

Years after that war had been won, the acclaimed book designer Bruce Rogers asked Lawrence to translate Homer's *Odyssey*. Lawrence was willing. He had often mused over the poem, which he read in Greek: "It goes with me, always, to every camp, for I love it." He felt himself specially prepared to do the job. For one thing, he had done archaeological excavations in the Middle East. Nor was that all. The Turk who wept would help him achieve verisimilitude! As he wrote to Rogers:

> I have handled the weapons, armour, utensils of those times, explored their homes, planned their cities. I have hunted wild boars and watched wild lions, sailed the Aegean (and sailed ships), bent bows, lived with pastoral peoples, woven textiles, built boats, and killed many men. So I have odd knowledges that qualify me to understand The Odyssey.

Does the resulting translation give us any clues to his state of mind, or soul, when he killed his Turkish and German prisoners? The task finally done, in a dismissive note to the printer he says of the poem: "Gay, fine and vivid it is: never huge or terrible." Compared to *The Iliad* with its myriad ghastly battle scenes this may be true, but parts of *The Odyssey* are terrible enough. In Book XXII, the revenge taken by Odysseus against the suitors who despoiled and tyrannized his household is described with unforgettably gruesome naturalism. Could it be that Lawrence ridiculed Homer as a mere bookish stay-at-home, "all adrift when it comes to fighting," who had never seen a single battle death because he, a self-proclaimed killer, found the destruction of the suitors to be physiologically or strategically implausible?

To me, at least, this book of the poem glows and glares with horrific power. Halfway through its retributory executions, while from the rafters Pallas Athene smites the suitors with supernatural fright, and our returned householder with his few companions drives them all back and back, crunching their skulls, shooting them in throat or liver, one named Leodes (who'd tried and failed to string the master's bow) seizes the knees of his enemy—or, as Lawrence renders it in his translation, in terms not dissimilar to the ones in his account of the Turk who wept: "By your clasped knees, O Odysseus, pity me and show mercy." Since he is gripping those knees, one must imagine that, like the wounded Turk, he was "sitting and weeping" to Odysseus—who heeds him not. Just as the Turk's dying heart beats out a tattoo of blood, like the neck of a decapitated chicken (I have killed those), so Leodes also meets death with the sad incongruousness of vain movement. Samuel Butler in his version has it: "Then he struck Leiodes on the back of his neck, so that his head fell rolling in the dust while he was yet speaking." Lattimore uses almost the same words: "And the head of Leodes fell in the dust while he was still speaking." The more recent translation of Robert Fagles puts it, slightly more inventively: "And the praying head went tumbling in the dust." In Lawrence's version, however, the matter goes beyond incongruity to approach the comic: "His head, yet praying for mercy, was confounded in the dust." We ought not to read too much into what might be something other than callous trivialization—after all, as his note to the printer makes clear, Lawrence had tired of the whole poem by now—as tired of "that cold-blooded egotist Odysseus" as of Leodes—probably more so, since Odysseus appears on practically every page. In Lawrence's life, everything had a tendency to turn to ashes. He had loved *The Odyssey* once; he'd loved war, and the Arab Revolt; but now it all sickened him, and he importuned his commander, Allenby, to be discharged, "pointing out how much easier the New Law would be if my spur were absent from the people. In the end he agreed; and then at once I knew how much I was sorry." Thus ends his famous *Seven Pillars of Wisdom*.

Lawrence was cracking up, his own mental instability now often betrayed by laughter, as when the sick and dying Turks in that hospital had begged him for pity. Did he recollect the begging of the Turk who wept? It has been said that the laugh reflex derives from consciousness of some logical or emotional disjunction—often a disjunction between persons, as when somebody is degraded in the laugher's eyes. I think of Caesar after his victory over Pompey, flittering all over the Roman world, conquering and pardoning, ascending rapidly now into his sterile godhead. Everyone is beneath him. In his revealing words, "I myself am never happier than when pardoning suppliants." He sees King Pharnaces charging toward him at the head of a hostile army and is "amused at his vainglorious display." Lawrence's translation of *The Odyssey* passage, and likewise his account of the Turk who wept, both echo with such pathetic chuckles of would-be omnipotence. When he saw the Turks in the hospital, his anxious superiority must have cracked in two: he was living, they were perishing; he was victorious, clean, successful, and they vanquished and physically loathsome; they had fought in a bad cause, for bad war aims— and now, as it appeared, so had he. "There was something which made me laugh at their whispering in unison, as if by command," he writes. He laughed—but he helped them, and later suffered nightmares about the jellied cadavers he'd found there and conveyed to a mass grave. A British medical major arrived the next day and, not knowing how much worse the hospital had been, called Lawrence a "bloody brute." Again Lawrence laughed, and the major slugged him. Earlier on, "a Turkish colonel from the window fired at me with a Mauser pistol, cutting the flesh of my hip. I laughed at his too-great energy, which thought, like a regular officer, to promote the war by the killing of an individual." How then could he have promoted justice by sparing one from retribution?

The Torment of Expediency

This brilliant and sensitive man—both more literary and more solitary than Trotsky (more akin to Caesar in both regards); capable, unlike Stalin, of admiring others, but almost as merciless as Stalin on the occasions (rare in Lawrence's case) that he undertook some retributory resolution; sardonically tormented; illegitimate; perhaps homosexual; guilty over everything—knew that his countrymen had lied to the Arabs, promising them independence if they fought for it; meanwhile, they'd secretly partitioned Arabia between themselves and the French. (Stalin, taking such maneuvers as matters of course, would have grinned, puffed his pipe and derived whatever advantage he could.) "In this hope" of self-sovereignty, Lawrence later wrote, his irregulars "performed some fine things, but, of course, instead of being proud of what we did together, I was continually and bitterly ashamed." (Stalin was never ashamed, as far as we know. Maybe shame is in inverse proportion to murderousness.) Meanwhile, Lawrence promoted British interests so well that he was decorated with medals he refused to wear; for as he wrote at the beginning of *Seven Pillars,* in a passage which Villa, Caesar, Trotsky and Stalin would never have penned, "the only thing remaining was to refuse reward for being a successful trickster." He took his job description to an almost parodic extreme of blatantly cynical manipulation in the "twenty-seven articles" he composed for "handling Arabs":

> 4. Win and keep the confidence of your leader. Strengthen his prestige at your expense before others when you can. Never refuse or quash schemes he may put forward: but ensure that they are put forward in the first instance privately to you. Always approve them, and after praise modify them insensibly, causing the suggestions to come from him, until they are in accord with your own opinion. When you attain this point, hold him to it, keep a tight grip of his ideas, and push him forward as firmly as possible, but secretly so that no one but himself (and he not too clearly) is aware of your pressure.

This is politics. This is what politicians do, but the lesson which Lawrence left unlearned is that the politician himself is to supposed to be unaware of, or at least companionable with, the pressure he puts. Pancho Villa was all grandiosity, and Stalin knew that everything he did was right; but Lawrence despised himself. That is why he had a growing death wish. In one of his war notebooks he'd written: "I've decided to go alone to Damascus, hoping to get killed on the way . . . We are calling them to fight for us on a lie, and I can't stand it." In 1918, surrounded, as he thought, by the enemy, he rode straight toward them "to end the business, in all the exhilaration of that last and terrific and most glad pain of death," because "when combats came to the physical, bare hand against hand, I used to turn myself in. The disgust of being touched revolted me more than the thought of death and defeat." (His aversion to flesh had metastasized within him after his capture and rape by Turkish soldiers in 1917.) But once again he won neither death nor defeat. The supposed enemy were friends.

The war over, and the Arabs more or less sold down the river, Lawrence, now famous, was invited to meet King George. The good soldier said to the King: "Your Cabinet are an awful set of crooks." He did what he could to help Prince Feisal get the sovereignty that he deserved, and was rewarded with the following compliment from the Foreign Office: "We and the War Office feel strongly that he is to a large extent responsible for our troubles with the French over Syria . . . the India Office hope that Lawrence will never be employed in the Middle East again in any capacity." I am sure that the India Office's assessment was correct: Lawrence remained incapable of becoming a professional employed in the calculus of expediency and loyalty. His loyalties were of the personal kind. He worshipped Allenby, his former commanding officer. Feisal liked and appreciated him for his efforts. But they drifted apart: Feisal was a King, and Lawrence, who in terms of his power over government resources (as opposed to his reputation) was now a postwar nobody, further degraded himself to become "Private Shaw." He continually wrote and spoke of being filthy inside, of longing to commit some hideous act which would make people feel the contempt for him that he deserved. I presume that this means he'd already committed it—perhaps by being "touched" by his Turkish rapists, perhaps also by being touched a little by the death of the Turk who wept—he was no Eichmann; in that passage don't you also find a secret spring of pity? Or is it all stone sadism to you? "The blood came out with his heart beats, throb, throb, throb, slower and slower." Is this merely clinical? Why did he watch—why write it? What was he thinking? How many other men did he kill directly and indirectly? I have never met a witness to violent death who hasn't been corroded by it.

Surely he thought to put the episode out of his mind. In the article on guerrilla warfare which he had been asked to write for the fourteenth edition of the *Britannica*, Lawrence proved himself to be capable of disavowals after all, assuring students of the Arab Revolt that "the members had to keep always cool, for the excitement of a blood-lust would impair their science, and their victory depended on a just use of speed, concealment, accuracy of fire. Guerrilla war is far more intellectual than a bayonet charge."

Between 1923 and 1935, John Bruce, his mate in the Tank Corps, is said to have flogged Lawrence nine times at the latter's request. Very probably he rediscovered what he had already learned in Arabia when a scorpion stung him, that "pain of this quality never endured long enough really to cure mind-sickness."

In his uniform and in his Arab dress there is little of him to see, except that like Napoleon he was short. Later portrait photographs show him to have been quite handsome, with a smooth face and rather hypnotic eyes. Peter O'Toole did a good job playing him in *Lawrence of Arabia*.

Deterrence at Tafas

If we set aside the unjustifiability of the act as retribution, and consider its expediency as deterrence, we cannot forget the significant possibility that other Turks, hearing how and why their fellow column had been wiped out, were in fact deterred from committing further atrocities—or, perhaps, simply deterred from engaging Arabs where possible (this being the classical sense of military deterrence, as when the Moghul dynast Babur put to death "several" of his prisoners, "to strike terror into the enemy").

We agreed that a good end cannot be validated by a bad means. But if the end of deterrence is good—*to prevent unjustified violence*—and if its means follows the proportionality principle—that is, if the number of people harmed by the act is less than the number saved—then we must suspend our condemnation until we have finished considering the moral utility of the act.

My first thought on the matter is that perhaps Lawrence could have deterred the Mezerib Turks in a less sanguinary way. During the American Civil War, President Lincoln was very careful to distinguish deterrence from revenge. In his order of retaliation against Confederate troops who were dispatching unarmed colored Union soldiers, he invoked, as Nuremberg would eighty-two years later, international law and custom as sufficient warrant to denounce that practice. *Violent deterrence is justified when it enforces a legitimate social contract—in short, when it is an instrument of legitimate authority.* "It is therefore ordered that for every soldier of the United States killed in violation of the laws of war, a rebel soldier shall be executed." In short, if the thing must be done, it would be done judiciously and judicially, without malice or excess; the retaliation would be one to one, not ten to one or a hundred to one. *[See pages 369–70.]*

Numerically equitable though it might have been (Lawrence did not bother to establish any preconceived ratio between his victims and their own civilian victims at Tafas, but it would have been on the order of ten to one), Lincoln's retaliation order would still have failed to dispense fair justice to the Turk who wept, either. I imagine that doomed soul as a conscript, a weak, hangdog fellow who could barely lift his own rifle, who hadn't been paid in months, or issued rations, perhaps, since before Tafas; whose training was poor and whose morale was worse; who pillaged when he could, in order to get a good meal once in awhile. The habit of pillage might have insensibly guided him into the habit of rape. Perhaps his colleagues, like Lawrence's, were afraid of keeping prisoners on the march. Surely he'd looked into the villagers' eyes when he was chicken-stealing, and saw their hatred. When his column began spearing children to death, could that have been intended as retribution and deterrence for something, too? Could an old man have refused to give up his gold? Had some raped girl bitten off a man's ear? We don't know, nor can we know; nor can it matter; nothing excuses what the Mezerib Turks did at Tafas. Lawrence, with perhaps too glib explicitness, writes that the massacre took place by order of Sherif Bey, the commander of the lancer rear guard, upon perceiving that the Turkish forces were being pushed back by the Arab irregulars. Were this the case, shouldn't the retaliation have been limited to executing Sherif Bey once they caught him? And if the atrocity had been a popular measure carried out with relish by the Turkish column, as Lawrence seems to imply in another place, we are still left to wonder whether the Turk who wept was one of the men who forced the pregnant woman down on the saw-bayonet, or whether he had stood aside, weeping even then, unavailingly invoking the Qur-'An's strictures of mercy, or whether he'd been sick with dysentery? Until we know that, how can we determine whether he got justice?

The sad law of collective violence: Collective justice (or not) sometimes disburses individual injustice. Imminence, ignorance of actual circumstances, miscellaneous collective necessities, especially in war and revolution, bring about this result. All we can really say is that misfortunes do fall upon the undeserving, and that human justice, like Fortune herself, cuts corners. When, like Stalin, we contentedly aim at committing worse unfairness than fortune, we're unjustified. In the meantime, expediency reassures us that we'll never know who's undeserving in cases such as Tafas, that deterrence must be exercised, that our first duty is to our victims and our own side, that the debased version of the Golden Rule, *Do as you are done by,* is the only plausible strategy for changing the enemy's policy. Maybe the next Sherif Bey will think twice.

Having reflected thus, we can go on with pleasure to remark upon Lincoln's humanity in the American Civil War: *He never had his retaliation order carried out.* The following year, being informed that Confederates had murdered a number of colored prisoners of war at Fort Pillow, he delayed putting the order into effect, on the commendable grounds that "blood cannot restore blood, and government should not act for revenge." He then gave the Confederates six weeks to promise that no other such massacres would occur, in which case he was willing to suspend the retaliation order. Otherwise he would "take such action as may then appear expedient and just." In short, his statement of impending retaliation was a restrained (and very decent and principled) employment of deterrence. *Deterrence approaches justification (or at least mercifulness) when it forbears to execute retribution.*

Instead of killing every man, Lawrence, like Trotsky, could have shot every tenth man—and for better cause. (This still would not have safeguarded any innocent Turks.) He could have turned them over to the surviving villagers (in which case the results would have been the same). He could have sent them to the rear with instructions that they be tried. As we've said, he could have shot Sherif Bey alone (had the latter been taken alive). In Lawrence's case, it is true, expediency raises its formidable head: he possessed neither Lincoln's authority, nor his fortresses, safe cities, guards and prisons. His nomadic camel-cavalry could not have conveniently sent two thousand captives to the rear, nor could they have traveled with so many prisoners. Still, he had taken prisoners before.

I cannot condemn him completely. The self-control of his guerrillas had been tested. Natural, then—however unjustified—for that self-control to give way. In *Seven Pillars,* when Lawrence recalls seeing one three-year-old girl in Tafas die from a Turkish neck wound, trying unavailingly to scream, his grief infects the reader, as does his horror, pity and rage. I would not raise a finger to save the Turk who did that, although I would hardly gun down his brothers. Lawrence, of course, calls *the Arabs* his brothers. Some of them hailed from Tafas; and one, Talal, the Sheikh of Tafas, went mad and galloped into the machine guns of the enemy. Lawrence did the brotherly thing, by their standards and (he being a self-described chameleon) by his: he took revenge for them. Remember: Arabia's social contract is maintained in part even nowadays by the blood feud and vigilant defense of honor. How much more must this have been the case in wartime? Expediency again: by so doing, he must have furthered his bond with the Arabs, and thereby augmented his powers as a commander.

CALCULUS OF RETALIATION: HISTORICAL EXAMPLES

For Every Person of Ours Whom the Other Side Harms, How Many Persons of Theirs Should We Harm?

RETALIATOR	CAUSE OF RETALIATION	RATIO OF RETALIATION (OURS:THEIRS) KILLED	REMARKS
1. Julius Caesar, in the Roman Civil War, 48 B.C.	The Pompeian commander, Marcus Petreius, kills Caesarian troops caught fraternizing with his own.	?:0	Refusing to retaliate, Caesar sends the Pompeian fraternizers back.
2. John Brown at Pottawatomie, Kansas, 1856.	Proslave men kill 6 free-state men in separate incidents and threaten further violence.	6:5	Total executed: 5, by Brown and his raiders.
3. President Lincoln in the American Civil War. (Deterrent threat only.)	Confederates kill disarmed colored soldiers at Fort Pillow.	1:1	Total executed: none. Order suspended. Persons executed would have been POWs.
4. Cherokee war-raiders, 17th–19th centuries.	Enemy raid. War was revenge-motivated, hence perpetual.	1:1	Total killed: perhaps hundreds.
5. Nissar, an Indian Muslim "soldier" in communal riots against Hindus, 1990s.	Hindu violence against Muslims, same riots.	1:2+	"If I hear that two of our people have been attacked and killed at the wooden bridge it takes me just five minutes to knife five of them."[F]
6. Jehovah (alleged).	Deterrent threat, to protect the fugitive manslayer Cain.	1:7	"Then the Lord said to him: 'Not so! If any one slays Cain, vengeance shall be taken on him sevenfold.'"

(continued)

RETALIATOR	CAUSE OF RETALIATION	RATIO OF RETALIATION (OURS:THEIRS) KILLED	REMARKS
7. The Persian King Cambyses in Egypt, 525 B.C. (alleged).	Persians invade and conquer Egypt. Egyptians tear to pieces a Persian herald calling for their surrender, along with the crew of the herald's ship.	1:10	Total executed: 2,000, all nobles.
8. The black American militant H. Rap Brown, late 1960s.	Following Martin Luther King's assassination, black-white race riots continue.	1:10	Total executed: unknown; few if any. Brown was an orator, not a military leader.
9. T. E. Lawrence at Tafas.	Murder of 60+ civilians (women and children) at Tafas.	1:10+	Total executed: probably 600+ (including those killed in battle).
10. The Germans in Yugoslavia, World War II.	Resistance and Partisan activity.	1:100	Total executed: thousands, men, women and children. In one occurrence for which Field Marshal Keitel was later held responsible, 7,000 were shot, including schoolboys.
11. Ahuitzotl, Aztec Emperor, ca. 1497, in Tecuantepec area of Mexico.	Aztec merchants (who also serve as heralds and spies) are murdered in this half-conquered region.	1:2,000??	Total executed: probably thousands. 1,200 captives taken for sacrifice.
12. Otanes, deputy of the Persian King Darius, on the isle of Samos, ca. 521 B.C. (alleged).	After agreeing to restore a Persian favorite, one faction suddenly turns upon the Persian delegation and murders some of them.	1:∞	Total executed: unknown. Persians massacre all the males they can catch.

Nor can whatever blame there was be exclusively assigned to Lawrence. He says that he ordered the massacre, and perhaps he did, but it would be in keeping with his masochism to take all the defilement upon himself. By his "twenty-seven articles," and the realities of his situation, he actually controlled less by discipline than by exhortation. On many an occasion—this might have been one of them—the Arabs did as they listed. *Surely this was no unpopular order.* Two days later, in Deraa, some had not tired of vengeance. We read (but not in *Seven Pillars*) that they boarded a trapped Turkish hospital train, ripped off the patients' clothes and slit their throats. Lawrence, ice-cool or crazed, struggled (unavailingly) to *prevent* British troops from stopping the carnage; but one hesitates to hold him responsible: nobody was in charge at that moment, and he, having already taken his retribution and probably giving little thought to deterrence, was quite simply an incompetent moral agent.

Ending Retaliation

If the most just action is that which harms the fewest people on either side, then justice means ending mutual retaliation; and the only way to end it is through restraint, which is the logical application of the Golden Rule. In 1994, during the Yugoslavian Civil War, one Croatian fighter described to me how the restraint of his Muslim enemies had freed him from the burden of revenge. Doubtless the Muslims who had offered that restraint had been accused of cowardice and unmanliness; but somehow or other they had been able to control their vengeance lust. The Croatian and I had been talking about cutting enemy throats, and he said to me: "My aunt and my sister told me, if you catch someone, don't do that. You understand, my sisters were in a prison in Zenica. There was an exchange. I asked them: Were you raped? They said they were not. And the women they were exchanged for were not raped by us. When it was good between us like that, I lost eighty percent of my hate. I have no hate in myself. If I were to cut someone's throat, I would lose my soul." —From this I take it that if his sisters had been raped, he would have retained 100 percent of his hatred and slit throats. But they hadn't been raped; and so he too was impelled to be decent. Such is the reaction that Gandhian tacticians rightly bank on.

And the moral actor who sincerely desires to shut off the retaliation machine can go further than restraining himself from retaliating. Employing the Golden Rule, he can offer compensation, making restitution for his own prior violence. That was Gandhi's way. In this situation, we must stand aside and praise the potential superiority of nonviolence.

Otherwise, we can use friendship or force to establish (or reassert) a social contract between enemies, calling into play retaliation against violence on either side, as administered by a functionary or agent of that contract. "For the family of the murdered man," wrote a twentieth-century British penal reformer, "for the girl whose health has been permanently broken by brutal rape, for the skilled workman who can no longer follow his trade, the simple fact that their hardships had been specially recognized would help to assuage the bitterness of their lot." In a way, the Icelandic system provided that "special recognition" admirably. The offender, or his kin, paid an agreed-upon restitution to the victim's family. Failing agreement, the victim had easy recourse to the blood feud, which afforded that special recognition in the more spectacular way beloved by Fulvia, Hitler, Lawrence and the Arabs, the Athenians . . . But with the establishment of the centralized state, revenge became the domain no longer of the victim, but of the sovereign power, who, bedecking it with legality, magically transmuted it into *punishment,* the subject of our next section.

II.

PUNISHMENT

The great mass of humanity abstains from evil-doing only because of the penalties of the law and the retribution that comes from the gods.

DIODORUS OF SICILY, first century A.D.

My prayer to God is for the police to commit unlimited atrocities upon young Muslims. Whenever I hear about Muslim boys being tortured, I feel like dancing with joy. Unless these boys directly experience oppression on their bodies, they will never be able to stand up against it.

"AKBAR" (Indian Muslim *pelwan,* or organizer of communal violence
Against Hindus during riots), ca. 1990

The Meaning of the Noose

The two epigraphs for this section exemplify two entirely opposed conceptions of the value of punishment as a deterrent. Diodorus claims that punishment deters; Akbar, that it radicalizes—in other words, actually incites. Diodorus is speaking for the law-and-order faction; Akbar represents the side of transgression. In old Vienna, prisoners were corseted with thirty kilograms of shackles. Was that sufficient weight to bear out Akbar's and Diodorus's respective theses? Engravings and woodblock prints of postmedieval tortures sicken us with their axes, swords, chains and wheels. Upon a brick-built mound, one figure is hanging; another kneels blindfolded, about to be beheaded; a third, already broken on the wheel, waits, disjointed, for death. We see women screaming at the stake, the crowd's hands raised in malediction. They are dragging witches down into the torture chamber, holding them as ranchers grip calves at branding time.

The neatest case, of course, is when the criminal spontaneously embraces his own punishment. A sergeant in Singapore who obeys the white-lit hallucinatory voice commanding him to "chop" his paramour to death now stands at the bar. He tells the court that "he hoped the judge would sentence him to death. He wanted to say sorry to his parents whom he could not serve until their old age." In several of the Qur-'Anic hadiths or commentaries gathered together in the famous *Sahih Al-Bukhari*, an adulterer enters a mosque, approaches the Prophet and in default of the statutory four witnesses bears witness against himself four times. The Prophet, who'd first turned his face away, finally utters the necessary command. Punishment begins. "When the stones troubled him, he fled, but we overtook him at Al-Harra and stoned him to death." "The Prophet spoke well of him and offered his funeral prayer." Hence this rule in our moral calculus: *Punishment is justified when the transgressor agrees to, or belongs to a culture which subscribes to, the rule by which he has been judged, and when he can be proven to have violated that rule.* Fourteen centuries after the adulterer fell bleeding and broken at al-Harra, the Oklahoma City bomber, sentenced to death, waves and nods to his jurors, while the prosecutor labels his act "the crime that the death penalty was designed for." What could be more satisfying to the sadism of public symmetry?

But, embraced or not, is the penalty just? A British soldier who fails to pass muster at parade gets flogged to death. A mutinous felon is sentenced to be "flogged with a boatswain's cat until his bones were denuded of flesh." Even if the felon begged for it, would that make it right?

Juridical fairness owns slow-grinding wheels. The defendant, his crime long since cooled and staled, is hauled in shackles before its bar. No matter how monstrous his deeds, he stands harmless now, his body and mind a tabula rasa upon which a long-calculated sentence can be engraved to a nicety. But self-defense is attended by different circumstances than legal punishment. In the former case, to preserve himself (or what he considers to be a higher object of his loyalty—say, my comrades over myself or my child) the victim is obliged to act hastily—which means without the benefit of the full knowledge required for a truly Platonic decision. (Jewish law in fact *insists* that he act hastily: self-defense is acceptable under this code *only* "when the act is carried out without premeditation and when one's life is in imminent danger." So too with Roman law.) Because the aggressor has forced this obligation upon him, it seems fair to correspondingly restrict consideration of the aggressor's rights and motives during the crisis. This is not to say that they must be ignored altogether. (After all, the social balance will not ignore those of the defender. "For if his sole purpose be to withstand the injury done to him, and if he defend himself with due moderation," says Aquinas, "it is no sin, and one cannot say properly that there is strife on his part.")

For law to partake of justice, it must codify its penalties into limit and consistency. But consistency is not enough. Dead legal forms lead us to death.

PUNISHMENT FOR FAILURE TO MAKE BED PROPERLY
Ravensbrück Concentration Camp for Women (1940)

First offense: Punishment standing without food.

Second offense: Solitary confinement in the dark cell.

Third offense: Twenty-five lashes.

Legal Retaliation Must Be Moral Expression

Why did the *Oberaufseherrinen* at Ravensbrück choose to be so strict? —Because she wanted subjection to her to be unquestioningly perfect. A badly made bed represented incomplete obedience; therefore, stern punishment gave her authority full measure of self-defense. Judicial retaliation (applied law), being public, and being applied for a given reason, always insists upon being taken as a lesson—notwithstanding Tocqueville's maxim that law seeks to apply justice to a given crime, not to create a new standard. When Tocqueville made this remark, he meant it to be taken in the sense that judicial power does not and cannot make its own laws, they being the prerogative of the legislature. But we already saw how Stalin's judiciary usurped legislative functions (being itself but the expedient tool of the executive), its busy procurement brigades, Committees of Unwealthy Peasants and firing squads injecting justice into millions. (In China during the Cultural Revolution, one elderly prisoner's interrogator contemptuously explained to her that "the victorious proletarian class makes the law to suit its purpose and serve its interest." The victorious class had already thrown her daughter out a window. She didn't learn about that murder for years.) Thus law at its crudest, making and remaking itself.

But even when it's not crude, doesn't law by the very nature of applying a standard reinforce and deepen it? Aren't all codes, all memories, like those lines which children trace into the ocean's edge, washed away by the world again and again, hence defensively rescored into the wet beach?

The Atonements of John Brown

Let us bring to mind again that famous story of how old John Brown kept an account book of whippings due for infractions of familial discipline—lies, laziness in assisting the tannery's blind old horse to grind bark, and the like (the penalty being six or eight strokes for each such sin); how one Sunday John Brown brought his scared but resigned boy out to the tannery to (as Hitler would have said) settle accounts; how John Brown administered a third of the settlement—"masterfully laid on" as his son later told it—and then suddenly stopped, stripped off his own shirt, handed the boy the switch, knelt down and commanded that his own bare back be striped! How must John Jr. have felt? Sad, relieved, grateful, ashamed, repulsed, horrified, moved to love? His father said that he was not punishing hard enough. I can almost see the boy now gritting his teeth and perhaps crying, desperate to get this over with, obediently striking his father with all his might until the blood flowed; no doubt that tough old man made no movement, showed no pain, uttered nothing except further commands to flog him harder. Very likely the instrument employed was a whip constructed by old Brown himself. In a third-person autobiography, the father recounts that as a boy he'd quickly learned "the entire Process of . . . Skin dressing . . . he could at any time dress his own leather such as Squirrel, Raccoon, Goat, Calf, or Dog Skins: + also learned to make Whip Lashes, which brought him some change . . . & was of considerable service in many ways." Did those sessions in the tannery constitute one category of that service? Oh, otherworldly, inflexible old John Brown! Strike, and strike again! It was the youth's first illustration, as he later put it, of the doctrine of the Atonement. By what might be more than an interesting co-incidence, Brown himself uses the same word in that same long autobio-graphical letter. His main vice as a child, he confesses, was lying,

> generally to screen himself from blame; or from punishment. He could not well endure to be reproached; & I now think had he been oftener en-couraged to be entirely frank; by making perhaps a kind of atonement for some of his faults; he would not have been so often guilty of this fault; nor have been obliged to struggle so long with so mean a fault.

In other words, corporal punishment was felt by Brown to be a kind-ness, because it granted quick instant release—not, obviously, in the sex-ual sense that it had for the Marquis de Sade a century earlier, but rather as moral catharsis: some pain, and all was cleared away! We are almost back in the era of the German mirror punishments. As with the Christian Atonement to which John Jr. was referring—that is, the notion that Christ's suffering is the solvent in which (if we but submit) our inborn sins can be dissolved—this equation between stripes and righteousness consti-tutes no more of any moral universal than the preference shown by Captain Nolan of the Light Brigade toward honor over self-preservation. Let's therefore interpret the concept of punitive purification purely as a didactic or magical measure on John Brown's part, like the condemnation of a stone. As Hobbes says, for a punishment to be more than revenge, it must be publicly witnessed and sanctioned by authority. The only public in the tannery was John Brown and his son, but punishers and offenders can be each other's public, especially when they switch roles. (Besides, a child may be a parent's most important public.) In one of his famous Ninety-Five Theses, Martin Luther insists that inward "penitence is null unless it produces outward signs in various mortifications of the flesh." The outward signs are for the benefit of the penitent—and the audience. Hence also the remarks of some of John Brown's enemies, an association of Confederate property owners, on the subject of slaves running away to the Yankees: "A few executions of leading transgressors among them by hanging or shooting would dissipate the ignorance which may be said to possess their minds and which may be pleaded in arrest of judgment."

That sounds evil; and an anarchist presents the case for edifying punishments in an even worse light when he bitterly complains: "Governments need police to produce criminals; because the mass of people are so frightened of criminals they willingly give away their rights and freedoms to obtain protection." The analogy with slavery doesn't hold up; the slaves never gave away their rights but were robbed of them. But perhaps it works for people like John Brown. He was not afraid of criminals, but he must have been terrified of sins. Is it too far-fetched to say that his conscience was his policeman, causing him to be whipped or to humble himself before his own children in order to protect him from invasive thoughts, little lies? Can we posit that for all his great principles he might have suffered from unfreedom of thought, his tethered soul struggling round and round his political and religious obsessions, like the blind horse in his tannery? Practically everything he tried failed, including the Harpers Ferry raid. —And yet, he *was* a bold man; he *was* free; he scorned the laws and punishments of others . . . Strange old Brown! With other figures of deterrence and retribution, the anarchist has a better case: his maxim explains precisely why Stalin harped so much on counterrevolutionaries, kulaks and wreckers; which is to say, why his secret police had to keep devouring all the Rudzutaks. After a while it becomes a miracle of perpetual motion: I must destroy Comrade Rudzutak in order to remind the masses that they depend on me to save them from him; and I must remind the masses that they need me so that it will be easier for me to destroy the next Rudzutak. *Violent punishment is unjustified to the extent that the punishment, which may be just or unjust in and of itself, furthers authority's power beyond the minimum necessary for enforcing the social contract.*

John Brown, on the other hand, never crushed his victims through the aid of moral-ideological machinery moving in smooth circles, but, like Lawrence liquidating the Mezerib Turks, acted with desperately illogical stabs of rage against what he hated. Unlike Lawrence, more fortunate than he in obsession, John Brown was certain that what he did was ordained by God. What we see as convulsive acts of violence he interpreted as chastisements writ in the bloody ink of meaning. In part, the tale of his career is a warning to us against self-righteousness and inflexible antibigotry carried to the point of bigotry itself, as when he murdered his prisoners on that dark cold night in Kansas; and one must likewise wonder regarding the whipping how he knew (or did he know?) that God demanded eight strokes for some particular lie of his son's, not seven or nine; but if we grant (as he would) that fathers are given latitude to administer reasonable penalties for the offenses of their children, and that those penalties, having been once explicated, earned and noted in that dreaded account book, must be carried out in order to avoid still another sin, namely the sin of a lie, of a broken promise, of (more to the point) a failure to wholesomely correct a child given into one's care, then suddenly that account becomes an absolute thing in and of itself, as universal and inevitable as the principle described by Newton, which dictates that the great boulder in Plato's never-never Country of the Laws must, once dislodged from its matrix, fall without respect to the living flesh below.

Love's Duty

Because his public life became so spectacular, John Brown's life as a family man holds less comparative "interest"—that is, offers less sensationalism. But the most cursory reading of the man's private letters, with their even lines of script, their capitalized nouns and capriciously underlined phrases, their news of calving lambs and oat fields, prove him to be either surprisingly home-centered, or else an excellent actor. "I am unable to pray for any thing better than a good Log House hewed inside, of peeled logs (with a good Cellar under it, about two feet longer outside than the old one we lived in)." And he proceeds to build his dream house line by line, at one point laying down his pen and resuming on the same subject two days later. It is strangely moving to observe this restless, distant, peripatetic murderer striving through unassisted will and imagination to create and consolidate in his image a world for his distant family. Brown was a would-be biblical patriarch, with his many children whom he instructed to regard and copy the wisdom of his letters, his increasing flocks, his potatoes and corn—but unlike Jacob or Laban, he remained a poor wanderer, a Moses born in Canaan, struggling to overthrow heathen ways, shepherd of an insignificant few. In his bankruptcy inventory of 1841 we find, among other sad flotsam, a mirror valued at ten cents, eight chairs valued at two seventy-five, two braining knives valued at a dollar twelve and, of course, eleven "Bibles & testaments" valued at six dollars and fifty cents . . . "There is a peculiar music in the word" *home*, he writes his wife (and typically enough—I love him for it—adds the mass revolution-ary's touch: "Millions there are who have no such thing to lay claim to"). Moses died before he even came into Canaan; one recalls that Martin Luther King compared himself to Moses shortly before he was assassi-nated; and John Brown shared with King not only zeal for defense of race but also the same manly mournfulness about oncoming doom. At the end of his long invocation of the ideal home we read: "These are my general ideas of a Log House but should you go on to build one you had better ex-ercise your own good judgment about it considerably for I may never live to occupy it." This was written in 1853; Brown, a year older than his cen-tury, still had half a dozen years left to live before the rope cut him off. We have seen him in his role of revolutionary know-it-all; but though he com-prehended full well the path of righteousness, and the misdemeanors of his family who sometimes strayed from that path, Brown was quick to confess that he often likewise failed to follow it. "Yesterday I began my fifty-fourth year," he writes in this same letter, "& I am surprised that one guilty of such an incredible amount of Sin & folly should be spared so long . . . I still keep hoping to do better hereafter." He *deserves* to be whipped, then—so perhaps he feels. When John Jr.'s strokes flew down upon his back that day in the tannery, did old Brown feel that he was expi-ating his son's guilt or his own? —*Both*, I would guess: he, who will soon become the avenging angel, can never be chastised enough. This may be the secret source of his strength: whenever life strikes at him, he accepts and glories in the punishment. —Both, I said; for Brown's logic, like Stalin's, forms a circle with its corollary: If I am hard with myself, then by a sly sub-version of the Golden Rule I have the right to be hard with you. —He whips young John; young John whips him. He kills proslavers and is killed.

To this difficult son of his, old Brown at one point pens a long epistle of witty, angry sarcasm, which must have mortified the recipient's soul, since it was unable to become a whip and mortify his back:

In your Letter, you appear rather disposed to Sermonise; & how will it operate on you and Wealthy [John Jr.'s wife] should I try to pattern after you a little, & also quote some from the Bible? In choosing my texts; & in quoting from the Bible I may perhaps select the very portions which "another portion" of my family hold as "not to be wholly received as true." I forgot to say that my younger sons (as is common in this "pro-gressive age") appear to be a little in advance of my older ones; & have thrown off the old Shackles entirely, after thorough & candid investigation. They have discovered the Bible to be all a fiction. Shall I add? that a Letter received from you some time since; gave me little else than pain and sorrow.

Old Brown then goes on for page after page, quoting maxims against backsliders, covenant-forsakers, father-dishonorers, and with an underlined amen and a final biblical shot: "And I beseech you Children 'Suffer the word of exhortation.'" In other words: Permit me to deter you from your ways.

The following month, "Your Affectionate Father" is writing to all his "Dear Children" at home that he hopes that through God's mercy "you may soon be brought to see the error of your ways; & be in earnest to 'turn many to *righteousness*' . . . I do not feel 'estranged from my children' but I cannot flatter them; nor 'cry peace when there is no peace.'"

It was as if he could not break himself of his harshness, merely direct it—lovingly against those he loved, or lethally against his enemies, or, lovingly or lethally we'll never know, against himself, like Seneca's simile of the horse-breaker's whip sizzling down angerlessly, "in order that by pain we may overcome their obstinacy." Despite their similarities of convulsiveness already noted, his tannery punishment sessions in no way equate with Lawrence's execution of the Mezerib Turks: in the latter case, the improvement of the recipient was no object, whereas for Brown, at least in the case of those who were dear to him, *punishment was love*. "Forgive the many faults and foibles you have seen in me," he writes the entire family, "and try to proffit by any thing good in either my example, or my council." To his wife he writes, in a richly affectionate and intimate letter which again allows us to set his murderous deeds momentarily aside, that he never forgets her, that she is truly his "better half." Then he gets down to the business of administering punishment long-range through her proxy:

If the large boys do wrong call them alone into your room, & expostulate with them kindly, & see if you cannot reach them by a kind but powerful appeal to their honor. I do not claim that such a theory accords very much with my practice; I frankly confess it does not; but I want Your face to shine even if my own should be dark, and cloudy. You can let the family read this letter.

The violent man (who venerates the mother who in keeping with the fashion of the times had whipped him) is trying Gandhism! Possibly he did not think it practical for Mary Brown to be whipping almost grown men of superior physical strength . . . But in the last year of his life, shortly before setting out to raid Harpers Ferry, he addressed his little daughter Ellen:

> I want very much to have you grow good every day; to have you learn to mind your Mother very quick; & sit very still at the table; & to mind what all older persons say to you; that is right. I hope to see you soon again; & if I should bring some little thing that will please you; it will not be very strange. I want you to be uncommon good natured. God help you, my child.
>   Your Affectionate Father,
>   John Brown

From such a man, this letter seems almost shockingly gentle.

He had his way: his children venerated *him*. The result? The killer-martyr father raised a crop of sacrificial sons in his own image. (A proximate result: blows struck on the proper side of the slavery question.) When he wrote his wife a year after murdering those proslave men at Pottawatomie that "as regards the resolution of the boys to 'learn, & practice war no more;' . . . it was not at my solicitation that they engaged in it at the first," he was surely being mendacious—even if only he believed that "little lie" which added to his whip-deservingness. Under whose solicitation could they have otherwise grown militant? For Brown was, by his own wry admission, "a King against whom there is no rising up." That is why by 1858, having proven himself at Pottawatomie, John Jr. that flogger and whipping boy from the tannery days, had also become, however ineffectually, his father's deputy, sent off on sensitive missions of what the CIA would call "stroking," garnering support for covert operations, "traveling slowly along, & enquiring out every man on the way." John Jr. obeyed. In 1859, old Brown led his sons Watson and Oliver to death at Harpers Ferry. (Their brother Owen escaped capture.) As usual, from the letter he sent home, one would never suspect that his party had been the aggressors. At least he continued to bear himself without pity:

> My dear Wife + Children every one I suppose you have learned before this by the newspapers that two weeks ago today we were fighting for

our lives at Harpers ferry: that during the fight Watson was mortally wounded; Oliver killed; Wm Thompson killed, + Dauphin slightly wounded[,] that on the following day I was taken prisoner immediately after which I received several Sabre cuts in my head: + Bayonet stabs in my body. As nearly as I can learn Watson died of his wounds on Wednesday. Also [illegible] on Thursday the 3 day after I was taken Dauphin was killed when I was taken + Anderson I suppose also. I have since been tried and found guilty of treason, &c; and of murder in the first degree. I have not received my sentence . . . Under all these terrible calamities, I feel quite cheerful in the assurance that God reigns; + will overrule all for his glory, + the best possible good. I feel no consciousness of guilt in the matter, not even mortification on account of my imprisonment; + irons . . . Be sure to remember + to follow my advice and my example . . .

    P.S. Yesterday Nov 2 I was sentenced to be hanged on 2 December next. Do not grieve on my account. I am still quite cheerful.

    So bless you all Four Ever,

    J. Brown

A terrible heaviness falls on me whenever I peruse this letter. My heart goes out to the shackled, bloody-scabbed old man in his prison, trying to do what little he can to prepare his blighted family for a fresh double loss, and for the loss of its patriarch inevitably to come. We have already asked the question: Did he do right or wrong as a terrorist and an insurgent? The question remains: Did he do right or wrong by his slaughtered sons? Were they martyrs or dupes? I can't really say, but one thing is certain: loved, admonished and punished into obedience, the boys did not universally obey. When Watson and Oliver were killed, they joined in a violent grave their brother Frederick, killed by a proslave man in retaliation for Pottawatomie; John Jr. had gone temporarily insane after Pottawatomie, which may have been why he didn't accompany his father to Harpers Ferry; the other three surviving brothers (four had died of childhood diseases) refused to go with him. Brown was grieved but accepted this decision. Perhaps I was wrong, and he wasn't entirely the king against whom there is no rising up, in which case one cannot hold Brown accountable for Watson and Oliver's participation in the doomed raid; perhaps, on the other hand, the dissenting brothers simply happened to be as stubborn as their father.

The Hanging of John Brown

If he was so sure he had divine right on his side, then why did he win only to the scaffold? The answer was simple: "God is no respecter of persons," Brown said again and again. The ancient oracle of Delphi would have concurred. Back to the punishment of rocks. We are told that a man who asked the Priestess whether he could perjure himself and keep money which did not belong to him had already sinned by requesting divine approval for the crime. Furthermore, "an oath has a son, nameless, without hands or feet, but swift to pursue until he has seized and destroyed utterly the race and house of the perjured one." I am haunted by the remark of one scholar that in the mind of the ancient Greeks, Zeus made us but does not care for us, that, unlike John Brown's God, Zeus is not our mainstay; and following His every commandment will not necessarily benefit us. (Indeed, He never does lay out the explicit commandments of which Jehovah is so fond; He only renders judgment after the fact, based on His own sacred, hidden calculus.) But, though He cannot be counted on to reward us, Zeus's greatest gift to mortals is "that 'violent grace' by virtue of which he punishes, late or soon, a man who has done injustice to another, either in his own person or in that of his descendants." In short, He is authority, upholder of social contracts. (Does John Brown believe in this mechanism? Probably, for it's in his favorite book.) In ancient Greek history and literature, just as in the Old Testament, we can scarcely turn without encountering the notion of transgression as a living monster, armed and fanged with the power of retribution over the sinner's descendants, who themselves never did anything wrong. Why? Perhaps because ancient societies tended to regard their basic atom as the family, not the individual. A jurist explains that "as the family group is immortal, and its liability to punishment indefinite, the primitive mind is not perplexed by the questions which become troublesome as soon as the individual is conceived as altogether separate from the group." "So there is no way to avoid what Zeus intended," writes Hesiod. "Often a whole city is paid punishment for one man."

"And We have made every man's actions to cling to his neck," says the Qur-'An, and the biblical book of Leviticus speaks in a similar vein. Sin is disease; above all, it is pollution. Julius Caesar ascribes to the Gallic Druids he conquers the belief that "unless for a man's life a man's life be paid, the majesty of the immortal gods may not be appeased," and when they run out of guilty people to burn alive inside their twig-woven mannikins, they turn to the innocent. Those Druids had fellow travelers throughout history. Phythius the Lydian, that antithesis of John Brown, asks that one of his five sons be excused from military service. To punish Phythius, not the unoffending victim, King Xerxes has the man's favorite son cut in half, "and the two halves hung upon the road for his armies to march between." The principle is not unlike that of Brown in the tannery with his shirt off, paying the penalty for his son's misdeeds.

Although the Diamond Sutra proclaims the opposite, Buddhist texts frequently preach the notion that evil in this life will be punished in one's own successive reincarnations into new bodies. We read that in India the traditional purpose ascribed to capital punishment is "not to inflict pain but to eradicate evil." How can we deny the cousinhood of this doctrine with "the sins of the father shall be revisited on the son"? My new body is still me, just as my son (at least in a culture which prizes bloodlines) is me, or partly me, or a stand-in for me. Therefore I am he; I can accept his punishment. In homage to this creed, John Brown would have placed himself on the block in place of a slave to whom he was no biological relation: his vast expansion of local norms of kinship was his most radical quality.

POSSIBLY VALID JUSTIFICATIONS FOR PUNISHMENT

1. To isolate (render harmless) an offender.
2. To improve him.
3. To make him accept, or at least to charge him with, responsibility for his crime. NOTE: This will free others from responsibility for his crime.
4. To restore a social balance.
5. To restore a spiritual balance.
6. To restore a balance of honor.
7. To assert a social norm or moral calculus.
8. To make him pay the price of readmission to the social contract.
9. To make him pay, period.
10. To compensate, gratify or soothe the victim.

Justifying some of these ends and effects would require adding to or modifying our axioms about the fundamental violent rights of the self (see 5.1.1–3, 5.1.8). Others are probably already justified in practice; their formulations here are based on the ethos (5.2.G.2) of a particular society.

To pay the penalty in this life, then—for oneself or for another—can be fitting, even honorable. In his *Phaedo,* which unlike his *Laws* is eerily sublime, Plato has the condemned Socrates refuse to choose exile over execution. The cup of hemlock is what he owes the state. He is a citizen. Here stands his obligation and his pride. Whatever the state demands of him, he will cheerfully render it up. All the same, like John Brown he has chosen to break those laws. And like John Brown, he thanks the jailer for kindnesses received, and drinks the cup of his own accord. He ennobles his own punishment by embracing it and participating it (Phythius the Lydian's son had no such opportunity, and I suppose he screamed pitiably when he was being cut in half). John Brown accepts with equanimity the fact that he owes the state of Virginia his life. He never possessed Socrates's choice of death or exile, but he will essay to infuse his execution with the same voluntarism—in part because he is a brave man, in part because he continues to be certain that he is right, in part to exercise the Christian meekness which so ill befits him—a mocking sort of meekness, perhaps; until the very end, John Brown continues to thumb his nose at secular authority, toward which he feels inextinguishable contempt.

Can Punishment Be Transferable?

The episode in the tannery leads us to consider the eerie supposition that an executioner can become as Christ, by taking on himself the death legally required of his victim.

Stop for a moment. By a paradox beloved of authoritarians, the executioner already *is* Christ. With his typical polemical determination, which strikes us as violent and unstoppable, like Lenin's, Martin Luther insists that our Savior could have been a hangman without compromising His mission one iota. The acts He never committed are hardly by that token prohibited. He never married, did He? But does that mean that marriage is wrong? He was a carpenter, not a soldier, but (unlike Tolstoy) He never told the soldiers to go home, did He? And what about all of us who aren't carpenters? Can't we be saved, too? For that matter, didn't carpenters make crosses for the crucifiers? Christ and His earthly father might thus be thought of as the executioner's occasional wholesaler. For that matter, didn't He scourge the moneylenders from the Temple with whips? Thus Luther, whose doctrine of judicial punishment at least can be most simply expressed as *What is necessary must be good.* (Its controversiality comes from humankind's continuing disagreement over what is necessary.)

Should the state in fact be sacred—a notion that Bakunin indignantly rejects—and if the state is, as Luther and Bakunin agree, founded on co-ercion, then the state's coercer must be worthy. Look upon him. He is the eighteenth-century executioner of Salzburg, and his name is Franz Wohlmuth. A portrait allows him a calm, resolute, slightly ruddy face in his forty-eighth year of life, mouth firm, pale eyes a little distant, as is of-ten the case with subjects who have to sit for paintings. The cover of his daybook, which is earth-brown or red-brown with two soft leather ties near the fore-edge, contains within an apple-shaped border a scene of burghers gazing up at the execution ground, upon which the condemned man kneels, gazing at the priest's upraised cross; while forming the third element of this trinity stands Wohlmuth himself with his upraised sword. The sword without the cross would be mere cruel murder by the standards of the time; for that cross reifies the common purpose, or at least the com-mon ideology—to the extent that the criminal gazes upon it in his final

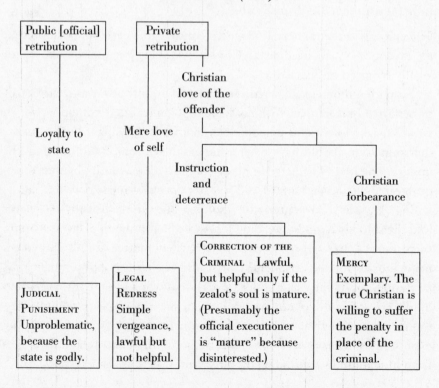

JUSTIFIED RESPONSES TO WRONG

Martin Luther (1519)

instants, he partakes of the social contract—but the cross without the sword would allow authority no recompense: the condemned presence is raw material upon which justice will be hewn.

Next comes the full title page, upon which we see citizens happily hastening through the greenery to watch the punishment, while in a calèche the condemned and the priest make up a sort of military procession. On the cover we've already seen their rendezvous with Wohlmuth. The verso side of the page shows its aftermath: the criminal's head hangs upon a pole, vaguely smiling, while hungry crows approach, and a rabbit bounds from a bush. The legend reads "Memento Mori." Remember that you must die. Should you fail to remember that, and thereby, privileging and desiring too greatly the things of this life, transgress the law, then I'll kill you.

Should the state *not* be sacred—and here, of course, John Brown stands with Bakunin—and should insurgency's cause be sanctified in its place, then he who rises up, coercing and killing for his own reasons, snatches away the executioner's cross of legitimacy, seizes his axe and goes into business. Give place again to the anarchist Berkman, whose story we'll shortly tell, and who, hating authority as he does, and rejecting Martin Luther King's maxim that "you can't murder murder," seeks to execute people's justice upon a capitalist exploiter while all the while retaining in his consciousness this conceptualization, fashioned from boyhood terrors, of the executioner in his Russian homeland:

> There stood the powerful figure of the giant palátch, all in black, his right arm bare to the shoulder, in his hand the uplifted ax. I could see the glimmer of the sharp steel as it began to descend, slowly, so torturingly slowly . . .

And Berkman has become the *palátch*. He's resolved to kill.

Thus precisely John Brown. The sin was that of the slave society, he argued, not his. He had explicitly said: "Those men who hold slaves have even forfeited their right to live." And his was the gallows, his the fate—like that of the Buddhist monks who burned themselves alive to protest religious repression in twentieth-century Vietnam. Of course, as one biographer so properly wrote—and others have stated in different words—"John Brown always found it very easy to believe anything he himself said. He was interested in putting his case before the world in the most favorable light possible, and he did not recognize the least scruple as to how he accomplished it." His intention had not originally been to go south and get hanged but to be a new Spartacus. "I want to free all of the negroes," he'd announced at the height of his temporal glory. "I have possession now of the U.S. armory, and if the citizens interfere, I must only burn the town and have blood." Once he was dispossessed of that armory, he retreated to the paradigm of the whipping in the tannery and quickly found it a crowd-pleaser.

But the fact that John Brown's motives were not unmixed need not bar us from considering the question of transferred accountability in its pure form. Recall that after being kidnapped by the Israelis, Adolf Eichmann had offered to publicly hang himself to atone for his crimes. What if during the Hitler regime almost three decades earlier he'd donned an armband of the yellow star and publicly hanged himself the first time that he had been ordered to deport a Jew? —Deterrence and retribution with a vengeance that would have been, almost, satyagraha! —What then if in 1960 Eichmann's interrogator, somehow, impossibly, able to forgive and accept, like John Brown in the tannery, had put on Eichmann's death's-head cap and hanged himself? What would the John Browns of this world say? (Never mind the prosecutors.) Should Eichmann have thereby become free to go back to Argentina? John Jr. was free to put his shirt back on even though he'd only been halfway whipped. Sinful Christians (so I am told) can yet hope for Heaven by virtue of Christ's sacrifice. —Well, how about it? Would the suicide of a stand-in have let Eichmann off the hook, or would six million people, Jewish or Gentile, have had to voluntarily, lovingly hang themselves first, in order to pay off all that dull demon's victims? What if one short of six million went to the gallows for Eichmann, and then the prosecutor demanded that the murderer be neck-elevated after all? Such absurdities illustrate, I believe, why it is that John Brown's notion of retribution should never be institutionalized: if I am free to take on myself your penalty, I may be equally free to reject my own.

Must My Hangman Think As I?

But the episode in the tannery is not without a certain savage moral beauty, and may inspire certain people in their personal relations, *provided that transgressor and punisher share the same moral absolutes*. Does he who actually received the stripes understand (whether or not he accepts) the equation between them and his criminal deed? That question is more fundamental, and far more important, than the issue of whether the administration of justice ought to be a private matter or a morality play.

Until we've answered it, we cannot rightly condemn even the tall King of Ugarit (now missing his neck and shoulders in the crumbled, ancient tablet), standing serene and farseeing above his supplicating enemy whose topknot he grasps in his left hand, while in his right the taper wedge of a sword begins to go into the enemy's eye. Had the enemy transgressed by his own lights, or only by the King's? To John Brown, of course, and to any politician or revolutionary who is determined to get something done, that just doesn't matter: the Law is absolute. The rock must be punished for a homicide of which it can never even be conscious. The proslave men in Pottawatomie can't get out of Brown's clutches by invoking any counterright to believe that blacks are beasts of the field: wrong is wrong; they must die.

Of course any executioner would prefer that the condemned agree with him about the rules (whether or not rule-breaking is admitted). In ancient societies, which were more isolated and homogenous than mine, harmony of belief was likely. It is in the context of such an agreed-upon Law—a Dharma, a Sangha—that the Buddha, who focuses as much upon the done-to as upon the doer, advises: "Where there is much suffering there is also great bliss"—regaling us with the tale of a courtesan who, having arranged a murder, was executed in a particularly slow and ghastly way: "Having taken refuge in the Buddha, the Dharma, and the Sangha, she died in pious submission to the punishment of her crime." This sounds rather more edifying than convincing, but it's what the executioner loves to hear, and in certain cases may comfort the condemned: better that I die for good reason, if die I must. Among the few, half-ruined questions to the ancient Greek oracles that survive we find this one: "The Dodonaeans ask Zeus and Dione whether it is on account of the impurity of some human being that god sends the storm." —Through such inquiries we approach astrology and ritual propitiation, for if one accepts as I do the notion that storms are not caused by crimes, then whoever will be condemned for this bit of dark weather (should the oracle of Zeus return an affirmative answer) will be condemned unjustly, as was the case with the supposed custom of the Spartans of arraigning their kings as a result of the appearances of shooting stars and other divine omens. But if the condemned believes and affirms, "Yes, I was impure; I am responsible for the storm," does the retribution thereby become fair? And if he doesn't, must we call it unfair?

Even Gandhi accepted the ugly necessity of imposing moral-political actions upon the unwilling, arguing that in Jesus's career "he did not count the cost of suffering entailed upon his neighbours whether it was undergone by them voluntarily or otherwise." Suppose, therefore, that the transgressor and the punisher do *not* agree. Told that he would be hanged and not honorably shot, Hermann Göring wrote in one of his three suicide notes: "I have no moral obligation to submit to the justice of my enemies. I have therefore chosen the manner of death of the great Hannibal." And this brutally evil man was, for once, morally correct. He deserved to die, and was doomed to, but why not at his own hand? *Retaliation which is not accepted as legitimate must be perceived as repression.* Perhaps this is the source of Cortes's assumed sadness when, having sentenced two rebels to be hanged, and the third to have his feet cut off (the prisoners might have disagreed), "he exclaimed with a deep and sorrowful sigh, 'It would be better not to know how to write. Then one would not have to sign death sentences.' "

The Hanging of John Brown (continued)

John Brown, of course, has not been asked whether he follows the State of Virginia's moral calculus. Strange! He always chooses the punishment he fails to deserve. When his son whipped him, he voluntarily took on the latter's sins; when he was condemned to be hanged, he accepted the penalty most "cheerfully," as his letters keep saying, as recompense for a bloody deed he'd committed with equal élan. On the Sunday before his execution he writes his family: "Nothing could be more grateful to my feelings than to learn that you do not feel dreadfully mortified and even disgraced on account of your relation to one who is to die on the scaffold." A century later, the British Royal Commission will conclude that there is "some evidence, though no convincing statistical evidence," that capital punishment deters; but because deterrence presupposes calculation, crimes of passion cannot be much deterred, whereas it exerts a most powerful effect upon "professional criminals."

Well, which is John Brown? His raid was nothing if not calculated, and the fact that he'd raided at least twice before makes him a professional of sorts. Of course he bungled; he calculated poorly. But the deterrent effect of capital punishment upon him seems to have been slight. And certainly the public deterrent value of his execution, at least vis-à-vis his intimates, will be nil. Quite the contrary. A page later, the handwriting shrinks a trifle and begins to hurry as Brown goes further, insisting that the rope will not only be no disgrace, it will be his glory:

I feel so astonished that one so exceedingly vile, & unworthy as I am would ever be suffered to have a place any how or any where amongst the very least of All who when they come to die (as all must:) were permitted to pay the "debt of nature" in defence of the right: & of Gods eternal, immutable truth. Oh my dear friends can you believe it possible that the scaffold has no terrors for your own poor, old, unworthy brother?

Replying to his cousin the Reverend Luther Humphrey, who's just now addressed him an epistle of pitying horror, he explicitly states that there is no necessary relationship between punishment and crime: "The fact that a man dies under the hand of an executioner (or otherwise) has but little to do with his true character, as I suppose." He insists that "no part of my life has been more hapily [sic] spent; than that I have spent here [in prison]; and I humbly trust that no part has been spent to better purpose."

When it comes to divine will, as opposed to state authority, Brown is all obedience. In 1846 we find him writing his wife that they have been chastised by God once again. "The sudden, & dreadful manner in which he has seen fit to call our dear little Kitty to take her leave of us, is I Kneede not tell you how much on mind; but before Him; I will bow my head in submission and hold my peace." Why? As usual in such cases, because of perceived commonality: "Whatever judgment God may hereafter pass on us as individuals; will also be reasonable, & will be fully sustained by our own sense of right and wrong."

So there is for John Brown a ranking of obedience due to whippers of all species, thus.

JOHN BROWN'S HIERARCHY OF PUNITIVE AUTHORITY (1844–59)

1. The chastisements of God
   AUTHORITY: Incontestable.
2. The chastisements of family
   AUTHORITY: Fairly incontestable, it would seem from the tannery.
3. The chastisements of government
   AUTHORITY: Nil, when they violate divine law as interpreted by John Brown.

Sources: Brown's letters.

The Christian lamb thus retains his discretion to become a wolf. He dies triumphantly principled; but he dies because he was convicted, and he was convicted only *because he was caught*.

Sade's Dungeons

What is the function of defiance? Why, to make martyrs! Thoreau refuses to pay his poll tax and proudly goes to jail (if only for a night). The young militants in Vietnam's new Self-Determination Movement get arrested by French or American puppet gendarmes and are greeted by applause from their colleagues in the cells. John Brown becomes eager to be punished precisely because he feels he's noble—which translates (or pretends to translate) as "he doesn't deserve it."

But the more common logic is to assert that since I don't deserve it, I ought not to be punished. Such souls aren't pulled up serenely into Heaven at the rope's end, like old John Brown; rather, they're dragged screeching (or cursingly drag themselves) into the sacrificial victim's sainthood-by-necessity.

Rigged Judgments

Sade being one of the dragged, it behooves us to remind ourselves that so deeply does it lie in society's interest to affirm the equations of justice that the opposing advocates in a court of law frequently reconstruct the circumstances of a crime in terms not of what is known, but what is "supposed" to be known—what *ought* to be true. In 80 B.C., the eloquently mercurial Cicero, defending Sextus Roscius of Ameria against the charge of parricide, whose statutory penalty is particularly hideous, gives the evidence itself scarcely a disdainful mention. Instead, he exhibits the defendant's character to the public—or, I should say, paints an expedient portrait. Wouldn't a person capable of such a terrible impiety have shown himself up in other ways? Wouldn't he be either a debauched and confused youth, or else a hardened old criminal (this latter category corresponding exactly to that of the "reprobates" in the British government's *Report of the Commissioners of Prisons*)? By easily excluding Sextus from these two groupings, which Cicero pretends are as accurate as they are facile, he claims to have proved his client's innocence. He "led a life that was quite the opposite of vicious," he concludes, and the imputation is that men don't live lies or act out of turn, that an otherwise exemplary life demonstrates innocence because it is consistent with it. Once again, Symmetry has been so well sanctified that it deserves a capital letter. Sextus Roscius is acquitted.

The modern reader remains unconvinced. Boy Scout leaders and Chamber of Commerce big shots who turn out to have been child molesters all along, nobleness-spewing politicians of evil, and all the rest shatter by their very existence Cicero's harmonious chain of logic. And the case of Sade twists the matter into deeper strangeness, because the defendant claims that *conviction alone* (fair or not) brands him as guilty in a Ciceronian sense, that imputed wrongdoing permits the advocates of consistency-as-proof to believe him guilty of everything. And it gets stranger still: through a perhaps unequaled act of macabre genius, Sade pens his very infamy into something exemplary, something that can teach us something, something "quite the opposite of vicious"—an act which gives the deathblow not only to consistency but to any number of notions of moral value. No John Brown submissiveness for him! He eloquently rages; he bottles his soul's bile and paints masterpieces with it, just as Turner, so they say, painted sunsets using the piss and menstrual blood of whores . . .

"He Must Have Been Guilty Since He Has Been Punished"

Despairing in his prison cell in Vincennes, Sade writes his wife, in an exact inversion of John Brown's equation: "People will merely say, '*He must have been guilty since he has been punished.*' " Shades of Ruby Ridge and the old witchcraft trials! (Well, *was* he guilty? Never mind—he's not interested in that.) If guilt demands punishment, and if only the guilty are punished, then this sheep logic follows—oh, they should all be beaten to death! If not only the guilty are punished, if the law has mistaken itself, then he stands a martyr like John Brown, and indeed his modern literary admirers claim so.

He is (as he believes) a distant descendant of Petrarch's Laure, who also bore the name de Sade; Laure was also the name of the girl he loved; but in 1763 at his father's demand he married the rich Renée-Pelágie de Montreuil instead. (His only daughter is named Madeleine-Laure.) Thus a single drop of his blood is worth more than every vein's worth from plebeian carrion! Aristocrat above all, he swears that defense of class alone ought to justify his release into perpetual immunity! Aesthetician, sad masturbator, he writes his wife (doubtless hoping to extort her pity's bounty) that Petrarch remains his only comfort. What other solace *could* he have? —Certainly not Luther's doctrine, so comforting to the condemned, and so expedient to the executioner, that the jaws of the Law can devour only our bodies, which are hardly significant, while our souls remain free and untouched. "For no human being can kill a soul or make it alive, conduct it to heaven or hell." —Sade might or might not have read Luther, but he's an atheist—and not only that, but perhaps the ultimate materialist, for whom reality lies almost exclusively in the corporeal realm, in the glance and glitter of light upon a droplet of blood, in the slow scarlet darkening of a fresh cut, in the jewel-like sparkling of a drop of whore spittle.

When we look in upon him, he is dreaming of ancestral Laure. (Compare him, if you will, to Caesar, who at victory erects a temple to ancestral Venus.) He dreams that she emerges still beautiful from her tomb, invites him to embrace her in death, vanishes into air. He scribbles endless philosopho-pornographic manuscripts, the content of which we shall consider in another chapter. Dead Laure never returns. After the first half-decade has gone by, he becomes hardened in his defiance, writing: "You refuse to understand that since vices exist, it is as unjust for you to punish them as it would be to jeer at a one-eyed man." In other words, the rights of the self supersede all other rights. The practical result of this doctrine is the same as that of John Brown's: he holds himself under no obligation to follow the law. John Brown justifies himself with his favorite strands from the self-contradictory Bible; Sade is more frankly the wounded animal. Soon enough his snarls increase in pitch: "I have always been inclined to favour vice[s], and I regard those who have the capacity to persist in them as great men." At the same moment, he begs his now implacable mother-in-law for pity; he implores her to see that he has repented, will cleave to his wife, will never go astray again. (His letters to Madame de Sade vary between querulous or paranoid reproaches and heartbreaking tenderness. Faithful to him throughout this first long stretch of imprisonment, she'll divorce him immediately upon his release.) He returns to the attack. "Ask Madame la Présidente de Montreuil whether there is in the whole world a better method than that of bolts and bars to lead to virtue?" he scribbles in desperate anger. That is the crux of it, of course: the meaninglessness and uselessness we can always find in penal suffering. I think again of that musty old *Report of the Commissioners of Prisons and the Directors of Convict Prisons with Appendices, for the Year ended 31st March 1902,* with its table of floggings. I think of the Kriminalenmuseum in Vienna. Three and a half centuries after Sade, another convict will write: "I cannot fathom the reason of a prison system keeping a man isolated with nothing but vengeful and vindictive fantasies to sustain him for years and then one day releasing him upon an unsuspecting community." —Very good, replies Sade's prison system, then we *won't* release him! Not ever . . .

His wife assures him, no doubt believing it, that he won't be imprisoned a moment longer than necessary. "It is charming," he replies, "and truly, those who guide your behaviour have every reason to congratulate themselves on the progress you are making in their profound art of poisoning the wounds of hapless victims." He hates her as he now does almost everyone. *He will not accept his punishment.* Finally he cries, just as Joan of Arc had done: "I would not change even in the presence of the scaffold."

Follies of a Libertine

Well, even though the *justice* of his immurement may be murky, the *cause* of it remains clear enough: sexual gluttony, accompanied by sharp-toothed mastication. (Dante would have punished him by having him eat mud in Hell, but, as we have seen, Sade does not believe in that place—or, we might say, he is already there.) He enjoys causing pain. He's repeatedly compromised the family honor by flagellating, pricking or half-poisoning prostitutes—or, I should say, he's wounded honor not by doing these things but by being arrested for them: getting caught transformed John Brown, as we saw, into a pseudo-Gandhi, and it made Sade into a resplendidly true and naked Satan.

His social and financial position picks another hole in Clarence Darrow's half-true assertion that the prevalence of crime is directly proportional to the price of bread, that "men would not explore their neighbor's houses at dead of night, if their own were filled; and women would not sell their bodies if society left them any other fairly decent and pleasant way to live." Granted, he's buying bodies, not selling; but why? In his case, what would be another "decent" way to live? Nowadays a person with his tendencies can very easily find discreet and willing partners; but the "divine Marquis," class snob that he was, never was attracted by consensuality; and his impulses did impel him beyond the rights of others into outright aggression. He *was* a criminal; he deserved to be, at the very least, restrained. The ethos of his time left small place for the notion that violence's

evil could be extenuated by sickness; and the asylum in which he eventually perished greatly resembled his various dungeons.

In retrospect, it started mildly enough, when, going wild with his in-
laws' money, he merely brought too many girls to his *petite maison* in
Paris; and police got involved; other aristocratic husbands committed the
same peculations, and Renée-Pelágie didn't seem to mind; her mother
laughed it off, and broke him out of prison, certain that he'd learned his
lesson. He continued to keep actresses and courtesans. Forgiving, sullen or
maliciously complacent, we don't know, Madame de Montreuil remained
willing to subsidize mistresses if he would only be discreet. He wasn't.

Rose Keller

We find foreshadowed in Rose Keller's legal deposition (April 22, 1768) the
lineaments of Sade's impending novels: luxury asserting itself over
poverty, cruel class "quality" (remember, he is Counte Donatien-Alphonse-
François de Sade, *Count* de Sade, that is—Captain of Cavalry in the Régi-
ment de Bourgogne) devouring helplessness in a monstrously "aesthetic"
fashion. Madame Keller, a widow "of thirty-six years or thereabouts,"
emerges from Easter Mass, and in the Place des Victoires, where prostitutes often rent themselves, meets a dandy in a grey redingote, who wears
a hunting knife at his side and holds a cane. He offers her an ecu should
she go with him, "and she replying that she wasn't what he thought her"—
an assertion made to her interrogators, and hence quite possibly false;
most commentators believe she *was* what he thought her—"he told her
that it was for her to be his chambermaid, and that she had but to follow
him, which she did." Then, inevitably, we look in upon the "interview" in
the room of yellow damask, the coach ride to his secluded country house
in Arcueil (fatal words: the poor creature had said that "it was all the same
to her where she made her living"), then, as in a dream, the little green
door, the garden, the "petit cabinet" into which he ushers her and whose
door he closes. Now for the second act. He demands that she undress.
"She asking why, he replied that it was for pleasure, and when she represented that it wasn't for that that he had brought her hither, he said that if
she didn't strip he would kill her and bury her himself." She strips. Now
for the bed, on which he throws her belly-down, tying her to it by the arms
and legs, with another cord cinched about her middle. The third act begins. Delighting in her cries of pain and terror, he makes "different inci-
sions" with a tiny knife, then pours hot wax, red and white (for his

scenarios require *elaborateness*) into the wounds. He also beats her with a knotted whip and a rod. She begs him not to murder her, for the pathetic reason that she hasn't yet made her Easter confession, whereupon, in a reply which wouldn't have been out of place in his *Juliette* or *Sodom,* he jeeringly offers to be her confessor himself. Finally he unties her, giving her bread and a restorative cordial. Does he plan to repeat the performance? She cleans her wounds; the cloth is saturated with blood.

She escapes. Sade's mother-in-law has to pay to keep her quiet.

In his own deposition, her assailant (whom I believe even less than I believe her) denies that he forced her into anything. Rose Keller agreed to go with him for a "partie de libertinage," he says. (That much I do believe.) He never tied her, he said. As for the hot wax, well, that was simply a helpful "pomade" to heal her wounds—for everyone recognizes the kindness of sadists to the unfortunate.

How It All Turned Out

Imprisoned for a few months at Pierre-Encise, he got a *lettre d'abolition* which conveniently "exempted him from crimes punishable by death." Then he ran away with his wife's younger sister.

A Pervert's Conscience

He disproves the naive axiom that "no man can draw a free breath who does not share with other men a common and disinterested ideal." He buys the bodies of others, although he has a wife; he bullies, tortures, threatens, rapes. Through it all, he breathes quite freely, thank you! Undeterred by the prospect of any legal penalties, certain that his mother-in-law will always buy him out—or else utterly self-destructive—he struts and spends, the only full human being in a world of pleasure puppets and two-legged trash!

France in Sade's time was, in one jurist's words, "smitten with the curse of an anomalous and dissonant jurisprudence beyond every other country in Europe . . . the stratum of feudal rules which overlay the Roman law was of the most miscellaneous composition." How could one in such times not hold the supposed universality of law in contempt? We're far, far from Cicero and the Twelve Tables! Up until the Revolution, in certain arrondissements of Paris, police power could be exercised only with the cooperation of the seigneurs concerned. So why can't Sade be arbitrary, too? In 1772, he feeds Spanish fly to half a dozen girls whom he keeps busy whipping and being whipped. They don't know what they're munching; they help themselves to his pillbox, thinking that these pastilles are only candies. Oh, what a joker he is! As his Japanese kinsman in aesthetics, Mishima, will imagine the scene two centuries later, "he, [the prostitute] Mariette, and the manservant joined in a fellowship of pain like galley slaves rowing their banks of oars in a trireme across the sea. The sunrise glowed like blood." For Mishima, sunrises always did, and that was precisely why he adored them. But the whores fall dangerously ill and file charges. Sade finds himself condemned in absentia to death, his property seized. His mother-in-law, losing patience at last, gets him imprisoned for a time in Chambéry . . .

In 1775 we find him choreographing an orgy at Château de la Coste, "possibly, it appears," says one commentator, "with the co-operation of his wife," whom he sodomizes, as he does his manservant. It's all going well, with his mother-in-law's money lubricating every orifice. But the girls grow discontented with their isolation; meanwhile, neighbors hiss that he's conducted murderous scientific experiments on women whom he's buried in his garden. One prostitute, Du Plan, did in fact carry human bones in her baggage to "decorate a little room" for him, so he later tells the tale to his wife. Would their hue have set off his yellow damask to aesthetic advantage? Was his plan to terrify children with them? The joke having worn off, Du Plan inters them in the garden; hence that discreditable neighbor-gossip. What will come of it all? Nothing; he's the Count; his pleasures will *never* have repercussions! He dreams of the "glorious" days of the ancestral Sades, "when France counted in its borders a host of sovereigns rather than thirty million vile slaves crawling before a single man." He couldn't care less about the other vile slaves, who very soon will make the French Revolution; he simply doesn't want to be one of them. But the bones? He explains again to the personified forces of justice. It doesn't help that in his wallet he's carrying a recipe for criminal abortion, which I'm sure he's made use of, another for poisoning swords, and a criminal confession—someone else's, he claims, but it's in his own handwriting! (Could it be the germ of one of his novels?) . . . Did he ever poison any swords? I doubt it. He had neither the goals nor the energies of John Brown. He must have kept that recipe only for its macabre novelty.

In prison his procuress-wife will write him, in the approved style of Justine or the other submissive heroines of his blood- and semen-drenched tales: "I shall never be able to stop adoring you, even if you heap insults upon my head." Well, that's between them. But the business with his sister-in-law Madame la Présidente can't forget. He's known to have spread venereal disease—and how will it all affect the poor girl's marriage settlement—and her sister?

His twaddling justifications: "I am a libertine, but I have saved a deserter from death . . . I am a libertine, but I have never compromised my wife's health."

Not impressed, his mother-in-law gets a lettre de cachet to put him away for life.

A Historical Note

Call him lucky. As far as we know, he'll never face physical torture. We saw the sorts of punishments that the Germans inflicted. One gloomy author of a history of corporal punishment concluded that "every form of cruelty which the law allows is practiced in a wholesale manner and with gusto by the public." During the French Revolution, our Marquis will need to pretend to be an energetic atom of the masses he despises, in order to avoid such a public and summary fate. But he avoids it. He's lucky, isn't he?

Georges Bataille will write: "Sade endured this life, and endured it only by imagining the intolerable. In his agitation there was the equivalent of an explosion which tore him apart but suffocated him nonetheless."

As an anonymous polemic against lettres de cachet insists, "it's for the social body to define if one of its members is to be declared an enemy of all his associates for his crimes"—the social body, not the King, not the *lieutenant-de-police,* not his mother-in-law. Either way, punishment is punishment. From a rebel's point of view, it remains unjustified. Bataille again: "The only way to respond to the possibility of overcoming horror is in a rush of the blood."

The Moral Effects of Endungeonment

He will be locked into eleven different prisons over a period of twenty-seven years. (I am fortunate enough not to be able to imagine what one year in prison would do to me.)

His earlier spells in prison suggest that such punishment, like the executions of Rudzutak and John Brown, will scarcely deter him or by society's standards improve him. Plato prescribes: "We should neither inflame the culprit by brutal punishments nor spoil a servant by leaving him uncorrected, so we must adopt the same course with the freeborn." —Sade agrees—with the first half of this, at least: "Any punishment that does not correct, that can merely rouse rebellion in whoever has to endure it, is a piece of gratuitous infamy . . ." —Well, what would correct him, then? —Nothing. —Sade's behaviorist definition of virtue—"our responsibility is limited to not spreading the poison and seeing that those who are around us not only do not suffer but are unaware of our weakness"—stands, like his relativistic one—"for a very vicious soul a lesser vice can be considered a virtue"—frank testimony to ethical impotence.

What's the point of confining him, then? His mother-in-law can't care less about giving satisfaction to the prostitutes in Marseilles he'd almost killed; as for those ladies, they've received justice according to the classical standard of torts: they've been paid off. Moreover, not being the omnipotent fiend he paints her, the mother-in-law possesses neither power nor desire to liquidate him, but she'll accomplish the next best thing: his removal from circulation. Meanwhile, insulted kinsfolk speak the forthright language of expediency, which will be so dear to Napoleon and Stalin. Although some of them pity Renée-Pelágie, who pleads and battles for her terrible husband's release, they're staunch for defense of family, of bloodline, of the now joined clan of Sades and Montreuils: —"Misplaced pity must not disturb our plans, which are dictated by prudence and necessity. My nephew's freedom cannot and should not reward anything other than his good conduct." I dislike the first sentence but approve the second.

Sade will never acknowledge this calculus in others—because he follows it himself. His immense self-centeredness scarcely comprehends the effect or rationale of any measure, except upon himself—a trait which will now serve his art. *Justine, Juliette, The One Hundred and Twenty Days of Sodom:* In these books we watch a procession or succession of dominant characters; but although they scheme together, or undermine each other, at any given locus within the oeuvre there reigns but one will, one intelligence enacting shrilly, snarlingly monotonous cravings. Each one is, in turn, Sade himself, and rarely do they meet with any answering humanity in the Other.

Even more than Stalin, Sade remains the quintessential inhuman—or, if you prefer, the unfettered (*in* fetters) state-of-nature human. Herewith, a typical passage from the steadily more schematic *Sodom,* the only narrative progression being composed of procedural escalation: "First a finger-twister, he currently breaks all her limbs, tears out her tongue, gouges out her eyes, and leaves her thus to live, diminishing her sustenance day by day." Sade denies the Golden Rule. He pleads for himself, cursing friends and enemies alike, that they don't serve him more expertly; but he never pleads for another. Projecting himself into another's life, he arrives within voyeuristic striking distance of the body, the intellect, above all the consciousness; but he never apprehends the soul. Nor does he want to. —"Adieu, my angel, think of me sometimes when you are between two sheets, your thighs open and your right hand busy . . . feeling for your fleas." He is very funny and brilliant and elegant sometimes; he writes sentences as delicious as a spoonful of vanilla icing; but he is one of the most selfish people on earth.

"The Divine Marquis"

He stands for *totality*.

Ernst Becker once wrote that "the ideal of the innovator must remain pure . . . we cannot compromise on an ideal of maximum individuality." For Becker, the alternative was Stalinist dullness. For Sade, the alternative was respect for law and for other human beings. Thus ever the artistic dilemma, and, like Nero, who died murmuring, "What a great artist the world has lost in me!" Sade was ever the aesthete, not merely with his books but with his red and white candle wax, his bones in the garden, his room of yellow damask. *He aestheticizes his rage*—not merely on the Rose Keller he tortures but in his continual petitions for release, which scamper mercurially back and forth between rage, pathos and sarcastic humor: *"To the stupid villains who torment me,"* he pens from his cell in Vincennes (1783): "Vile minions of the tunny-fish vendors of Aix, low and infamous servants of torturers, invent then for my torment tortures from which at least some good may result." What tortures might those be? He proposes one for his mother-in-law: "This morning as I suffered I saw her, the strumpet, I saw her flayed alive, dragged over thistles and then thrown into a barrel of vinegar. And I said to her: Execrable creature, that is for selling your son-in-law to the torturers! Take that, you procuress, for hiring out your two daughters!"—that is, the wife he married for gain, and the sister-in-law he himself seduced. What need has he to be fair? "Take that for making him hate the children for whose sake you supposedly sacrificed him!" Is it her fault he hates his children? No, but it's her fault he's incarcerated. His sentence proves as arbitrary as his own acts and desires—a *contrapasso* of sorts. Is it justified? No. Why not release him and cut him off from the family? —Not that he'll ever be a good citizen now! He rails, vituperates, gloats, fantasizes, chuckles, masturbates, dreams: His mother-in-law is screaming in vinegar! Juliette brutalizes her "good" sister and sends her naked into the rain, laughing to see her struck by lightning! In this book of mine, already so long, we can scarcely pause to do justice to Sade the artist. Suffice it to say that he dares, he searches, he casts the lamplight of his intellect into the dark unknown tunnels of self-obsession (no matter that those passageways usually represent merely his own anus).

PUNISHMENT AS ILLICIT JOY, CATHARSIS AND *CONTRAPASSO*
The aesthetic calculus of Sade (1783)

And I increased her tortures and insulted her in her pain and forgot mine.

My pen falls from my hand. I must suffer. Adieu, torturers, I must curse you.

Many pages ago, *Rising Up and Rising Down* asserted that the self may do violence under the following condition, which remains controversial in all times and places.

IN IMMINENT DEFENSE OF FREEDOM OF SPEECH
[SEE MORAL CALCULUS 5.2.E.2.]

The self retains the inalienable right to express itself as it chooses, on any topic that it chooses, the right to empathize with friend or foe (shall we call that treason?), to assent and to deny, to offend, to express its conscience and to express no conscience, to be offensive, vulgar, vicious and even evil in the object and manner of its expression, at any and all times.

As an artist myself, I offend people, and not always by choice; I resent authority; I *need* to express myself, and this need becomes almost a sickness which most of us who are not artists find it difficult to understand. Where do my rights end? If my nature is predatory, should I be allowed to express that? We must each of us decide how far we're willing to let authority's ocean wave rush up our shore, and where, if anywhere, we choose to build our pathetic doomed dykes of wet sand, to keep authority from overrunning us while we can. My grandfather, who as my mother always says "had a very hard life," used to say, "Bill, those sonofabitches who talk back to authority *have no rights!*" His solution for better engaging me with society: If I'd been his child, he would have punished me more often (his punishments were on the same continuum as John Brown's). And here for my part I stand, condoning Gauguin's abandonment of his family and his so-called marriages to thirteen-year-olds, in part because I believe in "different standards, different times," and in part because I love the art which resulted. As for Sade the artist, I don't know whether or not to call him a "genius," but I believe with all my heart that art and experience are both richer for his books, precisely because they terrify and disgust me, methodically, gleefully, with the same consistency and proportion which one feels when standing in the cathedral of Chartres.

What this section has been trying to say is that punishment must somehow be meaningful to be right. I pity Sade to the extent that he was ill, incapable of controlling his actions. I pity him as a human being who suffered. I admire him for creating art from his punishment and at least nourishing himself on that sort of meaning. I uphold his right to express whatever gorgeous filth and filthy gorgeousness he wants. And I would defend his right to use lethal force against whoever tried to destroy his manuscripts. But what he did to Rose Keller went too far beyond self-expression. Within the limits of his corrupt and stagnant era, his confinement expressed this basic meaning: The social contract prohibits us from raping people or hurting them without their consent. His punishment was just.

If Not Endungeonment, Then What?

Back to the issue of giving satisfaction to those prostitute-victims. More than one commentator has argued that by discarding the ancient legal practice of direct restitution, enforced either by the victim's kin (as in ancient Iceland) or by the community at large, "the modern criminal legal process" has been rendered "an inherently destructive one, because its aim is not to restore the injured party but to punish the guilty one." For the fine of goods, liberty or life now gets paid not to the injured individual but to the sovereign power. Imagine John Brown as being sentenced not to hanging but to working for the rest of his life at prison wages, some going toward his maintenance, some toward his family's support and the rest toward restitution for the victims of his raids. Would he be a martyr then? Sade's is altogether a different case. Thanks to the immense wealth he'd married, he could easily have made restitution to all the prostitutes he'd harmed—and, as we saw, this is exactly what his mother-in-law did. The result: He thinks his violence can be bought and paid for; intimidate and occasionally injure members of the vile underclass, and then compensate them at above the market price. This does not feel like justice. And yet the ease with which he can discharge such debts might be tolerable. Consider the notion, so well propounded by the utilitarian Jeremy Bentham, that if justice is equity, then restitution to the victim must be the proper way to repair the social fabric—at least in cases of theft and suchlike offenses where the logic of the specific assessment would be incontestable. As we have seen, other proponents of restitution propose its extension in cases of violent assault (Sade's specialty) to reimbursing medical bills, lost work, et cetera.

There's the matter of his wife's sister. How could he possibly pay compensation for that? His income derives from the family he's insulted. But suppose that he did compensate her, if she wanted to be compensated—or, more likely, suppose that her mother wanted compensation. How could he compensate her to whom money meant so little? *By being punished.*

That is another reason why I believe that (in the beginning, at least) Sade's imprisonment was justified. It remanded him to the principle that ignoring the Golden Rule—nay, trampling on it—subjected him to the operation of the debased, political Golden Rule: as he had done, so was he done by. He might never have understood this as a lesson; but, with or without that understanding, it rightly constrained his future acts.

Herbert Spencer, the Adam Smith of penology, as it were, proposed in the nineteenth century to let the invisible hand of hunger do its work in turning the convict into a productive citizen: deprive him of his liberty for society's sake, not for punishment; and pay him, if he works—and require him to pay for his food and keep. In the overcrowded prisons of my own time and place, where inmates rape and brutalize each other, the practical effect of the system, as of most systems, would be to starve the weak at the expense of the strong. But Sade got his own cell. What if they'd forced him to become an artisan and work at artisan's wages to compensate Madame de Montreuil? Could this possibly have "reformed" Sade? It seems very unlikely. Indeed, if the purpose of punishment were only reform, then most instances of punishment throughout human history would not be justified. We remain what we are.

"There Is No Safe Place"

Unimpressed by any Inquisitorial sophistries about his culpability, Sade escapes.

He flees to Italy. He writes his agent words whose sentiment, if not their overt self-centeredness, mirrors John Brown's: "When the court denies me my rights, I shall make my own rights . . ."

Contrast him with Gandhi, who wrote:

> If my life were regulated by violence in the last resort, I would refuse to give an inch lest an ell might be asked for. I would be a fool if I did otherwise. But if my life is regulated by non-violence, I should be prepared to and actually give an ell when an inch is asked for.

Miserable, broke, police-anxious and above all at loose ends, he returns to France. Why didn't he sneak off to America or something? Then he might have died free. Did he need wealth that badly? An ambiguous listlessness prevents him from concealing his whereabouts from his mother-in-law, Madame la Présidente, who promptly sends gendarmes to seize him again. His return to prison under such circumstances leads me to wonder whether Sade is merely lazy, impractical, indiscreet, or whether he actually connives at his punishment, which would almost begin to justify it . . . Or has he begun to realize the awful truth that he might be "happier" in a dungeon?

As we've noted, his barred life there won't begin to compare with that of an inmate in a late-twentieth-century American prison, where, as one rapist-murderer writes, "there is no safe place"; this rapist must fight off other rapists (*contrapasso,* anyone?); at mealtime he sees one convict beat another's brains out. Sade, on the other hand, will have books, sweetmeats, even custom-made leather merkins in which to sheathe his aging penis. His situation strikes me as not unlike one of the strange prison paradoxes so common to Ho Chi Minh's poems: outside of jail one can be arrested for gambling but inside one gambles as one pleases; inside of prison it is safe during air raids, but prisoners brought outside during those times, even if at greater risk, are happy to be free. Certainly Sade is safer in prison: he can't get into any worse trouble than he is already in; he doesn't have to face the family he antagonized and abused; in place of sordid deeds, he's free to imagine triumphal monstrosities, ritual slaughters, delectable sex murders, tortures of the powerless; and because they occur only in his head, or, at worst, on paper, there are no consequences; he can dream up the next scenario, masturbate again, eat yet another pastry . . . "He was capable of wolfing down frightening quantities," writes Maurice Lever, "and in the solitude of his cell he sometimes indulged in veritable orgies of meringues, biscuits, macaroons, preserves, marmalades, jellies, syrups, marshmallows, fresh and preserved fruits, and candied chestnuts." If other human beings are not real, then why can't he get along just fine with his own characters: cruel Juliette, the ogre Minski and ever so many young peasant boys and girls to eat for dinner? He does perhaps miss the taste of real flesh, the smell of a real whore's farts; but what he loses in realism he can make up for in giganticism, penning exhaustive orgies which must be staged as carefully as an ambassador's dinner parties. He munches on, excreting what one commentator calls "a raw passion, whetted by the imagination, without any frills—that is . . . what we find so unbearable." No justifications, says this commentator: defense of class and race, all the excuses valid and invalid of *Rising Up and Rising Down*, are irrelevant; flesh and chestnuts are the same; he munches on. Since the paradoxically indulgent Montreuils own the resources to pay for any number of desserts, over the years he grows stout.

A Punishment Suitable to His Class

The fact that he has access to those macaroons and jellied chestnuts, when poorer prisoners are lucky to get stale bread, hardly seems fair. Punishment is arbitrary enough as it is. Shouldn't it at least be uniform?

But practically speaking, it never has been and never will be. One study in Saint Louis, Missouri, conducted in 1962 found that three-quarters of all defendants charged with felonies could not even afford the bail bondsman's 10 percent of the bail.

Caveat

We might also remind ourselves that the lack of fairness implicit in Sade's being able to gobble macaroons in no way entitles anybody to belittle his punishment's endless, almost hopeless pain.

In Vincennes prison he replies by letter to his wife, who wants to know how he is. "I am in a tower, locked behind nineteen iron doors, receiving daylight by two small windows, each provided with a score of iron bars. For about ten or twelve minutes of the day I have the company of a man who brings me my food. I spend the rest of my time alone and in tears." He writes his mother-in-law, his "tyrant" as he calls her: "I would like to share your belief for a moment that a *lettre de cachet* is indispensable to avoid a lawsuit which is always disagreeable, but need it have been so severe, so cruel?" —"My mother calls out to me from the depths of her tomb: I seem to see her open her bosom once more to clasp me to it—the only refuge I have left." "Oh! my dearest one," he writes his wife, "when will there be an end to my horrible plight? When, in the name of Heaven, are they going to release me from the tomb in which they have buried me alive?" "Get me out of here, dear wife, get me out, I beg you."

A Holiday

In this seventeen-year stretch he writes (so he claims) fifteen volumes, many of which will get destroyed in the sacking of the Bastille. Come the Revolution, he benefits for once from the populism toward which he expresses such furious contempt: they actually liberate him! Herewith, his second chance of escape. What will he do now? I imagine him blinking like one of those prisoners led out of Plato's cave—but dazzled by the glare not of reason but of impending debauchery. What will he do? He's older, remember, and the times aren't so ripe now for libertinage. His beloved mistress of a sister-in-law died long ago. The revolutionaries call for a new republic of Roman virtue. They demote and imprison the King, then execute him. Aristocrats flee; others lose their heads. Robespierre shrills louder and louder. The *sans-culottes* hang class enemies from lampposts. What will Sade do? He takes (spurious) credit for having incited the crowd outside to conquer the Bastille; but any knowing firebrand would grin to recognize that our divine Marquis, for all his nihilistic posturing, remains first and foremost—an aristocrat,

> angry over losing a great deal, still more angry to see my sovereign in irons, baffled that you gentlemen in Provence do not feel that it is impossible that good should be done and continue when the monarch's authority is constrained by thirty thousand idlers under arms with twenty cannon.

Absolutism was bad enough, but *fraternity* is worse. With so many masters, where will he find slaves? To quote Sartre's protagonist in *La nausée,* he finds the world "stale and dismal" but he fakes his way into be-coming a good facsimile of a witch-burner. After all, the characters in his manuscripts love to talk—he himself is a great letter-writer—after years behind bars, maybe he enjoys talking . . . Soon Citizen de Sade is a leader in his section, making fine radical speeches to a portion of the thirty thou-sand (I imagine him chuckling deep in his paunch—extremism of any kind comes easily to him; politics is a game, just as sex used to be when he was young and potent). First he's the secretary, then the president. To his credit, our sadist never uses his new influence to avenge himself upon his in-laws, upon whom class suspicion now falls. His wife has divorced him; he does nothing against her. His father-in-law pleads with him for protec-tion, which he graciously accords. "If I had said a word" to the section meeting, "they would have been treated severely. I kept quiet: that's how I avenge myself." But hasn't his obsession always been with *randomly* swirling energies? In the end, too flamboyant, he slips; and, denounced by the Robespierrists, goes home to prison again. Among condemned aristo-crats he enjoys the odd lust-intrigue, probably finding the atmosphere not unlike that of the sealed castle in his salaciously ferocious *Hundred and Twenty Days of Sodom.*

Now for defense of the Revolution: zealots erect a guillotine in the gar-den. Sade saves his head at the last moment, when Robespierre loses his. But his liberty will never come back. "Justice," insists Darrow, "is not the function of the state; this forms no part of the scheme of punishment. Punishment is punishment."

Meditations in the Punishment Museum

At the end of his life, confined to the mental asylum at Charenton, and confirmed in that confinement by Napoleon's order, Sade will very mov-ingly write: "If I am what I ought to be, and I am, what is the use of mak-ing me suffer so long? And taking the second horn [if I am not what I ought to be], why torment me if there is no hope?"

He no longer shouts. The Montreuils are dead. He only tries to under-stand, reasoning heartbreakingly against the Providence he denies. He wants to understand; he strives to postulate. He's tired. He only goes through the motions. Maybe that's all he ever did. When he'd tied Rose Keller to the bed and threatened her with death, he could have murdered her, but he didn't. During the Revolution he resigned the presidency of his section in protest against a decree he thought too cruelly violent. Now he waits to die. He waits. He waits.

Meditations in the Punishment Museum (continued)

One begins to yearn, not for the *cruelty* of that father-skinned chair of Cambyses' Egyptian judge, but for the *logic* of it. And, indeed, it is to such neat punishments with attached messages that retributors love to refer. Thus one twentieth-century Indian *sadhavi*—half holy woman (she consecrated herself to virginity), half militant politician—who rabble-rouses Hindus against Muslims, indignantly informs her constituents that in Kashmir, "slogans of 'long live Pakistan' were carved with red hot rods on the thighs of our Hindu daughters. Try to feel the unhappiness and the pain . . . The Hindu was dishonored." Whether or not the story is true, what could be more perfect? The crime is its own message: *I was perpetrated on this innocent flesh by Muslims. By the Victim's Maxim, I hereby give license to retaliation upon Muslims.* If only Sade had committed such a crime, which he could tally against his punishment! (Would he have ruefully laughed if they'd compelled him to eat Spanish fly pastilles until he died?) Whatever transgressions he might have committed, surely he's paid them off by now! (Or is that not true? And wouldn't he commit more if he could?) What more does anyone want of him? —Why, they want him buried! —Their new, impersonal justification: deterrence. Sadean libertines will think twice before they emulate the "divine Marquis"! —"He is an unnatural being," reads the police report given to Napoleon, "and no effort should be spared to keep him out of society." They try to deny him pen and paper, to keep him from speaking with more than three persons, but a sympathetic doctor helps him. For a while he's even able to direct plays. In his last winter of life, 1814, he is seventy-four years of age, and completes his ninety-sixth copulation (probably, like so many others, an act of sodomy) with the sixteen-year-old Madeleine Leclerc, daughter of a nurse who has evidently been prostituting her to him since she was fourteen or thereabouts. A typical diary entry: "Mgl. [Madeleine] came to do her 88th of the total and her 64th *chambre*. It was easy to see that she had been sick; she was still feeling the effects. She had cut the hair on her cunt." Is his behavior wrong? I don't know. The girl evidently liked him and was willing. In any event, this would have gotten him locked up in my country at the time of writing.

The Meaning of the Cell

T. E. Lawrence obeyed his government, or tried to, and as a result his conscience bled for the rest of his life. We've seen how, always high-strung, he occasionally went crazy. Sade rarely did his duty to anyone, was probably never sane. He searched for ciphers and "signals" in his correspondence, convinced that some providential code would whisper to him the number of days remaining until he regained that freedom which he longed for but for which he had so little use. Through disobedience he created his integrity. Without his punishment, he might never have written the books and letters for which we remember him today. Without his punishment, without his dreary, meaningless suffering, he might never have made meaning for himself. This fact alone cannot even begin to justify it.

AND CAN THEY MAKE MEANING FROM THIS?
Some Soviet political prisoners and their crimes (1982)

VYTAUTUS ABRUTIS, *restorer*
Renounced Soviet citizenship, expressed intention of emigrating, met with foreign journalists. Tried under Article 190, Part 1: "Circulating deliberately false fabrications defaming the Soviet political and social system."

YEVGENY MIKHAILOVICH ANTSUPOV, *historian*
Wrote works "attempting to divide history into periods," demanded to emigrate, distributed "photographs of a demonstration with the same demands." Tried under Article 70: "Anti-Soviet agitation and propaganda."

IVAN MARINCHENKO, *driver*
"Attempted self-immolation on Red Square . . . as a sign of protest against being evicted from his home." Placed in special psychiatric hospital.

NADEZHDA PANTELEYEVNA SIDOROVA, *printer*
Worked for "The Christian" underground printing press. Tried under Article 162, Part 2: "Engaging in forbidden manufacture."

Education of an Anarchist

One more prison story, which we'll tell at far less length than it deserves: imprisoned for almost fourteen years of his twenty-two-year sentence for attempting to assassinate Henry Clay Frick—the revolver misfired, like the bomb before it and the dynamite cartridge in his mouth afterward, and the dagger was improperly aimed—Alexander Berkman, anarchist and denouncer of "false tolerance," wrote a long, strange book, and in places a very powerful one. Berkman's character was fundamentally revolutionary—which is to say he was a murderously rigid romantic.

WHO DESERVES TO LIVE?
The moral calculus of Alexander Berkman (1892)

The People —the toilers of the world, the producers—comprise, to me, the universe. They alone count. The rest are parasites, who have no right to exist. But to the People belongs the earth—by right, if not in fact. To make it so in fact, all means are justifiable; nay, advisable, even to the point of taking life . . . I had always taken the extreme view. The more radical the treatment, I held, the quicker the cure.

Source: Berkman, p. 9.

But his years of confinement, of monotony, anguish, false hopes and brutality, of stench and darkness and petty cruelty, awoke his capacity to be what Trotsky and Sade never could—an empathetic bridge. Political criminals whom he once scorned as "parasites" became his friends and sometimes even the objects of his passionate erotic love. That empathy never extended to his victim, of course, or if it did, only so far as to allow the contemptuous remark that Frick the "mere man" scarcely warranted an assassin's trouble:

The Homestead developments had given him a temporary prominence, thrown this particular hydra-head into bold relief, so to speak. That alone made him worthy of the revolutionist's attention. Primarily, as an object lesson; it would strike terror into the soul of his class. They are craven-hearted, their conscience weighted with guilt.

Thus Berkman's act of stupid fanaticism—and we must call it stupid, for not only did it fail by any standard to advance his immediate end, but it also prohibited him from carrying out any other useful labor for almost fourteen years—was meant as proactive self-defense of class, a combination of deterrence, through which the capitalists' "strangling hold on labor might be loosened," and retribution, a punishment for the Homestead incident, in which Frick's Pinkerton strikebreakers (to say nothing of eight thousand National Guardsmen armed with machine guns) had shot down strikers and a little boy. Most of all, it was as usual an act of aesthetic violence: didactic, propaganda theater. Round-faced, bespectacled Emma Goldman, then Berkman's lover, muse and confederate, agreed that "a blow aimed at Frick would re-echo in the poorest hovel." This was the decade of international anarchist murders: the King of Italy, the Empress of Austria, the President of France, the Prime Minister of Spain—and, of course, the American President McKinley. —So much for the crime—or, if you prefer, the illegal punishment. Rising up, rising down!

The *legal* punishment, we must presume, was actuated by precisely the same motives: retribution for the act; deterrence, both of Berkman himself and of other anarchists, from committing similar acts; and propaganda. The judge "spoke of making an example of me. The old villain! He had been doing it all his life: making an example of social victims." (The word "victims" is reminiscent of John Brown and Göring both; they reject responsibility; punishment is oppression imposed on them. But it reminds me of Plato, too, who argued that "correction must always be meted to the bad—to make a better man of him—not to the unfortunate; on him it is wasted." Once again, consider the previous section's exposition of deterrence through moderation and the counterdeterrence of excess and desperation. Who is bad; who is a victim? "The old villain" can never know.) Bitterly the prisoner repeated to himself that the sentence was not legal; since Frick hadn't died, he should not have been sentenced to more than seven years—a strange complaint for a martyr-anarchist to make, if he truly believed that all law was nothing but the arbitrary and cynical application of expedient force on the part of the ruling class. It would have been interesting to know whether a more merciful sentence might have softened him *civically,* as it never could Sade. The original meaning of the nineteenth-century word "reformatory" was exactly that. The prisoner was supposed to meditate, repent, become better as a result of commingled kindness and firmness. Berkman was never to find out whether that might be possible. Indeed, in yet another chilling *contrapasso,* his punishment was as stupid as his crime; for retribution never scratches the soul which wears the crystalline armor of ideology and thereby holds any perception of guilt at bay. How can that armor be cracked? Through "pressure," as the Stalinists would have said. The pressure brought to bear against him by the state of Pennsylvania included solitary confinement in "the hole" and "the basket"; deprivation of food, exercise, medical care and contact with the outside; beatings, verbal abuse, intimidation, et cetera—a far cry from the methods of the Cheka, but pressure, nonetheless, *deterrence,* in short, and it did not deter; and *retribution,* which might well have followed the local moral-social calculus but which, as with Sade, merely sharpened this criminal's defiance.

Toward the end of his fourteen years, the warden asked Berkman if he had changed his views. This was what deterrence was meant to do. Berkman replied that he had not.

In a letter which he wrote around the same time to his revolutionary beloved, he said: "Daily contact with authority has strengthened my conviction that control of the governmental power is an illusory remedy for social evils. Inevitable consequences of false conceptions are not to be legislated out of existence." Yet he had changed a little, disapproving of the assassination of President McKinley because "the background of social" as opposed to personal "necessity was lacking," even as he continued to justify his own attack upon Frick. Return to "Akbar's" epigraph at the beginning of this section: *Whatever motives retribution can't dissolve into repentance, it hardens.* "Magnificent was the day of hearts on fire with the hatred of oppression and the love of liberty!" The only remaining expediency stake which authority had in his imprisonment, namely, propaganda-making, could probably have been served by commuting his sentence earlier than it did. The jail stretch of Alexander Berkman, then, like that of many of his fellow inmates, was a costly, cruel and above all useless affair. "All soon grow nervous and irritable, and stand at the door, leaning against the bars, an expression of bewildered hopelessness or anxious expectancy on their faces."

Having said this much against his punishment, I return to social symmetry. For whatever reason, Berkman attacked a fellow human being with intent to kill. Even though his long misery improved him scarcely at all (his developing empathy might have come with experience in any event), I believe it to have been justifiably inflicted. Frick deserved justice, too.

Did Frick get justice? His own complicity in the shooting down of the Homestead strikers rendered him despicable, and worthy of class justice—perhaps even of assassination, should the rigged "legal" justice of which Berkman was so contemptuous have failed—which it almost certainly would have. Berkman's *Attentat* was arguably justified by a revolutionary calculus, which contradicts and supersedes the calculus of law. We agreed that rising up against the state is justified when that state's defense of authority aims at permanently excluding or debasing a portion of the governed, when it offers no release from obedience in the event of disagreement with it and when it invokes more violent power than it needs to in a given case. All three of these conditions applied to the vicious crushing of the Homestead strike.

Berkman, however, acted almost alone. He didn't seek out "the toilers" and fashion his violence into a tool of mass mobilization. His was the self-sufficient calculus of a Julius Caesar or a Raskolnikov. In terms of the power available to him, he was closer to the latter than the former. We've agreed that violence without hope of result lacks justification. He was another John Brown, but further removed than the latter from any consensual delimitation between authority and liberty of conscience. Many abolitionists supported Brown, and even the President of the United States agreed that slavery was wrong, although he didn't emancipate the slaves until the war required it. Berkman and his anarchists had behind them no influential people to argue their case in the nation's drawing rooms. Acknowledging no law but his own, then, renouncing the social contract, no matter what his ends, Berkman had no business complaining about his own judgment and punishment, which were arguably proportionate to the injury which he inflicted on Frick. Berkman got not death, but suffering and deprivation. It is easier, perhaps, to spend one's death, as John Brown did, than to waste one's life, like Sade and Berkman.

Any serious consideration of punishment makes one's heart ache. But he who breaks the contract extremely, that is by violence, may well be obligated to pay fearfully, no matter how justified he might otherwise be. (That is one of the reasons why the Moral Calculus of *Rising Up and Rising Down* is little more than a series of sometimes mutually exclusive lists.) Will he face the price and pay it, like Brown? Then *perhaps* he may be justified indeed. Take punishment away, and we're left with the easy violence of a street thug, a wife-beater, a totally unfettered Sade (whose unexpected kindness to the fallen in no way inclines me to trust solely to that kindness), or even an Alexander Berkman, any of whom could lean on the bully stick of some convenient moral calculus.

PUNISHMENT IS JUSTIFIED:

1. When the transgressor agrees to, or belongs to a culture which subscribes to, the rule by which he has been judged, and when he can be proven to have violated that rule. [Alternatively, when the transgressor

and punisher accept the same moral values which apply in the given case; and when the transgressor has in fact breached those values such that the law calls for the stipulated punishment.]

2. When its purpose is to prove that a legitimate social contract will be honored by authority.

3. When its penalties are codified into limit and consistency, and respect the rights of the self.

4. When it is proportionate to the original injury.

5. When it helps heal the victim, those who care for him, or society generally.

6. When it is the most practical means of isolating an unregenerate violent offender.

PUNISHMENT IS UNJUSTIFIED:

1. By tu quoque alone.

2. When the person suffering the punishment does not understand why he is being punished.

3. When the punishment is inconsistently applied to penalize similar acts committed under similar circumstances.

4. When there is no separation of powers among judges, executioners and sovereigns.

5. When proof of guilt is logically faculty, or when the judicial process is dishonest.

6. To the extent that the punishment, which may be just or unjust in and of itself, furthers authority's power beyond the minimum necessary for enforcing the social contract.

7. When deterrence remains possible but has not yet been tried.

JUSTIFICATIONS

Fate

I.

MORAL YELLOWNESS

Iago very precisely identifies his purposes and his motives as being black and born of hate. But no; that's not the way it is! To do evil a human being must first of all believe that what he's doing is good, or else that it's a well-considered act in conformity with natural law. Fortunately, it is in the nature of the human being to seek a justification for his actions.

SOLZENHITSYN, 1973

Trotsky's colleague Krestinsky once remarked that Stalin was "a bad man, with yellow eyes." After that, Trotsky thought to perceive what he called the *moral yellowness* of Stalin. (Krestinsky, by the way, was liquidated by Stalin, a few years before Trotsky's turn came. And some people might have seen moral yellowness in all three of them—or at any rate moral redness, they being so complicit in the atrocities of "Red Terror" which Lenin launched in 1918. "I plead not guilty," Krestinsky said at the end. "I am not a Trotskyite." He'd thus achieved the distinction of denouncing each of the antagonists to the other.)

Being able to spy out moral yellowness would certainly simplify our task of determining when violence is justified; for that very reason, a misperception of moral yellowness would be a very serious error. Stalin's belief that he saw it in the class of kulaks or rich peasants—for the science of Marxism-Leninism proved that it must be there—gave him the confidence to direct the repression and outright extermination of millions. In my experience *there is almost never any moral yellowness.* (I say "almost" because no one's experience, including mine, is wide enough.) When I set out to meet Pol Pot, I knew that I would search for moral yellowness in his laughing face if I found him (I didn't), and cast upon some perfectly innocuous trait which in my opinion betrayed and signified his evil. That is the artist's job, and the second-rate journalist's. And, indeed, it's superior to the tasks demanded by mere superstition. In life as in art, beholding commences or continues the search for wholeness, whose aim is to make meaning cohere with appearance. At its highest, this striving is expressed by souls such as the Canadian painter Emily Carr: "Search for the reality of each object, that is, its real and only beauty," she writes in her journal. With noble obsessiveness she wonders: "What is that vital thing, in ugly as well as lovely things and places, the thing that takes us out of ourselves, that draws and attracts us, that unnameable thing claiming kinship with us?" There is a significance, which we can call spirit, to a British Columbian cedar; and Carr's painting of one of those trees convinces me that she portrayed its outward form in a manner consistent with its inner character—or rather (crucial qualification!) with what she perceived as its inner character; for another painter's rendering of the same tree, successful or not, would be different. Meanwhile, her image owns life and truth because it is *fitting.* Most everybody searches for the secret, the summation, the innerness of things. Watch a child, a stranger in a new place, a person falling in love. The pupils widen; the face thrills, growing mobile like clay worked in the potter's warm hands; the consciousness within exercises itself, straining to identify with what it sees, to bind itself to the world with perception and memory.

"The thing that takes us out of ourselves" need not be happy. If that were the case, one would never find anyone at funerals. Whether the casket is open or closed, the mourners' perceptions surge forth, seeking the dead body inside that they will never see anymore. To reject the pain, turning away from this concentration point of grief which wounds them afresh, would be expedient but inhuman: the loss must be embraced in order to be understood. Even death is a "vital thing."

This is how we live, taking in, correlating, organizing our experiences in ways which express our varying personal needs for reference. When violent actors perform before us, whether they be victims, perpetrators or tools, then (if experience or professionalism has not yet made us inhuman) we tend to crave understanding almost desperately, understanding being the offering we lay down on the altar of every force of power—and in its transformative abilities violence is debatably the most powerful entity of all. Earth falls upon the coffin. Why did the addicted mother's boyfriend drown the three-year-old in the bathtub? Why did my friends have to meet a land mine? Why did Hitler want to kill the Jews? So the searching and seeking goes out, alert and cautious, like fingers toward a naked bloodstained razor—be it Trotsky's razor of terror or Sherman's razor of war or any other variety. Now, the most important part of the razor is the blade. When we face a human razor, we want him or her to have a blade, too, something that reveals itself instantly, something that explains. Many of us expect our mass murderers to somehow look like mass murderers, to glower, to be frightening or eerie in appearance. If only they were truly this way, then we could recognize them and be protected! Or at least we could somehow *know* them, which might spread the balm of rationality upon the shocking mind-wounds they give us. The same need applies to the murderers themselves—oh, not all of them; I've spoken just now of how inhuman it would be to turn away from the funeral of a person with whom one shared a life, but not all bipeds called human from a biological point of view *are* so from any other category; enough to say that *most* of them seek to create categories—especially the ones who justify (and it is, after all, with them that this book is concerned). They want to find a characteristic in their victims which will set them safely beyond the pale. Hence all stereotypes (the one-in-all being the furthest opposite on the continuum from the all-in-one of Emily Carr); hence the stone-throwing and cries of "Monster!" directed at a keloid-riddled girl who survived Hiroshima; hence the laborious reifications of Nazi movies in which all the Jews have shifty eyes and hooked noses, the ideal being to convince the uninitiated that Jews are the murderers, not the other way around; fool, can't you *see* the shining moral yellowness of the Jew?

MORAL YELLOWNESS is the outward appearance of evil or violence in the attitude or expression of a human being.

VIOLENCE BASED ON MORAL YELLOWNESS IS JUSTIFIED:

Never.

VIOLENCE BASED ON MORAL YELLOWNESS IS UNJUSTIFIED:

Always.

Moral yellowness is the aesthetic handmaiden of violence. It can never be a worthy justification. Although we may imbibe it unthinkingly, sooner or later, all of us who actually meet the morally yellow must experience the uneasy sense that they may be grey underneath. From that moment on, we can be said to worship the fiction of moral yellowness *by choice.* Be warned by the career of Field Marshal Keitel, who did Hitler's bidding because that was profitably easy. Loyalty and compulsion—much less inertia—cannot exculpate us from committing acts of injustice. A person is always more than a member of a category.

For such reasons, we very often overtly discredit the whole notion of moral yellowness—nobody owns or is only *one* vital thing! Keitel himself, for instance, reveals as many sympathetic traits as Napoleon: he took care to express "personal esteem" and "sympathy" to the head of the French delegation who surrendered to Germany in 1940, and in 1946 he displayed a textbook stoicism at Nuremberg in the face of a dishonorable death—nor is he evil-looking. How can we believe in moral yellowness, really? —But here it is in Telford Taylor's famous memoir of the first Nuremberg trial. This truth-sure jurist reproduces a group photograph of several of the first trial's defendants, the big fish; and in that image the most striking figure initially is Rudolf Hess, on account of the thick dark diamond-shaped eyebrows in his strange pale face; his chin is squared up, possibly due to clenched teeth, so that his head has become a cube upon that aloof white neck. His arms are folded. He glares into space. Moral yellowness? Taylor thinks so, claiming that the close-up is "accentuating his beetlebrows, sunken eyes, and grim expression." Beside Hess, but seemingly in another world, is stiff old Ribbentrop, his throat tight as if the trial were already ended and Master Sergeant Woods had applied the noose. He strains, as always in his career, to express resentment and fury. "Ribbentrop as usual has his chin raised and eyes closed," remarks Taylor. Between and behind those two we find Baldur von Schirach, formerly the leader of the *Hitlerjugend;* he's an ordinary, pleasant-looking man who gazes down at a pencil in his hands. Taylor is quick to tell us that he "is attending to his own writing rather than the proceedings." Moral yellowness? If I were shown an uncaptioned photograph of this man alone, I would never think him any kind of criminal. Hess is half-mad and looks it, but as a matter of fact, since he flew to England to try to negotiate a peace, he had no time to accrue much war guilt. Accordingly, he'll not be hanged, but at the insistence of the Russians (against whom he proposed an Anglo-German alliance) he'll be kept in Spandau until he finally commits suicide at ninety-three years of age. Even Taylor has to remark: "such long-continued incarceration, especially in a huge prison where he was the sole inmate, was a crime against humanity." That leaves Ribbentrop, by all accounts an eminently dislikable person. And that is how he looks. Can one tell from his expression, however, that he is also morally and politically dislikable, having been involved in the deportations of French and Hungarian Jews? Could the circumstances under which the photograph was taken (on trial for his life, in a court of his victorious enemies) have anything to do with his expression? (On account of exactly those circumstances, Admiral Raeder in the background is covering his face from the photographer.) I say again: There is no moral yellowness. Or, rather: The perception of moral yellowness is learned. "The first time I saw dead Germans they looked just like Americans, except for the uniform," an American soldier recalled fifty years later. "And then you started to think of them as animals." Moral yellowness is visual prejudice, and so is its opposite: the tendency of any given category of humankind to see good in its own image. Thus one American slave boy, who always ran away from white men when they looked at him, in case it might be their intention to sell him in Georgia, shared the conviction of his fellow slaves that Queen Victoria must be black. "Accustomed to nothing but cruelty at the hands of white people, we had never imagined that a great ruler so kind to coloured people could be other than black." Hence the Nuremberg judges' "gestures of bewilderment, readily explicable," when *Einsatzgruppeführer* Ohlendorf gave his hideous testimony. Clean-cut and polite, he just didn't look the part of somebody who'd murdered ninety thousand human beings! "No one could have looked less like a brutish SS thug such as Kaltenbrunner," in whom Rebecca West saw moral yellowness, which is why she wrote that he reminded her "of a particularly vicious horse." To me, Kaltenbrunner appears rather bored and neutral in his photograph, not vicious—and what should a brutish thug look like? I have met several. It's not how they look; it's how they act.

"Ohlendorf was small of stature, young-looking, and rather comely. He spoke quietly, with great precision, dispassion, and apparent intelligence. How could he have done what he now so calmly described?"

I grant the obvious fact that people's appearance may on occasion reveal their intentions, their emotions, et cetera. The man in the bar to whom I have said nothing, who sneers and glares at me, puts me rightfully on my guard. In that sense there are in fact physiognomies of aggression. But that is only because these souls act out of rage which shines through their flesh like fire behind a paper screen. However, should their moral spectrum be laid out differently than mine, their feelings as displayed by their bodies may be connected to different behaviors than I might expect. What if it makes the stranger tranquilly joyous to contemplate murdering me? What if, like de Sade's protagonists, they delight in caressing before they destroy? Then their friendliness is what I must fear. Among the indications of antisocial character disorder (in which category Göring has been placed) is this one: "Often a charming, likable personality with a disarming manner and an ability to win the liking and friendship of others. Typically good sense of humor and generally optimistic outlook."

We read that when Himmler came to Minsk on an inspection tour, *Einsatzgruppe B* demonstrated its shooting skills on a hundred Jews. One of the doomed had blond hair and blue eyes. Himmler was miserable. If, as his ideology insisted, biology justifies all, and if the measure of biology is phenotype (hence the skulls and pickled heads harvested from concentration camp inmates for scientific specimens), then why didn't this boy have a hooked nose? Where was his moral yellowness? Group B took aim. Two women survived the first volley, and Himmler screamed! He longed to understand his violence as much as we do. It seems to me that at that moment his understanding must have been unable to evade recognizing his dishonesty. What did he do afterward? Did he talk with racial experts who reassured him with maxims about the cunning mask of the Jew? Or did he retreat into one of his rationalistic metaphors about cleaning, fumigating, sterilizing—all processes which require overkill for their effectiveness to be guaranteed?

The moral is this: Never judge a person solely for what he is. We already know that we ought not judge him solely for what he does: if the defendant is insane, or if he had reasonable cause to believe, mistakenly or not, that the man he shot meant to shoot *him,* we treat the act of homicide differently from the professional or expedient acts of a Himmler, a Bluebeard, an Elisabeth Báthory. Judge him for what he is and what he does together. The insane man who kills not, and the killer who is not insane, each deserve differently from the crazed murderer. Clear—evident—banal. And in discarding moral yellowness we need not deprive ourselves of the concept of manifest intent. Look into those glaring yellow eyes, or those red ones: My Jamaican friend, Pearline, was sure that one "crew" of ghetto men was sinful because their eyes were all bloodshot—probably from ganja-smoking. As a matter of fact, Pearline was not wrong, for at least some of those fellows were gunmen. The red eyes she seized on were a kind of shorthand for moral yellowness—a metaphorically expressed intuition, à la Emily Carr. In this she was poetically justified—justified in every other way, too, for she didn't plan to act on her perceptions. (What do *you* see? *Whom* do you see?) And Telford Taylor would have had every right to remark on Hess's beetlebrows—had he not been simultaneously working to convict him. Metaphors ought to be left outside both courtroom and battlefield; metaphors and political action (to say nothing of metaphors and violence) make a dangerous mix.

ADDENDUM:
August Sander's Photographs of Persecuted Jews

For his immense *People of the Twentieth Century* series, the photographer August Sander, obstructed and menaced but not quite silenced even though his Communist son died in a German prison, quietly continued his project of depicting human types by, among other things, taking photographs of the people very accurately called "The Persecuted." It is 1938, and in an armchair against a grey wall sits old Frau Michel, a Jew, her thinning hair neatly combed back, her eyes half-closed behind the round spectacles on her round face. She grips the curved handles of her twin canes. She gazes at nothing. Her lips are pursed. She is wary, weary, pale and sad. Turn the page and see Herr Fleck—1938 again. All the portraits of persecuted Jews are dated 1938 or ca. 1938. 1938 was the year of *Kristallnacht,* remember, when with official sanction thugs and zealots smashed in the windows of Jewish businesses; the following year began World War II, whose course led on greased tracks straight to ghettos and gas chambers. At any rate, Herr Fleck, sallow and professional, folds his palms on his crossed legs and gazes anxiously through his too brilliant spectacles, while shadows crawl on the wall behind him. On the facing page sits Herr Leubsdorf, hale and clean, not fear-expressing like Herr Fleck but definitely pensive. File him under "Aristocrats" and you wouldn't know his case was serious. Frau Oppenheim, fiftyish but still pretty, with her necklace just so, draws her pale arms tightly inward, lowers her eyelids and glares at Sander (and us), her head bowed a little, as if she were awaiting a blow from behind. On the recto page, her elderly husband, his mouth grimacing almost insanely, gazes pop-eyed through his glasses. What has he seen? These two images glow with a pain which seems to be embedded in the very emulsion. Next comes a young persecuted Jewess who looks unremarkable, perhaps a little saucy; she could be refiled under "The Small Town" or "Working Women" or "Painters and Sculptors" and I'd never know, and then we see Herr Doctor Philip, who on the other hand looks crushed and ruined, as he probably is. We see a plump, submissive girl and a bewildered man (they could both go under "Servants" or "Families"), then middle-aged Frau Marcus in her butterfly scarf, clutching her coat-edges nervously together, then at last Dr. Kahn full on who stares at us with wet anguish filled with comprehension.

Many of Sander's other subjects, even some of the vagabonds, throw their shoulders back, raise their heads high. The persecuted Jews do not. Did Sander say, "Please, Herr Doctor Philip, I would like to take your photograph," or did he say, "Well, to get right down to it, Herr Doctor Philip, I'd like to use you in my series of persecuted Jews"? Knowing the context would be useful in evaluating the expressions on the portraits. And yet it is fair to say that the majority of these victims resemble victims.

Turning for comparison to Sander's photographs of National Socialists, we first discover a *Hitlerjugend* lad in 1941, dressed in his uniform best, the swastika armband proudly displayed, the black tie almost touching the belt—he stands serious and self-important there in what is probably the family backyard; he's blond and freckled, just a boy, but he knows how to stand with his feet apart in the tall boots, how to look confident. He does not resemble a persecutor. The National Socialist of 1937–38, fat and coarse, might be hard, but not necessarily vicious (I wouldn't have been surprised to see him categorized under the rubric of "The Circus"); facing him we see a portrait of an effeminate blond boy in Nazi uniform who squeezes his hands together just like the persecuted Jews, but his clenched, open-eyed young face inclines toward us in an even-tempered stab at resolution. The next two youths could be anyone, clean-cut, faraway-gazing. (Call them "Students." Recall this: "Ohlendorf was small of stature, young-looking, and rather comely." It's not so easy, is it? It's not that there's nothing there, but that the soul of a likeness is perhaps too complex for

these categorizations.) Finally comes a pair of uniformed, swastika'd officials evincing the hardness so fashionable during the period; they have power
and are conscious of it, especially the right-hand one, the ruthless-looking
chief of Cologne's cultural department. Call them Nazis, to be sure; but
Sander's other rubrics of "Businessmen," "Officials" or "Lawyers/Judges"
would also have fit—and of course Nazis became all of these things.

What can we say about the National Socialists as a group? Again,
they're not really evil; there's no moral yellowness; if there were, then the
Nazis themselves, who looked so hard for it, would have found it in the
mirror . . .

EVALUATIONS

I.

FOUR SAFEGUARDS

What signifies the massacre of twenty thousand unfortunates? Twenty thousand miseries less, and millions of miseries saved in advance! The most timid ruler does not hesitate to dictate a law that must produce misery and the slow agony of thousands and thousands of prosperous, industrious, even happy subjects in order to satisfy a whim.

Jose Rizal's Protagonist SIMOUN, 1891

However useful and necessary it may have been to divide self-defense into categories, we inevitably did violence to the concept thereby— and to events. When Gavrilo Princip took aim at the Austrian Emperor and Empress in Sarajevo in 1914, his bullets were probably weighted with as many motives as grains of gunpowder: defense of homeland for the South Slavs, defense of authority (or against imposed authority), defenses of honor, race, creed, ground and possibly class. But if we subdivide that one lethal instant into half a dozen, we misrepresent it, our verbose analysis failing to respect the taciturnity of the deed. Still, we must categorize: *Why did he do it?*

Of Multiple Justifications

But respect the deed too much, privilege one category too exclusively, and you'll risk becoming either a brutal simplifier, like the Stalinists, or else an ineffectual if sometimes admirable reductionist like our meditator-pilot Saint-Exupéry. In his memoirs, the Burmese insurgent Aye Saung describes being tortured with electric shocks administered through his toes. The current literally sears away the vestiges of his patriotic nationalism. "Henceforth, I vowed, I would recognize only the boundaries of class." In other words, he commits himself to the Burmese Communist Party. The remainder of his autobiography demonstrates (to me, at least) the incorrectness of this decision. Aye Saung's life of struggle, founded on noble inflexibility, continually precipitates its own disappointment. By his lonesome calculus, most of his fellow moral actors prove self-serving: they go to brothels, try to get rich and allow other nonrevolutionary topics into their minds. In the hot midafternoon before the night fair, a lady in an apron is dribbling noodles in her hand from a pan into a plastic bag, and boys are watering the red-earth lanes between stalls while women stand whisking the flies away with spatulas. What are they doing but living and making a living, hoping that politics will pass them by? To the Aye Saungs of this world, such individuals (moral actors in their own right) stand not to the side but near the bottom of his hierarchy of well-intentioned urgency. Incredibly, even after joining the Shan State Army and learning from local Shan how cruelly the Burmese treat them, Aye Saung continues to insist that nationality is nothing, class everything. Isn't he, the token Burman in an anti-Burmese insurgent band, best proof of that? Again, we can't dispute that his position is sincere, well-meant, even self-sacrificing. His years in the SSA will not prove easy ones. He complains of suspicion and persecution, of the humiliations with which the SSA reward his uncompromising views and his Burmese nationality. Finally he resigns in failure.

Why didn't he take better note of his neighboring insurgents to the south in Karenni State, who, rising up against the Burmese regime's lies, extortions, rapes, corvée labor and village-burnings, embraced national self-defense? In 1994 I saw one of their bases, trenched and palisaded with outward-leaning bamboo like some movie of Africa, and in the front gateway, which was the only gateway, they even had a little barbed wire. Inside it was hot and quiet and almost empty. Five pigs basked in the shade.

A woman soldier said that everybody else was out on patrol. Two boy soldiers showed off their Kalashnikovs for me. When their comrades came back, they were all eager and full of fight. They were defending their tormented homeland as best they could. —I don't mean to criticize Aye Saung's objectives, only his narrowness. It is not that defense of class as such was ever an unimportant consideration. Should the Burmese ultimately succeed, as at this writing (1996) they show signs of doing, in conquering all the hill tribes, their victims will all be in the same boat as oppressed Burmans. Too many of the insurgent groups, forgetting this, have wasted opportunities by fighting each other, while the Burmese gobbled them up. Why couldn't the Shan and the Karenni have better coordinated their resistance? The populations whom they ought to have defended were ill served.

I propose, then, the following rule: *The greater the number of categories an act of self-defense can legitimately invoke, the more justified it will be.* When proactive self-defense also fulfills the dictates of self-defense of race, honor and class, it is more likely to be good and decent than when it doesn't. Aye Saung followed class alone. He became no tree of reason, but a narrow, fragile stick.

The case of Gavrilo Princip's bloody ball of motives might seem to disprove such a principle. Perhaps it does. But was Princip justified? If not, then obviously his self-defense was never legitimate. If so, then he would have been more justified by being *multiply* justified. Does Aye Saung agree by now? I hope so, for the Burmese Communist Party has been dead and hollow for many years.

Of Diverse Actors

The second and related rule: *The greater the variety of participants an act of self-defense attracts, the more justified it is likely to be.* Let us briefly consider one more time the case of Lincoln versus Trotsky. These two men necessarily sat in judgment on others when they undertook to defend their respective systems. Indeed, Aristotle defines citizenship as participation in "judgment and authority," which strikes me as more reasonable from a descriptive point of view than from an ethical one. Would it be mere circular logic to argue that the authority is legitimate in which one partakes, of which one is a "citizen," a judge? In any event, the *morality* of such a definition does not hold up. Any S.S. *Gruppenführer,* any one of Trotsky's bloodthirsty Chekists, could have defended his position by hauling out the tired argument of the Nuremberg defendants that for him it was legitimate merely because he had been appointed or commanded to it! Lincoln would have been in this sense a "citizen" by election and conviction; Trotsky, a citizen by appointment and revolutionary necessity (for which read again "by conviction"). We saw that the two men exercised their mandates very differently. This is why I propose the following equivalent (and more useful) rephrasing of our second rule: Authority (and the defense of that authority) approaches legitimacy when it predicates itself on a commonality between leaders and led, *the led including the group against some of whose members violence is employed*. At the end of the American Civil War, almost everyone was glad that it was over, even if hatred and resentment necessarily remained on both sides, especially the South. Lincoln wanted to include the vanquished in government, avoiding reprisals except against those who would not swear loyalty. But at the end of the Russian Civil War, the losers were simply terrified. They had begun to understand their doom. Trotsky would have sneeringly replied that *of course* his war communism wasn't legitimate for the Russian aristocracy, nor was it meant to be: they were to be "eliminated as a class." We need not deal with that particular chestnut again. Set the aristocracy aside for now; talk about the peasants. Trotsky wanted to "lead" *them*, at least—under the fraternal guidance of the proletariat. But, as we saw, most peasants ended up hating the regime. "Most peasants" were most Russians. Whom then had the revolution been for?

Of Praxis

The third rule: *Experience alone, and theoretical grounding alone, are insufficient foundations for any moral calculus.* Consider Trotsky's classic distinction between war and revolution: namely, that the latter destroys state power from below, while the former temporarily strengthens it—but then (so he insists) undermines it. Trotsky is speaking from experience: the experience of World War I, which shattered many nations, particularly his own Russia, and weakened the rest. But his experience is inadequate. In spite of his visit to the United States, he had failed to see how war actually consolidated the U.S.'s international power, which in the long run strengthened the country internally. Trotsky has already arrived at his rules, which he pretends to establish on the basis of his experiences. Or again, the fact that the general strike of 1905 brought the Tsarist economy almost to a standstill proves to Trotsky that the revolutionary leadership of the proletariat is "an incontrovertible fact." But after the establishment of Soviet power, strikes were made illegal, and any group who dared to oppose the victorious revolution did not thereby prove itself to be revolutionary, but, on the contrary, reactionary—and the more dangerously so the more successful its disruption.

Mere experience, especially in a doctrinaire mind, produces equally parochial conclusions. Aye Saung's torture conversion from patriotic nationalism to international classism might well be "objectively" correct for a Burmese intellectual. It bears little reference to the realities of a Shan peasant.

Of Context

The fourth: *Context must inform the act that we judge, but ought not to predetermine the judgment.* Nor, remembering our maxim that both the perpetrator and the deed must be judged as one, ought we to rush to judge someone's entire career in one brief summation—a case in point being that wholly human, hence less than completely admirable, character Cicero, who reverenced the divinity of the tyrant he'd vainly opposed and evaded, but later showed himself to be in possession of courage, of true honor and therefore of justification when he spoke out against the new tyranny of Antonius, a deed of antiviolent greatness for which he was wrenched out of life.

Overreliance on context might lure me into the false assertion that the functionary of an evil regime must be evil—or, more vulgarly still, that the "objective" nature of that context allows for only a certain moral decision. Trotsky tells us that he was prepared from childhood to be a revolutionary, simply as a result of seeing around him so much injustice. But his parents, who saw the same things, did not become revolutionaries. Context does not determine; it only contextualizes.

Underreliance might, by limiting my focus only to the functionary's personal reality, make out his decisions to be more or less justified than they were: How much could he control? What was the institutional standard against which he was being measured? Did a given act actually comprise vacillation, compromise, acquiescence or rebellion? Go back to Cicero's address to the now triumphant Caesar, by whose war the Republic and

Cicero's own patron lie dead. He flatters him, you remember, with his saga-city, gloriousness, invincibility, mercy. Then he dares to say: "This is the program to which you must devote all your energies: the reestablishment of the constitution, with yourself the first to reap its fruits in profound tranquillity and peace." Was this heroic? It depends on whether anyone else felt comfortable telling "the deified Julius" the same thing, how brave Cicero himself had been in the past, how pure, good and useful his ends were, et cetera. Without describing and defining people's moral environ-ment, how can we know enough to characterize them as the crazed dream-ers of martial gallantry, the resolute minions of a just cause, or the armed chessmen of *Realpolitik?*

The aesthetics of context are of course closely related to issues of moral yellowness. Djilas describes the case of a "tall, dark-eyed" girl cap-tured by the Partisans; she'd been an Ustasha camp counselor. She refused Djilas's suggestion to come over to the Partisan side, insisting that "it would be immoral to change one's views." It is difficult not to see a sad no-bility about this girl; and yet the Ustashi were essentially torturers and murderers whose crimes sicken any decent person. Djilas had given her a chance; she'd refused it; that was and had to be the end of her story. "She stood up for herself bravely," he recalls. "However, Rankovic later re-ported that she weakened at her execution, and was weeping and trem-bling." Strictly speaking, these details are irrelevant. The dark-eyed girl was an enemy. I do most sincerely believe that ethical behavior as we best construe it ought to be followed by us throughout our lives, even on the last day of life, and that if we have made a bad or even evil choice we are not barred (or excused) thereby from continuing to live the last moments or years given us in whatever way we consider to be most right. Being safely removed by time, space and nationality from the Yugoslav Partisan War, I can in this quiet room of mine which looks out upon the undis-turbed darkness of a night street afford the luxury of being a human being and of seeing the dark-eyed girl as a human being, of admiring and pitying her on her journey from the interrogation room to the firing squad to the mound of carelessly shoveled dirt from which her hands and feet probably stuck out. But word pictures and emotional updrafts do not change the fact that under the circumstances of imminent collective defense, of justi-fied defense of homeland, however infected that might have been by preex-isting ethnic and local sectarianism, of obedience to an order given by the Partisans' legitimate command, *she had to be killed.*

A Warning Against Doctrinairism

Multiplicity of justification, diversity of participation, context, praxis—I freely admit that these and all such qualifications and limitations are the hallmark of someone who can't even be called an armchair revolutionary—rules which come perilously close to washing their hands of reality, like Plato or Pontius Pilate. War, revolution and indeed *most violence quickly produces its own imminence,* as a result of which these four hedges transform themselves into dangerous obstructionism. Consider as an example the class revolutionary type, or at least the class revolutionary public mask. "To her comrades, Res was a model guerrilla. She was organized, industrious, steadfast and firm in her determination." And shouldn't every guerrilla live and die as a model guerrilla? Che Guevara wrote that "the guerrilla fighter will be a sort of guiding angel who has fallen into the zone, helping the poor always." What if they don't want to be helped? The Unabomber wrote: "We don't mean to sneer at 'plantation darkies' of the Old South. To their credit, most slaves were NOT content with their servitude. We do sneer at people who ARE content with servitude." Poor contented people! It was they who received his bombs in the mail. And presumably the Unabomber was not sorry. Had he been, he would have stopped. A model guerrilla does not stop. Whenever she became despondent at others' unwillingness to believe in her, Joan of Arc would go aside and pray. Then very often she'd hear a voice which said: "Daughter-God, go, go, go, I shall be at your aid, go." It is the aim of *Rising Up and Rising Down* to help us decide whether our voices are offering good counsel or not. A true revolutionary will not be much affected by this book. He hears the voice; he knows, believes; he must go, go, go! Woe to the people against whom the voice directs him! He knows that he is right, and he will act accordingly. "And as for the angels," says Joan to those who will burn her, "I saw them with my own eyes, and you will get no more out of me about that." Master Jean de La Fontaine, who did as much as any other Frenchman to get her condemned, insisted with equal sureness that the Church Militant on earth, to which he, of course, belonged, was "well-composed" and could not err.

I defend these four rules. I urge violent moral actors to consider them carefully, to avoid falling into murderous excesses of doctrinairism. Perhaps it's not entirely impractical to follow the strategy summed up by the pacifist anarchist slogan "Minimize violence by emphasizing politics"—that is, to treat one's adversaries as human beings who share at least some of the same pains, hopes and goals as ourselves.

II.

REMEMBER THE VICTIM!

... and Judas said: "If it was prophesied that I should commit the world's greatest sin, is it then my fault?"

VILLY SØRENSEN

Did I ever believe that the most terrible ordeal guaranteed the most solemn wisdom?

MALRAUX, 1967

This book has dwelt, perhaps excessively, on shining or tarnished ends and on their violent means, which hang on the moral actor's wall, subject to all the principles of aestheticizing weapons. The bleeding objects of those ends we've seen in plenty. But each victim is also a *subject*. Violence being inflicted both by someone and on someone, its students often focus on the former, in hopes of understanding and controlling it "at the source." To Freud, violence is but the honesty-loving fellow who strips us naked, baring "the primal man in each of us. It constrains us once more to be heroes who cannot believe in their own death; it stamps the alien as the enemy, whose death is to be brought about or desired; it counsels us to rise above those we love." (To rise above them is, of course, to rise down.) He does not see how we can surmount war, only be less disillusioned by it through being willing to face our own deaths and the egotism with which we arm ourselves along the way. —And what about the deaths of others, violent or natural or in between?

In our three meditations on death we began in the catacombs, where death "natural" and "unnatural" reminds us of its universality, then we moved on to overhear the hard-nosed jests and bitterly compassionate seeking of the autopsy room, and finally bowed before the immensity of angry grief which deliberate violence inflicts, tearing each wound deeper, hovering over its victims, drinking in their screams. Thus we came closer and closer to the form of pure Violence itself. I spoke in that place of death's inimical human forms. But what of life's incarnations—the ones death kills? To put the question another way, what should this book have been about? Should I have devoted two hundred pages to one of Stalin's victims instead of to his agrarian policy? In my "Three Meditations on Death" and my many cameo depictions of victims, I've striven sincerely to remember violence's objects. One reader, Mr. Eli Horowitz, advises me that this chapter "needs a more explicit and direct focus on its own insufficiency. Currently, it seems like almost an afterthought, rather than an acknowledgement of the central counterpoint to the entire book."

When is violence justified? This is the concern of *Rising Up and Rising Down*. But it is all too easy to answer this question without remembering what violence *is:* not a shining weapon, but a person loathsomely, deliberately *hurt*. What of violence's incarnations?

To seek them out, let's make another journey.

Closer and Closer

"For me, death is irrelevant," said a Soviet lieutenant wounded in Afghanistan. "While I am, there is no death; when it comes, I won't be." Call that the farthest remove—or the extremest numbness—for, after all, he saw death, inflicted it, and half-suffered it. My companion D. had a friend who was a big bug in the police station in Yala City, and since that place lay in Thailand we could wander in unannounced, and her friend came right away, a uniformed old man with a generous helping of "fruit salad" on his chest, bowing, smiling; he seated us at his desk and brought us a stack of the latest multicolored newspapers (on the topmost, a color photo of somebody with a drowned girl in his arms); and a policewoman brought us two chilled Cokes; and every time the phone rang, D. picked it up for her absent friend and answered so helpfully, *"Kaa, kaa, kaa"* (yes, yes, yes); and we waited for her friend to come back to take us out to lunch, not disturbed by the presence of the drowned girl at all. Underneath her likeness was another newspaper proudly bearing a color photo of bloody corpses being dragged out from a smashed automobile. What were we to do about those people? And when we started meeting bomb-wise and machine-gun-wise killers and interviewing the families of their victims, it felt the same as finding more gruesome images. There *harm* was, and it would go on, and we could not stop it. We might have paid respect by being sad, but then we would always have to be sad. What to do?

Get a little closer, and you may become like my bank teller in Sacramento. In the fall of 1996 a robber ran in and shot somebody dead before her eyes. Shortly thereafter, her branch was bought by another bank, and she and her colleagues moved across the street. Two weeks later, the new bank was hit. No one died that time, but the robber was at her window. I asked her what she had thought and felt as she stood looking into his gun's steel snout. "I just did what he wanted," she said dully. "My husband and I watch thriller movies all the time. We know that if you don't do what they say, they kill you. I just gave him the money and tried not to think about what was happening." Closer still, you'll become the young woman from Sarajevo I met, the girl who had lost so many of her friends to snipers and shelling that she'd become "cold," as she put it; she just wouldn't, couldn't grieve anymore. Emmanuel Ringelblum, the chronicler of the Warsaw Ghetto, writes: "Almost daily people are falling dead or unconscious in the middle of the street. It no longer makes so direct an impression." Six months later the situation is worse, and he writes: "One walks past corpses with indifference." The author of a monograph on military Renaissance art confesses: 'We are not to expect that wounds, executions or burials were found 'pathetic' then."

For the year 1340 we read this entry in an Armenian chronicle:

The villainous Emir of Alep, under orders from Melik-Nacer the Sultan of Egypt, secretly invaded the territory of Sis and sacked it from top to bottom, massacring some [outright?], burning the others [alive], and carrying a portion of the inhabitants into slavery. The country of the Armenians, so rich in population, he left an empty waste.

We maintain our distance from the mass grave. The fourteenth century has receded into fabulousness; who can imagine the destruction of Sis, let alone believe in it? A little closer still to the lip of crumbling soil, and we meet Erich Maria Remarque with his empty trench dawns and rat-riddled trench nights where soldiers lie with their gas masks on, waiting for the poison clouds. Dead soldiers lie in blood and dirt, their faces smeared with blood and dirt. "We are deadened by the strain—a deadly tension that scrapes along one's spine like a gapped knife." Numbness need not mean indifference; often, it's repression of terror. Listen to my Bosnian friend Vahida, who when I met her during the siege of her home city, almost paralyzed by apprehension and grief, whispered only: "It's too difficult to explain." Four years later she sent me this letter:

> Until June '96 I may stay here in Germany, but after that, it's almost certain that I'll have to go back to Bosnia, back to Sarajevo. On that account I'm very ill at ease. You know already, I don't want that. I have so much fear about going back there to live. This is perhaps difficult to understand. Sometimes not even I myself can understand it . . . I ask myself what we'll all do, when I come back. No one can make any money there . . . I don't know if you've sometimes felt this way, that everything is giving way under your feet.

Difficult to explain, difficult to understand—numbness, hopelessness! She wanted to keep violence at a distance; thinking about it made her want to scream . . . A quarter-century earlier, it was no different for the Vietcong: "Caked in dried blood and sweat, we dragged our rifles and our dead on our backs . . . We marched, stunned by exhaustion and despair." But still those soldiers eat, play cards and defecate; they cannot exist in suspended animation; they too must live, numb to the smell of rotting bodies. Some become strangers to pity; others achieve an almost Buddhist freedom from attachment, fighting, killing and dying in a state of shell-shocked silence, madness, indifference or fatalism serene or otherwise. Closer still—don't be afraid!—come meet the *Sonderkommando* of a concentration camp. They pull apart the heap of blue corpses, break out gold teeth, hose the piss, puke, shit and menstrual blood out of the gas chamber, then haul blue flesh to the crematoria. That's all they do—their lives are nothing but death, and for them there's not even a soldier's chance: at regular intervals the entire *Sonderkommando* is liquidated. —What do they think about (aside from food)? How do they feel? I suppose that the key word must be expediency, as in the case of the Japanese soldier who during the same epoch of worldwide slaughter kicked dying Chinese out of his way. "I didn't harbor any ill feeling toward them," he recalled. And when such people did harbor ill feeling, as recounted in Tadeusz Borowski's concentration camp tales, no matter how personally it might be expressed against some victim, it was in effect merely the accidental expression of an impersonal animus of fear, frustration, hatred, sadness and bitterness—how can mass murder be personal? "Part of our existence lies in the feelings of those near to us," says Primo Levi. "That is really why the experience of someone who has lived for days during which man was merely a thing in the eyes of man is non-human." —Closer still, and you'll see your family die at Hiroshima, which just might make you numb "sometimes within minutes or even seconds," or maybe instead you'll be packed inside the gas chamber yourself (one person per square foot)—then, when one of the on-rushing deaths is indisputably yours, you'll probably be pricked out of your numbness by the needles of terror and agony, but only for a moment; then you'll be numb forever.

The Source

It is perhaps *only* aesthetics, the sensual apprehension of the results of violence, which can prevent us from being numbed, like genocidal bureaucrats whose "apparent cynicism," it has been written, "involves psychic maneuvers . . . that permit them to know very well about, and yet never really *feel,* the drastic implications of [nuclear] deterrence." This is why I, a novelist, took it on myself to write this book. But whatever talent I have should *frame,* not translate, the victims' speech. Let them speak. They experienced violence. They know. We must respect their knowledge.

One teenage girl, T., who'd been gang-shot at a traffic light in Los Angeles wrote me:

So you may see since the incident everything has turned, and like i've been telling everyone since the beginning of the year "This isn't going to be my year." You may say that i think negatively but these are the sort of images that i see in my dreams and one thing that bothers me is that they have to come true . . . And it was so funny when i read your letter and you said "try not to get angry or scared", because i actually felt really angry. Mostly because for some dumb asses reason i'm paying for the consicuences [consequences] not him/her. All i've wanted to do is finish school and graduate and since this has happened i've fallen behind.

More than half a century earlier, a hungry, friendless Soviet citizen who'd served more than one sentence in the Gulag camps and would later be shot was writing in his diary:

They dig up from somewhere an awful evaluation from Vishera, stating in no uncertain terms that I am an incorrigible prisoner . . . I immediately sense I'm not going anywhere, not now, and not after I've served my time either. This new way of lying, this collusion of actions against a man when he is to be destroyed, hit me so hard that I just crumbled psychologically and aged several years, right on the spot. But it is so natural: they sense the truth and can't forgive us our protests against their violence.

These two paragraphs express identical feelings. My friend T. never knew the gangsters who shot her, nor they her; she suffered what might almost be called an accidental assault. It could have been anyone at that intersection. Citizen Arzhilovsky, on the other hand, happened to belong to the wrong class. His shooting would be equally inevitable—because it happened—and perhaps equally impersonal, although his tormentor-murderers knew him and planned his liquidation in advance; they'd already dekulakized him. The moral ends of the two sets of shooters could not have been more different. And yet these two hopeless, negativistic, bitterly blighted hearts are brother and sister. Means and end—aren't they nearly always irrelevant to those who must suffer the agony of their infliction?

THE MORAL CALCULUS

The dull empiricism, the unashamed, cringing worship of the fact which is so often imaginary, and falsely interpreted at that, were odious to me. Beyond the facts, I looked for laws.

TROTSKY, *My Life*

But if ye will need have the law, I also have my law.

MARTIN LUTHER, "Commentary on Galatians"

Robespierre was not above using what Marat called "a very simple calculus."

MONA OZOUF, Essay on Marat

. . . Genius . . . raises itself above all rules. . . . but when we reach those ranks where we can look for no other notions but those which the regulations of the service and experience afford, we must help them with the methodic forms bordering on those regulations. This will serve both as a support to their judgment and a barrier against those extravagant and erroneous views which are so especially to be dreaded in a sphere where experience is so costly.

CLAUSEWITZ, *On War*

The greater part of what my neighbors call good, I believe in my soul to be bad, and if I repent of anything, it is likely to be of my good behavior.

THOREAU, *Walden*

An excuse is as good as gold.

A SERB ON THE TRAIN

To conjure up a conscience in others is tempting to anyone who wishes to extend his control beyond the legal limits.

GARETT HARDIN

You refuse to understand that since vices exist, it is as unjust for you to punish them as it would be to jeer at a one-eyed man.

MARQUIS DE SADE

Blessed are those who hunger and thirst for righteousness, for they shall be satisfied.

JESUS CHRIST, The Sermon on the Mount

Being noble isn't important. Saving lives is important.

"VIRGINIA," Animal Liberation Front Member

If I were at the place of execution, and I saw the fire lighted, and the faggots catching and the executioner ready to build up the fire, even so I would say nothing else, and I would maintain what I have said at this trial until death. I have nothing more to say.

JOAN OF ARC

Contents

Apology and disclaimer

The two kinds of justice *vs.* the two kinds of injustice
After 3.16: General violence scale
 Severity scale for violence inflicted upon the vanquished
 Retaliation: A continuum of severity

[4.0] When is nonviolence unjustified or insufficient to achieve its aims? [1–3]

[5.0] When is violence justified? [1–4]
Debatable justifications listed here in subsections appended to each relevant category.
 [5.0] The Machiavellian Caveat
 [5.1] Definitions for lonely atoms [1–8]
  The fundamental violent rights of the self [1–3]
  Some fundamental collective rights [4–5]
  Guides to individual and collective justifiability [6–7]
  The right to individual and collective freedom of expression [8]
 [5.2] Justifications: Defense of [a–m]
  a. Honor [1–3]
  b. Class [1–5]
   1. Justifications which may or may not be justifiable [a–d]
  c. Authority [1–2]
   1. Preexisting ("legitimate") [1–4]
    a. When may it enlarge itself? [1–2]
   2. Revolutionary [1–4]
  d. Race and Culture [1–5]
  e. Creed [4]
  f. War Aims [1]
  g. Homeland [1–2]
  h. Ground [1]
  i. Earth [1–3]
  j. Animals [1–3]
  k. Gender [1–5]
  l. [against] Traitors [1–2]
  m. Revolution [1–2]
 [5.3] Justifications: Policy and choice
  a. Deterrence, retribution and revenge [1–3]
   1. Deterrence [1–4]
   2. Retribution [1]

3. Revenge [1]
b. Punishment [1–6]
   1. Justifications which may or may not be justifiable [a–j]
c. Loyalty, compulsion and fear [1–2]
   1. Compulsion and fear [1]
   2. Loyalty [1–2]
d. Sadism and expediency [1]
e. Consensual sadism (S/M) [1]
[5.4] Justifications: Fate [a–b]
a. Moral yellowness [1]
b. Inevitability [1]

[6.0] When is violence unjustified? [0–4]
[6.0] General rules [1–12]
[6.1] Definitions for lonely atoms: [1]
When is violent defense of self-justified?
[When is violent defense of others justified? See 1.2.2.a.]
[6.2] Justifications: Defense of [a–m]:
a. Honor [1–5]
b. Class [1–9]
c. Authority [2]
   1. Preexisting ("legitimate") [1–9]
   2. Revolutionary [1–5]
d. Race and Culture [1–4]
e. Creed [2]
f. War Aims [1–4]
g. Homeland [1–3]
h. Ground [1]
i. Earth [1]
j. Animals [1–2]
k. Gender [1]
l. [against] Traitors [1]
m. Revolution [1]
[6.3] Justifications: Policy and choice
a. Deterrence, retribution and revenge [1–3]
   1. Deterrence [1–9]
   2. Retribution [1–3]
   3. Revenge [1–2]

b. Punishment [1–7]
c. Loyalty, compulsion and fear [1–2]
   1. Compulsion and fear [1–3]
   2. Loyalty [1–3]
d. Sadism and expediency [1]
e. Consensual sadism (S/M) [1]
[6.4] Justifications: Fate [a–b]
a. Moral yellowness [1]
b. Inevitability [1]

[7.0] When is violence unjustified but excusable?

[8.0] A Checklist for Revolutionaries

Definitions

Aloofness, of a race, culture, bloodline or organization: 5.2.D.2

Animals, defense of, legitimate: 5.2.J.3

Animals, dismissal of (absolute and relative; Mary Midgley's def.): 6.2.J.1

Animals, identity of: 5.2.J.4

Animals, imminent physical harm to: 5.2.J.3

Authority, illegitimate (descriptive defs.): 6.2.C.1.9

Authority, preexisting, legitimate: 5.2.C.1

Authority, revolutionary, legitimate: 5.2.C.2

Authority, rights of: 5.2.C.1.4

Carrying capacity of the environment: 5.2.I.1

Class (function, status by function or merit, property, rank, origin): 5.2.B

Creed, and defense of creed: 5.2.E

Creed, morally opaque: 5.2.E.1

Creed, morally transparent: 5.2.E.1

Defense, legitimate, indications of: 5.0

Deterrence: 5.3.A.1

Deterrence threshold (Herman Kahn's def.): 6.3.A.1.9

Discrimination: 5.2.F.1

   and *tu quoque* defense: 6.3.A.3

Dismissal of animals (absolute and relative; Mary Midgley's def.):
   6.2.J.1

Earth: 5.2.I

Ecological threat: 5.2.I.1

End: 2.0

Ethos: 5.2.G.2

First Law of Violent Action: 5.1.2.A.2

Futurity [of homeland]: 6.2.G.2

The Galapagos Maxim: 5.2.D

Gender (inner, outer): 5.2.K

Gender, aggression against aspects of: 5.2.K

General Will [vs. particular will and will of all; Rousseau's def.]:
   5.2.M.2

Golden Rule and variants: 1.2.1–1.2.6

Ground and defense of ground: 5.2.H

The Herdsman's Calculus: 5.2.I.2

Homeland: 5.2.G

Homeland, futurity of: 6.2.G.2

Honor (inner, outer, individual, collective): 5.2.A

Honor, illegitimate: 6.2.A.4

Identity of an animal: 5.2.J.4

Identity of a place: 5.2.I.3

Imminence, "ordinary": 5.1.1

Imminence, proactive: 6.3.A.1.6

Imminence, scientific [applicable only to defense of earth]: 5.2.I.1

Imminent physical harm to animals: 5.2.J.3

   Unjustified: 5.1.1a

Interest: 6.2.G.1

Justifications: 2.0

Apology and Disclaimer

The following principles of conduct were all extracted (verbatim whenever possible) from the text thus far. Ethics not yet being a circumstantially exact science (should it ever become so, free will and cultural variability might be compromised), we shouldn't expect that this or any moral calculus will of itself permit every rational user to arrive at the same judgment of a given case. Benjamin Franklin used to divide a sheet of paper into two columns, one in favor of a decision, the other against. "And tho' the Weight of Reasons cannot be taken with the Precision of Algebraic Quantities, . . . I have found great Advantage from this kind of Equation, in what may be called *Moral* or *Prudential Algebra*." Much of this procedure indeed makes common sense, but its sums, variables and formulas necessarily or unnecessarily rests upon vaguely defined terms. Plato's moral calculus differs from Cortes's, not least because their definitions of piety are different. Moses's Ten Commandments leave Lenin cold, in part on account of disagreements over the defined range and domain of that variable called Man: Does it include or dominate Woman? May it be substituted for God? Do its characteristics alter with its productive class?

Should you find fault with the calculus, as you ought to (I do my best to find fault with everybody else's; and my chapter on defense of animals remains especially unsatisfactory), I respectfully ask you not to leave a vacuum, but to construct your own. The translator of two old collections of Zen koans has noted that there is no "correct" answer to a koan, and, indeed, one student's right answer may be wrong if uttered by another. Which does one put first, defense of gender, which might repudiate female circumcision, or defense of culture, which might demand it? When does defense of race (one's own family) supersede defense of homeland? My moral calculus cannot tell you that. However, what it can do is to remind you that if you consider only one of those two categories of defense, your judgment will remain superficial, unfair, and therefore unrealistic. Can defense of gender meet defense of culture somewhere? I hope and believe so, provided that both sides respect each other by applying some approximation of the Golden Rule.

More generally, I believe that along the continuum of answers to moral-political koans we can hope to find a broad and sometimes generous but not excessive width of reasonable consensus. Yes, the divergence may at times widen far enough to allow for more than one specific "right" choice—for example, in the case of Caesar *versus* Pompey—for people and situations less frequently dazzle us with the pinpoint light of self-evident truth than with the diffuse glare of ambiguity. Still and all, the question of when violence is justified need not be left entirely unanswered.

On the subject of consensus, please note that this quality, on which I've tried to found my definition of the legitimate authority [5.2.C.1] to carry out many acts of violence, simply does not exist for the following categories: ethos of homeland [5.2.G.2], identity of race [5.2.D.2], place [5.2.I.3] and animals [5.2.J.4], ecological threat [5.2.I.1], inalienable qualities of creed [5.2.E]. More traditional categories such as class inevitably provoke irreconcilable differences of opinion, but it remains possible to argue out those differences based on common presuppositions about fundamental human rights [5.1.1–3, 5.1.18]. Such presuppositions have scarcely begun to evolve for the categories mentioned here. I would be very proud if *Rising Up and Rising Down* encouraged anyone to add a mite to the long process of establishing some broad or minimal agreement on such questions as: What right do we grant an ancient redwood grove to remain as it is? Which alien ethos of creed, homeland or race can we tolerate; and when do customs which some people consider abhorrent, such as hunting, justify violent intervention? Does a white separatist have the same rights as a black separatist? I have done my own poor best to wrestle with these questions; if the results are half-baked, please heap your own most inflammatory prejudices onto the fire, and help with the cooking.

The best way to apply this calculus to a particular act is to examine the rules for every sort of justification which might possibly be applicable to it. What claim to righteousness might a Palestinian suicide bomber possess? To evaluate that claim, one could apply the calculus to him—and to his enemies—regarding (1) the *justifications* concerning (a) homeland, (b) creed, (c) war aims (not neglecting proportionality and discrimination), (d) ground, (e) honor and (f) authority; (2) the *policies* of (a) deterrence, (b) retaliation and (c) punishment; and (3) the *fate-invocation* of inevitability. Then, and only then, can one begin to employ Franklin's moral algebra.

When one commits violence, it is more likely that it will be unjustified than justified. Therefore, I would advise that if an act seems by the rules of section 6 to be classified as evil, it should be treated as suspect at best. On the other hand, if the act seems to obey all the rules for justification listed in section 5, it should be treated as—somewhat less suspect. At its most noble, an act which passes all the tests of section 5 can only be said to *tend* toward being justified. Since these rules necessarily remain vague, and their interpretation open to opinion, no one test is sure; and **5.1.6** should be kept in mind. Calculus-lessness reliably produces amoral brutality; but, as Clausewitz reminds us, methodicism easily becomes stupidity. We must seek out the truth of each particular case.

[1.0] What Is the Best Way to Seek the Truth?

1. In solitude. A member of any organization can hardly without visiting the darkly mysterious world of nonorganization comprehend the truth about his organization—that is, the truth of what *he* has done and caused. I have seen and applauded Julius Caesar's clemency to my fellow Romans, but have I taken counsel with myself to see whether the purpose in whose service he so leniently fights is equally applaudable?

2. . . . And in diverse company. A hermit may come to know himself, but unless he listens to others, and sees the happiness and suffering of others, he cannot know if what seems right for him will also be right for others. Moreover, a witness *knows* (even if he misunderstands what he knows). How could a Spaniard fairly judge the Mexican Conquest, without first inquiring of remnant Aztecs?

3. . . . And through history. The world was different once. Learn what today's truth has in common with yesterday's. Hitler invokes defense of homeland. So does Lycurgus the Spartan. My President invokes it today. Which of those two predecessors, if either, does he more faithfully resemble?

4. . . . And through service. He who helps not, cares not. He who cares not, possesses no right to guide other lives.

5. . . . And through the commission of error, and through patient revision. "No organic law can ever be framed with a provision specifically applicable to every question which may occur in practical administration." This moral calculus is the best I could do. I hope that studying its successes and failures may help you to do better than I have done.

6. . . . And by eliminating the redundant terms and categories which make it difficult to distinguish a locally valid axiom from a universal one— or from a tautology. "A war of the Soviet Union against an imperialist aggressor would be a just war" really means "a war against an aggressor would be a just war."

Experience alone, and theoretical grounding alone, falter. Hence the two parts of this book. Context must inform the act that we judge, but it cannot predetermine the judgment.

[1.1] How to Form a Moral Code

1. Follow your own inner logic and feeling in order to postulate laws of conduct which seem to you good;

2. Follow those laws if they correspond to local norms, and reconsider them if they violate those norms; but

3. Above all, choose the right regardless of local authority or custom, and then act accordingly, with due regard to:

The First Law of Violent Action: *The inertia of the situation into which we inject ourselves must always be given the benefit of the doubt. Look before you leap.*

which can be restated:

Assume any potential victim of your violence to be as worthy of self-preservation as yourself, until that assumption has been disproven by the remainder of your moral calculus.

4. Follow the Golden Rule where possible. And give it the most generous possible interpretation. In other words, follow the Empath's Golden Rule [1.2.b].

a. The Golden Rule becomes more valid than ever in reference to one's dependents.

b. We bear an obligation to study and intuit the identity of the other, his rights and needs, his appropriate mode of self-expression, his ethos. That is the only way to know how he wishes to be done by.

[1.2] Variations of the Golden Rule

1. **The Golden Rule:** *Do as you would be done by.* But in the event that I would wish others to do unto me something which others would not wish for themselves, then the Golden Rule would not be justified. In fact, it would become the Zealot's Golden Rule. [Mostly justified.]

COROLLARY: Personalizing a situation may help prevent violence: the Golden Rule warns and guards. However, personalizing an already violent situation could make it worse because witnessing outrages committed on the Golden Rule inclines us to bitterness.

EXAMPLE: In the Yugoslavian Civil War I may resist the temptation to cut throats if I realize: It will be my neighbor's throat that I must cut! But once I've cut my neighbor's throat, my violence has surpassed the limit; I've done worse than cut a stranger's throat; my neighbor's children may never forgive me.

CAVEAT: The Golden Rule is justified only when applied to acts which all parties affected agree will contribute to their conception of goodness, or when the dissenting party is a bona fide dependent of the moral actor.

Otherwise it easily becomes the Zealot's Golden Rule.

[Throughout *Rising Up and Rising Down,* this caveat will be assumed.]

2. **The Empath's Golden Rule:** *Do unto others, not only as you would be done by, but also as they would be done by. In the case of any variance, do the more generous thing.* [Justified.]

3. **The Zealot's Golden Rule:** *Do unto others as you are doing for yourself.* Cortes exemplifies this fallacy: I am a Christian, so I'll force everyone else to be Christians. "Do unto others" can be justified only when applied to acts which *all* affected parties agree will contribute to goodness as they define it, or when the dissenting party is a dependent of the moral actor. [Unjustified.] [Compare with **1.3.2.**]

(VARIANT A) **The Missionary's Golden Rule:** *Do unto others as you convince yourself they would be done by.* [Unjustified.]

EXAMPLE: Cortes again: "Truth to tell, it is war and warriors that really persuade the Indians to give up their idols . . . and it is thus that of their own free will and consent they more quickly . . . accept the Gospel."

(VARIANT B) **The Marxist's Golden Rule:** *Do unto some others as you convince yourself they would be done by, and do to the rest whatever your end requires.* [Unjustified.]

EXAMPLE: The Bolsheviks "give" land to "the people" by forcibly enrolling them in collective farms while expelling and repressing rich peasants.

4. The Soldier's Golden Rule: *Do unto others as you are done by.* He shoots at me, so I'll shoot at him. This reduces moral actors to moral reactors. [Always justified in situations of imminent self-defense. Unjustified as a general moral code.]

5. The Terrorist's Golden Rule: *Do as your end requires.* This places the moral actor beyond anyone else's judgment. [Unjustified.]

6. The Golden Rule of Greek City-States: *Let others do unto others whatever doesn't affect me.* [Unjustified or not? Certainly very callous.]

[1.3] Maxims for Murderers

The following propositions are of a rough-and-ready character; a murderer needs no others. Other murderers can add to them, and ought to, to help them feel righteous afterward. The rest of us may consider them as beacons warning us away from evil shoals.

1. The Antichrist's Maxim: *If you were once an enemy, then you will always be.* By making reconciliation impossible, this perpetuates violence.

2. John Brown's Maxim: *If you refuse to follow the Golden Rule, then I have the right to use terror to impel you to follow it.* Very similar to the Zealot's Golden Rule [1.2.3].

3. Caesar's Maxim: *Should I extend mercy beyond expediency, then I have right to commit whatever aggression I please.*

4. Cleon the Athenian's Maxim: *"It is a general rule of human nature that people despise those who treat them well and look up to those who make no concessions."* This too makes reconciliation impossible. It approaches the viciously literalist Marxist-Leninist interpretation of the class struggle.

5. Cortes's Maxim: *In order to secure and defend my ground, I have every right to conquer yours.*

6. **The Crocodile's Maxim:** *If we lost the last war, it's a grievance. If we won the last war, it's the status quo.*

7. **Hitler's Maxim:** *Your homeland ought to belong to me, so I have the right to defend it against you.*

8. **Field Marshal Keitel's Maxim:** *"For a soldier, orders are orders!"*

9. **The Klansman's Maxim:** *If I believe your race or culture threatens mine, I have the right first to threaten you back, then to remove your threat by violence.* In its readiness to give sole discretion for judging means and ends to the perpetrator of violence ("If I believe . . . I have the right"), this maxim recalls Trotsky's [**1.3.12**].

10. **Napoleon's Maxim:** *Once I reify collective honor into standards and monuments, you must bleed for them. [The short form: "All honor is honorable."]* This translates into **The Terrorist's Golden Rule.**

11. **Shaka's Maxim:** *"If a foe were worth conquering at all, he was worth crushing out of existence once and for all."*

12. **Trotsky's Maxim:** *No one who disagrees with me is allowed to judge me.* Again, this is a variant of the Terrorist's Golden Rule [**1.2.5**].

13. **The Victim's Maxim:** *If any members of your side harmed any members of my side, then your side is completely in the wrong.*

    a. **The Victim's Corollary:** *Any moderate on my own side is an enemy.*

    b. **The Second Victim's Corollary:** *If you are not "one of us," I need neither trust you nor recognize your service.*

[1.4] Maxims for Tyrants

These may not necessarily be as lethal as the Maxims for Murderers, but they still promote violence, injustice and death.

    1. **Plato's Maxim Made Politic:** *No man will prove a creditable servant— unless we can keep him a servant for all time!*

    2. **The Slavemaster's Maxim:** *If I was born better than you, I have the right to rule you.*

Practically speaking, this is indistinguishable from Cleon the Athenian's Maxim.

[1.5] Maxims for Self-Defenders

In my opinion, these can be trusted, provided that each word is employed with honest literalness.

1. **The Shepherd's Maxim:** *As authority enlarges itself, its obligation to protect from violence the individuals it controls increases, and the ability of those individuals to defend themselves from violence correspondingly decreases.*

COROLLARY: Because the right to self-defense remains inalienable, each of us can and should maintain a self-reliant distrust of authority.

2. **The Weapons Owner's Maxim:** *When authority cannot protect me, I must protect myself.*

[2.0] Means and Ends

• An **end** is the goal of, or reason for, one's violence. It may be very simple and practical (for instance, the right of the self to defend itself from violence, or not), or it may hover in the sky like the dreams of most religions: close or distant prospects of improvement, revolution, salvation, security, etc.

EXAMPLE: When John Brown's son Watson lay captured and dying, a proslavery South Carolinian asked him why he had participated in the raid on Harpers Ferry. —"Duty, sir," said Watson.

Ends are just or unjust, but they are only ends; they harm no one until their disciples lift the cudgels of means.

EXAMPLE: Hitler's end can be judged (and found wanting) according to all the rights of the self [5.1.1–3, 5.1.18]. Simply stated, it is: "The people I define as Aryans will conquer as much of the world as possible and use it as their living-space." Hitler begins to put this unjust goal into unjust execution, and the Allies declare war. On the other hand, when neo-Nazis march through the streets of Skokie, Illinois, the American Civil Liberties Union rightly assists them; a march is only a march; suppressing speech is *always* less justifiable than permitting it. (Jefferson: "The opinions of men are not the object of civil government, nor under its jurisdiction." No matter that civil government protects those opinions by applying Turnbull's Maxim [5.2.D.5].)

• A **means** no one can be sure of in advance, because it belongs to praxis, to implementation, to the interaction between strategy and an unpredictable world. After its enaction, the means becomes the act we've judged: the dead body, the revolution or burned city.

• **Justifications** are the links between ends and means. "I committed this act for that reason." A justification may be justified, unjustified or debatable.

EXAMPLES:

1. Imminent self-defense, if true, is always justified by the rights of the self [**5.1.1–3**].

2. Defense of homeland is Leonidas's justification at Thermopylae, and also Hitler's in Russia; in the first case it is justified, in the second, unjustified.

3. Advancing society is one justification for class warfare which is justified or not depending on one's presuppositions.

• **Rising up:** A just act of violence. Both means and ends are legitimate.

• **Rising down:** An unjust act of violence. Means, ends or both fail to meet legitimacy's standard.

1. An unjust means or an unjust end equally invalidates all derivative moral enactions.

2. A just end may be served by a just or by an unjust means. Either way, the end itself has not been compromised in and of itself.

EXAMPLE: The fact that Trotsky might have shot innocent people for the noblest reasons cannot degrade those reasons from their nobility.

But an unjust end possesses no just means. And an unjust means, deliberately carried out [**see 5.2.A.2**], decreases the relevance of any end to the justifiability of the act which invokes it, and may nullify even the best end.

EXAMPLE: No end, noble or base, could justify the Holocaust.

3. The effects of any revolution, crime, rescue, or war cannot be anything but temporary and local. Therefore, every end remains (in its immediate expression) temporary and local. All the more reason for its means to be finite and limited.

a. An inconstant end is a warning: *Danger of deceitful or outright evil expediency.*

b. Precisely because these effects are local (finite), they may well be delayed. They may also cause temporary ill effects in the service of the greater good. Patience is required to determine their success and ultimate justifiability. At the same time, the moral actors who've caused those ill effects must stand accountable, and offer us proof that the good will indeed outweigh the bad.

EXAMPLE: Churchill writes about the 16.5 million people murdered in Stalin's collectivization drive: "A generation would no doubt come to whom their miseries were unknown, but it would be sure of having more to eat and bless Stalin's name." That generation never arrived. Peter L. Berger wrote: "I see no possible moral calculus that would retroactively justify the nightmares of the 1920s and 1930s in terms of the Soviet gross national product of the 1960s . . ."

c. Collective justice (or not) sometimes disburses unavoidable individual injustice. (The same goes for attempts at individual justice.) Imminence [5.1.1], ignorance of actual circumstances, and miscellaneous collective necessities, especially in war and revolution, bring about this result.

EXAMPLE: Applying deterrence and retribution to a Turkish atrocity, Lawrence of Arabia refuses to take prisoners at Tafas. Whether or not his massacre was in any sense justified, some of the individuals he cut down might have been innocent of the crime he was punishing.

4. "One must scrupulously avoid the temptation of a desire for results," says Gandhi, referring to *nonviolence*. [*Very limited case.*]

CAVEAT: This is *only* true (for both violence and nonviolence) if:

a. one's attachment to the end is absolute [in which case lack of results is only a disappointment, not a deterrent],

EXAMPLE: One side fights on in a lost war. Antoine de Saint-Exupéry: "War is not the acceptance of danger. It is not the acceptance of combat. For the combatant, it is at certain moments the pure and simple acceptance of death."

and if possible

b. the means harms only those people who stand ready to be harmed.

CAVEAT: Authority usually compels its subjects to sacrifice themselves, ready or not. In short, in daily life (b) gets violated.

Far more often, achieving results, or holding the reasonable expectation of achieving them, is essential to justify violence.

* * *

GENERAL RULE: Violence cannot be justified, even by the noblest end, should the means be ineffective.

> EXAMPLE: The nuclear bomb dropped on Hiroshima, morally dubious though it was, might have been at least arguably justifiable (by imminent self-defense), but not without reason to believe that its use would save lives by shortening the war.

Possible motivations for dropping the bomb:

> a. To save American and Japanese lives. [*Justifiable.*]
>
> b. To prevent the USSR from entering the war and claiming too great a share of the spoils. [*Unjustifiable.*]
>
> c. To field-test the weapon. [*Unjustifiable.*]
>
> d. To overawe the USSR. [*Unjustifiable.*]

5. The most illuminating way to perceive the shoddiness of your own ideals is to witness someone else practicing them.

6. Insofar as a cause is just, it ought to be open to all. To the extent that a cause is exclusive, it loses worthiness. (I repeat these words in the specific sections on defense of race and gender [**5.2.D.2 and 5.2.K.2**], because adherents of those causes in particular, which have to do with biological specificity and exclusion, sometimes forget that *every* just end includes all of us.)

[3.0] What Factors Need to Be Considered in Judging Any Violent Act?

1. What is the relationship between the aggressor and the victim?

The same physical act will have very different meanings if committed in wartime or in peacetime, by authority upon a criminal or by a criminal upon a householder, etc. How many victims are involved, and how were they selected?

> CAVEAT: In evaluating the aggressor and victim's judgments of one another, remember that there is almost never any "moral yellowness," any physiognomy of good or evil. [See **5.4.A** and **6.4.A**.]

2. Is the aggressor acting on his own behalf or is he an agent?

Is he acting under compulsion, loyalty or fear [**5.3.C.1–2, 6.3.C.1–2**], or is he acting of his own free will? Does he understand the end? Does he control the means, or is he merely someone else's means?

CAVEAT: When a deed is committed under the aegis of a hierarchy of authority, we who judge must superimpose a corresponding hierarchy of moral responsibility. Scared and ignorant triggermen are not as culpable as their commanders. This supplements rather than contradicts the principle that we ought to judge each other as individuals, not as members of various categories.

3. Has the victim been attacked for no reason at all, for no personal reason, for reasons connected intimately with who he is, or what he does, or in his capacity as an agent?

Is he simply, like so many casualties of gangland shootings, in the wrong place at the wrong time? Does the attack occur simply because he appears elderly enough to rob, because she is alone enough to rape, because they are of the wrong color or class? Or is the motive one of hatred for this particular individual? Does the victim fly the colors of an enemy state?

REASONS TO HARM A SPECIFIED PERSON

[1–6: Possibly justified, but progressively less likely to be so.]

1. What you've done. (You physically attacked me.)

2. What you are: allegiance. (You wear the uniform of the enemy army.)

3. What you haven't done. (You evince neutrality toward my behavior when I need your help.)

4. Whom you associate with. (Your best friend is in category 1.)

5. What you might do. (You could conceivably end up in categories 1, 2, 3 or 4.)

6. What you have. (You are rich and I am not, so I'll rob and kill you.) [See 5.2.B and 6.2.B.]

[7–8: Never justified.]

7. What you are: biological, religious or ideological identity. (You are a Jew, and I hate Jews.) [Hence this formation of Trotsky's, while not proven to be equivalent to Rule 7, is very suspect: "It is not only a question of what is being done, but also of who does it."]

8. The fact that you are. (You exist, and any victim will do.)

These reasons would be located thus on the Lutheran diagram of justice.

THE TWO KINDS OF JUSTICE VS. THE TWO KINDS OF INJUSTICE

1. RECEIVED GOODNESS	VS.	1. RECEIVED EVIL
You are what I consider good.		You are what I consider evil.

[nos. 7, 8]

[nos. 2, 4, 5, 6]

2. ACTIVE GOODNESS	VS.	2. ACTIVE EVIL
You do what I consider good.	[nos. 1,3]	You do what I consider evil.

4. *What is the victim's judgment of the act?*

A victim's consent or even fervid participation (for instance, that of a minor upon whom statutory rape is committed) may not necessarily render the act justifiable. Contrariwise, a victim's extreme anguish and condemnation of the act (as in the case of a robber who dies in a lawful homicide) may not make the act unjustifiable. However, the victim's circumstances and feelings remain relevant. Cutting off the hand of a thief will be more acceptable in a Muslim country which follows the Qur-'An's law, the shariat, than in a western country which follows the Geneva Conventions. [See **5.3b** and **6.3b.**]

5. *What is the victim's judgment of the aggressor's judgment of the victim's judgment and probable response?*

The necessity of admitting this seemingly arcane point is borne out by requoting that extract from the Babylonian Talmud: "What is the reason for the [permission to kill the] burglar? No man controls himself when his money is at stake, and since he [the burglar] knows that he [the owner] will oppose him, he thinks: If he resists me I shall kill him, therefore the Torah says: If a man has come to kill you, anticipate him by killing him!" This projection by each antagonist of the other's intentions may be extended as relevant.

6. *What is the victim's response?*

Has the aggressor correctly anticipated it? If so, then certain types of violence, such as proactive self-defense, may perhaps be justified in this case.

7. *What is the aggressor's end?*

Is it moral? Is it good? Is it justified? If not, or if there be no end, the act is unjustified. If so, the act may or may not be justified.

8. *What is the aggressor's means?*

In actual fact this will be the first question answered, for it translates as: What is the violent act itself? Does it cause death or harm? Does it involve torture? How imminent is the victim's right to violent self-defense?

　　9. What is the aggressor's judgment of his own means?

Does he extenuate or justify himself? If not, what does that say about the act?

　　10. What is the victim's judgment of the aggressor's means?

Do the answers to this question and the previous one correspond with my own judgment? If not, why do they differ, and whose assessments ought to be followed?

　　11. Is the aggressor's end justified?

If not, then acting against it is probably justified.

　　12. Is the aggressor's means justified in relation to the act?

Homicide, for instance, may be justified in the defense of one's life. It is not justified merely out of loyalty to some authority (although some circumstances, e.g.; a war, may render the loyalty defense more justified).

　　13. Could the means be unjustified but excusable? [See 7.0.]

　　14. What is the aggressor's judgment of the act?

If the act is punishable by the victim's standards, is it punishable by the aggressor's standards also? [See question 7, this sec., above.] The answer to this may possibly determine the quality of retribution, judicial or otherwise, which will be called for.

　　15. What is the context of the act?

Whether or not it is immediately justified, does it comprise a part of larger act, and if so, is that justified or not? To what extent does this war comprise a continuation of the last war? Is imminent self-defense acceptable in the context of an aggressive act?

　　16. How violent is the act?

How may violence be quantified? What is violence? Does it include, as householders and corporations insist, and ecodefenders deny, destruction against property? How severe is it? See the three scales immediately following.

SCALES USED IN PLOTTING CONTINUA AND CHARTS

GENERAL VIOLENCE SCALE

　1　Never acceptable. (Gandhi.)

2 Wrong as a rule, but not necessarily blameworthy if caused by intolerable provocation. (Late M. L. King.)

3 An acceptable last resort. (Lincoln.)

4 Acceptable against aliens, but against one's own kind. (Caesar, Leonidas?)

5 An acceptable way of achieving one's end. (John Brown, Cortes, Robespierre, Trotsky?)

6 Generally the most appropriate means. (Hitler, Stalin.)

7 An end. (Sade.)

SEVERITY SCALE (FOR VIOLENCE INFLICTED UPON THE VANQUISHED)

0 Full liberty to the surrendered.

1 Hostages / fines required.

2 Exemplary executions of "ringleaders."

3 Mass enslavement, mutilation, or pillage.

4 Mass executions.

5 Extermination.

CAVEATS

1. This scale represents only acts of physical violence. It cannot represent acts of territorial or political violence, such as Caesar's installation of Cleopatra on the Egyptian throne, or the intimidation tactics of the Animal Liberation Front.

2. Atrocities committed in combat, even on probable noncombatants, are not represented.

3. Proportionality forces us to give to the massacre of 30 out of 30 prisoners a higher severity score than the massacre of 500 out of 1,000.

[4.0] When Is Nonviolence Unjustified, Deficient or Insufficient to Achieve Its Aims?

When it is directed against violence *and:*

1. When the sacrifice entailed by the practitioner of nonviolence does not have sufficient intellectual or emotional justification.

EXAMPLE OF SUCH A JUSTIFICATION (from an American anti-nuclear pamphlet): "It is important to remember that we have made a positive choice to act in the way that we see as best, and to maintain faith in ourselves, each other and our non-violent actions."

EXAMPLE OF THE LACK OF SUCH A JUSTIFICATION: A child tries to "be good" and passively suffers an adult's unjust violence.

or

2. When the sacrifice is unlikely to limit the violence of the aggressor.

EXAMPLE: Gandhi's absurd advice to the victims of the impending Holocaust: "But if the Jewish mind could be prepared for voluntary suffering, even the massacre I have imagined could be turned into a day of thanksgiving and joy that Jehovah had wrought deliverance of the race even at the hands of the tyrant."

or

3. When nonviolence will sacrifice people who do not want to be sacrificed, while violence will save them.

EXAMPLE: In the Peloponnesian War, the Melians surrender at discretion to the Athenians, who then slaughter all adult males and sell the rest as slaves.

[5.0] When Is Violence Justified?

Begin by respecting the Machiavellian Caveat: "How one lives is so far distant from how one ought to live, that he who neglects what is done for what ought to be done, sooner effects his ruin than his preservation."

If we describe rather than prescribe human behavior, justice appears largely irrelevant. Most violence will always be unjustified, and we need not expect to "improve" it. Worse yet, *rights are often unenforceable.* If our means remain insufficient to accomplish our just ends, then what's the use? [But see 2.4 above.] Still and all, violence is justified in legitimate defense and self-defense.

INDICATIONS OF LEGITIMATE DEFENSE AND SELF-DEFENSE

- The violence is more reactive than proactive.

  CAVEAT: Proactive violence can be justified as self-defense against an imminent threat of aggression so massive or dangerous that a "second strike" would be futile.

  EXAMPLES:

  1. A man aims a gun at me. I shoot first, and so I live.
  2. A nuclear regime menaces my country. I launch a massive nuclear strike. This second example is obviously very problematic, and one hopes that the menace has been assessed fairly.

     [See **6.1.1**. See also **5.3** and **6.3** for various types of justified and unjustified proactive violence.]

- Nonviolence in this or similar cases already proved ineffective or even provocative.

  EXAMPLE: "How in the name of common sense do Christians propose to do away with this enormous sin [of slavery] if not with John Brown's method?"—Sarah Everett. She was right, at least from the point of view of a solitary abolitionist in that violently deadlocked epoch of the slavery debate.

- The violence is limited; it will cease if a given concrete result is reached; it shows mercy.

  EXAMPLE: Lincoln ends the Civil War when Lee surrenders.

- Whatever advantage the violence gains is limited to the restoration of a safe status quo, plus conservatively reasonable compensation for injuries suffered.

  EXAMPLE: At the end of the Gulf War, the U.S. leaves Saddam Hussein in power, but makes Iraq pay reparations to Kuwait for having invaded that country.

[5.1] Definitions for Lonely Atoms

[The fundamental violent rights of the self are listed in 5.1.1–3.]
More generally,

VIOLENCE IS JUSTIFIED:

1. In legitimate self-defense or the defense of other human beings against imminent physical harm.

• **Legitimate self-defense** means that the provocation and thus the initial threat lie largely on the other side.

• **Imminence** will often be asserted by someone who wants to justify violence. It applies to a threat of violence so immediate and so dangerous that a reasonable person would agree that violent defense, resistance, or even proactive action would be justified. Imminence extenuates many errors of perception and judgment.

> EXAMPLE: A police officer is justified in shooting a teenager who brandishes a realistic toy gun, because if the officer waits to verify the weapon's actual capability, he may well be dead.

> Imminence is the rule on the battlefield, and excuses conscripts from killing enemy combatants even if the war aim for which they fight is evil. Imminence is often confused with, or pretended to be, other quantities which may be debatable or outright wrong, for instance, the consolidation of legitimate or illegitimate revolutionary authority, the despairing zeal of John Brown, the urgent expedient need for Cortes to complete his wicked conquest.

> NOTE: This "ordinary" imminence applies to all cases in this book except for defense of earth, where **scientific imminence [5.2.I.1]** may apply. The overlapping, contingent category of **proactive imminence [6.3.A.1.6]** may be either ordinary or scientific. Obviously imminent defense of individual or collective rights will always be justified. Strictly speaking, therefore, the justification of imminence as applied to any of the categories in this calculus is redundant. However, I have included imminence occasionally and advisedly, when it might not necessarily occur to us in connection with certain categories [**e.g., 5.2.A.1**], or when it is the essence of an ostensible category [**as in 5.2.H.1**].

[1a. In legitimate defense of nonhuman beings against imminent and unjustified physical harm.]

• **"Unjustified"** has NO consensualized definition beyond the human context.

2. In defense of individual rights;

RIGHTS OF THE SELF:

• To violently defend itself, or not.

• To violently defend another, or not. [**See 5.1.7.**]

- To destroy itself or preserve itself.

Suicide is permissible whenever uncoerced (that is, whenever it is actually suicide), but most noble as an act of assertion in defense of a right.

EXAMPLE: "Caesar's troops beset the city gates, yet Cato has a way of escape; with one single hand he will open a wide path to freedom."
—Seneca.

- To violently destroy another who would be better off dead.

If suicide is not wrong, then consensual euthanasia cannot be wrong, either. In extreme circumstances, people may legitimately coerce the deaths of dependents or incapacitated strangers, in order to spare them from suffering (physical torture, a miserable death, abandonment which would lead to the same, mental torture such as permanent dishonor-grief or defilement-stigma, etc.).

EXAMPLE: Lawrence of Arabia shoots his wounded servant Farraj. "We could not leave him where he was, to the Turks, because we had seen them burn alive our hapless wounded."

Such actions ought never to facilitate the advantage of the euthanizer, but can be justified even should he not wish them applied to himself in a similar case.

- To violently defend its property, or not.

CAVEATS:

1. By proportionality itself [see **5.2.F**], the right to life supersedes the right to property.

EXAMPLES:

1. Others may exercise their right to self-preservation by confiscating excess property if they are in dire need. [See **5.2.B and 6.2.B.**]

2. A householder is not entitled to shoot a fleeing burglar in the back.

3. Legitimate authority [see **5.2.C.1**] may confiscate excess property in the interest of the social contract [taxes, the Muslim *zakat* tithe, etc.].

A. Circumstantial Conditions for 5.1.1 and 5.1.2 to be valid:

1. Full self-sovereignty.

EXAMPLE: We wouldn't allow a small child to destroy himself by drinking household poisons, or to carry a loaded pistol for self-defense.

2. Proportionality must be maintained [**5.2.F**]. The violent response must be of equal or lesser force than the injury—making due allowance for the ambiguities, mistakes and passions of urgency.

EXAMPLE OF AN ALLOWABLE MISTAKE: A man shoots and kills the stranger whom he discovers in the process of assaulting someone; he doesn't first inquire what lethal force the stranger plans to employ.

[See **5.1.7, 6.0.7** and **7.0.2**.]

3. Discrimination must be respected [**5.2.F.1**]. The violent response must be directed against the immediate aggressor—again, making allowance for imminence.

EXAMPLE OF MISTAKE ALLOWED BY IMMINENCE: A soldier's bullet inadvertently kills a civilian in the field of fire.

CAVEAT: Discrimination is obeyed according to one's presuppositions. [See **5.2.F.1**.] In one early-sixteenth-century campaign, the Aztecs liquidate everybody more than nine years old. Two years previous, when they'd attacked another kingdom, the criterion for execution was an age of more than fifty, "because they were the ones responsible for this rebellion," as an anthropologist explains. (To us they'd be civilians in their declining years; to their contemporaries they were respected elders, war leaders.)

B. Ideological Conditions for 5.1.1 and 5.1.2 to be valid:

1. No attachment to nonviolent creeds. *(No nonviolence condition.)* Adherence to nonviolence would prohibit us from exercising many of the above rights.

EXAMPLE: Tolstoy on a pact of mutual defense between Russian and France: "From the Christian point of view one can never admit the justice of war."

2. No allegiance to collectivity or authority which might prohibit the self from removing itself from "the line of fire." *(No allegiance condition.)* Interpreted by some to include allegiance to an implicit social contract. Allegiance might prevent us from exercising the rights of self-preservation, ethuanasia, etc.

EXAMPLE: Robespierre refuses to save the Girondin deputies from the guillotine: "There are periods in revolution when to live is a crime and when men must know how to yield their heads if demanded."

CAVEAT TO (1) AND (2): *So-called involuntary attachments* (among which revolutionaries include prior social contracts) *are not binding. Voluntary attachments may likewise be withdrawn at any time.*

In short, both conditions may be overridden—at which point one returns almost to the state of nature, with one exception: *The Golden Rule should always be respected.* Because the Golden Rule is always in force, except during emergencies, even if an entire regime should be smashed, an *implicit* social contract resumes at the cessation of violence.

EXAMPLES: By the rights of the self one may justifiably refuse to fight a war, or one may renounce nonviolence in order to defend oneself, or one may violently rebel against authority provided that one's cause is just [5.2.C.2], etc., etc. Of course there may well be dire consequences to the decider.

3. In defense of self-respect [see 5.2.A];

RIGHTS OF THE SELF:

- To violently preserve its honor, or not. [See 5.2.A.]

- To violently defend its personal authority, or not. [See 5.2.B–C, F, K.]

- To violently defend its expression of creed, or not. [See 5.2.E.]

EXAMPLE: *Joan of Arc:* "My victory or my standard's, it was all in our Lord." [See 5.1.8.]

- To violently defend its own particular choices of: nonviolent behavior *or* mutually uncoerced (consensual) violent behavior: sadomasochistic sexual, ritual or medical practices. [See 5.3.D.]
[The fundamental violent rights of the self end here. As a member of a society, the self may also take its part in exercising the following collective rights (5.1.4–5):]

4. In the *construction* or *maintenance* of legitimate institutional authority. [See 5.2.C.] This relates to the right to enter into or withdraw from any social contract [5.1.2.B caveat].

5. In *obedience* to legitimate authority; provided only that there is ethical commonality between the giver of the orders and the one who is ordered, and that the indications in (1) and (2) apply. [See 5.2.C, 5.3.C.1–2.]

[The next two fundamental "rights" [5.1.6–7] are not really rights at all, but recapitulations of other principles in this calculus (I apologize for the redundancy, which seems advisable here). They are in essence beacons of justifiability for both individual and collective action.]

6. When a number of categories of self-defense can be legitimately invoked (e.g., self-defense of race is more likely to be justified if it also comprises individual or national self-defense). The more conditions in this section satisfied, the better.

   a. When a variety of groups or individuals participate in that defense.

7. In defense of proportionality.

• **Proportionality** means to save from harm a number of people greater than (or equal to?) the number of people who will be harmed by one's violence. [See **5.1.2**: Right of the self to violently defend another, or not. See also **5.2.F**: Proportionality in war aims.]

   a. PROCEDURAL COROLLARY [particularly but not exclusively applicable to individuals]: Where practical, the amount of force employed for justified self-defense should not exceed the amount required for that end, although it may exceed the amount employed by the original aggressor.

   EXAMPLE: When Bernhard Goetz fires a fifth shot at his assailants after they have stopped being a serious threat, he is unjustified in doing so because he is violating this corollary.

   CAVEAT TO 7 AND 7A: A disproportionate response may be extenuated when imminent self-defense prevents methodological calculation.

   EXAMPLES:

   1. Goetz was justified in beginning to shoot when he is threatened with sharpened screwdrivers.

   2. Babylonian Talmud: "If a man has come to kill you, anticipate him by killing him!" But true knowledge of his intention is impossible; we have to guess. [See **5.1.1.A.2.**]

[The last fundamental violent right I posit produces some rather controversial corollaries, so I have invoked it as little as possible in this book. I personally believe in it strongly. This right may be exercised either individually or collectively.]

8. In imminent defense of freedom of speech. [See 5.2.E.2.] The self retains the inalienable right to express itself as it chooses, on any topic that it chooses, the right to empathize with friend or foe (shall we call that treason?), to assent and to deny, to offend, to express its conscience and to express no conscience, to be offensive, vulgar, vicious and even evil in the object and manner of its expression, at any and all times.

Artistic expression, political expression, pornography, hate speech, blasphemy, etc. should all be protected.

CAVEAT: Direct incitement to violence is action, not speech, and may be considered illegitimate to the extent that the violence it incites is illegitimate.

[5.2] Justifications: Self-Defense

[5.2.A] WHEN IS VIOLENT DEFENSE OF HONOR JUSTIFIED?
For our purposes, honor is *the extent to which the self approaches its own particular moral standard of replying to or initiating violence.* Honor is neither good nor bad without a context. It has four categories. Every type of honor falls into one of the first two *and* one of the last two:

• **Inner honor:** the degree of harmony between (a) an individual's aspirations, deeds and experiences, and (b) his conscience. As such, it remains unknowable to others.

or

• **Outer honor:** the degree of esteem in which someone is held. It derives either from his status [5.2.B def], or from the amount of consonance between (a) his *professed* aspirations and *known* deeds and (b) the values of his judges.

EXAMPLE: Cortes, in a pro forma reference to Montezuma, whom he has not yet met, speaks of "the honor and authority of such a great prince."

and

• **Individual honor:** one's honor as a person.

or

- **Collective honor:** one's honor as a citizen or member of a group.

EXAMPLE: Jung Haegu: "Korea's modern history is stained with dishonor and disgrace, and the people have been forced to accept frustration and shame" because of President Park's abuse of power.

Outer collective honor comprises the group's official face; inner collective honor is its esprit de corps as well as its degree of actual adherence to the ideals it professes.

VIOLENT DEFENSE OF HONOR IS JUSTIFIED:

1. When honor is altruistic—that is, when honor demands the deliverance of a third party from imminent violence. [See 5.1.2.]

2. When defense of honor perfectly corresponds with other justified defense.

NOTE: This rule is weak almost to uselessness because defense of honor is so often unjustified. Best to limit this excuse for violence as much as possible!

COROLLARY: When defense of honor is in accordance with the fundamental rights of the self.

EXAMPLE: During the Cultural Revolution, Nien Cheng refuses to bow to Mao's portrait or to confess to imaginary crimes. Imminent self-defense would have justified her had she taken the course of acknowledging authority's outer honor. This is Dwight Edgar Abbot's course [see 5.2.A.3]. Instead, she defends her own inner honor, a course which is allowed by the fundamental rights of the self to defend itself or not [5.1.2, 5.2.D.5].

3. When the defender's peers would agree that dishonor is equivalent to, or worse than, physical harm, and when the dishonorer willfully disregards that standard.

EXAMPLES:

1. A raped woman in Afghanistan may very possibly be killed by her male relatives. The rapist becomes therefore her proximate murderer, and can be treated as such. Killing him before he dishonors her, or killing him later to keep the dishonor secret, may save her life.

2. Julius Caesar: "Prestige has always been of prime importance to me,

even outweighing life itself." In fact, his prestige, his outer honor, is his power, without which he'd become anyone's prey. Regardless of the injustice of his war aims [**6.2.F.4**], to this simple extent Caesar's defense of honor is justified as imminent self-defense.

3. Dwight Edgar Abbot in juvenile hall: "There was never a doubt I had to retaliate. I had to save face. My honor and ability had been questioned. A punk had made an unusual attempt to hurt a straight. No mild retaliation would save face for me or my clique. I had to cut Blinky." Otherwise Abbot will be despised and treated with violence indefinitely after.

[5.2.B] WHEN IS VIOLENT DEFENSE OF CLASS JUSTIFIED?

Class may be any one or combination of the following attributes:

- Function.

  EXAMPLE: An ant caste is a group which carries out a specified type of behavior.

- Status by reason of function.

  EXAMPLE: In some hunter-gatherer societies, successful hunters have the status of "the best men," while "old and infirm people are treated with severity, and when dependent upon others for their food they are summarily disposed of by strangulation or left to perish when the camp is moved."

- Status by reason of merit.

  EXAMPLE: A seventeenth-century Iroquoian enjoys high status because he is proficient at amassing wealth and is generous with it.

- Property.

  EXAMPLE: In preconstitutional Athens, one of the main qualifications for an official appointment is wealth.

- Rank.

  EXAMPLE: "The noneconomic character of the institution of 'slavery' is revealed," says Leslie White, "when a Kwakiutl chief, for example, will kill a slave merely to demonstrate his high status."

  EXAMPLE: Burke insists that "The occupation of a hair-dresser, or of a working tallow-chandler, cannot be a matter of honour to any person."

• Origin.

> EXAMPLE: A Japanese Burakumin belongs to the Untouchable class because his ancestors half a millennium earlier performed labor which was considered defiling.

VIOLENT DEFENSE OF CLASS IS JUSTIFIED:

1. When it is truly defense against the exactions, impoverishments, oppressions and humiliations imposed by other classes—not proactive self-defense.

> EXAMPLE: "By 1908 the seventeen owners of the thirty-six major haciendas in the state" of Morelos "owned over 25 percent of its total surface, most of its cultivable land, and almost all of its good land." Violent efforts to equalize this situation might well be justified.

2. When it is directed against class structures and their active or official representatives, not against individuals who happen to be members of opposed classes only passively, through biological or social accidents.

> EXAMPLE: The Korean insurgent Manjok cries: "Why then should we only work ourselves to the bone and suffer under the whip? . . . If each one kills his master and burns the record of his slave status, thus bringing slavery to an end in our country, then each of us will be able to become a minister or a general." Justified as far as it goes, but don't then, as Bolsheviks would, liquidate the master's family without imminent cause.

3. When class equals function or status by function, and when that function is essential as the society is currently consituted.

> EXAMPLE: In a precontact Amerindian band, violent discrimination against old or otherwise unfit people by the hunter class, the "best men," may be justifiable during a famine in the interests of saving as many people as possible.

4. When class equals status by consensually defined merit.

> EXAMPLE: People may choose to give a priest or shaman a disproportionate share of their resources, and they may violently defend his right to receive this.

5. When the defense promotes classlessness.

[5.2.B.1] VIOLENT DEFENSE OF CLASS MAY OR MAY NOT BE JUSTIFIED:

> a. When it aims at "advancing society" [see 5.2.C.2, 5.2.M, 6.2.C.1, 6.2.M].

> b. When its purpose is to benefit the most emiserated class.

> c. When its aim is to end relative as opposed to absolute poverty.

> d. When it increases equality at the expense of liberty, or vice versa.

Justifying these ends and effects would require adding to or modifying our axioms about the fundamental violent rights of the self [see 5.1.1–3, 5.1.8].

[5.2.C.1] WHEN IS VIOLENT DEFENSE OF PREEXISTING LEGITIMATE AUTHORITY JUSTIFIED?

Legitimate authority means that it has been delegated by the highest political power available *and* that "most people" legitimize that power and that authority by uncoerced participation or acquiescence in its politics. Legitimate authority displaces and directs violence toward the justified goals listed in this calculus. Legitimate authority is constrained by, but not solely defined by, law.

> *[One of the "principles of 1789": The state does not exist for its own benefit, but for its sovereign citizens.]*

INDICATIONS OF JUSTICE

- The violence seems to promote nonviolent stability (and therefore probably proceeds at a moderate tempo).

    COROLLARY: Consensual authority ordinarily needs to employ violent deterrence [5.3.A.1, 6.3.A.1] on a smaller scale than illegitimate or revolutionary [5.2.C.2] authority.

- It is in accord with authority's stated conscience.
- It is in conformance with law.
- It enjoys a consensus untainted by

    > a. false consciousness, or

    > b. the exploitation of third parties.

    EXAMPLE OF CONSENSUS: "The word of the Chief [of the Mangeroma cannibals] was law and no one dared appeal from the decisions of this man . . . the natives believed him invested with mysterious power which made him the ruler of men . . . The Chief took no active part in the fight whatever, but added to the excitement by bellowing with all his might an encouraging 'AA-OO-AA.' . . . this had a highly beneficial effect upon the tribesmen, for they never for an instant ceased their furious fighting until the last Peruvian was killed."

[On the problematic nature of consensus, see Turnbull's Maxim, 5.2.D.5.]

- It respects the rights of the self. [See 5.1.]
- Its necessity is accepted by some members of the group against whom it is directed.

Rights of Authority

- Self-defense

    a. Defense of sovereignty and command

      i. Defense against opposition

      ii. Defense against factionalism

  CAVEAT: If and only if opposition and factionalism are imminently dangerous to authority's LEGITIMATE operation.

    b. Defense of homeland

    c. Defense of ground

- Enlargement [A conditional right, per 5.2.C.1.A.]
- Deterrence [See 5.3.A.1.]
- Retaliation [See 5.3.A.2–3.]
- Punishment [See 5.3.B.]

1. When the authority has not been proven unjust, and when failure to defend it will injure or destroy it. [Incumbency has a lower standard to meet than revolutionary authority. See 1.1.3.]

2. When mutual affection exists between authority and its subjects, and when the defense is motivated by that affection.

3. When the leaders' authority is peacefully revocable on the part of the led.

4. When authority directs its defense so as to commit the least possible harm. [In other words, when it obeys proportionality and discrimination. See 5.1.2.1, 5.1.7, 5.2.F.]

[5.2.C.1.A] WHEN MAY PREEXISTING LEGITIMATE AUTHORITY
ENLARGE ITSELF?

> 1. As imminent self-defense requires.

> EXAMPLE: Lincoln's defense of the U.S. during the Civil War leads him
> to temporarily violate such U.S. legal limitations as habeas corpus. The
> justice of the federal government's enlargement since then remains de-
> batable.

> 2. As consensuality permits.

> [In my opinion, most of the time, authority's self-aggrandizement is
> unjustified.]

[5.2.C.2] WHEN IS VIOLENT DEFENSE OF REVOLUTIONARY AUTHORITY
JUSTIFIED?

Legitimate revolutionary authority may be created when the preexisting
authority arguably fails to meet the criteria for legitimacy, either obviously
or behind the screen of false consciousness. Given the initial dominance of
preexisting authority, it is almost inevitable that at some stage, "most people" will NOT legitimize revolutionary authority by uncoerced participation or acquiescence in its politics. Revolutionary authority cannot be
constrained by law. Defense of its revolution may require it to engage in violence ordinarily forbidden to preexisting authority. Therefore, revolutionary authority must strive to bring out its own replacement within the
shortest possible time by an established authority whose power will be
normalized according to the same limits as any legitimate preexisting authority. Revolutionary authority is impermanent, as limited and legal as its
emergency permits. Its violence obeys the principles of proportionality
and discrimination. [See **5.2.F def.**, **5.2.F.1.**] Above all, revolutionary authority displaces and directs violence toward the justified goals listed in
this calculus. Given the almost unlimited license it temporarily seizes, revolutionary authority bears a terrible burden of proving the justifiability of
its ends and means.

INDICATIONS OF JUSTICE:

> • The violence aims at a nonviolent future. It may proceed at any tempo
> required to bring that future closer.

> [Possibly justified rephrasing of the above, **per 5.2.B.1.A**: The vio-
> lence will "advance society."]

- It is in accord with authority's stated conscience.

- It will someday bring about a decent rule of law.

- It enjoys a consensus *on the part of its adherents.*

- It acts in the ultimate name of, but may indefinitely disregard, the rights of the self.

- It will destroy false consciousness.

- It will rescue oppressed people from prior emiseration.

of which only the following need not be taken on faith by third parties:

MEASURABLE INDICATIONS OF JUSTICE:

- It is in accord with authority's stated conscience.

- It will rescue oppressed people from prior emiseration.

RIGHTS OF REVOLUTIONARY AUTHORITY:

The same as for preexisting authority. [See **5.2.C.1.4.**]

VIOLENT DEFENSE OF REVOLUTIONARY AUTHORITY IS JUSTIFIED:

1. When the goal and the means to attain that goal are consensual on the part of (a) the revolutionaries who constitute that authority, and (b) the people on whom the revolution is being imposed. When the revolutionaries who constitute that authority and the people on whom the revolution is being imposed agree on the goal and the means to attain that goal.

2. To consolidate the authority's power, and stabilize the area under its control. (What may be moral in seizing power may not be in exercising it.)

EXAMPLE OF JUSTIFICATION BY IMMINENCE: *Trotsky, on his actions during the Russian Civil War:* "Exceptional measures were necessary; the enemy was at the very gates."

3. To bring the revolution into conformance with the norms and limits appropriate to incumbency.

EXAMPLE: A purge of violent extremists.

4. To carry out the revolution.

CAVEAT: So long as the revolution continues, either authority must remain incompletely consolidated, or else **5.2.C.3** applies.

EXAMPLE: It may conceivably be appropriate to kill kulaks in 1917, if they are resisting the Russian Revolution. It would be inappropriate to kill them in 1977, when revolutionary authority is supreme and has been institutionalized for decades.

[For a justification of the rising up which creates revolutionary authority, see 6.2.C.]

[5.2.D] WHEN IS VIOLENT DEFENSE OF RACE AND CULTURE JUSTIFIED?

Defense of race and culture is highly problematic. "Does the concept of human rights mean that" minority groups "should be treated equally under given laws, or that they should have a communitarian right to sustain their own identity and way of life separate from the dominant culture to which they remain subject?" wonders a South Korean sociologist. I myself would answer that question with—

• **The Galapagos Maxim:** *Diversity is best served by local homogeneity and global heterogeneity.*

• One working definition of race and culture: expression of identity. Hence justified by the rights of the self [5.1.1–3, 5.1.8].

1. When it is simple imminent physical defense of self or others in response to an attack based primarily or solely on affiliation.

EXAMPLE: A black slave uprising against white slaveholders in the nineteenth-century American South would have been justified by defense of race, defense of class [5.2.B.2], etc.

2. When it is (a) directed by a minority against a majority whose actions are causing imminent danger to the minority's justified identity and expression; moreover, (b) nonviolence has already failed and (c) the violence offers a very convincing probability of effectively achieving its stated result while obeying proportionality, discrimination and limit; finally, (d) individuals within the group toward which the violence is directed are implicitly and explicitly considered to have the same fundamental rights as those who carry out the violence.

EXAMPLE: The seventeenth-century Powhatan Indians ("Pocahontas's people") rose up against the English colonists in Virginia who had been stealing their land and sovereignty bit by bit. The rebellion was cruel—it targeted all whites, even children—and it failed, thereby bringing immense punishment upon itself. It was still at least somewhat justified by near-imminent self-defense. This imminence, and the fact that the English had themselves disobeyed proportionality and discrimination in their massacres, makes me reluctant to condemn the uprising on the grounds of clauses (c) and (d).

3. When its cause lies open to all—in other words, when its purpose is to defend the possession of rights which ought to be applied irrespective of race and culture. *Race itself need not be relevant to defense of race.* To the extent that a cause is exclusive, it loses worthiness. [See 2.6.] Self-defense of race (or gender, or culture) is most frequently the simpler self-defense of human beings whom the *aggressors* have persecuted on the grounds of race. [See 5.2.D.1.] This rule permits violence against authorities and organizations which are unjust by Martin Luther King's Maxim.

Martin Luther King's Maxim: *A law is unjust which requires from the governed acts or allegiances not required from the legislators.*

4. Absent imminent defense, when its end does not go beyond defending the minimal aloofness which is the right of every culture or bloodline.

The Whale-Hunter's Maxim: *What is forbidden, allowable, or compulsory in one group need not be in another.* [The fact that Inuit kill whales, or that Muslims abstain from pork and endorse polygamy, in no way entitles, compels or forbids other people to do likewise.]

CAVEAT: The Whale-Hunter's Maxim is justified in inverse proportion to the proportion and influence of those who practice it in a given instance.

NOTE: A bloodline, organization, race or a culture can best maintain itself through some minimal degree of **aloofness**.

• **Aloofness** is the preservation and expression of individual, collective, inborn or acquired difference. Aloofness is the acts and manifestations which will keep difference distinct. Aloofness is a subsidiary end, not a means. It may be defended by justified violence, but it may not employ proactive violence.

EXAMPLES:

1. Traditional Inuit culture has been predicated on low population density in an unpolluted setting. If enough people settle in the north, that will be the end. Immigration quotas are probably justified. Would violence against new arrivals be justified? Maybe, if the threat to Inuit life were extreme enough.

2. A small professional organization might justifiably exclude members of the majority group, although such exclusion would hardly be noble. The majority group might perhaps exclude members of the minority, but only should there be no significant class or social cost to the latter. Any organization, popular, obscure or loathsome, has the right to bear its emblems and make its presence known in any nonviolent way. [See 5.1.8.]

Too much aloofness, and xenophobia will incite violence; not enough, and it will get swallowed.

CAVEAT: A minority group may justifiably maintain a greater degree of aloofness than an majority group. Defense of bloodline must come second to defense of individual choice.

Individual choice is partly determined by structural considerations. A job or a spouse may be chosen in the absence of another choice. Hence defense of bloodline is best accomplished in the structural arena, that is by regulating and predisposing choices.

5. When the defender exercise the rights of the self to express who he is. Should violence ensue, he is not culpable, provided he adheres to his justified ends and means.

In effect, the defender has chosen the left horn of—

The Pelasgian Dilemma: *Do I express who I am, and thereby cause harm to myself or others, or do I protect myself by becoming one of them?*

NOTES:

1. By the rights of the self [5.1.1–3, 5.1.8], either choice is correct.

EXAMPLE: Greek women kidnapped and impregated by the Pelasgians "had numerous children, whom they brought up to behave like Athenians and to speak Attic Greek. The boys as they grew older would not mix with the children of the Pelasgian women, and all supported one another when it came to blows . . . The situation gave the Pelasgians something to think about . . . They decided in consequence to kill the Attic women's children; then, having done so, they murdered the mothers as well." The Greek women would have been justified either in raising their children as Greeks, which they did, or in assimilating with the Pelasgians in the interest of imminent self-preservation. What the Pelasgians did was therefore utterly unjustified.

2. Potent and legitimate authority [5.2.C.1] renders the Pelasgian Dilemma unnecessary by following—

Turnbull's Maxim: *"In larger-scale societies we are accustomed to diversity of belief, we even applaud ourselves for our tolerance, not recognizing that a society not bound together by a single powerful belief is not a society at all, but a political association of individuals held together only by the presence of law and force, the very existence of which is a violence."*

[5.2.E] WHEN IS VIOLENT DEFENSE OF CREED JUSTIFIED?
Again, problematic.

Creed is part choice, part identity. As identity, it partakes of a nature similar to race and culture [5.2.D] and has all the same justified and unjustified defenses. (Its invocation is often a specious mask for intolerance. This category is very dangerous because such faith, by way of proving itself, so often refuses to descend to the level of logical proof. This leaves the end itself unsusceptible to our judgment.) Creed defines itself by including its present members and enrolling new ones, by enticement, compulsion or both. Creed also defines itself by excluding others, again by enticement, compulsion or both.

A creed is not an end. The means-end combination is a verb; a creed is a noun or even an adjective. The end is the goal; the creed is the standard in whose name the goal is chosen.

COROLLARY: The content of a creed is irrelevant to defense of creed.

1. When it does not violate the Golden Rule [1.2.1–2]. From this I derive:

2. More generally, when it is morally transparent. Defense of a "transparent" creed may or may not be justified, depending on the means and ends employed by that creed. Transparent axia are always justified in and of themselves, by virtue of their innocuousness. The Golden Rule is morally transparent.

• By **transparent** I mean that the creed does not in and of itself call for any act which supposedly defends that creed.

EXAMPLES:

1. "The Kingdom of Heaven is a mustard seed" says nothing about violence at all. It is irrelevant to violence, hence transparent.

2. The Golden Rule [1.2.1] includes all of us, so it likewise refrains of singling any of us out for violence. It is almost tautologically transparent.

• An **opaque** creed demands something of other creeds. It is not satisfied with accepting all differences of outlook. Its end is menacingly violence-specific. It disobeys the Golden Rule.

EXAMPLE: "The Qur-'An is the word of God" is transparent, but it becomes opaque when explicated as follows: "The Muslims need to hear from the Christians that there is no God but Allah and Muhammed is His Prophet, and then we will be friends."

3. When it is directed against the aggressive enactions of an opaque creed.

4. When creed is simply speech, transparent or not [2.0, 5.1.18], and the freedom to utter that speech is under imminent attack.

CAVEAT: Direct incitement to violence is action, not freedom of speech.

GENERAL NOTE: As is the case for legitimate, consensualized preexisting authority [5.2.C.1], the less rigorous the creed, or the more widely it is embraced, the less cruel the violence of its defense needs to be, and ought to be.

EXAMPLE: "For I am gentle and lowly in heart, and you will find rest for your souls. For my yoke is easy, and my burden is light."—*Christ.*

[5.2.F] WHEN IS VIOLENT DEFENSE OF WAR AIMS JUSTIFIED?
A **war aim** is any end whose defense, achievement or active prosecution is the justification invoked for a given military conflict. General considerations of means and ends [2.1–3, 2.5] are highly relevant here.
1. *When the war aims themselves are legitimate . . .*

A legitimate war aim may be derived from analogy with the rights of the self [5.1.1, 5.1.2, 5.1.8. All indications of justice in 5.1.1 apply]. A homeland or a command authority may violently:

a. Defend itself, or not [this requires its own subcalculus; see 5.2.G].

b. Defend an ally, or not [5.2.G also applies].

c. Destroy itself or preserve itself [although this option is very susceptible to coercion's abuse].

EXAMPLES:

1. The mass suicide of the Jews at Masada was probably justified since the defenders were zealots and had nothing good to look forward to at the hands of their Roman besiegers. (I say "probably" because it is difficult to judge the means of killing one's children for their own good.)

2. When the Athenians besieged the Persian-installed governor of Eion, the governor's disposition of the people over whom his authority exercised coercive control was this: "He made a huge pile of timber, set it on fire, and then, cutting the throats of his children, wife, concubines, and servants, flung their bodies into the flames." This seems a bit unjustified, to say the least.

3. On Takashiki Island in 1945, the "crushing of jewels" decreed by the defeated Japanese army against Japanese civilians was similarly gruesome, coercive, unjustified.

    d. Defend its right to nonviolently express its identity, in accordance with the rules for defense of race and culture [5.2.D.1, 2, 4, 5].

EXAMPLES:

1. The seventeenth-century Powhatan Indians "seldome make warrs for landes or goodes, but for women and Children, and principally for revendge, so vindictiue and ielous they be, to be made a derision of, and to be insulted upon by an enemy." Depending on its context, this war aim might be justified.

2. Oath of the Athenian defenders before the battle of Plataea: "I shall fight as long as I live, and I shall not consider it more important to be alive than to be free . . ."

A legitimate war aim may also be derived from analogy with the rights of the collective [5.1.4, 5.1.5]. A homeland or a command authority may violently . . .

    e. Construct or maintain legitimate preexisting or revolutionary authority [5.2.C.1–2].

EXAMPLE: The war aim of Wu Tzu: "Suppressing the violently perverse and rescuing the people from chaos."

    f. Obey a higher legitimate authority.

CAVEAT: Loyalty, compulsion and fear frequently do not extenuate war's violence and require their own subcalculus [5.3.C.1–2, 6.3.C.1–2].

. . . *and their enacted violence is limited.*

No one agrees as to how a limitation of war should be defined.

EXAMPLE: Moltke the Elder prefers to limit the war's *duration*. "Rapid conclusion of a war undoubtedly constitutes the greatest kindness. All means not absolutely reprehensible must be used to accomplish this end." This brings him into potential conflict with all other limitations, and would seem to justify a blitzkrieg or nuclear attack, since he never defines reprehensibility. And the Aztec "flower wars," which could drag on indefinitely, don't seem to have been necessarily very cruel. Therefore I reject Moltke's definition, and define limitation in terms of the intensity of the violence itself.

Michael Walzer's Axiom: *It is less important for the justice of a war that any particular item be on the list of limitations than that there* be *a list.*

In spite of Walzer's Axiom, I propose that *all* the following limitations be respected:

• FIRST LIMITATION: The violence of war should be employed only by and toward combatants. [Respect the Discrimination Principle.]

Discrimination Principle: *The greater the percentage of war victims who are combatants, political leaders, or otherwise directly associated with the war's aggression, the more moral, or less immoral, the war.*

EXAMPLES:

1. A suicide bomber is more justified in killing soldiers than children.

2. Geneva Conventions: "It is prohibited to attack, destroy, remove or render useless objects indispensable to the survival of the civilian population, such as foodstuffs, agricultural areas . . . , crops, livestock, drinking water installations . . .

COMBATANT: What makes him one we all know: He fights. But what emblematizes his status varies almost infinitely.

[Local examples of noncombatant status: sex, age, ill health, absence of a uniform, tokens of a herald, etc.]

• In Vigny's tale "The Russian Guard-Post," a French captain justifiably stabs a Russian boy in his sleep; the Russians employed children as officers in those times.

• FIRST COROLLARY: A just war must aim toward a just peace. We further the justice of war to the extent that we can persuade our enemies not to be combatants.

• SECOND COROLLARY: The violence must be employed only in war zones, and only during wartime.

EXAMPLE: "Once our soldiers had broken the enemy's ranks and put them to flight they would not stab another Indian: it seemed to them mere cruelty." —A sixteenth-century conquistador, who of course goes on: "What chiefly concerned them was to look for a pretty woman or find some spoil."

• THIRD COROLLARY: The unpersuaded are noncombatants.

• FOURTH COROLLARY: The uncategorized are combatants, if they occupy an active war zone. Justification: Imminence.

EXAMPLE: A British history of the Zulu War reports: "Dense masses of the enemy were seen about a mile off, and against these masses shells and rockets were directed with good effect." Some of those people a mile off might conceivably have been Zulu women and children. But since they were in the belligerent column of march, shelling them was not unjustified.

CAVEAT TO FOURTH COROLLARY: We must give the uncategorized the opportunity to categorize themselves, whenever we are not overruled by imminent self-defense. [See 5.1.1–2.]

EXAMPLE: A person who seems to be a civilian approaches me. If imminence allows me, I should search him to make sure he's no threat, rather than killing him.

EXAMPLE OF OVERRULING BY IMMINENCE: A Soviet lieutenant in Afghanistan machine-guns civilians after an uncategorized person killed his predecessor. "What was I supposed to do when all these *kishlak* [village] women started coming down toward our sentry post? How was I supposed to know who was hiding underneath the yashmaks? . . . They could have come right up to the post and shot all of us . . ."

• FIFTH COROLLARY: Prisoners of war who seek to fight on after capture are combatants.

EXAMPLES:

1. Julius Caesar's justified moral calculus: Kill all prisoners captured twice, unless they can convince you of prior compulsion. This is because he mostly released his prisoners, having no facilities to imprison them.

2. World War II: "Going through a group of dead Japanese required caution, because one might be feigning death and try to kill you. We were quick to make sure they stayed dead."

Otherwise, once disarmed and in our power, they are noncombatants.

EXAMPLE: The Plataeans to the Spartans: "To grant us our lives would be . . . a righteous judgment; if you consider also that we are prisoners who surrendered of our own accord, stretching out our hands for quarter, whose slaughter Hellenic law forbids . . ." Unfortunately and unjustifiably, the Spartans put them to death just the same.

SECOND LIMITATION: The violence of war should be employed against no more people than is needed to accomplish a specific justified result, and the number of people harmed by the violence should be lower than the number of people helped by it. [Respect the Proportionality Principle, **5.1.7.**]

EXAMPLE: Huong Van Ba, North Vietnamese Army: "To save fifteen million people was the highest moral obligation. To kill a few dozen people in the fighting was nothing important. Of course sometimes we were deeply touched by certain situations." In real life this is probably as close as a combatant can get to following the Second Limitation.

THIRD LIMITATION: When it is employed only by legitimate command.

Aquinas: "It is not the business of a private person to declare war, because he can seek for redress of his rights from the tribunal of his superior." [See the definitions of legitimate authority, **5.2.C.1–2.** Imminence may in fact justify ad hoc military command systems unacceptable to Aquinas, for instance, guerrilla insurgency or secret organizational "cells," as in World War II Yugoslavia. These would be ethically analogous to legitimate revolutionary authority.]

[5.2.G] WHEN IS VIOLENT DEFENSE OF HOMELAND JUSTIFIED?
Homeland is the ground on which "we" dwell. Homeland is also an ethos, whose actions justified and unjustified are *our* actions.

"We" is highly problematic.

(1) If we are Xerxes' Persians, does "we" include the Greeks who have not yet sworn allegiance to us? (2) Does "we" include the unwilling conscripts who happen to be dwelling in the heartland of the homeland? War will determine such questions from a practical if not an ethical point of view.

1. When the aliens [people from outside the homeland] are the imminent violent aggressors.

   EXAMPLE: Leonidas, when asked whether he has any plan other than to hold Thermopylae against the Persian invaders: "In theory, no. But in fact I plan to die for the Greeks."

2. When the aliens seriously threaten homeland's fundamental rights [based on the rights of the self, **5.1.1–3, 5.1.8**; the resulting rights of homeland are racial and cultural rights, **5.2.D.1–5**] to express its own ethos and follow its own lifeway, and when all nonviolent means for neutralizing the threat have failed.

EXAMPLE: Ho Chi Minh justly invokes defense of homeland against the French and the Americans: "Nothing is more precious than independence and liberty."

Ethos: Unknowable to third parties except through material standards. Wherever our common rights of the self permit, people have the right to determine what does and does not define, injure and preserve their well-being. The attempt on the part of third parties to redirect or redefine a group's ethos is usually unwarranted. In the political arena it is frequently associated with, or leads to, aggression. Nonetheless, an ethos may cause or countenance unjustified violence. The ethos of another should be approached with the utmost caution.

EXAMPLES OF ETHOS-DRIVEN INSTITUTION: Pederasty among the ancient Greeks, hunting among Inuit, patriarchialism in the Muslim world, female circumcision in parts of Africa.

NOTE: As stated, this rule is very dangerous and subject to abuse. Hitler invoked it to murder Jews. But he did so falsely. The Jews did not threaten the "Aryans," but in fact contributed to the German economy. No "negotiations" had taken place. But I believe that this rule is valid when its preconditions are literally true. The Aztec uprising against Cortes's Spaniards in 1520 was justified defense of homeland because the Spaniards meant to enslave them, had massacred Aztec nobles in the marketplace, kidnapped their Emperor and refused to negotiate.

COROLLARY: A local injustice *of which the locals do not complain* never invalidates local defense of homeland.

EXAMPLE: Afghan patriarchialism did not justify the "progressive" Soviet invasion of Afghanistan.

[5.2.H] WHEN IS VIOLENT DEFENSE OF GROUND JUSTIFIED?
Ground is the territory on which we find ourselves, rightly or wrongly. Because invoking defense of ground as an excuse for violence so frequently

avoids the larger question of how the moral actor came to occupy the ground that he did, this justification tends to be suspect.

1. By imminent self-defense, even during unjust aggression—but *only* by imminent self-defense.

EXAMPLE: Besieged by the Aztecs he's come to conquer, Cortes instructs his men, and so far imminence justifies him: "The Mexicans and their allies are now determined to kill us all. Let us then, with all our Indian allies, defend ourselves." Now for the unjustified part: "Indeed we can do no less in our defense than kill them, take from them their kingdom, and make them our slaves . . ."

[5.2.1] WHEN IS VIOLENT DEFENSE OF EARTH JUSTIFIED?

Earth is the ecosystem which sustains us and whose other members have no less a right to life than we do.

1. When needed to avert a scientifically imminent ecological threat. Proportionality especially applies. [See 5.1.7.] Be your own scientific expert, but be right—or follow one you can trust.

Scientific imminence is a term which applies to defense of earth only. For every other chapter of *Rising Up and Rising Down,* the only kind of imminence considered is "ordinary" imminence [5.1.1]. Scientific imminence refers to a threat to health, well-being or even existence, a threat which may affect one person [EXAMPLE: a rural well poisoned by PCBs] or every person [EXAMPLE: global warming]; a threat which may or may not be perceptible by the ordinary senses, as "ordinary" imminence is, a threat which may affect only human beings or other organisms as well [see the calculus for defense of animals; 5.2.J.1–3]; above all, a threat which meets reasonable scientific standards of proof for its harmfulness and its certain to highly probably onset, unless certain specific measures for defense of earth are undertaken. These measures must in turn meet their own scientific standards for effectiveness and relative harmlessness; if not, they are unjustified.

EXAMPLE: "The emission of greenhouse gases in distant lands is warming the Earth and causing the sea level to rise. The coastal fringe where my people live is but two meters above the sea surface. We are trapped . . ." Thus Kinza Clodumar, president of the Republic of Naura. If what he says can be proven to be true, the Naurans would arguably be justified in using violence as a last resort against the greenhouse gas producers. But its proof must meet the standards of scientific imminence.

GENERAL NOTE: Both pro- and antienvironmentalists are habitually guilty of making assertions which do not meet scientific standards.

An ecological threat can only be defined according to the presuppositions of the definer. For this reason, it is vital that each moral actor who cares to address this daunting issue articulate these presuppositions and attempt to give them some legitimate authority [5.2.C.1] by consensualizing them. Otherwise, one runs the risk of following our Maxims for Murderers [1.3.1–1.3.13], which selfishly reserve to the moral actor all evaluation of ends and/or means. At this point in time (2003), ecotage has little mainstream support and therefore resembles revolutionary authority [5.2.C.2] in its extreme character and the resulting very high burden of moral proof required.

EXAMPLE: A society which ignores or refuses to admit the obvious truism that our environment does have a carrying capacity has no business asserting that ecotage is always unjustified. If our demands on the environment grow without limit, then sooner or later we must reach a point of scientific imminence; that is a simple fact. But where does the emergency begin? When there is no longer enough food for all human beings? When there is no longer enough red meat for all human beings? (Was there ever?) When scarcity of ecological resources is directly responsible for pulling the per capita income below a certain number? Carrying capacity must be honestly and explicitly defined by all parties who invoke it.

2. As an agent of mutually agreed upon compulsion [in other words, legitimate authority; 5.2.C.1] to interrupt the self-destructive loop of the Herdsman's Calculus.

EXAMPLE: A government uses force to neutralize a polluter.

The Herdsman's Calculus: Problem: *What is my utility in adding one more animal to my herd on a common pasture?* Solution: Buy another animal, let it overgraze, and be damned to everybody else.

3. As a last-ditch defense of a place's justified identity [5.2.D.2, 4, 5]; by analogy with defense of the minimal aloofness permissible to a race, culture or creed [5.2.D.4]; again, by analogy with the ethos of a homeland [5.2.G.2].

EXAMPLE: Earth First! saves a redwood grove through ecotage. The justifiability of this is arguable and context-dependent.

Identity of a place: [modeled after def. of ethos] Undefinable to human beings except by consensus. Wherever our common rights of the self permit, people have the right to determine what does and does not define, injure and preserve the well-being of a place. This refers both to what is now called "aesthetic values" and also to whatever agreed-on right to existence and health a specific ecological niche may possess. For the foreseeable future, most attempts to establish a consensus on this matter will fail. Therefore, two opposing risks face us: Allowing the identity of a place to be destroyed forever (for example, by a developer); or else becoming judge, jury and executioner in carrying out ecotage according to one's own private calculus. In short, this category remains an ethical danger zone.

[5.2.J] WHEN IS VIOLENT DEFENSE OF ANIMALS JUSTIFIED?

This category remains largely undefined and unexamined in the common mind.

1. When demanded by imminent defense of earth. Scientific imminence applies [**5.2.I.1**].

HYPOTHETICAL EXAMPLE: Violence committed to preserve against human greed an animal species which is vital to the ecosystem.

Justifications [2] and [3] derive from the debatable 5.1.1a.

2. To save a species against extinction. Scientific imminence applies. [**5.2.I.1.**]

3. To save an organism from the unjustifiable violence of another organism (most probably a human being). This is nothing but a restatement of **5.1.1a:** Violence is justified *in legitimate defense of nonhuman beings against imminent physical harm.*

EXAMPLE: Someone kills an elephant poacher to save the life of the elephant. More extreme example: Someone kills a slaughterhouse employee to save the lives of a feedlot's beef steers. Justified, or not, by one's presuppositions.

- **Legitimate defense:** Remains undefined.

- **Imminent physical harm:** In this context, there exist various disputed and undefined exceptions.

EXAMPLES:

1. Experimentation which inflicts violence upon animals is not justified if it can be shown not to possess the possibility of benefiting humans significantly and directly, or if its goal need not be achieved by the particular violent method in question. Otherwise, it may well be justified by human imminence, no matter what the animal suffers.

> CRUCIAL AND UNRESOLVED QUESTION: Must scientific imminence apply to justify human use of animals, or is human convenience sufficient? The answer depends on one's presuppositions.

2. It would seem entirely justified by imminence for hunter-gatherer societies to eat animals and wear their skins.

3. To protect the identity of an animal against imminent and unjustifiable harm.

• **Identity of an animal:** Unknowable to human beings except by analogy with ourselves. Wherever the rights of the human self permit, people have the right to determine what does and does not define, injure and preserve the well-being of their identity. By extension, animals are entitled to our respect and consideration in whatever physical, behavioral, cognitive, psychological or other aspect of them in our good faith judgment defines and preserves the well-being of their identity. Identity carries with it the inherent right of any organism, barring necessity, for it to express its organism-ness. This right must at a minimum include the same basic rights of self-defense and defense of others which we allow ourselves; it should also take into account the differing identities of species and individuals: the right of an otter to express otterness.

> HYPOTHETICAL EXAMPLE: The Animal Liberation Front violently frees a monkey from a laboratory cage.

Other justifications may develop as the newly expressed cause of animal rights and the ancient axia of human ethics continue to shape each other.

[5.2.K] WHEN IS VIOLENT DEFENSE OF GENDER JUSTIFIED?
Points 5.2.K.1 and 5.2.K.2 are modeled after those for defense of race and culture, 5.2.D.1 and 5.2.D.3.

Gender in this context refers not only to the physical, sexually differentiated body and its rights, which are the rights of the self, but also to cultural, personal and spiritual expressions of that body. In short, gender is an inalienable aspect of the self. I assert, as many people in my society would, and many people outside my society would not, that one's gender and its manifestations of all kinds need no justification.

• **Outer gender** is the gendered characteristics of otherness which attract us, and our own characteristics which complement them.

• **Inner gender** is the gendered incarnation of the other with whom we're intimate, and our own incarnation which complements him or her.

• Aggression against gender consists of any or all of the following, which overlap:

   a. Attack against gender's embodiments.

EXAMPLE: The serial killer Danny Rolling rapes and murders someone because she is a "once-a-month bleeding bitch."

NOTE: The best long-term, nonviolent defense against attacks on gender is insure that each gender has not only its embodiments, but its perogatives.

   b. Attack against gender's traditional perogatives.

EXAMPLE: Igbo tribeswomen in Southeast Nigeria own their husbands' fields, and all domestic animals. When colonial authorities promise not to tax them, yet levy a tax on these categories of property, the 1929 Women's War breaks out.

   c. Aggression against inner gender. Namely, nonconsensual violence within a consensual or nonconsensual intimate relationship.

CAVEAT: We must take to differentiate violent aggression against gender from consensual sadomasochistic practices. [See 5.3.D–E.]

   d. Aggression against outer gender. Namely, a violent attempt to establish a nonconsensual intimate relationship.

EXAMPLE: Sexual predation.

   e. Sex-selective infanticide.

EXAMPLE: *Slavey Indians, 1807:* "It is a great deal of trouble to bring up girls, and . . . women are only an encumbrance, useless in time of war and exceedingly voracious in time of want."

VIOLENT DEFENSE OF GENDER IS JUSTIFIED:

   1. When it is committed (most likely by a minority against a majority) in the face of imminent agression against gender (which it need not prevent),

and the violence is directed exclusively against members of the other gender whose actions constitute physical aggression.

EXAMPLE: During the Babylonian uprising described by Herodotus, in which the men planned to put to death most of the women to save food, any woman, including one of those spared, would have been justified in killing any man to save herself or other women.

HYPOTHETICAL EXCEPTION: The destruction of all embryos, or perhaps of female embryos (which some social activists refer to as femicide) *may* someday be justified, a least arguably, by imminent ecological self-defense (defense of earth).

2. When its cause lies open to all—in other words, when its purpose is to defend the possession of rights which ought to be applied irrespective of gender. [See 2.6; 5.2.D.2.]

EXAMPLE: Imminent self-defense of a woman against her rapist.

3. When directed against a gender-class system whose unjustified categories place the subservient gender at imminent risk of harm, when the defensive violence would clearly diminish that risk, and when proportionality applies.

EXAMPLE: A Thai brothelkeeper who illegally imprisons Burmese girls for his own profit in conditions of sexual slavery could, I believe, be violently attacked were that necessary to help the girls escape. Were that brothel system legal and hence protected against nonviolent redress, I believe that any weak link in the exploitative chain—for instance, the man who drove truckloads of these prisoners from a collection point to a brothel—might be attacked with equal justification.

4. When it seeks by otherwise justified means to stop an attempt to violently transform gender into, or violently maintain it as, class.

5. When it is directed against gender-class structures and their official representatives, not against individuals who happen to be members of the gender-oppressing class only passively, through biological or social accidents.

EXAMPLE: An influential cleric or educator who called for cruel measures aiming at the domination of women, or for female infanticide, *might* arguably be a legitimate target for violence, if and only if the attack on him would provably neutralize his influence. [See 5.3.A.]

6. To the extent that the gender it protects is legitimate authority. [This is a response to (b): Attack against gender's traditional perogatives.]

[5.2.L] WHEN IS VIOLENT DEFENSE AGAINST TRAITORS JUSTIFIED?
A **traitor** is:

* Someone who threatens or embarrasses *personified* authority (a common ancient and totalitarian definition).

* Someone who threatens or embarrasses *generalized* authority, "the people" (a modern definition employed by totalitarianism and mass democracy).

* Someone actively or passively in league with the enemies of authority (a definition to be met with in wars and revolutions).

VIOLENT DEFENSE AGAINST TRAITORS IS JUSTIFIED:

1. Against a deliberate or accidental agent of danger—in other words, as imminent defense.

EXAMPLES

1. "Whosoever seeks to put law in chains and the state under control of faction by subjecting them to the domination of persons, and further serves these ends and foments civil strife by revolutionary violence, must be counted the deadliest foe of the whole state."—*Plato*.

2. A "horizontal collaborator" has a boyfriend who wears the uniform of the enemy occupation. His visits endanger a local resistance cell. [See 5.1.2.A.2.]

CAVEAT: Imminence implies responsibility on the part of the traitor-liquidators. Did they try to prevent the hideous necessity, by warning the dangerous person to stop being dangerous, before the potential danger became active? Less imminence is needed to justify the elimination of a deliberate traitor than an accidental one. A girl seen in a bar with an enemy boyfriend may not be culpable. When she begins to inform on her neighbors to him, she's become deliberately dangerous. Any defense against traitors which fails to distinguish between such cases is unacceptable, doctrinaire, murderous.

2. Against a deliberate agent of danger, as a personal, punitive, or didactic act.

EXAMPLE: an extortionist or informer. The caveat "deliberate" rules out such abuses as deterrent executions of hostages. "But suddenly, as we glimpse strand after strand in the web of support, we begin to sense the whole, and apprehend the truism that *nobody whatsoever should help the enemy.*"

Against a *rodef,* violence may justify itself as impersonal imminent self-defense. Against a *moser,* violence may be additionally legitimized as personal and punitive.

- **Rodef:** A community endangerer.

  EXAMPLE: A man who overburdens a ferry, putting other passengers at risk of drowning.

- **Moser:** An informer.

[5.2.M] WHEN IS VIOLENT DEFENSE OF THE REVOLUTION JUSTIFIED? *[Per def. of revolutionary authority; see* **5.2.C.2.***]*

Defense of the revolution means protection of the revolution's right, perceived or real, to develop from an initial recognition of grievance all the way into the maintenance of incumbency's power. Defense of the revolution allows means and ends to alter, provided that "justice" will ultimately be done in the name of some legitimate super-end.

> NOTE: Our moral calculus already contains rules for defense of revolutionary authority. Why do we need this section? Because in a revolution, rival authorities fight for the legitimacy which alone makes defense of authority worth anything. What happens when the revolution does not yet possess any authority? When is violent defense of a weak revolution justified?

> 1. When the ends of the revolution are explicit and legitimate. Whenever those ends change, the legitimacy of defense of the revolution must be reevaluated.

> Insurgent Subcommander Marcos, Zapatista Army of National Liberation: "The principal characteristic of this rebellion is that it seeks a voice. Having exhausted all legal means of enabling that voice, indigenous Mexicans had to use the voice of guns in order to be heard." Once it has been heard, what next?

> 2. When it is defense of the General Will.

> DEFINITION (BY ROUSSEAU): "There is often a great deal of difference between the will of all and the General Will; the latter regards only the common interest, while the former . . . is merely a sum of particular wills . . . ." And again, "the particular will naturally tends to preferences, and the General Will to equality."

COROLLARY TO DEFINITION: The General Will is best served by equally maximizing liberty and equality in accordance with the Golden Rule.

CAVEAT: Unfortunately, in a revolution the General Will is often knowable only after the fact. Therefore, the moral actor must continually attempt in good faith to define each local manifestation of the General Will as he sees it.

[5.3] Justifications: Policy and Choice

Revenge, deterrence, retaliation and punishment can only be justified by the meaning they express. Otherwise they become unmeaning *violence.*

[5.3.A.1] WHEN IS VIOLENT DETERRENCE JUSTIFIED?

Deterrence is "do unto others to discourage them from doing unto you." More precisely, deterrence is the infliction of terror for the purpose of disheartening the victim or his people from acting in a way which the deterrers have proscribed. Deterrence is expedient, although it may act in the service of ethical ends.

1. As proactive defense against imminent harm.

EXAMPLE: Our enemies, who enjoy quantitative superiority, mobilize their armies against us, disregarding all warnings. We may launch our missiles first if second-strikers will be losers. [For an analogy with individual self-defense, see 5.1.1.]

CAVEAT: Too much of the time, the politicians who employ this justification pretend that a merely strategic loss constitutes imminent harm. In such a case, the sacrifice of noncombatant populations in the name of deterrence cannot be expiated, let alone justified.

2. Against the narrowly defined imminent threat of a specified foe, especially when the deterrence is itself specific and limited. [See 6.3.A.5.]

EXAMPLE: John F. Kennedy, 1962: "It shall be the policy of this nation to regard any nuclear missile launched from Cuba against any nation in the Western Hemisphere as an attack by the Soviet Union on the United States, requiring a full retaliatory response upon the Soviet Union."

3. When it prevents unjustified violence; when it seeks to prevent violence generally.

(Julius Caesar's calculus: *Retribution is useful as deterrence's last resort.*) When it allows various retributive possibilities to be modulated, escalating itself only as needed.

EXAMPLE: The Aztec "flower wars."

4. When it enforces a legitimate social contract. When it is an instrument of legitimate authority [5.2.C.1, 5.2.C.2].

[CAVEAT: See 6.3.A.5.]

Deterrence approaches justification (or at least mercifulness) when it forbears to execute retribution.

[5.3.A.2] WHEN IS VIOLENT MILITARY RETRIBUTION JUSTIFIED?

Retribution is "do unto others as they have done unto you—or else do worse." Retribution may have expedient deterrent effects, or not, but it is moral or bureaucratic; it operates within a larger system of means and ends. Revengeless retribution is not personal.

1. To deter new atrocities by punishing old ones.

[The retribution must not itself be an atrocity except under imminent conditions; it must stay well within the limits of proportionality (5.1.7) and discrimination (5.2.F.1), and it ought to follow judicial forms as well as battle conditions allow.]

EXAMPLE, ARGUABLY BUT NOT CERTAINLY JUSTIFIABLE: Lawrence of Arabia enters Tafas, where the Turks had murdered every inhabitant, including "some twenty small children (killed with lances and rifles), and about forty women. I noticed particularly one pregnant woman, who had been forced down on a sawbayonet." When he gets this group of Turks into his power, "We ordered 'no prisoners.'"

[5.3.A.3] WHEN IS VIOLENT REVENGE JUSTIFIED?

Revenge is retaliation or retribution carried out for the satisfaction of the revenger; or for the benefit of a victim or offended party. Revenge is highly personal.

1. When it follows judicial forms, or when no judicial forms are available; and when it respects proportionality, discrimination and the Soldier's Golden Rule.

EXAMPLE: In medieval Iceland, there was no centralized authority to check infringements of the social contract themselves. Hence measured, discriminating revenge carried out by the injuried party after legal judgment had been obtained could be justifiable as it would not be in twenty-first-century America.

[5.3.B] WHEN IS VIOLENT JUDICIAL RETRIBUTION (PUNISHMENT) JUSTIFIED?

1. When the transgressor agrees to, or belongs to a culture which subscribes to, the rule by which he has been judged, and when he can be proven to have violated that rule.

EXAMPLE: A murderer in Singapore "hoped the judge would sentence him to death. He wanted to say sorry to his parents whom he could not serve until their old age."

Alternatively,

When the transgressor and punisher accept the same moral values which apply in the given case; and when the transgressor has in fact breached those values such that the law calls for the stipulated punishment. When Solon's Maxim applies.

Solon's Maxim: *The best possible city-state is "that where those that are not injured try and punish the unjust as much as those that are."*

John Brown's unauthorized version of this runs: "If I am hard with myself, then by a sly subversion of the Golden Rule I have the right to be hard with you." [See 1.3.2.]

[What are those moral values which all concerned parties must accept? Must they be universal? No. Montesquieu: "If the people observe the laws, what signifies it whether these laws are the same?"]

EXAMPLE: When a Muslim citizen of a Muslim country which follows strict Islamic law, *shariat,* commits theft, it is justifiable to cut off his hand. On the other hand, a fine or a prison term is appropriate to punish a Swedish thief in Sweden.

2. When its purpose is to prove that a legitimate social contract will be honored and obeyed by authority. This is especially important when a member of the ruling class does wrong.

EXAMPLES:

1. The government sniper who killed the white supremacist woman Vicki Weaver at Ruby Ridge ought to be tried and punished in a fashion commensurate with due process for other murderers. Not doing so serves extremist assertions that the government acts arrogantly and

evilly above the law. That is why Robespierre advises: "In order for the government to keep in the closest harmony with the law it is over its own head that it must wield the heaviest stick."

2. *Al-Bukhari:* The Prophet Muhammad assures the people: "By Allah, if Fatima, the daughter of Muhammad, committed theft, Muhammad will cut off her hand!"

3. When its penalties are codified into limit and consistency, and respect the rights of the self. [See 5.1.1–3.]

EXAMPLE: *Qur-'An:* "O you believe! Retaliation is prescibed for you in the matter of the slain: the free for the free, and the slave for the slave, and the female for the female." But compensation may be offered and accepted. "This is an alleviation from your Lord, and a mercy."

4. When it is proportionate to the original injury.

EXAMPLES:

1. *Code of Hammurabi:* "If a seignior has destroyed the eye of a member of the aristocracy, they shall destroy his eye."

2. *Plato:* "We shall neither inflame the culprit by brutal punishments nor spoil a servant by leaving him uncorrected; so we should adopt the same course with the freeborn."

CAVEAT: Predetermined equations between crimes and penalties have always been dissimilar in different times and places.

5. When it helps heal the victim, those who care for him, the criminal, or society generally.

EXAMPLES:

1. Robespierre and Cicero, among many others, assert the balmlike power of justified revenge. Hobbes suggests that punishment should forbear to dwell upon the evil already committed, but to approach the good we hope for in the future.

2. *Al-Bukhari:* "The Prophet added: 'And whoever among you fulfills his pledge, his reward is with Allah; and whoever commits something of such sins and receives the legal punishment for it, that will be considered as the expiation for that sin; and whoever commits something of such sins and Allah screens him, it is up to Allah whether to excuse or punish him.'"

6. When it is the most practical means of isolating an unregenerate violent offender.

[The Romans had no jails. Thus their penalties were limited to banishment, rapidly inflicted measures such as torture, or death.]

[5.3.B.1] VIOLENT PUNISHMENT MAY OR MAY NOT BE JUSTIFIED

   a. To isolate (render harmless) an offender.

   b. To improve him.

   c. To make him accept, or at least charge him with, responsibility for his crime.

   d. To restore a social balance.

   e. To restore a spiritual balance or purify evil.

   f. To restore a balance of honor.

   g. To assert a social norm or moral calculus.

   h. To make him pay the price of readmission to the social contract.

   i. To make him pay, period.

   j. To compensate, gratify or soothe the victim.

Justifying some of these ends and effects would require adding to or modifying our axioms about the fundamental violent rights of the self [see 5.1.1–3, 5.1.8]. Others are probably already justified in practice; their formulations here are based on the ethos [5.2.G.2] of a particular society.

[5.3.C.1] WHEN IS LOYALTY VIOLENCE JUSTIFIED?

   1. As such, never. It must be otherwise justified.

[5.3.C.2] WHEN IS COMPULSION VIOLENCE JUSTIFIED?

   1. By true necessity, individual or group salvation, and practicality.

Violence by command and without explanation is justified only by imminence [see 5.1.1]. In the case of an order which seems to be evil and cruel [EXAMPLE: kill all civilians at My Lai], whoever carries out such orders ought to use his reason and his conscience to see whether imminence can possibly apply. If not, he must refuse to carry out the orders. If so, he may carry them out, and the command which issued the orders without explanation becomes morally liable for the acts consequently committed.

EXAMPLE: The Persian navy were warned: "If they did not get command of the sea, they might fail to take Miletus and be punished by [King] Darius for their failure." What would their punishment consist of? And how would the people of Miletus be treated upon capture? These are the two things we need to know to determine how justified the excuse of compulsion would be in this case.

2. When only the sacrifice of the part will save the whole.

In 1620, upon consent of a learned Rabbi, the Jews of the Polish ghetto of Kalish give up one of their number in order to save themselves from a pogrom. [See 7.0.2.]

[5.3.D] WHEN ARE NONCONSENSUAL SADISTIC VIOLENCE AND EXPEDIENT VIOLENCE JUSTIFIED?

1. Never.

[But even here, as with all other motivations for violence, imminent defense or self-defense could conceivably in some rare or extreme case overrule unjustifiability.]

[5.3.E] WHEN IS CONSENSUAL SADISTIC (S/M) VIOLENCE JUSTIFIED?

1. Always, assuming that prior negotiations were detailed enough to make it truly consensual.

EXAMPLE: "Will you play with me?"—*"Beatrice Black"*

[5.4] Justifications: Fate

[5.4.A] WHEN IS VIOLENCE JUSTIFIED BY MORAL YELLOWNESS?
Moral yellowness is the outward appearance of evil or violence in the atttitude or expression of a human being.

1. Never.

[5.4.B] WHEN IS VIOLENCE JUSTIFIED BY INEVITABILITY?

1. Never, except when inevitability comprises a shorthand for some other justification [such as imminent self-defense].

[6.0] When Is Violence Unjustified?

1. When it is directed against someone based solely on who he is without reference to what he has done.

2. When it is directed against someone based solely on what he has done without reference to who he is.

3. When it has no limit.

4. When the Golden Rule has not first been applied.

5. When it is in the service of no end.

6. When it is called for solely on the basis of obedience to orders.

7. When (absent extenuating circumstances) it is based on insufficient data. Any sort of self-defense, proactive or otherwise, attempted without information of the target of our defensive efforts, is both inexpedient and immoral. *The inertia of the situation into which we inject ourselves must always be given the benefit of the doubt.* [See 5.1.2.A.2.]

COROLLARY: The practitioner of proactive violence remains morally responsible for both the intended and the unintended result.

8. When it is based on deliberate misstatements of fact.

9. When its justifications cannot be verified in the present generation.

10. When its definitions are obscure or illogical. When it is judged according to an inconsistent standard.

EXAMPLE: What is class? Lenin says one thing and a rich peasant says another. Unless both definitions are available, how can we evaluate each side's violence in defense of class?

11. When the cause does not lie open to all. When it is defined according to an inconsistent standard. Violent defense of any group is unjustified as such if the group defended has been privileged over other groups which could face comparable aggression.

12. When any one kind of violence insists on morally superseding all other kinds; and specifically when the violence insists on superseding the victim's right to violent self-defense.

[6.1] *Definitions for Lonely Atoms*

[6.1.1] WHEN IS VIOLENT DEFENSE OF SELF UNJUSTIFIED?

• When any one or more of the following fails to be met: the two circumstantial conditions (full self-sovereignty and proportionate response [see 5.1.2.A.1–2]) and the two ideological conditions (the allegiance condition and the nonviolence condition). [See 5.1.2.B.1–2.]

• Proactive defense is unjustified in every case when the likelihood of serious danger to ourselves from the source we intend to strike has not been absolutely verified. [See 5.1.1, caveat.]

[6.2] *Justifications: Self-Defense*

[6.2.A] WHEN IS VIOLENT DEFENSE OF HONOR UNJUSTIFIED?

1. When it is defense of collective honor alone, and when that collective honor is its own justification.

> EXAMPLE: "Can one American watch another die in his cause, by his side, without realizing that that cause must be worth while, and, therefore, must be pursued to a victorious end, whatever the cause?"

2. When it is defense of collective honor, from whose collectivity perpetrators of unjustified acts have not been excluded.

> EXAMPLE: Somebody feels called upon to defend the "honor" of the S.S.

3. When it is expressed as aggression against a nonviolent victim.

4. When it is derived from a standard which we cannot control [although this can become justified by imminent defense of self or others even in an arbitrary cause].

INDICATION OF INJUSTICE:

Dishonor to another dishonors oneself.

> EXAMPLE: In Afghanistan, my raped daughter must be put to death to save *me* from shame.

> CAVEAT: Although we must always be vigilant regarding this trap, the truth is that we usually do fall into it—or rather that we were born ensnared in it. If you and I are agreed that our honor lies at least in part in each other's keeping, then there is not much we can do about it. By no. 5.1.2 above, I possess the right to violently defend you, or not. If I care for you, I will do it, and I will be justified in so doing. [EXAMPLE: In Afghanistan, I kill my daughter's rapist, and thereby restore both her and myself to honor.]. What can we say then? Defense of another's honor must be consensual and must respect the other's rights in nos. 5.1.1–3 above. Above all, I must refuse to accept a demagogue's or murderer's honor into my keeping.

5. When it is linked to another end (e.g., defense of homeland) so as to render dishonorable any questioning of that end.

> EXAMPLE: Soviet patriotism gets expressed against dissidents.

[6.2.B] WHEN IS VIOLENT DEFENSE OF CLASS UNJUSTIFIED?

1. When it fails to distinguish between unequal human capacity, unequal luck and unequal goodness. Due to those three inequities, equality of circumstances can only be created and maintained through unending repression, which requires a class of repressers.

EXAMPLE: Stalin represses kulak peasants whose only sin was getting richer than their neighbors.

2. When it defines class solely in terms of origin.

EXAMPLE: Twentieth-century Japanese discriminate against Burakumin "Untouchables," sometimes driving them to suicide, solely on account of the occupation of their ancestors.

3. *[Similar to #2.]* When class is merely status without functionality. [*Alternate formulation:* When class expresses itself as worth instead of function.]

EXAMPLE: Masters defend themselves against emancipating their slaves.

4. *[Similar to #3.]* When the thing defended is merely class privilege.

5. When class equals nothing but strength.

6. When class equals property, and another's right to life supersedes the defender's right to property.

7. When its end or means violates the fundamental rights of the self [5.2].

8. When it is predicated on any one definition of class. [Having said that, let me give you one definition which covers many "bad" cases of class, excluding pure functionality: *Class is the local determinator of social inequality.*]

9. When it does not steer fairly between liberty and equality.

[6.2.C.I] WHEN IS VIOLENT DEFENSE OF PREEXISTING AUTHORITY UNJUSTIFIED?
That is, when is it justified to rise up against it?

1. When that defense in and of itself permanently aggrandizes the authority, as opposed to merely maintaining it.

EXAMPLE: Lincoln's victory in the American Civil War was justified certainly by the abolition of slavery it brought about, and arguably by the fact that the South attacked first. But one result of his victory, and the main point for which he fought—federal control—was not justified.

2. When the dispute does not physically endanger authority *and* when authority nonetheless refuses to entertain the idea of reconciliation.

3. When authority has no "empathetic bridge" to the masses or the opposition.

4. When that defense aims at permanently excluding or debasing a portion of the governed.

5. When authority offers no release from obedience in the event of disagreement with it.

6. When self-defense comprises mere defense of unity.

EXAMPLE: The Bolsheviks vote to make "factionalism" illegal.

7. When it does not generally take place at a steady and moderate tempo (revolutionary and emergency authority *briefly* excepted).

8. When authority invokes more violent power than it needs to in a given case.

9. When authority is not legitimate in the first place. [See 5.2.C.1.4.]

INDICATIONS OF ILLEGITIMATE AUTHORITY:

When authority can unilaterally abrogate the social contract.

[NOTE: Authority's subjects may, however, do just that. See 5.2.B caveat.]

DESCRIPTIONS OF ILLEGITIMATE AUTHORITY:

- When the officials are not assistants of the people, but constitute a ruling class. [In 5.2.D.2 we quoted Martin Luther King's Maxim: *A law is unjust which requires from the governed acts or allegiances not required from the legislators.*]
- When the government performs its duties by force, not by love.
- When the state does not enrich its citizens, but makes them poorer.
- When the state does not enhance liberties, but restricts them.
- When people do not feel safer under the government, but more threatened.
- When we cannot peacefully revoke the social contract.

REMINDER: Authority cannot legitimize itself merely by refraining from violence, or even by rewarding its dependents.

EXAMPLE: *Julius Caesar:* "I myself am never happier than when pardoning suppliants."

[6.2.C.2] WHEN IS VIOLENT DEFENSE OF REVOLUTIONARY AUTHORITY UNJUSTIFIED?

1. When by virtue of its own assumption of infallibility through future justification, revolutionary authority cuts itself off from any check or correction, and so operates increasingly in a moral and logical vacuum.

2. When its ends rather than mere military cut off subjects and bystanders cut themselves off from their ordinary attachments.

EXAMPLE: the Khmer Rouge.

3. When it revolutionizes the masses against their will for a prolonged period of time.

4. When it sunders prior civic allegiances without creating new ones.

5. Above all, when it assigns its violence no limit.

[6.2.D] WHEN IS VIOLENT DEFENSE OF RACE, GENDER AND CULTURE UNJUSTIFIED?

1. When it is based solely on the defense of a prohibition, privilege or compulsion in one's own group.

2. When it precludes defense of individual choice. [This rule derives from the priority which my own culture and epoch places upon the rights of the self [5.1.1–3, 5.1.18]. Other groups continue to emphasize bloodline over choice.]

3. When it is retroactive. Once the aliens move in, the land quickly becomes theirs, too.

EXAMPLE: The KKK's defense of race was doubly unjust, first because it was directed against people who had never invaded, but had been dragged there as slaves; second, because those ex-slaves had become no longer black Africans but black Americans.

4. When it considers alien habits and characteristics to be proof of inferiority or evil, and acts accordingly; when it forgets the rights of the self and the Golden Rule.

EXAMPLE: *Catechism of the Knights of the White Camelia:* "Are you opposed to allowing the control of the political affairs of this country to go in whole or in part into the hands of the African race, and will you do everything in your power to prevent it?"

Proactive defense of race is highly suspect.

[6.2.E] WHEN IS VIOLENT DEFENSE OF CREED UNJUSTIFIED?

1. When the essence of the creed is nonviolence. Imminence may still justify a limited emergency self-defense.

2. When creed is a mask for another means or end.

EXAMPLE: Joan of Arc's judges burn her alive in the name of Christianity. In fact they've condemned her because she was a threat to their authority.

3. When the creed defended against is nonviolent or morally transparent.

EXAMPLE: Giordano Bruno is burned at the stake for asserting that "infinite worlds . . . exist beside this earth."

[6.2.F] WHEN IS VIOLENT DEFENSE OF WAR AIMS UNJUSTIFIED?

1. When the war aims are not legitimate.

Nos. 2–4: When the violent means and ends are not limited:

2. When the violence of war is directed by or against noncombatants. *(Violation of First Limitation to 5.2.1.)* When discrimination is not respected [**5.2.F.1, 1st Lim.**].

FIRST COROLLARY: When we could persuade our enemies not to be combatants, and use violence against them instead.

EXAMPLE: *Deuteronomy 7:1–2:* "When the Lord your God brings you into the land which you are entering to take possession of it, and clears away many nations before you . . . and you defeat them; then you must utterly destroy them; you shall make no covenant with them and show no mercy to them."

SECOND COROLLARY: When the violence gets employed outside of war zones, and outside of wartime.

THIRD COROLLARY: When the violence gets employed against the unpersuaded.

CAVEAT: Practically speaking, this is impossible to live up to.

FOURTH COROLLARY: When the violence gets employed against prisoners of war who are in our power.

3. When the violence of war is directed against more people than is needed to accomplish a specific justified result, or the number of people

harmed by the violence is greater than the number of people helped by it (*Violation of Second Limitation to 5.2.1*). When proportionality is not respected [**5.1.7**].

> EXAMPLE: King Shaka orders his army of Zulus to kill the entire Kumalo tribe. Women "can propagate and bring forth children, who may become my enemies."

4. When the leader's authority is not justified; when the violence is employed by illegitimate command [**5.2.C.1–2; 6.2.C.1.9**]. (*Violation of Third Limitation to 5.2.1.*)

> EXAMPLE: *William Pultney, speech to the House of Commons, 1732:* "Where was a braver army than that under Julius Caesar? Where was ever an army that had served country more faithfully? . . . yet that army enslaved their country."

[6.2.G] WHEN IS VIOLENT DEFENSE OF HOMELAND UNJUSTIFIED?

1. When it is mere prosecution of homeland's interest.

Interest is advantage, not right. It may be unjustified or merely value-neutral, but when advanced by violent means it becomes aggression.

> EXAMPLE: Regarding the partition of Poland, Napoleon remarks that "Vienna . . . felt great satisfaction . . . at acquiring several million souls and enriching its treasury by many millions."

2. When it is nothing but defense against futurity.

By **futurity** I mean the inevitable obliteration that awaits every homeland, given enough time.

> EXAMPLE: In 1939, Germany holds a four-to-one advantage in materiel. "In order to maintain it," Hitler reasons, "we would have to go on producing four times as much. We are in no position to do so." The solution: Attack Poland while we can.

3. In any civil war, unless this defense can be shown to uphold legitimate authority. Otherwise, both sides can claim to represent the homeland.

> EXAMPLE: Pompey says to his legions: "Surely we may trust in the gods and in the righteousness of the war, which has for its noble and just object the defence of our country's constitution." But when his rival Julius Caesar begins to march, the senate "in its panic repented that it had not accepted Caesar's proposals, which it at last considered fair, after fear had turned it from the rage of party to the counsels of prudence."

[6.2.H] WHEN IS VIOLENT DEFENSE OF GROUND UNJUSTIFIED?

1. When that ground may be shifted at will for the sake of expedient or aggressive advantage.

[6.2.I] WHEN IS VIOLENT DEFENSE OF THE EARTH UNJUSTIFIED?

1. When scientific imminence remains unestablished:

a. Because the presuppositions of imminent danger on which it is based remain open to good faith scientific disagreement.

CAVEAT: Dissenting perspectives always exist. Still, from a practical point of view we can speak of a "general scientific consensus" on a question.

EXAMPLE: The Darwinian theory of evolution continues to be more plausible than both Creationism and the Lamarck-Lysenko notion of acquired characeristics.

and/or

b. Because the defender is neither a scientific expert on the issue in question, nor capable of showing why the experts on his side are more correct than those of the opposition.

In short, when there exists a danger that what is called scientific fact may simply be a murderous assumption.

2. In the absence of an explicit calculus which allows the defender to—

• Weigh benefits to an ecosystem against benefit to the human economy which harms it. [For comparison see **6.2.J.1.**]

• Define an imminent or scientifically imminent threat [**5.2.I.1**] to a place in terms of which losses are acceptable [examples: the extermination of a species, the destruction of "scenic values"; the justifiability of a specific risk to human health]

• Publicly judge and be judged on the criterion of *results* [**2.4**].

[6.2.J] WHEN IS VIOLENT DEFENSE OF ANIMALS UNJUSTIFIED?

1. In the absence of an explicit calculus which allows the defender to weigh benefits to animals against benefit to humans. [By analogy with **6.2.I.2**, all three of whose subclauses apply.] Miscellaneous exploitation, extermination and cruelty [EXAMPLE: the boiling alive of lobsters] has not yet become unjustified by most human norms. Moreover, if humans and

animals are ethical equals, those who would prohibit human violence against animals must fit the violence of animals against each other into their moral framework. This calculus should include:

• A detailed categorization of the spectrum of animal use, from food to research to entertainment to maintenance of ethos.

• Descriptions of the human and animal identities involved, with estimates as to the likely suffering or positive effects to all parties for each moral choice being considered.

> COROLLARY: Animal defenders rightly accuse others of advocating absolute or relative dismissal of animal rights without justifying the basis of that dismissal. They must be careful not to be guilty of the same sin in regard to human ethos [**5.2.G.2**].

> DEFINITIONS (after Mary Midgley):

• **Absolute dismissal** means that animals have no rights at all.

• **Relative dismissal** means that they have some, but not as many as we do.

• Definitions of all undefined or badly defined terms:

Animal identity

Human ethos and identity

Imminent and unjustifiable harm

[6.2.K] WHEN IS VIOLENT DEFENSE OF GENDER UNJUSTIFIED?

1. When it is merely the violence committed by one gender on another for reasons which have nothing to do with gender.

> EXAMPLE: A woman who murders her abusive husband does not thereby automatically defend her gender, only herself. Her self-defense may be entirely justifiable as such, without being so as defense of gender.

2. To the extent that it violates freedom of expression. [See **5.1.8**.]

3. Against infanticide which furthers scientifically imminent defense of earth [**5.2.I.1**]. Fortunately, scientific imminence does not now exist.

4. When gender becomes a mask for the violent maintenance of a class system.

> EXAMPLE: In Honolulu in 1932, two Asian men are assaulted, one fatally, in after-the-fact "defense" of a white woman named Thalia Massie who falsely claimed rape.

[6.2.L] WHEN IS VIOLENT DEFENSE AGAINST TRAITORS UNJUSTIFIED?

1. When the acts defined as treason are the same as the acts committed by the supposed anti-traitors. [A rule violated no less for its obviousness.]

[6.2.M] WHEN IS VIOLENT DEFENSE OF THE REVOLUTION UNJUSTIFIED?

1. When the acts defined by the revolutionaries as treason are the same as the acts committed by them before they came to power.

2. When the revolution's immediate ends change but legitimacy fails to be reevaluated.

EXAMPLE: Robespierre begins by calling for freedom of speech, then muzzles the press. Why? For him to be justified, he must offer satisfactory reasons.

3. To the extent that it fails to explicitly and consensually define the grievances which it seeks to address.

EXAMPLE: "That the price of bread on July 14, 1789, would have been of less significance to Robespierre than his belief that men, on that day, set out to destroy tyranny . . ." Do we have a consensus as to whether we are correcting the price or bread or overthrowing a tyrannical government?

[6.3] Justifications: Policy and Choice

[6.3.A.I] WHEN IS VIOLENT DETERRENCE UNJUSTIFIED?

1. Absent imminence, insofar as its effects are not foreseeable and controllable.

EXAMPLES:

1. Nuclear "deterrence," which may destroy the entire world.

2. When Seneca's Maxim operates.

Seneca's Maxim: *Violent deterrence becomes inexpedient, although not necessarily unjustifiable, when its severity corrodes loyalty and fear into desperation.*

Thus, harsh deterrence often defeats its own object, in which case it was unjustified by the crucial test of *result* [2.5].

2. When directed against persons who have broken no code and are actively or passively loyal to the deterrer's authority. When its violence does not fall entirely upon those who made the choice to undertake the proscribed behavior.

CAVEAT: This case may be justified nonethless by very rare situations of military imminence, or the imminent proactive defense of a legitimate revolutionary authority [**5.2.C.2**]. Still, it is not excusable as a routine transaction of authority [**6.3.A.1.5**].

3. By mere symmetry without discrimination. *Tu quoque* is not a justified defense for unethical acts of violence unless those acts have been consensualized into an ethos of acceptability.

Undiscriminating symmetry of unjustified acts [+ *tu quoque*]: If I commit an illegitimate act of violence upon A, it is no excuse that you who judge me have committed the same illegitimate act upon B. (However, if you commit that act upon B, then I may deter or punish you by committing that act upon you [**5.3.A.2**].)

EXAMPLE: Nazi war criminals ask for acquittal on the grounds that their Soviet judges also committed war crimes.

4. When it harms more people than those harmed by the deterred act. That is, when proportionality has been violated. [**See 5.1.7.**]

5. When its main purpose is to overawe people into routine or perpetual compliance with authority (i.e., when it has not been crafted to deter the specific and limited violence of a narrowly specified group). [**See 5.3.A.2.**]

CAVEAT: Deterrence is, however, justified when its main purpose is to overawe people into routine or perpetual compliance with the *laws* established by legitimate authority [**5.2.C.1–2**].

NOTE TO CAVEAT: Since legitimate authority is consensual, legitimate authority's laws, to be just, must be revocable at the will of the governed.

6. When it is not didactic.

EXAMPLE: A biological warfare attack which its victims believe to be a natural epidemic will not deter them from carrying out their own violence against the aggressor; therefore, although the biological warfare attack may be justifiable by other categories, it cannot be justified as deterrence.

7. When it is justified by proactive imminence alone, and the justifiability of the violence which invoked proactive imminence is debatable.

Proactive imminence: The more people I kill, the more I need to kill, in order to deter or prevent others from killing me. Frequently invoked in defense of ground, war aims, revolution and revolutionary authority, proactive imminence need not be unjustified if the original violence which brought it into being was justified; still, it is obviously of a lower, more contingent order of justifiability than ordinary imminence alone. Proactive imminence may be either **ordinary** [5.1.1] or **scientific** [5.2.I.1].

8. When it is executed proactively as both deterrence and retribution.

EXAMPLE: Napoleon kidnaps and slays the Duc d'Enghien to deter assassination attempts. He could have simply imprisoned him as a hostage, and issued a deterrent warning of his liquidation in the event of another assassination attempt.

9. When the act deterred remains undefined, when there has been no deterrent warning, or when the deterrer's retribution proves to be more severe than was indicated in the deterrent warning.

10. When the deterrent violence knowingly exceeds the deterrence threshold.

Deterrence threshold: Herman Kahn invented this term, which refers to the minimum level of severity whose threat or execution will be required to deter.

[6.3.A.2] WHEN IS VIOLENT MILITARY RETRIBUTION UNJUSTIFIED?

1. By tu quoque alone. [See **6.3.A.1.2.**]

2. When it is not didactic. [See **6.3.A.1.5.**]

3. When the degree of imminence is low enough to allow judicial retribution (punishment).

[6.3.A.3] WHEN IS VIOLENT REVENGE UNJUSTIFIED?

1. By tu quoque alone. [See **6.3.A.1.2.**]

2. When it creates a new wrong equal to or worse than the wrong it has revenged.

[6.3.B] WHEN IS VIOLENT JUDICIAL RETRIBUTION (PUNISHMENT) UNJUSTIFIED?

1. By tu quoque alone. [See **6.3.A.1.2.**]

EXAMPLE: Because A punishes B does not give C the right to punish D.

2. When the person suffering the punishment does not understand why he is being punished.

EXAMPLE: "Correction must always be meted to the bad—to make a better man of him—not to the unfortunate; on him it is wasted."—*Plato*

3. When the punishment is inconsistently applied to penalize similar acts committed under similar circumstances. (When it comprises the expedient or slapdash employment of arbitrary means.)

4. When there is no separation of powers among judges, executioners and sovereigns.

5. When proof of guilt is logically faulty, or when the judicial process is dishonest.

EXAMPLES:

1. "In each organization about 3 to 5 percent of the total must be declared 'the enemy' because that is the percentage mentioned by Chairman Mao in one of his speeches."

2. *Malleus Maleficarum* on plea bargains with witches: "After she has been consigned to prison in this way, the promise to spare her life [if she confesses] should be kept for a time, but after a certain period she should be burned."

CAVEAT: Punishment of objectively innocent persons, such as witches, might conceivably be extenuated, although not justified, were a fair judicial process applied to their case, and were there a widespread presupposition of the imminent danger they represented.

EXAMPLE: The Huron Indians believed in witches and sometimes put one of their number to death on this basis. Huron witches were, in effect, selfish or antisocial people who often might have saved themselves by following tribal norms of generous sociability. Witches investigated under the *Malleus Maleficarum*, on the other hand, had little hope of escape from condemnation.

6. To the extent that the punishment, which may be just or unjust in and of itself, furthers authority's power beyond the minimum necessary for enforcing the social contract.

EXAMPLE: "Governments need police to produce criminals; because the mass of people are so frightened of criminals they willingly give away their rights and freedoms to obtain protection."—*John Myhill*

EXAMPLE: The imprisoned Marquis de Sade writes his wife that people will say of him: *"He must have been guilty since he has been punished."*

NOTE: Both of these accusations may be in their own context disingenuous and even untrue. That is not the point. The point is that the fears they raise must be addressed in each case.

7. When deterrence remains possible but has not yet been tried. A statutory penalty is its own deterrent. However, in more fluid cases, a warning or less severe penalty should be tried first. This is why the law treats juveniles more leniently than adults. And this is why Stalin's application of the death penalty to twelve-year-olds was wrong.

[6.3.C.1] WHEN IS LOYALTY VIOLENCE UNJUSTIFIED?

1. When its justification is loyalty alone. [In such a case, obedience needs no compulsion, and the fact of superior orders becomes irrelevant to the order-follower's role as a self-determining moral agent.]

EXAMPLE: The Nazi war criminal Otto Ohlendorf, explaining why he murdered 90,000 people: "To me it is inconceivable that a subordinate leader should not carry out orders given by the leaders of the state . . ."

2. When the loyalty derives its only justification from commonality between leader and led. [Ethical identity between leader and led is necessary for justice, but not sufficient.]

Imminence may create commonality. Commonality alone, however, can never create imminence.

3. When the loyalty is defined only as a synonym for achieving the political end.

[6.3.C.2] WHEN IS COMPULSION VIOLENCE UNJUSTIFIED?

1. When one cannot demonstrate that one would have been severely punished for not committing it.

2. When what gets defined as compulsion is in fact only a requirement for achieving an end.

EXAMPLE: The Japanese vivisect Chinese POWs without even an anesthetic "because in a war, you have to win."

3. When the compulsion derives from the moral agent himself.

[See 6.3.C.1.]

[6.3.D] WHEN ARE NONCONSENSUAL SADISTIC AND EXPEDIENT VIOLENCE UNJUSTIFIED?

1. Always.

EXAMPLE: Life among the Ik of Africa: ". . . men would watch a child with eager anticipation as it crawled toward the fire, then burst into gay and happy laughter as it plunged a skinny hand into the coals. Such times were the few times when parental affection showed itself; a mother would glow with pleasure to hear such joy occasioned by her offspring, and pull it tenderly out of the fire."

[But as noted in 5.3.D, even here, as with all other motivations for violence, imminent defense or self-defense could conceivably in some rare or extreme case overrule unjustifiability.]

[6.3.E] WHEN IS CONSENSUAL SADISTIC (S/M) VIOLENCE UNJUSTIFIED?

1. Never.

[6.4] Justifications: Fate

[6.4.A] WHEN IS VIOLENCE UNJUSTIFIED BY MORAL YELLOWNESS?

1. Always.

EXAMPLE: "The first time I saw dead Germans they looked just like Americans, except for the uniform. And then you started to think of them as animals."

[6.4.B] WHEN IS VIOLENCE UNJUSTIFIED BY INEVITABILITY?

1. Always, except when inevitability comprises a shorthand for some other justification [such as imminent self-defense].

[7.0] When Is Violence Unjustified but Excusable?

1. When it is based on sincere misperceptions of fact which, had they been correct, would have justified the violence. [See 5.1.2.A.2 and 6.0.7.]

2. When it is carried out under the direct threat of extreme violence. [See 5.3.C.3.]

[8.0] A Checklist for Revolutionaries

1. Do postrevolutionary conditions resemble the prerevolutionary conditions which we objected to?

2. How accurately does revolutionary theory predict events?

3. How reductionist is the theory? Does it permit most people and things to exist for their own sake?

4. How gigantic a task ought the revolution set for itself?

5. Does the revolution allow nonrevolutionaries to inform it of its errors?

MORAL QUESTIONS FOR A CYCLE OF REVOLUTION

1. Sense of grievance
   Should I be angry? Should I hope for a different future?

2. Polarization
   Should I join?

3. Escalation of violence
   Should I fight? Should I kill?

4. Triumph and consolidation
   Now that I can see the future, does it justify me?

5. Maintenance of power
   Should I continue? Am I satisfied? Am I justified?

From a Letter of Comment from Prof. Bruce Trigger

Department of Anthropology, McGill University (14 September 2002)
There is, however, something missing which you may wish to deal with in another book or not at all. When I was younger I thought there was little to be said for the superiority of the Golden Rule in its Christian form (Do unto others . . .) over the far more widespread negative version (Don't do unto others . . .). Indeed Shaw's observation that tastes differ made me think the negative version was probably the better one. It seems to me now, however, that one can formulate lega-style rules about what people can and can't do about defending their rights but self-interest will go on construing those rights to mean whatever the construer wants. What is needed is an underlying consensus about how modern societies should be run . . . Curiously we already have this standard in that most ignored and reviled document *The Universal Declaration of Human Rights* (1948), which set out minimum standards for the legal, political, economic, social, and cultural treatment of human beings everywhere. No country has ever lived up to the standards of this declaration but I find it a most remarkable statement of ideals we should be living up to. I also believe that if there are still people around a millennium hence who can read and write they will honour this declaration as the supreme accomplishment of the 20th

century and the one that made the survival and growth of civilized life in the third millennium possible. John Humphrey and the other people who drafted it will be remembered by the general public when Hitler, Churchill and others are known only to specialists who study the Pre-Really-Civilized era. I believe in cultural diversity but I also believe that this diversity must be grounded in respect for each human being and each human being's right to develop and flourish—the first aspiration of the Enlightenment and the first to be abandoned by those people whose political power grew from the Enlightenment. I don't believe such universal values undermine cultural pluralism; on the contrary they can enhance it by counteracting the hegemonic forces that are economically and socially corroding the basis on which cultural pluralism flourishes and hence are limiting freedom of choice. What I think I am trying to say is that it will only be when people can be brought to agree about issues such as these that your calculus will really take hold and provide a basis for judging human conduct. How to get issues of this sort even discussed is of course a bit of a question. But until this happens my terrorist is going to be someone else's freedom fighter.

Everyone deplores violence. So why do so many of these people seem so happy?

518. Boy with knife "for defense," central Madagascar, 1994.

519. Boys and knife, Peshawar, Pakistan, 2000.

520. Boys with toy gun, southeast Thailand, 1996.

521. Rock-and-roll star Ted Nugent with his son and a hunting rifle, Michigan, USA, 1997.

522. Afghan Mujahid's son, with toy rifle carved for him by his father, near Parachinar, Pakistani-Afghan border, 1982.

523. Afghan Mujahid with Kalashnikov, near Jalalabad, Afghanistan, 1982.

524. Boys with toy gun by bullet-pocked wall, East Mostar, Bosnia, 1994.

525. Basque volunteer who fought with Muslim side, East Mostar, Bosnia, 1994.

526. Policewoman in women's prison, Bogota, Colombia, 1999. She loved guns.

527. My government-appointed Iraqi interpreter with his pistol, Baghdad, 1998.

528. Iraqi soldiers raising their Kalashnikovs on Saddam Hussein's birthday, Tikrit, 1998.

529. Karenni insurgents, Karen State, Burma, 1994.

530a. Boy with toy machine gun, Japan, 1995.

530b. Boy with squirt gun, Louisiana, USA, 1994.

531a. Boys with toy gun, southeast Thailand, 1996.

531b. My friend Craig, with my Desert Eagle .50 caliber, California, USA, 1995.

532a. Young Mujahideen with guns and rocket launcher, near Jalalabad, Afghanistan, 1982.

532b. Military parade, Vienna, Austria, 1996.

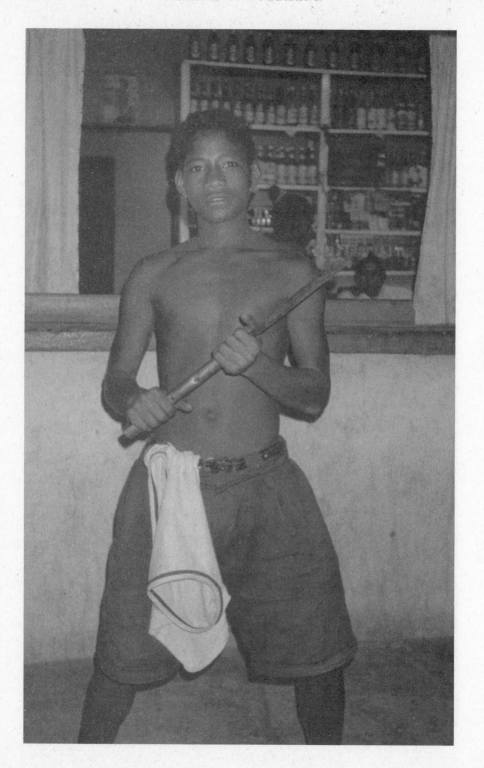

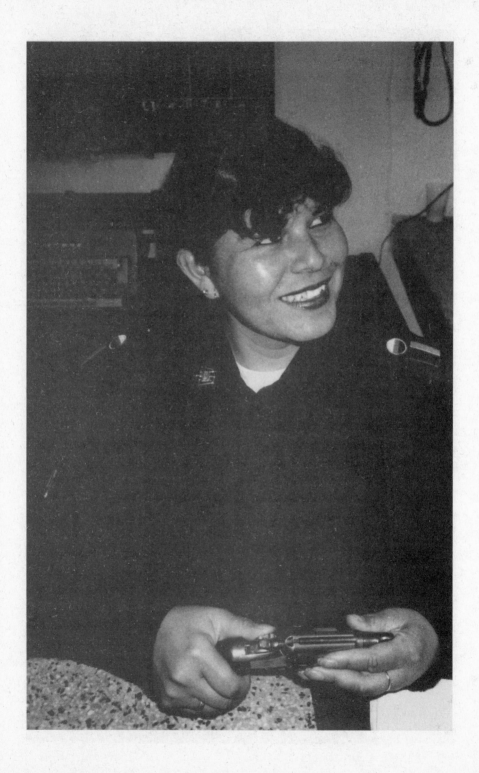

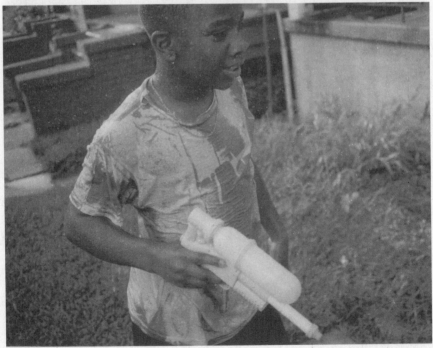

PART II

Studies in
Consequences

Note on Inconsistencies

You will find minor stylistic differences in the case studies. For instance, some chapters, such as "The War Never Came Here," deny themselves the convenience of quotation marks in direct speech. This so-called innovation, which I have employed in my novels for some years now, was a source of some distress to my patient editor, Mr. Horowitz. Other chapters show the influence of market pressure. For instance, the Somalia essay was handwritten in Nairobi, in a composition book which I bought in a little pharmacy. I then sent it by courier express to *Esquire* magazine. Because I would be out of reach of copy editors, I inserted quotation marks for clarity. Should I have standardized these inconsistencies? I recall Lawrence of Arabia's comments to the proofreader who warned him that he had spelled the name of this favorite camel every which way in *Seven Pillars of Wisdom*. Lawrence replied simply, "She was a splendid beast."

SOUTHEAST ASIA

INTRODUCTION

Need I explain why it is that in a book that purports to help people judge excuses for violence, the case studies are accompanied by introductions only, not conclusions? The main reason, of course, is that I don't trust my knowledge and competence to apply my own calculus, which like all human productions must be awfully flawed anyway. If I reject the calculus of conquest in Deuteronomy, how dare I hold up my own moral calculus for your dismissal—especially when I admit that it could be better applied by those who know more facts than I, and differently applied by those who weigh any justification more or less heavily than I? Of course in my own second-rate world of armchair declamations, I get as opinionated as the next hindsighted or walleyed prophet. *I* know who's right and wrong in Colombia, and I'll tell you—if I can only trust you not to embarrass me with the shoddiness of my ideals and arguments. But I try not to put my foot in my mouth on the subject of Southeast Asia, where Buddhism blunts the edges of right and wrong, and tradition devalues *Rising Up and Rising Down*'s presuppositions—in particular, the rights of the self, on which my requirement that legitimate authority be consensual are founded.

Khmer Rouge Cambodia, considered in "The Skulls on the Shelves," did derive from the European tradition of Marxism, but took the long way around, reinterpreting itself through and receiving moral support from

Mao's China. Remember, it was Mao who said that half of his population, or three hundred million, would be an acceptable price to pay in a decisive war against the capitalist world. No matter what, my moral calculus will never be fair to Southeast Asia on its own terms; I will never "understand" this region as I do my own. All the same, Pol Pot's new order can be judged quite easily by almost any moral calculus. The rights of self, creed, class, culture—you needn't seek them here! (Rule number one on the blackboard at the Tuol Sleng torture-murder center: *It is absolutely forbidden to speak.*)

Rising Up and Rising Down insists that given the almost unlimited license it temporarily seizes, revolutionary authority in particular bears a terrible burden of proving the justifiability of its ends and means. "The Skulls on the Shelves," which was researched in 1991 and 1996, is less of an attempt to define the already glaringly definable moral issues of the Cambodian situation than to meditate upon the human how and why of a *limiting case,* by which I mean a point at the practical end of a moral continuum. What Pol Pot did bears comparison with what Hitler did. Mao to the Khmer Rouge: "You, comrades, have won an amazing victory. You have gotten rid of all classes at one blow!" Hence the skulls on the shelves, the skulls stinking and yellow (almost nine thousand of them at Choeung Ek Killing Field alone). If you are a moral relativist, I urge you to study these murderers' example and then rethink your position. "The Skulls on the Shelves" proves that anybody who thinks and cares about the world bears an urgent necessity to construct a moral calculus.

The brother of my friend Vanny was tortured to death at Tuol Sleng, now a "genocide museum" where Vanny sought his face amidst the crowds of wall photographs of tortured faces. I asked her what she would want me to demand of Pol Pot, and she replied, "Just I want to know why. Why he kill the people when he is Cambodian like them." This case study suggests several possible answers to that question. None of them are good enough to justify the skulls on the shelves. *An unjust means or an unjust end equally invalidates all derivative moral enactions.*

So Cambodia became hell, and Cambodians fled when they could. What then? "The Last Generation," set in southern California in 1996, raises issues of imminent self-defense, and particularly defense of race and culture. Most Cambodians are rural people; frequently they're illiterate. The lucky few who escaped the camps in Thailand to arrive in the United

States came to rest in a predictable niche: the inner city. In the schools their children encountered black and Latino gangs who invoked defense of ground and racial self-defense to attack them. Hence the eighth-grader who was attacked by "Mexicans" with screwdrivers: "I didn't know them," he said. "They didn't know me." As you read this story, ask yourself what you would have done if you were a Cambodian schoolchild with no one to protect you from such violence. Why do gangs spring into being? This case study tells why. And, as you will have seen in "The Skulls on the Shelves," Cambodia itself is rife with robbery and warlordism, starving soldiers deserting on both sides, men gunfighting over a fish in the market, vendors kidnapped by royalists or Khmer Rouge for a little money. Where would this eighth-grader or his mother have ever witnessed an incumbent, potent, legitimate centralized authority? Not in the U.S. The President of the United States, the principal of the high school, the teachers who failed to preserve him from harm in the institution where they ostensibly exemplified and led—what kind of leaders were any of these? A Cambodian mother: "My boy, he get beat so many times by Mexicans. Teacher they can't do nothing. They don't want to do nothing. Sometimes American way is not so good."

Would you abolish gangs if you could? Then you must figure out what you would have done in that boy's place when the "Mexicans" came after you. Or else you must conceptualize some interventionist protective authority that can save children from being attacked with screwdrivers. When is violent defense of race and culture justified? Certainly it is when the racism of others imminently requires self-defense.

When racial self-defense continues without end, institutionalizing itself into an attribute of race and culture itself, then the next chapter of the story begins. Set in the decidedly unwealthy city of Stockton, California, in 2000, the case study "Kickin' It" looks in upon two gangs whose memberships are primarily Cambodian; in defense of honor and defense of gangland culture they fight each other. In the undying words of a certain Mr. Scarface, "All here, all the Asian people have Asian enemies. Why we gonna make enemies with the other races?"

And if this weren't strange enough, these gangbangers copy and idolize black gang culture more than their own. Why? Because in their view, blacks know the most and have suffered the most in ghetto America. Overlooked aliens, children of people who literally can't speak the language of the new country, with nothing to look forward to but menial drudgery at best, these Cambodian teenagers go for what they can go for: gang pride. "Well," said one young man, "I felt like I was strong 'cause I had friends. It made me more of a man since people were more afraid of me. I remember one guy in my class who tried to fight with me, but then he learned I was kicking with a gang." Is someone who thinks in this way exercising the fundamental right of any self or group to express its identity, or has violence merely forced him into the conformity of counterviolence? What is manhood, and can it justify or be justified by Cambodian ganghood? If the soldier in Cambodia who extorts a fish with his machine gun is justified by desperate hunger, is the friendless young Cambodian in an alien country justified in making gang friends to be strong?

In Burma, or at least in Burma's rebellious province of Shan State, such disempowered individuals might have joined the private army of Khun Sa, better known as the Opium King. Meeting this eerie, charismatic figure in 1994 was one of my greatest experiences as a journalist. In defense of race, homeland and culture, he sold a substantial proportion of the world's heroin (the Cambodians in "Kickin' It" sold street drugs to make pocket change). I have never been able to refute Khun Sa's words: "I do sympathize with the addicts, but also with the growers and traders. Not just one group, but three."

When the Burmese rape your sister and burn your village and you have no way of making a living but selling opium, what are you to do? Hence the title of this case study: "But What Are We to Do?" This is what they always asked me in Shan State, and I never had an answer. When Khun Sa employs the profits of his heroin trade to defend your zone with his private army, what will you say against him? If he keeps any portion of those profits for himself, does that render him less justified? What constitutes imminent self-defense? Does defense of homeland allow the Shan tribes to secede from a Burmese federation in which they never wished to remain? Khun Sa said: "This is legally our country. According to the Panglong Accord we should have been independent more than thirty years ago."

Rising Up and Rising Down's moral calculus proposes that defense of homeland is justified *when the aliens, the people from outside the homeland, are the imminent violent aggressors.* Are the Burmese aliens in Shan State, or are the Shan breakaway renegades? The American Civil War and the Yugoslavian Civil War posed their own versions of this question. Who defines homeland? What equilibrium would you propose between authority and liberty? What are the rights of a sovereign state, and what if they conflict with the rights of an ethnic minority? Should Burma, or Yugoslavia, allow its own dissolution down to the subatomic level? Or must the Shan, the Karenni and other insurgent minorities abandon their own dreams? What else could or should the Shan people have done?

"Yakuza Lives" (1998) deals with the "Japanese Mafia," the Yakuza. This case study bears obvious comparison with "The Last Generation" and "Kickin' It." The ethical questions, the violence justifications, are similar. However, the American gangs described in the latter two studies are ad hoc organizations whose traditions, such as they are, go back only a few years, and whose members remain powerless to influence more than a few square blocks of their own neighborhoods; whereas men who enter the Yakuza may stay in it for life, with all the adult employments of corporate extortion, money laundering, strikebreaking, "protection," prostitution clubs, et cetera; furthermore, Yakuza claim an indefinitely long-standing presence in Japan, and indeed, even now the police afford them a certain respect and tolerance; they're right-wing superpatriots, defenders of this and that, Robin Hoods (in their own minds, at least). And the fact that they continue to insist on this image of themselves with such conviction casts a hint of doubt on other claimants to that role, such as Khun Sa. "What we do is help the weak," said one very powerful and frightening man. "And if the weak are so appreciative and bring money, then we refuse to receive it unless they insist."

These heroes are also well instructed in the finer points of deterrence, retribution, revenge and defense against traitors. "My policy for living in this organization is to throw myself away," one Yakuza informs us. "The organization is always first. This is my belief. I must always come second." Put this way, it sounds almost beautiful.

"I'm Especially Interested in *Young* Girls" is set in Thailand in 1993. It deals with prostitution, particularly child prostitution. Although this case study is, in effect, a confession about a kidnapping I committed, I'm not sure that what I did was violence. If it were, I still would be proud of it. When is violent defense of gender justified? For one thing, when its cause lies open to all—in other words, when its purpose is to defend the possession of rights which ought to be applied irrespective of gender. That little girl was sold against her will, locked up, and essentially raped for profit. This chapter really belongs in *Rising Up and Rising Down* on account of the very fundamental issues it raises regarding consensuality and the rights of the self. The fact that her slavery was sexual, gender-associated, is in my opinion irrelevant to imminent self-defense. But violent defense of gender is also justified when it seeks by otherwise justified means to stop an attempt to violently transform gender into, or violently maintain it as, class. Would you agree with me that nonconsensual prostitution constitutes precisely such an unwarranted violent attempt?

Meanwhile, the ethos of Southeast Asia shimmers weirdly over all this; prostitutes clasp their hands and bow to Buddha when they get a nice customer; beggars *wai* in the same fashion; people tend to submit to their destiny. When is submission justified? What does the child owe the parent? By the Confucianist creed, everything. If, as in this case, the parent sells her in order to get a new roof for his house, by his creed and hers is she entitled to complain at all? You think so, and I do, too. But how much right do we possess to interfere with an alien society? Speaking strictly for myself, I would do what I did again. But, also speaking for myself, I dislike missionaries; I'm outraged by the harm they've wreaked on native societies down the centuries. A seventeenth-century French Jesuit would have happily undermined tribal authority and religion among the Huron Indians, because he was certain that in so doing he was saving their souls. I am not so sure that he was. When I prevent a cat from killing a bird, or when I rescue a child prostitute, how certain will my own certainties remain to "posterity" five hundred years from now?

THE OLD MAN (1995)

"So Near the Border"

Statement of Governor Chunchart Poonsiri, Yala City, Yala Province, Thailand

The Provincial Governor believed that tobacco led to marijuana and heroin. He had studied among Mormons in Utah before becoming an alumnus of the Drug Enforcement Administration; needless to say, drug interdiction was his foremost hobby. Following the style of Southeast Asian officials, he wore an immaculate military style uniform with many decorations. I felt him looking at me with piercing eyes, his hands in his lap, not quite smiling, not quite weary or severe. His dark stare reached me from the sofa, or from behind his vast desk where the King's portrait stood on an easel. Call him a very nice man. We chatted about the cold turkey method, and herbal emetics, to which he was patriotically inclined, and his bête noire, the Opium King, whom I never let on that I had met. He was far less interested in the terrorists, who in his estimation comprised only 120 to 130 souls.—The people living outside of Yala Province, they say we have a war with guerrillas and like that! he cried while two TV cameras whirred. It's a myth. Let me give you an example of the criminals we caught. The ones we caught this whole year, it's very few compared to the other provinces. If you don't believe you can go to the police station. Our people over there are very kind people. It's not fair to the people who come to Yala for investment. —I asked him if he could give me any written reports on the problem, and one of his assistants presented me with a white pamphlet tricked out with the following words of gold: EXECUTIVE SUMMARY REPORT: INVESTMENT OPPORTUNITY/PLAN OF YALA PROVINCE. The two TV cameras filmed that, and then they filmed my press card, and then they filmed the piece of paper on which the Governor had asked me to write my address.

When at last the Governor allowed me to turn the conversation to the bombers, he began, of course, by mentioning the drug addicts. They placed the bombs and delivered the threatening letters in exchange for money so that they could buy heroin. (This topic led us most naturally back to those emetic herbs, which were, it appeared, a sort of natural Antabuse. He said that the vomiting and retching disturbed naive observers, but in the end most addicts were gratefully cured.)

The Governor's second category of bombers was the jobless. —They live with their family and they make something against the law, he shrugged. I admired the way he downplayed the political nature of the attacks, ascribing causation to sickness and economic desperation, to isolated flaws and negatives which could be solved through his government's beneficence.

But now he had exhausted his categories of misguided and ignorant individuality, and had to admit the third group, which in his opinion made up considerably less than half of the total: the ideologues, the principled ones, the deliberate ones who desired to protect what he called "the PULO idea."

And who are their victims? I asked.

Just people who live in the forest. Maybe when they go for the lumber from the upper tree, the tree in high place, then maybe some bomb, but not so often, because for PULO and for the other group, the BRN, it's very difficult to give them the bomb.

Who gives them the bombs?

I don't know, the Governor said.

How many victims would you estimate are killed by the PULO every year in Thailand?

Maybe twenty. Not more, he said, and I know that he spoke truly, for the PULO is not what it used to be.

What's the best way to solve the problem? I said.

We have to make the population feel very warm toward the government. For example, some villages still live isolated in the jungle. They have no roads . . . All Muslim villages?

Yes. That's why I decided to have the government make the roads. Don't leave them alone.

If you were to catch the PULO leaders, what would you do?

If they do as a criminal, we have to follow the law. If not, then we have to rehabilitate.

A Partial Alphabet

Acronyms often represent extraneous words, for the sake of making vowels, and I think that this was the case with the word "PULO," which stands for Pattani Unification Liberation Organization. The "U" could have gone; unification in this context was almost tautological. But then, of course, we might have confused the PULO with that other social club of Islamic do-gooders, the PLO.

As far the BRN, their name meant *Barisan Revolusi Nasional Melayu Pattani*—National Revolutionary Coalition of Pattani. Their aims were the same as the PULO's. They wanted independence for the four southernmost provinces of Thailand: Satun, Pattani, Yala and Narathiwat—realms of pepper-smelling forest, cows and goats, heat and brightness, steep low hills like jellied blue mist, emerald jungle on slope and hollow, wet grasses, bowed backs and cone hats in the yellowing rice fields; villages of wood (heaps of wood slowly seasoning), villages of concrete, villages of stilt-legged, grey-bleached bamboo huts roofed with corrugated sheet metal; kingdoms of stickiness; malarial territories; countries of barefooted people shading themselves in low treehouses; nations of small white mosques, grand mosques domed by moneyed pride, and more mosques (in Pattani, cradle of the PULO, there was the Matsayit Klang, the second largest mosque in Thailand); in the four provinces (so a prominent Muslim told me) there currently existed more than a hundred persons who had the entire Qur-'An memorized. Were independence to be achieved, the bombers would fashion of this material an Islamic state, which anciently it had been before. If they could not break away, they'd continue to use terror.

Until recently, as is the fashion with extremist groups of similar persuasion, they'd been enemies. Now they were in love, I heard. BRN and PULO were all PULO together. Just imagine what good deeds they'd be able to do!

'NEW PULO' UNDER SUSPICION

The police suspect the New PULO, a separatist movement, may be responsible for last Wednesday's bomb blast at a police booth in Narathiwat's Su-ngai Golok district . . . Two teenagers on a motorcycle threw a grenade at the police booth on Takbai-Sungai Golok highway on Wednesday night. No one was injured. Pol Gen Pote said about 200 border patrol police would be deployed to help local officials maintain peace and order in the predominantly Muslim region.

Statements of Three Railroad Workers, Hat Yai, Songkhla Province

In the small train station the loudspeaker echoed commandingly and the noise of fans, trains and motorcycles made a deep bass hum over which people's voices barely carried, proving what everyone already knew, that flesh is weakness; and two small boys passed through the crevice between gratings with their arms around each other's shoulders; the khaki-shirted ticket-taking girl, whom ticketless souls were supposed to pay one baht to go to the platform, did not look up. Such was security; such was sleepiness. The hot sky had paled to white. My phony-copper Malaysian watch glittered in the sunset. People wearing light-colored T-shirts in obedience to the laws of coolness swarmed toward the grey train horizon, the ticket-taking girl looking weary. A barefoot monk in saffron-orange robes joined the queue at Window 5, where, playing the role of an innocently worried *falang,* I asked through the mesh if the train to Yala were safe. I'd heard that it had been bombed by the PULO, I said.

The clerk flashed his sparkling white choppers. —He said no problem, safety, D. translated. But I think he couldn't know about the PULO.

D. had told me that a year or so ago, half a dozen people from the northeast were sleeping here waiting for their train when a PULO bomb went off and killed them. —They want to do something bad in every province in the south last month, she went on. Because maybe they get some money from Libya and they must show something to Libya. They have big meeting in Malaysia, and then they come and bomb here. No more night train, because a little afraid for the PULO.

I had her ask the ticket-taking girl if it were safe, and she yawned and said: I wasn't working here when it happened. Anyway it's very safe. And if you want to die, it can happen just the same on an airplane.

At the trackside we found the "Chief of the Looking for the Train Go Forward and Back," as D. described him in the glory of his official position. He wore a navy blue uniform with three stars and one crescent. When I asked my question with due shy mournfulness, he looked at me through huge spectacles and patted my arm. —He says, now is safety, safety. He says no problem. And now is the end of Ramadan, so is spection (special) safety, because he tell me Muslim always do the bad thing in Ramadan, when other Muslim all at home and then easy for kill only the other religion.

Why do they do those things?

He say, Muslim here have lower level of education. Not hardworking like Chinese. Chinese love land—work, work until rich.

She laughed. —Now he worry maybe I am Muslim.

He say, last year same like ten five years ago he find bomb in luggage on train, disarm by himself. But he says safety, safety. Very funny, eh?

Hat Yai to Yala

The train went south through low jungle, the mountains and sky as white as steam. The people seemed more Malaysian to me than before. One had to address them with *salaam alaykum*. Across the aisle from D. and me were four Marines in khaki. The train was very full, so D. had to sit on my lap. The Marines hated me for that, and tried to stare me down. It was the first time I had encountered unfriendliness in Thailand. D. had told me that when a PULO boy and a PULO girl fell in love, they had to leave the organization. Men and women could not work together. The Marines kept glowering and sneering at me, until finally I thought to offer them water, which they refused with gracious smiles; then they offered me dried bananas (ignoring D.), and we were friends. Two of them kept their caps on; one nibbled at his; the fourth, bareheaded, gazed out the window. They patted each other's knees, laughed, flashed laminated photographs of themselves with weapons. I showed them my knife in its quick-draw "belt buddy" from Colonel Bo Gritz, and they liked it. Then I took D.'s hand, after which they hated me again.

A Small Village in Pattani Province

She said now doesn't have too much problem, D. was translating. She is head of village. In the mountains so difficult to contact them now. Now many is run away from PULO. They don't bring so many gun here. When they come to their family, police come with walkie-talkie.

When the woman took her leopard-colored headscarf off, she looked younger and prettier. A head of village, yes: three gold bracelets on her arm. We'd met her on her motorbike coming back from the market, with a plastic bag of fishes so fresh they were still twitching. She had lovely white teeth and dark eyes. When she raised her voice and clapped her hands, people came quickly in to bring us coconut juice. D. had been the first woman to become a head of village in the south. Now there were two others, and this woman was one of them, which was why D. called her friend.

Before, was the PULO a big problem? I asked.

She said not too much problem, but some.

This was, I thought, a generous understatement. A decade before, her husband had been shot dead by the PULO. On the way D. had told me how this woman used to cry, how D. had been so sad for her and tried to comfort her; they'd never caught the man who did it because he'd run to the mountains. She'd told D. that the man was known to be PULO.

This year not too much member of PULO in her area, D. translated. Because people have problem and they run away to Malaysia to become PULO, so never see them.

The woman rapped on the armrest of her sofa when she spoke, her brown toes splayed.

In the last ten years, how many people have the PULO hurt and killed? I asked.

She say, before have a little bit, but not now.

And what does she think about the Old Man? What does she think about Hadji Amin?

The woman smiled quickly at the name, a brittle twist of lips. She was missing a couple of teeth.

She don't know about Hadji Amin. She know just name.

OK, then what does she think about the PULO? Are they a hundred percent bad? Fifty percent bad? A hundred percent good?

It began to rain now with a noise like grapeshot. —She says, for her idea, she don't say PULO is good or bad, but PULO never help her. And bad, she doesn't know.

She doesn't know! But they killed her husband!

She smiled again and chopped the air with hand-edges swift like knives. —She said the man who kill her husband, she doesn't know PULO or not. He ran away.

Why did he kill her husband then?

She don't know why.

This interview was proving less than informative, I thought. —Does she think the Thai government treats Muslims the same as Buddhists in the south?

The government treat the same. If the people need something, they must tell the government and then OK, the government do the good thing.

The rain stopped, and a man wailed thrillingly, slowly, calling people to prayer.

What about the Malaysian government?

She has never been to Malaysia.

Then D. had to go to the toilet, and the woman went to show her the way. As I sat there looking out at the half-wild jungle (rubber trees attended by coconut bowls to catch the sap; birds and mosquitoes; low pineapples like grenades—All this village also member of *them!* D. had assured me in a whisper. If they run away, can always eat some fruit . . .), the woman's new husband came in. He was from Yala, a placid, handsome, good-natured fellow who spoke a little English. What did he think about Malaysia? Oh, he liked it. He went often . . .

With your wife?

Of course. My wife comes with me every time.

Ah. You speak English so well. Where did you study?

In the Middle East.

And what do you think about the PULO?

Five years ago they had more power, three years ago a little, now not so much.

Because everybody run away to another place.

And what do you think of Hadji Amin? I said.

He don't know too much about Hadji Amin, D. interpreted from the doorway.

I don't agree with all of Hadji Amin's ideas, I said carefully.

Instantly the man's eyes flashed hatred, and he said: Why? Why you say that?

Statement of an Important Person, Yala

The important person sat across from us under the slowly turning blades of the fan, which he had activated in our honor; and, long-faced and skinny, with long skinny teeth, gestured with the flats of his hands as if he were swimming or maybe pushing history away. Unlike the Governor, he was Muslim, a native son. D., who admired him, said that over the years the important person had done many good political deeds, but now he was tired and just wanted to go into business in Malaysia. He had deep, dark, rather sweet eyes. I liked his gentleness. He sat in the middle of his thin green carpet, which resembled pool table felt, in his concrete ante-room which was open to the street of white sky and palm trees, the motor-bikes snorting just beyond his family's fleet of shoes; and an immense china cabinet halfheartedly partitioned off the room; behind it a woman lay on her side, with her buttocks facing us, her fingers groping slowly at the lattice of a closed window. A muscular, unsmiling man brought us sug-ared rose water with ice.

He think sometimes government do something wrong about people in the south, D. translated, because they doesn't care about Islam, and now when Malaysia come to help PULO in the south, maybe Thai government come to help, too late.

What is the wrong thing that the Thai government does?

They doesn't give high education for them; they doesn't take care for them.

This was the crux of it. This was what they usually said. And the im-portant person expanded and expounded. —He is very nice idea, D. en-thused. —Here lay the thesis: discrimination against Muslims through neglect. The important person said that thirty years ago the price of rub-ber had been very high, so the southern provinces made good revenue, but the Thai government took the money away to use elsewhere.

What percentage of the population do Muslims make up?

About eighty percent. Before, was ninety percent.

Why did it change?

Because somebody leave from here, because economy here are not good. And other people came here to make good money here, because they have good education.

I knew which "other people" he meant. —Are Muslims and Chinese equally rich here? I asked.

Chinese is higher.

And are Chinese friendly with Muslims or not?

No problem with Muslims.

And how about the PULO? I heard they bomb Chinese.

He laughed nervously. —I think we don't talk about PULO, he said. (He could speak a little English.) PULO is not yet a big trouble, he said, but government need to highlight the PULO, to get money for military.

So the PULO is good for government, eh?

He laughed.

He say, sometime the PULO does something wrong, too.

Statement of Governor Chunchart Poonsiri (continued)

How would you characterize the relations between Muslims, Chinese and Thai in these provinces?

Oh, very good. We can work together in all these areas.

Does the PULO target Chinese more than Thais?

I never heard that. Let me tell you one thing frankly. The Chinese get angry if you call them Chinese. They want to be Thai. Thailand welcomes everyone. Wonderful thing in Thailand.

Statement of a Muslim Taxi Driver, Pattani

What do you think about the Chinese shopkeepers?

They talk very friendly, same like friend, but then they stab our heart. Always take more money from Islam people. Because we Islam is stupid doesn't know. But now we begin to know.

Statement of an Important Person, Yala (continued)

And Qaddafi—good or bad? I hazarded.

He's a good person. He wants to have a system in his country to make Arabs strong. And the Western people look for Qaddafi because he makes Muslim people too strong, so they look for something bad against him.

The United States government says that Qaddafi pays terrorists to do things such as blowing up the Pan Am jet over Scotland, I said. Is that true or false?

He laughed. —I cannot comment. Qaddafi's country is not steady. So why do like that and cause trouble?

So who do you think blew up that airplane?

The other men in the room began to murmur and glare at me angrily.

Qaddafi has a lot of enemies, he said. Maybe Israel.

He smiled, and added: Maybe Qaddafi.

I asked if I could use his name, and he said that if I did, the next time he met me he would not be able to greet me.

Another official in the room laughed and said: He could not greet you because you would be in the next world!

I considered this joke to be in poor taste. Nor could I see any reason for the important person's refusal to be cited—what had he said that was so revealing?—until D. explained on the way back to our hotel with its warning sign against bringing in weapons—a grenade with a slash through it (actually, a durian fruit, because it would have stunk up the hallway)—that during one of his long soliloquies to her in Thai (which she'd translated: Oh, he say his family all OK no problem), the important person had been giving her detailed directions on how we could meet the Old Man, the secret one, the feared one, the head of the PULO.

There was only one way to do it, the important person had said. If we did it any other way then the way would be closed to us forever. He said that he himself wanted nothing to do with the PULO anymore. He was sick of politics. He just wanted to get rich. Dealing with the PULO was bad for business.

Kabong Yaha, Yala

Nets and webs of low mountains warped around the horizon. The official in the slate-colored uniform (who had just finished slowly signing documents in an immense green dog-eared accordion folder) said that there were no bomb blasts here—only in the cities. When D. asked whether the group in this area were Old PULO or New PULO, he replied that the government never learned those things.

Sad, said D. Very poor (she meant sorry) for him. Thai government so weak, not yet strong! And so many government official, they go to school with PULO; they know them, but can never do anything . . .

And I thought of my old *Britannica*'s remark: *The relative political stability Thailand has maintained in the face of continual Communist guerrilla warfare inside its borders since World War II is largely the result of Western support.* Now the Communists had mutated into something else (with the exception of one jungle militia, so they told me, which had once been and might still be funded by China, and continued to lurk and train and occasionally plant ambushes not far from here); Western support was not so sure now, had decayed ever since the closing days of the Vietnam War, and other symptoms previously masked by the Communist pox were remarked once more by the body politic; Muslim insurgency, so one official in Yala (also unwilling to be named) told me, had existed here for ninety years or more. (He made notes and diagrams for me when he explained; afterward he shredded them carefully.)

This is Area Number Three of BRN, another official said. Area Number One is in Narathiwat Province. Area Number Two is between here and Yala. This area is head of Area Number Three. *Yala Father* was name of head of BRN for forty years, but now *Yala Father* is dead.

There was a walkie-talkie on his desk. Static came out of it, and he tapped it and the antenna quivered. He estimated the BRN's strength at several thousand persons. He said that the PULO was weaker than that and that it was based more in Narathiwat than in Yala. He said that Qadhaffi was a very good person.

He showed us a pink binder with his plan for fighting against the BRN. I asked for a copy, but he was afraid that then it would fall into BRN hands.

They use M-16 and AK-47, he said. When they come to the government, they never talk about where they get. Maybe from the dark market. They never say where.

Do you have any opinion as to where?

From Laos.

Statement of a BRN Defector, Yala Province

He had dark brown eyes in an undernourished face—the classic mercenary look.

Scared and helpless, he flashed big dark rodent eyes, twitched his moustache, showed teeth. He never stopped watching me. His tense brown face was a sculpture of fear. His fingers dug into his knees.

And were his father and mother in the BRN? I asked.

No, just only him.

So how did he come to join?

Head of BRN in Yala tell him BRN is the good support for you, good money, good money and good food.

What was the first thing that happened next?

Training. Everything training first. Training gun, looking map, running away, like that, thinking about what place to attack and like that.

Was it easy or difficult?

Difficult.

How old were you? I asked the man.

Twenty-one.

The man's lips opened, and he said something wearily to D. —Always in the jungle, in the jungle, she translated.

How many years?

Four years.

Did you ever go home to see your family?

He afraid people know he was BRN, so he never go. Sometimes he write to his parents. Give somebody to arrive his parents. Never get answer.

Were you lonely for them?

Yes, but cannot walk out anymore.

In this dark dirty boy clasping his own hands, stretching his forefingers together, I saw now what I had seen when I interviewed Khmer Rouge cadres: the ignorance, the apathy, the fear, above all the *weakness* of this human being made me want to excuse him in advance, to let him off for whatever he'd done.

How many people were in your group?

Fifteen in small group. A hundred in big group. Sometimes in small, sometimes in big.

Did you have many good friends?

All friendly, smoking together.

What did you think about the Thai government at that time?

He smiled, brown-toothed. —He said we want to separate Islam from Buddhist and Chinese.

And what did he think about the King and Queen of Thailand?

He doesn't think about the King and Queen.

And what did the BRN say to him about Malaysia?

He doesn't talk about Thailand and Malaysia.

And what does he think about Chinese people now?

He clenched his fist and smiled. —He doesn't think about Chinese and some Buddha.

Did he ever participate in any attacks?

The defector hesitated, but the government man behind the desk nodded at him encouragingly.

Oh, seven, eight, he finally said hesitatingly.

Tell him he's very strong, I said.

The boy smiled, a politely mercurial flash.

Tell us the story of one attack, I said.

In the Lao Village, in Narathiwat Province, he shoot the Buddhist who make the bridge. Dead seven persons. With M-16.

Were any BRN killed?

No. Because all the Buddhist no gun, only working.

And when he killed the Buddhist, was he happy?

Yes, so happy.

When did he do this?

In the nighttime.

Ask him if he can make bombs.

B.R.N. DEFECTOR'S SKETCHES OF HIS BOMBS

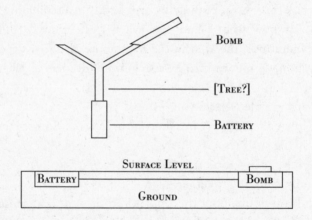

They make some bomb. He buy some equipment and make.

And the equipment for the bombs they buy from where?

He buy from our country but he doesn't know.

What's his opinion of Qaddafi?

He don't know.

And did he get good money?

No money. When he think about walking out, always the people following him.

And if he were to ask his commander if he could leave?

Would kill him! Cannot!

So how did he escape?

He run away in the nighttime. Half-half, maybe live, maybe death. Climb the mountain. And he walking until S. village. Then he run away to Malaysia by boat. One year in Malaysia he work make construction job and then can get money one hundred baht per day over. Happy! Have house, food, lodging.

And how much had the BRN given him?

Nothing.

And how did he return here?

Have one friend of him go to government in Yala and he follow him.

And since he killed one person, does he have any problem with the government now?

Government always say *ma pen lai* (never mind). Government cannot catch him.

So he has no problem at all?

That time, if police doesn't catch him, under law cannot do anything.

Why doesn't the BRN kill him for defecting?

Oh, now is BRN so angry! D. laughed. But BRN cannot hurt him, because he stay in government control. Been one year working with government like assistant of soldier. Already married with Muslim girl. Happy life.

Is it safe for him to visit his family now?

Yes.

And if he were to meet his former BRN commander?

Whenever he met him, he kill him! In control is much better, safety life!

Statement of Hadji Amin Tohmeena

Later, when D. and I had met the Old Man, I asked him: What are your views on the government amnesty for defectors?

Oh, they're just local people, chucked Hadji Amin. I don't worry about it. They'll never get the big people.

Statement of the BRN Defector (continued)

And does he still want to secede from Thailand?

No.

In this province, does the Thai government treat Muslims the same as other people?

Same.

The young man had told me that the insurgents in his group wore the same clothing as Thai soldiers. —Where did you get your uniforms? I asked.

Some Malaysian person come to visit BRN, he said, and the government man drummed warning fingers on the desk. His fingers were ringed, the bezels inset with stone bubbles of jungle darkness. —Officer a little afraid, said D., because so near the border.

"He Must Find a Way in Darkness"

Statement of a Pulo Defector, Yala Province

The PULO man was Christ's age, and very Middle Eastern looking, with dark and mobile eyes. The long shadows of the man's spread fingers seemed extensions of his long white teeth. He was moustachioed, could have been an Afghan or a Pakistani. The BRN man had seemed abject. This one was not like that. His face bore a cast of confidence which I found refreshing at first, but as the interview went on I began to dislike him for it.

Nine years ago he became PULO, D. translated.

Why?

Someone make trouble with him in his village, so he *must* become PULO and go away.

How did he know about the PULO?

Some people from Malaysia came to them in the jungle, people who told him about independence.

Did these Malaysians have uniforms?

No.

The officer who listened said something quickly to the defector, and he nodded and spoke to D., who interpreted: Sorry, he tell wrong. Not yet Malaysia people, but Thai people learning in Malaysia.

And then?

He become assistant to the big boss, Mr. Hamil.

So did he contact Mr. Hamil or did Mr. Hamil contact him?

He contacted cousin of Mr. Hamil first. He know about PULO and BRN and he think PULO is better.

Why?

Because Hamil's cousin was easy control. Easy life for him.

What was the difference between the PULO and the BRN at that time?

Different, Bill. More different! BRN is more different. PULO better. PULO should do for the rich people only Chinese, but BRN take even from local people. PULO they have system . . .

Extortion Versus Ideology

In his handbook on guerrilla warfare, Mao Zedong lists seven steps needful for "the creation of a national united anti-Japanese front," for which, if we were PULO or BRN, we might substitute "the creation of a transprovincial united anti-Thai front." Since Mao's grasp of guerrilla tactics has been, to say the least, well proved, it is worth examining the list as one measure of the PULO's possible success. Herewith:

1. Arousing and organizing the people.
2. Achieving internal unification politically.
3. Establishing bases.
4. Equipping forces.
5. Recovering national [here we would have to read "ethnic"] strength.
6. Destroying [the] enemy's national strength.
7. Regaining lost territories.

These steps are presumably to be followed sequentially. The seventh step is of course the aim of the PULO—namely, to recover the provinces Satun, Pattani, Yala and Narathiwat for their Muslim utopia. To accomplish that, they'll have to paralyze the Thai government's grip on those provinces (the sixth step), which means that they must gain sufficient force to do so (the fifth step). Bomb blasts here and there won't cut it—and of course Mao himself freely grants, as do Lenin, Che Guevara, and all the rest, that while guerrilla warfare may be necessary to achieve the final outcome, it is not of itself sufficient to do so. The third and fourth steps, by all accounts, have been and are continuously being achieved. PULO bands live and operate from ever-changing jungle camps for years at a stretch (Cook in valley, sleep up high in tent, a man told me, and if meet another group we must say *salaam alaykum* to them; if they no answer with password, we shoot!), and they all eat; they all have machine guns—but at the cost of the first and second steps, for the PULO is not some munificent terrorist octopus which can equip them; in point of fact the bands must equip themselves, which means that brigandage is the norm; there are thus many PULOs, every group for itself. Were the PULO to truly adopt Mao's idea of a "united front" which would give it the greatest chance of success, it would expropriate only "enemies of the people"—in its case, presumably rich Thai officials. Because its needs are greater than those actions could supply, and its powers weaker, it preys on any wealthy people it can reach—usually ethnic Chinese shopkeepers and factory owners. Now, as it happens, from the PULO's point of view even this may well be tactically sound in the short run, on account of the antipathy with which so many lower-class Muslims regard Chinese. It is a fact of life that most any poor person of minority blood will be convinced that "they" have made or kept him poor—and very probably he will in some sense be right. Nonetheless, the Chinese as such do not constitute the ruling class; they have no say as to whether the four provinces shall remain part of Thailand. True, the employment of extortion and terror against them does weaken the government's ability to govern; hence perhaps some measure of the dismal news of the Governor's "Executive Summary Report" on investment in Yala Province (and Yala, I was repeatedly told, is the *richest* of the four provinces!). Shaking down Chinese thus appears to be as popular among the PULO as shaking down Jews was among Hitler's Brownshirts. But in the long run, how beneficial can this be? Were the PULO to succeed someday in expelling Thai authority, wouldn't it be in their interest not to scare away their richest citizens until they could supplant them? But perhaps, seeing the plight of the new Muslim state, kindly Malaysia would step in . . .

Statement of the BRN Defector (continued)

Did you ever go to rich Chinese and say, You must give us money or we'll bomb you?

The boy grinned. —Chinese, even Islam people, if they are richest and we need!

Would you talk to them or send them a letter?

By letter. And we ask one hundred thousand baht per person, give for head of BRN.

Guerrillas of the Counterrevolution

It would seem, then, that by descending the path of undiscriminating banditry some PULO and BRN groups have left the lofty mountains of jihad, and become mere commandos of selfishness. About such people Mao writes: "They must be firmly opposed. They are easy to destroy because they lack a broad foundation in the people."

But, after all, they remain faithful to Islam, right? Isn't the whole purpose of this insurgency to nourish the religion of Muslims, to allow it to freely express itself?

Statement of the BRN Defector (continued)

And is there a mosque in the BRN camp?
  Yes. Some places.
  Does a mullah ever come there?
  No, no. Doesn't mean too much about religion.

Statement of the Pulo Defector (continued)

In his camp, did many people read the Qur-'an?
  Some. Everybody praying but some no have time.
  The man stroked his chin. Later he added: Sometimes everyone malaria.

Guerrillas of the Counterrevolution (continued)

But still, religious or not, weren't they at least fighting for a social ideal?

Statement of the Pulo Defector (continued)

Before he came to the PULO, did he believe that Muslims were discriminated against in his province?
  He don't know anything.

An Afterthought

Of course, even if he had thought so, this small spy who'd come in from the cold might not want to say it in the presence of his Thai government handlers . . .

Statement of an Islamic Studies Teacher on the Train From Yala to Sungai Kolok (Narathiwat)

Be that as it may, my chain of logic remained ill-forged. First of all, the fact that PULO cadres were not especially devout was irrelevant to their "audience." How would the local people know what they did or neglected to do in their camps? If they went into the jungle without the proper password, they'd never come back anyhow. As for the business of bleeding rich people, well, the victims didn't exactly spread around what had happened, for fear of incurring future extortions. Well-to-do Muslims merely bit their lips after a visit from the BRN. And the Chinese? The poor Chinese! Nobody liked them! Even D., cosmopolitan though she was, had imbibed enough local prejudice (she was from the south) to sometimes think them selfish. She was gentle and good; she would never have wanted anyone to suffer expropriation; but still she said: Chinese is just work work working, keep for self, never giving. —In short, as I've said, the PULO was not alienating its constituency through these extortions—no matter that in the long run they might reap the whirlwind. Every time I think about the PULO, I bring that hatred back to mind—steady fuel for robbery and murder, deep, distorting cause.

Another piece of anecdotal evidence: On one of our journeys to Malaysia to seek the Old Man (this being Southeast Asia, one had to go to some humid place to make inquiries, wait for the refusal, which meant going to another sweltering place to find some new card to play, return to present that card, go to another insect-ridden place while the request was slowly floated up to the next level, and so and so and so; in the three weeks that I tried to gain this elementary understanding of the bombers, for instance, my itinerary was: Penang, Hat Yai, Yala, Kota Baharu, Yala, Kota Baharu, Kuala Lumpur, Hat Yai, Pattani, Hat Yai, Bangkok, Hat Yai, Pattani, Hat Yai and Penang), the hot slow train wandered through a peppery morning, delving amongst palm trees and brilliantly blue jungle hills. Every woman except D. wore a cloth around her head and throat, only the face itself, naked of hair and context, gazing through, as if from a helmet. These coverings, called *hijab*, were of all hues from pink and blue to black. They removed the women from things, transformed them into discorporeal souls. One pretty young girl slid her *hijab* off for a moment so that it became a high pleated collar of blueness, caressed her baby, shook out her sweaty hair, and then pulled the boundary back around herself. D. and I were sitting across from a pleasant-looking, bearded young man in a prayer cap. I told him *salaam alaykum* and he smiled. D., who is plump, coffee-colored, and nondescript, can pass for almost any nationality other than her own. Today she felt like being from Peru. (If she had told the man that she was Thai, he would have clammed up.) One of the many benefits of working with D. was that I did not have to do much of anything except pay and think up my questions (which D. might or might not see fit to ask). Most of the time I sat looking stupid. It was a great life. D., meanwhile, wide-eyed tourist from Peru that she was, questioned the man at length in the local Yawi dialect. She asked him if she spoke his language well, and he allowed that she was not too bad for a foreigner.

He was a teacher of Islamic studies, so let us snoop a bit into his views, you and I, for in Asia teachers are respected; their opinions are as gold. He said that Malaysia was much better than Thailand because its strict laws made it safe. He liked Malaysia so much. He didn't mind the Thais, but ethnic Chinese bothered him because they always thought that Muslims were stupid; Chinese shopkeepers always gave Muslims short weight. (It was just like listening to an American ghetto black complain about Koreans.) Before, said the teacher, Muslims had kept quiet about these wrongs, but now they were going to do something.

Can't you teach the Chinese to be more fair? I put in.

He say, how can we teach them anything? We are low; they are high; they will never listen.

And what about the Chinese in Malaysia? They're low there, not high. Are they bad people, too?

Now he says that not all Chinese people are bad. Anyway, he don't know so much about Malaysia . . .

He was a very nice man. He was always rising to offer his seat to women and children.

Statement of the Pulo Defector, Yala (continued)

The PULO want to training him like BRN but he don't want anymore, D. translated. He never training about violence, but still he get lots of power, because assistant to Mr. Hamil. When people want to shoot someone, must use his name. If he says you shouldn't kill someone, then cannot do. Strong power. He have control for small person. If small person have trouble together, he can take away their guns for one month or whatever, so no problem with them. He take good care. After two-three years he become famous name and he wanted to leave from my country to Malaysia. But he stay in PULO six years, and then he leave to Malaysia stay there four years.

Did he have a girlfriend?

Hamil have two wives at that time, cooking for everyone. But he himself was alone.

Did any heroin addicts work for him? I asked, recalling the Governor's characterization.

Old Hamil he never have addict. Never sell heroin.

And as assistant to Mr. Hamil, did he write letters to Chinese?

Yes.

What did they say?

I need some money from you, about two hundred thousand baht in two week.

And what if the Chinese wouldn't give him any money?

He didn't like shoot bomb too much, because he don't like kill too many people, just one-one. And sometimes BRN so stupid; BRN kill themselves with bomb accident! Better shoot person or burn car. That is best way. He ever shoot. When he want to do something, he doesn't want to tell small soldier first, just bring him to the place and *then* say he should do that. Best way to protect secret. Shoot and shoot. One time he need four hundred thousand baht from some Chinese company in Yala. But owner of company doesn't know if he really PULO or not; how can owner believe it? So this one, to make him believe, he kill the wife of one of Chinese owner's drivers. Shoot her in car.

As the man told this tale, he flashed a brutal white smile.

When we do something, the owner of company should come to find us soon. If he doesn't come, then *we* must come again.

(Another smile.)

And how does the owner find the way to the PULO? I asked.

He must find a way in darkness. Because this one is very big name in Yala.

After he killed the driver's wife, did the owner pay?

A big grin this time. —Yes.

So how many people died by his orders?

One woman, two men. When they shoot, fighting against police, he have five person in group fighting with one police, and they kill that police after they tell him, You should support my way. —Police never can catch us, he added happily. —And the other time, you see, if someone talk the bad thing with him before he leave his village, he must remember that and kill him. He go together with his group, four people with him, to kill. He was the highest, the one with power.

The PULO man kept laughing and grinning, thrusting out his hairy lips and grinning. (Maybe I did him an injustice; maybe he was only nervous.)

What kind of weapon do they use?

M-16 or AK. (Like all the others, he pronounced it *Ah-Ka*.) Only PULO know where take gun.

And then what do they use the money for?

If they get one hundred percent of money every time, then thirty percent for him, ten percent for food for group, thirty percent for small person in group, thirty percent for gun.

And nothing for the PULO itself? I inquired, surprised. Nothing to send to the Old Man?

Nothing.

So when he was Mr. Hamil's assistant, how many baht did he get every year?

Too much. He don't know how much.

How many letters did his group send out each year?

Fifty-sixty.

What did he buy with the money?

He always give a lot to friends for good time. He do the good thing for the small one in his group; nobody angry with him. But he say now finish PULO, finish money now! Oh, but he say the Thai government give him one house!

As I remember him now, I also think upon a smiling, white-toothed boy whom I met in Malaysia; he had thick dark sunglasses tricked out with gold, and his hair was perfectly moussed. They looked much the same. They both liked karaoke singing. My readers might expect more appearance of cruelty than this in the defector's enjoyments, but there is no need to do so; in his account of how he earned them there is nastiness enough. He probably groomed himself well; it most likely pleased him to "do the good thing for the small ones," whom I can imagine him escorting to Yala to listen to long-haired girls singing Thai pop songs, holding microphones, behind them a painted background of waterfall—no headscarves here, gentlemen—and maybe some of the long-haired girls were elder sisters to the schoolgirls all in white I met who wore dark bows and smiled bareheaded and told me that Muslims were not so good—because it is truly a small world, as people generally say when they mean that life is all mixed up.

Okay, fine, I said. So he killed people and then he got famous and went to Malaysia.

Yes, always he go to Malaysia, to head of PULO, to the Old Man. He must have one card of PULO member. He must pay twelve ringgit and after three months must another three ringgit to head of PULO. He just make another job, like construction. Most Malaysians just like English people, only care for themselves. They don't care about PULO. But if you say, I am Islam, want independence for my country, then maybe they don't help you do the bad thing but still they let you easy, easy.

That's natural, I agreed. And then?

And then Hamil become wanted. Put on most wanted list. And this one talking to us now, Mr. A——, now his brother come to Malaysia to tell him Thai government open for him if he want. And brother Mr. A——bring him to this house, to this official (pointing to the government man who sat behind the desk). He bring nine person from PULO to this boss because he has power. And this official help him with guarantee. You know, he was born here; he cannot work another place. He never been back Malaysia, because the head of PULO angry him, the Old Man angry him. He afraid.

Because he went to the government?

Yes.

"He Didn't Care"

How many people has the Old Man killed?

No no. He just for independence.

But the PULO kills people! And the Old Man is the boss. So how many die?

He don't know.

And how many people are in the PULO?

His group was forty. Maybe in Thailand, his idea one thousand PULO now.

And what about Mr. Hamil?

Thai government always open. Now is head of village, same like me! D. laughed.

What's the best thing about the PULO?

He say nothing. Nothing interesting.

When he was in the PULO, did he believe in the cause of independence?

He didn't care.

The Old Man

That was the chilling thing, to be sure, that they did these things and didn't care. It all fell through. If they were killing and threatening people just for money, then what? And yet I couldn't deny they were squeezing the only ones within their grasp, the most appetizing and *convenient* victims—and the Chinese had few Muslim friends, it seemed; thus, mercenary though they were, the PULO cadres must remain uncompromised pawns for the Old Man—if he needed pawns, if *he* believed; if he had an Islamic cause. And *did* he believe, too, or was he just the mega-bandit that I had once believed the Opium King to be? I needed to meet him; I needed to find him and ask him some things. But the Thai soldiers said that that would be impossible, because the Old Man lived in darkness. Where was he? What lay in his heart?

Kota Baharu, Malaysia: "It's So Easy to Find Him"

I had a white, floating feeling, due in part to my accustomed fever, but also to the dreamy lowness of the pale buildings in relation to the pale sky. Two skinny files of traffic (cars, vans, unmuffled motorcycles and occasional trishaws) rolled magically past each other. Plump, *hijab*-wrapped, cotton-walled women sat in the street, one of them in trousers raggedly striped like a watermelon's skin, her thighs bulging like flesh of the same fruit; and they gazed into or through the worlds of their newspapers, their angels of news crumple-winged at the foot of a white wall of sunshine. A lonely long-limbed grey-haired Chinese hunched in a bus shelter. Caucasian tourists with their backpacks, moisture dripping from roofs, head-scarfed girl students returning from school, all wandered in such fashion that I finally comprehended the meaning of the U.S. Supreme Court's phrase "with all deliberate speed." Rows of windows cupped their shutters like hands, as if they'd been a thousand years begging for air, until they'd died and gone to Malaysia and then it no longer mattered. Down those long white streets the light strings of Hari Raya Aidil Fitri still hung, but glazed now, colorless, useless; that holiday had been over for days. Yes, yes, it was hot and I was back in Muslimville.

Ever since the important person in Yala had helped us, D. had been convinced that it would be "so easy to find him"—that is, the Old Man. Thus assured, she did something that boggled my mind. She telephoned the Thai embassy to ask his whereabouts. —Different thinking than *falang,* she explained patiently.

The PULO kills people, I said. He's the head of the PULO. Won't asking for him mean trouble for us?

Thai law is different law, said D. If he give order to kill and Thailand catch his order some cassette or something like that, then problem for him. But if no cassette, then problem only for man with bomb. Thai law is very open law, very gentle.

Anyhow, the Thai embassy didn't have the number. The helpful "young boy" there, as D. called him, advised us to try Malaysian Immigration, since the Old Man had lived in country for maybe sixteen or seventeen years; but I sensed imminent trouble and begged her to desist. We went out, and everything hurt my eyes, and I ordered four more orange juices.

It was 11:20, but the clock in the beauty salon said quarter to two. The beautician in his shiny black shoes shook his head.

Even my friend he don't know the way, said the ever-astonished D. He come from Pattani! What can we do?

In reply, I blew my nose like a walrus. By then—genius that I was—I'd already begun to sense that it would be a slow process discovering the Old Man, maybe even slower than waiting for breakfast in Penang on a holiday, where eventually, if one were very lucky, the chef or his unaccredited representative might shuffle out after half an hour and slam down a cup of coffee with a surly look.

"It's So Difficult to Find Him"

It's so difficult to find him! cried D. in amazement. Bill, what you want to do?

Find him, I guess.

In that street there were occasional shady book-haunts, Arabic calligraphy everywhere, and in one particularly inviting place I asked the old Yemenese—tall, skinny, and pale as a marble statue; white-haired; his skin as colorlessly white as the pages of his books; sunken-eyed and weary; half-blind, that one—if he knew where the Thais from Pattani congregated. I'd told him *salaam alaykum* at first, and his friendliness had blazed up, but after he questioned me and was disabused of his notion concerning my religion, he became listless again. (It was very hot.) So I had to ask him again. I could not tell whether he were considering or sleeping. A smell of fresh bread came in from next door.

In the big mosque, he finally said.

So it was that after following another false lead which brought us to the shore of the hot thick river like a coffee addict's spit, in which floated a weary fleet of houseboat shacks bare of doors, bare of windowglass, fruitful only in the proudness of their spidery TV antlers which carried their wishes and various greeds aloft and maybe transformed them into prayers, D. and I found ourselves back in Independence Square, in front of the grand white mosque with its domes dark and pale, and to me it seemed then that all the possibilities had shut like Kota Baharu's shops' metal accordion-gates on holy Friday, the windows of my future shuttered fast (the shutters paper on wood frames, like Japanese lamps, only the air gratings above, with their swarms of tiny diamond-shaped holes, allowing egress of a sort, of an exhalation's sort, of a hope's sort); and I asked her: Are you sure we're looking for the right person?

I tell you, Bill, in my country he so famous in south! But here in Malaysia nobody know him. Malaysia they don't take care, only think about themself same like Chinese.

O.K. Should we go in?

Better I go alone. If you with me, they ask too many question: Are we married? Am I Thai prostitute? and like that.

Sounds good to me, I said, blowing my nose on the grass.

"It's So Easy to Find Him" (Part II)

The man in the mosque introduced D. to a man who knew a man, and so the next evening we were in a taxi which whizzed importantly past a line of brilliantly hidden women, turned left, and passed a workshop crammed with bicycles, then a hotel, a ramshackle house from whose second-story laundry proudly dripped, and so and so and so, the taxi chittering unsteadily and reeking of the driver's Indonesian cigar. The sun was low, its disk dulled to egg yolk luminescence as it slowly melted down between palm trees. A stop at a gas station, another left, and then things began to get positively rural. A hooded driver peeped over her steering wheel at us as we stopped to ask directions. A girl, maybe ten or twelve, scuffed by, her sandals momentarily the loudest ruler of the road, and then a motorcycle burped. Banana trees spread their sweating green fingers over our heads. The houses were all wooden now; we'd left concrete in Kota Baharu. Giant trees, heavy white flower clusters dwarfed those houses, on whose porches children stood quietly staring. Now pavement gave way to dirt, the pathside heaped with rotting coconuts.

I think we find him, said D. Eighty percent we find him.

I blew my nose.

The sky was bled of almost all color. I heard a steady clinking somewhere of metal on metal as we turned into a mudpatch before a house badly in need of paint. Our driver was very proud. A wide-eyed little girl in a very dirty shirt rode her bicycle around us. Red cows meandered across the road, switching their tails. A deep voice scratched from a nearby mosque. Goats scratched themselves. Now the bare bulbs and incandescent tubes began to come to life. I smelled fresh sawdust.

You get out of the car go say *salaam alaykum* the Old Man, D. instructed. Already he coming. Look! Maybe a little afraid to see white person.

In the dusk, I spied a man's silhouette. But when I drew closer to him I saw that he was only about forty. I said *salaam alaykum* as I had been bidden, and he warily extended his hand. Now I was close enough to the doorway to read the nameplate, the abbreviation for "Haji" proudly displayed because not every Muslim gets to Mecca:

HJ. HAMID A——

"It's So Difficult to Find Him" (Part II)

No, no, no! cried D., sweating and exasperated, when I showed her. Hadji *Amin!*

Hadji Tahir? inquired the driver.

Amin, Amin, Amin! wailed D.

Now the driver felt extremely unappreciated. He had brought us to somebody who was *almost* Hadji Amin. Was it his fault that a couple of letters were different? Sullenly he ground and clashed his gears.

Never mind, said D. Malaysian people, Bill—I tell you already! Don't think about who is other people! Just stay at home, go to market, like that.

"It's So Difficult to Find Him" (Part III)

No need to report every move in our game of searching. Back to the mosque, where at two o'clock in the afternoon we awaited D.'s friend in the stream of men in white shirts and white prayer caps who began to issue from the mosque, whose towers clenched themselves behind the trees. Men, and men, and more white-clad men under white parasols swarmed at the base of the immense arch, with its central hemispherical blade pleated to a fan, the sky so pale and hot. It was extremely hot, and old men sat upon tree-shaded benches, greeting one another with handshakes and *salaam alaykums*.

Some of them I think from Libya, said D. See, look Libya face!

And when we went into the place where we were to meet D.'s new acquaintance, I saw for the first time in Malaysia a woman whose face was covered to the very eyes.

A little later, we got into a car with two men and left town.

They had studied certain procedures in Libya, they said. Qaddafi and the Old Man were both liberation fighters. They asked me to write a letter of introduction for myself and D., so we stopped at a roadside stand and did just that. They were tall men, dark, skinny and bearded, and they'd ornamented themselves with dark sunglasses so that I could not see their eyes. They did not stand over my shoulder when I wrote; I could not tell if they were watching me or not. I tried to make the letter as gracious, positive and truthful as I could. I said that the press often told only one side of the story, and that I wanted to know his side, that I was a friend of Muslims, all of which were correct statements. The PULO men took the letter, and left us to wait.

I watched two young women in a rustic swing, giggling at one another, sipping sodas from straws. D. drew pictures of flowers, singing old American songs. I popped a thousand grams of paracetamol.

After two hours they came back. They returned our letter to me, the envelope now unsealed. They said that Hadji Amin had a lot of visitors just then.

I think they was a little bit afraid, D. said, because they don't know us. And he have big security, many many bodyguard. So I believe in Malaysian support sure! Because you cannot stay here fifteen years with security if Malaysian government don't like. Illegal to cross border with even one security.

I wonder if the Old Man ever got our letter? I said.

Me stupid no good you lose your success! D. wailed. What can I do? Maybe you is big problem. But what can I do?

"It's So Difficult to Find Him" (Part IV)

And so we went back to Thailand to beg information from D.'s friends once again, back to Thailand where they laughed at my stupid jokes, and motorcycles and painted minibuses crawled round and round the block in a current of smog and cigarette smoke. Malaysian and Singaporean tourists liked it, too. They came for Thai food, Thai shopping bargains, and Thai pussy (even prostitute they know how nicely to tell money, money, money from Malaysia people! laughed D. gleefully, one thousand five hundred baht spection price!) Beggar boys in grimy oversized shirts bowed and cupped their hands most hopefully; I gave them coins until all my coins were gone and then I didn't give them anything. Girls rode sidesaddle on the backs of motorcycles; or they rode in front with boys behind holding

them tight; men walked with their arms around women; it was all so different from Malaysia, where they glowered at me because I held D.'s hand.
People smiled in the minibuses; their mechanical breezes cooled them and
left the smog behind. —And there in Yala I saw my second woman
wrapped in black from head to toe, only her eyes and upper nose showing;
she was like a three-dimensional shadow in front of the mango stand's hot
colors; she was like doom.

Statement of Another Pulo Defector, Kabong Yaha, Yala

He stay in Saudi Arabia three years, make business selling turbans. It was
good.

How old were you when you first got there?

Seventeen.

And when you joined the PULO?

Twenty.

Why did you join? I asked this slender, gentle-looking dark boy. He was
dressed in loose grey cotton, and he wore a beard no thicker than his upper lip. He kept his hands at his sides, and stared straight ahead with candid eyes, like a student wanting to make a good impression upon his thesis
adviser—who, I suppose, was that same officer, here again listening; every
time he insisted on taking D. and me to lunch. Today he would bring us to
a roadside stand for fish-egg soup; the eggs were yellow and tasteless and
resembled eyeballs.

About ten person in his group go first to contact, D. interpreted. He
don't know about PULO, but his friend say, We go to training, get good
business.

Where were you trained?

Tripoli. He passed from Saudi to Syria and then go to Tripoli.

What was your position in the PULO?

Soldier. When he come back, he is very good training from Libya, come
back very strong soldier. They teach: You must take care for your country.

Who first came to you in Saudi Arabia to tell you about the PULO?

He don't know who, but he know is Thai people.

What did he say?

"Come to PULO, help country for Islam."

At that time, did you know who Hadji Amin was?

When he come, the Libya government tell him Mr. Hamil was head of
Thai people.

And did you ever meet Hadji Amin later?

He just meet one time with Hadji Amin. He never talk with him, because Hadji Amin big, big like Prime Minister. This one just small soldier training to do the bad things. Now he tell me he didn't even know that Hadji Amin was the leader of PULO. He thought was only leader of BNPP. He didn't know they were the same.

Okay. So after you said yes to the recruiter, what happened?

First he think for two months, good or not. But he is young, want to fight, and want to know about Tripoli. He like to have nice uniform.

So you said yes, and then . . . ?

He stay in Saudi one week more.

And then?

Fly from Jeddah to Syria.

How long did you stay in Syria?

Two hours flying. Stay in Syria about three week, wait for ticket to Tripoli.

Who gave you your ticket to Syria?

Mr. T—— B—— from Pattani. About forty years old.

Did you fly alone?

Ten person from group in Thailand fly together.

How many passengers were on that flight in total?

Syria Airlines. Not so big.

And then someone met you in Syria?

Have another person from Thailand.

And what did that person say?

They have one house to rent for group training.

And did you stay inside this house while you were waiting, or could you look around like a tourist?

He had good food. Could go anywhere. Very free.

Were you happy or afraid?

No, no, no afraid anything. They have big group.

And after three weeks in Syria, what happened?

From Syria they take from Tripoli by bus to camp.

How did you feel?

Yes, happy.

Can you describe the camp?

He just came for the PULO camp. That camp is near a camp for Somali and Morocco.

Was it very hot?

No. Air-conditioned!

And what did you do?

Training for system same same soldier. Use AK.

How many bullets a day did they give you?

Just take gun. Never shoot.

In your training you never shot?

Never. And training for bomb, but never use.

What time did you get up?

Five morning.

And then?

First praying, then training, run-run-run about three hours.

PULO Defector's Sketch of His Bombs

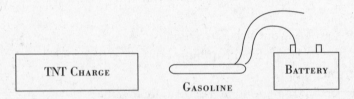

TNT Charge   Gasoline   Battery

*[Note that while the defector took the trouble to draw in the battery termi-
nals and two wires, there is no proper circuit. One suspects that he did not
plant bombs very often, if ever, and certainly not without supervision.]*

And then.

Wait for lunch.

And then?

After that, training for gun. Where to take materiel for gun, what to
do. One hour. Then finish. Relax. He has holiday Saturday-Sunday and
can go outside. One month he could get about twenty dinar, about four
hundred baht. So just looking, shopping in Tripoli. And three o'clock
come back to camp.

How far by bus from Tripoli to the camp?

Two-three hours walking. One hour by bus.

What is the name of the camp?

Suba-ifran. Seven-Apple.

And did you want to stay in Libya and marry a Libyan girl? I asked
him.

LOCATOR MAP OF CAMP SEVEN-APPLE

CAMP SEVEN-APPLE
[Suba-ifran]   "MANY SHOPS"

TRIPOLI CITY CENTER   OCEAN

From the city center to Seven-Apple
is about 1 hour by bus, or 2–3 hours walking.

Source: Defector Interviews

No, never.

Why?

So difficult to go in Libya. Even him also Islam cannot make friend there. Libya don't like someone else go in his country. But some things more relaxed. All of Libya's citizens like Qaddafi, but have many poor people, too. For the women, for the poor people, do not have to cover everything in black color. In Saudi, you don't cover face in black, maybe they rape you, you die.

Was it difficult to have no girlfriend while you were training?

He don't think about it.

What did you think about the King and Queen of Thailand?

No, no, doesn't think about them.

And did you see any BRN?

ROUGH SKETCH OF CAMP SEVEN-APPLE

NAMIBIA	[sometimes Moroccans] THAILAND & SOMALIA	PHILIPPINES
(more than 100 persons)	(about 30 Thais and about 15 Somalis, the latter all wounded insurgents)	(about 50 persons)

(Approximately 5 km. end to end)

Source: Defector Interviews

He don't know. At that time no BRN.

How long did you stay in Libya?

One year. Then he come to stay with Mr. Hamil. He pass from Tripoli to Syria to Pakistan, stop flight. After training, have about thirty person Thai from training. Whatever Mr. Hamil order, he doing. He is bodyguard for Hamil, security. In group, many AK machine guns from Russia. Buy from Thailand. He contact somebody in village of assistant to Hamil.

Did you ever kill anybody in Thailand?

No, just working with PULO. One time fighting with police on the back side of this mountain, J—— D—— W—— village. No camp, just stay in jungle like that. About five minute fighting, because police know them. He shoot M-16. His group was seven person that time. Police about fifteen.

And did the police chase you?

No, no. Stop. Don't follow. Maybe police afraid.

So every day you just sat with Hamil doing nothing?

Just only that other defector Mr. A—— is famous, Bill. Because in Saudi this one he stay a long time, doesn't know so much about Thailand. Maybe other one is better.

And where did you meet the Old Man?

He meet Hadji Amin with two person in Malaysia.

Why did you go to Malaysia?

He's very bored in jungle Thailand after one year. So he go to Kelantan, Kota Baharu, make construction job. Then the other one, assistant to Mr. Hamil, he contact him and they go together to Thai government.

And what's your opinion of Hadji Amin?

He don't know him. High, so separate from him.

And of Qaddafi?

People like him. Qaddafi give TV, everything in camp.

Do you still want independence? Yes, he thinking want independence, but how can he do? Not much power, eh? He say if he have money maybe he must go back to Saudi Arabia: better life than Thailand. All is Islam and better to find job.

I took the hint and gave him a hundred baht. —Why not go to Malaysia? I asked.

Cannot. All of *them,* all member *them* angry him, because he come talk to government.

"It's So Easy to Find Him" (Part III)

Meanwhile, D. kept sighing and worrying about me. She was afraid that my magazine would be angry.

Finally she called a certain royal person—or, I should say, a relative of a practicing royal person. In this region and at this time, royal persons, as a rule, prefer to be kept safely above politics. Even if no Opium King, for instance, were to lurk or parade in a royal person's domains, it would be better for the royal person not to comment, which might entail doing what D. would call the bad thing. D. herself, however, was a very impressive woman, and she made the royal relation tell all. And he *knew* all. Hadji Amin was not in fact surrounded by security men, he said; he had only one cousin who took care for him. His star was waning, the royal person said. Hadji Amin's followers had taken too much money from mosques. —Now he has donate money from eleven countries, about two hundred million baht, for memorial to his father, but he keep for him, D. reported.

He said that all Thai taxi drivers in Kota Baharu were members of *them*—which I don't believe was true at all. He said that from Pattani just now thirty commandos of *them* had gone to Libya for training "to learn how to take money"—which sounded more than plausible. He said that the BRN had exploded into three factions now, and only one had merged with the PULO. But the fact that the BRN and the PULO had mixed at all rendered them inconceivably more dangerous.

He named a restaurant in Kota Baharu where the PULO met. He named a village and a neighborhood.

Yala to Kota Baharu Again

Back on the train again, I popped two fever pills and a stomach pill, watching the Thai stations creep by one by one, the train creaking past shaded waiting rooms and laundry hung between banana trees . . . —This jungle I like so much—tree tree tree and bamboo so wonderful! D. enthused.

Malaysia again. D. and I crossed the border separately, as usual; it wouldn't do to get in trouble for not being married. We went back to the same hotel.

Have you ever been to Thailand? I asked the woman in reception.

Never.

Why? You live so close.

I don't like.

Why?

I don't know.

Kota Baharu to Kampung Y.

Taxi drivers, all grinning in a row, slapped gleeful palms with each other because D. and I, poor stupes, had just agreed to pay fifty ringgit for three hours. The village that the royal person had named, which we'll call Kampung Y., was three hours away. —Round the world! our driver yelled out the window to a colleague. —Your friend or your wife? another one whispered into my ear. —Maybe both, I said. He giggled slyly. I held the door for D., and a man glared.

In Kampung Y. nobody knew him until at dusk we finally turned into a weed-grown courtyard where a tall scarred man was sitting. The man said that he was not a member *of them* anymore because he needed money to eat. He said that the Old Man was always moving around, but right now he was in Kampung Z., which was near Kota Baharu.

Kampung Z.

It was a hottish night of cooking fires on the roadside and between stilt houses, square darknesses with open doorways of light in which I could sometimes glimpse people or faded posters of mosques. Motorcycles putted by as I sat in the stopped taxi brushing away almost silent mosquitoes, D. and the driver silhouetted in doorway after doorway as they asked after the whereabouts of the Old Man; and sometimes I could see people's clotted shadows coming or going in the road, the men's wider and leggier, the women's all of a piece within their long cotton dresses which shape-shifted around their narrow forms so strangely; and at last the driver and I went to a large and silent house which we were sure was the Old Man's, and the driver knocked respectfully on the wall and called *salaam alaykum,* but no one answered, and I knocked and he knocked again until finally the old woman next door poised her white-cotton-bordered head at the window and after long colloquy explained that she had never heard of the Old Man but he might well be nearer or farther, and my hot stale shirt was heavy with sweat. It was unpleasant to nerve myself to approaching house after house, each time wondering if scared or jangled bodyguards were waiting with ready M-16s or AKs; but then I reminded myself that this was Malaysia where they always water down the fruit juice; probably the gunpowder in the bullets would be weak, too. We met a man who knew D. by name and reputation although he'd never seen her before, and he guided us to a gated mansion, told us to wait, and vanished into the darkness. At last he came back to the taxi and said: If you come in the nighttime, people afraid.

"He Must Be a Bad Man"

D. said: I think maybe he's not so powerful. The Opium King he never do like this. Just stay always one place with many bodyguard. But Hadji Amin no.

But he's the head of the PULO! I said. How can he not be powerful?

Because he come old, Bill. Before was maybe more power. Now, must share with another. And he always do the bad thing, so always afraid. I don't like him. Even that royal person said, "If he fight by killing Prime Minister or something, then OK, but why kill the poor people?"

And how will we find him?

You remember Kampung X. where we go the first time? Now somebody tell me he living back there again. We try again.

And the taxi driver said: Why does he hide like this? He must be a very bad man.

The Bodyguards

The next morning we found a small grocery store in Kampung Y. whose owner told us that the Old Man came there every day. He hadn't come yet that day. We asked another ten or twenty people where he was. Nobody had heard of him. Then we reached a roadside stand packed with grim and ruffianly individuals. D. approached the man behind the counter and spoke to him. I saw him begin to rage. She came back and reported: He say why we want to meet him? I think this his cousin who take care for him. All these his bodyguard.

We drove around the corner and I wrote another letter to Hadji Amin. I told him that we didn't mean to harm him and wanted only to understand his ideas, that we had tried to meet him many times, and that it would be in his interest to let us see him. Then we drove back to the roadside stand.

I got out of the taxi and approached the tall man behind the counter. I greeted him with *salaam alaykum* and he bowed slightly with immense dignity and salaamed me back. He shook my hand. I said to him in Malay: For Mr. Hadji Amin, please. —Then I thanked him and walked away.

We returned in two hours. Again I approached the stand alone. The tall man was gruff this time. He pointed down the street. —The green house, he said. That made sense, I thought. Green was Islamic . . .

"It's So Easy to Find Him" (Part IV)

As I walked down that dirt lane alone, D. and the driver sitting motionless in the taxi behind me, I charged my mind with questions, chambering all my varied alertnesses and needs to understand like bullets; and the house ahead was very hot and silent. This was always the bad moment, like the instant of leaving a friendly checkpoint in a war zone and beginning to traverse that too open space between oneself and the hostile checkpoint; this was the time when panic-stricken improvers of the world could take their opportunity upon me. My heart was pounding. There was a fence around the house, and a gate. I opened the gate, which slowly squeaked open, entered, and closed it behind me. The taxi had begun to follow at a hearse's pace. The door was widely ajar. Ascending the stairs, I called out: *salaam alaykum!* and waited to face the gunbarrels of his bodyguards . . .

The Old Man

He was a stoutish, kindly faced old man with round glasses, a round head, a receding hairline of grey. I gazed around the room. No bodyguards. He had massive bare feet. There were strange growths or calluses on his ankles. With his pallor and smoothness he reminded me of a grandfatherly turtle. Sometimes he gazed into space, and sometimes he leaned forward and looked into my eyes with a smile into which I could have read anything; I was probably inclined to feel more friendliness in my welcome than was actually the case, as a simple result of my pleasure in actually being able to meet him; but he was cordial enough, though wary. I was sorry to distress him. He said that he didn't speak English, which was my cue to jovially call to D., a proceeding which he didn't like, but D. quickly put him at ease. His maidservant brought D. and me iced orange drinks in glasses on little saucers. Sometimes he sat back in his chair and smiled at me tranquilly and coolly, and I sensed that he was at peace with himself. He had done what he thought was right; he had sacrificed his happiness and

security—to say nothing of the unwilling lives of others. This was the man whom the PULO defector who'd trained in Libya called "big like Prime Minister." And indeed he bore himself with highborn regal patience.

On one wall hung a sword which had been given to him by King Fahad of Saudi Arabia. On another hung a photograph of his murdered father. There were fresh flowers underneath.

The fan was spinning quietly in that tiny house of white sunlight bleeding in through drawn curtains, a house that reminded me of the inside of a bleached seashell. I saw a small television, a Chinese fan with depictions of cranes, a few books, some Arabic hangings and medallions, stared again at the Old Man with his big glasses on his big egghead—

Statement of Hadji Amin Ben Hadji Sulung

Before, the south of Thailand—Patani, Satun, Narathiwat and Yala—was independent of Malaysia, began the Old Man. The Thais conquered us in 1786. There was fighting six times, and the Thais finally won.

My father, Hadji Sulung, wanted to regain independence for the Muslim provinces, but could not, because at that time, Prime Minister Luang Phibunsongkhram was a bad person regarding Islam. The government wanted to change everything for Muslims, to take away sarongs and *hijabs* and like that. All must be Thai.

I was in secondary school when my father started fighting the Thai government in 1945. In 1948 they caught my father. He was imprisoned in Bangkok for four years, and then they had some meeting in the Prime Ministry, after which the new Prime Minister, Mr. Kuang Apaivong, helped my father and secured his release in 1954. The second time they caught my father, they put him in the ocean, and he was never found. My father, my brother, and two of my father's friends—four persons—all died.

Extract from a Booklet Published by the Prof. Haji Sulong Abdulqadir Tohmeena Foundation

On the date of August 2497 B.E. (A.D. 1947) Haji Sulong and his two friends and his eldest son Ahmed Tohmeena (with pregnanted in Makkah) [conceived in Mecca?] went to see the investigation police at Songkhala province by ordered which his eldest son was his translator, but all of them disappeared, the government inform that, the investigation police released them by released memorandum of signed.

After that time, became to know about that case from the clearance board of committee which establishing by field Marshal Sarit Thanarat the Prime Minister said that, Haji Sulong and his two friends and his eldest son killed by the police on that day, by neck tightened, and operated the death bodies fastened with cement pole, sinking in the Songkla lake.

Statement of Hadji Amin (continued)

What did you think when you heard that news? I said.

Hadji Amin's reply was very soft and quiet.

D., who loved her country, hung her head. —He talk about his government, she said.

Did your father begin the PULO movement or had it existed before his time? I asked him.

In his day it was not called the PULO. It was called GANPAR. GANPAR was founded in 1947–48. In that period all of our Muslim citizens were angry at the government, and formed a group to fight it.

What was the worst thing that the government did?

In Coconut Village in Province Narathiwat, in '48 and '49, the government burned Muslim houses—a hundred of them. And four thousand Muslim died. It was kill, kill, kill.

Why did the government kill these people?

They were GANPAR.

D. clucked and shook her head. —You know, Bill, before I never know that. I'm so poor for him. So sad.

I myself thought: How could one be completely unsympathetic to the Old Man? His accusation concerning Coconut Village was a pretty serious charge, although of course the massacre had occurred several administrations ago. And if the government killed my father I don't know what I'd do. No doubt Hadji Amin truly believed he was being just. A lawyer lives next door to me in California, an older, very kind, wise, soft-spoken man. I asked him whether in his career he'd ever met somebody who came out and said: The other side is right. I'm in the wrong. —The lawyer smiled and scratched his chin. —No, Bill, he said, I don't think I've ever run into that . . .

Interjection

There did not seem to be any point in going to the Thai government to get official denial or confirmation of the Coconut Village story. No Thai official who valued what D. would have termed his "take it easy life" would have wanted such a hot potato. Did this atrocity actually occur or not? Unfortunately, by this time my resources were almost exhausted and I could not visit Coconut Village. I can say only that almost all the old people whom D. and I asked—even one Chinese-Thai man as far away as Bangkok—confirmed and believed the Old Man's tale, as they did his account of the liquidation of his father. (About that latter event, D. herself told me that when she was younger she had spoken with some elderly folks who claimed to have seen the four bodies go into the water.)

One old headman, who might have been Buddhist or otherwise "disaffected" from the PULO, stated that Hadji Sulong's organization had itself killed the Muslims in Coconut Village because that area was such a "very nice economy" with precious stones that GANPAR wanted to use it as a base, and the victims, mistakenly preferring their take-it-easy lives, had refused. After that, the headman said, Hadji Sulong blamed the atrocity on the government. —Impossible, another PULO man responded curtly. The government do it. The people have the power, want to make independence, stay there, so the government do the bad thing.

I am inclined to agree with the PULO man, at least regarding the impossibility part. (For one thing, if Hadji Amin's dates are correct, his father would have been in prison during the burning of Coconut Village. For another, it is very difficult to believe that any perpetrator could have hoped to remain incognito forever. Such an act would deeply prejudiced the PULO's cause, and Hadji Sulong does not appear to have been stupid.) I think it very likely that something bad happened at Coconut Village.

Statement of Hadji Amin (continued)

What was your reaction after you heard that your father had been murdered?

I tried to talk with the Minister [of the Interior] and the Prime Minister. I was a Member of Parliament two times. What did the government say? The government wanted to close my mouth and give me more power— "please, you keep quiet and I'll make you big"—but I didn't need that. And after that, Phibunsongkhram went down. His successor tried to meet and talk with me; that Prime Minister was the best.

And then?

The Old Man laughed. —I tried fighting.

Statement of Hadji Amin (continued)

GANPAR was finished in 1957, said the Old Man. The BRN was formed in 1960. The BNBP began in 1963. By then I was already marked. They caught me and someone else, and they put me in prison from 1961 to 1964. I was with a hundred other "politicals": Communists, Socialists . . .

Could you make friends with them?

So-so. *Comme ci comme ça.*

Since you were Muslim, did any Communists make trouble against you in prison?

The only ones who made trouble against me were Thai people.

Could you do any work?

I learned French and Arabic. I taught Malay . . .

And when you were released?

I went underground. I had a different mentality after prison; I saw that I would have to fight in another way.

In Thailand?

Yes. I was able to get some work in the government again, but a less powerful position than Member of Parliament. I taught religion in the mosques. And I worked underground with the BRN.

You were the head of the BRN?

Yes.

And when the PULO appear?

In 1968.

And then?

In 1981 I came here, because the government wanted to kill me again.

What happened?

In 1980 the government bombed my house. The Ministry of Soldiers [Ministry of the Interior?] had the order. Soldiers and police came to bomb my house. Even now, Thais think that Islam is only stupid, like an adopted daughter, not a true daughter of Thailand.

And the Chinese people in the south, what do you think about them?

The Thais and the Chinese have the same ideas about us, said the Old Man, studying me with a steady smiling look.

Statement of Some Buddhist Schoolgirls in Yala

Muslims are some good, some bad. Not so good. We don't like them so much.

Statement of Hadji Amin (continued)

And what's your opinion of the King and Queen of Thailand? I asked.

The King and Queen are no problem, he shrugged. All of the citizens love them. It's only the government which is the problem.

And the Opium King?

A very nice person. He tries to do the good thing for his people.

Looking into his eyes, I asked him: When is violence justified?

I must use it if there is danger for me, he replied at once. I don't hesitate to use it. Last year, ninety-five police over three provinces were killed at my orders.

What had those police done?

They did bad things against Islam. Some were corrupt, and they took money from local people.

And that bomb in the railroad station in Hat Yai, was that PULO or not?

PULO. But the police will never know. Because the police are stupid—*lazy* and stupid, he laughed.

Statement of Some Low-Level Policemen in Pattani

How harsh was that particular characterization? Buddhists and ethnic Chinese were burning incense at the place where half a thousand years ago a Chinese girl had hanged herself because her brother had married a Muslim and converted to Islam, after which he did not want to return home to China anymore; her grave could work miracles, and so, someone told me, the PULO often "made trouble there." Not so far from there was Hadji Amin's old house, once his grandfather's. His son Azmi (who'd been a year and a half old when his grandfather was murdered) lived there now, and when I asked whether he thought that the PULO were good or bad he smiled tenderly and stroked my arm and said: Here in this place it's so dangerous to talk about the PULO! —No doubt that was true. Surely the Old Man sent out his spies, and the Thai government sent out its spies, which the ancient Chinese sage Sun-tzu had formed lovingly into five categories, saying: *They are a ruler's treasures.* But Azmi had just been to Kota Baharu to celebrate Hari Raya Aidil Fitri with his father. His mother also went back and forth at pleasure. That was the Thai way. The government knew where Azmi was, so they surely knew where his father was—indeed, Hadji Amin said that the Prime Minister had contacted him recently, to invite him back into the government; that rang true because it would have been the Thai way, the open, easy way. But Hadji Amin said that he told the Prime Minister: I don't need it. —Meanwhile the police didn't pounce on Azmi; they didn't much menace the Old Man; they wanted just to appease him and bring him back, as they'd done with those PULO and BRN defectors in Yala. No doubt they considered their attack upon his house a mistake.

That old house lay in one direction, but in another, and much much closer to that shrine of the Chinese suicide, squatted a concrete hut with two faded blue and white flags in which skinny-legged policemen and policeboys sat barefooted and gently stuporous in shorts, big black boots awaiting them from the rack. Tiny birds hopped and cheeped in their cages. Their boss, the "big police," slumbered thunderously behind an almost closed door.

On 24 February of this year came just two person, member of *them,* said a policeman. They had M-16, one M-16 coming, in the nighttime, 2:10 minute A.M. About five minute shooting, and then fighting about five minute, and then run away. They shot at the checkpoint. They want to kill police on the road but they don't succeed. And then they bring the stamp of New PULO here, so we know.

In the last two years, in your idea, how many victims have there in been?

In Yala too many people die, but here in Pattani I don't know.

And how many victims of the PULO would you say there are in all Thailand every year?

He said he don't know.

Well, very roughly—twenty or two hundred or two thousand?

He cannot account anymore. About two-three years ago they bomb Pattani Town but he forgot where. I so poor for him, Bill! The Old Man speak true—Thai police so stupid never know anything! Now this police he say he think PULO never finish. Because always training in the Middle East. If you knock one down, another come up, like that.

On the Other Hand

I do have to confess that when I walked around the police hut and inspected the checkpoint barrier (now dragged off the road since it was daytime) and the surrounding trees I could find no bullet holes, not one. And no police had been killed in that episode. And everywhere I went in those southern provinces, I'd ask the police to show me captured PULO bombs or weapons but they never had any; it was always the next province over that had the problem. Was it possible that the Governor of Yala was correct, that, like many terrorist organizations, the PULO possessed a reputation exceeding its competence? Could it be, as the woman head of village had suggested, that its powers were simply on the wane? Later the Old Man had a heart attack, and he lay weak at home near Kota Baharu, with his wife attending him; the Thai government didn't stop her from going;

then he had another heart attack and had to go to the big hospital in Kuala Lumpur; but there were new PULO men ready to take over. D. laughed sadly and said: Now is very quiet, but never go away. Same like cancer . . .

Statement of Hadji Amin (continued)

Which Muslim countries do you like the best?

Before, Fahad in Saudi helped me. Then Khunying Songdau Sayamvalo from Bangkok visited him, and requested that I stop. And now Libya has stopped also. Syria has stopped; Brunei has also finished.

Do any governments still help you or are you alone now?

Malaysia gives me aid, but they gave ear to the Thai government, and now they also have begun to stop.

What would be the best thing that someone could do to help you?

Talk to the O.I.C. Tell them to help me again.

Statement of a High Police Official in Hat Yai

How many terrorist attacks have there been here in Songkhla Province in the last two years?

Just only three, including that time when the railroad was destroyed. Another time in the Chinat district. Then on the third of January this year, two New PULO died in a bombing accident. Not so many victims. Terrorist just put for show off and like that. I never live in Narathiwat Province. Maybe more trouble in Narithiwat than here. Where the three province come together is Budo Mountain; many PULO there.

Statement of a Former (and Possibly Current) Pulo Man in Southern Pattani

Oh, Budo Mountain is very safe for you now. Today you can walk there in jungle no problem.

On the Other Hand Again

So had the Old Man's orders really been responsible for the liquidation of ten police? Impossible to say, and in a way it didn't matter. (Are there any PULO in prison here? I'd asked the political official in Yala. —Oh, many, many! he replied.) The primary purpose of terrorist violence, as I've said, is to instill fear; and if people were already afraid, why, then, the PULO was home free!

Statement of a Low-Level Policeman in Pattani

One of the policeboys who lounged on a motorbike under the trees was a "special police to fight PULO." I asked if he had fought the PULO many times.

Oh, many times, in K———.

And what happened?

He laughed merrily. —They are upstairs on mountain with many gun; we are downstairs, so we run away. If not, maybe we die!

The Reason for Murder

And why did you place that bomb in Hat Yai? What did those six or seven people do?

Nothing, answered Hadji Amin with a gruesomely cheerful smile. We placed the bomb to make police afraid, just to make trouble in general.

How many members do you have?

Many, many! But I cannot talk about that.

Are the Old PULO, the New PULO and the BRN united now, or separate?

They all follow me. And now the Prime Minister tried to call me back again, but I told him I don't need it. I don't need to work with those people anymore.

The Old Man As Gandhian

What's your opinion of Gandhi? I asked him.

Good! he replied.

Why is it acceptable for you to kill people when it wasn't acceptable for Gandhi?

Because Gandhi's citizens weren't bad like the Thais, explained the Old Man. They were Indians. But Thais are bad people. Some must die.

Statement of Hadji Amin (continued)

Is there one sura of the Qur-'An in particular that makes you feel strong?

Ya Sin, replied the Old Man. It's so cooling and quiet.

An Excerpt from "Ya Sin"

In the name of Allah, the Beneficent, the Merciful.

O [perfect] man, By the Qur-'An full of wisdom! Surely thou art one of the messengers, On a right way. A revelation of the Mighty, the Merciful, That thou mayest warn a people whose fathers were not warned, so they are heedless. The word has indeed proved true of most of them, so they believe not. Surely We have placed on their necks chains reaching up to the chins, so they have their heads raised aloft. And We have set a barrier before them and a barrier behind them, thus We have covered them, so that they see not. And it is alike to them whether thou warn them or warn them not—they believe not. Thou canst warn him only who follows the Reminder and fears the Beneficent in secret; so give him good news of forgiveness and a generous reward. Surely We give life to the dead, and We write down that which they send before [their actions] and their footprints, and We record everything in a clear writing.

What It All Meant (Penang, Malaysia)

And what might Hadji Amin's ideal Islamic state resemble? What course his revolution? *Use and wont will now no longer direct any man,* offers Carlyle, *each man, with what of originality he has, must begin thinking; or following those that think.* And when I think, for some reason (I really can't imagine why), Malaysia comes to mind. (When I asked the important person in Yala whether there were any differences between Muslims in Malaysia and in Thailand, he replied: No, because we are all one unity.) In Malaysia, of course, in Malaysia lazing rich behind her palmtrees, all the differences between Malays, ethnic Chinese, and Indians had long been solved. —It was the first day of Hari Raya Aidil Fitri; Ramadan had ended at last. Men whistled songs in a Chinese café, watching the dogs, motorcycles and foreigners go by. They were happy that the long fast was over. The doorway was hung with a row of red cloth squares, each sporting a golden ideogram. Sometimes these moved vaguely in the breeze. Beneath them lay Penang's low skyline of rust-bricked roofs, the shutters down on all the Muslim shops. D. and I had in fact had some difficulty in finding a money changer that morning so that we could pay our hotel bill for a second night—not that we really wanted to stay in Penang, but the buses and trains were all overbooked for the holiday and we were not yet desperate enough to take a taxi to Thailand. Finally we found a hardware store proprietor in the Indian quarter who was willing to transform dollars into ringgit. The next morning a Muslim approached us on the street and asked if we wanted to change money. When I said that we had done so yesterday, he flew into a terrific rage. —Illegal! he shouted. Who is this

money changer? Where is he? —I refused to tell him. He hated that Indian
for taking the bread from his mouth, and yet I am sure that if I'd met that
Muslim on the previous morning he would have refused to make the transaction I needed. Somehow that man reminds me of Hadji Amin. Had he
expressed racism? Had he engaged in "discrimination"? —Surely, but no
more than that of the man of Chinese extraction whom D. and I met at a
bus stop on the other side of the border; he was lethargic and missing
many teeth; D. believed him to be an addict. That man announced: Islam
is no good, is lazy. They want only to make the bad thing. All rich people
here in Thailand are Chinese. Sometimes Islam come to them and say, you
must give money or we do the bad thing. —The man clutched a long
smoky cigarette in his skinny fingers, and wrapped his other hand feebly
about his bare feet. —One could not really call his remarks discrimina-
tory, for he had no power to discriminate against anybody. What would
the Old Man have made of him? Was he too a bloodsucker, a rich sur-
charger of Muslims? Why not live and let live, then, as everyone did in
Penang's ancient buildings whose shutters were as warped as peeling paint
chips, whole windows gaped like the shells of boiled clams, whose sodden
curtains sagged? Ah, Hari Raya Aidil Fitri, a happy time; even the Chinese
musicians sang and tapped their wrists, maybe because they lived there,
too, and because the Muslims weren't working, so business would be especially good for the Chinese. Where would they fit in the Old Man's theoc-
racy? He'd never really answered me. If he won, would he expel them or
tax them or convert them or what? I didn't trust him to leave them alone.
Sausages and barbecued chickens hung from hooks, lethargically twirling
while below the girl lethargically chopped, about two cleaver strokes per
minute, her jaws entrancedly chewing; I met a man studded with square
gold rings and gold bracelets and gold necklaces who raised his chin from
his hands to sing a Chinese song with D. . . . Around the corner, a Hindi
trishaw driver waited for business, his forehead gashed by praying, his
hands and wrists scarred with circular silver burns from his welding job. I
asked him if Hindus were treated the same as Muslims in Malaysia. —Not
the same, he said. And there was a silence, and then he quickly said, I don't
know if out of fear or fairness: But me cannot be jealous! No jealous! Because Muslim work hard, hard, hard, and also pray very good . . . —That,
after all, was true.

   One citizen after another assured me that Malaysia was better than
Thailand—that Malaysia was the best country in the whole world, in fact;

because it was clean, quiet, beautiful and peaceful. (The assurers were all ethnic Malays, Muslims.) Why were D. and I so unenlightened as to refuse to convert to Islam, take up residence and become citizens? If we did we'd certainly be welcomed. I met many Chinese and Indians who loved their country, too. But the citizens who complained about their country were more likely than not to be Chinese and Indians—that is, to be non-Muslims, like the old man, a sixth-generation Chinese immigrant, who said to me mildly that Thailand was more open-minded. He said most people didn't treat him well. If he wasn't so poor he would have left Malaysia long ago, perhaps for Thailand, maybe for Australia . . . Would Hadji Amin have encouraged him in that resolution? Probably it didn't matter—not only because secession of the four provinces was unlikely to be realized in the Old Man's lifetime; but also because life will have its revenge over ideology. The low-level defectors whom I'd interviewed—the assistants, the triggermen, the Libyan trainees—wasted few thoughts on Islam. They were poor; they were ignorant—very well, they'd become bandits. These were the malleable souls—the Nazi street thugs of the 1920s; the *sans-culottes* of the 1780s—whose destiny could be altered by any puppet master. There was an excellent chance that the Old Man's insinuation of their insignificance was correct—but by virtue of that very fact, they were the majority. Counterinsurgency had won over some of them, at least. When I asked the important person in Yala if life were improving for Muslims, he replied: I think maybe better than before. Because the economy is going up, and there are more Muslim officials. —The vast majority of the Thai Muslims I met agreed with him. The only question was: Were things getting better fast enough, far enough? And here a gruesome parable comes to mind. The story goes that in Penang there was a Kung Fu master named Da Sa Lim, who was caught selling heroin; and in those days Malaysia had a penalty which seemed stiff enough: hanging by the neck for two hours! — But Da Sa Lim was able to tense up the muscles of his neck in some special Kung Fu way, and so after the statutory two hours they had to set him free! He, so they say, was intelligent enough to depart from Malaysia quickly; he went to Singapore, and then to China . . . After that they changed the law as follows: hanging by the neck until *dead*. It would be easy for Thailand with its smiling lazy policeboys to think that the two-hour approach to the PULO was enough . . . But, as far as I could tell, Hadji Amin had no approach at all: insurgency alone was his department. What about educating the faithful, or constructing decent jobs? Perhaps this isn't fair. Nowadays we don't ask the four-star generals what the Prime Minister's policy ought to be. For whatever reason, however, the Old Man's ends remained as shadowy as his means. Closing my eyes, I can see him again, smiling, opening his mouth wide, chuckling soundlessly in darkness.

"Sympathetic Support"

Not far from the ice cream parlor in Pattani which D. informed me got extortion letters from the PULO every year because it was successful and Chinese-run (D. said they'd never been bombed because they paid; sometimes her friends would intercede with the PULO to reduce the amount by 50 percent) there stood a taxi stand where we hired a Muslim to take us into the hot green palmy maquis. D. wasn't sure of the exact way, so she did what any logical person would do when searching for a big fish in the PULO; she stopped in a government office, visited an old friend, and came back with a detailed map and a letter of introduction. —You happy? she said proudly.

The driver said that people were afraid to drive this particular road after six at night because "members of *them*" might do something bad.

How long has it been that way?

Long time. Long time until now, even now.

The man we'd come to see had a dark, almost characterless face, missing teeth, a wooden brown man, a true guerrilla leader, immensely strong and resolute. He wore a pistol in his sarong. He brought us into a concrete anteroom like that of a head of village. Five small boys and two little girls sat on the floor quietly listening. Outside, in the covered courtyard, many people were sitting on benches or leaning on the rear wall, looking in at us. From time to time somebody brought the dark man something to sign. They always bore their documents on trays and stood waiting while he signed. He sat in his chair, with that small pistol at his side.

. . . And then he have trouble and run away, D. was saying. He run away to become PULO. He have one son, and he thinking about his parents, and police come when he go to his parents, and then government do the bad thing to his mother and his father.

What kind of trouble did he have?

Before, they fighting with the government two times a day, and his wife miscarried from fighting.

And then?

The government send police always make problem with his family. All his family run away, and many citizen here. They make a big group, eight, one hundred person, and the village keep quiet. All of citizen give money, hold hand together, and then they have food, have gun and something. Always he giving the people. Always helping the people. Never do anything bad, only helping. Only government do anything bad.

D., have you heard of this man before? Oh, yes, Bill. In the south he so famous. Big general. More than one hundred PULO in his group. And what do you think about what the Governor of Yala said, that there were only a hundred and twenty PULO in all Thailand?

She laughed. —I think maybe Governor don't know, never see.

And how was this general able to come back to the village? Did he accept an amnesty?

Now, police do always the bad thing, and he become bigger, because the people like him, and because he can stop the bad thing. Police get afraid of him.

What kind of bad things?

Before and now is the same. When they want to catch the drug with some person, they plant the drug. Take innocent person. Or maybe they looking for PULO. If cannot find, police take somebody, anybody, and they hitting. Hit them to tell for information even if they never know. But hitting is now not so bad. Now government is more OK about hitting.

I understand. But did he get an amnesty?

Yes.

So they amnestied him, but he's still PULO.

Yes.

And those PULO and BRN defectors we met in Yala, do you think they're still PULO and BRN?

Maybe, said D. Sometimes I think like that . . .

Where do you get your weapons? I asked the man.

All the gun he buy from the corrupt government. The government buy cheap from Vietnam War and sell expensive to him, sell maybe for ten thousand baht. And the people who come to sell all have star on shoulder, not yet small person! —D. laughed as she translated this accusation of Thai military corruption, and she added: I believe.

How old was he when he became PULO?

Twenty-one. In the jungle for ten years.

Statement of a Counterinsurgency Warrior

As Mao's translator and enemy writes:

> Historical experience suggests that there is very little hope of destroying a
> revolutionary guerrilla movement after it has survived the first phase and
> has acquired the sympathetic support of a significant segment of the pop-
> ulation. The size of this "significant segment" will vary; a decisive figure
> might range from 15 to 25 per cent.

Statement of the BRN Defector (continued)

The people in village give us everything.

Statement of Another Muslim Taxi Driver

As we rode back toward the city of Pattani (about which my guidebook
remarked: *The town as a whole is as dirty as Yala Town is clean,* I said
to D.: Ask the driver who he thinks will win, the government or the
PULO.

He don't know, she reported.

Who does he want to win?

He don't know, but he don't like so much the government.

Why?

Must always pay something to corrupt police. If only a little, is no
problem, but must always pay big, big.

Statement of the Dark Man (continued)

When he first went into the jungle, was the PULO separate from the BRN?

Both BNPP together.

And now?

All together.

It was very bright in the window outside with giant leaves drooping and
glistening like chili pods, and sweat shone on everyone's faces. The children
had stopped listening by now and were lolling on the cool linoleum of the
main house, watching television, from which blasted the stupidly sinister
music of some American cops and robbers program.

What percentage of the people in this area are members *of them*? I
asked.

The dark man replied flatly: A hundred percent.

"You Must Be a Bad Person and Help Yourself"

All well and good, but the dark man didn't much care for Hadji Amin's ideas and often went his own way. So how many PULOs were there really? Could any extortionist, ideologue or provincial savior just call himself PULO? It might have been thus in eighteenth-century France with those peasant insurgents who called themselves Chouans. The republicans had won their revolution and shattered organized opposition, reducing the Chouans to atomized individuals and small groups carrying out their petty attacks. After that, though, the Revolution never rooted them all out . . .

What actually constituted the miniature PULOs? From what the defectors had told me I already had a sense of the answer, which was confirmed in another village near Narathiwat whose shacks and houses were hung with multiple round birdcages, in each a single cheeping creature; and sometimes there were pale monkeys chained to coconut trees. Men bare to the waist lay drowsing on shady platforms of bamboo. D. asked a group of these lords where we could find the one we sought, and they crowded around. A man who'd studied in Saudi Arabia took my arm caressingly, gazing into my eyes with authority rather than self-importance; he was perhaps the village headman. —He come from Saudi, D. said to me later in knowing tones. Sure he is member of *them*. —And, still disbelieving the dark man's words, I wondered: Could there really be that many of "them"? Was the PULO, was the Muslim disaffection in these four provinces (for it was perhaps of too desultory a nature to be called a resistance), so widely seeded and rooted?

During the Vietnam War, this area had been partly controlled by the Communist Party of Thailand, since suppressed by a deal involving the Thai military, the Khmer Rouge and Red China: Chinese arms could go through Thailand to Cambodia; in return the Chinese would abandon the CPT. So that insurgency, once popular, had almost died, and another insurgency whose ideology was entirely different had expanded to fill the vacuum. Did so many people want out? If so, someday perhaps another Bosnia would take place here. What might Hadji Amin's five-year surprise be? More than one Thai Buddhist had told me that if Malaysia continued to train and arm the PULO then there might be war. (As a wag said: There are two ways of making enemies. A contiguous enemy is made by a *territorial claim*. A non-contiguous enemy is made through an alliance with the *enemy's contiguous enemy*.) I remembered one hot afternoon in a very hot park in Yala when

D. and I, having just drunk iced sugarcane juice at a Muslim girl's stand, were drawing sketches of trees; and ants of a dullish red nature busied themselves upon my flesh. I saw a man who by his clothes and demeanor could have been a Thai official off work, so I lured his children in by flashing the box of watercolor pencils that my parents had given me for Christmas—for journalists must be as anglers, baiting and twitching their selfishly inquisitive hooks. Once the children had become addicted to my pencils, the man was forced to answer a few questions, although he looked at his watch from time to time and told his children that they had to go back to the office (at which they'd howl, compelling him to talk to us further). As it happened, he was a political officer—like C.I.D., explained D., who soon exercised her customary magnetism upon him. That afternoon she was from Indonesia, not Peru. —The political officer never knew what our job was. He said that although everything seemed quiet, in his opinion the PULO were more dangerous than ever. They had just planted a bomb in this very park last month, but a student had seen, and contacted the police. He said that the PULO were entering a new phase of insurgent tactics. Before, they had operated out of the jungle, sowing secret terror. Now they were moving into the villages. —Stupid Muslims sometimes, said D. angrily at this news. Because we don't want to have problem with them. (These were almost the same words that Hadji Amin had used about the Thais.) —D. cried: Always Muslims say I am good, good, good and Chinese no good! —The political officer said that they were coming and going to Libya by means of Bangkok; and Malaysia was behind them, too, of course . . . The Thai government had sent a spy to follow people who went to Libya, but the spy was Muslim (this detail he said with contempt), so of course they never got any information. —Well, what's the best way to end it? I had asked. —Seal the borders with Malaysia, the man said. We're too soft with them. They always take, take, take. They're so dangerous. They deny that they give the PULO support, but it's not true. If we close the borders, Malaysia will starve for supplies. They're smaller than we are; we can defeat them. —His harshness shocked and frightened me. The four provinces seemed so sleepy. But of course the cancer remained. The political officer must have seen it every day.

Meanwhile, in the village near Narathiwat, the man who'd studied in Saudi Arabia lifted his hand from my arm and pointed. We were right across the dirt street from the house we were looking for, the home of the man in the white prayer cap, who invited us in, and sat cross-legged with us on the floor because it was cooler there. He had a fine intellectual face, slightly tending to weariness.

Before, he think that independence for Pattani is the best, D. relayed. For *idea* independence is best, but now he think that some people like Hadji Amin want independence only for themselves, not yet for him; they want only money. When the government say PULO bad, that's OK, because yes, many thing bad. But PULO always here, never go away. Before he was born, PULO always have member everywhere, like Mafia. BNPP, BRN, PULO all same. BRN before doesn't hold hands with PULO. Just PULO show off because Hadji Amin is *money money money* mentality. But then they all come together. All same. Not want independence for citizen; just want power for themselves. Same until now, even now.

The man's wife came in on her knees and served us iced orange drinks on a tray.

But PULO and BRN do sometimes good, something for small people, the man continued. And soldier in the jungle, he don't do bad things with the people; he just fighting the government.

Does the Thai government listen to Muslims or not?

Before, government doesn't open too much about Islam people. They don't need too much the people. But now it's OK.

It was very hot. The shutters were all slanted in parallels in the wide windowhole. Mosquitoes danced in.

So now you don't want independence from Thailand anymore? I asked him.

Now unless the PULO change their idea he want to stay with Thai government.

Did the government kill Hadji Sulong?

The man lit a cigarette. —He listen people talk but he don't know. But, Thai government afraid Hadji Sulong because he have big power with Islam. And maybe the government do the bad thing.

So you can trust the government?

Maybe.

If you don't want independence, what's the best way to help the Muslim people here?

We must give Islam high education first. Just only education first. If you don't have education, you don't know the way for fighting for the good thing.

When we talked with the Governor of Yala, I said to the man, he told us that only about twenty people a year are killed by the PULO, but Hadji

Amin said that last year he killed ninety-five police. In your estimation, how many actually die from PULO activity?

The man smiled. D. smiled, too. —He said PULO is always the winner.

Can you be more specific?

Ten years ago PULO always shooting, fighting together. So die one-one. Kill one police, die one PULO. Five years ago, stop for fighting. Get more strong for PULO. PULO come up, up. This year maybe more than one hundred people PULO kill. But now cannot fight with the soldiers with guns. Try to absorb with the people. And now a different kind of PULO. Before, you can go to the PULO anybody; it's easy if you have problem of your life. —He speak true, Bill, same like PULO defector who run away from village just for fighting, you remember? —So now they change: to be PULO you must have secondary school education, and you cannot be addict. Better.

So the PULO is trying not to fight anymore? What about those bombs last month?

The man in the white prayer cap grappled and groped with the hot air. —Not too much bomb now, because change PULO style. And who knows everything? He tell sometimes burn school, you know. People say PULO, but PULO say government do. Now he's bored about bombing like that. Anyway, PULO cannot do, because we need the people.

And that bomb in Hat Yai that killed those half-dozen people in the railroad station, I asked, was that a PULO or a government action?

He say government do and then show off about PULO.

Since the Old Man himself had accepted responsibility for that bombing, this answer effectively discredited the man's accusation that the Thai government blew up schools—unless, of course, the Old Man had taken the credit to magnify his power. Who knows? Either way it was an atrocity. Perhaps reading my look, the man dropped his head a little. —He don't agree with the bomb from PULO sometimes, because PULO do like stupid thing.

I nodded. The man looked at me wistfully and said: Hadji Amin no good. He always move outside my country and want only to show off to get money from another country. If Hadji Amin want to fight for independence really really, maybe can do. But he don't want.

So he did still want independence, then! (Hadji Amin did, too, I thought; he seemed more sincere than this man gave him credit for.) And he talked about a "different PULO" . . . I felt again, as I had with the dark man, that Islamic separatism continued to thrive here, if not to grow, that perhaps someday it would rise again into its bloody flowering season. D. had told me: Royal person he said PULO more dangerous than before, because they go underground. And the local people don't know. PULO always working, working underground, but other people they doesn't know too much about Hadji Amin . . .

That too was natural, I reflected, for the Old Man lived and worked in darkness.

Statement of Hadji Amin (continued)

Do you have any message to the world? I'd asked him at the end.

Yes, he said. (He was tired by then; his heart disease was bothering him.) Number one, we are Islamic in origin. Number two, Thailand wants us to follow everything Thai, and we cannot. Number three, please grant us the independence that we had before.

If you succeed, should the Thais in your new country stay or go?

If we live together, the Old Man replied, for us it's no problem. We never started the trouble with them.

He wanted us to go; he was tired and unwell. The anxiety of being hunted down by us had probably been bad for him. D. had already risen. I closed my daypack and said: And you think that independence is possible?

If Allah wills, then tomorrow it can happen. Everything is from God. But we ourselves never know what we do.

As D. and I were leaving the house, he smiled and added: Five years from now, something big is going to happen, a special thing. I cannot talk about it now.

Statement of the Man in the White Prayer Cap (continued)

The man in the prayer cap was smiling at me now, a wise and strangely kind smile. I said to D.: Please ask him if it's possible to do any good things with gun and bomb.

He have many experiences that make him think now PULO no good. The first, he doesn't have high education. Just do the same thing all the time, the stupid thing. The second, even if he die fighting, he get nothing. He always in the jungle, Bill. Two years he always move in the three province. The first time he come to PULO, they say no problem with money, and then no money. So you must be a bad person and help yourself. He never buy gun. His group already have. He do in Hat Yai Province, Songkhla Province. So he take some money from Chinese.

A Chinese Restaurant in Hat Yai

It had been very hot all night, so early the next morning D. and I went to the nearest Chinese restaurant and ordered a long tall bottle of chilled sugarcane juice which we poured over ice. I had pork and egg and chili rice for breakfast. The Chinese family was keeping itself busy. The old man and his wife were taking fresh vegetables out of plastic bags and inspecting them carefully. A middle-aged woman with curled hair piled her just-made translucent noodles into the bottom level of the double-tiered glass case and walked around it, even inspected it from the street to make sure that it lived up to her standards. The youngest woman, evidently her sister, stood in a special booth of hanging chicken parts, slowly cleaving meat with a knife as wide as her thigh. As she labored she very slowly chewed.

—Very hardworking, Chinese, said D.

Are they rich, these people here? I asked.

Yes, yes! she replied.

Rich enough for the PULO to come?

Oh, yes!

Statement of the Man in the White Prayer Cap (continued)

When he catch the Chinese, he keep two or three of them in jungle, and let one Chinese back home, and if he don't come back with money, then the other two die.

Where did he catch them?

In the town. Nearly dark time. PULO come inside Chinese house. He take to jungle. Must do like that to support his group: twenty person.

How much did he ask for?

Two hundred thousand one time.

And if they were to say that they could give only a hundred thousand?

Many time when he said five hundred thousand and they say please half price, then he said, yes, it's OK to support us; I never think about kill you. He is nice person, eh?

Oh, very nice, I agreed, looking into the terrorist's face. Does he believe that the Chinese always overcharge Muslims?

Always Chinese do like that even until now.

Can anybody make them stop?

Cannot. He said, we want to teach him to stop, but Chinese is very wise people, so how can we teach him? We must get education and then get wise like him.

And even though life is getting better for Muslims in Thailand, you still want independence?

Yes, yes. He not afraid of us now, Bill, so he speak true. He want.

I shook his hand, and D. and I went out. In my brain tolled a line of that favorite sura of the Old Man's:

Surely We have placed on their necks chains reaching up to the chins, so they have their heads raised aloft.

INTRODUCTION

All the case studies in this section have to do with one country—and the new nations and territories which broke away from it. Yugoslavia was never a nation as much as one of many experiments in confederation. We need only take a train across the central European plain to see that where Hungary ends and Serbia begins, to give but a single example, is from a topographic point of view arbitrary, subject to the vicissitudes of means and ends down the centuries. If some moral actor pushed his power across these flat fields, what would stop him from pushing further except for some local accident of defensive superiority? Regions seemed to preserve their identity more successfully than states and nations. The Austro-Hungarian Empire might come and go; Yugoslavia might assert its brief unitarianism; but a Montenegrin remained a Montenegrin. And within these regions, which during the Yugoslavian decades got called provinces, people attached themselves more fiercely than an American can readily imagine to the patch of homeland in which they were born. In the second case study you will meet a man who explains: "In this country, when you build a house you build for life. After you, your sons and daughters will live on in that house." You must keep this house-based, field-based, village-based conception of homeland in your mind to appreciate the anguish brought about by the forcible displacement of populations during the Yugoslavian Civil War.

Like all generalizations about Yugoslavia, this one is largely false. Unfortunately, the violence which wrecked Yugoslavia cannot be understood as readily as the violence described in the two African case studies, where poverty and class jealousy stand out with the utmost obviousness. The words "Byzantine" and "balkanize" associate themselves with the history of eastern Europe for very good reason! Accordingly, all I can hope to do here is convey the urgency with which historical grievances can sometimes cry out long after the original protagonists have become dust in the cemeteries of homeland.

For example, the Serbian emotionalism over Kosovo goes back to 1389, when Prince Lazar died in battle against the Turks. To Serbs, the Albanian majority in Kosovo descends from or derives from those same Turks. From the Albanian point of view, the fact that they are indeed the majority renders Serbian authority over what technically remains a Serbian province illegitimate.

Thus the conflict in Kosovo may be seen as opposing defenses of homeland ("Kosovo is our Jerusalem," say the Serbs, while the Albanians say, "*We* are the ones who live here!"), of race and culture—which in turn explains why that homeland cannot be shared; of creed (Serbian Orthodox *versus* Muslim) and of authority, which demands: Is Kosovo to remain a part of Yugoslavia, in which case it's a province, a dependency, or will it become its own country, or even perhaps, as Serbs fear, a dependency of Greater Albania?

Kosovo also raises the grimmest questions about proportionality, discrimination, and the allowable limits of war aims, which have in turn been culturally conditioned by Yugoslavia's horrific history of war. Just as Kosovo cannot be understood without reference to 1389, the civil war described in the first two case studies takes its context from 1941–45. That is why you may wish to browse through Annex F: "Ethnic Relations in Yugoslavia During World War II." In the case studies, you'll find that people continually justify their hatreds on the basis of what the Croatian "Ustashas" did to the Serbs, what the Serbian "Chetniks" did to the Muslims, et cetera. In Yugoslavia, the past remains fatally alive.

Annexes G and H present two opposing points of view as to how the Bosnian war began. One is from a Serbian perspective; its complement is a Muslim's version. The Serb had a very high position of power at the time she explained her interpretation of events: In fact, she was none other than Biljana Plavsic, then the acting Vice President of the Bosnian Serbs. After the Dayton Accords stalemated the Bosnian war by means of a partition which seems unlikely to last down the ages, Ms. Plavsic briefly became an official leader in the new Bosnian Serb Republic; she now resides at the Hague, serving a stiff sentence for war crimes. As for the Muslim, she was anonymous and by her own request nameless. I met her in a camp for displaced persons in Croatia. Finally, Annex E is a letter from the inmates of the *studenski dom* in Sarajevo. Their plight receives discussion in the first case study. (What should I say about them here? My publisher, Mr. Dave Eggers, who is in fact a very bighearted, generous, empathetic man, read my account and inserted this comment: "At this point a reader wants to know more about why the students, as noncombatants, stay in this building, which seems extraordinarily dangerous." It is, and I also want to know why, and so did the students, but there was nobody to ask except God. Their plight was almost ordinary.) The letter itself is much shorter than its signature pages. The terrible year 1992 has dwindled away from these people now; they live on or they have died. This letter accordingly means nothing. Their names mean nothing today as they meant nothing before to the evil men and women whose policies locked them fast to the front line of a besieged city. Let them stand in for all the other people whose names have meant nothing to war criminals.

As you read these Yugoslavian case studies, ask yourself: What is legitimate defense of homeland here, and what pretends to be? What defines the ethos of each of the three sides, and to what extent does it exclude the ethos of others? How many of the Maxims for Murderers in our moral calculus can you see winking cynically at you from these pages? Who seems to be respecting the moral limits of warfare, and who does not? Above all, how much do you know and how much must you take on faith? One person sees so little in a war! What I have seen I will tell you. It remains your task as a citizen of this earth to weigh claim against counterclaim.

How much should history weigh on us in our judgment of a violence which constantly appeals to history? The first case study begins *after* Croatia and Bosnia, among other republics, have already declared independence from the republic called Yugoslavia, whose capital lies in Serbia and whose army and government seem to be increasingly dominated by Serbs. The official moral actors: Tudjman in Croatia, Izetbegovic in Bosnia, Milosevic in Yugoslavia. Milosevic has gone to the Kosovo battlefield monument, invoked Prince Lazar, and threateningly promised to protect the rights of Serbs. Tudjman for his part upholds the cause of Croatian rights a bit too stridently. Izetbegovic's stance on behalf of his Muslim constituency reminds his neighbors, irrationally or not, of the ancient nightmare of Turkish domination. On all three sides, defense of authority has become defense of race, a particularly absurd category in Yugoslavia, where strangers must sometimes ask one another's last names to know whether or not they are supposed to kill them. Polarization breaks out like an infection in ethnically mixed towns; neighbor rapes neighbor; neighbor cuts neighbor's throat.

Slovenia has already seceded from Yugoslavia, and gotten away with it. When Croatia announces the same intention, Croatia's old friend West Germany instantly recognizes her independence, thereby adding to Serbs' fears that the Ustashas will arise from the past like vampires and once again begin to collect jars of Serbian eyeballs—Milosevic decides not to let them go. War begins.

Impelled by his own fears, which Serbian threats in part justify, Izetbegovic also declares independence. War spreads.

"Where Are All the Pretty Girls?" takes place in 1992, during the height of the Serbian siege of Sarajevo, a city once renowned for its cosmopolitanism and now the capital and symbol of Muslim Bosnia. Meanwhile, the anti-Serbian coalition between Muslims and Croats has begun to fracture. Croatia, riddled with fear and quiet frenzy, awaits the outcome of its battles. On the streets of Zagreb one frequently sees members of the Croatian Party of Rights, which was founded in the Hitler era and carried out atrocities against Serbs and Muslims. (See Annex F.) One also finds people who still fondly remember their Serbian and Muslim friends, but there seem to be fewer and fewer of those. Meanwhile, the short-lived Serbian Republic of Krajina has given birth to itself just east of Croatian-held territory. The Croats will obliterate it in 1995.

"The War Never Came Here" is set in 1994, when the Serbs have begun losing the war in earnest, and the rift, in Bosnia at least, between Muslims and Croats is emblematized by the divided city of Mostar, whose less-damaged western half remains in Croat hands; the eastern, Muslim half was savaged twice, first by Serbs, then by Croats. In what remains of Yugoslavia, which is to say Serbia and Montenegro, militant defiance unites the people against the internationalists' "surgical strikes," while the struggle between moderates and extremists divides them. Relations between Serbs and ethnic Albanians deteriorate in Kosovo. In Croatia, the Party of Rights continues to profess its own extremist program and carry it out on the battlefield, but its influence seems to be waning as the military situation improves; it was never the ruling party in any event. In this case study even more than the two others, we can see how deterrence, retribution and revenge against ancient injuries inevitably creates new injuries to avenge—unless and until a moral actor passes up his own turn to do harm.

"The Avengers of Kosovo" was written in 1998, one year before a NATO offensive will strip from Serbia all but nominal authority over the disputed province of the title. The Civil War is over; Croatia is beginning to recover; Bosnia remains divided into ineffectual ethnic-based subrepublics, but at least the mass atrocities there are over; as for Yugoslavia, of which now only Serbia and Montenegro are left, that sad land, still impoverished and isolated by international sanction, continues to self-destruct, with the same ugly ethnic conflicts now taking place in Kosovo, Serb against Albanian, the Serbs outnumbered, the Albanians outgunned, the killings and mutilations continuing on, NATO's bombers about to come.

WHERE ARE ALL THE PRETTY GIRLS? (1992)

Zagreb, Republic of Croatia

Men in Uniform

One day in the park it was very hot, and the almost barkless state of the ocher-colored trees was like the paint peeling on the benches, like the ocher-colored leaves that scraped occasionally across the asphalt or just lay clutching with outstretched points. It was the middle of the afternoon. A boy stood calling to his playmate, staring and scratching his throat. The other boy came on a bicycle, and they went away together. A cloud of dead leaves blew suddenly with a sound like lizard skins being pulverized. Two pigeons pecked in the dead leaves that covered the steps of the bandstand. Across the street, a man in a blue-grey uniform lounged against a car, his foot welded to his knee. He called to another man dressed the same way.

At once a third man in blue-grey came walking through the park very rapidly with his walkie-talkie out and his hand on a holstered gun. Then he was gone. A man in camouflage fatigues passed more slowly, carrying a leather briefcase. There was a girl who rode her friend on the handlebars of her bike facing her; those two rode round and round. A woman with long tanned legs passed, smoking a cigarette. People in their summer clothes entered the patch of bleached light at the middle of the square, and an old man bowed himself over a drinking fountain. For a moment I thought that there were no men in uniform anymore. But then another one came.

Across from the bookstore where I'd once bought Communist-flavored children's books (eleven years ago now, just after Tito died), a young couple sat on a bench, the woman scissoring her knees to bring coolness inside her sweaty dress; and white-winged black bugs kept landing on me and crawling on my sticky skin, so I got up and walked away past quadruple-storied facades, one a bleached chlorine-green, the next pale yellow, the third chrome yellow, all as clean as if they'd been carved out of soap; and past the sloping grey awnings where people took their drinks in the shadow of a saber-pointing horseman long since petrified, I saw a campaign poster for the Croatian Party of Rights. Paraga, their leader, looked handsome, determined, somewhat effete. (Someone who'd known him in college said that he had been nice but perhaps a bit quiet.) Paraga's army was called HOS, the Croatian Defense Force. Their slogan was READY FOR THE HOME! A HOS poster two steps away showed two brawny tattooed men in black uniforms, their arms upraised in a Nazi salute. Of course the Romans had saluted in the same way. Maybe I ought to make allowances, as I already had for the T-shirts that said GOD AND CROATIA (I had nothing against either of those quantities). Anyway, Paraga had lost the election overwhelmingly.

That evening when I heard the organ notes twisting and rising through the green-oxidized doors of the cathedral I thought: Why not God and Croatia? The music in those old ocher walls, still warm from the sun, vibrated with a painful beauty like droplets of summer darkness dripping from copper flowers. (I remembered the flowers I'd seen in the empty restaurants. Not very many people in Zagreb had the money to eat out.) The sacristan watched me from behind his gratinged and arched window. I opened the door, and the music stopped. I didn't go in. I heard a page turning, and then the organ filled me with sweetness again as the sacristan closed the door in my face and bolted it. On the black steps which resembled lava, cool air and music issued from the cracks in the door along with the old mortar smell peculiar to churches. The music appeared to be talking to itself, ready for any death.

I don't remember this scaffolding, I said to a man in uniform. Is the cathedral being restored?

In a manner of speaking. The Serbs bombed it. They love to target monuments.

On one of the walls hung a great cross plaited with the barbed wire of agony, and fresh roses in a plastic cup. I thought again of the flowers in the empty restaurants. I thought of how written on a long yellow wall over and over I'd seen CRO and VUKOVAR (the latter sometimes inside a heart). I was glad I had not had to see the ruins at Vukovar. I'd kept walking until I saw the expected swastikas. The swastikas were a curse upon the Serbs.

Anyhow, the Serbs were not bombing Zagreb anymore. They never really had. Those blasts had been mere episodes, compared to the sniping. In short, the city was safe. You had to drive half an hour to get to the place where last week a Croatian girl had been found raped with her throat cut. In the street bulge in front of the church, frowning dark faces were vomiting pure water endlessly, and around them sat people undressed for summer and above them stood gilded angels holding crosses so powerfully. The brown water rippled yellow in the sunset. The bells rang. The church door opened. Old women in black came out. They walked down the street, past another HOS poster.

Later, when I was in the Serbian Republic of Krajina, my police translator claimed that HOS built and controlled concentration camps for Serbs, just like in Germany in the Second World War.

Have you seen those camps yourself? I said.

No, he said. How could I see them and not be dead? But one journalist told me he saw these camps, and the HOS commander said to him: Journalists are like soldiers. The less they know, the longer they'll live.

In Zagreb there were no concentration camps that I could see. There were only men in uniform. Greenish summer leaf light pressed coolly against the hot back windows of the flat's blocky rooms. Blocky rugs and furniture allied themselves with the huge rectangle of the TV which square religious pictures watched. My shirt glued itself to my back. On the TV the newscaster said *dobar dan,* good day, and then they showed the shattered flowerpots and broken glass of Slavonski Brod. They showed Sarajevo, a man running in the heat, a bird flying, smoke coming up, wounded people, a smashed roof. There came happy trilling music. Army boys and girls were singing at attention, machine guns at the ready.

Is this the song of all Croatia or just the army? I asked my friend Adnan. He was a Croatian of Albanian extraction.

Some not important song. It says we are saving our home.

At midnight the bleached sidewalks and windowed wall blocks formed a room of hot and tireless hardness, a single roofless night room of many wide corridors which were usually empty but down which cars sometimes moved, or a man on a bicycle with lights. A dreamy fellow with a beard and glasses stood with his hand on his arm looking for a long time into the window of a shop that sold women's dresses. Then he turned half away. He tried to walk on but could not. For a long time he stayed locked into alignment with one dress. Finally he took the first step, but his head only turned further back. Two military policemen stood at the corner watching, one with his hands on his hips, the other turning to face this bearded one who stood still, peering into another night window displaying Cro Army chocolate bars in a camouflage wrapper (the accompanying poster proud of its soldiers and tank). Slowly the policeman came forward, staring at him. The man looked up and began to run.

On another night Adnan took me to meet a blonde in a dark dress who sat with her hands clasped and her legs crossed. I'll call her Nives. She said: Well, I'm Serbian and Croatian. I'm mixed. And I haven't any problems with my job, with my friends in the town. I can say I am Serbian. I think it is not so difficult in the big towns. Maybe in a small town I might have problems.

Two men who might have been HOS or maybe Tigers swaggered down the street in camouflage uniforms. One threw a cigarette butt down. There was a new slang word in Zagreb; instead of "cliquish" people said "squaddish." These frequent shimmerings of squaddishness were hardly so grave a sin. What if those men *were* HOS? HOS were only squaddish; that was all.

How do you feel about the attacks of Serbians and Croatians upon each other? I said.

Well, I am cautious, said Nives. It is war, so everything is much more intense. Many people say to me: I hate Serbians, but you are OK.

I had heard people using the word "Chetniks" in accents of horror and hate. A man in uniform had told me that Chetniks were Serbian extremists. So I said to Nives: Do you know any Chetniks?

She smiled. I'm not sure, because it's a name somebody from here they call people, but people in Serbia, they don't agree. My father is in Yug Army. For all Croatian people, he is a Chetnik. But he does not agree.

What would happen to you if you went to HOS and said to them: I am one-half Serbian?

They will say: So what? So what you want?

They would never hurt you?

Probably not.

They never hurt anybody?

I think not. Never in Zagreb.

We were sitting in a cafe. Couples walked whitely in the dark park squares. I heard a noise like a hooting owl. Then from not far away a bell began to ring.

Some people tell me they commit atrocities on Serbs near Zagreb, I said.

Adnan interrupted, shouting: It's not true!

Well, maybe it's possible, Nives said.

Adnan grabbed his milk glass and stared at her. You don't write good! he said to me. Maybe it's true, but I have not experienced it and she has not experienced it.

The blue tram rounded the bend slowly, glowing yellowly inside. When it passed, a streetlight left its cool gleam on the track and then I could see the building block laced with darkness that used to be the artists' institute but was now HOS. A man in camouflage stood vigil in the doorway beneath a flag.

Tito

At midnight the Croatian flag waved endlessly on TV to the national anthem.

I'm sad about Yugoslavia, I said. Because I remember that when I was here before I could go anywhere, all over the country. There was no fighting. I would be sad if my country broke up into so many countries.

But your country has no history! said Adnan. Here we have always had separate countries. It was only the Serbs trying to dominate us who forced us into one country.

I'd say it wasn't the Serbs; it was the Communists.

No! No! Tito was not well educated; he was not a real Communist. He only set up the Serbs to dominate the non-Serbs.

But, Adnan, wasn't Tito Croatian?

So they say. But I don't believe. They have his birthplace in Croatia. But I don't believe.

So you honestly think Tito was a Serb?

I think so, yes. There were never any Communists here.

But when I was here ten years ago, I stayed in the youth hostel with seven other boys. And they were all Communists—Stalinists!

He looked at me in disgust. —They were stupid! They were liars! I don't believe!

I speak from my experience, I said.

Then they were Serbs.

Gypsies

I met a man who'd seen gypsies at the dump. It had been early in the morning, he said, but the stench was already intolerable. The gypsies were roasting a pig in a pile of garbage. While the meat cooked, they were gleaning among the trash.

I met a man who owned a book of old gypsy songs. I leafed through the book.

What does this song mean? I said.

The gypsy is asking God to make love to him.

And this song?

He asks God to give him meat instead of sauerkraut.

And this song?

He asks God to give him a red dress for his girlfriend.

I met an old gypsy who tried to sell me shoelaces. —No, no, I said. I don't want them. I need a gypsy wife before I can wear those shoelaces!

Take them, shouted the old man. Only five hundred dinars! I have a beer belly, as you see. I must have a beer.

No.

Three hundred dinars.

I don't want them.

Two hundred.

No.

Okay, take them for nothing. They're yours.

As soon as I had the shoelaces in my hand, the old man laughed in triumph and cried: Now they're yours. Now you must pay.

I met a gypsy whore who sold me her body, her tiny body blooming with tattoos. Her bluish-dark face, her little elf face, lived with her little gold Jesus. Her name was Dina. The first time a man told her to take her clothes off, he gave her five dinars on special green paper. She couldn't read or write, so she thought it was worth more.

How did you lose your teeth?

They fell out when I was pregnant. (Big eyes in the little elf face.)

Are you a gypsy?

I'm not a gypsy. Only my mother's a gypsy. My father is Croatian. My husband, I don't know about him. He's in prison for eleven years.

Why?

Somebody tried to kill him, but my husband killed him instead.

No, God had not given her any red dress, not to this tiny little gypsy in the green shirt with the gold ring and the name in the rectangular tattoo, the name in the flower tattoo. She had a mind like a bird.

How did you get tattooed?

My husband did it.

I don't believe it, said Adnan, who was interpreting.

I was hungry all my childhood, Dina said. I must sell my body because I haven't no food. Up until my sixth year I was going to school, but only two months at a time. Then my parents put me out on the street to beg. When I had something, I'd buy bread for my brother.

What's the war like for you?

I don't like Serbian people, but some of them are good. The war hurts my heart. I want to cry.

But I don't believe her, said Adnan. She says it with no emotion. She gnawed on her cross alertly, like a bird. —It's better you're alive than nothing, she said.

That girl, what she says, maybe I don't believe, said Adnan. In her heart is darkness.

What kind of darkness?

I don't know. Darkness. She is very intelligent, very bad inside.

I met another gypsy who also sold me her body. She had dark eyes and a pouting face. She said: I'm not a gypsy. My mother was a gypsy.

Do you know Dina?

We're friends, but not such good friends. (She was drinking from a green liter bottle of mineral water with three red hearts.)

Has she ever taken customers from you?

I don't know. I never steal anything, but maybe she's different.

At the next table, some men from HOS were pointing at her, and making farting noises and whistling. She frowned slightly. —The HOS men said: Hey, whore! —She said: They're fools. I've seen them in Italy. This chance with you is special and I don't want to say anything. —The HOS men said: Hey, whore! Up your mother's cunt! —She ignored them all with her brown face; she shut them out with her brown eyes.

You want to see me naked? she said. Her eyes were darkly glowing.

How much? I said.

You want to touch me?

How much?

Fifteen thousand dinars. (A wink of her gold tooth.) You're a foreigner. Foreigners pay the best. Germans pay me sometimes a hundred deutsche marks, sometimes fifty.

Hey, whore! said the HOS men.

Sylvana raised both shoulders, drawing them in toward her head.

The HOS thugs were leaning on their hands now, smoking cigarettes, sneering at her with bleary eyes. —You're a stinking gypsy whore! they said.

Fuck your mother! said Sylvana.

Summer darkness made the streetcars cooler now. Blue trains sped along the weird-angled streets, blinking their lights, and the people inside were not sweating anymore. What do you think of the Serbs?

Fuck all their mothers! They should go into their mother's cunts. If I saw a Serb, I'd bite his balls off. On the other hand, this war is good for business. When there's work, there's bread at home. I have children, but no husband, and I love bread.

How about Croatians?

Croatians are ordinary people. Gypsies have the Turkish religion. Gypsies are better than ordinary people.

She took me down a long, dark, stone hallway, then right at the first door, which was outlined in medieval light. She knocked. Inside was a huge kitchen of stone. An old lady and two burly old men stripped to the waist sat smoking cigarettes and playing cards. They were all gypsies. Other gypsies were standing. A man sat softly singing a song about a red dress.

Sylvana couldn't read, and neither could any of them. They didn't need to, they said. In Sarajevo I met a man named Nehro, and I never found out if he could read or not.

What makes a gypsy a gypsy? I asked him.

We come from India, he said. Our origins everybody knows.

Are some people ashamed of being gypsies?

I'm speaking for myself only, he said. I am not ashamed and I will never be ashamed. My father was a gypsy, my mother was a Muslim, and my wife is a Serbian. I don't allow anyone to touch her. If she makes a wrong move with the other Serbs, I'll kill her myself.

Nehro was the commandant of the gypsies, from a camp called Mahala. At the beginning of the war, he saw fighting going on just above the Presidency building. He was there with his men and two guns they'd bought with their own money.

So you knew war would come?

We had a hunch, he said.

Are you a good fighter?

Not bad.

How about with a knife?

Have you ever seen a gypsy who didn't know how to fight with a knife?

What's the trick?

Be the fastest.

Why are you living in this apartment block? I asked.

When our houses were burned down, we heard there were empty shelters here. And this land was ours before the apartments were ever here. We came in and took over.

Nehro brought me into the smell of greasy garbage, where people with dark brown faces milled in the shade, never going outside where a sniper might get them. Kids in worn clothes ran from shadow to shadow, dark-eyed and skinny.

There was excrement on the floor. Past the open space under the stairs where eight people lived, we entered the shelter's arch. A baby was crying. Great shadows lived on the cracked wall, attacking the single candle. Deeper inside, women and children sat in darkness. —Sometimes an attack comes here, a grandmother said. We don't trust anybody. —She had a hand like leather. The floor was made of cardboard. The pipe overhead was from the toilet and it leaked.

Why is it so quiet today?

Maybe they're cleaning their weapons.

Do you ever sing songs here? I asked her. In Zagreb they sing the song about the red dress.

I'm too sick to sing songs. I'm too sad to sing songs.

I met a gypsy who said to me: I like our people because we are always very happy or very angry. We work only for ourselves, and not for anyone else.

What do you think of the Serbs? I said to him.

I'm a gypsy and I'm a Croatian, he said. Slit all the bastards' throats!

But I also met a man who wasn't a gypsy, and I told him I might go to Belgrade to interview the Serbs. —You're going to Belgrade? he said in disgust. That's a dirty gypsy town.

The Details Killed Everybody

Outside of Zagreb, there was a camp for Bosnian Muslims without documents. It was hot and dusty, and gravelly. People walked between white barracks.

Beside the hospital room, which smelled like vomit and had no windows and no electricity, and no doctor, an old man was leaning, staring. He had hairs in his nose.

The details killed everybody! he shouted.

He speaks without meaning, the interpreter said.

From here to this place everyone is going down, cried the old man. It's hard for me to talk; my throat hurts.

But it makes no sense, said the interpreter. Anyway, I see here ten nice girls. They haven't documents; with them one can do anything.

Because I Am a Muslim Girl

A pubescent girl came and asked: Can I talk?

Sure.

She said: They started to shoot at the place where we were. Then we fled to another nearby town. We took grenades and everything.

What did you think the first time you saw a grenade?

I didn't think, she said. The Chetniks found me and put me in prison for twelve days. They came when we were making coffee and they said: You must make us coffee.

And then what?

They said: You must stay. Don't leave this place. Only a few will have enough food to go away.

And then?

Soldiers said: You must leave this village in half an hour. If not, we kill everyone here in half an hour. We were all afraid, and there were twenty-six of us in the cellar. They began shelling. Then we didn't have a house any-more, because of the shelling. The houses were all on fire and it was ex-tremely frightening.

Why did the Chetniks want you to leave?

Because a second army was coming to kill everyone.

Why don't the Chetniks like you?

Because I am a Muslim girl.

Why don't they like Muslims?

Because they want all our territory.

What would you do with them if you could?

I would kill them, because they want to kill us, the girl said joyously.

What's it like here?

It's not the same as a concentration camp, but it's similar. If you go to eat, if you go to the bathroom, you must wait in line. But you get some-thing to eat. Nobody beats you.

Tito

An old lady in a whirling flower-leaf dress was stringing peppers. They were all women in that room, all Muslim women without any documents.

There are four generations here, the old lady said.

What are your memories of Yugoslavia?

It was nice the way it was before. I'd like to live in the house of peace again.

(Into my mind flashed a phrase from Lucan: *Rome's inability to bear herself.*)

What did you think of Tito?

He was very, very good to us.

Did he always respect religion?

Yes, of course.

Lies

In Zagreb there was a man who sat in a bar. The town he'd escaped from, the town where he'd been born, was called Bosanka Gradiska.

He said: I was sitting in a cafe when a Serb came in. I am Muslim; it was a Muslim cafe, so I was causing no trouble. The Serb said to me, "I could kill you, but I won't. I'll kill that man instead." That man was the man next to me. The Serb fired two slugs into his head.

That was the story the man told me. That was one reason that he hated the Serbs. One of a thousand reasons.

What about the Serbs in Zagreb? I said. Do they hurt anybody here?

They may be hidden under another cloak, he said. Even if they haven't done anything against us, they have not stood up against the injustice.

I said: How can they stand up? What can they do?

The man looked at me and said: There is a mountain called Duboki Jarak. The Serbs took girls aged ten to thirteen from my town. They took them all to Duboki Jarak. They raped them all.

I left the bar and went back to where Tudjman was talking on TV, saying: Despite the attacks of the Serbian imperialists and their Yugo-Communist allies . . .

My friend Adnan turned the channel to Serbian TV, shimmering, staticky. There was a red star and crescent moon on a purple screen. There were Cyrillic letters.

What are they saying? I asked.

Lies, Adnan said.

Life Put Me Here

Behind the barracks of the "Drop of Goodness" shelter, a boy sat drinking, pursing his greasy lips out into a snout. Women sat in old chairs reading and drinking amidst the hot summer smell of armpits. The old man was drinking, too. His breath stank of slivovitz. The boy with the greasy lips was his son.

I have to live in this place because life is hard, he said to me. Life put me here.

He had a goat's-leather face. His narrow greenish-brown eyes were shelved by pinkish underlids. His moustache, thicker than grass, was black and silver.

My son uses drugs, he said. But I never use drugs.

Then what are those abscesses on your arms?

I worked for five years in a small town near Rijeka doing metal etching. Those are acid burns. It was illegal labor, so they gave me no gloves.

I believed him. I'd seen people like him all over the world, people born without luck or money or talent, the kind of people who live and die most horribly. He was the proletariat. He was the one that the Party had set out to save.

Are you sad that Yugoslavia is dead? I asked him.

For me it's completely the same. I have sixteen years working. In Yugoslavia I had nothing. In Croatia I have nothing.

What's your opinion of the Serbs? I said.

The Serbian people are not so bad. I had many Serbian friends before, I believe they're still my friends. I remember the start of war in one town called Delnice. I took a few boys from here to fight, because we didn't want Delnice to be in Serbian hands. I had an old gun, and the boys had some sticks. The police stopped us and sent us back. They said they didn't need us. About the Serbs I don't really care. About the war I don't care. Nobody cares except the people who are getting rich.

The boy with the greasy lips heard this, looked at his father, and spat on the dirt.

My son of course really wanted a weapon so much, said the old man, scratching industriously at his sores. He bought a machine gun from the gypsies for fifteen hundred deutsche marks. I don't know where he got the money. Maybe from selling heroin. Then he went to Bosnia and joined up. Since he was only sixteen, I was able to take the bus to get him out. I am his father. He must do as I say until he's eighteen. The judge made that a condition of his probation. Now he's angry, as you see. He won't speak to me anymore. As soon as he finishes school he'll be free to enlist, and I can't stop him. He'll go. He's a wild one. I expect he'll lose his life.

The old man was like a stone, an inert and sullen stone at the bottom of the creekbed called politics. Water and blood wash over the stone, but they cannot change it. Nor can it change the stones it lies against. The stone can do nothing. It is nothing.

Are people different in Zagreb since the war? I asked.

Yes, so much. Never before would they always ask: Where are you from? Who was your mother? Before the war, someone might help you. Now your best friend won't help you. Tomorrow maybe I'll help my best friend. But my best friend won't help me today.

But I knew by then that for the old man it had always been this way, that no best friend had ever helped him and none ever would.

Everything Was Waiting

At the Restaran Splendid, it was not yet six, and men sat at a table in the middle of the preordained echoes, saying *Sarajevo* while a small boy ran back and forth, slapping new echoes down on the tiles which descended all the way to the toilet where the toilet queen and her daughter waited for someone to urinate or defecate and then pay them, and the radio kept talking with an anxious twist of voice like the tightness behind your eyes when you haven't slept. Then the radio played country music, and the mirror filmed with stale cigarette smoke. It's only fair to say that I don't think I would have known from these indications alone that what newscasters call a "tragedy" was going on, which only proves that I am stupid or else that tragedies do not affect anything except themselves, as we all know anyhow—so my point ought to be quite obvious, but novelists and journalists who write about foreboding circumstances do too often do what cinema directors do when they instruct the composer to make the musical score sound ominous so that you'll get it. My friend Francis said: But it doesn't *feel* right in Zagreb! but I wondered whether it would have felt right to him without the men in uniform. Maybe Zagreb didn't seem so different because the only other time I'd been there (back when Croatia was still Yugoslavia), people were also quiet since Tito had just died and they were nervous about a Soviet invasion.

At a corner where someone had scrawled in wide fierce strokes VUKO-VAR, a lady in a blue hat stood waiting, I think, for the bus.

From the Gradska, music escaped past patrons at outdoor tables and impregnated each stone with the sky's luminosity. A little boy and a middle-aged man bicycled their separate ways over that light, which joined the ground to the sunset that the icecream man stood on. Three men in camouflage, U.N. insigniae on their shoulders, were peeping into a store that sold baby clothing. I heard a lady say to her friend: Vukovar and then Sarajevo, Sarajevo. —People's muffled calls took on a scuffed and polished quality in that cooling light. The bell sounded the half hour. It was a small and dissonant bell. Nothing was loud in Zagreb. Everything was waiting.

Sarajevo, Republic of Bosnia-Herzegovina

Cabbages

On the Muslim side of the first front there was a concrete building that used to be a youth hostel. It stood alone and apart from the apartment towers whose ragged windows and round shell holes were a good three-minute sprint across a very dangerous open place that used to be a busy street. Curtains hung out of the hostel's broken windows. The roof of the portico was spattered with fragments of glass. The white walls were scorched. There was garbage on the grass, because in Sarajevo carrying the trash out was less necessary and no less dangerous than getting water. Some people in Sarajevo did empty their trash, of course. What would life be without the freedom to empty the trash whether or not it kills you? And perhaps it will not even kill you if that is your one indulgence, and your other rules of conduct are drafted more prudently. A man named Darko told me his particular rules: When I walk, I am very careful in some cross-roads. I never go in open places. You always have to find some kind of shelter, some wall or building behind your neck. And always run. Never walk easy. If you hear some kind of bomb or shooting, don't move. Try to walk in the shadows. (This last bit of advice, I think, explains what I call "the Sarajevo pallor.")

The hostel was definitely one of the places to and from which you always ran (unless you were drunk on vodka), because it was only two hundred meters from the Chetniks (nobody called them Serbs anymore). To go by car you screeched across the sidewalk, weaving and dodging until you gained the safety of the portico. You jumped out as quickly as you could. As you ran into the lobby of the hostel you became lost in a wilderness of shattered chairs and planks. Behind a desk, soldiers from the Blue Thunderbolt special unit sat in the darkness, smoking cigarettes with their rifles ready beside them.

I remember the first time I went up the concrete stairs with half a dozen soldiers and crossed to the wing where no one lived anymore. The hall was black and it stank of burning because three days before a tank shell had come smashing and roaring in. The soldiers told me that when the napalm in a tank shell explodes, the snipers start shooting at that room to kill anyone who is still alive. Going down this hall terrified me because we had to run past every open sunny doorway, knowing that any Chetnik waiting and aiming at that doorway would be able to get me. Maybe a Chetnik was playing his binoculars across all the doorways and had just found me. He would be calculating my speed as I ran. He'd take aim at the doorway ahead, waiting for me to pass into its lethal openness and light (during this first visit I was too afraid and was running too quickly to see the smashed littered rooms and broken windows inside those zones of nakedness); and I also was aware that if the Chetniks were watching then they would know that I would be running back this same way. If I were a Chetnik, the logical thing to do would be to wait for the prey to re-turn. That was the worst, the knowing that every doorway would see me twice.

At one of the landings, a round porthole long since deglassed by war looked out at the Chetniks. The soldiers told me that there were about twenty of the enemy in that red-roofed white building which used to be an institute for the blind. To look out this porthole, you took a cracked mir-ror from the soldiers and sat to one side, holding the mirror at a forty-five degree angle to the still and shattered cityscape so that you could see the Chetniks and they could see your reflected face but they could not shoot you. When I tried this, a soldier looked down at my knees and I looked down and saw that they were trembling. The soldier smiled.

How do you feel now? he said.

Afraid.

The soldiers all laughed. —Try to spend twenty-four hours a day here, one said.

The desolate shining of the hostel's white walls in the twilight chilled me. It was a wrenched and twisted whiteness, so alone on the edge of life. Sol-diers and students were sitting in the darkening lobby. A seventeen-year-old in a swivel chair held a Kalashnikov between his knees.

The commander came in. He took me through a room barricaded with chairs and then up to a place on the second floor where a man sat reloading his Kalashnikov in the dark. The Chetniks were firing an antiaircraft gun right then, their shooting making the same idiotic rhythm for a time, then changing beat, then degenerating into randomness. —They are attacking from that house now, the commander said, showing me the place through a hole in the concrete not much larger than a coin. —That one, he said, that red-roofed one with the hole in the roof.

A soldier sat on guard on the steps, his face pale and calm, his lips gleaming.

To the right of that house there are eight bunkers, the commander said.

Through the loophole I saw a motionless kingdom, a grey zigzag of streets. White stars hung over green trees in the dusk. Then came the hiss and slamming boom of a shell.

On the left is a tank, said the commander. We cannot destroy it. In that tank there is a professional soldier from the ex-Yugo Army, maybe five or six hundred meters from our eyes. There they have their artillery. We cannot locate it. We have only *had* artillery, the greater part of which is under con-trol of UNPROFOR which cannot defend us.

They're only terrorists now, the commander said. They were Serbs. Now they're not Serbs. There are no more legitimate Serbs.

Another view through darkness. I saw the destroyed grey-white skulls of buildings, figurations of ghastly terror. Across that grassy courtyard heaped with garbage and rubble rose the weird vertebrae of a wigwag apartment building which had been heavily shelled.

There was a student, Adbel, who was interpreting for me. I asked his opinion of the soldiers. —I like them very much, he said. Because they keep me alive.

He showed me a black hole in the ground where a student had been killed. —We haven't any chance, he said.

One of the apartment towers next to us had just been hit by a shell. Fire glowed more and more brightly in the window. Smoke soared softly into the night while sparks fell. I wondered if anyone in that flat could still be alive. Some soldiers and students stood beside me watching. We heard the sharp crashing barks of a machine gun, and then an antiaircraft gun started. The students were as still as the weeds behind the smashed red Volkswagen beside the yellow station wagon whose roof had been patched with a sheet of plastic, whose side was spattered as if with mud; actually the spatterings were bullet holes. Flashes of light from a Chetnik-held building pinkened the sky, glowing until they dominated the stars, sullenly booming. A howitzer made a tremendous crashing noise. The sky lit up in an arc around the explosion.

We have to hold this building, a soldier said. If this building falls, they'll get us. We all live in Sarajevo. They'll get us all.

The students slept in an A-bomb shelter in the basement.

The shelling is almost continuous, a student said. From April we've slept underground since our rooms are too dangerous. It's very cold. Food is a great problem for us.

On their cots they lay still, some smiling shyly at me in the light of the white walls. Their pale glowing hagridden faces were transected by blue-grey shadows.

In the ventilation room, they took turns for fifteen minutes every hour turning the crank. That was what changed the air. This job was very strenuous. Some were stronger than others. The strong ones cranked for half an hour. It was concrete-grey in there in the beam of my flashlight (they themselves turned the crank in the dark), and the sand was grey. —We have eyes in the dark, a student said.

On a dark hill nearby, a spot of flame glowed up. —That's a house, Abdel said. When they destroy our children, our women, our fathers, our grand-mothers . . .

In the darkness, a shell exploded. A sheet of metal rattled.

The darker darkness of the camouflage-uniformed boys broke like the skin of a lake around a falling stone, because a man lit a cigarette. I saw a quick match-gleam on the upraised barrel of a gun.

Of the eighty-odd students, there were three who did not sleep in the shelter. The shelter was too dark and crowded, they said. They had beds set up side by side on the second floor landing in front of the elevators. That was the safest place except for the shelter. Sami, skinny and brown, lay on one side of the candle. The two girls and I were on the other. The flame caught warring crab's claws and crescent moons on the edges of their hair and faces, the rest of their heads silhouetted against the wall. I told them about California and Sami talked about the Sudan and Suzy began to say something about Kuwait but then she began to think about her parents, who didn't know whether she was dead or alive, and grew silent. Mica never said anything. She was a Serbian girl from Visegrad.

After Suzy blew the candle out there came the first of the autumn storms, and wind groaned terrifyingly through the shattered corridors, chilling our faces, opening and slamming doors, toppling barricades with sickening crashes, knocking out jagged pieces of glass that smashed loudly on the floors. I could hear rain falling inside the ruined hall. The sky flickered white and black, then suddenly red from a distant shell. Mica moaned in her sleep. I had taken the bulletproof vest off because I could not bear to lie next to them with more protection than they had, but all that meant was that I kept waking up wondering when a shell or a bullet would discover me. This fear was, like most fears, founded on inexact statistical analysis. Had I known that in World War I, for instance, it required on average five thousand bullets to wound or kill a single soul, I might have slept better, although in Sarajevo they probably harmed people more efficiently since so many of them were noncombatants. At any rate, I did sleep better every night, because after all I was there and my fear could not do me any good, so it was better to be influenced by fallacies of safety than by chimeras of extinction. At six in the morning, a soldier woke us. Six was the time at which one must leave open places, because it was getting light and the snipers would be able to see in. The girls got up one by one, rolling up their sheets and carrying them away. I could see the white roll of cotton fading down the dark hall as Mica vanished. By six-thirty, dawn was well established, the sky grey like a dirty sheet, raindrops tinkling down against glass shards on the floor, and the Chetniks beginning to fire once again with the antiaircraft gun.

In Sami's room the window was shattered, the wood splintered on the sill. Blue sky was cracked with greenish glass lines and tracked and sectored by translucent tape. Sami told me that he'd been lying on his bed a week before, at about 5:00, when the bomb came in. He'd had a bad feeling just before it happened. Shrapnel had shot up over his head and gone into the corner of the ceiling. He was knocked to the floor. —Thanks for God I tell you because until now I live!—Now he took an ice-cold shower in the dark bathroom, brushed his teeth and smoked a cigarette. Proudly, he showed me a fresh cabbage. That was the first vegetable I had seen in Sarajevo. I asked him where he had gotten it, and he smiled and said: Wait until tonight. At 8:00 I show you!

And what do we do right now?

We gonna make some tea. So nice for you!

He took me upstairs to the place where I'd had to run past doorways the day before. This time I was not quite so afraid, and was able to see inside the doorways. Bullet holes, shell holes, these the abandoned rooms wore for makeup, their faces splintered into weird and ugly terraces. We entered a door. Whoever's room this had been had left quickly or been killed. All over the floor lay rumpled clothing, shoes, photos, identity cards, even coins. Curtains blew back from the shattered windows. —You want sweater? said Sami. It will be very good for you. Always the girls go shopping here.

We entered another door. The room had many holes in the wall. —Sniper, said Sami. If you stand there you will die. —From a ruined dresser he took some scraps of wood as quickly as he could. Then we ran back downstairs. We walked quickly when we got to the open part where snipers might see us, and we came to a landing where the concrete wall was scorched black. From his kindling and some sheets of old physics exercises Sami started a fire almost at once. He put on the black cast-iron pot. The dresser wood crackled and flared. The landing filled with smoke. A soldier peered out at the Chetniks, yawning and gripping his Kalashnikov. He rubbed smoke out of his eyes. He squatted on the stairs, leaning on the butt of the gun. —If he see, he must shoot, said Sami. If no see sniper, he must not shoot. Because they always shoot back again. We must shoot only for control, to make them afraid.

The water was boiling now. The Chetniks were shooting from their house behind the parking garage. We had tea.

At a little before four o' clock, the shooting and shelling around the building had become intense. All the civilians except Suzy, Mica, Sami and me had gone down to the shelter. Sami said: From the first day of the war, I have never left my room. I will never leave my room.

Then the soldiers had to get their one rifle and go down and fight. The two women sat on the terrace drinking coffee. I brought Mica a vodka and she laughed and cried: Oh, no! and Suzy said: She don't like. So I left the shot glass on the table in front of her and went back to Sami's room to get my binoculars. I was going with the soldiers.

I could hear Mica laughing with Suzy on the terrace in between bursts of bullets because everything else was so quiet. Then I heard her walking past me down the hall. I heard her unlock her door. Then I heard firecrackers in the empty sky.

In the dark, people were going down to the shelter to get water. Sami was still asleep. Women kept calling Mica, and Mica would reply: *Molim?* Suzy came back with water. Mica was calling her. Then the noises stopped and I heard a dog bark, which sounded very strange. A thunderous purr of distant howitzer silenced that, but Mica and Suzy went on speaking to one another in the hall. A soldier came for me. He had a bottle of slivovitz in his hand.

To shoot Chetniks you go up a few flights of stairs and walk quickly down the hall heaped with plaster, old clothes, trash, scorched wood and broken glass, flitting as quickly as you can past the sunny doorways where students used to live and into which the Chetniks can see from their white house next to the destroyed newspaper building, and then you cross a corner terrace and run because it is very exposed and you go up a cement-walled flight or two of stairs until you reach the porthole of your choice, where there will be a couple of chairs and many many 7.62 and 30.06 shells golden and black on the floor. You turn the chair backward and straddle it, leaning against the back of it as you fit the rifle against your shoulder and line up your sights on one of the windows of the red-roofed white house and then you wait for movement. The soldier who's pointed out the apartment house where he used to live with his mother and sister and where a Chetnik shell struck when his mother and sister happened to be there (they lived) takes aim. He fires five careful shots. He says: I prefer to wait, you know, I can stay like this two days. I wait. I prefer to see someone dying.

You each fire. The Chetniks do nothing. You fire again. The Chetniks send machine-gun bullets against the walls. You wait until they stop and they fire again. The soldier who pointed out the apartment house where he used to live says: All Chetniks have beards. They never wash. When I come home, I wash. They, never. They stink. They are dirty.

They killed three of our men here, a soldier said, two from snipers and one from a shell.

At night Sami and the commander and two other soldiers played cards by the light of one candle kept low on the floor, and their breath clouded. They laughed. The besiegers played their usual music. After it was time to sleep we hid our faces under the blankets for warmth. Just after I got to sleep the enemy sent a shell. Their machine guns probed the walls of the hostel briefly from time to time, each bullet hoping to find not concrete but a window and then flesh. There was also a noise like some huge thing splashing. Then, once, a shell came very close and loud.

The morning was clear and cold, with shots, drumlike machine guns now extremely loud and nasty. Mica had taken a cold shower and washed her hair which was as black as the soot-galaxies that powdered the corner of Sami's white ceiling where the shell had exploded. In the cold shadows of distant buildings, people ran, carrying splinters of wood as something smashed fiercely and repeatedly. Mica carried the teapot back to her room, filled it from the bathroom, and the war continued to happen as the girls laughed and smiled. They played Ping-Pong and Tzeta was presented with a white rose from the old gardener outside and everyone teased Tzeta's boyfriend.

* * *

Suzy, Sami and Mica talked about escaping again, but no one could come up with a plan, so Suzy sighed and fell silent. I will always remember those dreary evenings of darkness, the candle on the floor or even extinguished, depending on our fear, and the darknesses of those motionless faces like coagulated misery. Of the three of them I worried the most about Mica. Sami was an organizer. Whatever was possible he would do. Suzy for all her depression seemed extroverted. She had friends. Mica, however, was shy and quiet. Even now she continued to study her subject, which was forestry. She seemed so often to be terrified and silent. And she was a Serb.

I called UNPROFOR to ask about the students. A woman told me: I wouldn't worry about them if I were you. They're foreigners. Nobody wants to feed them in the winter. In a few days we'll evacuate them.

Because they're foreigners?

That's right.

Then what about the Serbian students? I understand that there are seven.

This is only my opinion, but I don't think they'll be evacuated.

At that time the students did not seem to me to be sufficiently organized. It was very discouraging to me to see how passive they were. Their most important job ought to be preparing for winter. (The soldiers were better off. They had a twelve-hour shift and then they could go home.) Whenever I discussed the future with the students, they would say only: We will die. This seemed to me unnecessarily defeatist. If the siege was not lifted before winter, the chances were that some of them would in fact die, but without proper planning all of them would die.

First of all, I thought, they ought to be gathering fuel of any kind. Abdel and some others agreed with me that there remained at most two months' worth of furniture in the building to be burned. I had met several people in Sarajevo who were living in well furnished apartments formerly occupied by Serbs. That must mean that there were other empty apartments full of fuel. And what about the flats that had been hit by enemy shells? In some of them the owners must be dead and there must be splintered tables and desks which could heat enough water for many meals. The problem, of course, was making the trip to collect the wood. Just going as far as the other hostel building was frightening. —Get ready to run, Sami said as we were about to clear the shelter of the portico. Then we were running past shattered glassed structures which I had only the briefest time to glimpse; maybe they were greenhouses. Later I saw that they had been cafeterias. Inside the other *studenski dom* it was dark and cold. A girl paced, shivering. A soldier stood sheltered in a closet, the door opened, his Kalashnikov at his side. The windows were boarded up on the side facing the snipers. The plank nearest me had twenty-four bullet holes.

Inside the darkened sandbag concrete UNPROFOR offices where the ass-holes said no to everything and outside, amidst the rolls of concertina wire, a U.N. soldier sat in his idling APC with U.N. flag at half-mast for the people in the plane that had been shot down last week by Serbs or Mus-lims, depending on whom you talked to; inside and outside I went with Sami, Suzy and Mica. There was a general who'd promised Sami that the students would be evacuated.

They promised us so many times before, said Suzy quietly.

As we ran back from UNPROFOR, a shell landed not far away. I jumped. Mica bit her lip. Suzy just looked down at the ground, her face more grim and terrified each day.

In the middle of the afternoon Mica and Hazim were playing the game called Mica with dark stones and pale corn kernels, trying to get threes and cut each other off and diminish each other like armies. There came a terrible noise of shooting from the apartment next door, and looking out we saw sparks and smoke boiling from the windows. Suzy, who was sitting beside Sami on the other bed, folded her hands across her breasts and let her head sink down into emptiness. And I thought how many thousands of people there were like her in Sarajevo on that rainy day. Consider the red streetcar full of passengers who knew that at any time the Chetniks might send them a shell, but they were so tired and hungry and their feet hurt, so they took the streetcar anyway. Consider the old ladies who vis-ited their friends. After leaving their passports with the old lady in charge of each apartment building, they had to ascend ten or fifteen flights of pitch dark stairs, past people carrying their jugs of water wearily. At every landing, the shattered glass was boarded or cardboarded over. People squatted there and begged for cigarettes. The people they visited all lived the same life as Suzy. They could never sit out in the sun because if they did someone would shoot them. If they stayed in their rooms someone might or might not shoot them right through their curtain windows. Consider the people who stood in line outside the bakery that had no more bread.

The Chetniks had killed a crowd of bread seekers already. Consider the three men who went to a restaurant to eat but found it closed. They tried a second restaurant, which was also closed, and then a third, inside which it was sepia-dark and people sat at empty white-clothed tables. After a long time a waitress came. Because the men knew the owner, they were able to order a bowl of soup apiece and two plates of meat for the three of them. The other people watched them with hopeless greed. They ate quickly. The measures in their double vodkas seemed to grow grander each time. Cigarette ends whirred like glowing bees in the muddy darkness, and lighters flashed almost in time to the distant shells. One of the men said to the other two: I told you, Serbs in general are not bad. It's not my fault seventy-five percent of the motherfuckers are assholes. —I remember asking a Serb in Krajina his opinion on who the assholes were, and he said: Maybe the Serbs first started shooting, maybe the Muslims, maybe the Croatians. But it's possible that all this mess was organized by Muslims. They want their country, and they don't care about the price. —And I remember a Bosnian who said: The Croats are the worst. They made a secret deal with the Serbs to divide up our country. In five years there will be no more Bosnia. —The three men in the restaurant were trapped, and so were the local journalists who came out of the office of the Bosnian Dragons and had to duck between two trucks to wait for their colleague because the street was very open and went all the way to the hill where the Chetniks were well established in those red-roofed white houses, so two of the journalists stepped out into the street to make obscene gestures at the enemy as if they were small boys, and then before the shell came they rushed back between the covered army truck with the Dragons' insignia on it and the Mercedes-Benz van which carried a couple of bullet holes, where they lurked against the concrete wall of the Bosnian Dragons' office whose windows, comprised of green glass blocks, were occasionally bulleted or shrapneled, the holes white-frosted with white cracks weaving into the green. Equally trapped were the patients in the French Hospital, which had been so heavily shelled that half the windows were raggedly black; equally trapped was the teenager who'd drawn a skull and crossbones on the side of this apartment building and written WELCOME TO HELL; equally trapped was the soldier now walking past Suzy, another huge-headed crewcut Muslim fighter who wore a patterned handkerchief over his skull. His black vest bulged with pockets for pistol and rifle magazines (empty now; he wouldn't go back into action until the afternoon). He wore a ring in his left ear to signify that he had a girlfriend. (In the right ear meant no girl-friend; in both ears meant married.) —I have only twenty years, and I don't want to die, he said. I hate this gun. I want to be drinking and fuck-ing. My girlfriend is a Serbian in Belgrade. I have not seen her for half a year. But I must fight. For my mother and for my sister.

At seven o'clock it was getting cold. The apartments, tall towers of stag-gered length, their remaining windows shining gold in the twilight, were heavy like panic. In the dark landing, Suzy and Mica were fanning the smoke away laughing, jumping a little, Suzy biting her lip when the noises came too close, Mica hunched over the fire, her hair dark and striped. The smoke was getting worse. Sami fanned himself with cardboard, coughing and laughing. He wore a scarf over his head. I looked out to the right at the still apartments and the hills behind them. The sky echoed with can-nonades. Something jackhammered. Something unyielding and echoing went off as steadily as target practice; and there was a rocket, and then Suzy and Mica brought the little plate of halvah (greenish, soft, floury, sweet) and set it before us. I saw people running. Then the sky was empty again except for an unknowing cloud.

Tonight at eight or nine o'clock we will go out to the garden, Sami said. When we go out to the garden, we will make a great salad. It will be dark. For our organism, you know. To stay healthy.

It was eight, cold and dark, and we went down to the lobby where the soldiers smoked cigarettes among the shattered chairs (the words TO BiH made up of sanitary pads pasted into letters on the wall). Sami sprinted low to the dark ground, crunching broken glass under the balls of his feet until he could fade into the nightdarkness of dirt, crouching, embracing the dirt, clutching and gripping for cabbages. He could not find them. A shell exploded far away, fixing us in light for a forever second of terror like some slice of tissue stained in eosin on the microscope slide of God, and then we heard an antiaircraft gun and Sami was running to another place and coughing. —I smoke cigarettes too much, you know, he said. —I heard him digging again. —Ah, now I find the last two cabbages, he whis-pered gleefully. We gonna have too nice a salad, you know!

When we came back inside, he talked happily and quickly, wet with fear-sweat.

I tell you, we gonna make a nice food, a nice salad, he kept saying. Too nice, you know!

Mica stood with her wrist curved against her hip, looking down at Sami, smiling patiently, saying: I know, I know, I know.

Sami, that skinny brown boy, agile, happy and kind, scooped tinned meat into a bowl of soaking rice, added some tomato paste and vinegar while Suzy sat and mixed everything up slowly and carefully with the fork and outside the action was starting, so the howitzers and machine guns boomed sullenly and Sami lit another cigarette, Mica sitting next to me on the bed, cutting cabbage slowly and carefully with a big knife.

Sami was always cleaning, tidying, keeping the room in order. He liked to be correct, he said.

Mica's thin and sprightly movements were like a little cricket's, her black hair tied behind her head in a short ponytail.

Now I make everything to be clean, Sami said, sweeping the floor again. And I gonna make some nice food. I am so happy. But I'm so happy because I wait to do it nice.

When Mica had finished grating the cabbage, I put in my last tin of sardines, and Suzy added oil, salt and pepper. Sami took out a packet of vitamin-added cheddar cheese spread from UNPROFOR, kneaded it, tore open the packet, and slowly extruded the cheese as Suzy mixed with the big spoon. We were all very happy. Afterward we sat drinking Special Balkan Vodka, my treat (the man I'd paid had run through sniper fire to get it). Mica and Suzy had one glass apiece, to be polite. Sami and I got drunk. He laughed and said: Bill, what do you feel? I start to fly, I tell you!

The room smelled of cigarettes as always, cigarette ends the only light, trembling and jerking with the gestures of the dark figures against the pale unseen background, white darkness outside the windows, the soldiers drinking wearily, the noises going on outside. A soldier said: You know, we used to drink with the Serbs. And now all Serbs are Chetniks. —A thud and a sullen thunder roll echoed outside. I heard the high heels of the two girls coming down the stairs. I heard the sound of something crashing into echoing depths. A soldier rose, flickered into existence for a moment by grace of his cigarette lighter, then joined the darkness that snapped around him. A thud, an echo with many reverberations, and then a sharp echoing crack ached in our bones, but the soldiers began to sing. They told me: This is a song about a dead girl, very religious.

Then a soldier came in and ordered them to be quiet because the

Chetniks might be doing something under cover of the happiness. Everyone sat in silence.

At midnight there were no lights in the city, nothing but grimy darkness made more hideous by a reddish-orange moon.

A bullet struck somewhere, and a window shattered.

I miss something, Sami said. I don't know what. I feel so bad I tell you.

All morning Mica carried pots up and down the dark stairs or sat on those stairs feeding the fire with splinters of wood and pages from an old computer book. (That burned and smoky smell of Sarajevo is not the smell of gunpowder but rather the smell of burning chair legs and scorching paint where people are cooking.) At noon, it got quieter, the noises sounding almost happy like construction and from the terrace we saw two men walk slowly in the open street; it seemed almost shocking. Not long after, a man went the same way, sprinting with his head down. A moment later the machine guns resumed.

A soldier said that they had just thrown a bomb against the Chetniks, so the Chetniks could be expected to retaliate, and even at that moment we heard machine-gun bullets striking outside. After a long time they stopped. A man sewed and chopped wood outside. The ping-pong ball clicked between two paddles, and howitzer sounded. It was cold. For the second time the water was off. The soldiers in the hostel were shooting carefully, single shots spaced far apart that echoed coldly under the blue sky. A soldier fired five shots very close together, and a sixth.

There were loud smashing noises and later I found 30.06 shells all over the floor.

It was a quiet day because a VIP had arrived in a VIP plane, which was unfortunately too good to pack out the two new French bodies, and the inhabitants of Sarajevo sat in the shade in front of their partially destroyed flats (in the sun people were more visible, so they ran). I took one of my walks, which always began and ended with a run, and I came to a basking place between apartments. A man whose jaw had been bandaged with packing tape stared up the hill at the red roofed white houses. The boy whose girlfriend had no legs anymore sat next to the boy with a white bandage over his eye, and the man with his arm in a sling laughed as his militia friend shot him

with an unloaded pistol. The militia friend loved that pistol. He kept pointing at everyone and firing it. The old janitress walked by leering at the boys
and they shouted and imitated her gleefully. Then the shell came. It hit
around twenty meters from us. I went briefly deaf in one ear. —Run, run,
run! Everyone was shouting. We sprinted into the nearest apartment building. Standing in the dark and stinking lobby in that crowd, I saw that no one
had been hurt this time. The man with the bandaged eye said that the shrapnel must have gone into the grass. I had a couple of splinters in the palm of
my hand. The old lady who was in charge of passports for that building
wrote down the time of the attack in a notebook. Then we stood together
waiting for a few more minutes in case the Chetniks might send us some sur-
prises. No more shells came. —Well, my friend, said the man with the bandaged eye, I must go upstairs now. My wife will be worried about me on
account of that shell. —He winked. —And so will my girlfriend.

I had to make another useless phone call to UNPROFOR, so I walked
back to the TV station, where reruns of *Hogan's Heroes* played hellishly
and the canned laughter sometimes corresponded to the live shells and
they started drinking slivovitz and whiskey at seven in the morning. When
I got there, one of my colleagues was swearing. Forty-five minutes earlier a
machine gun had shot four holes into the window around the corner from
where I'd slept last week.

Maybe the non-Serbian students would be evacuated and maybe they
wouldn't. Because I could not bear to think about Mica being left behind
in the hostel to freeze to death, I went to UNPROFOR with Sami. A soldier and a British journalist had both told me that the best thing to do
would be to bribe the guards at the Serbian checkpoint to get her out. This
would cost between three hundred and fifteen hundred deutsche marks.
The problem was that this operation would deposit her in Kiseljiak, which
was in Croatian territory and where there was food in the stores and a
blonde girl told me: We have the nicest church in the world! —They told
me that there was a good chance that Mica would be raped or killed there.
So Kiseljiak did not seem such a good idea after all.

Past the first line of concertina wire and sandbags, a blue-helmeted soldier took my passport. I heard the smash of a shell not far away. It was a
good day. The electricity would be coming back soon, they said.

A German journalist had told me to ask at a certain office about brib-
ing the Serbs. The staff there had been very helpful, he said. I got a pass

and went there. A soldier escorted me and opened the door for me. I had no hope.

The lady at the desk would have helped, I think, but her boss interrupted, frowned, scratched her nose and said: I am not interested in this case. This case has nothing to do with me.

We're talking about someone's life, I said. I'm not trying to write a story. I just want to help this person out. You can't tell me whom to talk to?

I know nothing about such things, she said. We always follow the letter of the law here. You are proposing something illegal. I cannot advise you.

I'm not going away until you give me someone's name, I said.

She's a Serb, the woman said. You can try the Serbian attaché. I don't care.

I went to the Serbian attaché, who said that he would be happy to evacuate Mica if the Bosnian attaché would agree. I went to the Bosnian attaché, who shouted: Who told you that Serbs would not be evacuated? The evacuations are conducted without regard to ethnic origin. We help everyone equally! We are not like the Serbs. You must give me the name of the person who told you this information. I must have this name immediately.

I went back to the Serbian attaché's office with Sami, who was becoming increasingly tense. This time there was somebody different behind the desk, a man whose face was patient and whose voice was kind. He promised me that he would try to help Mica. He said to me: Why not bring her today?

When we got back to the hostel, everyone greeted me as usual. Sami seemed not to want me to talk with them. We called Mica, and I'll never forget the look of concentration with which she listened to us, because she knew that her life might or might not continue as a result of what we were telling her, and Sami warned her not to speak to anyone else, since it was clear we could help only her, not all seven Serbs. She nodded and agreed. Then Sami came rushing back. He closed the door.

Listen carefully, he said. I hope I can explain very carefully. If you are not very careful I will punch you like this! I am so worried, I feel very dangerous!

He told me that he didn't want to go to the Serbs again. Word might get around that he was a spy. Mica would go alone with me. But Mica had been afraid of me. She'd spoken with Mustafa, who Sami said had once been a private detective. Sami believed that Mustafa was a spy now. He wanted to call the whole thing off. He wanted me to leave the hostel immediately. He wanted to change his own lodging.

I'd had it. I agreed to go. I started walking out. Sami went out, then came back very agitated. —No, no, it is all right now! All correct! She has agreed to go alone with you.

Never mind, I said. I'm not going.

Please, please! If you go like this, I'll cry!

It was hard for me not to look on Mica without revulsion. She did not and never would trust me. I could not really blame her, but I, too, was very tense. Two days after my arrival on the UNPROFOR flight, an UNPRO-FOR plane had been shot down—whether by Muslims or Serbs was never established (UNPROFOR said by Muslims), and the airport had closed. I had come to Sarajevo for three days, with ten extra days' worth of food which I had given away at once, and now my food was long gone and there was no knowing when I would be able to leave. Every time I ran across the empty street to UNPROFOR I expected to meet my bullet. And Mica did not care. I was childishly hurt. So we ran to UNPROFOR in silence, look-ing away from each other. Sami ran beside us, and I did not look at him, ei-ther. We all three of us behaved very badly that day.

The Serbian attaché was still in his office. He spoke with Mica calmly, gently. She began to get very agitated. He spread his hands.

He says, he can take her out on a convoy anytime, Sami told me. She must only contact him when she is ready.

So she is happy? I said to him.

Yes. Mica sat staring at the wall.

Do you believe him?

I don't know, said Sami, and I saw that he was very tense.

If you and Suzy are evacuated, will Mica be all right?

I prefer not to be here, you know.

When I finally did leave Sarajevo in a BBC armored car, trying not to think about the weird injustice of life, that I could go where I pleased and they could not, I felt an awful sinking of my soul, and I wondered how many of the students and the soldiers would be alive at the end of the winter.

Serbian Republic of Krajina

Where Are All the Pretty Girls?

On the Croatian side, emboldened by the pornographic magazine in the cellar where the soldiers had tried unsuccessfully to shoot a hole through my bulletproof vest (I wasn't wearing it at the time), I asked what Serbian girls were like.

They stink, a soldier explained. They look ugly, and none of them ever washes. That's because they have no water over there. But they have plenty of vodka; you can use it as a disinfectant!

That was at the third and final Croatian checkpoint, just out of Karlovac, which half a millennium earlier had been the command center of the Austrian-financed chain of fortified towns called *Vojna Krajina*. Most of the soldiers of the old Krajina had been Serbs fighting Turks. The new Krajina was on the other side of the line, still Serbian, but its main enemy was Croats now, for it had carved itself out of Croatia. My translator and I drove down the road past the stop sign with bullets in it, the mines, the caltrops, the red and white pole as if for a railroad crossing, the house with the almost-square hole in the wall, tall grass, hot still air. Around us loomed houses under a cloudy sky with sky-chinks glowing through their roofs, houses speckled with shell holes and bullet holes, green walls pocked and holed, houses pimpled by nothingness, clouds oozing through the roof tiles that were missing in godlike patterns; roof frames and skeletons, a roof without a wall. Past the mines and the next stop sign there was a rusty fence in front of a house. This was the U.N. checkpoint. It was very quiet.

Where are all the pretty girls? I asked the U.N. soldier.

In the cemetery, he laughed. Just bring your own shovel. You can do whatever you want to them there.

At the next checkpoint the men wore the same uniforms as the Croatians, but their insignia were different. We had crossed the border.

I sat in a plump armchair at the side of the road, drinking Sarajevo water while the militiamen from the Serbian Republic of Krajina ate inside a house that was not too demolished. A militiaman sat next to me. He said: Everything they say about Serbs conquering is a lie. We are only defending ourselves. We accept the Croatian government. I worked in a firm in Karlovac and I got kicked out because I was a Serb. There are Croats living on this side, but we don't touch them. We get along with everyone. We don't attack Croatians. We don't attack children. We feed them.

We drove past destroyed houses and gradually came into another place: hills of ferns, brown cornfields, some houses untouched, more and more of them, their shutters down. There were hedges, geese on the grass, hills, red-roofed white houses. Then we saw two cows in a yard, an old man sitting. We had left the war.

Across from the police station, a black flag flew from a house where lives had been lost. Then came the cafe with dark walls open to the light, an almost Bavarian-looking place. Three Serbs, two in police uniform, one in a checked shirt, sat drinking. The waitress, seventeen and beautiful, would not marry me because I was too old.

Well, I said, can you find me a nice Serbian girl like you?

She liked that, I could tell. And I liked the way she laughed.

The police translator started talking about pretty Zagreb girls, but the waitress made a face and said that no Croatian girls could possible be pretty. The Croatian people were all wicked. She could never go there. If she did the soldiers would kill her.

And how about this country? What's the best thing about this country?

It's a *good* country! she smiled, raising her arm. It is a very, very good country.

The police were watching her. Can you give me a souvenir of your country?

She reached inside the cash register and handed me something golden. —Maybe this bullet, she said.

Rising Up and Rising Down

The case of Krajina was a microcosm for the case of Yugoslavia. Here was Croatia like a crescent; the Krajina Serbs had taken a bite out of it—or, if you like, kept all but the crescent. "Croatian authorities could not succeed with their ethnic cleansing only on those territories which subsequently became parts of the Republic of Serbian Krayina," ran a Serbian pamphlet that year. The Croats said that Krajina's existence could never be tolerated; the Serbs said that they would never give up Krajina.

Two years ago, when they started to blockade roads in Knin, civilians began buying arms, the man began, sitting across from me in his kitchen dusk in Zagreb, the ashtray full of cigarette butts. He cut the air like bread with his huge, knifelike hands. —At first they had permission to buy arms, he went on. It was then still Yugoslavia. Yugoslavia passed a law forbidding this. Naturally, then, they started to smuggle. Of course there were so many Croatians in Germany that they had many ways of importing them. So then the police started blockading roads in Krajina, in Knin. You know, Krajina is the path to the sea where the big ships are. Police are blockading roads in Krajina because there was an uprising in Knin and Krajina the summer before last. They purged the Croats from Krajina. They occupied that part of Croatia; they created the Serbian Republic of Krajina. At that time the Croats had no army. The Special Forces of the police in Zagreb went in to liberate. Then they started shooting, not too much. Then the Yugo Army got in the act, followed by the Serbian and Croatian regular police forces. Now civilians wanted arms more than ever, so they started blockading the various barracks, especially the Yugo Army barracks. Twenty to fifty people at a time would go, neighbors together, and attack the barracks before the police ever got there. In most barracks the army just gave up, although not in all. When they did give up, the civilians would go in, take over, sweep up arms, and walk out with two or three hundred grenades. They'd hand them out to whoever got there first. Boxes of pistols they'd take home. It wasn't organized at all. Eighty percent of the stuff looted went to the new [Croatian] army; twenty percent went to the civilians who proceeded to sell off big lots. By the end, people were just jumping over the fence, as in the town of Pestco. Now if you have money you can buy a hundred pistols! Of course, the police came in and confiscated many caches.

Someone of the People

Early in the morning we drove down the deserted foggy road. There were fields and houses with potted flowers on the terraces. We reached the Karlovac office of military police, the windows wisely taped and sandbagged. We got our permission to cross, and then we left Croatia and went back into Krajina.

Looking back at the sign for Karlovac, I saw that it was full of bullets.

The police chief in the Serbian town was a huge man in camouflage uniform with a deep voice. As he talked he sliced the air with his forearm.

Probably you know the story from the other side, he said. The misunderstanding between the Croats and Serbs is from the Second World War and before. We ourselves were fighting together with the English, fighting against Hitler. The Croatians were slaves of Hitler. They were against our way of life. Many many Serbs were killed in the Second World War, many, many civilians. I can show you five places where Serbs were massacred, all within thirty kilometers.

Well, as you know, we beat the Germans. We tried to put history out of our minds. Tito believed in equality for all nations. So we continued to live with one another. That was until the Croatian president, Franjo Tudjman, won the democratic election, if you can say democratic.

Tudjman tried to clean Serbs from politics, from government, from law, school, hospitals, and police. Because we were Serbs we must be dismissed. My wife got dismissed from her job. My colleagues got dismissed. Nowhere else in the world would policemen with twenty-four years of experience be forcibly pensioned off! Well, a new generation of police came in. They were literally criminals. I myself had arrested some of them before! That didn't matter; all that mattered was that they were Croats. Now I must work with these criminals. They threatened to kill me.

Here is the rule of the stronger, you see. The Croats have no respect for international law. They have killed Serbs just because they are Serbs. On 31 October 1991, the Croatian police came to a place near Karlovac. They were six people in camouflage uniforms with masks. They took three Serbs away with them in an unknown direction. Their names were Grujíc Marko, born February 18, 1950, a father of two; Ivošević Milos, born in 1946, the father of two; he lived at Subeliosova 1; and Pajíc Rade, born in 1956, the father of one child. After one month we found them in the fields of Pakrac. Their throats had all been cut. An inspector tried to investigate this. He was also a Serb. Now we have no more information about him.

Meanwhile the Croatian government established a new flag, the same as in the Second World War. Under this emblem, Serbs were killed.

So I came here together with my colleagues in the police force. We didn't have to be under the control of the Fascists.

After that the Croatian side went by force into a Serb village with the new police to put the emblem in our schools and everywhere. The Serbs are a proud people. We don't allow this. On this very territory forty thousand of us were killed. The graves are still fresh. We couldn't allow this again. So the people rose up and forbade the Croatian police to cross our territory. We police officers organized our citizens for fighting. We won't give the Croats permission to come here again.

What's your solution to the war?

Look. I can tell you my opinion. The end of the war can be. Our people don't want to live together with Croatians. We want a border. We want to have relations with them as with any other country. The Croats have Karlovac and Zagreb and other cities on their side. We have only villages. We are satisfied with that. If we allow again what happened during the Second World War, we will be eliminated.

Personally, I think Europe recognized Croatia too early. The Europeans don't understand what kind of state Croatia wants to make—a Hitler state. It's dangerous for all the world, especially with a united Germany pulling the strings.

May I use your name in my article?

Personally I have no problem, but unfortunately I do not have the authority to allow this. Just say you have talked with someone of the people.

AFRICA

INTRODUCTION

Had some accident taken me to South Africa and Morocco instead of Madagascar and the Congo, I don't doubt that the case studies here would convey a very different feeling. The notion of picking *any* two countries from the continent, and calling the result "Africa," is far more unfair than pretending that Yugoslavia with its history of violently shifting borders represents Europe—which it does. In short, the "Africa" I have selected (or which circumstances have selected for me) cannot be "the real Africa," but it may illuminate aspects of that Africa.

Talk about ancientness! It's said that the human race was born in Africa. The complexities of Balkan tribalism stretch back beyond 1389; but the kingdoms, customs and tribes which have come and gone in Africa extend beyond comprehension. All the same, you'll find little history in my African case studies. The reason is that the violence I studied in both countries tended to found itself on such imminent desperation (and despair) that the grievances of the dead approach irrelevance.

An occasional exception is ethnic violence. In the case of the Congo, the stink of Rwandan genocide hangs over the rebel-controlled area along the eastern border—and here is a good place to remind you that I will be describing two Congos: a republic to the west of the Congo River, and a "democratic" republic to the east, which was rather recently still known as Zaire; each of these nations in turn consists of a government-held zone and an area dominated by one or more insurgent factions. In the Democratic Republic of Congo, the clashing groups each known as the Rassemblement Congolais pour la Démocratie (RCD) are stiffened, and some people say commanded, by Rwandan troops. (You will meet the figurehead president of the larger RCD group.) Just across the frontier, in Rwanda itself, members of the Hutu tribe murdered Rwandan Tutsis, and vice versa—defense of race, of course. In each case, the killers pursued their victims into the Congolese jungle. And violence is infectious. Like the region once called Yugoslavia, the two Congos have seen their own borders and peoples migrate over the centuries. Thus many Congolese in the RCD zone are themselves Hutus and Tutsis. They hunker down in their huts, wondering when comparable tribal violence may break out among them.

But this fear constitutes a luxury, because it fails the test of imminence. Go westward into government territory. In Kinshasa, official capital of the Democratic Republic of Congo, it is as common as it is heartbreaking to see two women fighting over a rotten mango in the marketplace. Much of the food supply lies in RCD hands. A car comes, and people will come running out of nowhere to beg or demand a ride on it, because wherever it's going, the destination may be better than here. (From a balcony, they resemble ants swarming on a sugar cube.) Meanwhile, unwashed policemen, whose only claim to authority is their guns, shake down whomever they can, beat prisoners, threaten and extort; *everyone* extorts. In RCD territory, they might extort away your car or your daughter.

In the other Congo, whose capital is Brazzaville, people may be less hungry, but they remain no less ready to plead or threaten. The houses of Brazzaville are bullet-pocked from various civil wars. Government is weak, so crime is strong.

Both Congos teach me this lesson: Where there is no decent, legitimate, reasonably potent authority, the social contract remains incomplete.

When is defense of class justified? It would be difficult not to wish the people well in endeavoring to overthrow the weak and rotten authority which afflicts them with its "special taxes." But who or what would be better?

Sadism and expediency play their ghastly part in both Congos (just watch a skinny young fruit thief get kicked and beaten in a prison); so do compulsion, loyalty and fear. What precisely *is* compulsion? When does the extortionist lose his justification of imminent necessity? We enter the bullet-holed apartment of an official in Kinshasa. Of course he takes bribes. "I'm inspector of immigration; I'm a big person. And look at me," he says. "Look at this." He has a wife, a baby, and an existence which you or I might consider unendurable. Does this justify him in extorting "special taxes" from anyone in his power? All his colleagues think so. What constitutes necessity to you?

In Madagascar, authority is even weaker, and the street criminals and cattle rustlers proportionately stronger. Meet the woman who stabbed a pregnant lady in the belly so that she could sell the victim's clothing; meet the mother-and-son team of knife-wielding robbers. Enter a prison, where people starve to death if their relatives don't bring food or money. Look at the portfolio of beggar-women and note how pitiful they are; one poor old lady told me that she had been hungry as long as she could remember.

Here everything feels *personalized*. Every day, face-to-face social contracts get enacted between the haves and the have-nots. Whereas in the Congo a policeman will take you into a hot dark stinking room and run his hands over you, determined by virtue of his authority, which constitutes nothing but superior force, to rob you of everything he can, in Madagascar a beggar will approach you and calmly express his expectation of receiving, not everything, just something, an amount varying between reasonable and unreasonable; if you give it to him, he will be satisfied; if you refuse, he will become, as they constantly say there, "jealous," and he will stab you if he can. There is a strange fairness to it all, although it never ceased unnerving me. To be sure, in Madagascar you can also meet the predators who operate outside the social contract; they'll follow you in packs and start to flank you; if you don't get away fast, you're done. But these men and women constitute a recurring exception to the rule of pay-as-you-go, pay a little bit every day and you'll be allowed to live until tomorrow; to each one of us who lives within a social contract, which is to say most men and women on this earth, the procedure will feel surprisingly familiar.

AUTHOR'S NOTE: *Due to space considerations, all African case studies have been omitted from this abridgment.*

THE MUSLIM WORLD

INTRODUCTION

The "Muslim world"! This inevitably summons associations with defense of creed, and indeed that category cannot be escaped in these case studies. Islam speaks of a House of Submission, in which people have accepted God according to the precepts of the Muslim faith. Outside the House of Submission lies the House of Wrath, which, depending on whom one asks, includes either all non-Muslims, or else those non-Muslims who mock, challenge or actively reject Islam. The fact that it is up to those who dwell within the House of Submission to decide who deserves to be called an enemy troubles me deeply; most of the Maxims for Murderers in our moral calculus derive their unjustifiability from the fact that the maxim's practitioner reserves the exclusive right to define terms, set ends and means, and execute the resulting calculus. Many of my American friends and neighbors interpreted the terrorist attacks of September 11, 2001, in just this light. As far as they were concerned, these literal bolts from the blue seemed nearly incomprehensible. They didn't know the first thing about Islam, probably couldn't name more than one or two Islamic countries if they tried, and seemed to genuinely need the articles in the popular press which soon began to helpfully explain WHY THEY HATE US.

I feel as strongly about what happened on September 11 as do most of my fellow citizens. On several occasions I have publicly expressed my hope that the people connected with the attack will be hunted down and killed, in the interests of safety and peace. But that is not all I have to say.

If the moral calculus of *Rising Up and Rising Down* is valuable at all, it should be practical. Specifically, it should help us analyze almost any sort of violence one can imagine into its component excuses, analyze the excuses for justifiability, then leave us to the exercise of weighing those competing justifications according to our own predispositions.

I believe that the acts of murder committed on September 11 were un-justifiable, evil, wrong. The great majority of the people I met in Yemen a year later considered them justifiable. How can we build an empathetic bridge between us and them?

First of all, we can consider our un-justifications against their justifications. At the very least, we will have practiced empathy, which is always a good, and to my mind the supreme principle of human relations; at best, we may gain practical information as to what to do next. (Should the bridge remain unbuilt, we must either expect more attacks, or we must eternally police and obliterate.)

So, what do "they" think? In the hope of rendering a service to all parties here and now, I will devote the remainder of this introduction to topical matters which will quickly grow dated. But a hundred years from now, the same ethical principles will apply.

Many people in the Muslim world view us as practicing our own Maxims for Murderers. In particular, we stand accused of following:

JOHN BROWN'S MAXIM: If you refuse to follow the Golden Rule, then I have the right to use terror to impel you to follow it.

Our President continually speaks of "regime change" in Iraq. As I write this (January 2003), he is preparing to go to war to unseat Saddam Hussein. Most Muslims believe that if Saddam is to be overthrown, it ought to be by his own people.

Bush's father, the previous President Bush, also invoked John Brown's Maxim to strike at Iraq after that country unjustifiably invaded Kuwait and committed atrocities there. Bush Senior's true end might or might not have been as noble as he stated it to be: namely, to rescue a victimized nation and protect the Golden Rule in international relations. In *every* Muslim country I have visited since that Gulf War, I've been repeatedly told that the U.S. meddled unjustifiably for its own plutocratic ends. Did our airstrikes kill eighty-five thousand Iraqis for Kuwait or for American oil companies? (*Rising Up and Rising Down*'s moral calculus: *An unjust means or an unjust end equally invalidates all derivative moral enactions.*) The case study "The Wet Man Is Not Afraid of Rain" is set in Iraq 1998, with the Gulf War long ended and our sanctions against the Iraqi people still in effect. It is always possible that, like socialist "fellow travelers" who visited the USSR during the Stalin period, I was hoodwinked, and saw only the victim-image of itself that the regime wanted me to see. That is for you to judge. But if any of the suffering I observed, and the claims I heard, had any basis whatsoever, then the gravest charges of failure to respect proportionality and discrimination must be raised against the United States. Are we in fact war criminals? What responsibility do we bear for the deaths of so many children, deaths which might have been prevented by the medicines which our sanctions continue to deny? And when is defense of homeland justified? Surely the Iraqis had, and have, the right to self-defense. If they do possess these "weapons of mass destruction" to which our President refers, it must be incumbent on him, even after September 11, to prove that they mean to use them on us, so that our own defense of homeland can be justified. Furthermore, if we continue to hound Hussein until imminent self-defense entitles him to use weapons of mass destruction, it must be incumbent on us to prove that our hounding was right and necessary.

CAESAR'S MAXIM: Should I extend mercy beyond expediency, then I have the right to commit whatever aggression I please.

They are saying this about us now, regarding our invasion of Afghanistan after September 11. Whatever we might be doing to reconstruct the country (which actually isn't much), that can't get around the fact that we overthrew the Taliban regime.

Did the Taliban in fact bear responsibility for September 11? The case study "With Their Hands on Their Hearts" is set in Afghanistan during the year before that event, when the Taliban, although already sanctioned and getting hungry, still controlled almost all of Afghanistan. When you read this chapter, you will see that most Afghans liked Americans even then, remained grateful for the CIA's help against the Soviets—and believed Osama bin Laden innocent of all the American charges (he had, we alleged, bombed our embassies in Kenya and Tanzania two years earlier). The stupid arrogance of my government, which refused to prove its accusations and simply demanded that Osama be extradited to a non-Muslim court of law, reached outright culpability then—although, to be sure, whoever bombed our embassies was far more culpable. The worst disservice that our government did then to itself, and to its citizens, was to convey to the Muslim world that we set our own rules and expected the rest of the world to follow them. From many, many Muslims' point of view, that perception of us helped to prejustify the retribution of September 11. (Does that mean that September 11 was in fact justified? Not to me.)

(Was Osama in fact guilty of those bombings? You know as little as I. And this demonstrates another grave limitation in *Rising Up and Rising Down*'s moral calculus: it is worthless to the extent that its determinations rely on disputed facts.)

The next principle with which the Muslim world takes issue is:

CORTES'S MAXIM: In order to secure and defend my ground, I have every right to conquer yours.

This justifies the doctrine of "preemptive defense" which the U.S. adopted after September 11. Of course, it also can be used as an excuse for September 11 itself.

THE KLANSMAN'S MAXIM: If I believe your race or culture threatens mine, I have the right first to threaten you back, then to remove your threat by violence.

THE VICTIM'S MAXIM: If any members of your side harmed any members of my side, then your side is in the wrong.

These latter two maxims have been followed in equal measure by the U.S. and by the Muslim extremists who threaten us.

TROTSKY'S MAXIM: No one who disagrees with me is allowed to judge me.

The Muslim extremists seem more guilty of acting on that basis than we.

At this particular moment, it is not merely worthwhile, it is *urgent* that both sides evaluate each other's points of view. If, for example, the Muslim perception of us as practitioners of the Zealot's Golden Rule was *mis-taken*, based on the failure of the U.S. government to supply genuine information then in its possession about Osama's links with the two embassy bombings of 1998, then we can see that we ought to make that information public; even now it may change some minds, and thereby reduce violence. On the other hand, if, as so many Muslims allege, we had no such information, then surely we ought to reconsider the validity of our extradition demands. (As I write this, my President finger-points once again from his bully pulpit, showing "proof" that the Iraqis possess, or are hiding, "weapons of mass destruction"—proof which fails to convince the United Nations.) Either way, as a matter of expediency if nothing better, we ought to be trying harder to at least give the impression that we can follow the soldier's or empath's version of the Golden Rule, not the zealot's. In "Everybody Likes Americans," which is set in Yemen in 2002, it is instructive (and frightening) to see how deeply in the wrong we are considered. I sometimes reminded Yemenis of our services to Muslims in Bosnia in 1994, Afghanistan in 1980–89, and Somalia in 1992, but these were inevitably, infuriatingly discounted. It lies in our interest to alter this perception.

Enough about our interest. What about our rights? For one thing, we can courteously but firmly draw the Muslim world's attention to its own dangerous allegiance to the Victim's Maxim.

LET ME KNOW IF YOU'RE SCARED (1993)

The soldier bent, searching the car whose passengers stood hands up before a white cave whose weird ledges had once been steel shelves and now comprised a many-tiered steel fungus. Beyond the cave was a slope of white rubble which had once been a wall. The rear wall still stood, incongruous with its windows.

Orange-faced and brown-faced children stood in the shade, watching the search, clean-skinned but in dirty faded clothes. A seven-year-old girl was carrying a baby on her hip. The baby stretched out his hand at a passing tank whose Americans were throwing ration packets into that hot morning of shut gratings riddled with the wormholes of civil war while ladies washed clothes in the sea where the fish market used to be; and one Meal Ready to

Eat (MRE) landed at the young girl's feet. She snatched it up laughing and gave it to the baby to hold. She was skinny, but not skeletal; when I was in Mogadishu I saw only one child who resembled a brown skull on spider legs. To verify my optimistic impressions I drove every day past a certain cemetery where I invariably saw the same four gravediggers sitting under an awning by a burned-out transformer's mast, drinking sweet tea choked with cinnamon—"Somali whiskey," they called it. They were waiting for someone to die. They said that in the good old times thirty or forty corpses a day had been planted under the tiny markers among the cactus bushes and the poisonous *booc* trees, for a hundred thousand shillings apiece ($25); but now there were days when nobody died. The average was three or four deaths every twenty-four hours. So the gravediggers sat still in hot sand, almost out of work, because we'd called in the Marines.

The Marines, of course, had to share credit with the other branches of our armed forces, to say nothing of the French, Italian, Australian, Pakistani and Swedish soldiers, and the relief workers from around the world who literally faced death to do their jobs (just before my arrival in Mogadishu one Swiss man was murdered in Bardera); and the journalists who reminded others of what needed to be done, themselves taking great risks (a day or two before I came, a Chinese journalist was shot, though not fatally); and the politicians who made it all happen—but I never got to know the soldiers who weren't American, and as for the civilians, well, I have to admit that I did not like them all that much. The relief workers were as immature as the missionaries. They bent over backward to be cordial to anyone whose skin was brown, but cliqued and backbit among themselves. The journalists, even more curt and contemptuous than the relief workers with anyone who did not serve their turn, marred themselves with the additional sin of jargon-pride. A typical conversation between journalists went like this: "Drumroll, please. Okay, we're coming back up. Now hit control-alternate-T. You should get a level prompt."

"Now, do you have a form for TEMPS in your computer?"

"Yep. What are we gonna do for partly cloudy, chance of showers?"

"You just type partly cloudy, chance of showers."

As for the politicians, I cannot recollect any the smell of whose utterances is distinguishable from that of a fart.

Give me a soldier anytime. For straightforwardness a soldier cannot be beat. Like cops, doctors, mothers and whores, they've been through it, and they cannot be fooled.

The reason that the gravediggers were almost out of work was because the soldiers in desert camouflage were disarming everybody. The relief workers had been there all along, and they'd failed; they were almost helpless behind their high walls. (In an orphanage a man explained to me: "They were sitting here when the shell came in. The aunt head chop off, but the child die a little by little, after few minutes.")

The journalists and the politicians had been no better than Chicken Littles. "The actual Marines doing the job, those are the ones that should get the credit," a corporal said to me. "The other guys, the higher-ups, they're just trying to make things seem better than they really are."

Inside the ruined stadium where they lived, the Widowmaker Squad of the Peace Frog Platoon (motto: "Let me know if you're scared!"), which was in turn a limb of Charlie Company, passed the last minutes before going on noon patrol.

"I can't wait to get out of here, so I can get my coffee brewed by electricity," said a Marine, bringing his Java almost to a boil by means of a heat tab (which is to say FUEL, COMPRESSED, TRIOXANE RATION HEATING), setting down his spoon upon his machine gun.

"Shit, who cares about coffee? *I* wanna get back, buy a blender and eat some pussy."

These manly words were spoken by none other than Corporal Brewster, Michael S.—and here it occurs to me that a full listing of the roster of Widowmaker is in order, namely:

1. Corporal Baumgaurt, Jr., Robert P.

2. Lance Corporal Kalan, "Korky," Matthew A.

3. Corporal Diaz, Miguel A.

4. Corporal Brewster, Michael A.

5. Corporal Holsinger, David S.

6. Lance Corporal Manalato, John

7. Lance Corporal Mosley, Chuck

8. Lance Corporal Nilson, Troy

9. Lance Corporal Boltman, Joseph R.

"It's bad luck when I can't even beat the cards," said Baumgart.

"You know what we have for maps? Fuckin' aerial photos!"

"Aw, quit runnin' your mouth."

Snapping fingers, ruffling cards, chess pieces clicking down passed the last few minutes of sitting on those benches which were actually broken marble slabs set on sandbags.

"You know, I think my dad smoked marijuana before he joined the Corps."

"As long as he didn't inhale."

"As long as he didn't exhale!"

"Five minutes, guys."

" 'Five minutes,' he says. I'd rather be humpin' broads. Let's act crazy 'til they send us back."

"Don't masturbate in the headshrinker's office."

"Aw, shucks, I was gonna blow myself."

Now the flak helmets went on, sweaty and grimy and wobbly.

"A flak helmet never stopped a bullet anyway, and that's a fact. The Marine that got dusted—"

"He had his helmet on backward. And he had it pushed up over his forehead, because he was got. Got drilled right in the forehead."

"What the fuck are you talking about? He got shot in the throat!"

"Okay, squad, move out. Happy hunting!"

"Is Shortwave ready?"

"He's takin' a piss right now."

They pulled themselves up into the back of the five-ton, slamming down long steel benches from the walls, locking the struts into place. They were still inside the stadium compound where it was safe.

"You guys chill out. Take off at about quarter 'til. Got about ten minutes."

"Okay, sir."

"Now remember, aim for the center of the ass!"

"Thanks, coach."

A Marine with a flashlight at his belt sat reading his Bible very quietly. I saw his lips move like those of the Somalis I'd seen sitting barefoot in the sand outside the hospital, waiting for water. (On the gate it said: ALL KINDS OF WEAPONS WHATEVER IS ARE NOT ALLOWED. INSIDE THE HOSPITAL IT IS FORBIDDEN.)

The five-ton started up, and they came to the first gate where a machine gun needled outward from a high nest of sandbags, and a Marine with a gun pointing straight up lifted the long pole (once red, now almost entirely silver-white, ringed with barbed-wire coils like an immense slinky), and the Marine swung the pole slowly outward.

The name of the Marine was Corporal Prato. He'd said to me: "We Marines are strictly military, but this is a whole new ball game. Now everything's fucking political. The fucking colonels are running around making everything clean and tidy. So when the higher-ups come, they don't see the real Africa."

"What's the real Africa?"

"You don't know where the enemy's coming from. That's the real Africa, and that's the scary thing."

The five-ton cleared the gate, and Corporal Prato lifted the pole and swung it inward again, and Widowmaker Squad was out in the real Africa.

The objective of the patrol was, as always, to find and confiscate as many weapons as possible. "We have an evenhanded policy here," explained the political officer, one Len Szensey, smiling wearily inside the sandbagged Conoco compound at all the relief workers, diplomats, journalists and other bathroom whistlers. "We don't want any faction to break the peace. We want all factions to turn in their weapons."

"But Marines are trained to kill, not to be policemen," I said. "This job must be hard on them and on the Marines."

"I'm a political officer, not a press officer," said Szensey. "I suggest you get together with the rest of the Press Corps."

It was, in other words, just one of those things.

In the five-ton one Marine was working the action of his M-16, listening with absolute concentration as he clicked it back and forth until he was satisfied. Another checked the top round in his magazine. When the five-ton turned a corner, they all chambered rounds.

"Just watch them kids with the rocks. I got hit in the face with one. Cost me three stitches."

Warily they descended deeper into the real Africa, their guns bristling outward through the long horizontal slits in the walls as the five-ton snarled and jerked. The two Marines in the back each sat with one foot up on the tailgate, the muzzle resting on the high knee, pointing out.

They passed a donkey pulling a rusty water can on wheels, an old man sitting on top, and the old man did not wave. But along the pale sand outside the stadium was a refugee camp of yurtlike domes from which children issued running to wave because they slept safely at night now. They waved whether or not the Marines waved back, and during my stay I saw so many young soldiers in yellow-green trucks or tanks going by that place, some waving at the kids, some stern and straight, riding on top, aiming big guns right at everyone until the soldiers were gone in a clatter of tanks or a buzz of truck tires and then came new soldiers, dusty yellow-green, pointing guns at the windows. The children never got tired of waving. Partly it was that they were truly grateful, I think; partly it was that they hoped for MREs; and mainly it was that inside those domes was nothing but oven heat and green light from the ceiling plastic; when I myself went in one I couldn't stand upright or lie full length, and three or seven people slept in each yurt. There was a mat on the sand, and both mat and sand crawled with ants, flies and fleas. There was a basket with the household's possessions: a wooden spoon, a metal spoon, cooking oil, a pot of porridge, a can of porridge powder. Rags or clothes hung from the ceiling where the branches met in a knot of wire. I think I would have preferred to go wave at soldiers, too.

The five-ton stopped in front of the cigarette factory that Widowmaker had raided once before; instead of weapons they'd found only stacks of bricks. Today they'd walk a few blocks down narrow sandy streets not nearly as crowded as the Street of Counterfeit Passports at the Big Market (they said you could get any kind you wanted, but all I saw were the green Somali passports, green like the prickly pear bushes that grew in the weird open spaces which had once been houses)—not especially crowded, as I said, so that would be a cinch; nor was it close to the Green Line that divided the city between the clan-enemies Mr. Aidid and Mr. Ali Mahdi, so there were very few empty windowless buildings pimpled and riddled here; almost all the trees had tops; there was only slow ordinary steady life here in the middle of this day, the canvas-and-burlap-covered stands having opened like shabby flowers long ago, and newsboys lethargically distributing a sheet called *Courier of Peace*.

The Marines jumped out of the five-ton quickly and steadily, spreading out along the white and sandy street.

"Set up. Security, point and rear, one man."

Shortwave was carrying the big green radio on his back. His buddies raised the antenna for him. —"Suicide, Suicide, this is Widowmaker. *Do you copy?* Come in, Suicide. Shit, this radio is a piece of junk."

Crowds of Somalis swirled around them like the golden and black herringbones in the lap of the barefoot woman who sat covering her mouth. A man in wool dress pants, a polo shirt and sandals was squatting on the broken pavement, patiently curling his fingers around his long teeth, which were patchily stained the color of camel bones; seeing the Marines, he stood up and came at them open-mouthed, losing himself among a constellation of spectating woman-heads (strangely egglike thanks to the garbashars which covered their hair and necks, so that each woman seemed a brown expanse of face floating in a yellow or crimson or purple sea of flowers); all these faces, too, smiled upon or studied the grim Marines; most numerous of all, however, were the children, who would have quickly surrounded each soldier had he let them, and who continually waved, begged, practiced English, tried to sell things, and pickpocketed.

"One thing you gotta watch out for is a place with no women and children," a Marine said. "That means they're setting something up."

They moved down the hot street, watching everything, ignoring the Somali welcomes, which were a distraction; they were always ready to shoot, and it was sickeningly hot.

"This is Widowmaker. Go. Be advised that you are coming in broken up. I'm having difficulty picking you up."

"Suicide, Suicide," the kids chanted.

"We got somebody up on a roof there. Watch your ass."

Everybody was smiling; everybody followed the soldiers, soldiers walking slowly down a hot and sandy road. Along the long low row of stands of thatch or canvas or corrugated metal shagged with burlap (trees above and behind them, behind a long white wall), everybody laughed at the Americans.

"Level one, this is Widowmaker."

Something flickered in a window.

"Get out of the way!" the Marines yelled. The children scattered; the Marines slammed themselves against house walls in a furious rush. They waited for a long time in the hot silence, and nothing happened.

A skinny man in a baggy shirt stood outside his house begging, and there was money in his hand.

"No," a Marine was saying patiently. "If you don't have a pink card, then we must confiscate the weapon."

"Okay. I get pink card. I come in one hour."

"Suicide, Suicide, this is Widowmaker. And we have confiscated an assault rifle. Over."

"You think he'll turn up with his pink card in an hour?"

"Pink cards haven't even been issued yet."

In the shade of a white wall, ladies with floral garbashars wrapped around their heads and shoulders sat and squatted by tables, selling tea. They washed the glasses from a dark green jerry can, rubbing soap inside with dirty hands. Then they rinsed the glasses again and filled them with tea from a thermos. When the soldiers came, they all stood up.

"Suicide, Suicide!" cried the children. They pointed eagerly at a house behind a gate, and a child said: "Many bang-bang in there."

"We can't check it out. We're not allowed to search houses."

After that I remember even more kids shouting, "Americans, welcome!"; then an old ebony-colored man in white robes and a white prayer cap, striding barefoot in the sand away from the soldiers, and then the crowd of giggling girls; and the girl in the violet garbashar said to me: "What's your name?"

"Bill. And you?"

"Asya."

"That's a beautiful name."

The other girls screeched with laughter. I saw Asya's face, pretty and blushing and happy; and then the sniper pulled the trigger.

"Get the fuck outta the way!" the Marines shouted, shoving aside the terrified people, sprinting to the wall, kneeling for cover, waiting for the next shot to come and it did not come.

As I too knelt in the dust, I wondered, as one always does in those situations, whether I would be dead at the end of the day. When I was in Sarajevo there were moments when I was certain that I was about to die, but this did not feel like that. Whoever had fired just now was either timid or indifferent or stupid, because he had not hit anybody and he was not firing again.

The Somalis had their hands over their ears, and they were quiet.

"From that high roof in the back," a Marine said finally.

"Watch that roof!"

"Let's get the fuck outta here!"

The children laughed hilariously to see the Americans duck and sprint one by one across the intersection ahead. I was last. When it came my turn, I expected to receive the prize. And again it did not come.

"Now I've lost my fucking calm," a Marine said.

Nobody likes to be shot at, but of course it was all routine. They were doing a job, and they would finish the job.

They stopped a CARE van and discovered a gun.

"You have ID? Which of you has ID? Bring the weapon up here."

"Two one six nine five . . . This number right here on your authorization form and this weapon, they're not the same. This is for an AK and this is an HK."

"I have another form."

"Let's take a look at it. No, that number doesn't match, either. We're going to take your HK in."

The Somali grew more and more angry, waving his hands. The Marine showed him the discrepancy again and again with stony patience.

"The serial number and the gun are different."

"Hey! Truck's here! Thank God!"

"Now here come the rocks."

As the five-ton pulled away, the children began to rain stones in among the soldiers, rattling off flak helmets, stingingly striking a wrist or a knee.

"Better rocks than rounds," a Marine muttered.

"It's because some men give small money to babies, tell them: 'Throw stones American!' Because Americans take their weapons."

My friend Abdi said this. He had lived through the worst in Mogadishu. In his house he uncovered a boy's nakedness and I saw a swollen plum-colored thing which I thought for a second must be an umbilical hernia, and then I saw how proud and happy Abdi was, and I understood that his son had just been circumcised.

"I have boy now," he told me exultantly. "Now I'm no more afraid! I can go anywhere. I am free! I have a son! They cannot kill me anymore!"

But the following night he and his family did not sleep, because bandits were shooting.

A soldier sat atop a tank, smiling caressingly to his companions inside. A white hill of rubble abutted a sea-green wall. We left the soldier behind and drove a long way, past the animal market, where children went playing, running, shooting an AK-47 into the air.

American soldiers were in attendance along the walls of a street with gunpoints out because a food convoy was coming.

Passing the almost naked children who were sitting in the sandy shaded Lenin Street (now a soup kitchen), we came to a pink wall with a hole in it, and then another road that was very quiet about which Abdi said: "That way very dangerous. They have knife, revolver! They take even your dress!"

There was a general store whose painted wall forbade entry with Kalashnikov or grenade.

The gate was open, and outside the city it was green on either side with dark green leaves, plants with white spiny fruits, prickly pears and reeds. Abdi said: "Bandit here. Bandit have no time. Day or night they always here. So we afraid. No gun."

"Thief is have knife, pistol, gun—all of them!" he said. "My gun is here in truck, hidden in *good* place. I afraid for Marines. If they find, how can I defend?"

"I'd feel the same way if I were you," I said. "But if everyone thinks that way, the problem of thieves won't be solved."

"Better to leave our guns, you know! When I see a thief I can do nothing. Thief is moving fast, two three persons. Some have gun, some have knife. If I keep my gun in sight, thief is afraid, because they no want to fight."

His logic was perfect. To validate it one had only to drive to the Green Line, where a gate was smashed to rusty twists and scraps, and the thick wall in front of the former ministry had been gnawed by some giant to show the barbed wire behind, then soldiers with guns and blue hats in the back of a U.N. Toyota pickup, a cave that used to be a building, yellow stucco ripped off a building, an apartment instantly transformed into an ancient ruin, hot bleached street of walls with holes through which a passing body sometimes flickered; and three children sat in a shaded alley of roofless buildings and barred windows (at which point Abdi said: "The first time that I come here! I don't like to come here!"), and a woman in tiger-yellow with black spots and black stripes who was carrying a jerry can of water up slopes of rubble-sand, her gold earrings jiggling in tune with her necklace, sweat starting out on her polka-dotted kerchief, set down the jerry can and said to me: "Very dangerous. Here in shadows many thief come running with gun." Then she picked up the jerry can again and walked on toward the sea, where the whitewash on houses had been blasted off, leaving their rough walls the color of beehives.

That was why a money changer I knew smiled and said: "We buried our best weapons in the ground before the Americans got here."

To make the Marines' job still more discouraging, there remained a weapons market where in stands on the street they sold M-16 magazines loaded and unloaded, AK-47s for eighty dollars apiece, M-16s for a hundred dollars, grenades and other toys. —"You see," beamed a Somali, "here is bombs!" —Beside a mango stand, strings of bullets hung from the rafters. Each bullet costs ten thousand shillings, which is to say one-tenth the price of a grave. A skinny man sat on the table smoking a cigarette, tinkling those pretty strings for the grinning buyers who drove slowly by. A man stood easily in the street, holding up two Kalashnikovs. Another man in sunglasses strode with machine gun pointed down.

"He's a thief," Abdi said. "I know him. Very bad, very dangerous."

"Don't the Marines come here?"

"Sometimes. When they come, everything disappear."

Why did so many people want guns in Mogadishu? Granted, the thieves and counterthieves needed them for each other, but it would be a shame to forget Mr. Wario Hukla Ali, of Kenyan nationality, who was nice, but very nervous; he jumped when I clapped him on the shoulder—doubtless because he had been to prison six times. Mr. Wario was a minister of the Northern Frontier District Liberation Front. He'd fled to Somalia when the magistrates said that they had many, many questions to ask him on many, many subjects. In a darkened house not far from the stadium, he explained his manifesto, his long skinny brown finger tapping each word which he chose to read aloud from the 1962 report of the Northern Frontier District Commission. "So we fought a liberation war in 1963. That war ended in 1967. Somalia was told to leave the NFD alone. However, later the NFD struggle was subordinated to Somalia. But we continue. Kenya is licking the boots of the colonial power. We want to have our own homeland, our own sovereign state. We want a roundtable discussion; we don't want to use force."

"Do you have many weapons?"

"Oh, yes, and we are trying to get more."

"We have no relationship with the Mau-Mau," he added reassuringly. "We are two different organs."

Then, of course, there were Mr. Mohammed Farrah Aidid and Mr. Mohammed Ali Mahdi, whose enmity divided the city between them. Not too surprisingly, neither one had time to see me. I did, however, get an opportunity to view the guards behind the steel gate at Aidid's, smoking cigarettes, jiggling twigs between their pouty lips, masturbating the barrels of their AK-47s. "Marines never come here," a man crowed to me. "This office Aidid!" A U.S. helicopter rattled and chonked overhead. Outside the gates, the sand was practically paved with spent cartridges.

These were calmly self-reliant faces that I saw here, faces that did not beg like so many others, but turned upon me the cool beams of their aloof dislike. I was an American; I was interfering with their murderous projects. Their power in Somalia can best be gauged by the fact that almost every day someone would ask me: "What is your tribe?" (I always replied: "My tribe is your tribe.") The grinning, strutting boys in Aidid's entourage were threads in the grand tapestry of idiocy into which were also woven the black and white racists in the U.S., the Serbian and Croatian ethnic detergents in Bosnia, and every other all-or-nothing. In the case of Aidid and Ali Mahdi, the stupidity was compounded by the fact that they were from the same clan; only their subclans were different.

No doubt the fighters in both factions believed that they represented a righteous rising up against the hated other. And what had they accomplished?

We drove through the city, and Abdi said: "There is military building. Now finished."

We drove a little further. There was the smell of shit by a wrecked car.

"Before, was industry for military car. Now, nothing. Here is university. Now it's not university. Now it's camps."

We passed a white sand-alley that reeked of decaying garbage. "From the town. Some people carry here. They throw here. No government."

Everyone blamed the thieves, of course. That was easier. They all had stories about them. I heard the tale of the Marine who had his Beretta 9 millimeter stolen instantly as soon as he left the compound, the lanyard cut by two children's daggers; and they were the good thieves; the bad ones pointed guns at you. Abdi had said: "But those who learn to kill the people, always they want to kill the people. Better to catch and kill them. This my idea." And I thought he was right.

So I went to the prison and talked to a thief, a skinny brownish-black man in a dirty yellow shirt who stood at attention for me, one guard holding his pipestem arms, and the thief regarded me with tired brown eyes.

"Why are you here?" I asked him.

"I steal a bed to sell. I was hungry. But police catch me."

"How long have you been here?"

"Three months."

"How much longer will they keep you here?"

"Another three months."

"When you leave prison will you steal again?"

"No," he said by rote.

"What if you are hungry again?"

"I want to live. I see many people die from hunger. If I don't steal, maybe I will die like these people. I steal for survival."

"With a gun?"

"Yes."

"Are you hungry now?"

"No," he said, but again (I thought) by rote, and when I asked him if he had anything further to say, he said: "The only thing I want to tell you is that most people eat three meals a day. I get only one meal a day here. That's what I want to tell you."

It was against all these forces, then, that Widowmaker Squad was struggling, in accordance with the United Nations mandate—or perhaps struggling is the wrong word, for they went out and did their job for a set length of time and then came back into the stadium behind the wall of rolled barbed wire, where the .50-caliber Browning machine gun pointed out of a hole at tall-humped sand-colored camels; they came whether the overall job was being accomplished or not. This is how armies must function, and there is nothing wrong with it.

"Go ahead an' clear 'em before we get in there!" Clickety-click-click as the men unchambered bullets.

"Well, that was a good patrol. We all came back!"

"Better luck next time."

"An' what is it next time, night patrol?"

"Just a roadblock. Six P.M. to six A.M. Checkin' for weapons."

(And I remembered Abdi, who'd admitted: "From these days a shortage of fighting. Now not much need for gun.")

Now it was mail call, and whoops echoed around the ruined stadium.

"Ho! Fourteen pages!"

"Pictures!"

"Hey, man, will ya let me look at my fuckin' pictures? Get the *fuck* away from me!"

"This one's from that stripper I was tellin' you guys about. She wrote back! Listen to this: 'I remember that you were very nice and intelligent.' "

"She must not remember you very well."

"Oh, my wife sent me an article. This is about some heavy fighting in Somalia. Four confirmed kills, it says."

"Doc killed a camel. Doc smoked a fuckin' camel! I wonder why *that* ain't in the article."

They sat in a pit of sandbags, running their fingers along the blades of their Gerbers, leaning over the dirty table, staring tenderly at their letters. "Okay, squad, move out!"

"Come on, guys, let's get in the track."

Inside the rack there echoed the clicking and rattling of rounds. A man was working a gun on a tripod, working the action back and forth until the belt of pointed bullets was ready to go in. Another belt, golden and black, found its place upon a man's shoulder. Camouflage-colored legs and ankles crossed the sky in the hatchway above me. A Marine tapped his M-16 magazine against the ceiling. A Marine reread his letter from home, sitting quiet among green protrusions.

"You got everybody in?"

"Check!"

In the front of this weird vehicle was a raised seat and a steering wheel like a pretzel. The hatchway above the seat resembled the dome of an observatory. A Marine's back appeared in the chair. A hand levered the chair magically down. The engine hooted and reeked of fuel. The Marines were grinning with their toys, cocking and chambering. The noise of the moving track was almost like that of a jet engine. Rigid legs slanted ceilingward; hard backs and buttocks braced against the tongue of metal that bridged the hatchway, all M-16s steady and level with the sky.

They passed the place where I had seen a boy in a dirty dark-green shirt running in the sand, and he had a gun, and Abdi was saying: "You see, a thief goes. He catch some girl hat."

"If this thing takes an RPG round, we're dead," a Marine grinned. "The gas tank will go for sure."

Downpointing belts of bullets faded into olive and brown uniforms. Faces happily took the evening wind. A Marine braced his boots against a squat black gun. All those brooding male faces, staring into their own dreams, rattled and lurched as the track carried them into the real Africa.

"Don't be surprised if you see tempers fray," a soldier said to me. "This ain't our job. We only know how to kill."

Marines waited in the shade at the end of the bright spot where the generator nourished two blinding lights. They stopped the truck loaded so high with green bananas on fronds that waved in the wind while kids chased each other in the darknesses between two stopped buses which the Marines were searching. Beyond the brightness loomed weird trees with flat tops and weird trees with oval tops like hot dogs skewered on toothpicks. The children teased and sometimes tormented the soldiers, trying to change money with them, dancing, imitating English. One soldier played Simon Says with them. Two other soldiers yelled: "Get the fuck away!"

When the headlights came, they raised their weapons and finger-beckoned each vehicle into the sand at the edge of the road. —"Hey! Hey! Open it!"

"Have a nice night," the Marine was saying to the former General of the Somali army. "Thanks for the weapon."

The Somali pulled out an incomprehensible document.

"What's this? What's this mean?"

The former General explained, smiling bitterly.

"We're gonna hold onto this, okay?" said the Marine as patiently as he could. "Put your name on this document. You can get it at the U.S. Embassy."

"What's your name?" said the former General.

"It don't matter," said the Marine wearily. "Just go to the Embassy Wednesday morning."

A skinny man started shouting at the Marines and showing his bullet scars. —"That just proves your stupidity," a soldier said. "Shut the fuck up or I'll put my boot on your face."

* * *

Again I remembered Corporal Prato, who said: "Like any military deal the U.S. does, we come in and sit around for awhile, and they are starting to get as restless as we are about being here."

In the middle of that long cool night of desert stars, the radio crackled, and then a Marine said softly: "Second platoon got hit. In the same place where we patrolled today and they shot at us."

"Shit. Shit. Who is it?"

"I don't know yet. He was a point man, and they heard a garage door open and then the sound of a weapon being cocked. I don't know how bad he's hit, but they say he's getting CPR."

The morning came, chilly with dew. —"He didn't make it," a Marine said. "He held on for a little while, that's all."

Unchambering rounds, they returned to the stadium in quiet weariness. The flag was not yet at half-staff. I felt sad and tired. When I saw Abdi I told him, and he sighed and said: "I tell you, there is so many thieves in the night, you know!"

ASSESSMENT OF RESULTS
OF OPERATION RESTORE HOPE

From the *Sacramento Bee,* Friday, October 21, 1994, page A28:

CONVOY PROTECTION TO END

UNITED NATIONS— . . . Threatened by increasing lawlessness and clan warfare in Somalia, the United Nations said Thursday it plans to withdraw troops that have been protecting convoys bringing food to tens of thousands of civilians.

NORTH AMERICA

INTRODUCTION

With a gun I'd say the peace of mind is as valuable as the safety it-self." This is a peculiarly (although not exclusively) North American attitude. In much of the world, guns are tools only of authority and of outlaws. In Colombia or Southeast Asia, ordinary citizens fear guns. But the Second Amendment in the United States, and the wild animals of the Canadian North, make for quite a number of armed citizens on my continent. The speaker I've quoted lives in Nome, Alaska, and he explains: "I have shot a bear in self-defense before, down in Kodiak. Without my gun, I would have been at the very least severely injured." It is very natural for this self-reliant man to see guns as tools of self-defense against animals in Alaska, and against humans in South Carolina.

And it also appears to be natural for Apache teenagers on the reservation to kill themselves. It is natural for young men in the ghettos of Jamaica to defend their neighborhood against rival neighborhoods.

North America is the Columbine massacre, where two despised school-boys took up guns to defend their own conception of honor and execute retribution upon a world they hated. North America is also the Guardian Angels, who employ the Wild West conceptions of patrolling gangs and citizens' arrests to form themselves into a "good gang," armed only with their hands, to make the streets safe. North America is the rock star Ted

Nugent, who glorifies guns and hunting. His watchword: *"KILL 'EM AND GRILL 'EM! WHACK 'EM AND STACK 'EM!"* Nugent and the Columbine shooters exemplify the extremes of the American gun culture. The man in Nome exemplifies its core.

How does North America look from the outside? I have been investigating violence in Africa from the standpoint, unavoidable to me, of an American. I'll never know enough to see myself from the standpoint of an African, but a European perspective may not be entirely beyond my ken.

The Europe of my case studies was limited to the former Yugoslavia. This is the Europe of Machiavelli and the Kaiser, the Europe of the Thirty Years' War and the Hundred Years' War. It is not, superficially at least, the Europe of 2003, which has now begun cohering into an economic power whose glue is a partially justified anti-Americanism. This Europe remembers the time when it burned its witches, broke its murderers on the wheel, buried its infanticides alive. Each state in the European Union must now renounce all capital penalties against its citizens, and Europeans note with disgust that when an American gets judicially electrocuted so incompetently that his face bursts into flames, an American leader remarks: "A painless death is not punishment. I think it's important that there is a deterrent and a punishment element." This Europe remembers all too well the violence invoked by its own various national sovereignties, and hates violent Americanism accordingly. The United Nations will someday (so Europeans hope, as do I) be powerful enough to mediate all international conflicts. The rhetoric of this body seems to express a philosophy of benign coordination, which may at times require "verification" (a favorite United Nations word). Hence this prediction from Major General Nils Carlström, who headed the United Nations inspectors in Iraq in 1998: They were monitoring many hundreds of sites, and "it is my belief that the Council will keep that system for many years." This is the European solution, and for Iraq, at least, it is certainly superior to the American solution of mean-spirited threats and unprovoked attack. But it makes this American uneasy.

From the standpoint of my European friends, the North American, and in particular the American, passion for firearms is a mark of barbarism. Europeans tend to live in social welfare states, within which the citizen is more politically opinionated and historically aware than his American counterpart. Health care, housing, safety, et cetera, have been more or less guaranteed by the state. In short, the social contract is both effective and efficient. Bureaucrats in Brussels now make certain that French cheese conforms to German procedures of pasteurization.

Rising Up and Rising Down has asserted the Shepherd's Maxim, namely: *As authority enlarges itself, its obligation to protect from violence the individuals it controls increases, and the ability of those individuals to defend themselves from violence correspondingly decreases.* In Europeans, the capacity for individual self-defense atrophied so long ago that it is not much missed. As a cause or result of this, Europe's streets are presently less violent than America's. (Again, forget Yugoslavia.) Hence the corollary to the Shepherd's Maxim, which seems so self-evident to a person with my prejudices, would strike a European as absurd and even dangerous: *Because the right to self-defense remains inalienable, each of us can and should maintain a self-reliant distrust of authority.*

Self-reliance is indeed the name of the North American game. The price we pay is one Columbine massacre after another. What some of us get in exchange, or at least what we strive for, is a sense of wholeness, pride, fulfillment best known to the hunter-gatherer. In the hands of a Colombian *para*, a gun is primarily a tool of terror, deterrence, retribution, revenge. For a Congolese insurgent, it may be any of these things, or it may be an implement of extortion. For an American, a gun is, for better or worse, an "equalizer."

North Americans are the quintessential lonely atoms. In Canada, where tolerance for social control approaches Europe's, and interhuman violence remains relatively low, there runs a narrow belt of densely populated cities along the U.S. border; this zone really belongs to Europe; but then North America resumes, running north all the way through the Arctic archipelago. Here the solitary woodsman stalks his moose; and the Inuit family summers at the floe-edge of the frozen sea, killing seals and defending themselves against polar bears. These people are one with the defender of Jamaica's Rema ghetto, who when I asked him whether Rema could ever reunite with its hated enemy neighborhood, Tivoli Gardens, replied: "Too much people dead already. We are turn a new page. Cannot *force* dem in Rema to live Sodom way. Dem *force* us live in certain things, but Trenchtown is *ours,* sir. Dem want take our glory and magnify." And so he stood ready to protect Rema with lethal force. "A man's home is his castle," runs the old English saying, and it is a North American saying, too. Defense of ground, defense of homeland, equal rights for sovereign selves, these principles are what we've been raised on, for better or worse. What if somebody wants to pasteurize us according to German procedures, or any procedures? We might be better off, but we won't do it; we just can't. After Columbine, the memorials to the murdered went up in Clement Park, and I asked a nonconformist woman, a Goth: "Do you think you'd have a hard time if you went to Clement Park in your Gothic clothes?" —"I could say a resounding yes. But I'm strong enough to ignore them even if they throw stuff at me. I think it's sad that people are taking one faction of society and blaming us. We're nonviolent. We never hurt anybody. You know what? This winter when I need a jacket, I'm gonna get me a black trench coat. Because this is *ridiculous.*" That is the North American way. Self-reliance equals defiance. That is why Ted Nugent insists: "In Vermont, anyone, anywhere, under any conditions, can carry anything that can go bang, and no bullets are hitting six-year-old girls in bathtubs." And that is why a Guardian Angel says, and this, I think wonderfully and nobly: "You have to encourage the good and discourage the bad. We Americans are the ones who want to have all the opportunity and not share it and at the same time we want other people like police to solve our problems for us. What can you say about a society in which a man or a woman can be attacked at two o'clock in the afternoon and no one will do anything? That's an indictment. I'm not against criminals. I'm against apathy."

A Parisian expects "other people like police to solve our problems for us." My friends in the Congo and Madagascar expect the "problems" to remain menacingly insoluble. North Americans solve their own problems. That is why I own guns, and it is also why those two despised boys at Columbine brought guns to school and solved their own problems, evilly and uselessly.

What are the rights of the self? Ask a North American, who worries about them the most. But many people on this earth might disagree with his answer.

"DEY BRING DEM BLOODSTAIN UP HERE" (1997)

NOTE: *My Jamaican friends have asked me, "in the interests of the island,"* *to remind the public that Jamaica is a safe and desirable playground for tourists. I would not recommend the Kingston ghettos to tourists, but I wouldn't recommend the ghettos of Los Angeles, either.*

My Neighborhood, My Prison

We read that Satan took Jesus to the top of a high peak, and showed Him all the kingdoms of this world, announcing their availability in return for the trifling favor of devil-worship. But when the two men from Rema brought me to the topmost story of the abandoned college, which had been mashed up by gangsters from Tivoli Gardens, with perhaps a little local help, the world they showed me from the unpaned windows was beyond their power to bestow, for it belonged to Satan alone, and they could not hope even to enter it. Wires flapped against the concrete walls now paragraphed with the utterances of an angry God as they led me through the echoing, urine-stained rooms, inviting me to behold the evil kingdoms: Plead my Cause o Lord, with Them That Strive with me: Fight against Them That fight me: Take hold of Shield and Buckler and Stand Up for mine help. The wind blew in. Remembering the youth hostel on the front line in Sarajevo where people ran past open windows, not wanting to give the snipers any bonus points, I was surprised that my new acquaintances could stand there at the very border of Rema, aiming their didactic forefingers first at the long flat hot weedy lot that had once been Boys' Town until Tivoli Gardens had mashed that up (in Tivoli Gardens, no doubt, they would tell me that Rema had done it); Boys' Town thus lay now as dead as the American Embassy in Phnom Penh after the Khmer Rouge had finished *their* spring cleaning; next my guides swiveled their forefingers left until they were marking no-man's-land at center stage where birds nested in the littered nothingness, with Tivoli Gardens in sight beyond; then they pointed farther leftward still at the long grey wall which marked Board Villa, which was likewise mashed up. (Mashed-upness can eat you up in your body and in your insides! preached one of the elders at the Swallowfield Chapel, which was safely uptown. Battling with the air, pugilistically gesturing, he cried out: *Perishing—shriveling—falling to the ground!* Ultimately, perishing accompanies people beyond the grave. *Do we believe this?* he asked. I think we need to decide whether we believe it. I tell you this: When God looks upon this world today, He sees it is PERISHING!) Back to center stage. At the edge of no-man's-land was another long wall, behind which weeds grew between the rotting roofs of Denham Town. My friend Philip's house stood there, or, I should say, the skeleton of his house. Gunmen had driven him into Rema, where he now cooked at Miss Lorna Stanley's school. Denham Town was no town anymore—this portion of it, at least. Near Hanna Town it wasn't so bad. —Dey call it Dead Man Town, said my tour guide, the security man, who liked his little joke. He went on: Ever since the Rema Massacre of 1984, everybody run away. Used to be so nice! (I *saw* dem go to work, dem Tivoli gunmen, mon.) Now look over dere, past Dead Man Town. See dem high-rise building up dere? Dat's Tivoli. Oh, so many people mashed up! Most of dem come here, we know dem *evil* . . .

I asked the question that had been irritating me: If it's so dangerous right here, then how come you guys stand at the windows?

Right now, dey under security force at Tivoli. Canna come here.

When will the soldiers go away?

We doan know.

He was referring to what the newspapers had predictably called an "operation" against Tivoli Gardens, in which four Tivoli residents had been killed and seven injured. A probe would be launched, explained the authorities blandly. "The investigations will also determine if shots were fired from an aircraft." —From an aircraft! What kind of "operation" was that? Did it bespeak repression, desperation, or both? Either way, it was a military act—not law enforcement but war.

How do you feel about what happened at Tivoli? I asked the security man.

Good, mon! They kill one gunman. Him was the hit man, the biggest murderer. Dem kind of people were *bloody* people.

Well, I said, then do you feel any safer now?

We are still weak ones, he quickly replied. Police help the strong ones.

But the police attacked Tivoli Garden, not Rema, I objected.

Brushing this off, the security man gripped my shoulder, brought my face almost against his face, and said: Dey bring dem bloodstain up here, sir, like water running up dem sidewalk. We never get a nice time. Just more distressed, 'cause of dem Tivoli gunmen.

Political Geography

By this time I had asked any number of men, women and children in Rema what would happen if they crossed no-man's-land. The answer was always the same: death by shooting. So, turning to the security man's tall, dreadlocked, shining-eyed friend, who was very good to me and whom I'm going to call Colin, I asked him to indicate what prospects awaited him at each of the four directions.

Pointing straight ahead out that gaping window toward Tivoli Gardens, he said: You canna' go there.

He pointed to the left, toward Board Villa. —You canna' go there, he said.

Toward the right, toward Trenchtown, he gestured: Can go that way a little.

He pointed behind us. —Can go that way.

What happens if you get in a taxi?

If go the wrong way, Tivoli gunman see, then shoot up taxi, kill everyone.

Can you go uptown?

Yes, but some place no good. At Halfway Tree one good friend got killed . . .

When the fact of what Colin was saying finally pierced my comprehension, I stared at him. It was one of the most hideous things that I had ever heard.

"We Just Try to Live Our Ghetto Life"

I ought not to imply that the situation of Rema was as terrible as that of a community besieged in wartime. Nor could the "Tivoli operation," ugly as it was, be equated with a typical moment of war. An *act* of war it undoubtedly was, but that act, with its eleven resulting casualties, remained an aberration. —Certainly since last week at Tivoli we're very close to seeing summary executions, Father Michael Linden, S.J., had told me. He added: Guilt by association can be a capital crime . . . —But Tivoli operations did not occur every day or even every week—not yet, at least. The texture of Rema life, I felt, was that of an imprisoned, wounded, interrupted peace, not of a committed war. Everyone said things had been worse last year; perhaps it had been a true war then. If Colin had really wanted to go uptown, or the security man to a supermarket, either foray could have been pulled off, given patience and knowledge, with a seasoning of luck scarcely needed. It was not a routine thing at Rema—or anywhere in Kingston—to see bloody bandages or war dead. Authority's tanks and jeeps went by, while a kid walked up the street singing: *On the road to Jesus Christ* . . . A man sat in his wheelchair, taking in sun. He'd been shot and paralyzed. Yes, the wounded were around, and one heard gunshots every day, but only as easy finger exercises, not as arpeggios, let alone full-scale orchestral works. The air didn't smell like gunpowder. Up in the abandoned college, which was now his sentry post, kicking the charred fibers and springs of a torched couch, the security man obligingly pointed out to me some bullet holes on a facade, but if he hadn't pointed to them I wouldn't have seen them. (Everybody wanted me to write good things about Rema, and so I am trying to oblige.)

We *not* robber, we *not* thief, said a stubby man named Mackel. We just try to live our ghetto life. —White chickens cheeped in an immense siding-roofed hutch (a church project), kids played basketball, clothes ballooned and wriggled in the hot wind, while fat ladies and skinny ladies pursued life with clothespins in their mouths. Colin, like the church workers I talked to, kept telling me not to emphasize violence in this story. Fair enough; as I said, it really wasn't as bad as it could have been. Life was getting better and better, Colin continued, leading me to a couple of fledgling shops (gasoline, soft drinks, cold juice) on the border strip which overlooked Board Villa: in the old days, he explained, when Tivoli Gardens ruled, the proprietors would have been taxed to financial death by gunmen. Miss Lorna, the gruff, determined old schoolmistress, made similarly optimistic claims, as did that white American Christian, the Reverend John Steigerwald (about whom more below), who first brought me into Rema. These people requested in the most forceful terms that I not make the community look bad. I think it no aspersion on Rema, which I came almost to love, to report the general consensus as to the extent of progress actually made—summed up by one man's cry: *Worse, worse!* We need *money* to spend! We need some training center; we need jobs . . . Miss Lorna, who several times told me not to write this down or that down, cried out: What I would *prefer* to tell you, what I would *love* to tell you, is that we have established peace in Rema.

And if you told me that, would it be true?

Yes! she cried.

But five minutes before she'd been saying to Reverend Steigerwald: And I started hearing gunshots over there, and I said: Let's get out! and the boy was insulted. He thought I'd dissed him. He threatened me . . .

And the gap-toothed security man in the abandoned college had insisted: Dey come regular. Daytime or nighttime. Heavily armed, man. They ambush us.

Well, that didn't invalidate her. In my country's ghettos also, there were gunshots and threats, which occurred occasionally enough for us to stretch the word "peace."

Politricks

Turn your back to Tivoli Gardens and ascend the gentle slope which leads you out of Rema into Jungletown and Jonestown; that's the one approved direction. Now go right, and soon you'll be in Hanna Town, where Paddy Boy is always ready for business and where Saint Anne's Church is by necessity fortified with gates and bars. (Is that such an aberration? I read in the newspaper just yesterday that Canadian churches are starting to do the same.) A sister turns a key, removes a padlock, and lets you in.

Tribes, I wanna call it, said slender, dark-faced old Deacon Patterson, whom Paddy Boy remembered from his own school days. A wooden cross hung around his neck. —Different opinions, he said. I've been here for a number of years, and this is the worst. You have drugs, and you have criminal activity, too. It's no use trying to blame it on any individual. It's only posturing bitterness. Quite a few people get shot . . .

How dangerous is it here? I asked.

I'd say it's not so dangerous, but I don't need any more trouble, you know.

Do they respect the church?

They respect the church. Some younger ones, oh, very very bad, very ignorant . . . When people get injured, nobody's willing to come forward. The thing is, people avoid being hurt.

(The columnist Dawn Ritch had proposed a countervailing axiom: *When they are not caught, it means that the community approves of their actions.* I see no reason not to accept both explanations. Devotion works as well as intimidation.)

So what do you do about all this? I asked the deacon.

We try to do our best to smother the anger, to let the anger wait for tomorrow . . .

We went for a walk, and at every corner there was someone to wave to Deacon Patterson. He ambled gently, with the listlessness of old age, smiling, murmuring sweet vague greetings. No one wanted to be photographed except for one street prostitute who stuck out her tongue. Some youths in a doorway shouted at me. —People said, you're an informer, Deacon Patterson explained. They don't like informers.

The walls said JLP or PNP. JLP was the Jamaica Labour Party. PNP was the People's National Party. The walls said this everywhere I looked.

Deacon Patterson, is the violence mainly politically motivated, would you say?

Oh, we don't talk about that, replied the old man. We call it politricks.

The Plantocracy Thesis

When you got downtown, when you got to Badtown, you found scrawled on almost every wall the initials JLP or PNP, sometimes with additions, as in: PNP A HYPOCRITE, or JLP MUST BE WIPED OUT. These letters and slogans *expressed* and *directed* the violence. They did not exactly *cause* it anymore: through habit and retaliation it caused itself. —*Examine the behaviour of some of the people who occupy the PNP and JLP garrison communities,* said one editorial. *We see the same pattern as existed among primitive bands and villages . . . We have graduated . . . from stones and spears to Glocks and M16s.* This was the tribal explanation, which to my mind explained nothing. It was the convenient tautology of those who were afraid, of those who lived uptown. (When I arrived in Kingston, people warned me not to go downtown unless I had to, and never to go downtown alone. I took that advice. I always went with my dear friend Pearline, who, not being from downtown, had no hereditary enemies there. She was from the country. Dawn Ritch looked Pearl's town up on the police report and said that it was a garrison community, too. Pearline was surprised to hear it; but it's true that she used to vote PNP because that was how her parents voted. Once a year, her family went to the National Arena for a PNP rally. Now, like almost everyone else I met in Kingston, she said that she no longer wanted to vote.)

Deacon Peter Espeut, an eloquent, high-powered, barrel-shaped uptown man, proposed a more plausibly sophisticated version of the tribal thesis. — I suppose a historian could make a case that Jamaica is a society founded on violence, he began. When the British came in 1655, not one Arawak Indian was left alive. The Spanish had killed them all. Of course all slave societies are based on violence. But this was not like the southern United States, where the populations of slaves and free were about equal. In Jamaica the whites were outnumbered by the blacks twenty to one. Jamaica was just

Britian's overseas garden. The kind of violence wreaked in Jamaica was more severe than elsewhere, since this island had jungle for slaves to run away to; so the masters had to make examples. They tried to avoid hanging, because if you hang a slave, you eat up your capital. So they used a lot of whipping. The word was: *plantocracy*. Even after emancipation there was an absence of justice. You tell people they're free, but you compensate the masters for the loss of their slaves—six million pounds! And people continued to work on the plantation for starvation wages. They had to pay rent for the houses they'd been in for generations. Until 1944 the only people who had votes were people who had land. It took a riot to get universal suffrage!

Was there the same sort of violence in the schools then as today?

No, said the deacon. The population of Jamaica then was eighty-five percent rural. Rural children even today are better behaved, more tolerant of bad treatment. Even today, fifty-one percent of the population are rural. And I can't think of any violence that happens in rural areas.

If slavery was responsible, I asked, shouldn't the violence have been as bad or worse just after emancipation as it is now?

Wait, said Deacon Espeut. The story's not over with emancipation. After 1944, the next sort of upheaval came in 1962. Out go the British, in come the brown Jamaicans to take up the mantle of power. *Emancipation from slavery simply freed the masters from having to care for the slaves.* And we *still* have elite rule, but now it's brown. Political office is still a way to enrichment.

It always is, I said.

The violence came in the 1960s as a route for ensuring power, Espeut went on, frowning a little at my interruption. First, guns were brought by the JLP before the 1967 election. Then the PNP brought in guns for the '70s. Before '67, it was just a few bruises. After '67 it was a matter of being killed. And the children learned violence from their parents, and it's been going downhill ever since.

"We Just Try to Live Our Ghetto Life" (continued)

At age fifteen I seen my first murder, a teacher at Miss Lorna's school said. I seen where houses was burnt down over there for the political violence. I seen men shot out of the tree, drop out of the tree like a bird.

When was the last murderer here? I asked a woman in the street.

Sunday morning time. A man just come from Tivoli, killing. Same way they kill my husband.

Statement of Father Michael Linden, S.J.

Eight hundred people have been killed in a single election. Politicians have so much as admitted that they used the gangs to do their work. But now it's linkages between families which is an engine of the drug trade. The cocaine traffic follows the same way as the old ganja traffic, only it's not provided here. The trade is all controlled by the Tivoli gang.

Statement of Ms. Dawn Ritch, Newspaper Columnist

Tivoli Gardens is the West Kingston seat of the JLP leader, Seaga. Three years ago, he admitted that he had lost all control in his district. He gave police the names of thirteen gunmen.

Statement of Another Rema Security Man

I saw dem go to work, dose Tivoli Garden gunmen, mon. Dey have *artillery,* man. Where dey get that from?

Why the Peace Was So Peaceful

We don't kill nobody from Tivoli Gardens, explained a Rema boy. The problem is we diss 'em, cause they stand for Satan.

　　And if you were to go to Tivoli Gardens?

　　Chop 'em up, mon!

Statement of Father Linden (continued)

Seaga and Thompson began it, said Father Linden. They were the leaders. As you know, Seaga was JLP and Thompson was PNP. There was a growing expertise in both parties in affecting drug trade, for which there would be payment in U.S. dollars or guns. In the late '70s and '80s, there was a lot of Cuban military training. So the JLP became more ideological. The '70s perfected a lot of the ideological stances.

　　(I thought of the Rema man who when I asked him about the JLP replied very calmly: We cannot vote for the devil. —Hard to be more ideological than that!)

　　Both parties have an official no-violence policy, the father continued. For the most part, they live by it, but the symbolism of violence is certainly not dying.

Political Geography (continued)

From downtown to Rema one went by way of funeral and automotive parlors past the wall that said PNP ZONE and JLP and LOVE. The cabbies who didn't refuse outright to go were usually nervous. For some reason I especially remember one whose radio blared an old American comedy show bristling with canned laughs, while the driver himself sat sweaty-faced and baleful, hating this job, hating us. Here came another broken wall, barbed wire, funeral homes, grafitti—GHETTO YOUTH, LOVE JAH (God) AND LIVE!—rusty sidings and half demolished houses, goats at Brooklyn Corner, a burned house full of burned and twisted things, a wall that proclaimed REVOLUTION, and then May Pen Cemetery, the burial ground for both Rema and Tivoli Gardens. The cemetery walls shouted JLP. (This place is designed to make criminals, said Miss Lorna. A lot of hideouts for the guys.) We were on Spanish Town Road, in sight of Tivoli Gardens, whose wall said FREE JIM BROWN. Jim Brown had been the Don of Tivoli. The story went that after he went to jail he was going to be extradited to the United States for murder, which worried his confederates, who would have sprung him if they could, but did the second-best thing, namely, to send him a smoke bomb with instructions to activate it at just the right moment, which would force the prison officials to open the windows, and then the confederates would come and get him. The smoke bomb, of course, was a real bomb, so Jim Brown blew himself straight to heaven, thereby easing the confederates' worries. Another story, which was less dramatic and hence more likely to be true, simply went that he had burned to death in his cell. Some said the police had done it. There were other stories. Pearline, for instance, often heard rumors that Jim Brown was still alive somewhere, just waiting his time, like Barbarossa or King Arthur, but she didn't believe it. Seaga had been one of Jim Brown's pallbearers. One Mr. Wayne Jobson, a Jamaican living in L.A. who was trying to market a screenplay treatment of Monsignor Albert's life, told me that when the BBC asked Seaga how he could show graveside support for a wanted murderer, Seaga merely replied: His community respected him, so I have to respect him, too. —Jim Brown's son Dadas was the Don now. His police report described him as *a short man with a short man complex*. The cab now turned onto an empty, weedy plain of ruins, which as I said reminded me of Sarajevo or Phnom Penh or Mogadishu; and we were back in Rema again, insects once again upon that bleakly sunny ruinscape which was so politrickally mashed up, idiotically wrecked—just like West Beirut, said one of the security guys who like me had never been to West Beirut; but his Adam's apple worked with emotion when he said it. From the Board Villa side there came a shot, then silence, and then a shot. —Them keepin' somebody from comin' in, said Philip with a smile. Keepin' the community safe from Tivoli Garden. —But hard-to-impress Pearline told me out of the side of her mouth that it was nothing serious—only three shots, after all! (For another had sounded now.) —Just trying to start something, maybe, she said. —(I remember how she was curling her hair uptown when a gunshot sounded, and when I asked her how that made her feel, she replied: Happens all the time. You can hear that everywhere.) The next day a Rema kid said that those shots had been let off by a soldier killing one of his friends. I said that I was sorry. Maybe the soldier had actually done it at a different moment, employing a fuller burst of shots; for we were only in Rema for three or four hours that day, and that kid could not have known which noises we'd heard. Maybe the kid was lying, who knows? The shots themselves were real enough. Pearline's sister sometimes dwelled across the border in Rose Town, I suppose for boyfriend reasons. That occasional address meant that she would not be very safe were she to visit Rema, because Rose Town constituted, in Colin's words, "Little Tivoli." She'd told Pearl: I love the music of the guns. —Pearl shook her head wearily. Her maxim was: *People mostly think of doing evil rather than doing good.*

Political Geography *(continued)*

Deacon Espeut headed a school, whose boys and girls, like their American counterparts, occasionally showed up with knives, ice picks and hacksaw blades. (Well, they will always tell you that they carry the knife for self-defense, he said with weary geniality.) In such cases it was the deacon's unenviable job to be present at the hearing. (So far, he confided, we haven't expelled anybody, because usually, unfortunately, there's some defect in the procedure.)

What Espeut said next was a complete sociogeography lesson:—The first question we ask the child is: What is your address? And we may get a violent address—Tivoli Gardens, Wilton Gardens. And we ask: Do you know your mother's name or your father's name? And then we know.

Two years before, while studying the "untouchable" Burakumin caste of Japan, I'd heard of a similar procedure. An employer or a university admissions officer asked the candidate's address, and then he knew. The Buraku—or many of them—lived in generations-old ghettos, partly out of inertia, partly from social pressure, and partly from a desire to be with their own. Such an address closed the file. The candidate would not be admitted.

Deacon Espeut, of course, put his question out of motives entirely alien to those of bigotry. What a Rema or a Tivoli Gardens address told him was not that the candidate was low, or subhuman—but rather that the candidate was unfortunate. Ghetto affiliation explained things.

Statement of Another Security Man

Mostly rifle, the man said. Dat's what dey use when dey come to Rema. Dem stand up. Dem come in car. Dem come any way. Dem used to drive all the time, but now dem stop. People kinda have eyes out. Dem use gun. Yeah, mon.

How many come at once?

Dem, six, seven, shoot and damage.

How do they dress?

Just normal. But dem kill anybody, even baby accidentally. Dem doan respect the baby. And woman shield them, so police cannot do to them. Dey is *violence*. Dem come and burn and kill, mon. If dem see we's not here, dem come here, dem Seaga gunmen, dem Tivoli types. We in fear. Every time somebody good come up here, dem Tivoli gunmen come here. Last week us find five dead bodies in Dead Man Town. As long as Seaga rule, it must be like that.

What were you doing in Denham Town?

The man only smiled.

The Wisdom of Three Thugs

Ten minutes away from Rema, in Hanna Town, the cabbie was asking still another ruthless man in gold-rimmed sunglasses: You seen Paddy Boy? and the man muttered: Up de road, up de road! and Paddy Boy came strolling alongside a wall that read YOU ARE NOW ENTERING PNP TERRITORY and at a fruit stand whose wisdom proclaimed MR. TRUST IS DEAD, MR. CASH TAKE OVER, my friend Pearline and I fell in with Paddy Boy, who for two thousand Jamaican dollars let us photograph another gunman with his pistol, which I first unloaded; then we took another very unwilling taxi back to Rema where they told me: Understand dem Tivoli Garden kill a guy dis morning. A little guy. Some guys passing the Rema Town border from Board Villa . . . —and then the next day we went back to Hanna Town again to meet Paddy Boy and two of his friends. I knew that the rendezvous would cost me, but I got receipts from Paddy Boy; instead of "bribe" I wrote in "community fee," because Paddy Boy wasn't the sort whom one wanted to disrespect.

Joint Statement of Three Thugs in Hanna Town

It started to change around 1976, said the PNP man (well, all three of them were PNP men, so let's call him the agitator—come to think of it, they were all agitators, so call him the gunman's friend). —Politics get more rigid, he went on. The CIA gangster arm the JLP government, because afraid of Communist. Well, violence became more rigid. Man from Tivoli come here, start firin' shots. PNP in Tivoli had to leave.

When was the last time you went to Tivoli Gardens? I asked.

During the peace of 1988, he said. We had a dance down there, a group down there for some police competition.

How did you feel about meeting your enemies?

We shake hands, laughed the gunman's friend. Those guys are those guys. I tell you straight up, you cannot trust 'em.

Did they pat you down for weapons?

No one gonna start anything. The Don of Tivoli was there . . .

Do you have a Don?

In Hanna Town we don't really have one. We have a *political adviser.*

All right. So you went to the dance. And now?

We can't trust Tivoli now. They doan love peace. They have to say dee [kill], you like it or not. We are on the corner. They shoot at us.

When was the first time you got shot at?

It all begin in 1980, said the gunman's friend. I was on the corner one night when a bullet come down the hill from the Tivoli Gardens. The bullet start to come from the Rema people. And if we see 'em now, gun or no gun, we have to shoot 'em back.

Beside the gunman's friend, lean and vicious and old, sat Paddy Boy himself, who said: For the 1976, election we go around the country. We campaign. Well, we were driving to a JLP community on the way to our office and a group of men just open fire at our vehicle. We tried to retaliate through the police. We never had no idea about what place it is. So we go to the polling station and the police listen to us, give them retaliation from us.

What kind of retaliation was it?

Oh, no one got hurt, he grinned, and the gunman's friend and the gunman both laughed.

(But I do not want to give the impression that these three violent man were swaggerers. They struck me, rather, as pathetic and fearful.)

Then the CIA started to come in, said Paddy Boy. We started to get aid from Cuba, so the CIA didn't like that, so they pump dollars into the JLP.

OK. So you're telling me the JLP was on the American government's side, I said. And what did the PNP stand for?

The gunman spoke for the first time. His gold-rimmed sunglasses dazzled me. He said: We care more for the poor people. We help the people.

And they shot at you, too?

Yeah.

Were you feeling pretty angry about it? I asked.

The gunman replied: This bit of town here, you have to fight pretty hard here. This section of town here, Seaga want to destroy.

Did Rema rise up against Seaga and Tivoli? That's what they tell me.

Well, they would say that, because they were with him, but he turn against them. Now they say one hundred and seventy dead in the war between Rema and Tivoli . . .

Why the Peace Was So Peaceful (continued)

Everyone agrees that Rema and Tivoli used to be under the same Don—the Don of Tivoli. The Rema people whom I interviewed always spoke of that time as the bad old days of dictatorship, but the bitterness of after-times may have contaminated memories. At any rate, the Rema people seem to have felt that Tivoli was keeping a disproportionate share of the resources. As one youth put it: We only get coffin and prison, but *dey* get develop. —Colin said much the same: We do everything for the Don, even be gunmen for him, but he give us only coffin when we die.

The first version of the tale was that one of the worst Tivoli gunman, whom I presume was so labeled by my storytellers because he had killed Rema people, stuck a pistol inside his pants as usual one fine day and accidentally blew his balls off. Tivoli, however, rightly or wrongly believed that the gun had discharged with assistance from Rema. And here I might want to insert what was told me by a member of a crowd of Rema "sportsmen" wall-sitting at the borderline—namely, that before this ambiguous death, Tivoli had put up placards throughout JLP territory advertising a dance, and once the dance was over, a Rema boy, thinking no evil, tore one poster down; but since it bore the likeness of that gunman soon to die, the gunman felt disrespected and gave the Rema boy an etiquette lesson by shooting him in the head six times. The Rema boy pitched forward on his face, which according to Pearline was a sign from God that the killer would soon die, as we know he did. This subplot of the poster, if true, certainly strengthens Tivoli's case that some Rema gunman might have taken revenge, because the Rema people, Christians though they were, never expounded to me on the virtues of turning the other cheek; but let's leave that alone and simply mention that after the Tivoli gunman died, one of his colleagues, the suggestively named Shotty Marks, rolled into Rema to uphold the law of vengeance.

Shotty kill one boy here for nothing, said the security man. When 'im dead, when 'im done, 'im Granny go an 'shout at Tivoli: *Blood for blood!* An' that's when the war come up.

The second version, which bore a finer ideological polish, and which commenced without reference to the events just described, was that Rema had won a liberation struggle—a veritable holy war. Rema had possessed only three guns against Tivoli's thousand, but because Tivoli was under Satan, God had been on Rema's side. —Down dere is de army now, you know, Colin said (and he wasn't the only one who said it). Not even de army can go dere now, you see—must shoot 'em from helicopter! *An' we stood up to 'em.* Dis system is God system. Deir evil system is de devil system. Dem *kill you, kill you.* When dem come up, dem do *anything* dey can do, especially if dem carry malicious feeling. Dem rob, dem kill, dem make de girl do oral sex like Sodom; dem is *WICKEDNESS.* So we take a stand dat time. Before, if we take any kind of stand, even make a youth club, dat's a PNP youth club, dey call it Communist youth club because dey is JLP. We supposed to live without *any* kind of system right now, not PNP, not JLP. Enough of my friends, me an' them, we're not gonna vote. No more politicians. *So us rise up.* The youth from this community gonna get locka up in the prison three-four years. 'Cause if we don't defend the community, we gotta run away. *We gotta rise up.* We gotta stop them by any means necessary . . .

Why couldn't you just go talk with their Don?

No chance! Colin cried in husky bitterness. I promise I will *not* no more JLP stronghold! Don is JLP politician. Must kill me. So we fight.

Dem come up and kill! We stand up against dem with three gun. From dat day dey don't dictate. It was thanks to de Almighty that we won . . .

The third version, the dry one, the cynical one, was propounded by Pearline, that sad forty-two-year-old country girl who knew a few things. —Dey want to switch from JLP to PNP, she said. Dat's all. So dey fight. And Colin with his story 'bout the three guns makes me laugh. Colin was Tivoli gunman before, I am sure. He must be. He *himself* must have dose three guns!

Statement of the Three Thugs (continued)

Did you help Rema in their uprising against Tivoli? I asked the Hanna Town gunman.

Well, we had a relationship, to be frank, the man replied, running a thumbnail along his sweating beer bottle. (His pistol was an old black Luger, so old that I almost wondered whether he might be fooling me with a licensed firearm, because it was not very shiny or showy [Oh, they love the Glock! Father Linden had laughed, particularly the *chrome* Glock . . .]. But when I photographed the weapon, sweat broke out on his face. He hid himself, all but his gun hand, crouching unsteadily behind a pillar.)

And that was justified?

Of course.

When do you think violence is justified?

Violence is justified if somebody try to hurt you, Paddy Boy recited quickly, knowing this lesson by heart. —You have to look out! If a man from Denham Town or even Tivoli, you can welcome them but you cannot trust them. Some people just bring politics up to the max. Election time is just gunshot. You don't take your eye off any minute.

And you agree with that? I asked the gunman.

Yeah.

And is revenge justified?

Yeah.

Have you done that?

A lot of that.

I heard that a seventeen-year-old girl in Tivoli got shot in the brain during that recent helicopter assault, I said to the three of them. How do you feel about that? Are you sorry for her?

Well, the violence is caused by them in Tivoli, you know, said the gunman jauntily. Tivoli really start it.

Statement of Father Linden (continued)

We used to baptize everything that walked, said Father Linden. After Vatican II, now a pastor has to make sure that the person has been raised in a proper environment. But I had a girl shot the other day. She was in our youth group. She's blind now. She's been baptized.

Why did she get shot?

Unknown. It's a security forces bullet in there.

Statement of the Three Thugs (continued)

Would you like to see the violence stop? I asked.

Paddy Boy said nothing, and the gunman's friend grinned sarcastically, but the gunman became emotional and his patois thickened and he said: Dey need unity. Can no have the peace, no peace. If most of 'em can't eat, what can dey do?

Statement of Sister Beverly, Saint Anne's Church, Hanna Town

You see some really malnourished people. I saw one man whose face was eaten away by hunger. I don't know if he died.

Statement of the Three Thugs (continued)

If your address is Kingston, Jamaica, insisted the gunman, even with twelve subjects in school, you can't get employment.

So what can be done about it? I asked him, bearing in mind one very bitter remark of Deacon Espeut's: You see your colleagues driving cars that you can't buy, and when you ask where they got them, they say: I'm carrying a gun for this politician. A gun becomes a ticket to prosperity.

But the gunman either chose to keep that axiom a professional secret, to avoid repulsing me, or else he really believed himself (as I hope he did) when he answered: In the ghetto, it has to start from some skill. From earning and learning. Police Youth Club is a good thing, too. I was even invited to their meeting. Maybe I should have gone.

Do they help you much at Saint Anne's? I asked.

Saint Anne's is a good school. Enough of them learn from it. Paddy Boy here, he went to Saint Anne's . . .

Well, do you see peace coming to stay? I asked.

The gunman curled his fingers into fists. —As long as Mr. Seaga have power, and 'im *comin'* and 'im *dealin'*, it's not gonna stop, he said furiously.

Dat *my* experience. If something happen in dat community, cannot even let police know. Is a *vicious* man.

Surprisingly enough, Paddy Boy thought differently about Seaga. He said to me: Once, we want to see 'im dead, but he start to show the kindness, aid us with things, pump money into Hanna Town. Him start to repair commercial center. Him start more from the old-time politics.

But the gunman in his patched pants and loose shirt raised high the beer in his hand and cried: Mr. Seaga just find a way for to kill 'em! Because him so big, you know! Seaga make the politics of West Kingston get *rotten*. Dem doan' want the government force, the good force, the security force to enter Tivoli Garden! Is like some guerrilla! Dem people doan think like us. Bullet whistle overhead, mon! Last July, big things go on. Big mens plot when big man of Tivoli get dead. Dey say is just fire gun salute over graveside, but dem gunshot two day, three day—and dem gunshot come into Hanna Town! Police kill 'im! It look to me like Seaga get 'im up for dead to get WAR, WAR, WAR! And I remember dem shoot up de police station at Denham Town . . .

The gunman paused for breath. Then he, who'd been shot in the chest at a recent dance (he'd spent his birthday at the hospital), turned his gilded sunglassy stare full upon me and said: Long as Mr. Seaga have dem blue breath of life in 'im, gonna be no peace.

The Uneasy Rule of Law

To help you visualize the kind of campaigning that Paddy Boy and his colleagues had engaged in (and probably would undertake again for the next elections, which would happen sometime between October and March, the date to be announced only two weeks in advance to reduce opportunities for violence), I can do no better than quote Father Linden: It's a secret ballot by law, but the mob goes to welcome the voters. So the voting is always unanimous. The other thing is, the police get frightened and disappear. And at some point the crowds might move in and steal the ballot box . . .

Political Geography (continued)

Bearing those words in mind, I asked a taxi driver how he planned to vote. The driver (who carried an ice pick for protection, because thirteen cabbies had already been killed by gunmen so far that year) stuck his head out the window and spat into the street. —Win-lose, win-lose; I don't care anymore! he growled. Last time I go down there, a man and a woman come in with a big long paper and say: What is your name? Okay, you don't have to vote. We vote you already.

In the country, Paddy Boy might or might not be able to boast of such impressive results. But in garrison communities such as Hanna Town or Tivoli Gardens, the sheep must follow their gun-wielding shepherds. The outcome was apathetic disenchantment. —You see, politics is sport, explained the elegant columnist Dawn Ritch. Vote early and often. Traditionally, voter turnout in Jamaica is very high. —And I am sure that many people did plan to vote. But I have to repeat that almost everyone I polled—the nature of my task, of course, skewed my sample, who were mainly Rema people, Hanna Town, and downtown people, with some cabbies and ministers thrown in—said that they didn't want to vote anymore. (I have already relayed Colin's view: No more politicians.) But it might well be that when polling day came, Ms. Ritch's prediction would be borne out once again—for Paddy Boy would vote, and our taxi driver would either vote or be voted for . . .

Police

There was a second factor that tended even more to alienate that portion of the electorate whose spirit was already imprisoned by violence. That was *authoritarian* violence. At literally the same moment as the radio droned on in anxious confusion about the attack on Tivoli Gardens, other people were telling me counterpart tales. One of Pearline's friends, the sister of a robber-gunman (who, by the way, had his own ethical code—seeing a strange man beating a strange woman, he at once shot the man in the leg; and it may also be placed to his credit—or not—that he regularly gave his sister gifts of stolen gold chains) put on her sandals late one morning while her brother slept on, tired from his night work, and she went out to the market. The neighbors led her home. Policemen had shot her brother in his bed. Pearline told me she would never forget her friend's wailing. Not long after, the authorities liquidated her other brother, who'd followed the same brutal trade.

Does she hate the police now? I asked.

No, because she know both brothers were gangsters.

But Colin, not so forgiving in his disposition, called the police "terrorists." —Just past the ruins of the old Ambassador Theater, which squatted, white and blasted, at the edge of more no-man's-land—Rema

land, really, all the way to the watchtower of the prison where five of
Colin's friends sat in payment for their efforts in the cause of community
self-defense, but all the same, it was not advisable to go much past the
roadblock of rusty and burned things because Tivoli Gardens might fire
wide, and a stray bullet was, in Colin's words, "the worst disease"—just
past the Ambassador (It were a *nice* place, eh? said Colin, shining-eyed
and guarded by his chest-length braids. Look, Bill—here were the screen
for the theater! Look, Pearl! The people just dismantle from both sides of
the community. Lick it down with sledgehammer!), a street ran in the one
direction that Colin could freely go; a street walled by metal sidinged
shanties and then by genuine concrete walls that were painted with
oceans, angels and bottom-waggling girls, courtesy of the youth arts project. This was Jonestown. Ever since Tivoli Gardens had lost its reputed
stranglehold, Jonestown and Rema, once politically divided, were united
in the emancipation of apathy: no more PNP or JLP! We sat on a Jonestown
stoop drinking Dragon Stout, my camera lens mobbed by uniformed schoolchildren. Then suddenly, rapidly, came a khaki-colored tank, bristling with
helmeted soldiers. People's faces closed. I wanted to take a photograph,
but they begged me not to. —They don't like, a man explained. Maybe then
they hurt us, mon. All the time they brutalize us.

Do they come here often?

They patrol here every day.

The police, of course, had their own plausible and reasonable version
of events. —I will stay here in the station and hear shots fired in Rema,
said Superintendent Lanval in his windowless office in the heart of the station, which stood a block from the Ambassador, with machine-gun-
gripping soldiers on the front steps. —And they'll say no shots were fired!

Which is more dangerous, I asked him, Rema or Tivoli Gardens?

Rema is as dangerous as Tivoli Gardens, although it is true that here
they are more exposed to us during the day, thanks to our armed patrols.
Once you come into close contact with the Rema gunmen, there can be no
hesitation about shooting back. Over the past two years, two police have
been killed in this area, six shot and injured, and four or five soldiers also
shot. Most of the shootings occurred last year. Right now, it's like a dor-
mant volcano. The criminal element within forces us to be aggressive.
There have been occasions when people who have been friendly with us
have been told by gunmen to stop. I don't want to imagine what this area
would be like without our presence here.

What's the worst thing you've seen?

Firing at the police station. They have attacked this police station three weeks ago—about eight men with M-16s . . .

When I asked Colin about this, he gave me confirmation, and there was mirth in his eye. Dawn Ritch gave me confirmation of another sort when she showed me a map that she'd recently printed in her column. It depicted the island of Jamaica, benignly blank except for the area around Kingston, which was heavily shaded with garrison communities. One-third of Saint Catherine Parish was garrison; that was next to Kingston. In East Kingston, the police knew of six discrete gangs; in Central Kingston, of twelve; and in West Kingston, of eight. According to the police report that lay on her desk, Rema had the second-highest number of gangs.

And the police's case was reinforced by the testimony of almost everyone I met, such as the little Rema girl who said she saw gunmen all the time; when I asked what they looked like she replied: Like Satan. —Are there gunmen here? I asked a strapping fellow in the mixed PNP and JLP town called Riverton, where boys jumped onto the garbage trucks to claim first ownership of what must be literally called the spoils, and where no one had been killed for a whole month. —I wouldn't deny it, came the reply. Just like any normal community.

If gunmen constituted normality, and the police were to perform their duties at all, then swift, ruthless action must sometimes be called for. —The vast majority are just spoiled kids, Father Linden had said. The worst I've seen are people who are lethally dangerous and also cocaine-addicted and in leadership. When you see mutilation it's almost always cocaine. There's a strong suspicion of irrationality. —Was Father Linden's chain of cause and effect accurate? I don't know. But how can I demand that anyone, police or not, negotiate and palaver with irrational gunmen?

I can, of course, demand that the police know what they're doing. Last month's victim, whom the strapping citizen of Riverton mentioned, had been a twenty-four-year-old mother accidentally shot by the police, who were after five men. I don't know if the men escaped or not. The dead woman left behind four children.

Obviously, the officer who had discharged his weapon into this woman was most to blame. But can we deny Paddy Boy and his counterparts all responsibility?

Statement of Sister Beverly (continued)

Yesterday I went to Tivoli to meet the parents of someone who was shot. He was probably killed by soldiers. He wasn't in the street; he was in his bed. A little kid. The brother of the dead child comes to our school, and he was crying a lot that day, so we visited the house . . .

What did you do? I asked her.

We introduced ourselves, she said. We let the father tell the story of how his son had died. We wanted just to be there with the family. Then we prayed with them.

And did the father feel better?

He was grief-stricken, but I think he felt a little better maybe, replied the nun without much conviction.

Politricks Triumphant

Thus the usual steady state, which one can find in any instance of prolonged violence (Serbs kill Croats, so Croats kill Serbs) had been achieved. The more Paddy Boys proliferated, the more violent the authorities became, which encouraged the perception that they were "terrorists," and gave the Paddy Boys all the more license . . . Hence that cliché, the "climate of violence." —The moral point for people in the church is, you have a culture that can easily undermine the morality of people, said Father Linden. There's a culture of subterfuge; there's a culture of get-rich-quick. And in the garrison areas, large numbers of parishioners have suffered violence. Once the violence does touch people, you have the revenge factor. Once you have a member of a family killed, you have it—or a girl from one turf mixes up with a guy from another part. Suppose someone from Hanna Town goes down and robs somebody under protection in another area; or someone is supposed to transport a gun and uses it instead. Or someone fails to transport a gun . . . —Thus Father Linden.

But in Rema everybody disdained such detached explanations and indignantly insisted: Look like we are the evil, but not true! Tivoli send someone kill by day or night, then run so police say from Rema gunman. But we only stand up to them so we can live nice. If we no stand up, they must mash up everything with fire and sledgehammer. —Such ran their justification. In other words, Rema gunmen were always right. And, after all, Rema *was* mashed up. If the police were unable to "stand up," how could one blame the locals for doing it?

Solutions

I firmly believe that it's not a behavioral problem that people have. It's a spiritual problem.

These were the words of the Reverend John D. Steigerwald, the executive director of Jamaica Teen Challenge, an organization self-described as "a Bible-based alcohol and drug rehabilitation program," whose unfortunately ambiguous slogan, "Helping Hurting People," might bring sarcastic smiles to the lips of the ungodly, but Reverend Steigerwald's urgently martial sincerity, which could be but the uneasiest of friends with the cosmopolitanism (some would say rottenness) in which I live, was perfectly in place in the ghettos of Kingston, where one's enemies received automatic enrollment into Satan's legions, and even weary, worldly Pearline could say, when I showed her an illustration of Aztec gods in a book I was reading: Better doan do that. Burn up too much money already. Idols are a waste of time and money. —Steigerwald's famous Catholic counterpart, Monsignor Richard Albert, believed that such religious typecasting was superficial and did not benefit anyone. About Teen Challenge he said, after a word or two of lukewarm praise: I think we have to be careful about overspiritualizing things. I want to help the people live their lives as they choose. I'm not out to make them follow my line. —How could anyone deny that Steigerwald's moral vision was black and white? But I admired this balding, bespectacled, squinting, uncomely man. He was here to do good at the risk of his own life—and his crusading ethos surely raised the risk to a level exceeding Deacon Patterson's. He was no cautious delayer or time-waster. On the morning I met him, we sat uptown in the townhouse of a mutual acquaintance, and after interrogating me as to my purpose and gazing deeply into my eyes he took Pearline and me straight to Rema, although the acquaintance begged him to be careful down there. Could Steigerwald find young people who needed him, and could he in some sense help them? It seemed eminently possible, for he had love and will in his heart. Colin appreciated him, too, which counted for a lot with me. Teen Challenge had joined in cooperation with two Kingston churches who for some time had supported Miss Lorna's school there within the high fence, catty-corner from the police station, and Miss Lorna was a bundle of furious, no-nonsense goodness with no time for me, so if she had time for Steigerwald that made me respect him all the more. (We never see NO ONE here! cried Colin passionately. No one help us except only this school! This lady, she's the first to give opportunity. —Did any Don ever help you? I asked, and got the usual answer: When somebody kill us, Don give us only coffin. Only this lady care about us so many years . . . And Pastor John, he new here, but he try and do the good thing. —When I heard that, my heart went out to him and to Miss Lorna, who two weeks after her first arrival in Rema—fifteen years ago now—saw two men approaching each other with upraised machetes, and in her deep, hoarse, shouting voice cried out: In the name of Jesus, what are you doing? and they stopped.) . . . Miss Lorna's school would be the place toward which Pearline and I would direct those uptown taxi drivers who were willing to go to Rema (one in three of them weren't). Kids standing outside the locked gate. Every time someone passed through the gate, they unlocked and locked it. Miss Lorna was sorting donated clothes inside, to the click of padlocks. Tanks and jeeps clattered past the fence.

Man has *choices* in life, Steigerwald told me. The Scripture clearly says that a man's bent is toward evil. These guys have made *choices*.

So your strategy is to get them to make another choice?

That's right, answered Steigerwald, seeking and searching for something in my face. —They talk about injustice. Well, the biggest injustice was what happened two thousand years ago. They want to stop the injustice. They never include the option of prayer.

You know, John, I said, the last time I was in Cambodia I met a kid who'd joined the Khmer Rouge because he was hungry. He was scared and he was ignorant. He killed innocent people—and government soldiers—because he was told to. He doesn't even know his own leader's name. How responsible would you say he is?

Steigerwald replied: I have to believe the Scriptures, where it says in Romans that God reveals Himself to all. People, even the Gentiles, know that to kill someone is *wrong*.

I understand, I replied.

As I write this now, considering Steigerwald's argument as closely as I am able—for the issue is a universal and desperately important one—I have to say that I disagree at least partially. *Necessity is murder's first defense,* and it is so easy to define necessity in expedient terms! As far as I can tell, it never entered that Khmer Rouge boy's mind that he had done anything wrong. As for the violent ones of Kingston, Dawn Ritch had— very insightfully, I believe—illuminated their moral actions when she told me: They come in search of better conditions, and don't find them. It's a social phenomenon. They don't see why they should be so weak, so poor. You wouldn't compare this with Pol Pot and Bosnia. You compare it with old Corsican banditry. These people are protected by their communities. They become outlaws. Rather than face the law, they retreat into their communities. The problem they have is of being a permanent underclass. *Their communities regard their first offense as an honorable thing.*

But on another level I think that Steigerwald was correct in asserting the existence of apodictic moral knowledge. When someone in Rema shot up the police station, say, and was applauded for it by his peers, he was applauded (so I like to think) not because shooting was good in and of itself, but because the police were perceived as the aggressors. In other words, he was applauded because his act was considered an important exception to a rule: Killing was bad, but the police had killed, or by confiscating neighborhood guns, had left us vulnerable to be killed by Tivoli gunmen; therefore in this particular instance, counterkilling was good. (That is why when I asked one of Colin's friends, a big man who declined to be photographed and who sat watching Board Villa from his box of zinc siding and barbed wire, how often the enemy attacked, he replied: This week they cool, mon. I'm a security officer. That my job. You see someone come. If they approach us the bad way, then we must do the same. But we don't want to destroy people. We are not animal. We are not cannibal. We are human being.) —The problem with making exceptions was that it left the gunmen free to make whatever exceptions they chose.

That's the whole message of Teen Challenge, Steigerwald said. It's a faith-based program. We're not preaching religion. We're preaching *relationship.*

This was one valid approach—the way of discipline, of pulling the recalcitrant camel through the needle's eye to bring it to Heaven. One reason, I think, Reverend Steigerwald and Miss Lorna could be colleagues was that in the gangland atmosphere of *take-take-take* they both laid down strict rules of creed or behavior, which could infuse backbone into certain lax individuals. Hence their colleague, the Reverend Bobby Wilmot, whose aggressive, nay, insatiable determination formed handholds out of its own bony hardness from which it pulled itself upward, aggrandizing itself, executing its purpose in small steps, leaving its undisciplined competitors in the dust. He told me: I must say, early on, when I came here seven years ago, dey would pass me skeptically and say: *Are you still there?* But we didn't come to play games. Dis used to be deir place to play football. We took it over for a school. I said, I will clean up de place dis month, and you clean up next month. Then next month dey didn't do it, so I cleaned it up and said: I have rights now. And de mainstream of guys support us now.

Hence also the teacher I met at Miss Lorna's school who was studying for purposes of refutation the heretical doctrine of evolution up at the All Life Ministry Bible Institution, learning how wrong Darwin was. I disagreed with her opinions, but the most important thing was that she was studying, and sometimes studying required direction. Even at the school itself the workers, most of whom had scars, might suddenly fly into a rage, and shout: *Doan argue with me!*

They have asked us to discipline their children, Miss Lorna said, rushing from room to room as usual, this time with an extension cord and a washcloth in her hands. —I mean, we are everything down here—doctor, nurse, hairdresser, mother . . . I closed the school down once. Closed it down last week, for discipline problems. The parents came within one hour. The first thing the parents said was: Grab them by the ears and beat them! Because they equate beating with love. It's true that if they don't see the rod, they don't behave.

Miss Lorna! cried a boy eagerly.

Hey, how you doin', babes? she said, kissing his cheek.

She entered the classroom and said: All right, children. I am leaving. Please do not frustrate the teachers. Respect Philip. Respect the others. All right; all the best now.

Statement of Monsignor Richard Albert, Saint Patrick's Foundation

Other individuals, who might not like being drilled in matters of conviction, found a patron in Monsignor Richard Albert, who, although he lived in that same personal relationship with the Father and Son that Reverend Steigerwald talked about, he could still say to me: There are a lot of good people who don't accept Jesus who are in Heaven.

His headquarters, Stella Maris Church, was way uptown. The taxi driver who carried Pearl and me up there for our first interview kept a licensed Colt six-shooter in his pants, which made me feel as if I were back in upstanding sections of my own country. We rang the buzzer, and from inside they unlocked the steel-barred gate just as they did at Saint Anne's

Church in Hanna Town; and then they held open the inner door to the air-conditioned anteroom where assistants worked at computer and phone; to the right was a nameplated door behind which, in an office ornamented by three English bulldogs that grinned sadly with their sharp little white teeth, Monsignor Albert himself sat at his desk, bald and red-faced and brawny like his dogs.

I'd like to meet some of the people you helped, I said.

Most of the people I've helped are either in jail or dead, he said.

Grimacing, he picked up the phone.

He got bail, huh? the priest was saying. Before the jailbreak? I didn't see his alias in the newspaper, so I wondered if he was in the jailbreak. He's up for some serious charges—murder and whatnot.

The priest chuckled. —What're we gonna do? He hung up. —Wacky Mikey's gone, he said. We can't get him.

I came to Jamaica in 1976 . . . he began to tell me, but just then the phone rang again. Another case. He picked it up and muttered into it: What I said was, I wanted him to get checked by a doctor as long as it's a genuine situation. I wanna help him. Not thousands of dollars, but a thousand dollars or so is OK. I understand he lost an eye and he's very depressed. I can help with two and a half, three thousand dollars. And I would pay it to the doctor, not to him.

He hung up. On his desk was a box of Cuban cigars. He put one to his lips, and made a face. —A lot of inferior cigars these days, he said. —He threw the whole boxful into the garbage and went to a cabinet to get a better one. —All right, let's go, he said. We got into his van, the cigar now puffing satisfactorily, and proceeded down to Waterhouse, where he had lived from 1983 until quite recently, when the death threats and the dead bodies thrown over his wall finally drove him uptown to Stella Maris. (Pearline's niece lived in Waterhouse from time to time with a man—shall we call him a gun collector?) On the way, Monsignor Albert gave me his autobiography, in a perfunctory sort of way, his impatience at being taken from his work less palpable than Miss Lorna's, but it was clear enough that here was one busy man. Everybody in Kingston seemed to know him (as was natural, for like any other sincere fund-raiser he tirelessly tooted his own horn), and most seemed to like him. —He's a great person, said neck-scarred Philip in Rema, slowly licking a spoonful of peanut butter. —A hero, said Colin, who insisted that he was Monsignor Albert's friend, and wanted to see him again, which was not so easy because the priest maintained no center in Rema: he couldn't be everywhere, after all. —He a good chap, said the friendly bartender at the Indies Hotel uptown who always charged me double. Even Paddy Boy's friend, that Hanna Town gunman, allowed: Well, a good pastor. Always try an' sort out any violence. —The Saint Patrick's Foundation, which he had founded, was the largest charitable organization in Jamaica. He ran women's centers, woodworking shops, schools, and the like, all locked and gated like everything else in Kingston. —Some guys would be interested in building up their churches, he said. I'm interested in building up centers.

One of the brothers at Saint Anne's had told me: I'm not trying to be critical of Monsignor Albert, but the infusion of foreign aid is not the best answer. —But what was? —The gangs are protesting the lack of opportunity, said Dawn Ritch. Once there is growth in Jamaica, the killings will decline. The answer is not simply to suppress them. —Monsignor Albert with his extraordinary budgetary powers proposed to provide a mite of that opportunity.

When is violence justified? I asked him.

As a pacifist, I would say, violence is almost never justified. As a Catholic, I think the same.

What about the death penalty?

The death penalty should die. Killing people to stop people killing people is crazy. I've walked some men to the gallows. One of the saddest times in my life was when I walked one guy, and he said he was innocent, and I believe him. Jesus had a lot to say about it. He said: *He who is without sin, let him cast the first stone.* Unfortunately, we're in a terrible situation in Jamaica. We're fighting for our survival. This area we're going through now, two small boys were murdered for reasons of donsmanship. We're on a PNP-JLP border. The inner city is coming up into the outer city. We're in a free-market economy, but the vast majority of Jamaicans are not capable of entering the free-market economy. Ninety-four percent of the kids in this city are born out of wedlock. Sixty percent of the kids who graduate from the schools can't read. The teachers are the last to arrive and the first to leave each day. And the gun problem is worse and worse.

Because of politics or because of drugs?

Don't let anyone tell you the gun problem is drug-related, said Monsignor Albert. It's the result of political donsmanship. I don't believe any man has the right to have a gun. Garrison communities have been armed by politicians. This is modern-day slavery.

How is that? I asked.

Dependence is slavery. Give a man a fish and you help him for a day. Teach him to fish and you help him for his whole life. The people in the garrison communities aren't free. They're trapped.

But isn't having your own gun like having your own fishing pole? I wanted to know. Give a man a gun and he can defend himself for his whole life . . .

(As I said this I was recalling the hot ghetto afternoons in Rema, one of Colin's daughters, the youngest, on my lap, inhaling secondhand ganja smoke while her father and the other men read American gun magazines, admiring the Para-Ordnance models P-12 and P-10, the Sig Sauer P220 . . .)

I lived for fifteen years in the ghetto, replied Monsignor Albert. I could go in and out—when the gunfire was quiet . . .

We came to a wall on which was written ANYONE FOUND HERE AFTER 12:00 PM WILL BE FOUND DEAD IN THE MORNING and Monsignor Albert, one hand on the wheel, the other clenched around the big cigar, was saying: Every night there's a major flare-up. Last August I had just finished dinner up in town with my Archbishop, and I radioed down to Waterhouse and they said: There are three guys on the premises with M-16s in their briefs, and nothing but shooting going on. We went to the police station for assistance, but we were also getting shot at *at the police station;* we were under siege. Finally we were able to get a policeman to come to our help. The policeman and I stood in the street. Eight soldiers had to come to get me on my property. Now, the three guys with the M-16s weren't out to attack me. They were just stationed there. The soldiers smashed down my front gate, lay down on the ground in combat position, and we watched as *nine* guys with M-16s jumped over my wall . . . As I watched eight black Jamaican soldiers knock down my gates, ready to kill other Jamaicans, I was so sad. I realized how entrenched the gun culture was. The inner-city communities have become so tainted now with this culture of death that they see it as the logical thing to have a gun, not only for self-defense, but also to get their way . . .

A Border Memory

He spoke with some truth. At the border between Rema and Rose Town, which was, the Rema crew told me, controlled by Tivoli, there stood a corner store where Colin, Philip and I left Pearl for the moment and proceeded with the crew into enemy territory, the young men all nervous, sweating and swallowing, which made me the same. Pointing back at the corner where Pearl sat, one youth said to me: If dem try come that shop, come and burn down everything. Gotta keep 'em out—boom-boom-boom! —*Why the black man cannot live together?* Philip soliloquized in anguish. —Metal sidings sported the occasional bullet hole, although I could not honestly say that this zone was as much weapon-devastated as simply neglected— well, mashed up, too, by sledgehammers and such, but the borderscape was merely ugly and sad, not hellish. Past the Seventh-Day Adventist church we transected hot squares of naked lifelessness, then arrived at the weedy ruins into which we all dropped, cautiously upraising our heads like prairie dogs. —You are a brave man, someone told me, which made me feel even less brave, but out of inertia and egotism I accompanied them over the wall, hearing one boy mutter: Very dangerous!—and now those black bodies were running through the weeds, and no one shot at us, and we came into Rose Town where they had me photograph a crazed old lady for proof that we'd done the dare; another woman, in youngish middle age, spoke with me civilly for a moment, but between her and the Rema crew no words were exchanged. They leaped back up over the wall, but I, feeling fat and old, had to run around it. No one shot at us. But Philip's question continued to roar as loudly as any gun.

Statement of Monsignor Richard Albert (continued)

Now, this is Mandela Terrace, the priest interrupted himself, pointing out another fine part of garrison Kingston, ugly like Colin's scarred gashes from an assailant's cane-bill—a hot and spread-out city it was, with high curving walls topped with fences or barbed wire or concertina wire. —These people living along the road are like refugees, he said. The government put the road in; I put the water in. And this is one of my centers: Saint Margaret's.

A gate was unlocked and opened, and people came running, crying: Yes, Father, Father!

How's the neighborhood? he asked the boy with the scarred arm. How's the kid? Everything quiet?

Yeah, mon! So far, so good! Both his brothers were murdered by the police right inside the house, the priest said to me.

With or without cause?

Without cause.

This is Tower Hill, he said. Half JLP, half PNP. During election time, I'm the only one who can move about, he said, in the same matter-of-fact way that Pearline could tell me how one of her friends, pregnant, had worked in the cane fields until the hot sun made her miscarry, got out of the hospital, went back to the cane fields, and worked until she hemorrhaged again—because people did whatever they had to do, or thought they had to do, and who knew the difference?

We drove on. —This is where I lived, he said to me, and from the crowd of well-wishers and assistants, whose hands he shook through the rolled-down window, he singled out the priest who had succeeded him here. —This is a different Jesus, he was saying, pointing to a fresco. I got some beautiful things in Rome. A black Jesus, a black Madonna and child . . . Yeah, that's great. What'd he charge you for that?

Eighty thousand, said the new priest.

Too high, said Monsignor Albert.

I thought it was reasonable.

No. That's too much. And I'll tell him he's got to do a free one for me.

Both men laughed, one heartily, the other a little nervously.

He did my Baptism of Jesus for six thousand, Monsignor Albert continued.

The priest grinned anxiously. I suspected that Monsignor Albert might not always be an easy boss.

Things quiet?

Last week they burned up somebody. A thief.

All right, said Monsignor Albert, shaking hands, asking: You still working? At the supermarket? You havin' fun? All right. Good. Fine. How's it going? I want to see your kid's report.

He hugged and kissed.

We drove out, and they locked the gate behind us.

This is the school wall, he said. I put a lot of sayings from the Bible on it, as you can see.

YOU SHALL NOT KILL, I read.

Anyone else, they would have crossed them out, the priest mumbled around his cigar. They used to throw dead bodies over my wall at night. It was pretty rough. I still don't go out alone. Say I had a flat tire . . . Now, this is the house that the Don, Willie Moscow, built for his mother. He never stopped anything I did.

Stretching his hand across the vista of shacks, he said: This is where Jesus Himself was.

You know, I grew up in the Bronx, he went on after a moment. I saw some tough stuff but I really wasn't exposed to it at all. I was trained to be a university chaplain but in 1975 I flunked my exams. So I had to go back to the monastery and study again, and by then the position was filled. Then when I did pass the exams, my superiors said go to Jamaica. I said you're crazy; I never worked with minorities; I don't want to do that; I said no. My superior tried to convince me and I said no. But on the subway car going home, it hit me that in giving you receive, in dying you're born. So here I am. When I got off the train I called him and said: Okay, I'll go.

I was overwhelmed by the suffering, but I was young and enthusiastic, and I dug in. I learned not only to offer spiritual consolation but also to remember that Christ lived among the poor. After Saint Catherine, where I set up the only leprosy hospital in Jamaica, I went to Kingston, and I've been there for fifteen years. I've lived through all the death threats, all the gunshots, all the abuse. The majority of the people love me, because I want nothing from them except their prayers. A guy had threatened to kill me; he's since dead. Satan the gangster came to me, very grateful for some help I had given him, and offered to take the man out. I said I was very grateful but let God take care of it.

Now this is Seaview Gardens, he said. The Don asked for thirty thousand dollars U.S. to allow us to build. We told him no. And here it is.

Rolling down the window, he let out air conditioning and cigar smoke, let in greetings, asking all the young men who came running up: Are you workin'?

Yeah, mon.

Quiet around here?

Uh-huh.

He slapped shoulders. —All right.

Have you gotten lots of people jobs? I asked.

Two and a half thousand kids a year go through our placement program, he said. At least thousands have been placed in employment. I'm not into handouts. I'm not into charity. I don't want anyone dependent on me.

Being Present

The Saint Patrick's Foundation, which Richard Albert headed, got to spend three hundred thousand U.S. dollars every budget year. Down on

Hanna Town, Saint Anne's Church had a little money for its school, but almost nothing to give for wages, so Pearline was less impressed with that organization. But what people like grey-haired, blue-scarfed Sister Beverly, who worried about rape and who had been bitten by gangsters' dogs so badly that she'd been hospitalized, could offer the desperate was themselves, their lives, their listening and witnessing.

I feel that I am part of the community down here, Sister Beverly said. I'm really happy down here. I think it's a privilege. It's like a dream of my life. I grew up feeling like I wanted to be a nurse, so I could help when people are hurt.

What's the greatest help that religion can provide in a violent community? I asked.

To help people be friends with one another and to be friends with other religions, replied Sister Beverly. God is the one who is mighty, not me. Let's be humble before God and recognize each other as brothers and sisters.

Her superior, Father Linden, was obviously gifted by the same sort of commitment as Sister Beverly; and as a result of his close, observant living, he perceived several weak links in the chain of influences that led people to violence.

The first link is obviously the individual, he said. All ministers see someone who they know is getting gangish. By the age of eight or nine, you may be asked to carry a gun inside a cooler. The next link, the next weak point, is working with the politicians. If word goes out that they don't want shootings, maybe the gangs will fear the loss of patronage. It's not the rule of life, but you just do it. The other area where it can be done is to address unemployment.

I guess that's Monsignor Albert's strategy.

Right, he said, although that's another kind of patronage.

Small Successes and Apparent Failures

Sister Beverly with her projects—helping teen-dyers make dolls to sell at the Devon House, establishing town meetings and dances; Deacon Patterson with his slow promenades past gangster-owned doorways; Father Linden with his excellence in talking and listening (of all the divines I met in Kingston he pleased me the most, thanks in equal measure to his wide, large-spectacled face and his cheerfully tolerant intellectualism), Miss Lorna down at Operation Restoration Centre in Rema, exuding gruff love and business; the two churches that helped her, with their hutch full of white chicks, maybe sixty of the cheeping little things on a Rema street; Reverend Steigerwald with his unnerving mix of compassion and doctrinal determination; Monsignor Albert with his learning centers; Junior Rowe with his twenty-two years of schoolmastering on a garbage dump; were they doing enough, or the right things, or the *appropriate* things?

Consider Junior Rowe and Monsignor Albert together, where at Riverton somewhere between four and five thousand people lived on or beside that garbage dump, and a Jamaican flag flew over greasy gravel in possession of a swing set without swings. A blue and white concrete building called itself CHRIST THE REDEEMER EARLY EDUCATION CENTER. Naked little kids rolled themselves on barrels; other kids kicked, laughed and stretched. That was on the midterm Monday holiday. A day or two before, when school was in session, Monsignor Albert had entered and the children had rushed around him and he'd taken them into his arms. All around crouched low shacks and dirt streets that were sometimes walled with scavenged sheet metal.

It wasn't like this, said Mr. Rowe, who was that center's director. We had a wooden structure. When Monsignor Albert came, we tore that down and built this with the assistance of United Way and some business groups. —When Pearline and I wandered into a soft drink stand that offered us a locked grate and flooring of stinking cardboard on which flies crawled, we met one of the men who had been hired to build it. He loved Monsignor Albert, said that constructing the school had been one of the best jobs he ever got. His cigar-smoking patron had, of course, no plans for resting on any laurels. The center must expand. When the van rolled past an idling bulldozer, the window shot down, the cigar came out of the mouth, and Monsignor Albert cried: Lord God, man, what's happening? Why isn't it moving? What's wrong with ———? I was hoping this would all have been done . . . Awright. Call me.

He give all kind of help, said an old woman who dwelled in the stench of garbage. He give me a house. And he help me and help my son. And he look out for him. All these houses down here is Father house. Her affectionate encomium moved me. Monsignor Albert had done good. And how much should it matter that the tiny concrete cubes he'd commissioned were not exactly up to the standard of my quarters, or of Monsignor Albert's? —They're good compared to what they had before, said Mr. Rowe, who estimated that each one had cost one hundred and forty thousand dollars. When I asked him to tell me one of his success stories, Mr. Rowe replied:

Recently, I gave twenty people recommendations for jobs. They all got jobs—security jobs and fast-food jobs. So they came to say: I'm doin' well. I was so happy.

Well, twenty people, out of five thousand or five billion it didn't really matter, was probably more than the number I myself had ever helped. And the soup kitchen fed fifty of the worst cases every day. And the others? Well, they weren't starving, as far as I could tell. But did I want to spend my life at Riverton? And what about the people in Rema? (The religious doan like us so much, said a security man there. Get timid. Even Father Albert come years ago, get timid.) Monsignor Albert simply could not be everywhere. —You have to live with a lot of apparent failures, Father Linden had said. I remembered those words at Riverton. Monsignor Albert had been there for fifteen years, and Mr. Rowe for twenty-two. —Father has changed people, said the old woman's son. People feel like if a white man can come down to our level, then why not change? —We used to use coal, said the school cook, but Father Albert give us gas so it much quicker . . .

What would Riverton be like today without the Saint Patrick's Foundation? I asked.

Monsignor Albert was about to leave for Washington and then Grenada. He sat cross-legged, swiveling a fat cigar in his mouth, his round face aimed down at something he was proofreading, then looked up at me and said: Well, I know that we've made a genuine difference, because kids are getting educated that would not have gotten educated. When I first went there fifteen years ago, we had a little girl who had never been to school. I put her through school. She's now twenty-four, about to graduate from the University of North Carolina, and plans to come back and work in the Jamaican tourist industry. We spend forty thousand dollars a year paying school bills, buying some books . . .

What's your idea of how Riverton will look ten years from now?

Well, I would hope that they would each have a house. I would hope that the kids would have an education.

A fine goal, I thought—but still only a goal. Meager results: that's life. Not to be deterred by meager results: that's a kind of nobility: steadily scrubbing a bloodstain or two off the sidewalk.

My Neighborhood, My Nation

Up here was PNP; down here was JLP, a Jungletown man said, raising his beer and clinking it against the beer of his Rema friend. —But it change now. We not supposed to unite. We supposed to be killing each other.

Rema and Jungletown, Rema and Jonestown people could mingle; I grant you that. But these were exceptions. The garrison communities continued to guard their frontiers. Pearline and I could go almost where we chose, and so, as she said, could Dawn Ritch, because we three were not Rema people or Tivoli Gardens people or whatever; Sister Beverly could go to Tivoli even though she lived in Hanna Town, because she was, as they used to say about the religious, "not of this world." But the Rema people tended to stay in the Rema tenements with their laundry hanging out to dry, their subworlds partitioned by zinc siding. They could go past the strange pale yellow ruins of the Ambassador Theatre and be in Jonestown, and thence uptown or even out of Kingston, but what about the other three directions at home? —When I asked Colin whether Rema could ever reunite with Tivoli, he replied: Too much people dead already. We are turn a new page. Cannot *force* dem in Rema to live Sodom way. Dem *force* us live in certain things, but Trenchtown is *ours,* sir. Dem want take our glory and magnify.

Fair enough; I've expressed Colin's point, probably too many times. (Christianity continues to challenge people to live respecting their neighbors, said Monsignor Albert.) Now for the other side. —People's vibes now are more positive than negative, Colin also said, and I think he was right. (Of course he couldn't stop there, and added: The negative vibes we get is just from Tivoli Garden.)

What do you most want? I asked the lady on the sidewalk.

Job.

What kind?

Dressmaker's.

Anything else you want?

Me want to see tourist in de community, and me want cut down dey violence 'cause it keep us apart. *The community itself is at peace.*

That wasn't what the police would say; and throughout this survey I have been using the word "peace" in an ironic way, but when I wean myself away from my irony I find that the word can almost stand. Gunshots every night, yes, but the Rema people weren't shooting each other (at least most of the time). Pearline and I were welcome around the rubbish fires; we greeted and were greeted by the ladies in curlers who were leaning on their machetes, cleaning up for Labour Day; we found tranquility in sitting out on a second-story concrete railing among the big-shouldered black boys who were reading *Guns and Ammo*, while the radio was saying at that very moment that somebody had just gotten shot by four gunmen in Norman Gardens; and a barefooted, thick-legged, busty, pretty young woman cradled a baseball, calling to her boyfriend, who was one of the security men, and then she literally danced down the street to find him, down that street of PNP and old JLP slogans, of paintings on walls, goats on littered grass. Evening, and peering down from the high steps into the zinc-walled zones of personal life, I could see dark naked boys pouring bucketloads of water over themselves, or men close together beneath a white cloud of ganja smoke, or women sitting in the light of open doorways. Old people came out of their houses for the first time since early morning. As darkness fell, the place became emotionally warmer in inverse proportion to the physical temperature, more intimate, somehow, beneath the peaceful dark humidity of the occasional banana tree; jazz played on the radio, and children called to their mothers; girls were laughing; stars came shimmeringly into the pale blue sky, while light oozed out from between stairs. —Blessed! Colin bade farewell to his friends, raising two fingers, out of habit, in the old JLP sign. I would have thought it was the peace sign. (JLP was the bell, PNP was the head, explained Pearl. Those were their symbols.) Now it was night. On the dark blasted concrete plain of Concrete Jungle, the watchers stood watching, still and wary. This place had the feel of unfriendly territory. When Pearline and I walked up there to buy our dinner through a cautious woman's door grate (roast pork for her and for me some of the best roast chicken I ever had), Colin felt obliged to come with us, holding my hand. We were happy to get back to Rema, where we felt safer among the now well-known murmuring of water taps and of street-loungers, rival boom boxes, some painted with iconographic pistols, meaninglessly glowing walls, silhouetted heads beneath the rare trees. On the way to Jungletown it seemed as if one could see farther away than one really could, because there was no traffic and one can spy people's silhouettes waiting and clustering on the road, as if some drama were about to happen. And there many of them remained, sentinels, until it began to get light at five in the morning, clouds of mosquitoes inside, bodies oozing sweat in the beds, smoke from rubbish fires seeping through the open windows to make people cough and wipe their eyes. By seven the asphalt and concrete plains were getting hot, and new silhouettes stood on the sidewalks, and the open sewer running down the street had begun to stink again while a boy who sported an upside-down backward sunshade and incipient dreadlocks like caterpillar heads erupting from his skull nodded to radio music from within a taxicab parked on the sidewalk with all four doors open; and on that day, the twenty-seventh of May 1997, while the taxi's radio announced that the fourteenth taxi driver of the year had just been killed by gunmen, ghetto women were already washing clothes, a line of young men were taking turns shaving outside, with one electric razor plugged into a storefront, each shaver holding up a mirror while he did it. I wanted to take a photo, and they all refused. —I scared dem camera, a man growled. Watch yeah face, boys!

What's yeah motive? another man once asked me then.

Ill prepared (he wanted a word, but I needed a paragraph), I returned: What's yours?

He said: *For us.*

And yet, this transcendent usness of theirs, pleasing, protective, and even inspirational though it surely was, scarcely hindered them, as I thought, from being violent to each other. —In the ghetto, when a man sees the next man get ahead, instead of applaudin', he wants to pull him back, said Reverend Bobby, shaking his head. You have to be willin' to help de next one of your brethren to rise up. —Deacon Espeut in his denunciation of what he (and also the superintendent at the Rema police station) had plausibly called "the culture of violence" had argued that the evil began at home. —Jamaican parents beat their children, he said. Often mercilessly. You walk and you hear: *Bam, bam, bam!* Do you agree? he asked Pearl, who nodded with a grin. Pearline, after all, was the one who bore on her arm a thick red angry scar that her stepfather had made with a pot lid when she was a baby. He hadn't let her mother take her to the hospital because he might have gotten in trouble. The earliest thing that Pearl could remember was being sent to her auntie's house for a month or two at a time because her stepfather hated her for not being his. He was always telling her: You doan belong here. —So Pearl grew up calling her auntie Mama and calling her mother Auntie. —I like your niece, I said to her, and she replied: Oh, dem all fine when me around. When me no around, dem talk different, I sure . . . —But at least her family never pretended, as far as I could see, that they were "for us." —Lick him down! I heard early one Rema dawn, and Pearl pointed. I saw a man punching a woman to the ground. The man was the woman's child. Sobbing, the woman stood up and went to the police station. When I mentioned the incident to Colin, carefully, so as to avoid launching one of his easy rages, he replied wisely:

Man doan own any of dem Rema girls. They just stay till you doan have more to give 'em, den dey go another guy. But to hit a mother, of course it's too bad, mon . . . —and I realized anew that my trying even to mention such things was as useless as trying to turn on the water taps in the daytime in Rema—although Colin, I am happy to say, had attacked a man who'd hit one of his daughters, and he bore cane-hook scars on his face to prove it. Over in Hanna Town, Sister Beverly told me about a mother she'd just met who'd branded her baby with a red-hot iron. I asked her how she planned to proceed with that one and she said: I'm sort of relating to her first. —That was probably the best way, the only way, the slow way. At Pearl's auntie's house way out in the country, where people were certainly friendlier and laughed more, I saw one of Pearl's nephews, eighteen, a pleasant, churchgoing boy who loved to draw pictures of Jesus in his Bible, strike his six-year-old sister down to the floor after she had poked him with her little finger, and no one said a word as she lay there wailing. When Pearl and I were outside under the mango tree, I asked: Why does he have to hit her so hard? and Pearl, who always had all the answers, replied: Maybe he doan like her, because not from the same father. Only mother same. I think same mother is stronger bond, she added bitterly, surely thinking of herself, but maybe he doan think so . . .

(What was the natural result of such treatment? On a hot afternoon in Rema, Miss Lorna said to me: One eight-year-old girl, her father got killed right in the cemetery, and she was in a rage; she wanted a gun to kill the murderer. I hear he's a dead man. Such a rage from her mother's womb!)

Pearline's idea of heaven was a three-bedroom concrete house like her auntie's, which at age forty-two she was no closer whatsoever to affording. So her fallback plan was to leave Jamaica forever, and find a healthier economy. —I remembered Dawn Ritch telling me: In general, social spending is down. This is how the government has balanced its budget. —I remembered a ragged Riverton youth pleading: Father, gimme a start, and Monsignor Albert peered out at him from the down-rolled window of his van and said: Paul, if you come up to Stella Maris I'll be happy to help. —I never give money, he said to me over and over. I give a job. A job liberates a man. Jesus was about liberating men. —All Pearl wanted, like Paul, was a start, not charity. And she could not get it. Her sister had inherited a sewing machine from a lady who never returned home, and when I asked the reason for her permanent absence Pearline replied dryly: Nobody want to come to Jamaica, if dey can get away. —For just this reason, Pearline had gone illegally to Curaçao, where she dwelled silently and desperately until she was deported. Her stereo, blender, television, the bicycle for her son, and all the other possessions she'd gained from her sweat, from cleaning Dutch people's houses, the immaculate houses of people who despised her and sometimes refused to pay her—all were confiscated by the police, who caged Pearline, gave her only a vague and useless receipt for her things, and then expelled her from the country. —People lose dem thing like me and become violent, she said.

Are you violent?

Not yet. Maybe someday, she steadily replied.

So there was more than one path into the Pit. I wondered: Is there something in humanity equivalent to the swarming impulse in ant colonies, a drive toward subdivision and exclusion? War was the norm for the ancient Greek city-states. War of sorts was the norm in Kingston's garrison communities. Or had the "normal" social element, whatever it was, simply been degraded (mashed up, I should say), into a mess of mutually repulsive atoms? In Kingston, even uptown, whenever I, walking alone, met a stranger, or, worse, a cluster of strangers, I had to prepare myself for insistent begging, discourtesy and threats. (For that matter, whenever I met someone new in Rema and asked how he or she was, the answer would usually be: Not as good as you! Buy me cigarettes! Buy me a cold juice!) The fact that these unpleasantnesses did not always occur was offset by the fact that they *did* occur often enough. Once when I was uptown I went out to buy some cold carrot juice for Pearline, who was feeling hot and weary; and almost immediately a man bicycled up to me and, assuring me that he was neither a beggar nor a thief, commenced to beg. The thieving part came when I offered him some coins. He unwrapped a machete and shouted: No coins! Give me paper! —For the sake of my own self-respect, I told him that I didn't want to give him paper, but that he could still have the coins. —Well, he finally grumpily said, it's enough for cigarettes. Without thanks he took the silver coins out of my hand and left me the almost worthless coppers. Then he rode off. I came to the juice place, where the man charged me double. I returned, meeting another beggar. —My white skin did render me a target, but the anger of Kingston could be turned on anyone. Whenever I shared taxis with people, I was saddened by their mutual unfriendliness—no greetings, pushings and shovings over room, occasional nasty words, no goodbyes. A few days after my meeting with the bicyclist, Pearl and I were eating patties at Halfway Tree when we saw one man stab another right outside, and the policeman soon appeared to arrest the stabbed man, who was bleeding from neck and face, like Philip had, I suppose, when he got his wounds; and a crowd began to shout and raise their fists, but already the policeman and his prisoner were gone, and so the scene was over. (I think the whole country is going to blow, Monsignor Albert said. —About the upcoming elections he said simply: I fear the worst.) Pearl most bitterly insisted: It'll come out to the country, too. In the last election, the violence came out there, because all the city people came out thievin' and killin' . . . —In Kingston, while I wasn't exactly afraid, I found myself becoming wary whenever someone I didn't know drew near. Dawn Ritch had assured me that she could walk anywhere she chose, provided that she took off her gold chain. And it was true that whenever Pearl kept me company my annoyances were vastly reduced; her black presence legitimized me in Rema, or maybe just made me appear less alone. But Pearl herself dreaded Rema, and never got over that dread. I think I was more comfortable there than she was. Colin and Philip and their friends knew us and looked out for us; but some of our protectors had red eyes, which Pearl considered to me a mark of sin, so I tried always to stay in her sight, for her sake and for mine, preferably holding her hand. —Canna trust any of them, she muttered, and she *liked* Colin and Philip. What she was most afraid of, as it transpired, was not so much the possibility that someone in Rema would turn on us as the chance of receiving a bullet earmarked from or for Tivoli Gardens.

But certainly there were paths out of the Pit, too. One hot grim evening I returned to that roofless polygon, the Ambassador Theatre, whose high shell concealed much of the damage, which was visible only when you entered, stepping between lumps and pats of human excrement: rubble above all, but also stripped ribs and stalls that reminded me of the ruins of Roman baths; and outside the Ambassador I met a fiftyish lady who said: The concrete is not damaged. Dem can fix it up good. —Deacon Espeut and Reverend Bobby and the others were always talking about giving hope to the garrison communities, but this lady already had it. Colin had it, too; his fond delusion was that I would write an article promoting tourism in Rema: Bob Marley was from Trenchtown, after all; wouldn't reggae fans want to come see his house? And maybe he was not so far wrong. I had come to love being in Rema; I really had. Pearline still dreaded the place; but the friendliness and energy of it (the nighttime carnival energy of competing radios and boom boxes) always gave *me* a kind of hope.

When I saw the kids slowly working with machetes and rakes on the barren grounds of Miss Lorna's school, moving rubbish for Labour Day, I felt hope, even as a jeep full of soldiers rolled by, and one soldier grinningly aimed his machine gun at the kids. Some of the American ghettos I had visited seemed far more damaged by anger than Rema, and more unsafe, too; Rema struck me as merely *formerly and potentially* dangerous. But the war with Tivoli Gardens went on, and they were resigned to it. —Dem's a different set, mon, said the hopeful lady. Shoot you up for nothing. Kill so many people all the time . . . —and she turned and pointed across the rise and the vacant border field toward Board Villa and Tivoli. The next morning I met a fellow eighteen or nineteen years old whose father and brother had both been killed by Tivoli gunmen within the space of forty-eight hours. (Dem are the WICKED ONES, he cried, See 'em bullet holes in the zinc up dere this side?) He took me to the borderline and dared me closer and closer while Pearline watched aghast, then pointed back to the window of an apartment where, he said, eight people had been murdered by Tivoli on May 8, 1984. That was long before the present war with Tivoli, of course, and when he showed me a hole blasted in another apartment and said that Tivoli had done it. I wondered if that was true, and if so, under what circumstances: Why did this professional victim's friend keep clicking and unclicking his switchblade at me, and why did the others not want their photographs taken? (We one big family. We doan like de photo, mon.) They weren't a crew, they assured me; they were just "sportsmen." Day after day I'd seen them lounging near the borderline, watching, protecting Rema. The knife-clicker said: Seaga, we doan want him to be our godfather no more. (Not many blocks away, the superintendent of police wryly told me: They say, you take our guns, but are you going to protect us?) They terrified Pearline, who implored me never to go near them again. But I gave them a thousand Jamaican dollars and rendered them harmless . . .

What yeah name, mon? the knife-clicker had said to Pearl when I was at the border.

Pearl. What yeah name?

Shootah. Just Shootah. What yeah full name?

Why you doan tell me yeah full name? asked Pearl very reasonably. If you just Shootah then me just Pearl.

Pearl knew how to deal with them. But she was still afraid.

You're taking your life in your hands sleeping here, said a teacher at

Miss Lorna's school, and when I laughingly repeated the remark to Colin, to show him how unafraid I was, he flew into a rage and told everybody and soon the women on the streets were howling that that teacher was "a Judas in plain clothes." (A lot of these guys are short-tempered because of a lack of education, which impairs reasoning ability, Reverend Bobby had said. You and me, we can agree to disagree. Politicians spoil them, because a man can get money without working. They don't have to know anything. You cannot agree to disagree with them. If you try, they say you're dissing them. I want to get them to see the senselessness of killing one another.)

At the Tuesday night dance the singers cried: *Rema! Rema! Rema!* and in abundance one heard readers from Ecclesiastes. A song attacked Seaga; an orator cried: I realize the politicians mash up our land! and at good parts of this speech, watched again and again on video by Colin's crew, some youths banged and boomed on the school desks with earsplitting enthusiasm. People swayed and clapped as at church. *Rema, Rema!* —The people in Jamaica have an inner joy you won't see in America, Monsignor Albert had asserted, and maybe this was a case in point; this was civic pride good and bad, the expression of people who would not give up on their neighborhood—and of violent defenders pounding the last nail deeper into the coffin of urban unity. This was neighborhood nationalism.

Well, this looks like a fine place, I said when I first got to Rema.

No! the little kids giggled.

Well, why's that?

Guns!

But I prefer not to end on that note. I prefer to remember Colin giving up his bed for me, and Philip the cook at Miss Lorna's, who always wanted to make lunch for Pearl and me, and whose neck and belly with scars from a stabbing (one of his assailants had been caught and went to court)—Philip my friend, who said he loved me; I prefer to remember coming downstairs out of Colin's flat early one Monday morning, with kids bouncing basketballs, shading their eyes, and a "sportsman" shouting at me: *Love the place, mon! Rema's the best, mon!*

Annotated Table of Contents to the Unabridged Edition

VOLUME II

Justifications

Justifications, Section One: Self-Defense

one's own homeland's futurity; Hitler and Lebensraum; Stalingrad changes hands; Leonidas's inexpedient nobility at Thermopylae.

VOLUME IV

JUSTIFICATIONS, SECTION TWO: POLICY AND CHOICE

EVALUATIONS

*{From a strictly logical point of view the Moral Calculus should go here. It is
comprised of extractions from the various "theoretical" chapters in volumes 1–4.
On the other hand, to save the budget of both publisher and reader, it has been
found necessary to bundle the calculus itself with the annexes and other end-
matter. My editor proposes that you consider it a "resource volume," which can
go anywhere or nowhere. —WTV}*

VOLUME V

PART II: STUDIES IN CONSEQUENCES (1991–2003)

SOUTHEAST ASIA (1991–2001)

*   *   *

List of Continua

    I. When is class stratification justified?

    II. When is forcible redistribution in the service of equality
justified?

List of Charts, Maps and Figures

Definitions for Lonely Atoms

Justifications: Self-Defense

Acknowledgments

So many people have done so many things for me and this book that if I detailed all the services, favors, jobs, etc., another volume might be required. As it is, I hope my gratitude comes through in the preceding text.

I would like to thank all my unnamed drivers, defectors, guides, pimps, prostitutes, psychics and translators—although I certainly did pay them. I also wish to thank the following: My friend and interpreter Mr. Abdi of Mogadishu, Somalia, Mr. Abdoolcarim in Sana'a, Yemen, Major John Abrant in Nome, Alaska, and his children Hallie and Dean; Ms. Kate Addiego of *McSweeney's;* the man in Abyan City, Yemen, who said to me: "Allah help you!", Ahmed in Yemen, Mr. Akbar in Afghanistan, Monsignor Richard Albert of Saint Patrick's Foundation in Kingston, Jamaica; Alex, who was the queen of the Queer Street Patrol; Mr. Mohammed Nagi Allawo, chairman of the HOOD human rights organization in Sana'a, Yemen; Arguriana in Kosovo, Mr. Anwar in Yemen, Imam Abdullah al-Aqa in Sana', Yemen; Mr. Rabih Aridi of Amnesty International in the U.S., various unnamed members of the Autodefense Union of Colombia, Mr. Awad in Aden, Yemen; Mr. Don Baldwin in Seattle, Ms. Haley Ball of *McSweeney's,* Mr. Safet Bandzovic, President of the Sanjak Committee for Protection of Human Rights and Freedoms (Novi Pazar, Yugoslavia); Mr. Jay Barmann of *McSweeney's;* Dr. Basri in Yemen, Mr. Red Beckman from Montana, Sister Beverly in Hanna Town, Kingston, Jamaica; Mr. and Mrs. John and Ann V. Bible, Group Leader Tim Bishop of the Aryan Nations, the dominatrix Beatrice Black, Mr. Will Blythe of *Esquire* magazine; Ms. Carla Bolte, my designer at Viking, who was sweet enough to give this project some help on her own time; Mr. Bonwut of the Ministry of Foreign Affairs in Phnom Penh,

Ms. Amel Boussoualim, Branka in Beograd, Ms. Susan Brenneman, Executive Editor of the *Los Angeles Times Magazine;* the late Will Brinton, Ms. Moira Brown, Mr. Ewen Buchanan, then in New York, of the United Nations Special Committee on Iraq (UNSCOM), several anonymous members of the Buraku Liberation League in Osaka, Mr. Ben Bush of *McSweeney's,* who made a number of long, hot scanning trips to my house; Richard Butler, then Chairman of UNSCOM, Pastor Richard Butler of the Church of Jesus Christ Christian (Aryan Nations), Mr. Ernesto Calderon, self-styled King of the Cartucho in Bogotá, Colombia (he deserves to be stuffed and mounted as the epitome of a menacing, disgusting individual); the villagers of Campo Dos, Colombia; Ms. Martha Carvajal and Mr. Pedro Betoncourt in Bogotá, Colombia, Major General Nils Carlström, who was then UNSCOM's director of monitoring and verification in Baghdad; Mr. Ralph Carter in Houston (who by the way was the happiest concealed carry instructor I ever met); Mr. Ray Carter, founder of the gays-with-guns Seattle organization Cease Fear, Mr. Mike Casados in Houston, Prof. Agim Çavardasha of Pristina, Kosovo; "Mr. China" in south Thailand, Mr. Sei Chong of *McSweeney's,* Chris in Seattle, the U.S.S. *Cole* detainees in Sana'a, Yemen; Colin in Rema, Kingston, Jamaica; the people who shared with me their painful memories of the Columbine Massacre, the "Special Services" cadres of Convivir in Currulao, Colombia; the Cost of Freedom antinuclear affinity group in Ithaca, New York, and Seabrook, New Hampshire; the Crazy Ruthless Kings tagger gang in Long Beach, several officials of the Criminal Justice Unit of the FBI, Ms. Madeleine Crowley in Seattle; Mr. Jim Cuff in Houston, Ms. Chheng Cuoch, who was my Khmer interpreter in Long Beach; D. (immeasurably); Ms. Kate Danaher, my vegetarian shooting partner; Diana in Colombia, Mr. Jacob Dickinson of Long Beach, Dina in Zagreb, Mr. Matt Dorville of *McSweeney's;* Mr. Dave Eggers of *McSweeney's,* who was kind enough to approach me after one of my readings and express interest in publishing a book which otherwise never might have gotten published; Mr. Brad Edmondson of *American Demographics,* Deacon Peter Espeut in Kingston, Jamaica; Pastor Joe Esposito at the Cambodian Baptist Church in Long Beach, California, Mr. Eric Falt, spokesman for the Office of the Humanitarian Coordinator for Iraq, Mr. Farras in Iraq, Mr. Feisal in Aden, Yemen, Mr. Max Fenton of *McSweeney's,* Ms. LeighAnne Fitzpatrick of SPIN magazine, Mr. Nathan Bedford Forrest in New Orleans, Mr. Bob Fletcher of the Milita of Montana, my bitter, brave, lecherous, belligerent, thieving, cocaine-addicted Congolese interpreter and friend, Mr. Franck, Mr. Jonathan Franzen, friend and debater; Mr. Matthew Frassica of *McSweeney's;* Mr. Joel Freeman, who told me about Norbert Elias; Ms. Mieko Fujioka, secretary at IMADR in Tokyo, Mrs. Fatana Isaq Gailani in Peshawar, Mr. Steve Gardiner of the Coalition for Human Dignity in Portland, Oregon; Gladys in the slum town of Ciudad Bolívar near Bogotá, Colombia; Mr. David "Militia" Golden, networker extraordinaire; his wife, Mrs. Keiko Golden, who translated a number of Japanese documents for this book; the courageous individuals in Goma, Democratic Republic of Congo, who told me certain truths at great risk to themselves, Mr. Craig Graham, who gave me Artyom Borovik's book, has gone shooting with me many times, and appears in the photo portfolios; the passionately sincere Ms. Lizzy Gray, animal rights activist; Gremlin in Stockton, California, Colonel James "Bo" Gritz of Sandy Valley, Nevada, and of Almost Heaven in Kamiah, Idaho; his then-wife Claudia, who was always very fair and gracious with me; Mr. Richard Grossman, who introduced me to *The Blue Cliff Record,* the Guardian Angels, Mr. Bob Guccione Jr., first of SPIN magazine, then of *Gear* (he owes me money, but was always generous with it when he had it; furthermore, he sent me to any number of interesting places—this book's case studies owe more to him than to anybody else—and he even published my views, with which he frequently utterly disagreed); Mr. Carvilio Guzman, who was displaced from Brisas, Colombia; Ms. Vesna Hadzivukovic at the Southeast Centre for Geopolitical Studies in Beograd; Mr. William Haines, who was then a philosophy student at Cornell; Mrs. Naur Salem al-Hakemi in Sana'a, Yemen; Mr. Rashid ul Haq of Darul Uloom Haqqania *madrassa* in Akora Khattak, Pakistan; Prof. Robert Harbison in London, for his friendship, constructive disagreement, whiskey and crisps (he will hate this book); Mr. Ben Hedstrom of *McSweeney's,* for especially persistent fact-checking in a number of areas; Mr. High Tech in Pony, Montana; Ms. Marlene Hines of the Montana Human Rights Network, Ms. Vahida Hodic in Sarajevo, Italy of the Guardian Angels, Mr. Eli Horowitz of *McSweeney's,* who worked intelligently and sincerely to improve this book, especially the moral calculus—he lost some arguments with good grace and he won some arguments with good grace; Mr. Andro Hsu of *McSweeney's*; Sergeant Jim Hughes of the Stockton Police Gang Violence Suppression Unit; the Hughes family in Teller, Alaska; Mr. Sarwar Hussaini, Executive Director of the Peshawar-based Cooperation Centre for Afghanistan, Mr. Hussein in Yemen, various doctors, nurses and patients in Saddam Hussein Hospital in Baghdad; Mr. Takahiko Inoue of the Inagawa Yakuza, the sinister Monsieur J. in Kinshasha, who taught me even more than I was hoping to know about police corruption, Mr. Sura Jirampaikal, Thai ruby deaker; Mr. Mark Johnson, who sent me (a piece of) the *Plain Dealer*'s article on baseball bats as Polish murder weapons; certain anonymous people in Kabul who trusted me with their anti-Taliban stories, and especially "the brave girl," Mr. Ken-ichi Kadooka of the Buraku Liberation League in Osaka, Ms. Sarah Kakaruk in Teller, Alaska, Detective Jim Kang of the Sacramento Gang Violence Unit, various unnamed members of the Karenni Liberation Army; my dear friend and interpreter Mrs. Takako Kawai in Tokyo; the Kentfield Crips and affiliates in Stockton, California, Khunying Khanitta, founder and proprietress of We Train Guest House in Thailand; Khun Sa, the "Opium King"; Ms. Robin Kirk of Human Rights Watch in the U.S., Ms. Suzanne Kleid of *McSweeney's;* Mr. Dave Kneebone of *McSweeney's;* Ms. Mayumi Kobana, interpreter, explicator and friend, Mr. Marinko Koscecs in Croatia (he was intelligent and brave), various unnamed members of the Kosovo Liberation Army; Ms. Cindy Kumano of *McSweeney's;* Mr. Kent Lacin in Sacramento, whose perspective as a commercial photographer contributed to my chapter on Columbine; Laura in Colombia, Ms. Devorah Lauter of *McSweeney's,* who worked diligently and effectively to gather a number of images from various sources, and who also headed the scanning team; Mr. Andrew Leland of *McSweeney's;* Mr. Gideon Lewis-Kraus of *McSweeney's;* Father Michael Linden, S.J., in Rema, Kingston, Jamaica; Miss Lara Lorson, who was then with NPR's "Talk of the Nation" and who remains a friend and guide; Mr. Jia Zhen Li of Sunnyvale, California, Ms. Rose Lichter-Marck of *McSweeney's,* Miss Christine Lim, Mr. William Linne, who worked hard for not especially good wages to make so many of the beautiful prints which have been reproduced in this book; the Croatian healer Lirija and her husband; Dr. Rasim Ljajic, who was Prime Minister of the Muslim National Council of Sanzak, Yugoslavia, and General Secretary of the SDA; Mr. James M. Lombino, shooting partner, devotee of airguns, mechanical engineer and free spirit; Mr. Loth Suong in Phnom Penh, who talked more freely than I would have expected about his infamous brother; Marcos in Bogotá, Colombia, the late "parent" of the Machiya Yakuza family in Tokyo, who was very hospitable and kind (he has since been murdered by a rival gang); the Manchester Blood gang affiliates—Moonlight Strangers, Tiny Rascal Gang and Crazy Brother Clan—in Stockton, California; the men I interviewed in Maifa'a, Yemen; Ms. Madeline Martell in San Francisco and New York, Masha in Beograd, Larry and Sinda McCafferey in California, Mr. Jack McEnany, Mr. Casey McKinney of *McSweeney's;* Ms. Emily McManus of *McSweeney's,* Mr. Brian McMullen of *McSweeney's,* Mr. Hazbo Medovic, who was Vice President of the Serbian Socialist Party (SPS) in Novi Pazar, Yugoslavia; Ms. Heidi Meredith of *McSweeney's;* Mr. Sebastian Metz of the Guardian Angels, Father Joseph Michael in Apartadó, Colombia, Mr. Ken Miller, for various tips photographic and otherwise (for instance: don't bet on the horses); certain unnamed cadres of the Taliban's Ministry for the Propagation of Virtue and the Prevention of Vice in Kabul, Ms. Elizabeth Mitchell, formerly of *Spin,* then of *George* magazine, Misha in Beograd, Mr. Taylor Morris of *McSweeney's,* Mr. Bradford Morrow, eminence of *Conjunctions;* my Pakistani foster-father Major General N., Mr. Brian Neff of *McSweeney's,* whose fact-checking caught several of my most embarrassing errors, especially in the realm of Norse sagas; Ms. Kellie Nelson in Montana, Nives in Zagreb, Mr. Khaled A. Wahed Noman, who represented Canon Products in Yemen, Mr. Ethan Nowosocki of Farrar, Straus & Giroux, Mr. Mark Novak of *McSweeney's,* Mr. Ted Nugent at World Tedquarters, not to mention his family and his assistant Linda; O. in Madagascar, Miss Vanny O., Sheikh Bin Ali al-Okaimi in Sana'a, Yemen; Mr. Bengt Oldenburg in Barcelona, Mr. Walt Opie of *McSweeney's,* Mr. Owen Otto of *McSweeney's;* Paddy Boy in Hanna Town, Kingston, Jamaica; Deacon Patterson in Hanna Town, Kingston, Jamaica; Mr. Dobroslav Paraga of HOS and HSP in Zagreb, Mr. Adam Parfrey of Feral House Books, Juan and Kathleen Park in New Orleans, Mr. Richard Parks of *McSweeney's,* Mr. Ben Pax, who was the manuscript's first reader and who supplied illustrations of Cu Chi; Pearline in Jamaica, Mr. Robby Peckerar of *McSweeney's,* Mr. Warren Pederson of *McSweeney's,* Philip in Rema, Kingston, Jamaica, Mr. Seth Pilsk of Oracle, Arizona, Miss Biljana Plavsic, then Vice President and later Acting President of the Bosnian Serbs, now serving a prison sentence at The Hague; Ms. Kara Platoni of *McSweeney's* (her contacts and information for "Defense of Animals" and "Defense of Gender" greatly improved those chapters); Mr. Chunchart Poonsiri, Governor of Yala Province, Thailand; the people of Priluzje and Glavotina in Kosovo, and especially the brave doctor in Priluzje, Ms. Miriam Posner of *McSweeney's;* Mr. Garth Pritchard, then a resident of New York, with whom I frequently discussed the concept of Same Day Liberations; Mr. Michael Pulley of the *Sacramento News and Review,* various unnamed members of the Pattani Unification Liberation Organization in Thailand and Malaysia, El Raton of Medellin, Colombia; Mullah Abdul Razzaq, then the Taliban's Minister of the Interior, Ms. Vanessa Renwick, who runs the Oregon Department of Kick Ass and has kicked ass in various unseen parts of this book; Reptile in Stockton, California, Mr. Noah Richler of BBC Radio, Junior Rowe in Riverton, Jamaica, Mr. David Roberts of Resolute Bay, Northwest Territories, and his wife, Ms. Elizabeth Allakriallak, Professor Michael Ryan, for a Marxism class a long time ago, and for a suggestion about Thoreau; Ms. Dawn Ritch, newspaper columnist in Kingston, Jamaica; Ron in Montana; Mr. Gabe Roth of *McSweeney's,* for a superbly careful job of copyediting; the Russian Special Forces man in Beograd, Dr. Janice K. Ryu, for a great number of helpful offices, Mr. Carlos Salinas of the Latin American affairs department of Amnesty International in Washington, D.C.; Mr. Brenden Salmon of *McSweeny's,* San, Sara and Scarface in Stockton, California; a few kind people on the San Carlos Apache Reservation in Arizona, Monsieur Roger Samba in Kinshasha, Democratic Republic of Congo (the "special tax" he extorted from me for not quite arresting me was reasonable, the subsequent interview and photos a bargain for the money); Mr. Paul Slovak at Viking-Penguin, who has done what he could to help this book; Mr. Don Smith in Nome, Alaska; Ms. Soeun K., my Khmer interpreter in Long Beach; Mr. Nabeel A. al-Sofe of the Central Committee of Yemen's Islah opposition party, "someone of the people" in the late Serbian Republic of Krajina; Detective Norm Sørenson of the Gang Violence Suppression Unit in Long Beach, the Spanish UNPROFOR soldiers in Drasevo, Bosnia; Ms. Srey S. of Phnom Penh, the S.F. Skinz, Mr. Curtis Sliwa of the Guardian Angels, Ms. Pamela Jean Smith of *McSweeney's;* Snake of the Guardian Angels, Mr. Speed of eastern Thailand, Ms. June Spencer in Nome, Alaska; Miss Lorna Stanley, a schoolmarm in the Rema ghetto of Kingston, Jamaica; the Reverend John Steigerwald, in Rema, Kingston, Jamica; Ms. Jean Stein, who gave me many wonderful books on Sade, the Soviet Union, Plains Indians & c, and to whom I could always talk and worry about violence; Ms. Ayoka Stewart of *McSweeney's,* Mr. Jeff Stoffer of the *Townsend Star* in Montana; the inmates of the *studentski dom* in Sarajevo, Sukanja in Thailand, Dr. Gloria Suarez and her husband Carlos, both of Bogotá, Colombia; Mr. Greg Sullivan, the Deputy Director for Press Affairs at the U.S. State Department's Near Eastern Affairs Bureau, Mr. Surat Suravich in Thailand, Ms. Susan Squire in New York, Mr. Ryuma Suzuki, second in command of the Sumiyoshi Yakuza (he was one of the most unpleasant people I have ever met), Professor Scott Swanson in Indianapolis, Indiana, Sylvana in Zagreb, Mr. Adnan T. in Zagreb, Mr. Ahmed T. in Zagreb, Mr. Sharif T. in Zagreb, Teo in Split, Croatia; Mr. Tommy Thornhill of *McSweeney's,* Mr. Alan Thuma of *McSweeney's;* the late Hadji Amin Tohmeena in Thailand and Malaysia (I will always be grateful for the interview he granted me), the late Mr. Francis Tomasic, Mr. Ken Toole of the Montana Human Rights Network, Ms. Deborah Treisman, once of *Grand Street,* now of *The New Yorker,* for her intelligence and gentleness, Professor Bruce Trigger, both for continuing to inspire my work through his own, and for kindly answering a few more queries on seventeenth-century Huron Indians; Ms. Jenni Ulrich of *McSweeney's,* a certain U.S. State Department official in the Department of

South Asian Affairs; the unnamed man from Noxon, Montana; Vineta in Serbia, Ms. Sarah Vollmann, Mr. and Mrs. T. Vollmann, Ms. Vicky Walker of *McSweeney's,* Mr. Ben Westhoff of *McSweeney's* (he was very helpful with information I haven't seen before on animal liberation and environmentalism); Ms. Nitsa Whitney in New York, Ms. Esther Whitby in England, who never liked any of my longer books but who always tried to make me work harder and better, the Widowmaker Squad (motto: "Let me know if you're scared!") of the Peace Frog platoon of Charlie Company of the U.S. Marines, then in Somalia, Professor Susan Williamson in England, Mr. Paul Wilner, then editor of the *San Francisco Examiner* magazine; Ms. Alison Willmore of *McSweeney's;* Professor Robert Winzeler in Reno, Nevada; the woman who was formerly in charge of the literary programs of Radio Kabul; the Freeman Mr. John Wright in the Montana Mountains, General X. in Cambodia, Doctor Adolphe Onosomba Yemba, Ms. Jayme Yen of *McSweeney's,* President of the Rassemblement Congolais pour la Démocratie; Yhon Yhone in Thailand; Yuki in Japan; and Zhalko in Beograd. I thank these people with all my gratitude, and in some cases my friendship and love.

Appreciative acknowledgment is made to the United Nations Department of Public Information (Cartographic Section) for permission to reproduce the following maps herein: "UNPROFOR Deployment as of July 1992" (map no. 3684), "UNPROFOR Deployment as of February 1993" (map. no. 3684, rev. 2), "UNPROFOR Deployment as of March 1994" (map. no. 3684, rev. 5), "UNISOM II Deployment as of September 1993" (map no. 3805). I would especially like to thank Mr. Miklos Pinther, Chief of the Cartographic Section.

I am very grateful to the West Virginia State Archives, Boyd B. Stutler collection for permission to study and quote from facsimiles of John Brown's letters—and to Professor William Plumley, University of Charleston, who very kindly obtained specified John Brown letters for me from that source.

Anybody browsing through the footnotes to the first "theoretical" part of this book will find a preponderance of references to secondary rather than primary sources. I am very grateful to the various scholars I have cited. No matter what they may think of my use of their material, this book is often more theirs than mine.

My great thanks to Mr. Jim Gullickson, Ecco's copy-editor, and also to E. J. Van Lanen, both of whom improved this abridgment.

I would also like to thank my agent, Susan Golomb, and her associate Sabine Hrechdakian.

Permissions

PUBLICATION INFORMATION FOR THE UNABRIDGED EDITION

"The Skulls on the Shelves" was originally commissioned by *Esquire,* but they ran my piece about Cambodian whores instead. *Common Knowledge* wanted it, but they wouldn't pay anything. Parts of it later appeared in *Spin.* "Where Are All the Pretty Girls?" first appeared as a series of four BBC Radio 4 broadcasts (somewhat cut to fit) and as a *Los Angeles Times* magazine essay, severely abridged, entitled "Welcome to Hell," both in the fall of 1992. "Let Me Know If You're Scared" first appeared in 1993 in *Esquire,* mildly abridged, as "Letter from Somalia." "I'm Especially Interested in *Young* Girls" first appeared in an amputated form in *Spin* magazine in 1993. "But What Can We Do?" "The War Never Came Here" and "Nightmares, Prayers and Ecstasies" also appeared in *Spin,* in that order, in 1994–95, as "The Opium King," "It's Not a War" and something else, respectively. "Yakuza Lives," "The Avengers of Kosovo," "The Wet Man Is Not Afraid of Rain," "Guns in the USA" and "You Never Know Who Is Who" appeared in *Gear* under other titles, and fairly drastically abridged. "With Their Hands on Their Hearts" appeared in the *New Yorker* in 2000 with only about 50 percent cut—fairly decent for a magazine. Each of these has been restored to its original glory and sometimes further polished.

"The Old Man" first appeared in *McSweeney's* in 2002, unabridged.

The description of the Rajasthani daggers in the chapter "On the Aesthetics of Weapons" was published in a cut form in *Esquire* (1996) under the rubric of "My Favorite Weapon." I like the daggers very much. They are not, however, my most favorite weapons. I cashed the check.

The chapter on moral yellowness first appeared in *Conjunctions* in 1998. An abridgment of the chapter on "Defense of Ground" was published in the same journal in 2001.

My visit to the San Francisco County Medical Examiner's office was arranged by the *San Francisco Examiner* in 1997, which published an abridgment of the relevant pages that same year. *McSweeney's* later published the "Three Meditations on Death" (one of which the *Examiner* abridged).

The following case studies were commissioned and killed by magazines ranging from the *New York Times* to the *New Yorker* to *Men's Journal* to *Gear:* "Kickin' It," "Snakehead Fear," "Special Tax," "Murder for Sale" and "Papa's Children."

Some excerpts from "On the Morality of Weapons" and "Means and Ends" first appeared in *Grand Street* in 2000.

I am grateful to the magazines who gave me the money and press accreditation which made most of the journeys for this book possible.